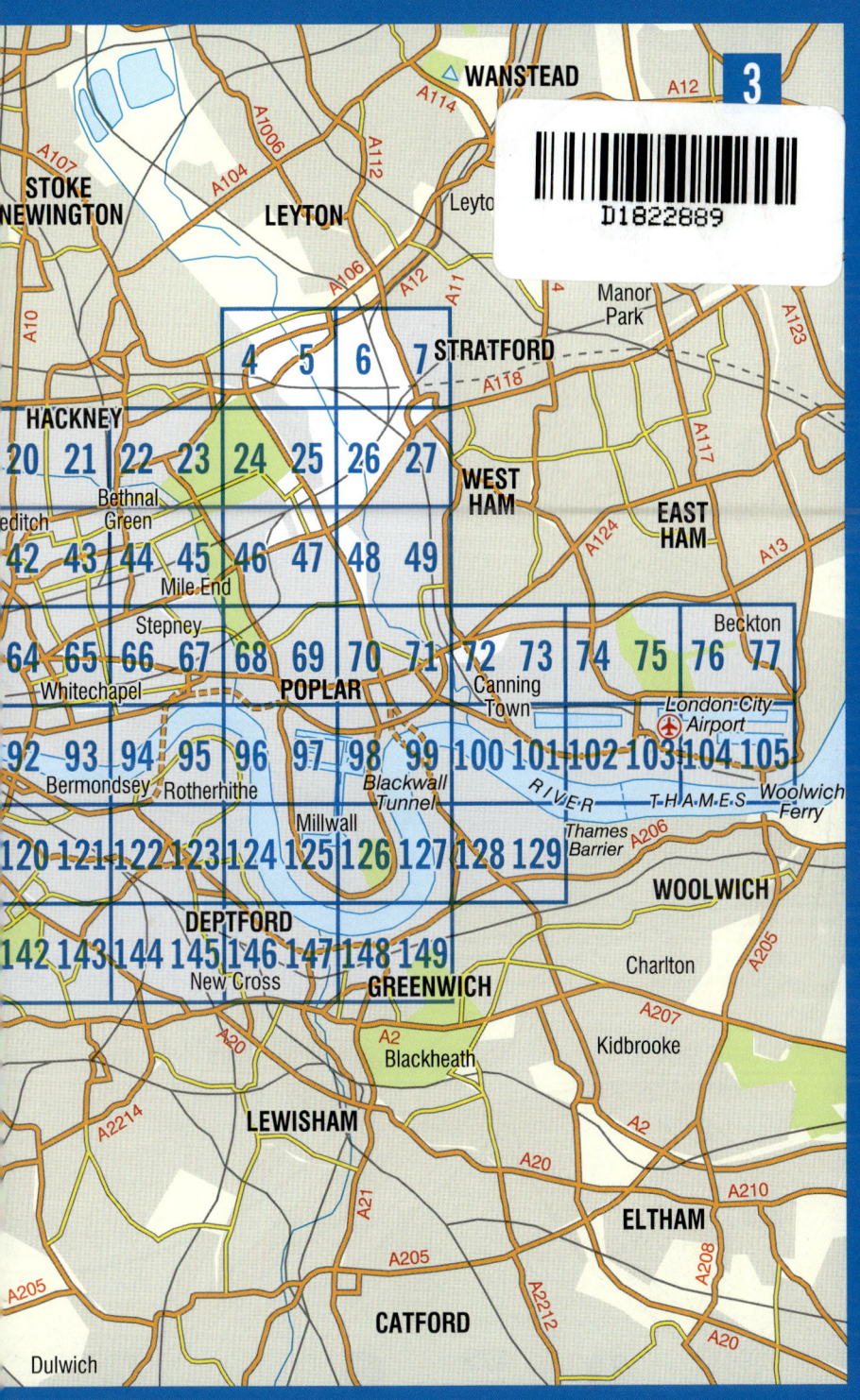

CONTENTS

Key to Map Pages	2-3	Index to Stations	252-253
Map Pages	4-149	Congestion Charging Zone Map	254-255
Index to Streets	150-249	West End Cinemas & Theatres Maps	256
Index to Hospitals etc.	250-251	Underground Railway Map	Back Cover

REFERENCE

A Road	**A40**	Cycle Hire Docking Station	
Tunnel		Fire Station	
B Road	**B502**	Hospital	H
Dual Carriageway		Information Centre	
One-way Street		National Grid Reference	⁵29
Road Under Construction Opening dates are correct at the time of publication.		Police Station	▲
Proposed Road		Post Office	★
Inner Ring Road	R	Red Light Camera	
Junction Name	MARBLE ARCH	River Boat Trip	
Restricted Access		River Bus Stop	
Pedestrianized Road		Safety Camera with Speed Limit Fixed and long term road works cameras only. Symbols do not indicate camera direction.	30
Congestion Charging Zone		Theatre	
Railway Station		Toilet:	
Railway Station Entrance: National Rail Network Overground Underground Docklands Light Railway		without facilities for the Disabled with facilities for the Disabled Disabled use only	▽ ▽ ▽
Borough Boundary		Educational Establishment	
		Hospital or Healthcare Building	
Postal Boundary		Industrial Building	
		Leisure or Recreational Facility	
Map Continuation	14	Office Building	
		Place of Interest - Public Access	
Airport		Place of Interest - no Public Access	
		Place of Worship	
Car Park (selected)	P	Public Building	
		Residential Building	
Cinema		Shopping Centre or Market	
		Other Selected Buildings	

SCALE

1:7,040   9 inches to 1 mile
14.2cm to 1km   22.86cm to 1mile

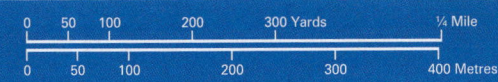

| 0 | 50 | 100 | 200 | 300 Yards | ¼ Mile |
| 0 | 50 | 100 | 200 | 300 | 400 Metres |

A-Z A'Z A toZ
registered trade marks of
Geographers' A-Z Map Company Ltd

www. az .co.uk

EDITION 5 2014
Copyright © Geographers' A-Z Map Co. Ltd.
Telephone: 01732 781000 (Enquiries & Trade Sales)
          01732 783422 (Retail Sales)

© Crown copyright and database rights 2014 Ordnance Survey 100017302.

Safety camera information supplied by www.PocketGPSWorld.com.
Speed Camera Location Database Copyright 2014 © PocketGPSWorld.com

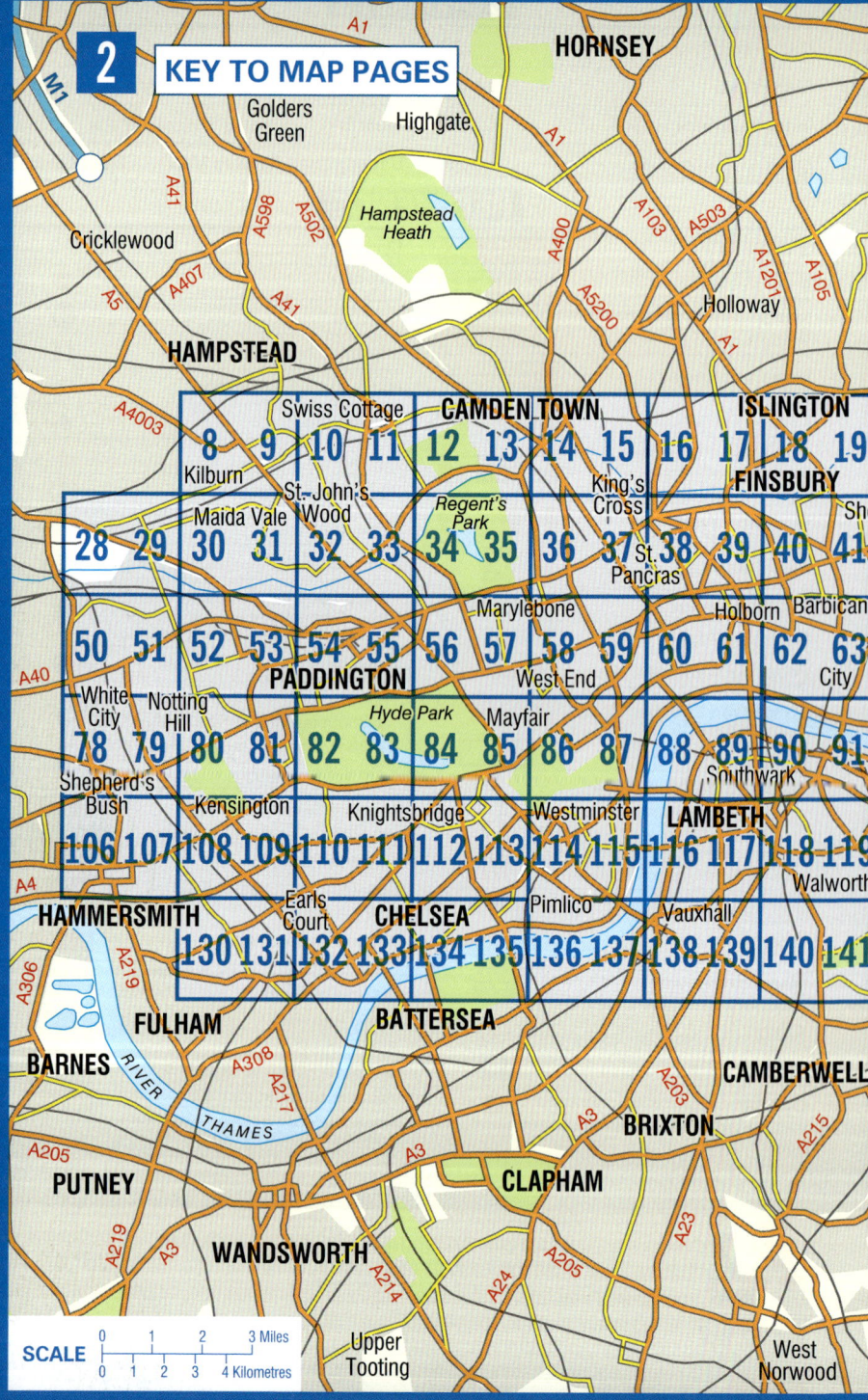

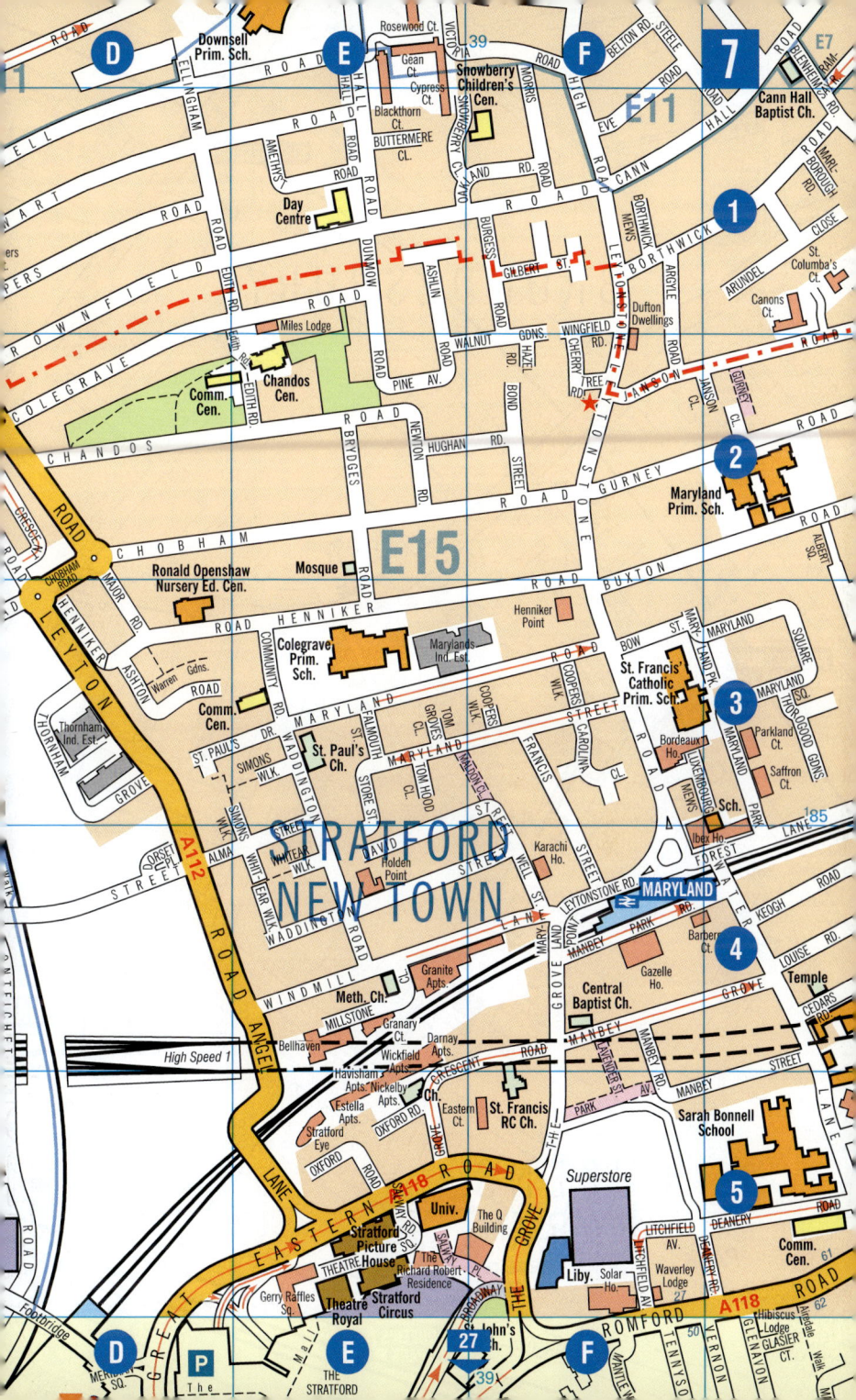

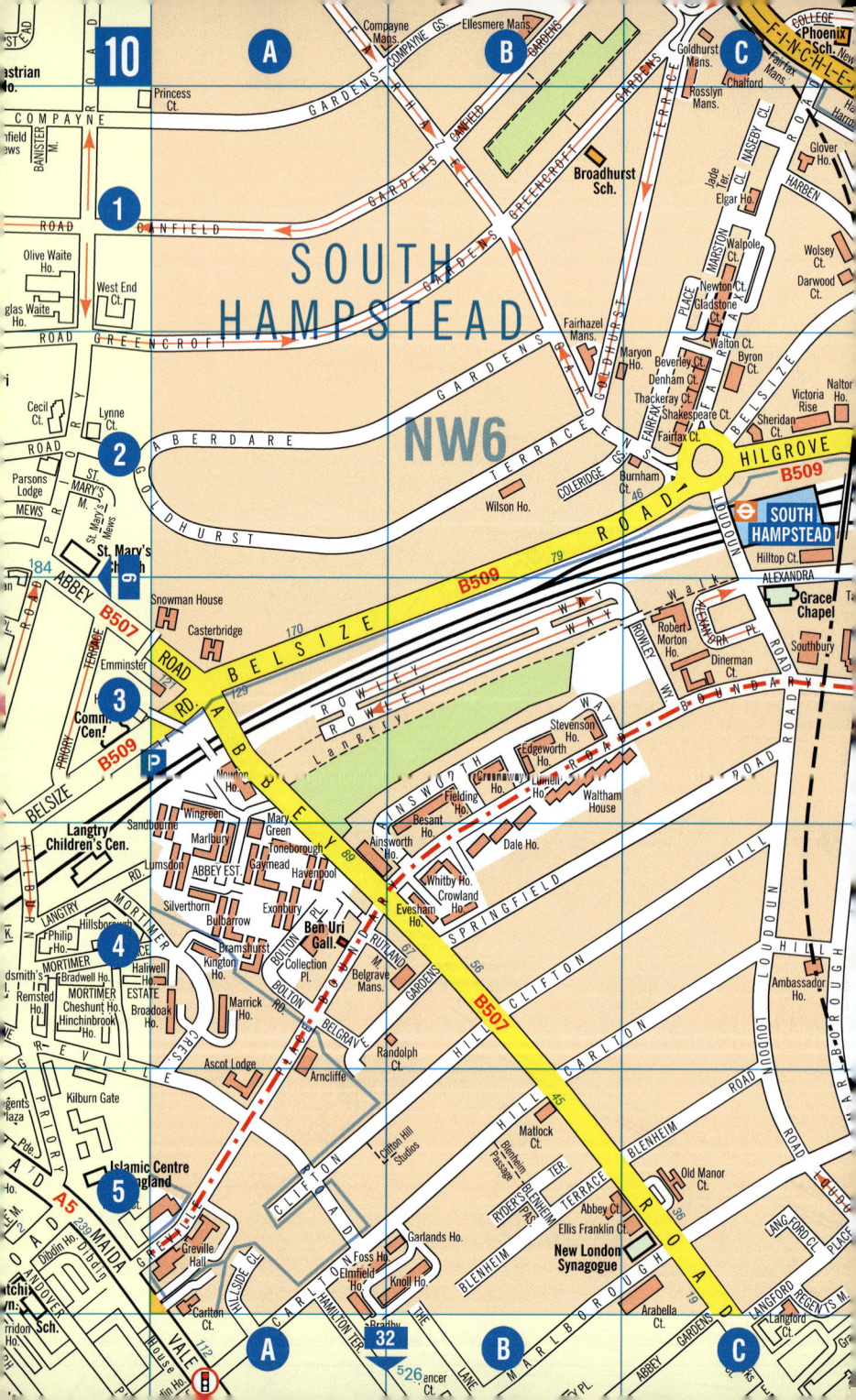

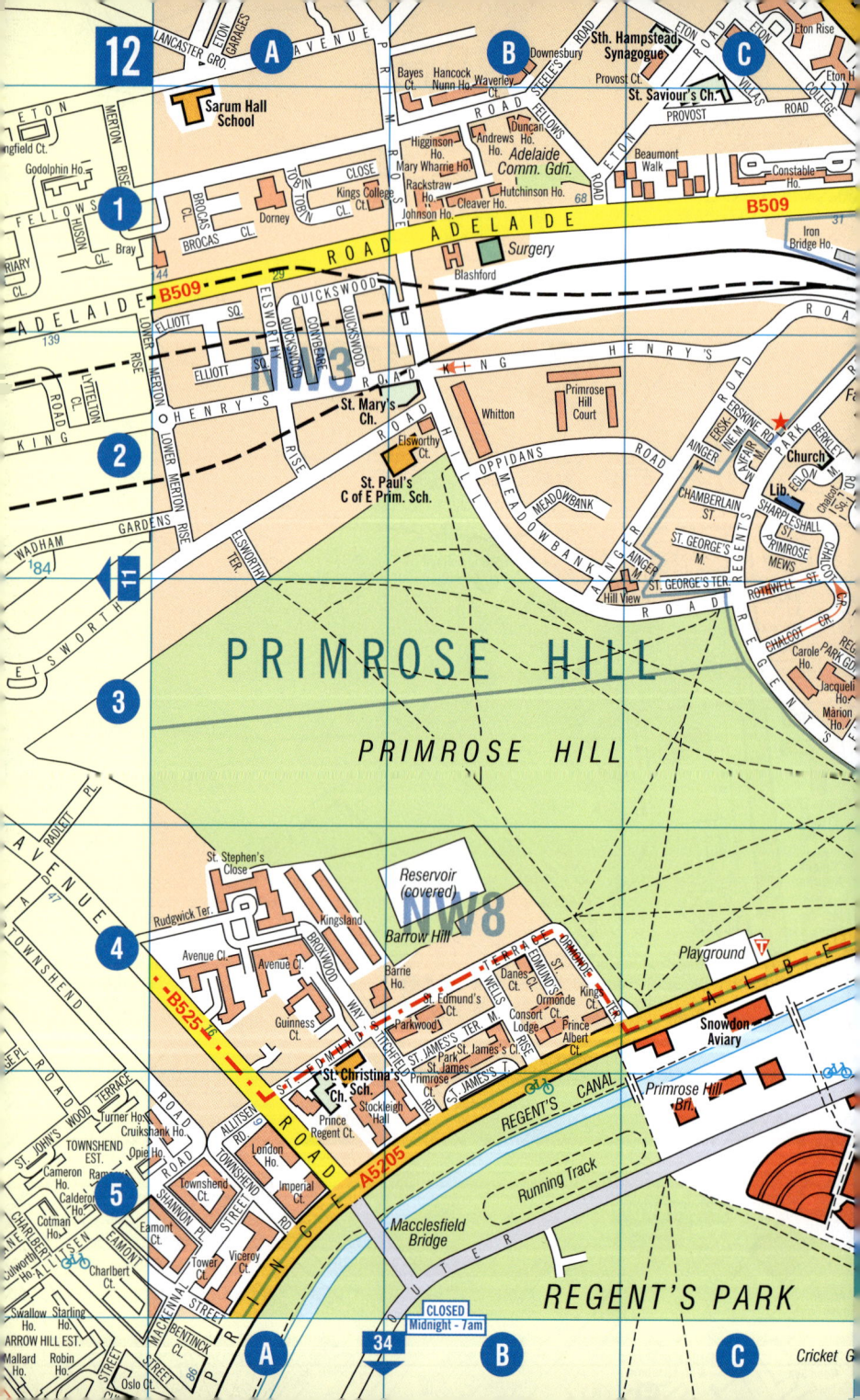

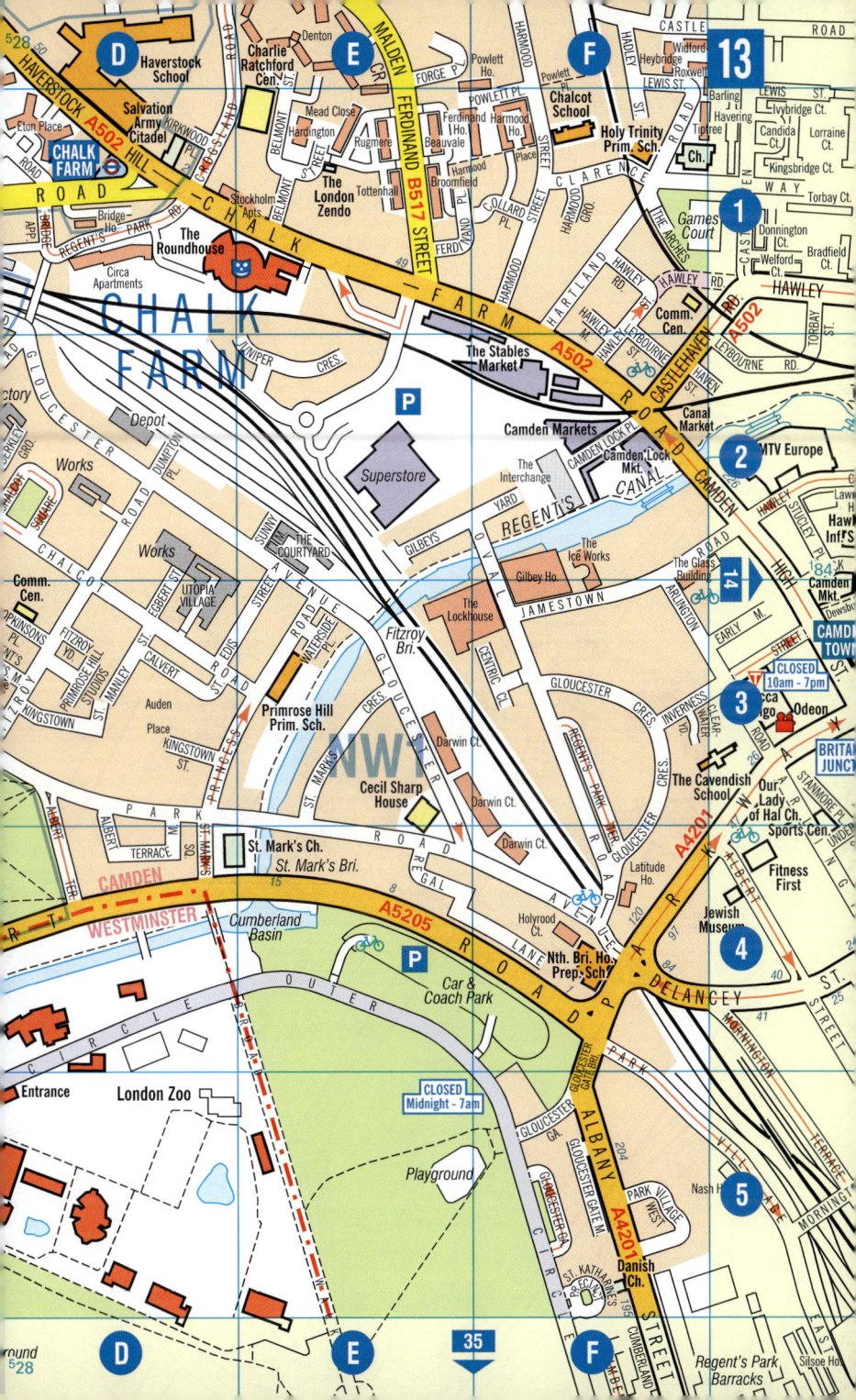

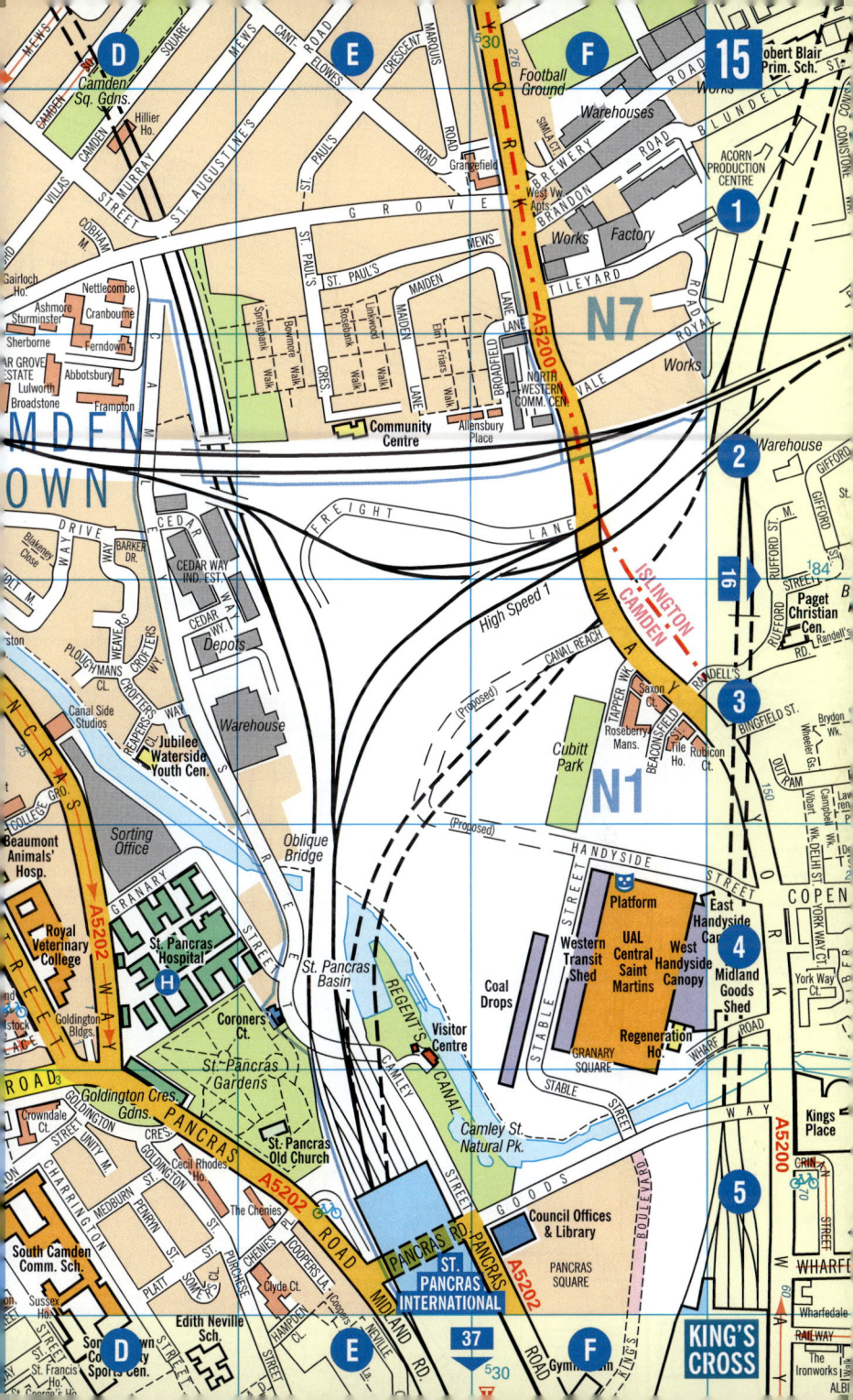

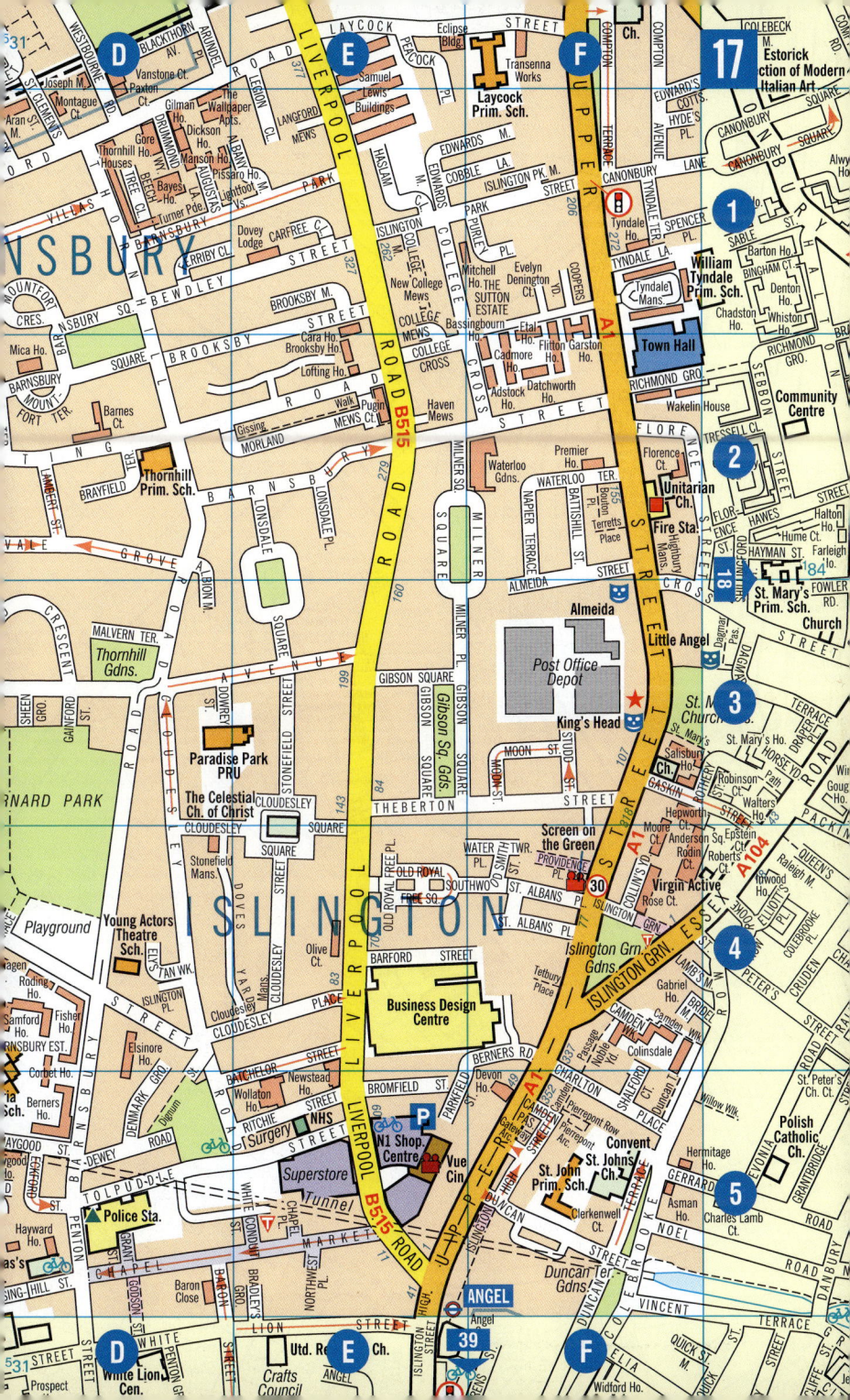

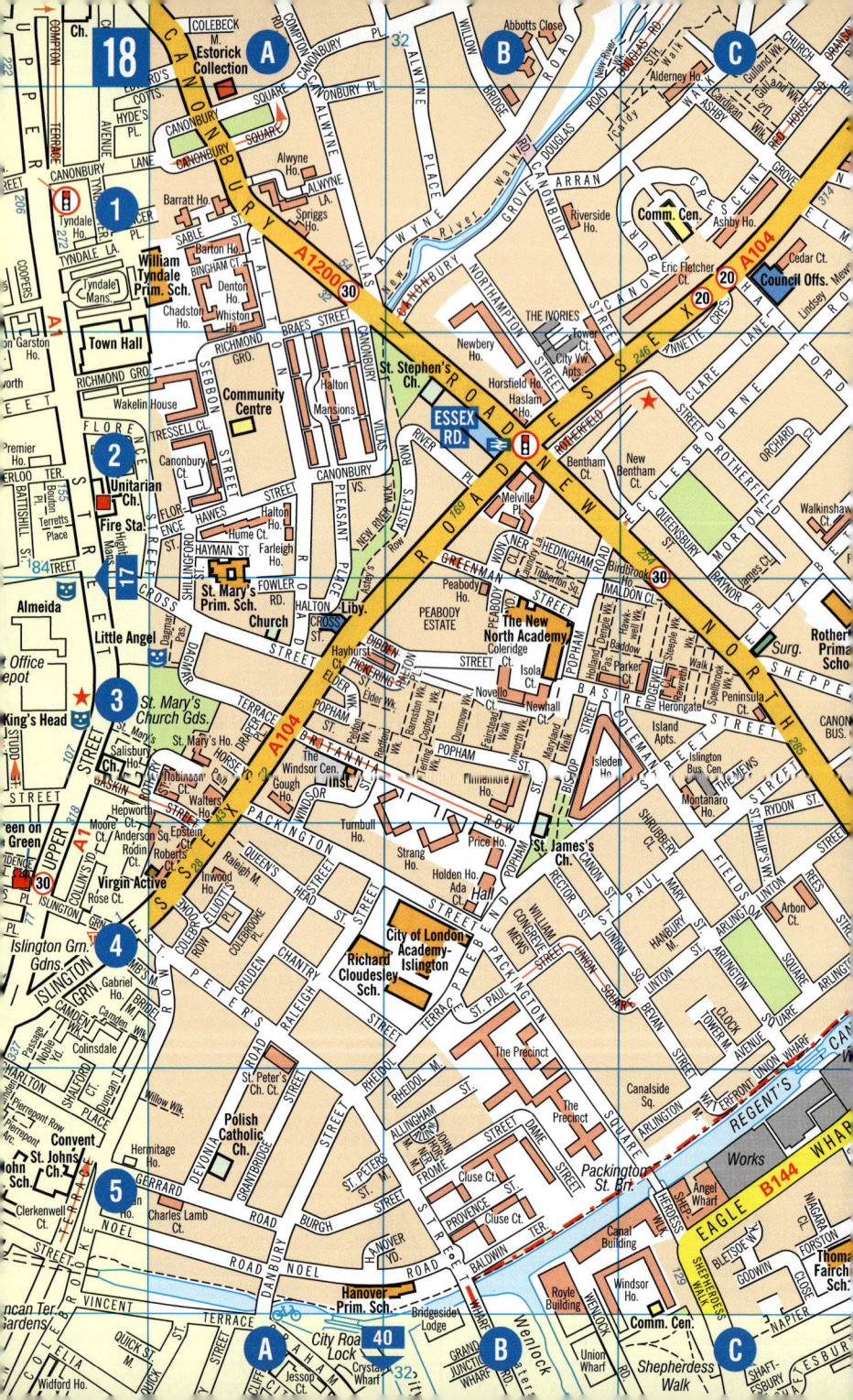

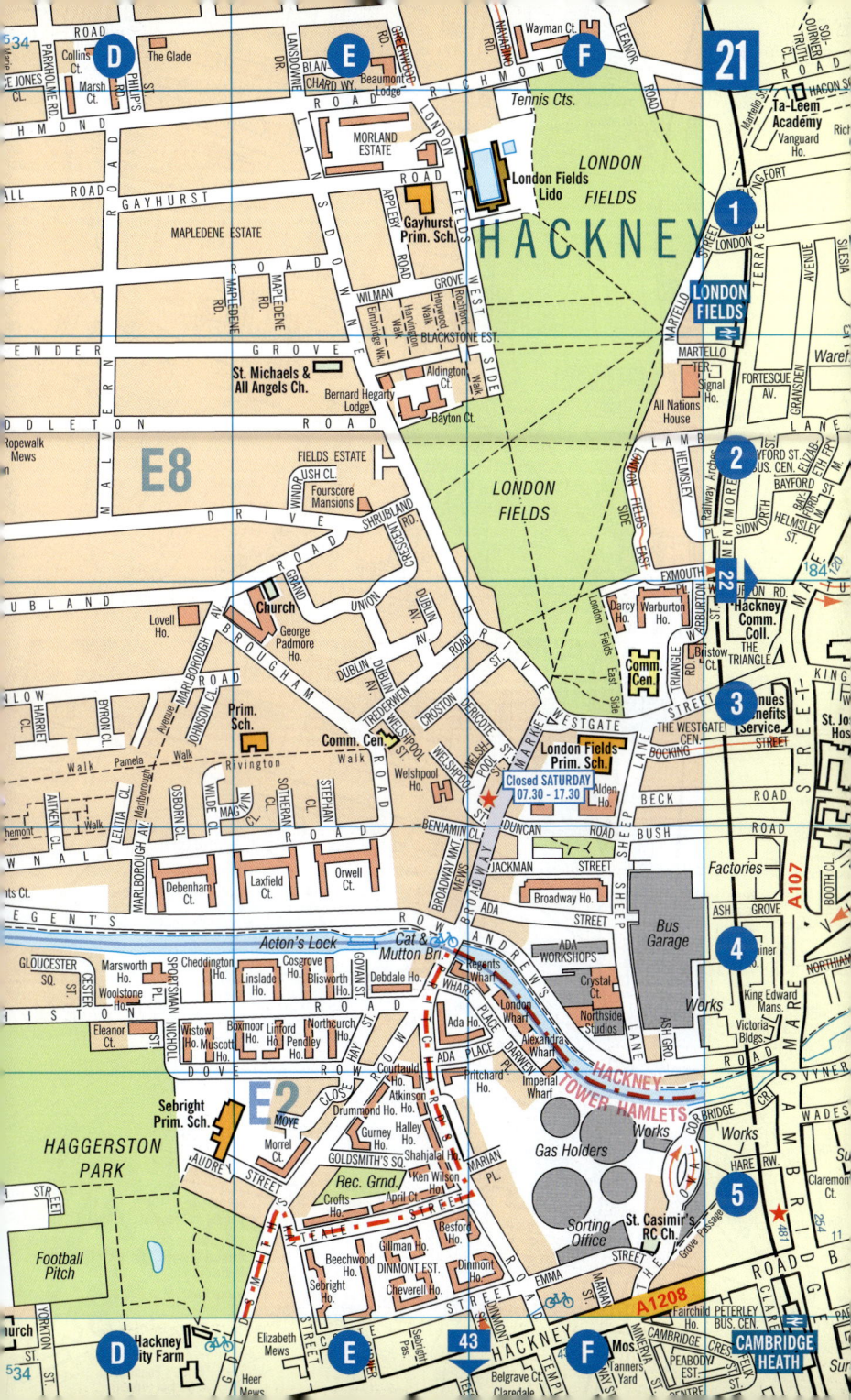

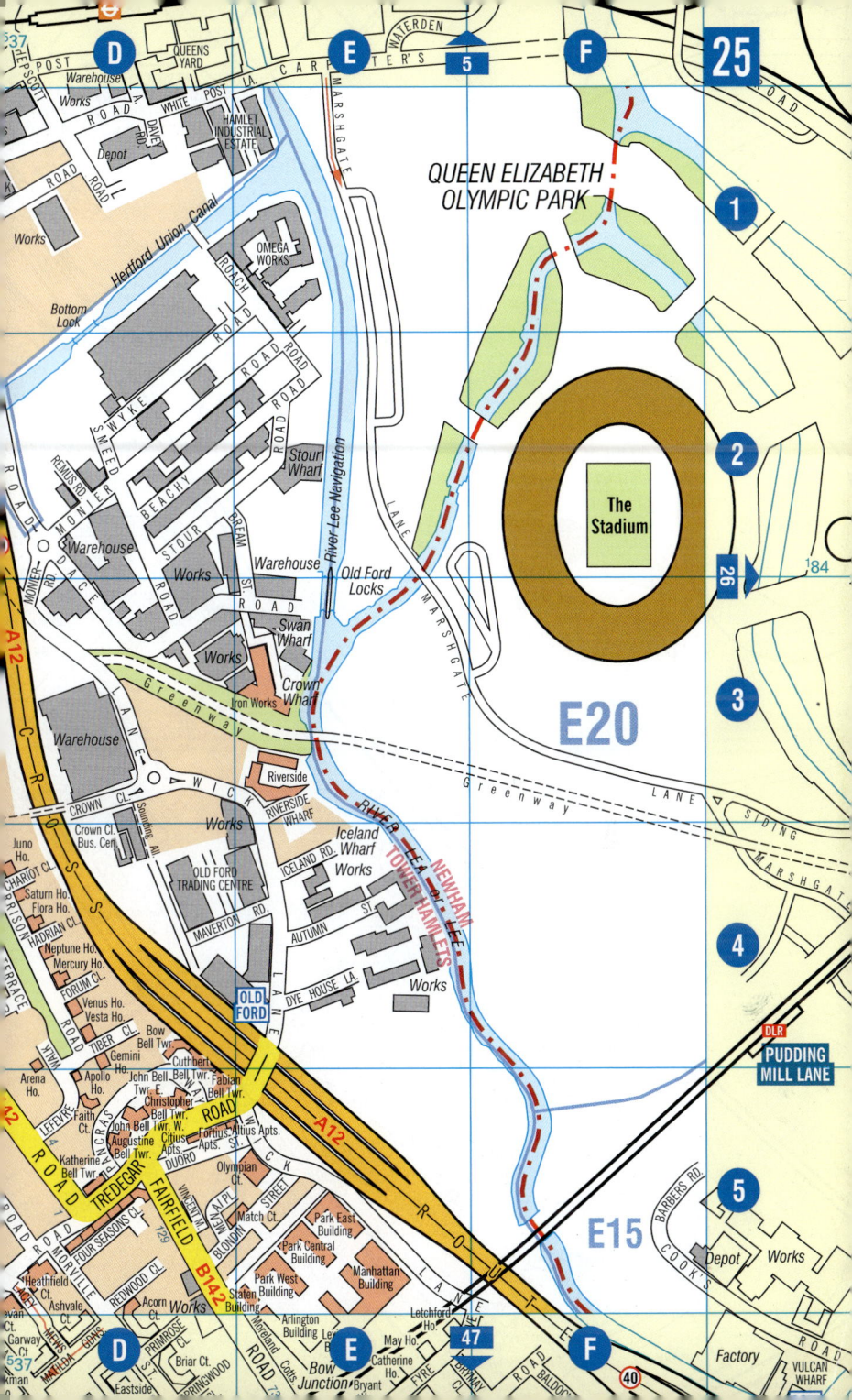

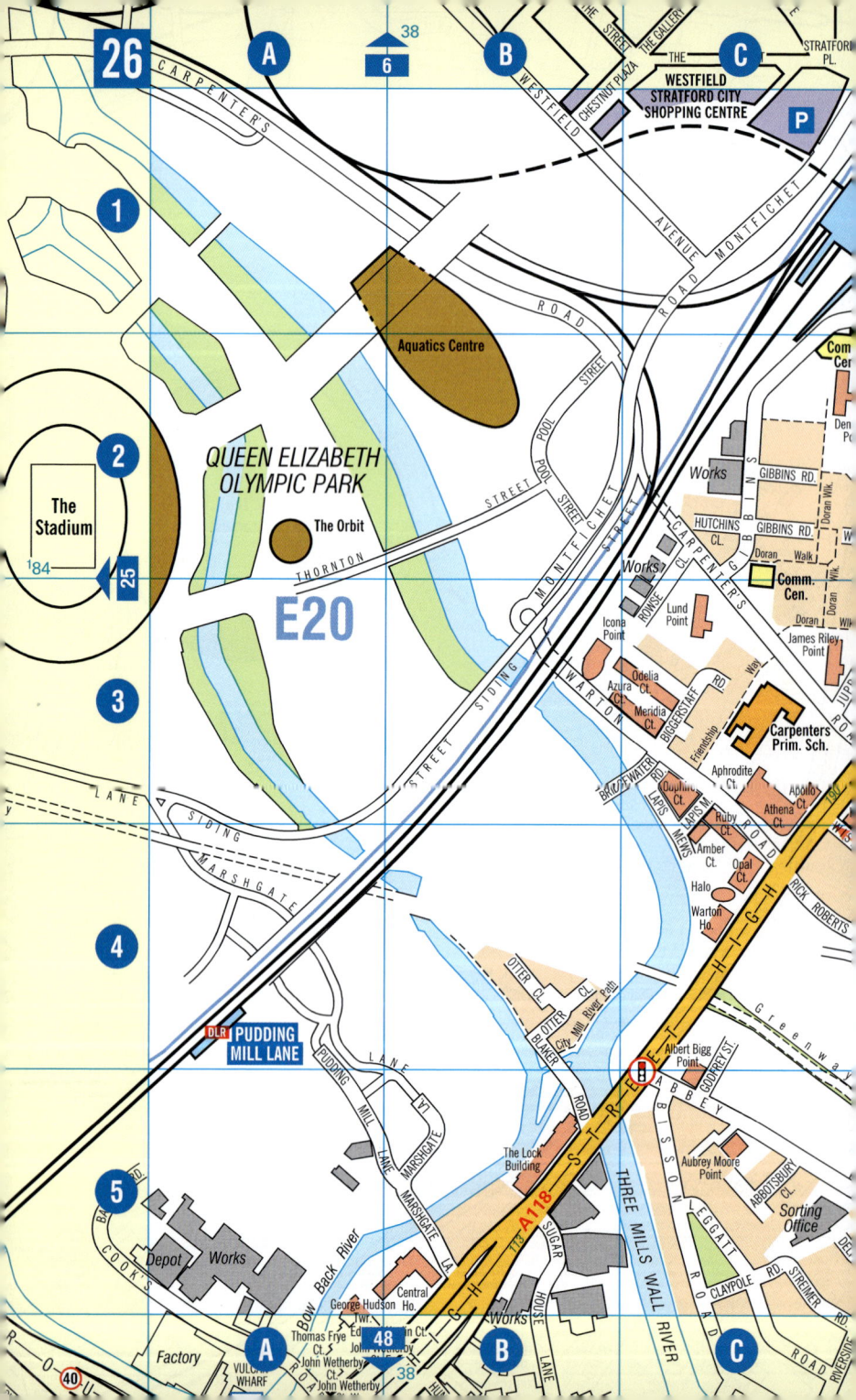

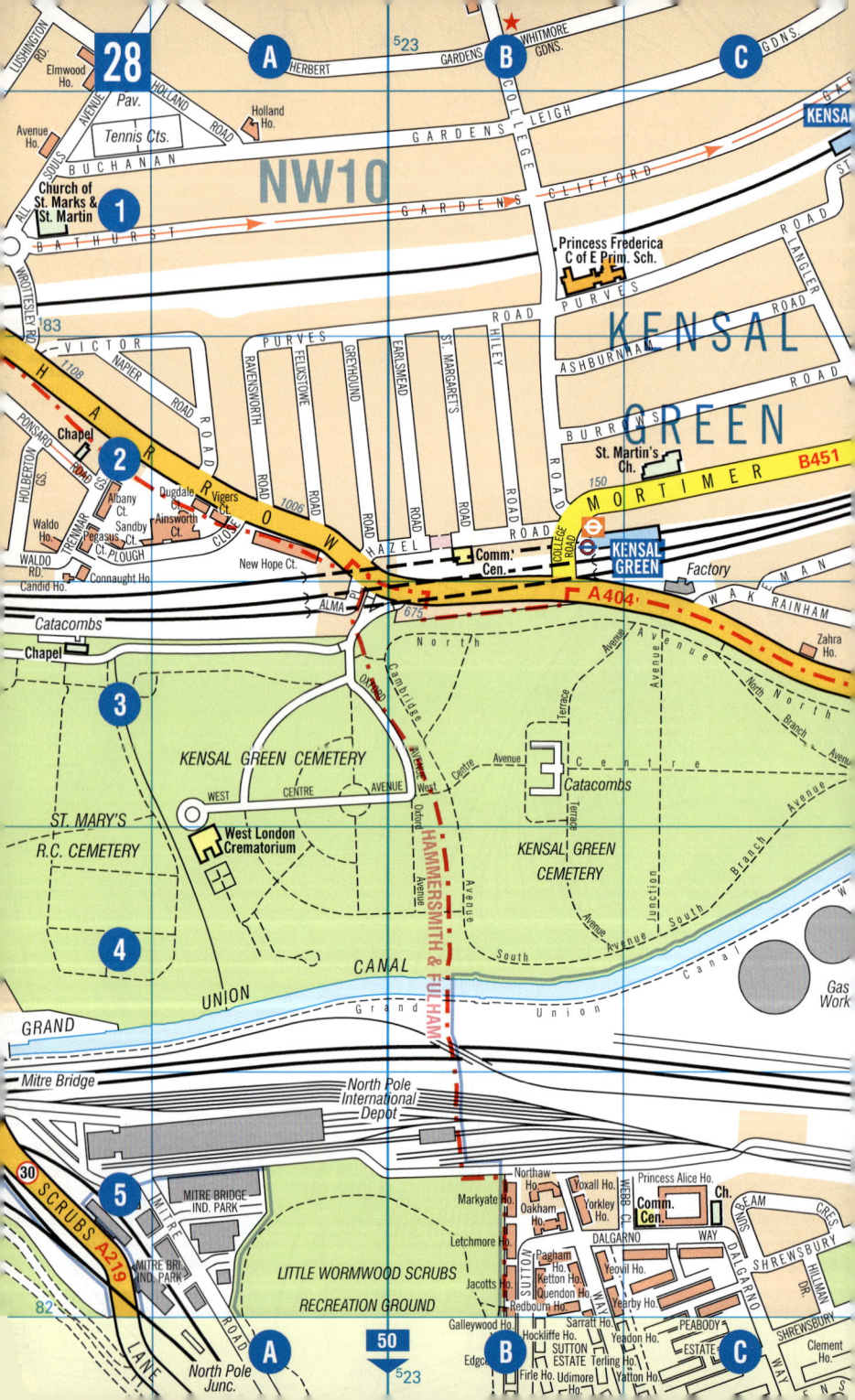

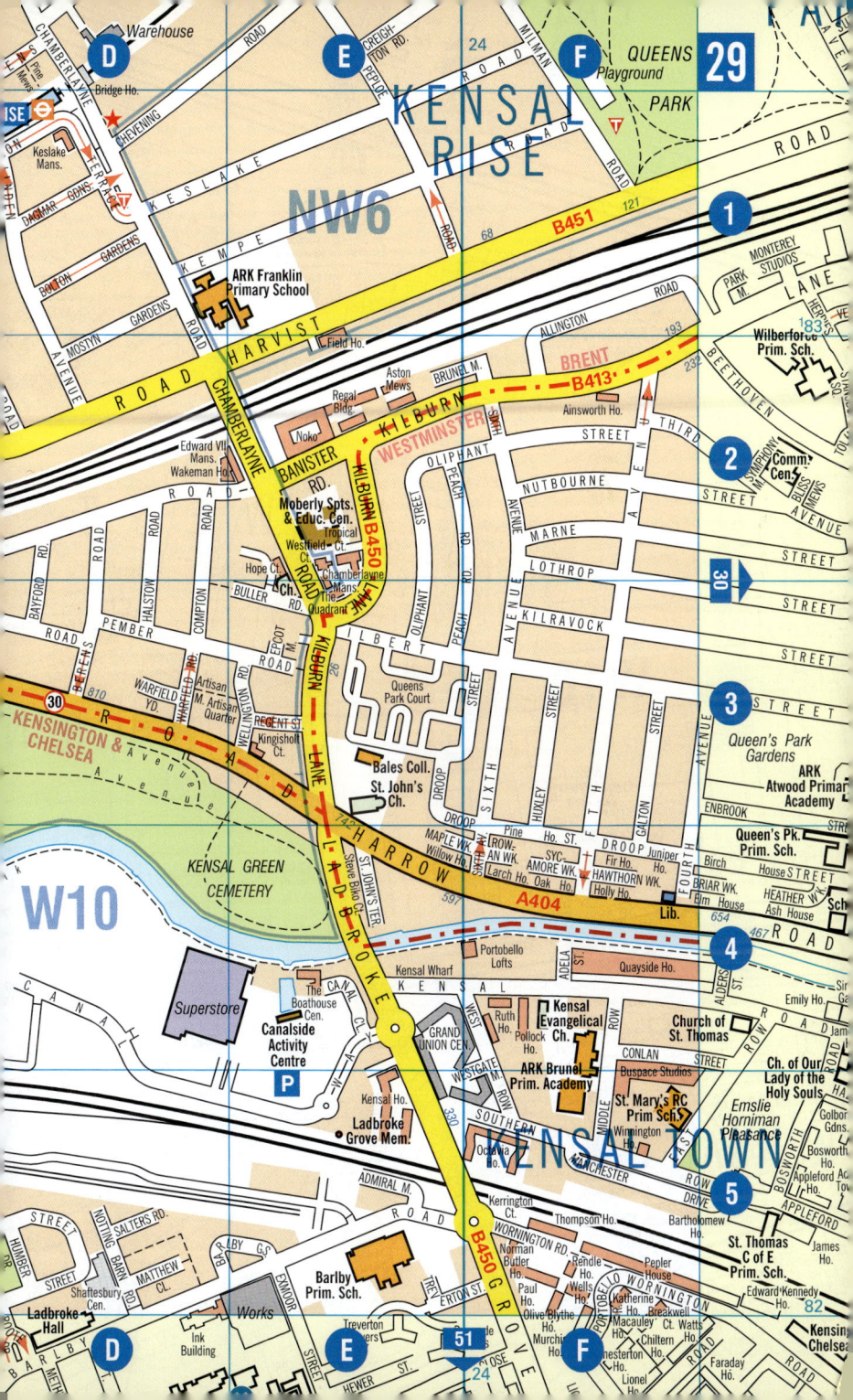

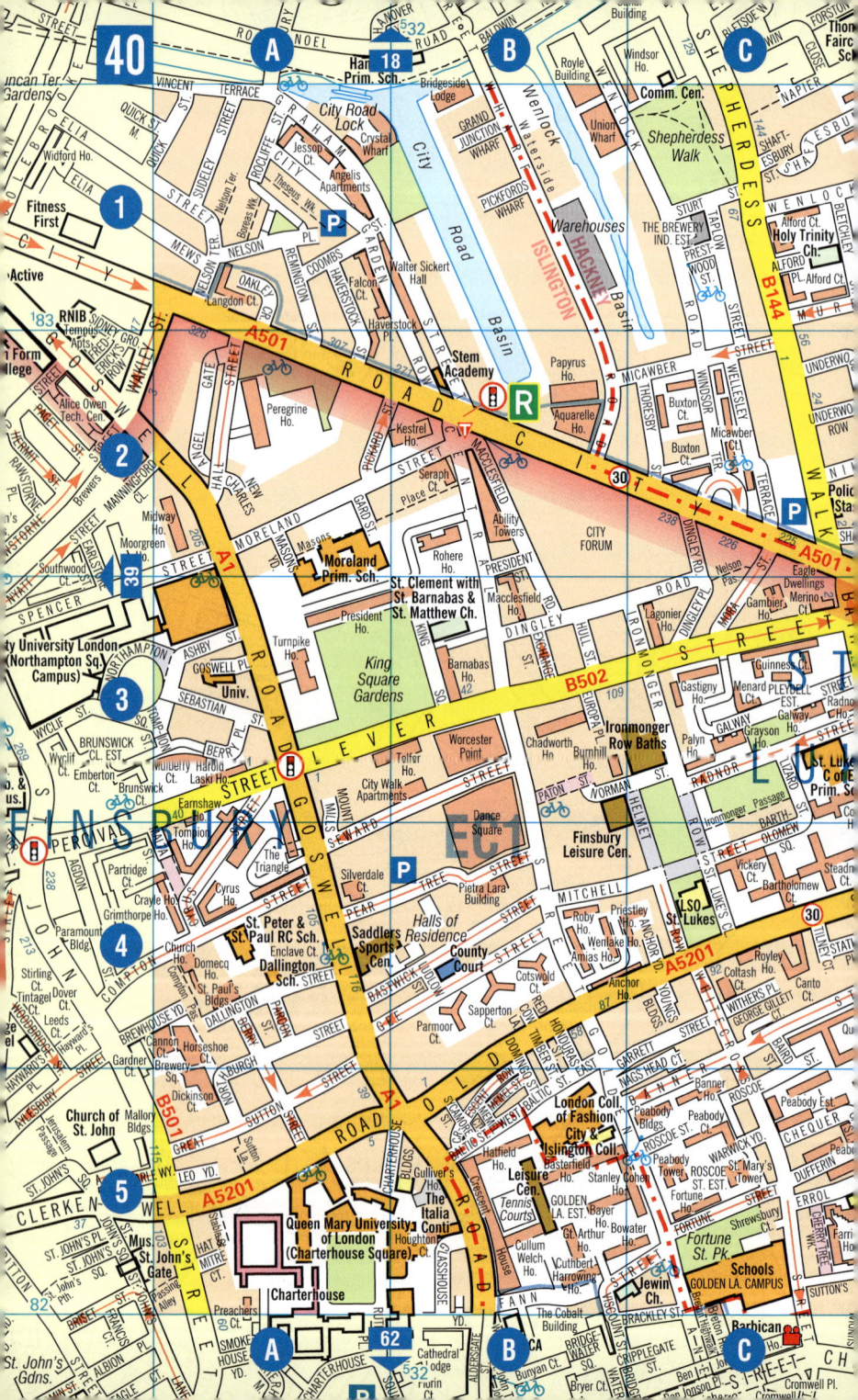

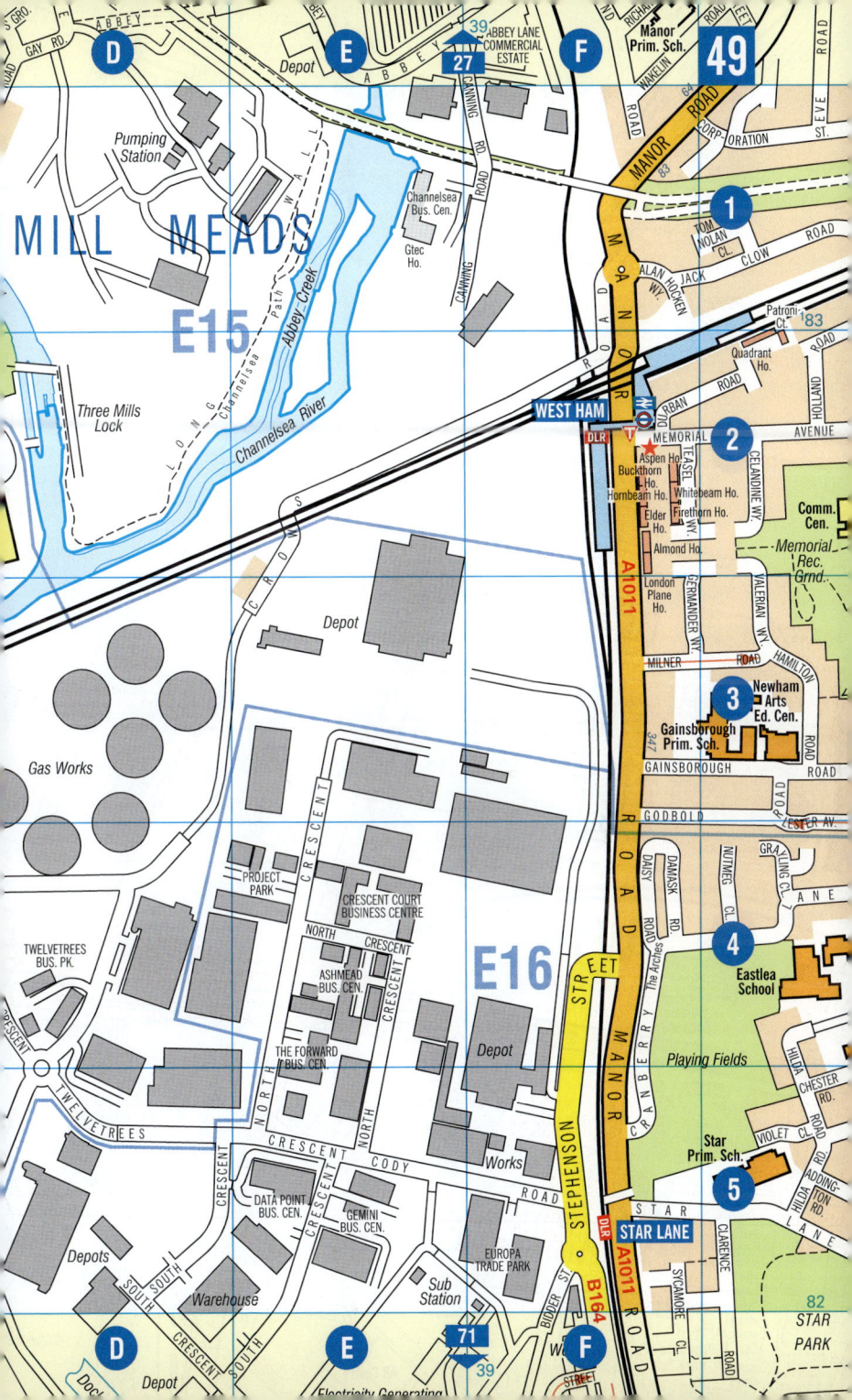

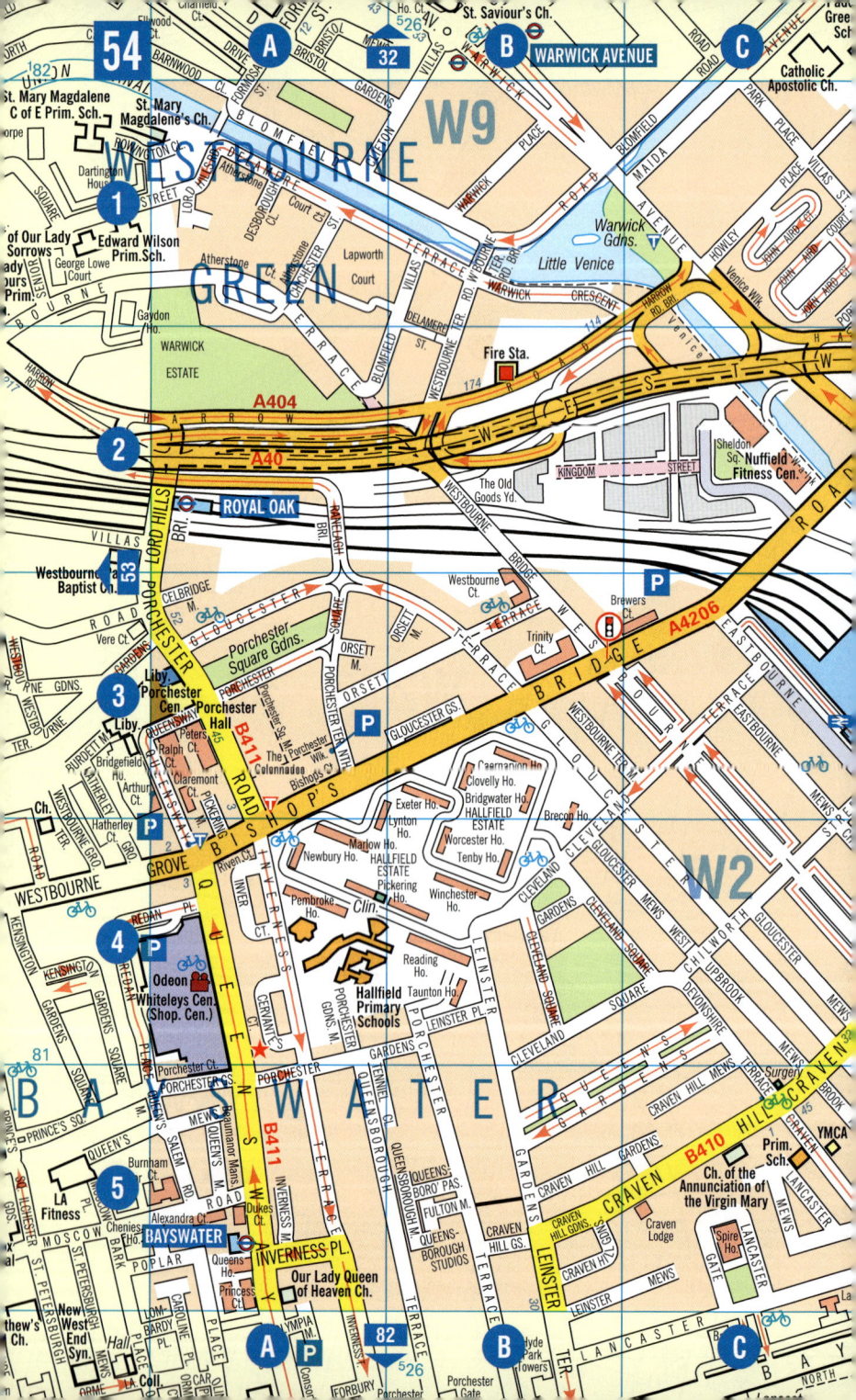

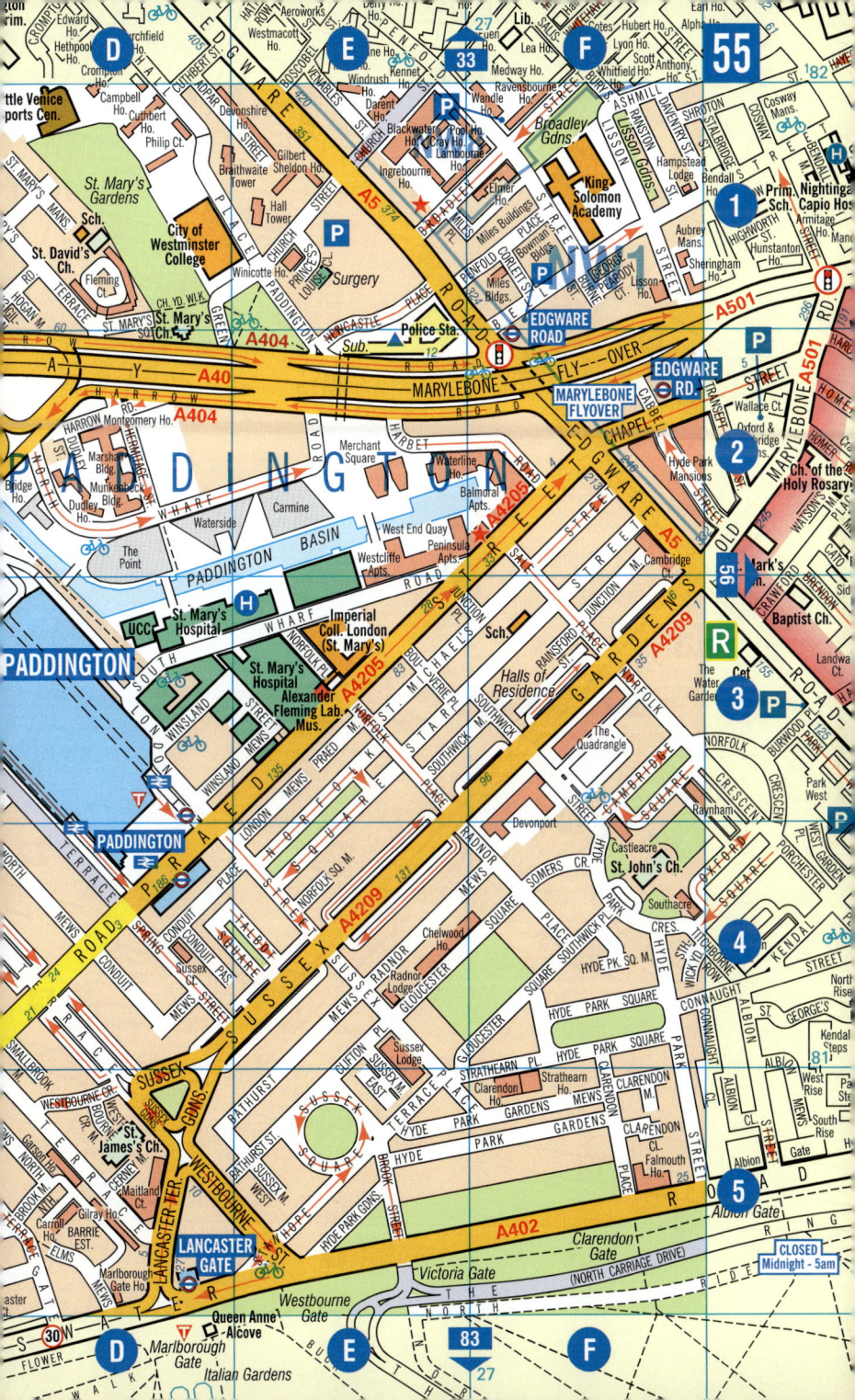

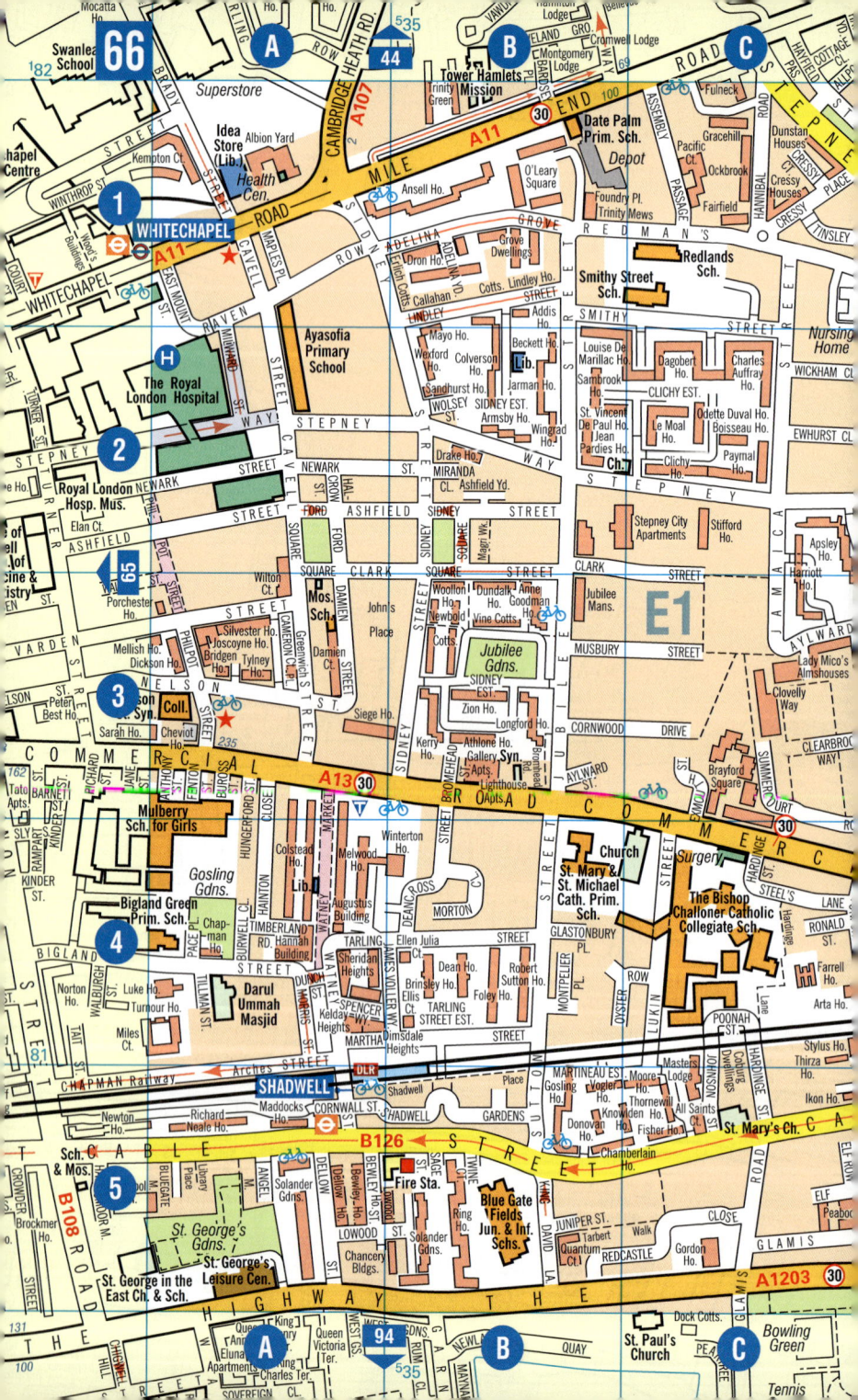

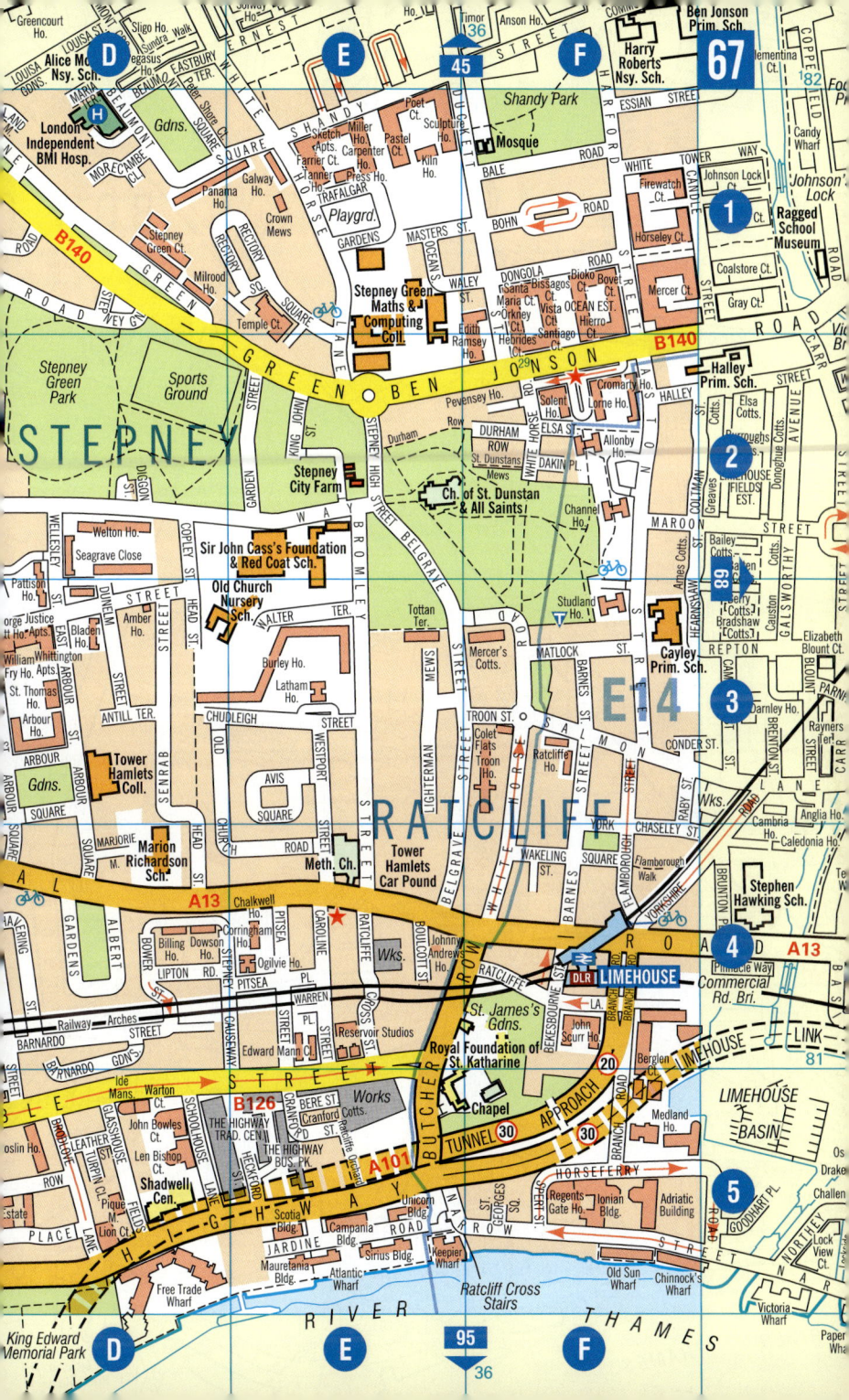

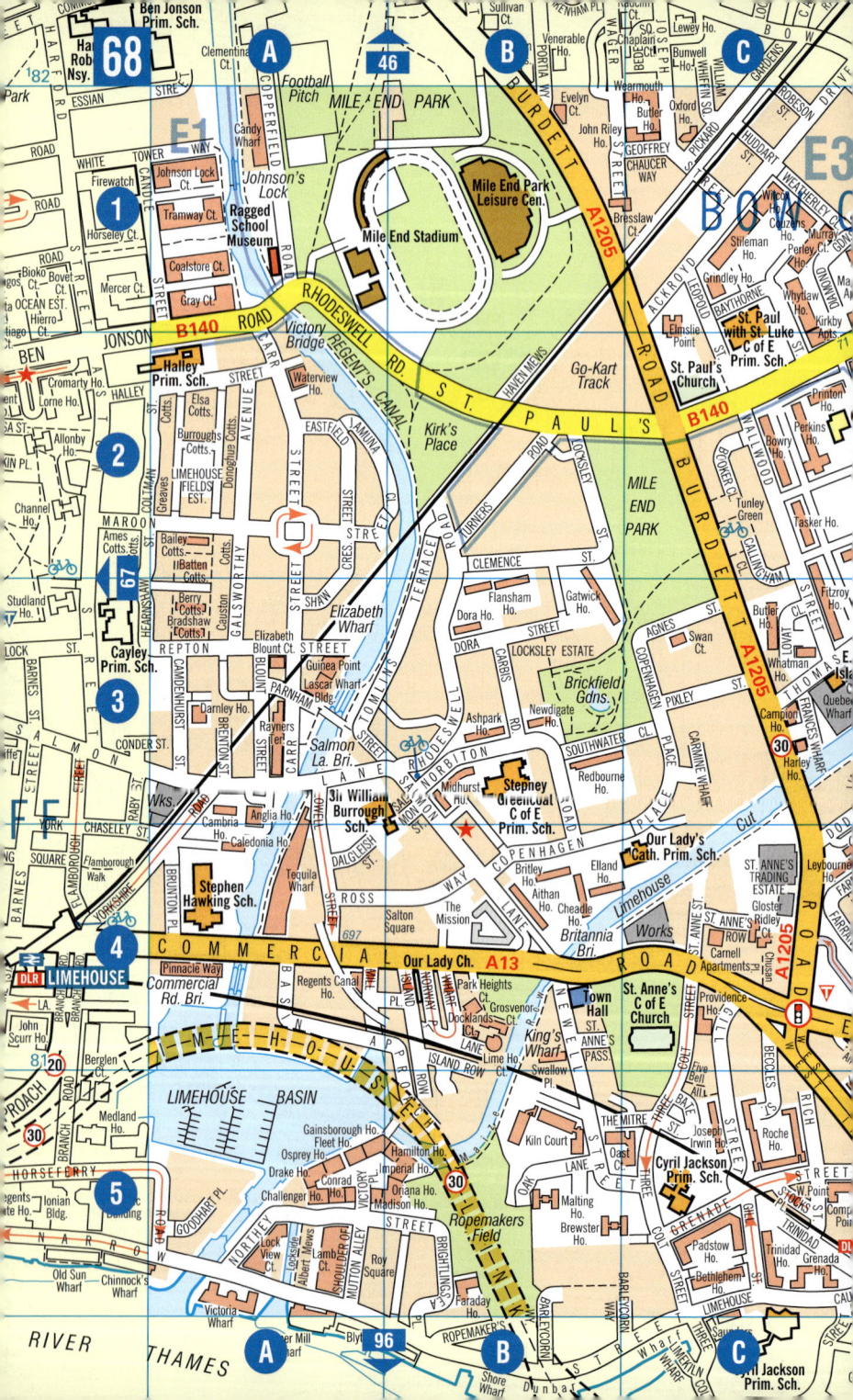

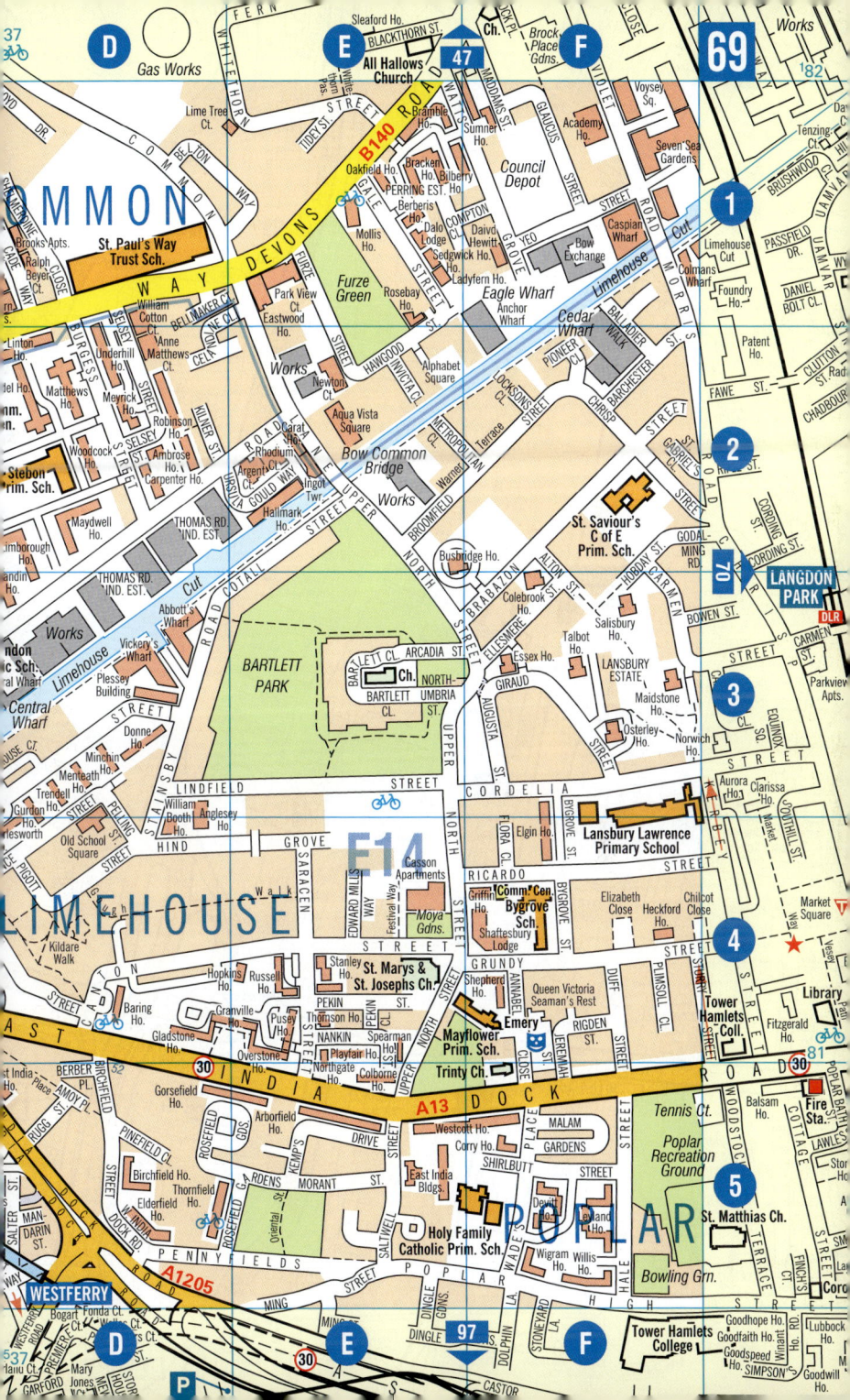

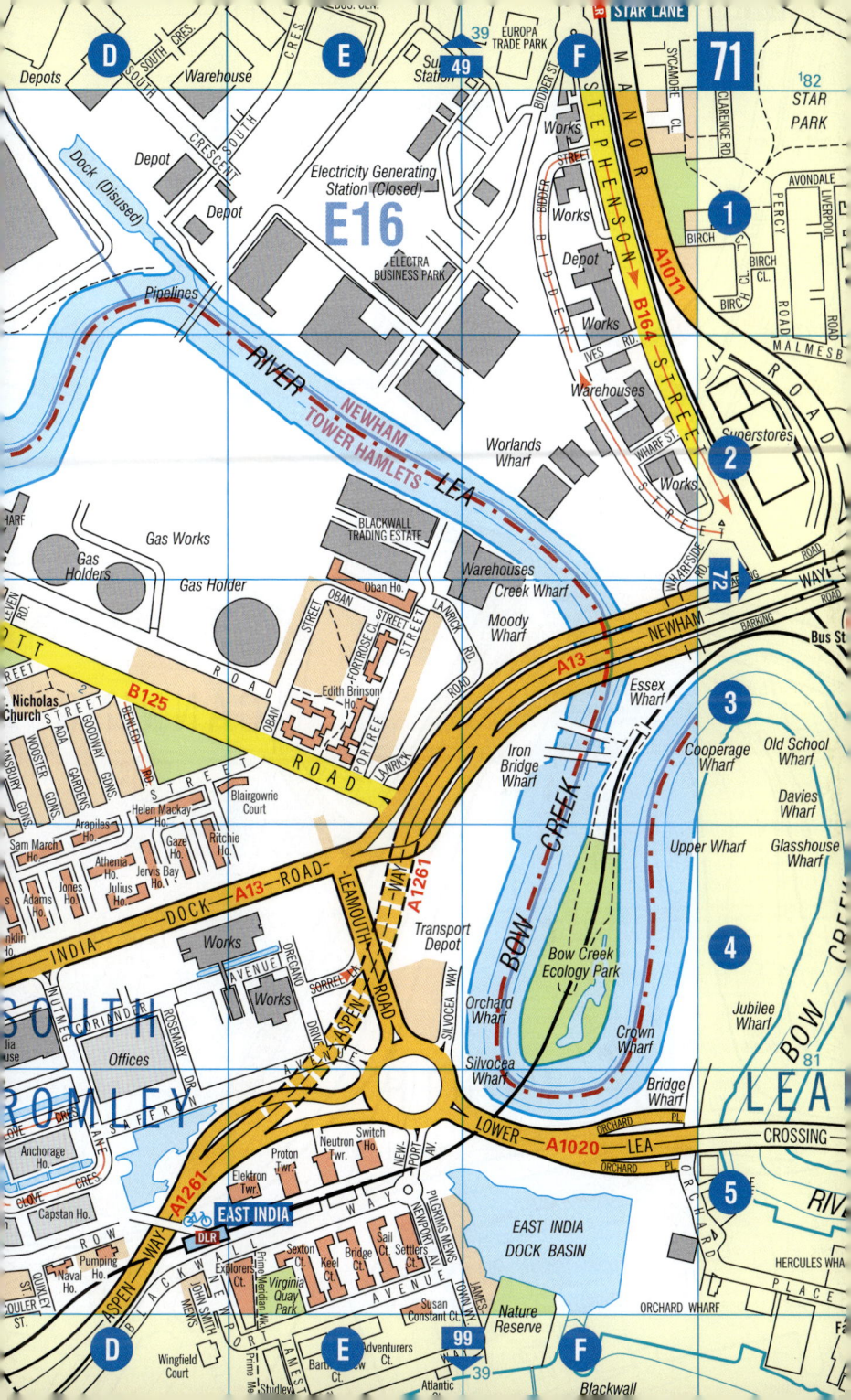

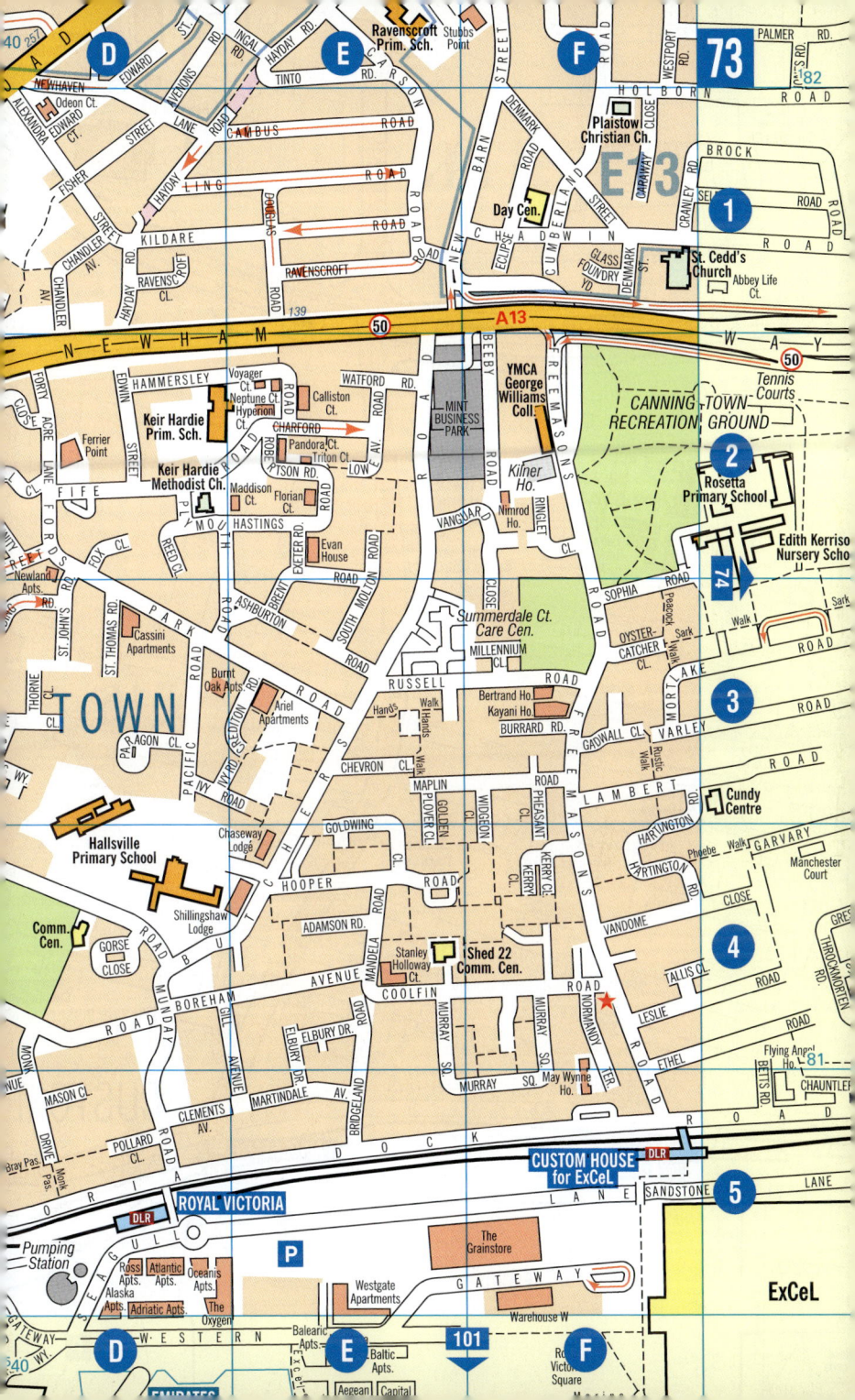

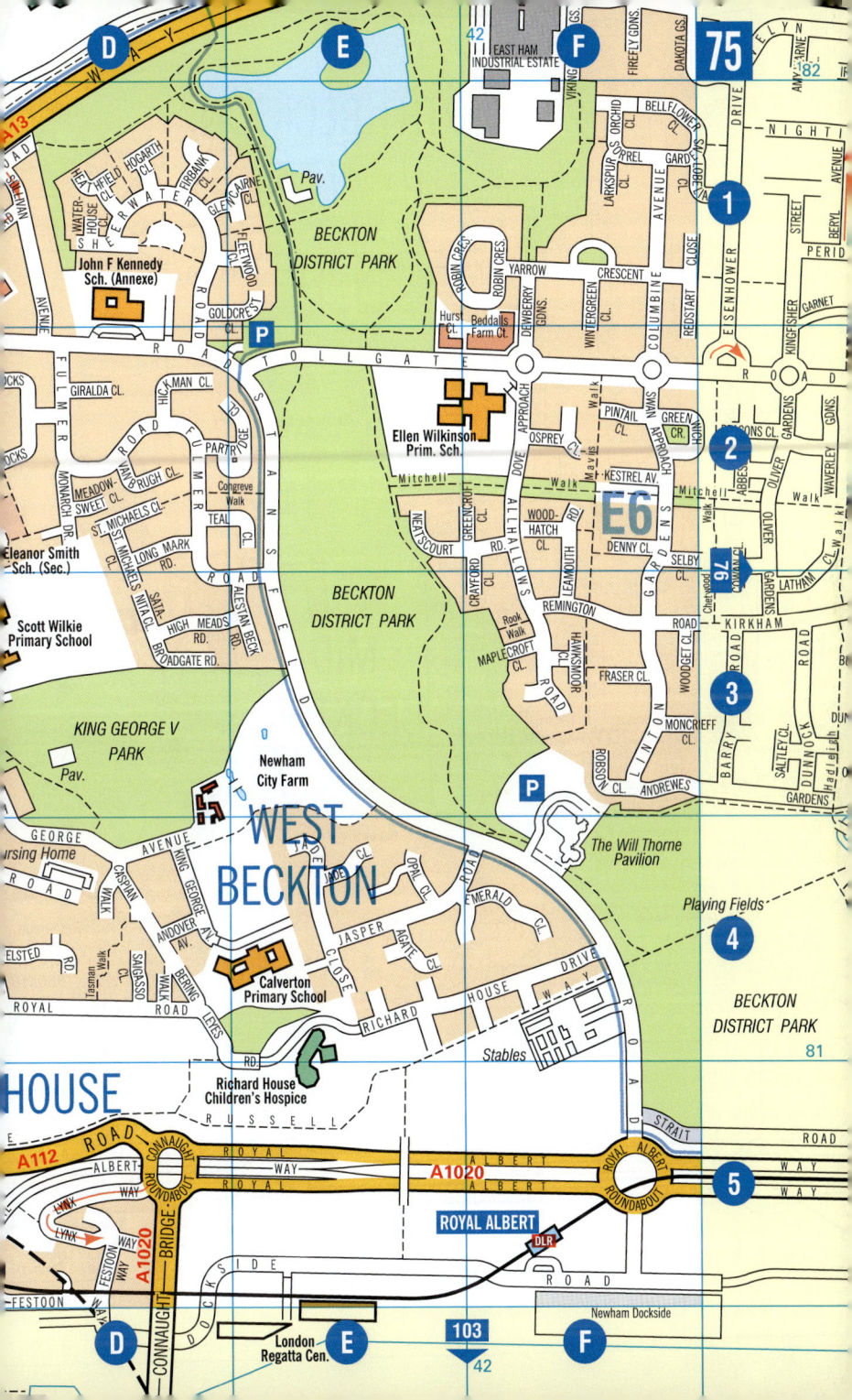

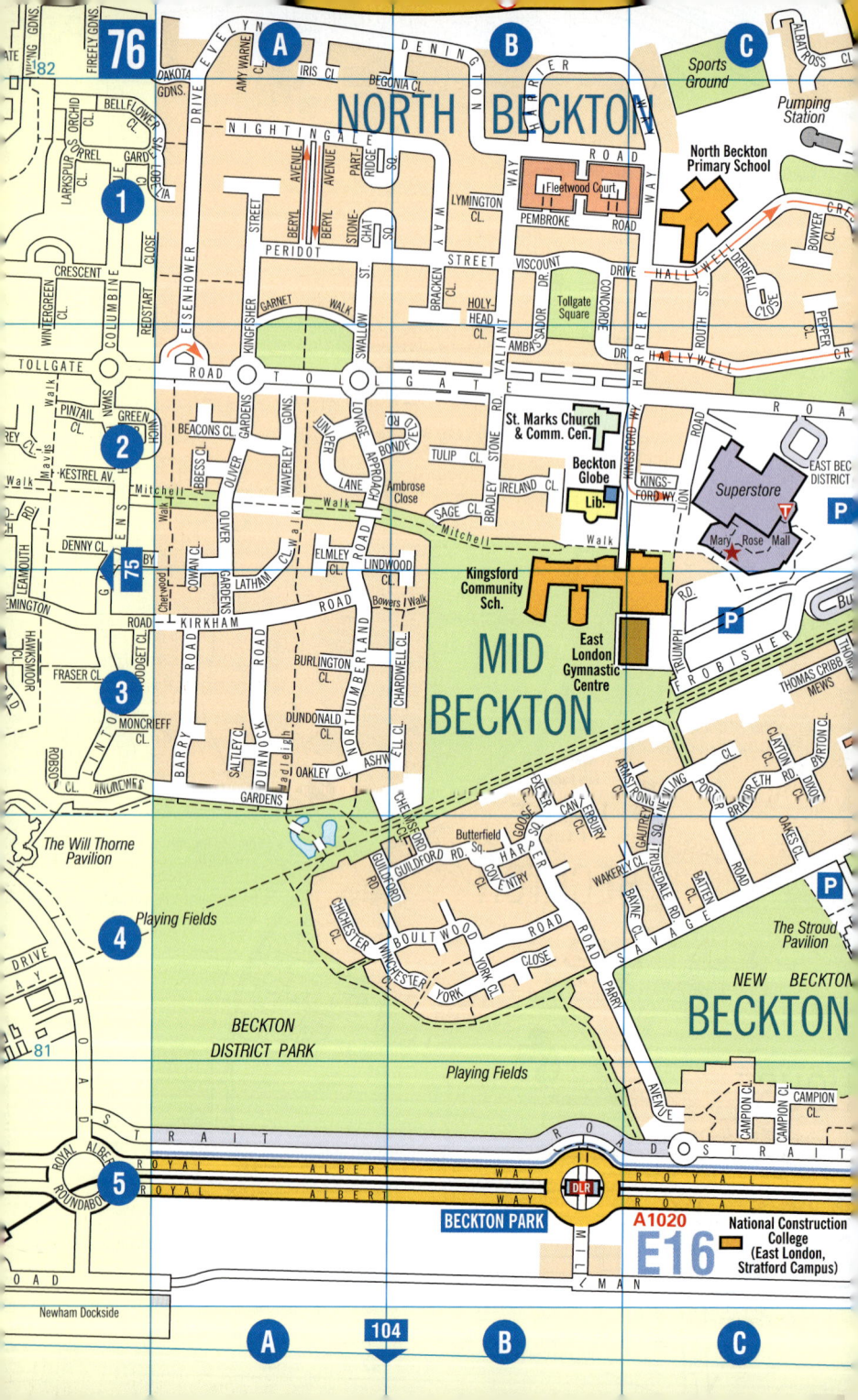

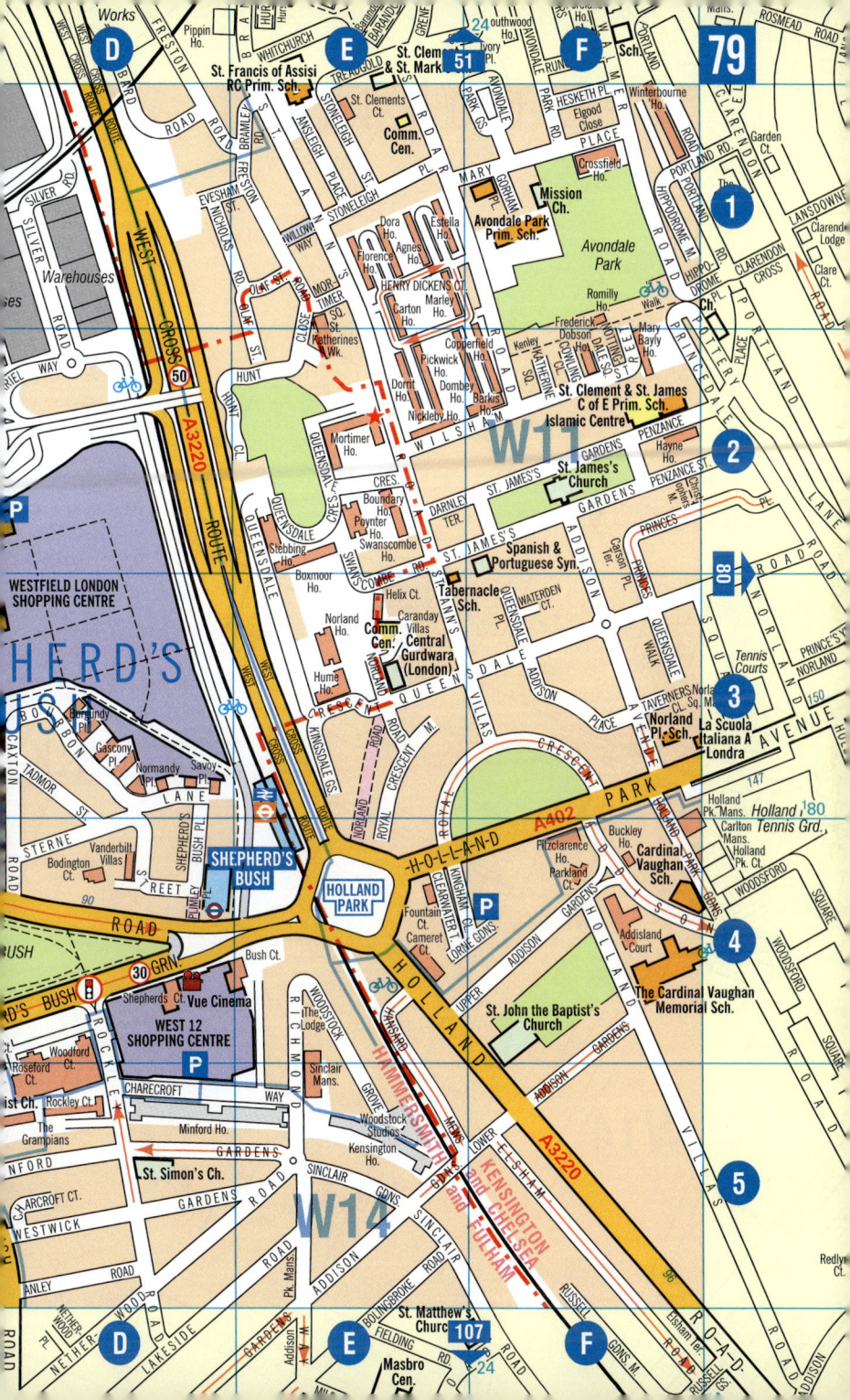

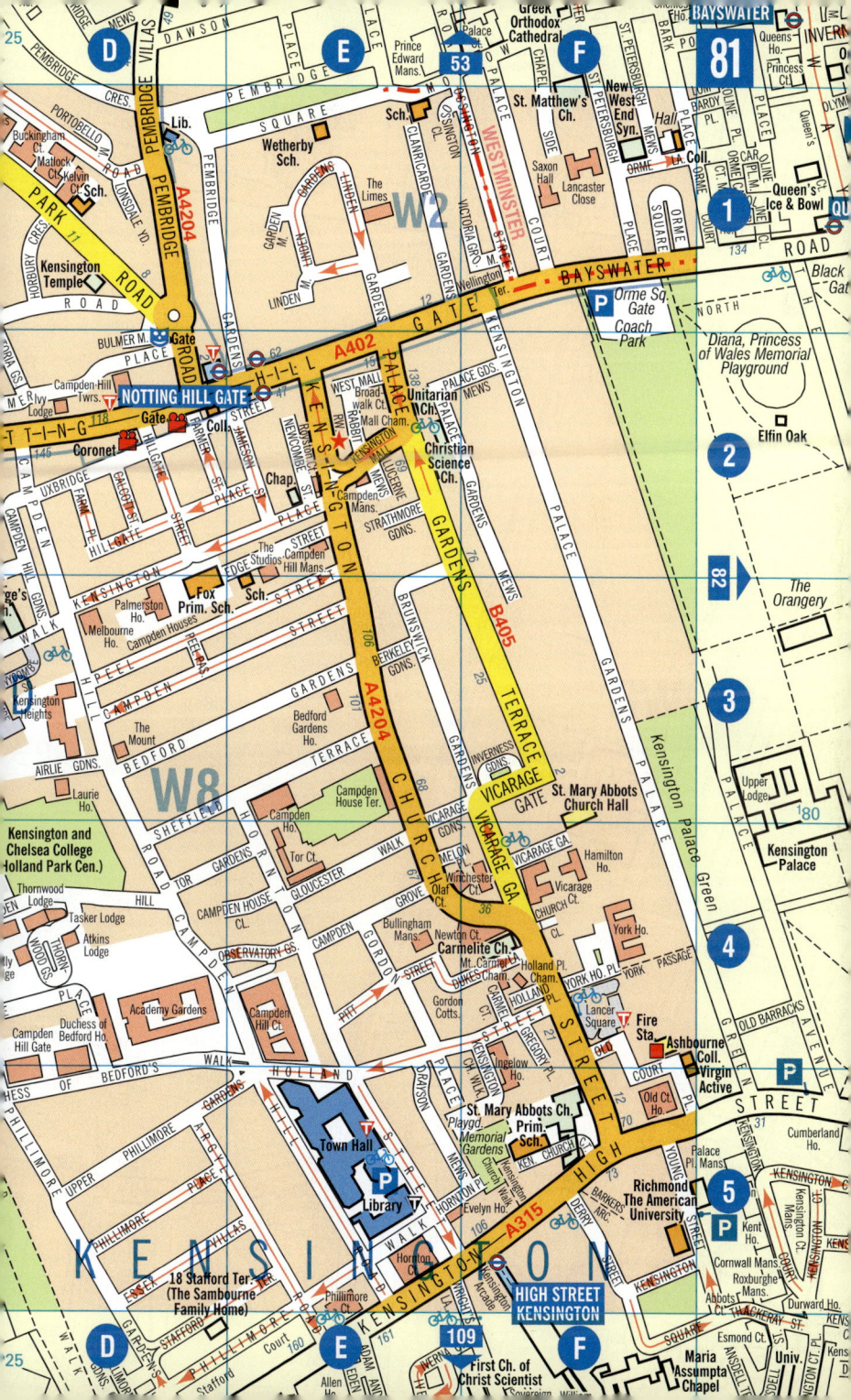

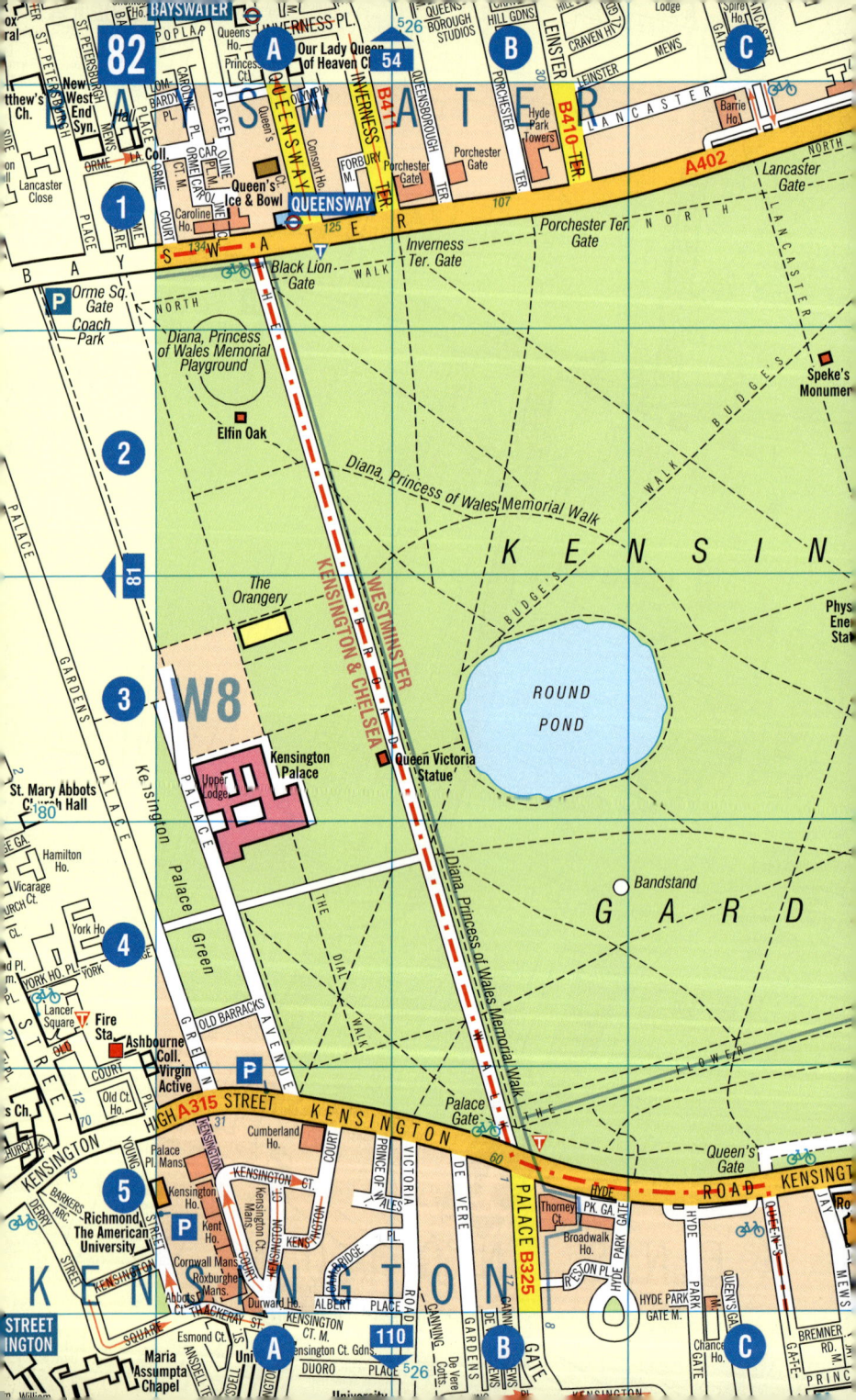

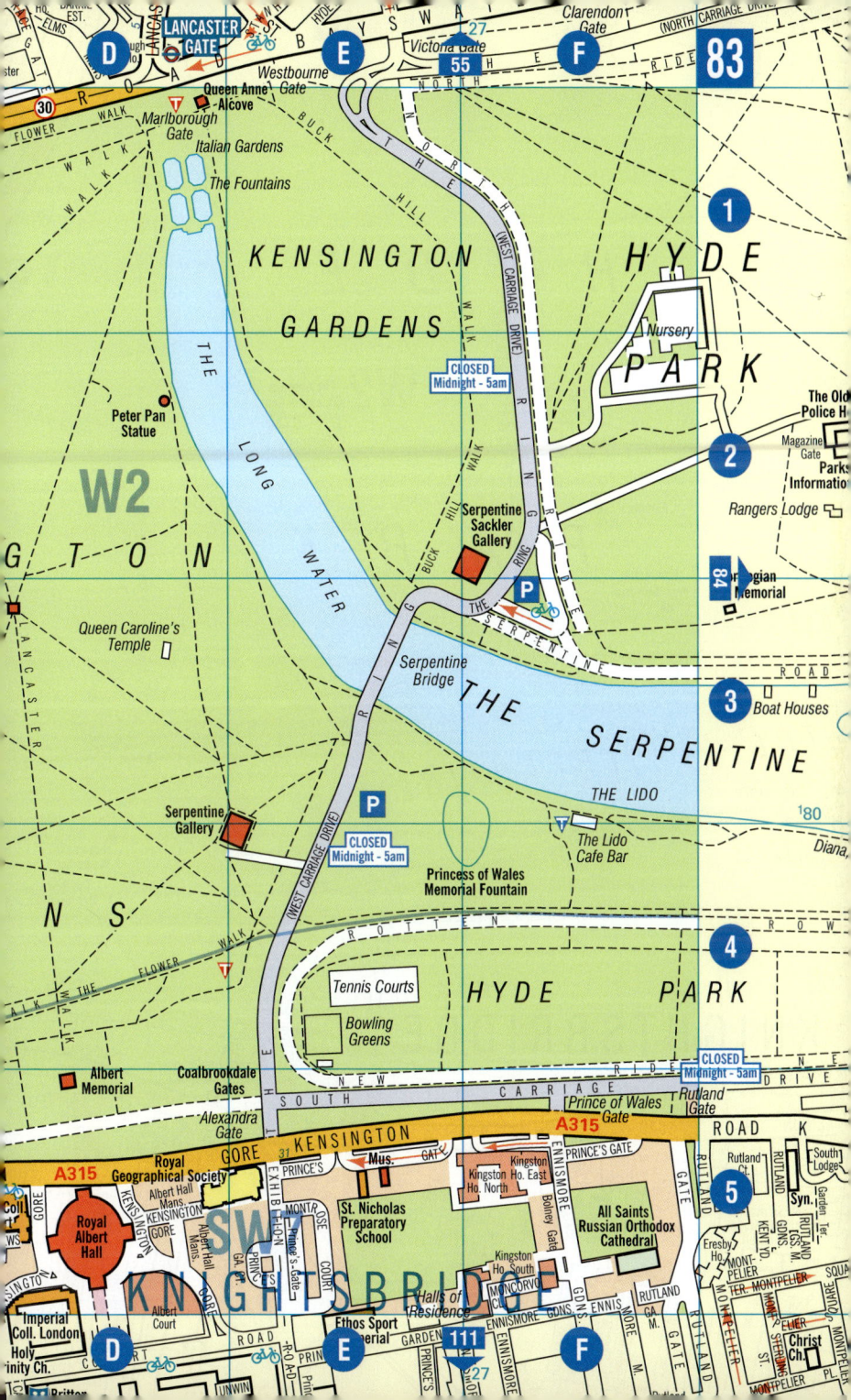

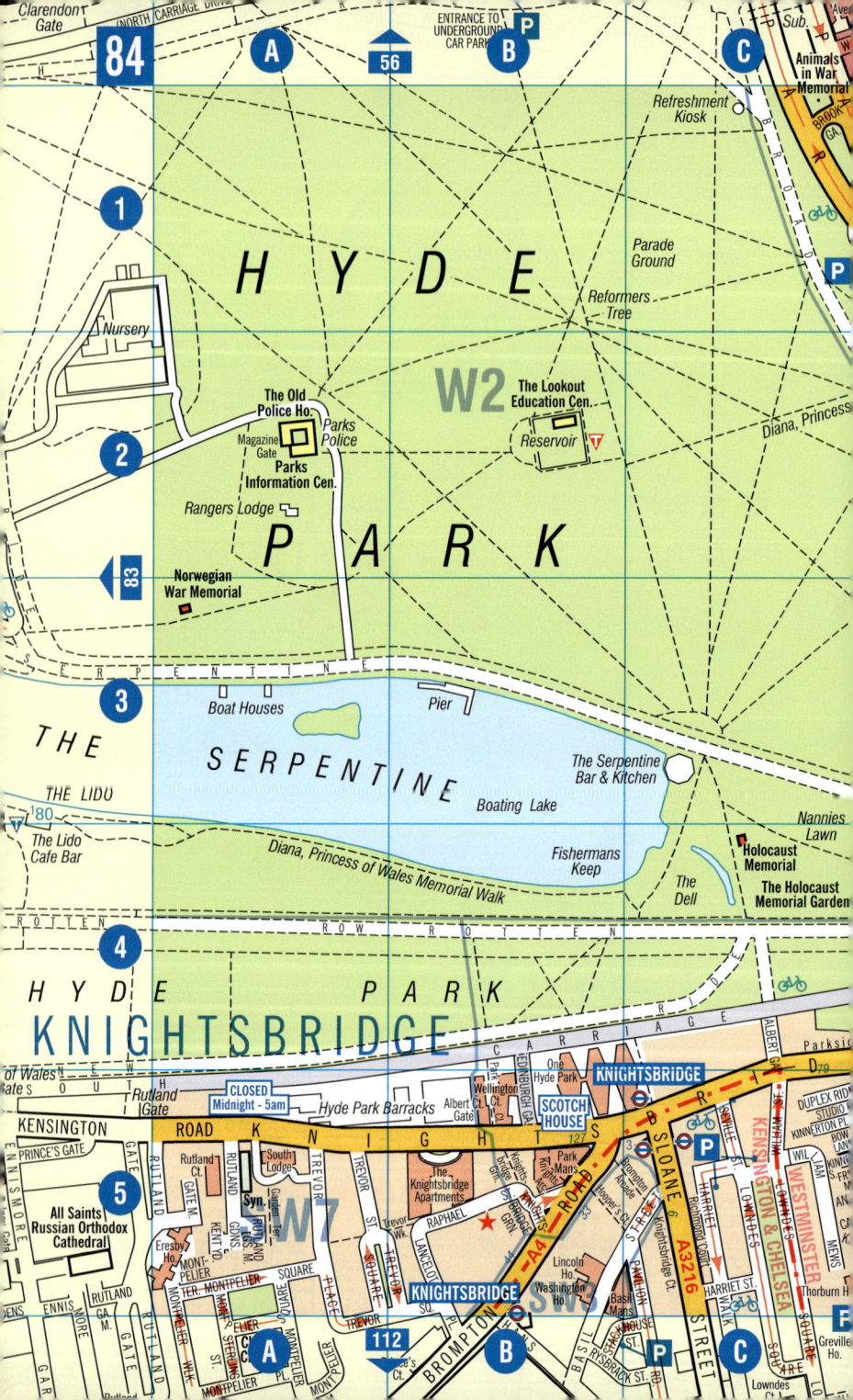

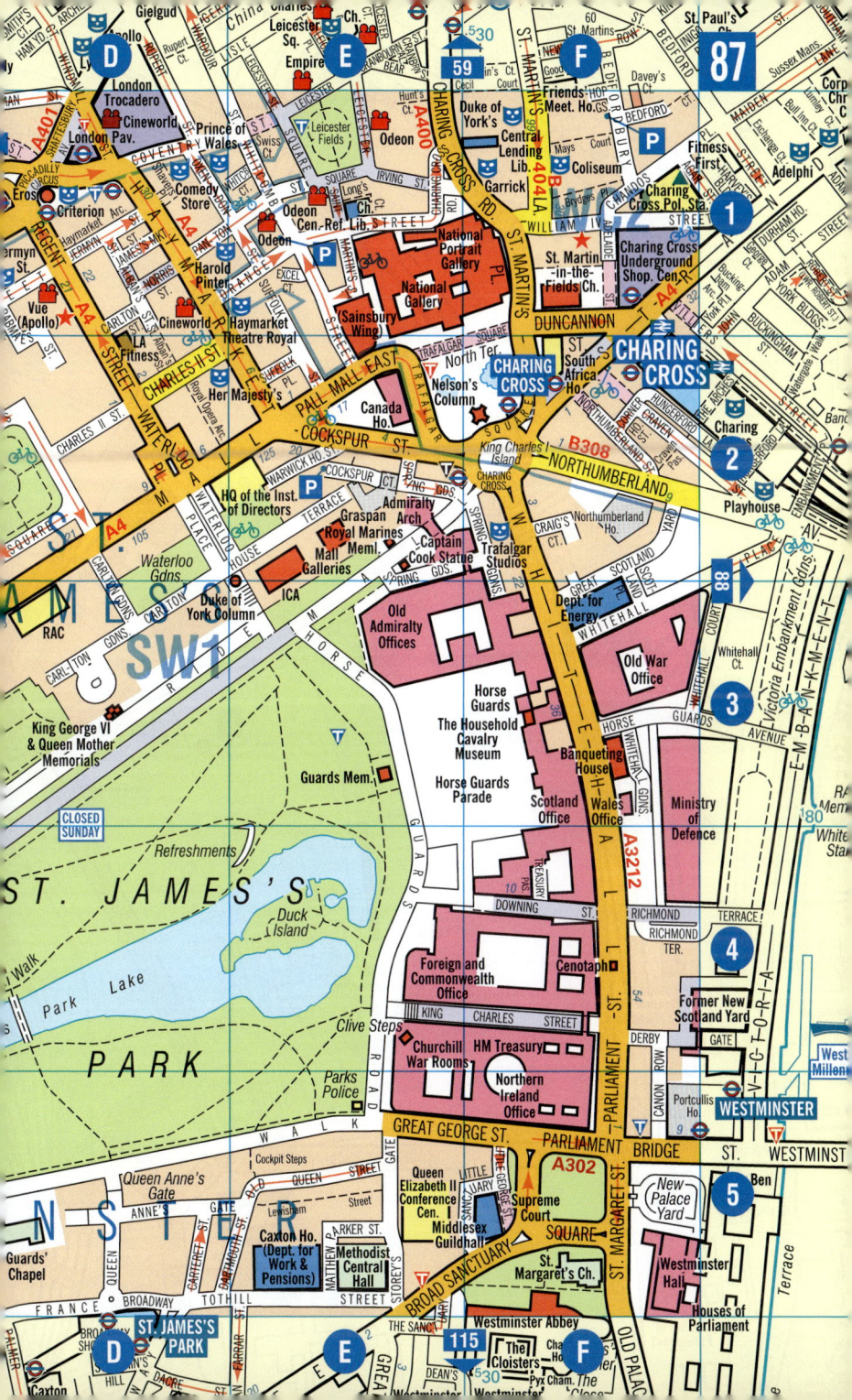

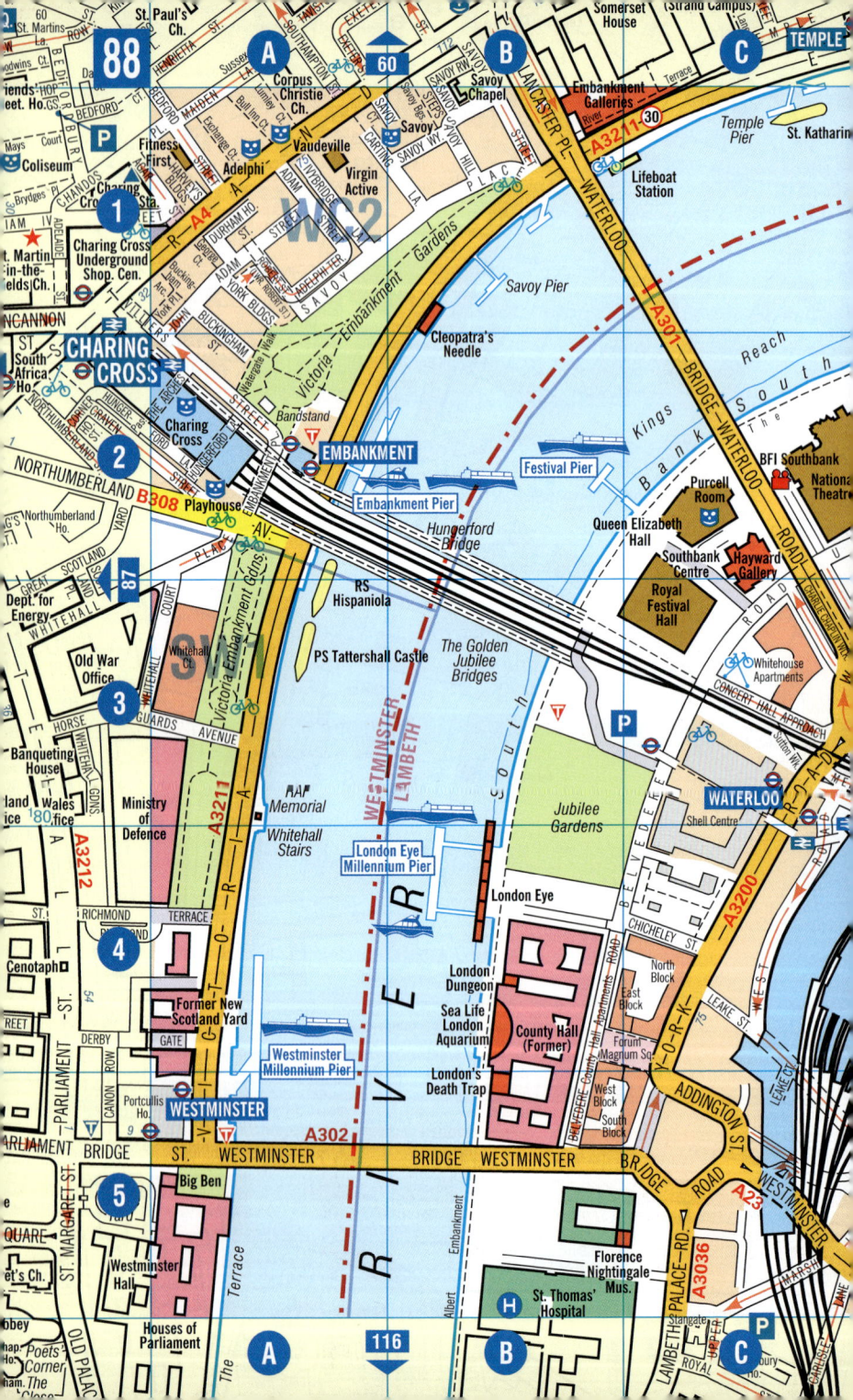

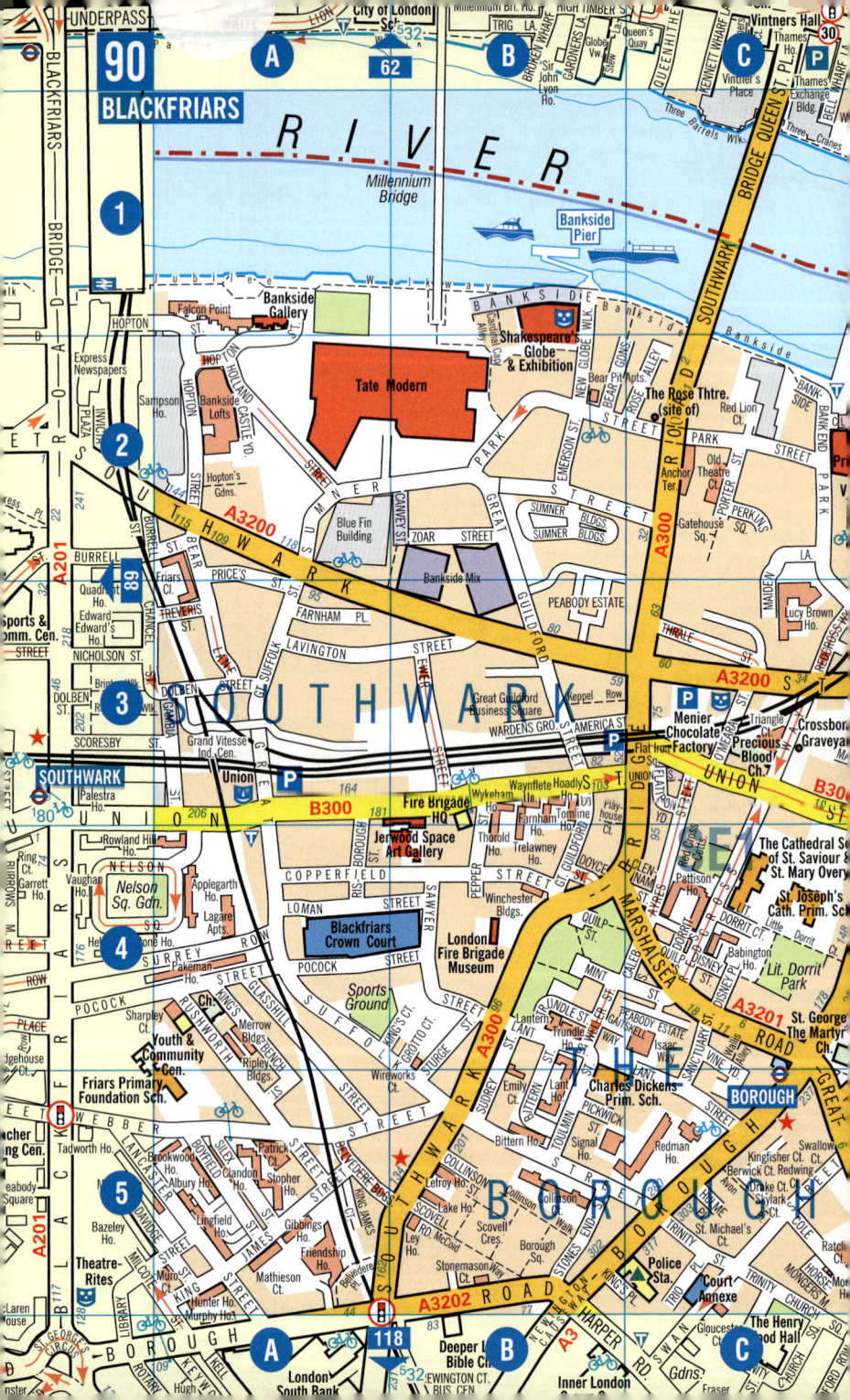

ROYAL ALBERT

D

E

42

75

DLR

F

ROAD

Newham Dockside

FESTOON

WAY

LYNX

A1020-BRIDGE

DOCKSIDE

London
Regatta Cen.

ROYAL ALBERT DOCK

1

CONNAUGHT-BRIDGE-C-O-N-N-A-U-G-H-T-

ROAD

A112

LONDON CITY AIRPORT

Terminal Building

2

✈

DLR

LONDON CITY
AIRPORT

104

D

CONNAUGHT

HARTMANN

CAMEL

DREW RD.

Royal
Connaught
Apartments

DREW RD.

Comm.
Cen.

ROAD

STREET

DREW

ROAD

ROAD

WHITES

DREW

ROAD

RD.

ROAD

SAVILLE ROAD

STREET

LEONARD

HOLT RD.

N
E
W
L

3

ROAD

A112

Works

Depot

ST MARKS
IND. EST.

ORIENTAL

ROAD

Brick La.
Music Hall

Lily Nichols
Ho.

William
Owston
Ct.

CONSTANCE ST

PARKER CL

PARKER

ST

Drew
Prim.
Sch.

ROAD

ALBERT

ROAD

80

George
Walk

Connaught
Heights

THAMES RD.

NORTH

WOOLWICH

ROAD

FACTORY

THAMESIDE
INDUSTRIAL ESTATE

SUGAR REFINERY

ROAD THAMES

ROAD

WARDS WHARF APPROACH

THAMES ROAD
INDUSTRIAL ESTATE

4

R E A C H

Conveyor

Jetty

T H A M E S

5

THAMES
BARRIER

NEWHAM

GREENWICH

D

E

42

F

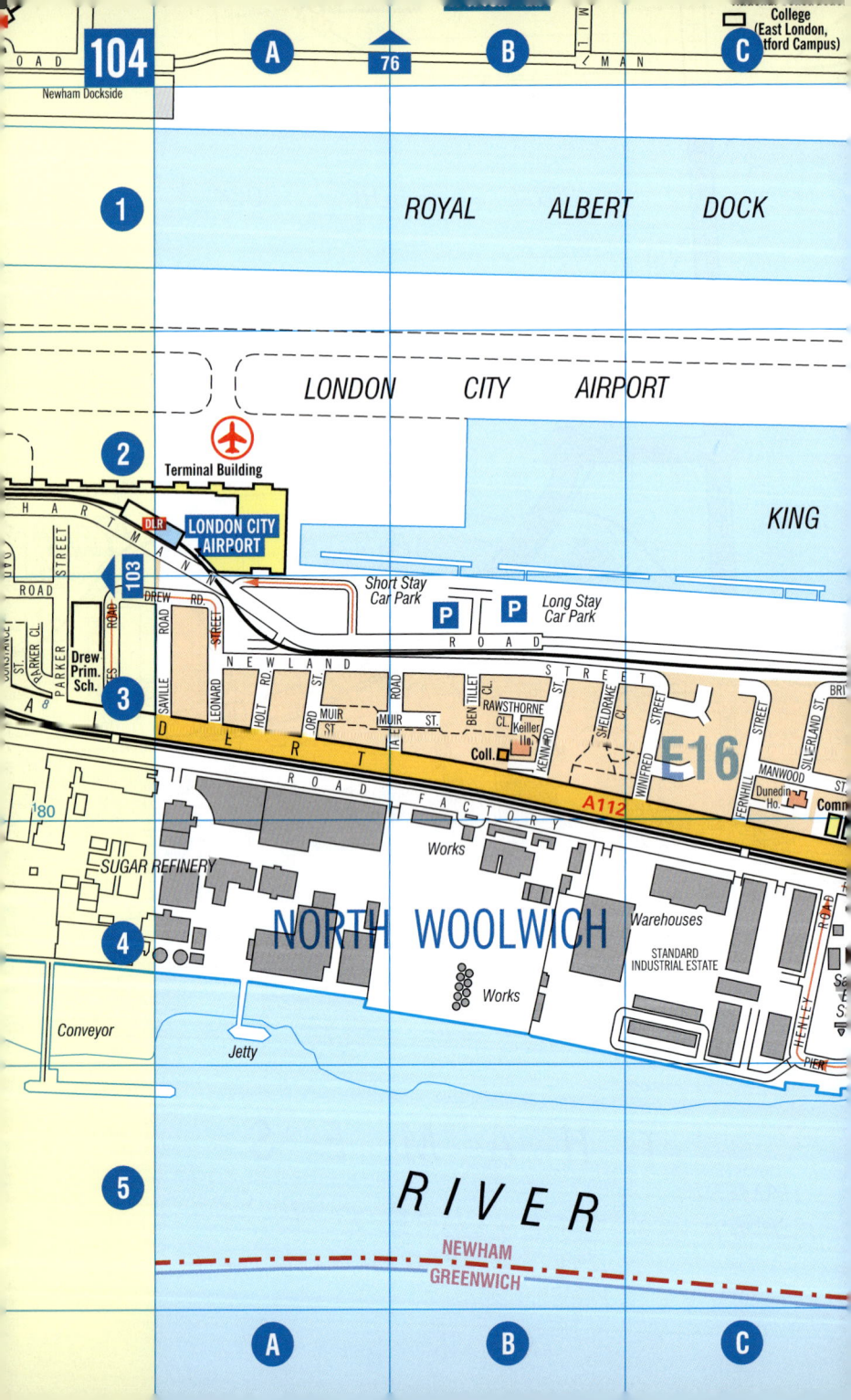

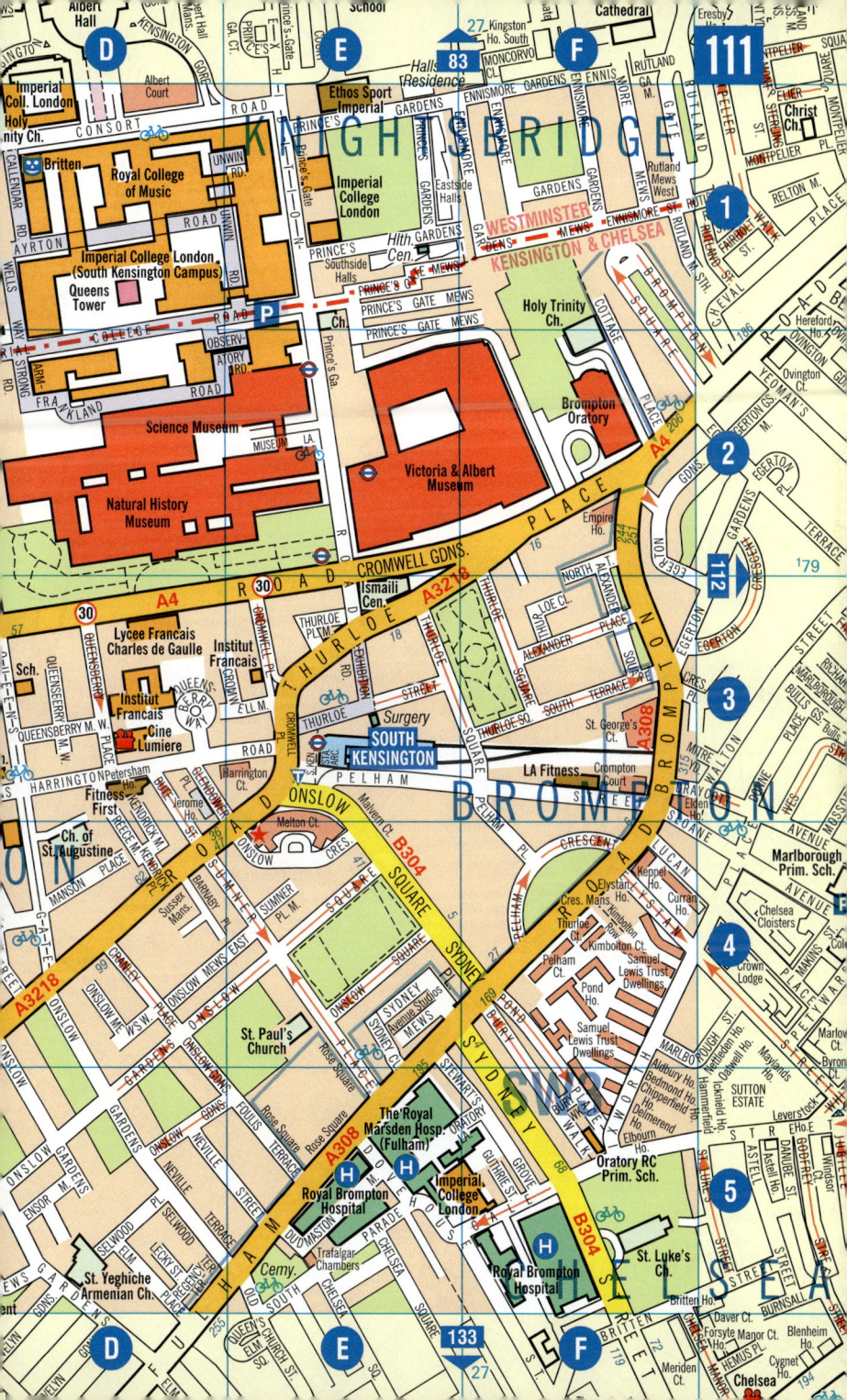

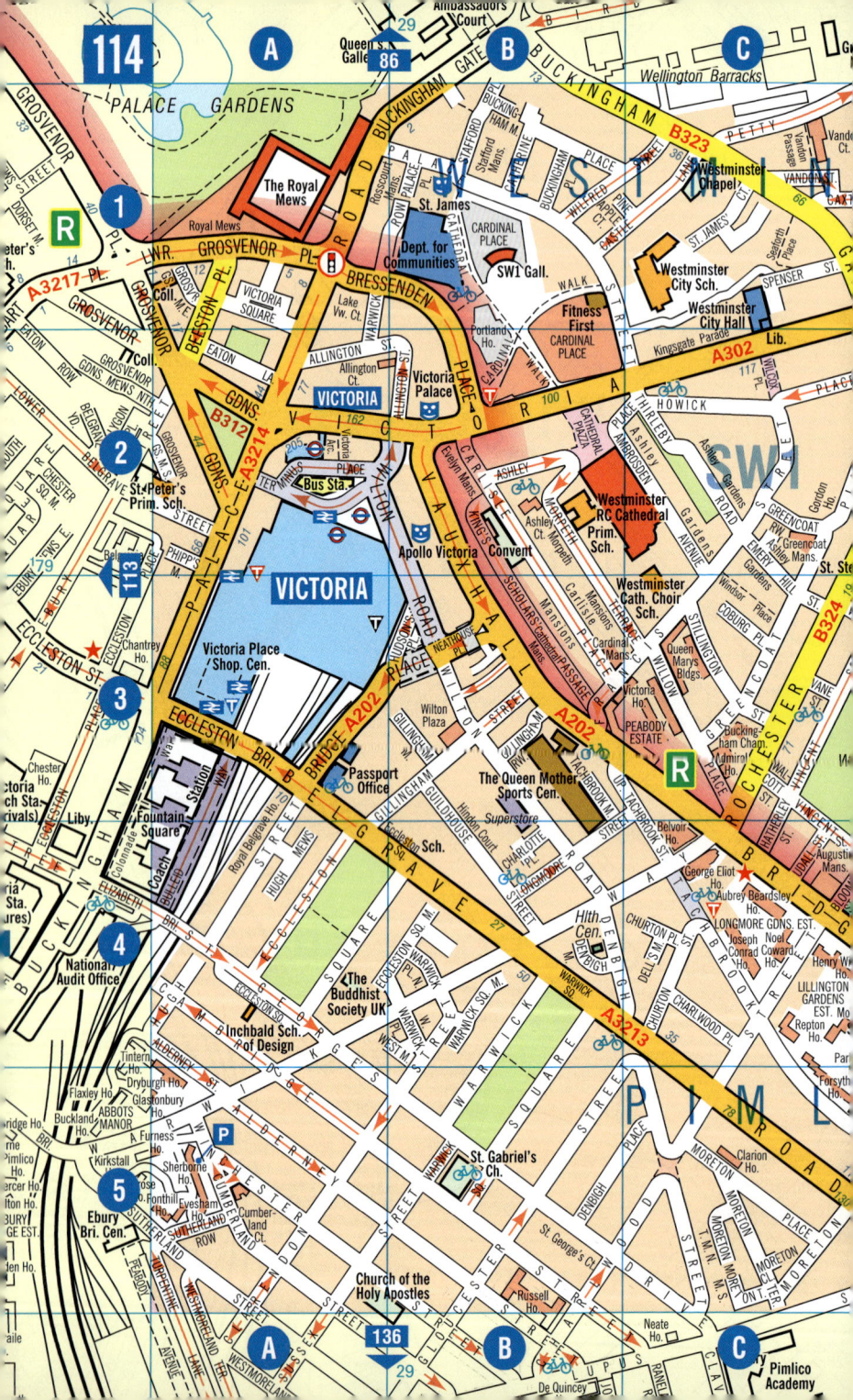

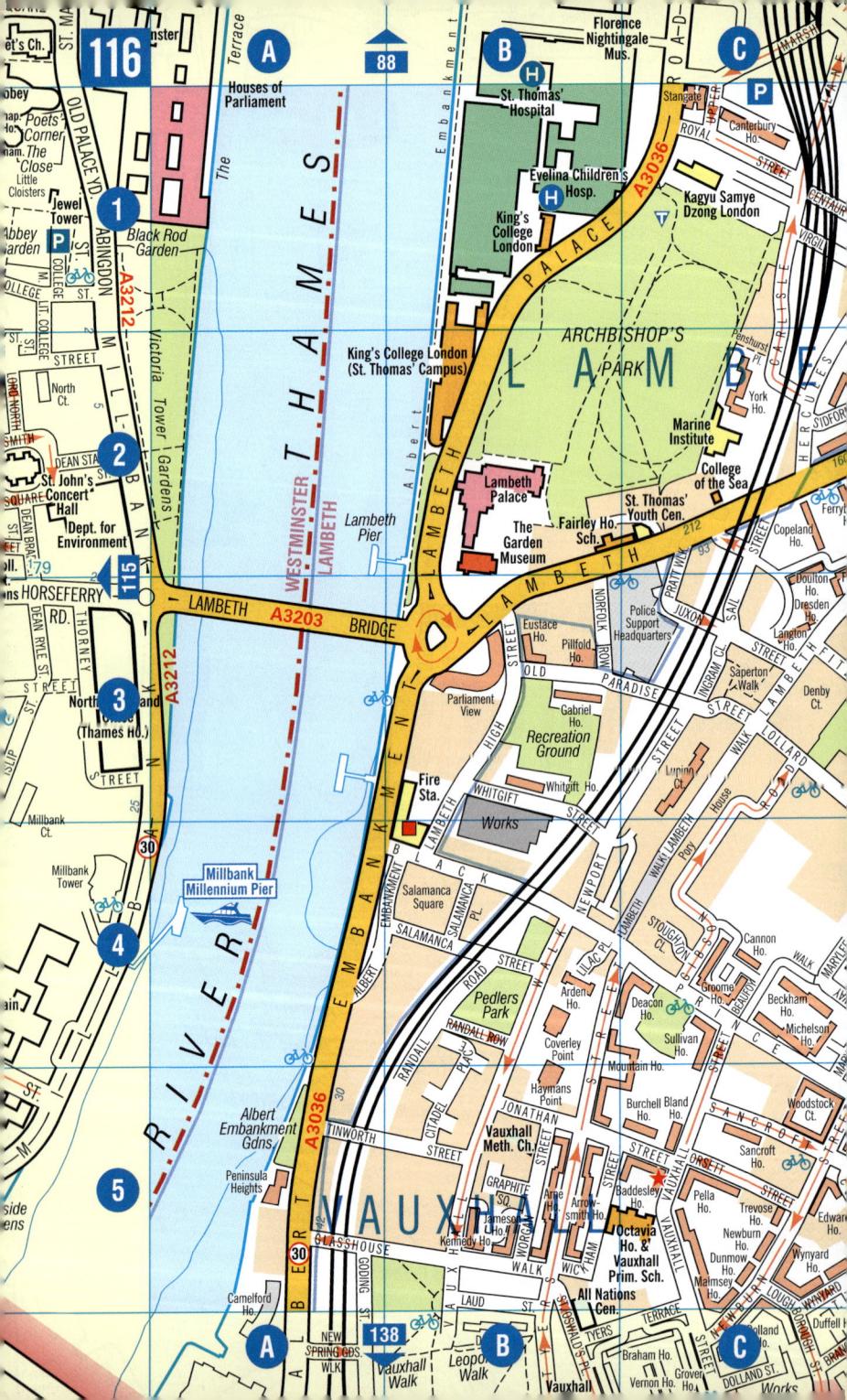

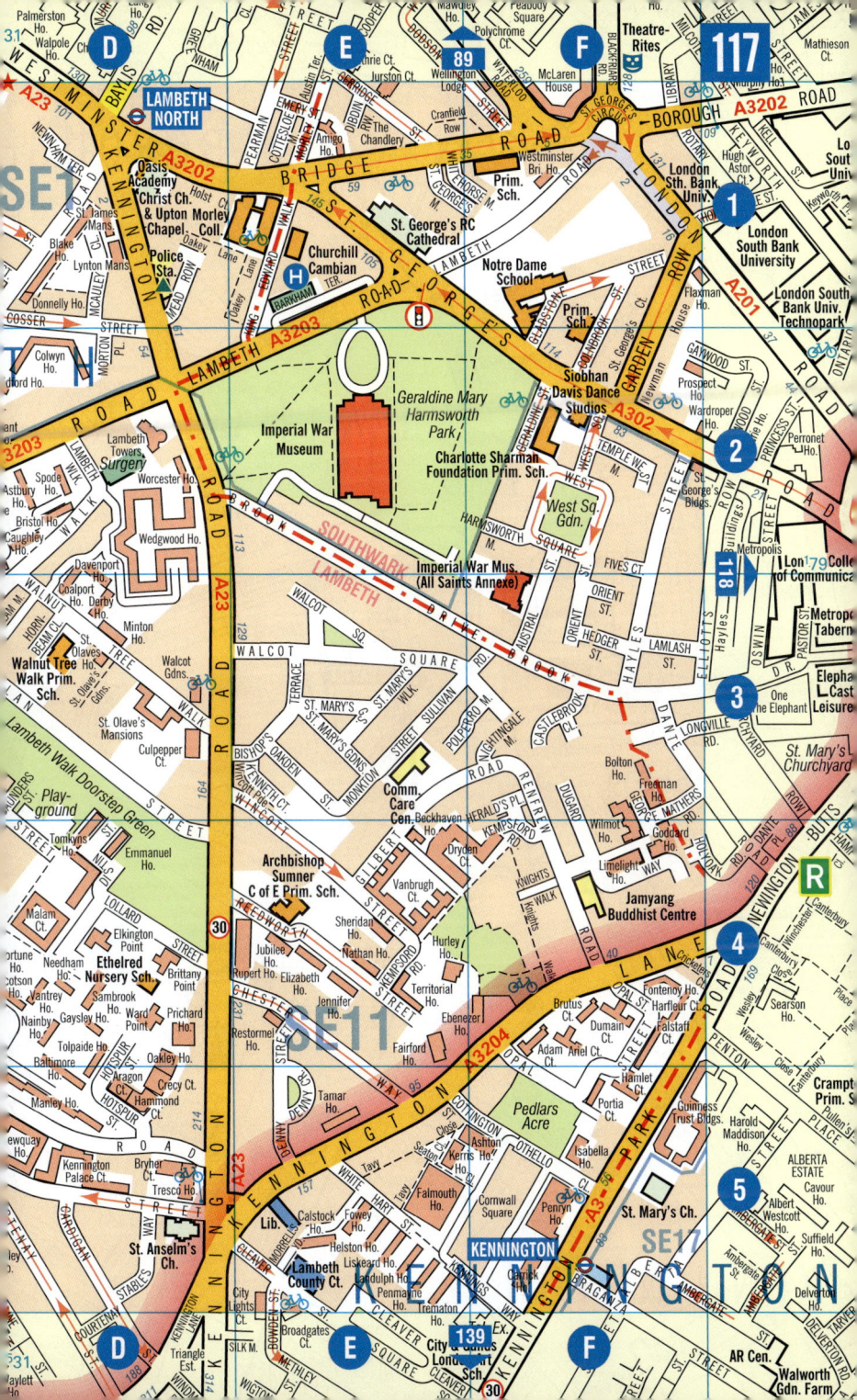

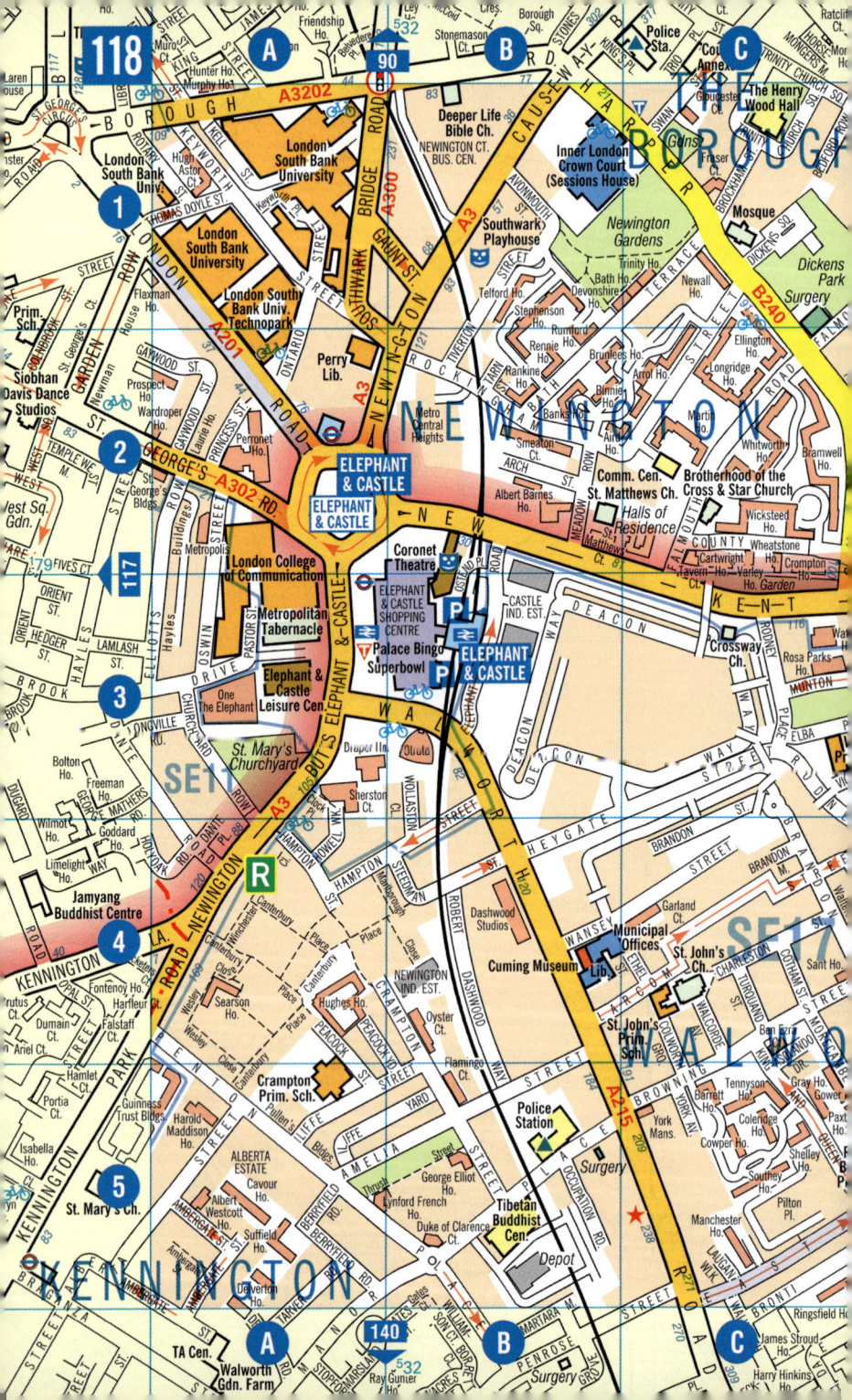

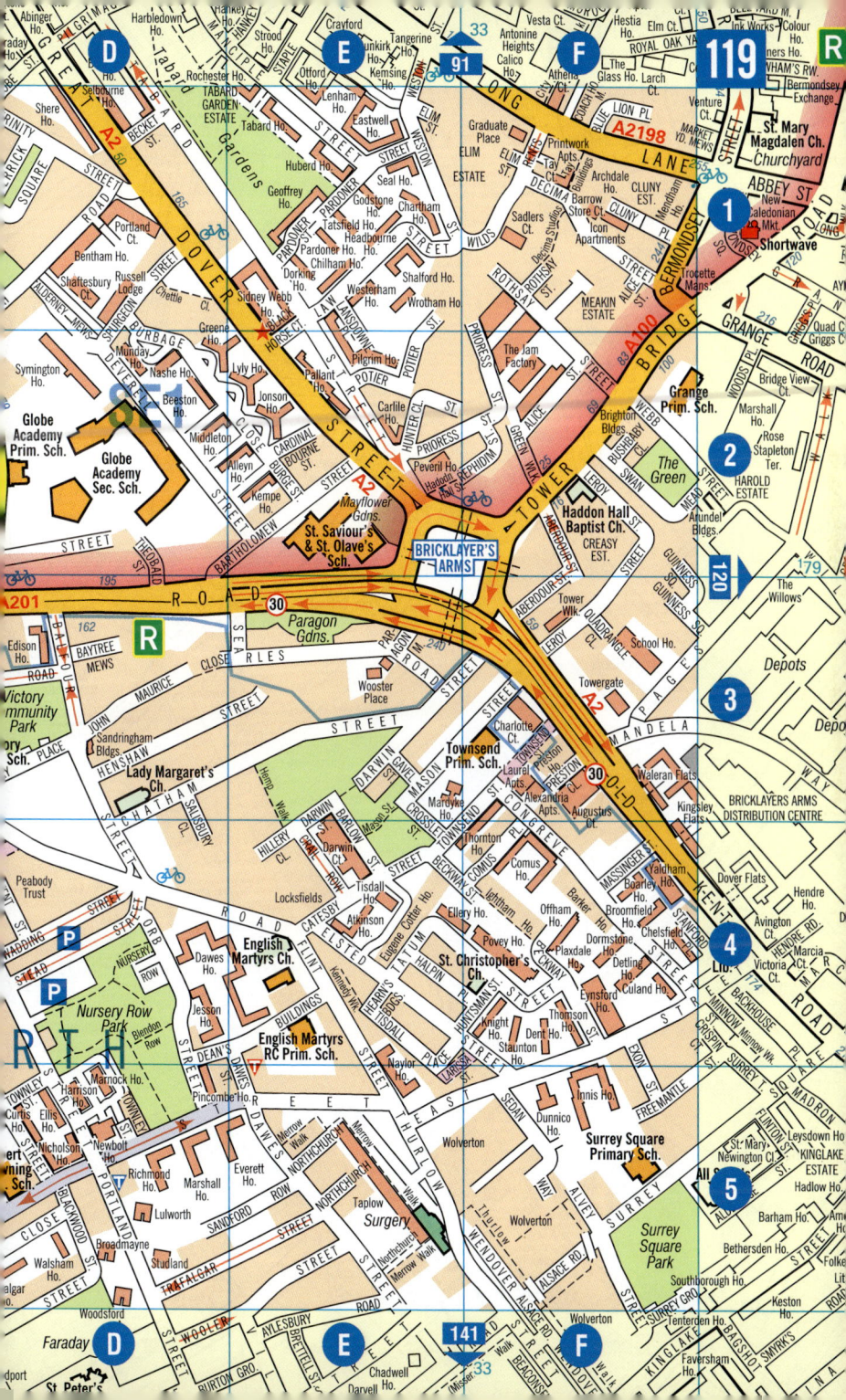

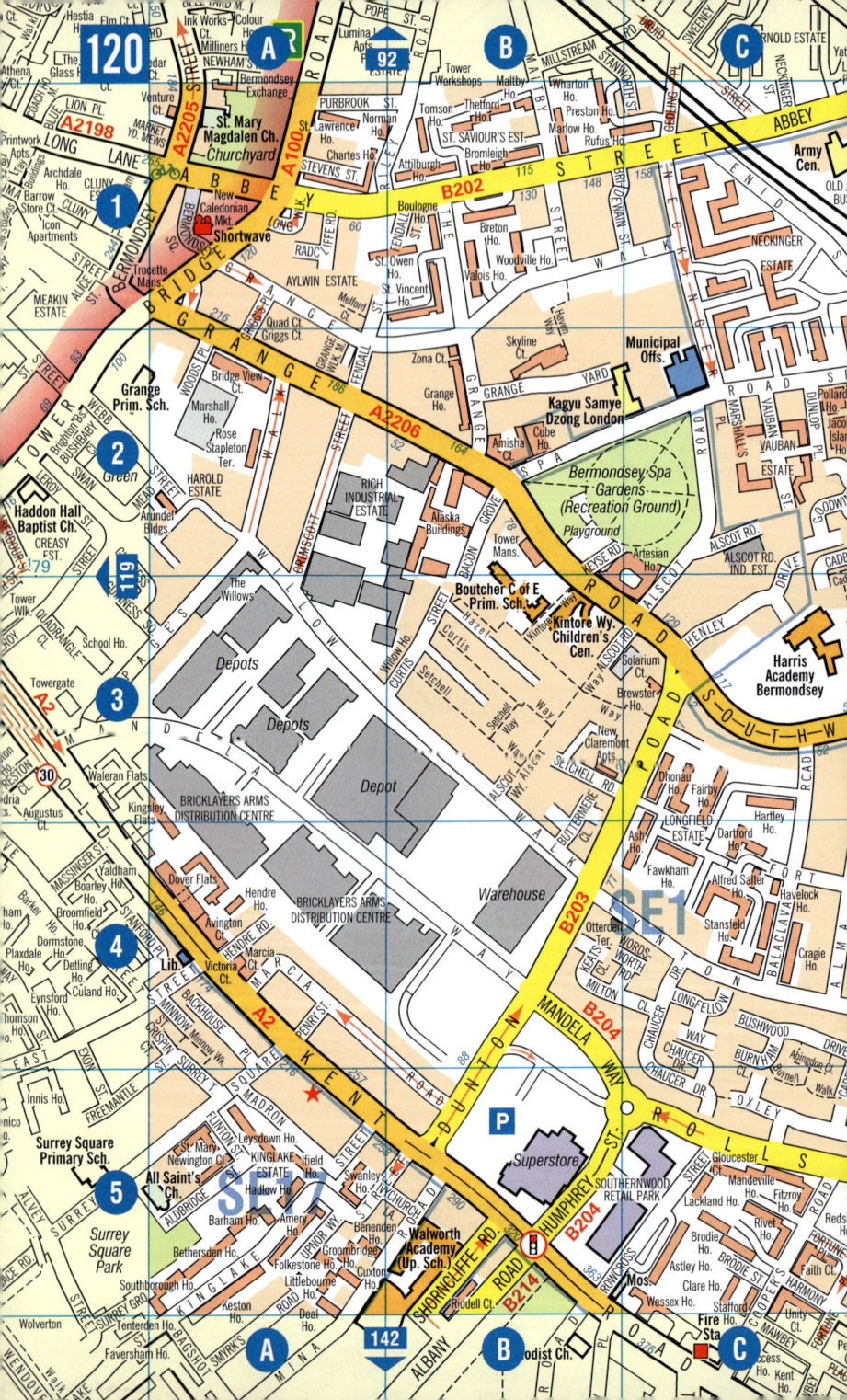

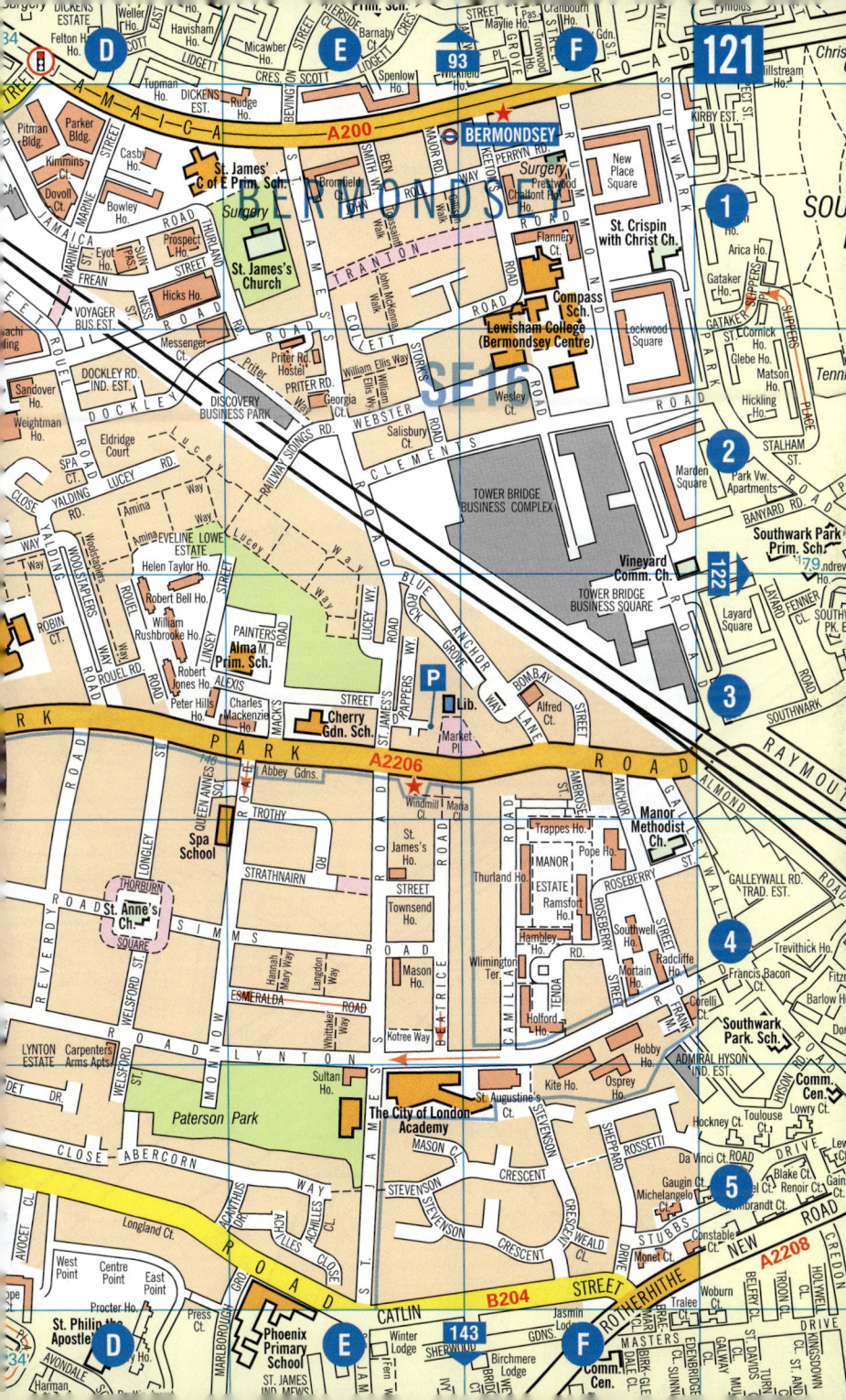

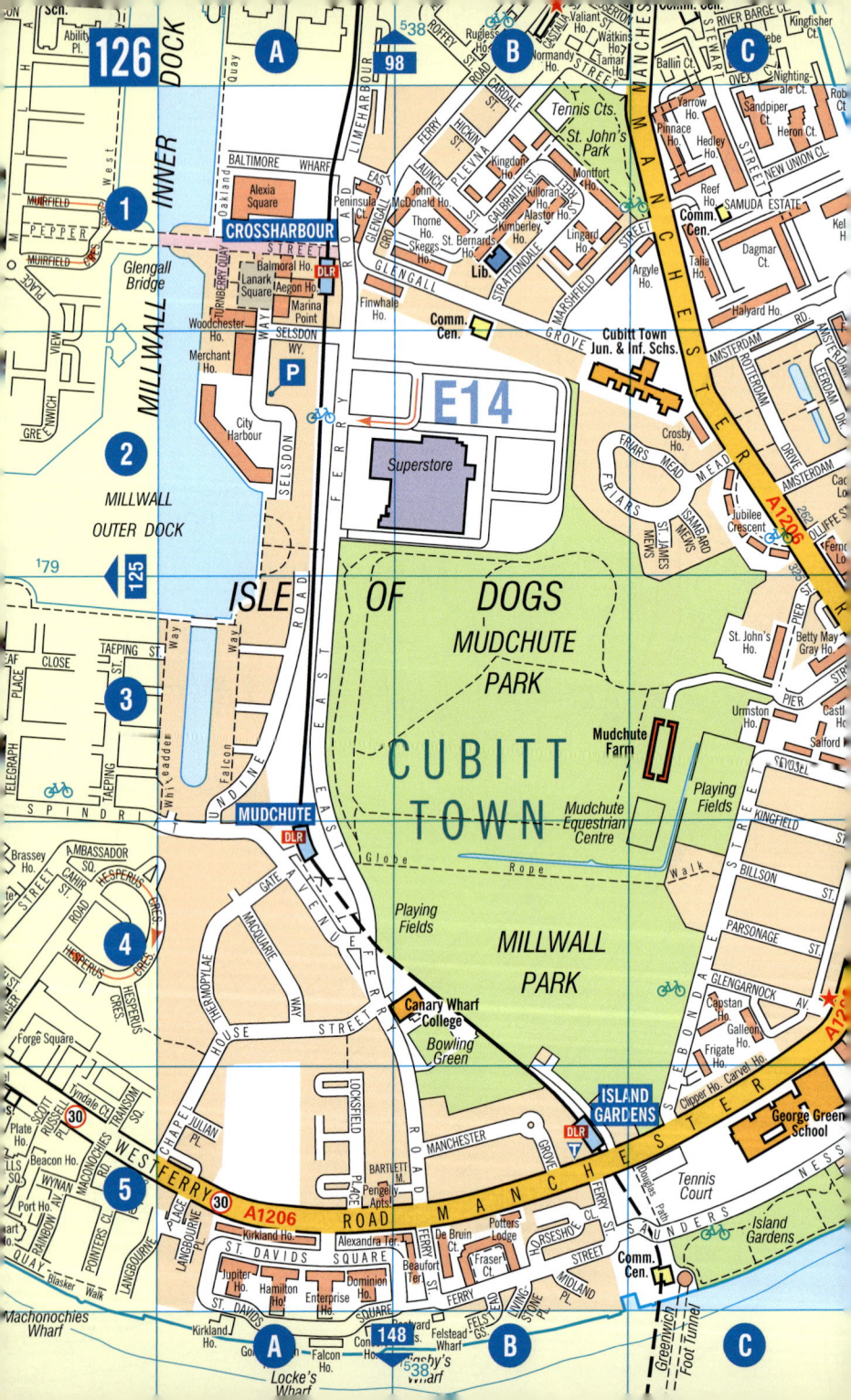

Gogh Ct.
Vermeer Cl.
EMBRAND CL.
MILLENNIUM
SCHOONER Cl.
Lymington Lodge
DRIVE
ulien dge ge
NNIUM
Lyndhurst Lodge
Fawley Lodge
th
CHICHESTER CL.
MARINERS WAY
BLYTH CL.
SAUNDERS
SEXTANT
NESS
MEWS
AVENUE
PLYMOUTH WHARF
FRANCIS CL.
ROAD
OBSER-
VATORY
MEWS
Pier

St. Luke's C of E Prim. Sch.
STORERS QUAY
Cubitt Town Wharf
CALEDONIAN WHARF
NESS
ROAD
GLENWORTH AV.
CALEDONIAN WHARF
Church rist and John
EMPIRE WHARF RD.
SAUNDERS
FRIC
GROSVENOR WHARF
GROSVENOR RD
ROAD
CUMBERLAND SQ.
Wharf
MILLS
Newcastle Drawdock

THAMES

TOWER HAMLETS
GREENWICH

RIVER

REACH

GREENWICH

Travelling Cranes

VICTORIA DEEP WATER TERMINAL

Slipways

Bay Wharf

Walk

Riverside

Riverside Walk

Enderby's Wharf

CRONDALL CRES
PAVILION
A-D-M-I-R-A-L-...
TUNNEL APPROACH
AVENUE
M-I-L-L-E-N-N-I-U-M
A102
BLACKWALL
30
TUNNEL
SOUTHERN APPROACH
TUNNEL
BOORD STREET
WAY
DR...

Gas Works
Lorry Park

1

Primrose Wharf

MORDEN WHARF ROAD
MORDEN WHARF

Glucose Refineries

2

128
79

Warehouse

SE10

3

SALU
CITY CROSS BUSINESS PAR

Wor

Piper's Wharf
Providence Warehouse

Samuel Wallis Lodge
Ernest Shackleton Lodge

Sir Walter Raleigh Ct.

4

MAURITIUS
AZOF
STREET
YELL M.
STREET
WAY
STREET
CALLISONS PL.

Christ Chu C of E Prim.

DERWENT ST.

Granite Wharf
Cadet
Place
Lovell's Wharf
Sir Francis Drake Ct.
RIVERSIDE QUAY
Anchor Iron Wharf
BALLAST
Merchants
STAIRS COURT
LINDON
DERRY
BALLAST QUAY

PELTON
BANNING
CARADOC
BRADDYL
ROWLEY
GIBSON

ST. HUNSDON
HADRIAN STREET
STREET

FLA
Depot Gdns.
St. Joseph's Prim. Sc
Earl
Ch

5

CHRISTCHURCH
WOOLWICH ROAD
ROAD
COMMERELL
EARL...

Comm. Cen.
Christchurch 'Forum'
★

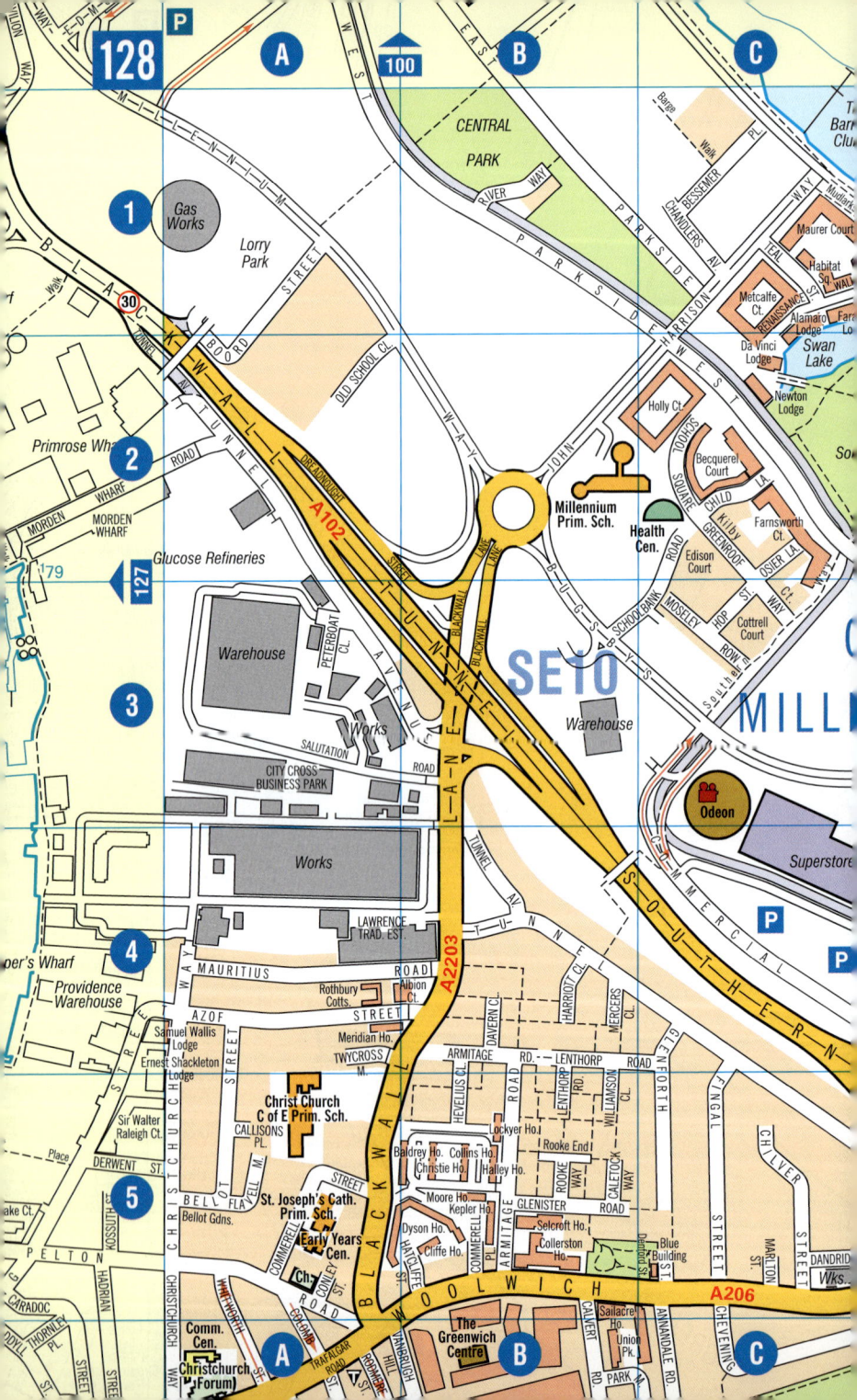

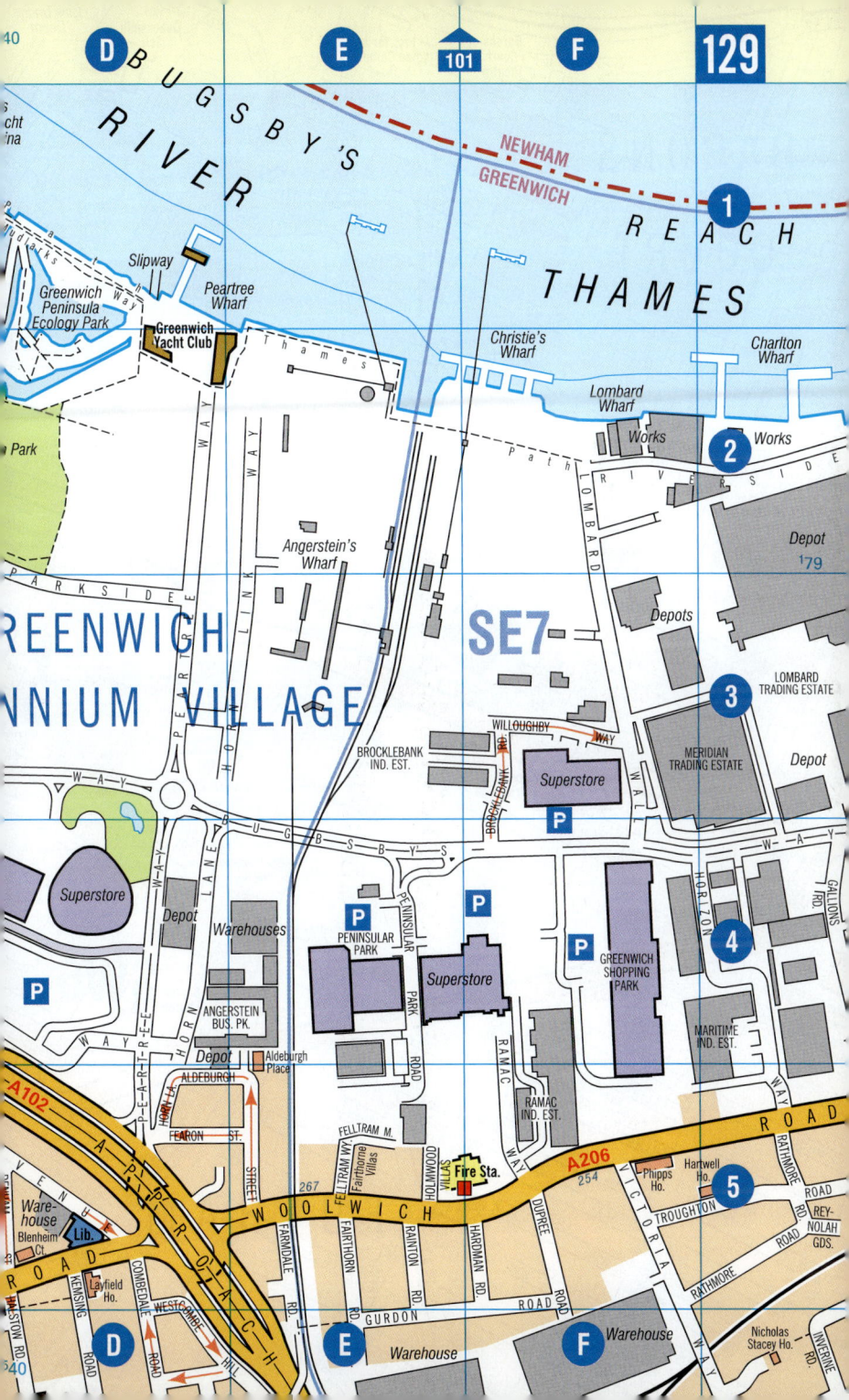

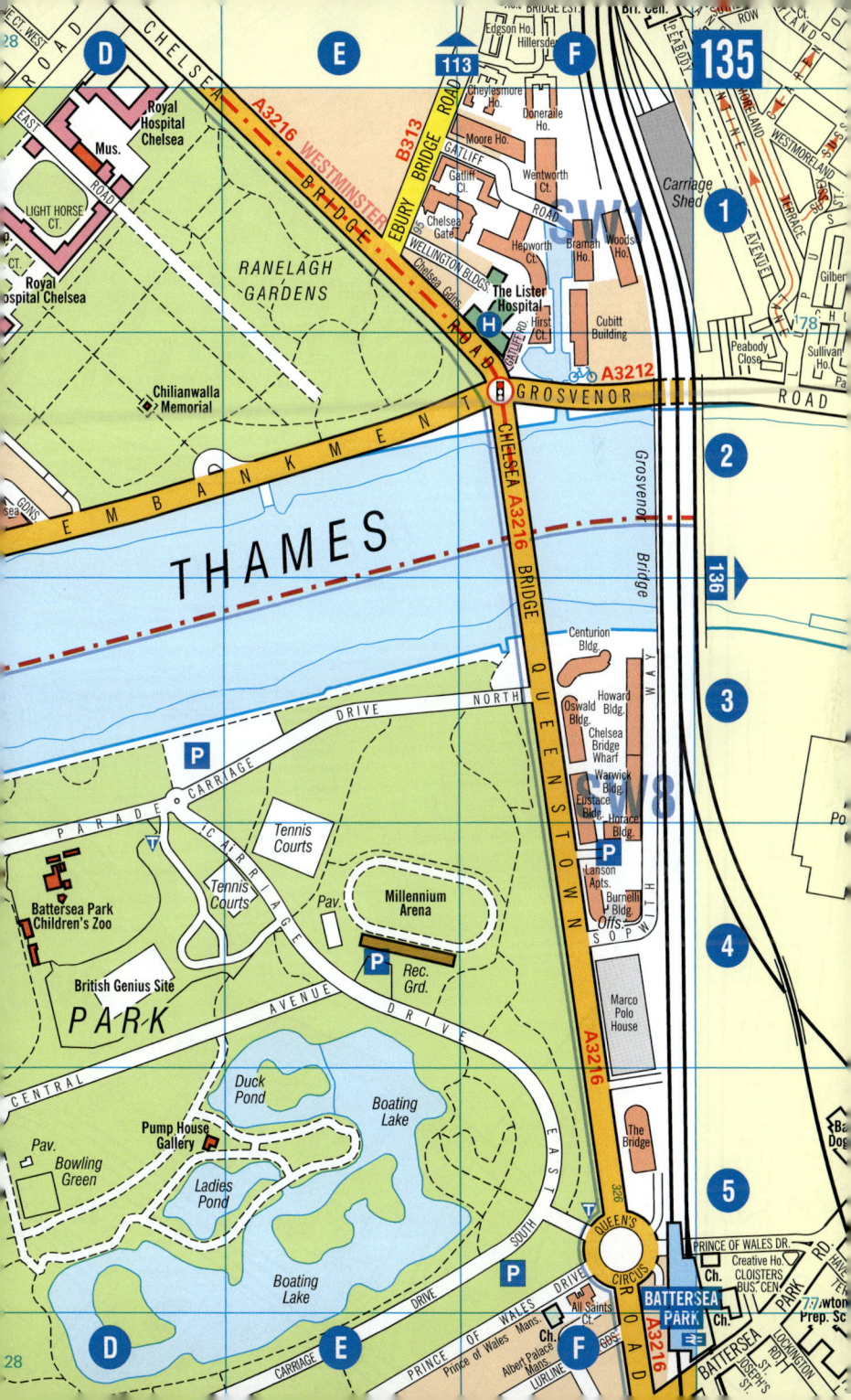

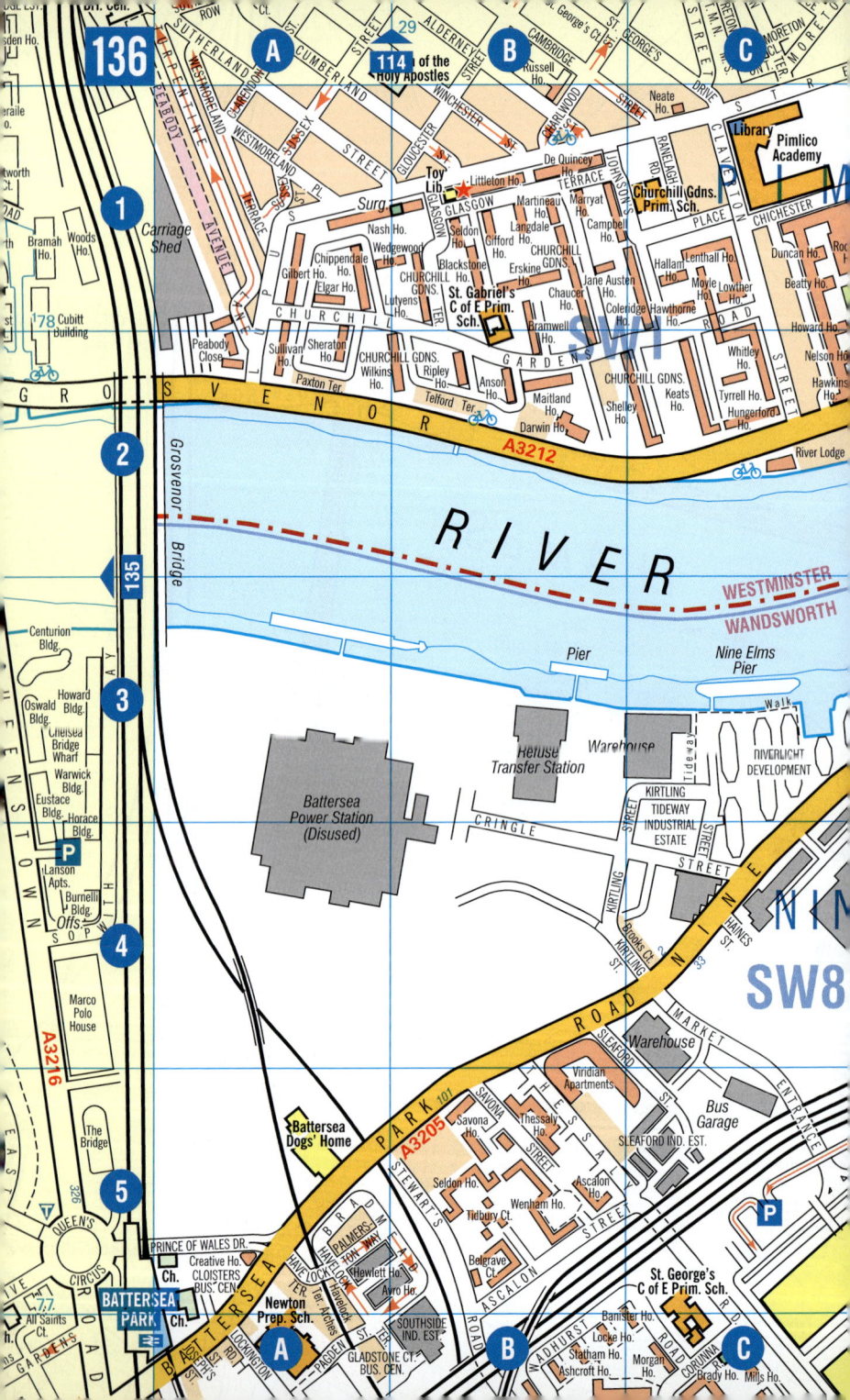

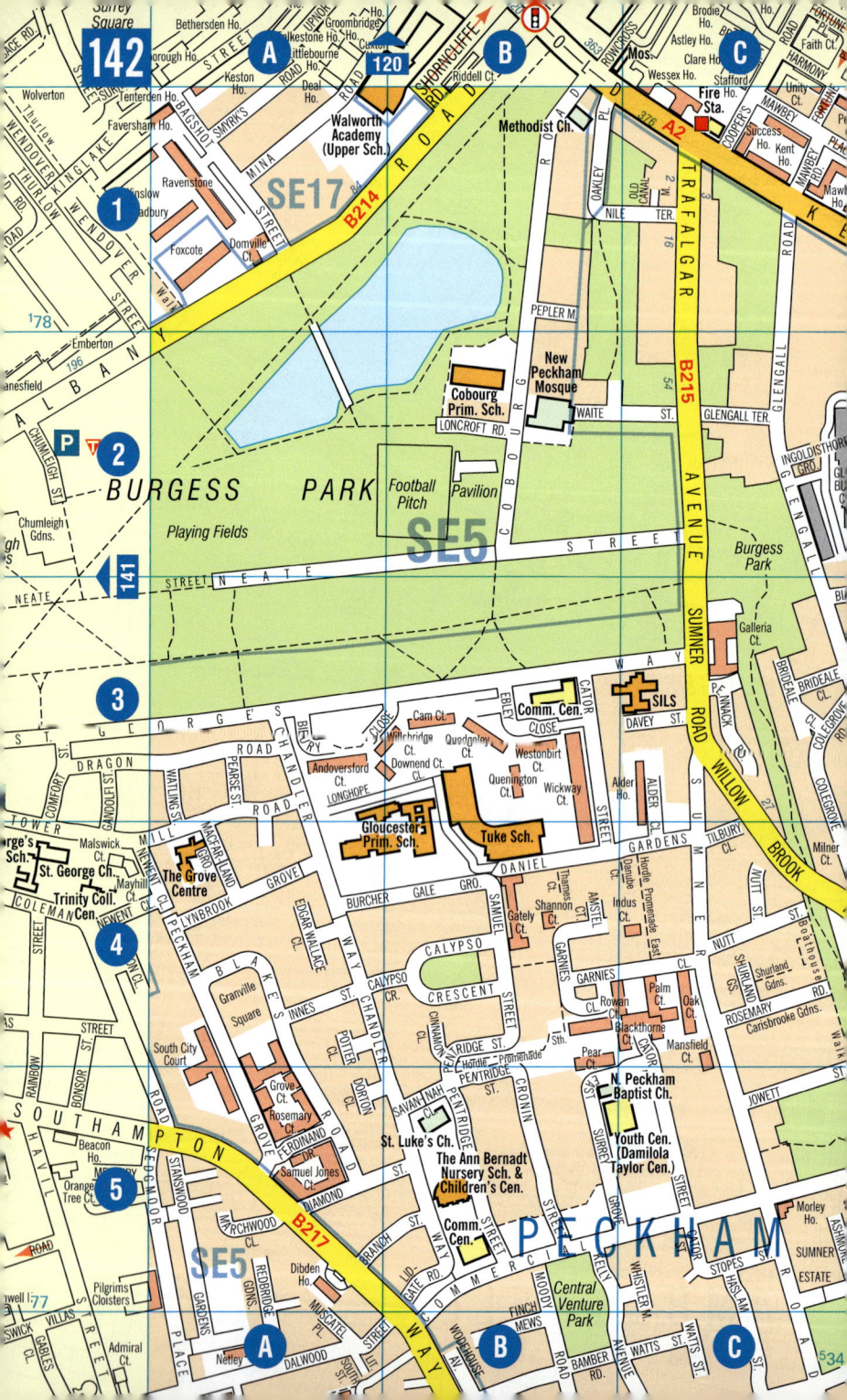

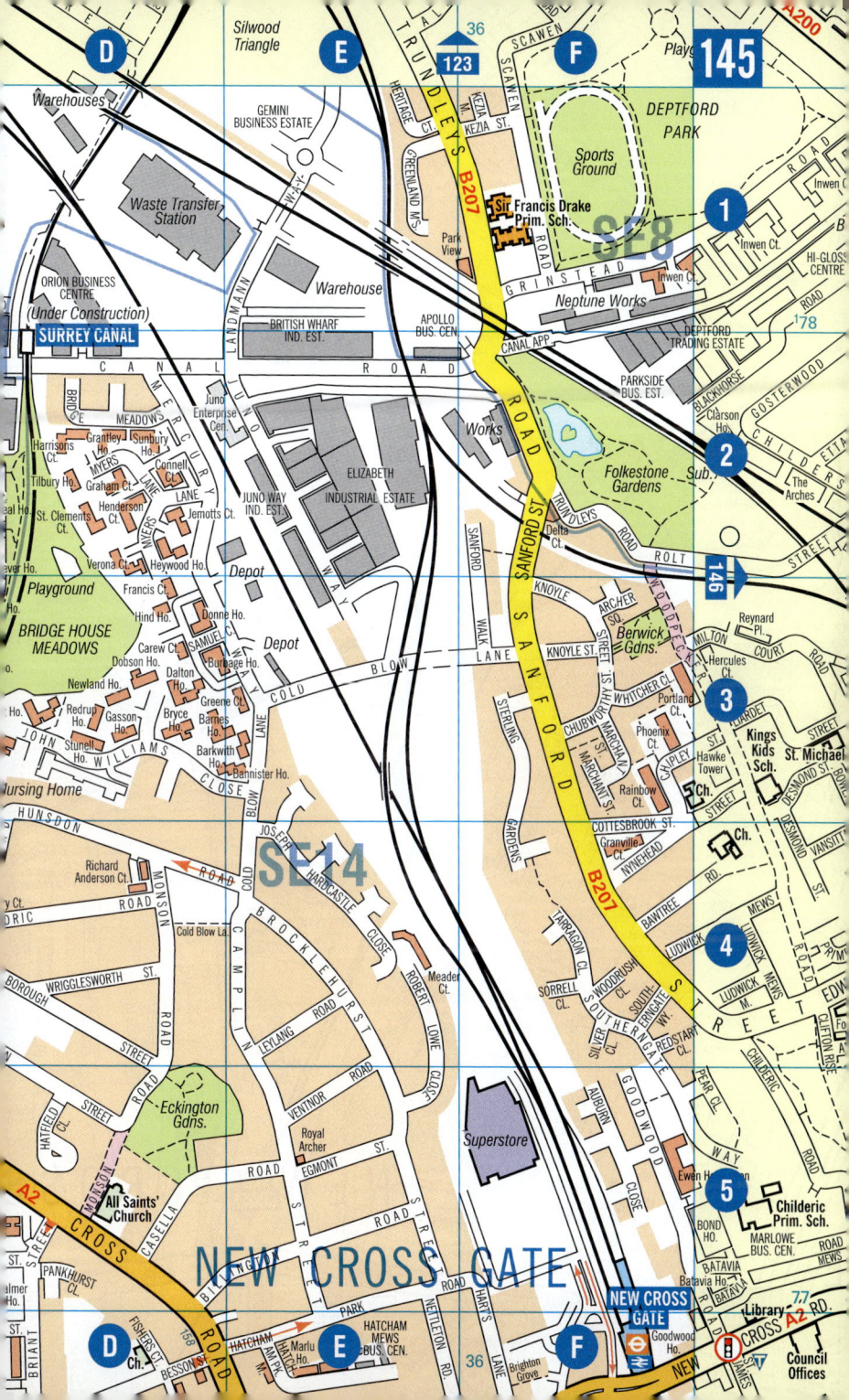

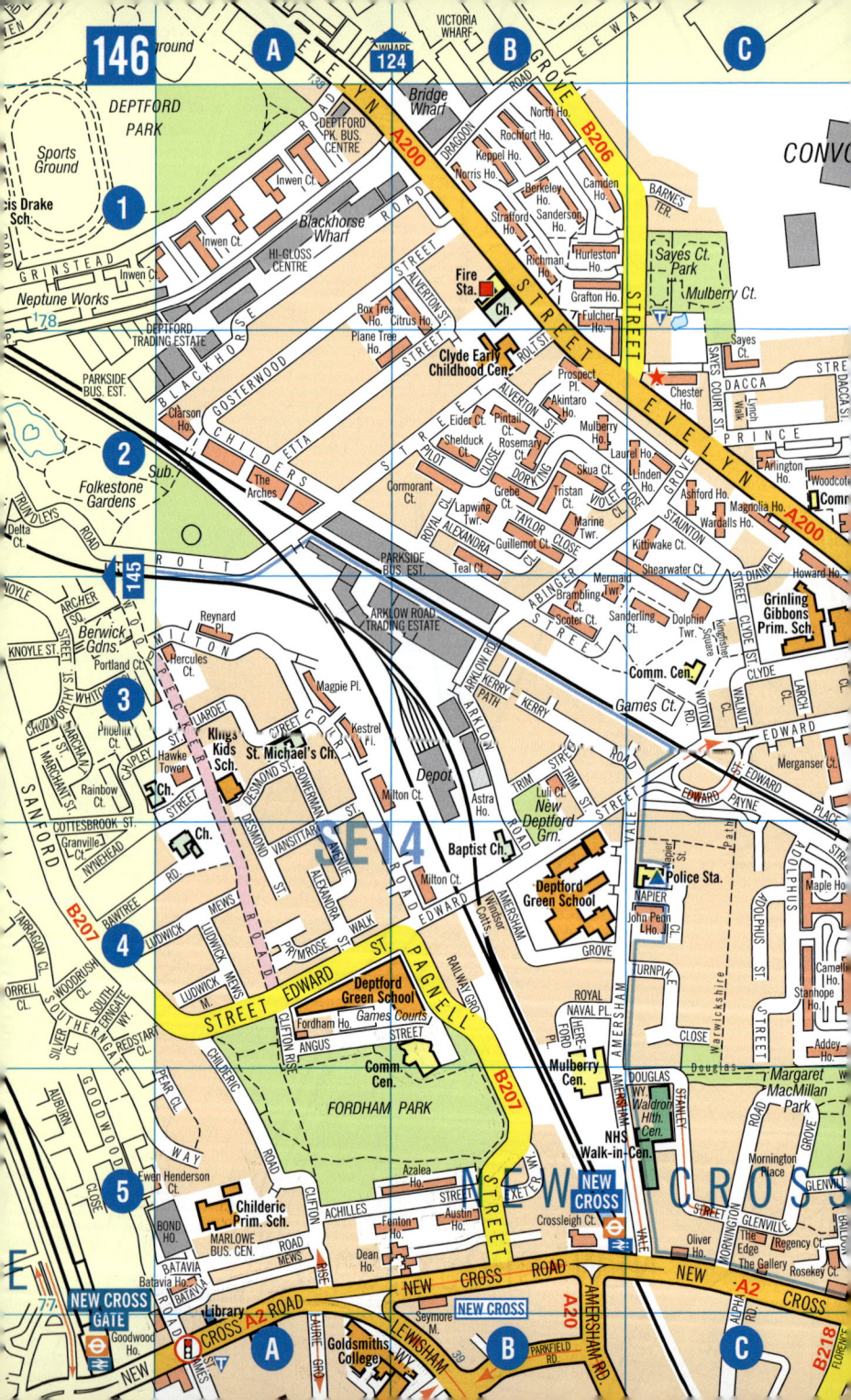

Including Streets, Places & Areas, Industrial Estates,
Selected Flats & Walkways, Junction Names and Selected Places of Interest.

HOW TO USE THIS INDEX

1. Each street name is followed by its Postcode District and then by its map reference;
   e.g. **Abbey Rd.** E15 . . . . .4F **27** is in the E15 Postcode and is to be found in square 4F on page **27**.
   The page number being shown in bold type.

2. A strict alphabetical order is followed in which Av., Rd., St., etc. (though abbreviated) are read in full and
   as part of the street name; e.g. **Allsop Pl.** appears after **All Saints St.** but before **All Souls Av.**

3. Streets and a selection of flats and walkways that cannot be shown on the mapping, appear in the index with
   the thoroughfare to which they are connected shown in brackets;
   e.g. **Ada Maria Ct.** *E1* . . . .4A *66* (off James Voller Way)

4. Addresses that are in more than one part are referred to as not continuous.

5. Places and areas are shown in the index in **BLUE TYPE** and the map reference is to the actual map square in
   which the town centre or area is located and not to the place name shown on the map;
   e.g. **BARNSBURY 2B 16**

6. An example of a selected place of interest is **Alexander Fleming Laboratory Mus. 3E 55**

7. Junction names are shown in the index in **BOLD CAPITAL TYPE**; e.g. **ALDGATE 4C 64**

GENERAL ABBREVIATIONS

All. : Alley
App. : Approach
Arc. : Arcade
Av. : Avenue
Bk. : Back
Blvd. : Boulevard
Bri. : Bridge
B'way. : Broadway
Bldg. : Building
Bldgs. : Buildings
Bus. : Business
C'way. : Causeway
Cen. : Centre
Chu. : Church
Chyd. : Churchyard
Circ. : Circle
Cir. : Circus
Cl. : Close
Coll. : College
Comn. : Common
Cnr. : Corner
Cotts. : Cottages
Ct. : Court
Cres. : Crescent
Cft. : Croft
Dpt. : Depot
Dr. : Drive
E. : East

Emb. : Embankment
Ent. : Enterprise
Est. : Estate
Flds. : Fields
Gdn. : Garden
Gdns. : Gardens
Ga. : Gate
Gt. : Great
Grn. : Green
Gro. : Grove
Hgts. : Heights
Ho. : House
Ho's. : Houses
Ind. : Industrial
Info. : Information
Junc. : Junction
La. : Lane
Lit. : Little
Lwr. : Lower
Mnr. : Manor
Mans. : Mansions
Mkt. : Market
Mdws. : Meadows
M. : Mews
Mt. : Mount
Mus. : Museum
Nth. : North
Pal. : Palace

Pde. : Parade
Pk. : Park
Pas. : Passage
Pav. : Pavilion
Pl. : Place
Pct. : Precinct
Prom. : Promenade
Ri. : Rise
Rd. : Road
Rdbt. : Roundabout
Shop. : Shopping
Sth. : South
Sq. : Square
Sta. : Station
St. : Street
Ter. : Terrace
Twr. : Tower
Trad. : Trading
Up. : Upper
Va. : Vale
Vw. : View
Vs. : Villas
Vis. : Visitors
Wlk. : Walk
W. : West
Yd. : Yard

2 Temple Place 5D **61**
7/7 Memorial
. . . . .3E **85**
18 Stafford Terrace
   The Sambourne Family Home
. . . . .5D **81**
60 St Martins La.
   WC2 . . . . .5F **59**

201 Bishopsgate
   EC2 . . . . .1A **64**

A

Aaron Hill Rd. E6 . . . . .1E **77**
Abady Ho. SW1 . . . . .3E **115**
Abbess Cl. E6 . . . . .2A **76**
Abbey Ct. NW8 . . . . .5B **10**
   SE17 . . . . .1C **140**

Abbey Est. NW8 . . . . .4A **10**
Abbeyfield Est. SE16 . . . . .3B **122**
Abbeyfield Rd. SE16 . . . . . .3B **122**
   (not continuous)
Abbey Gdns. NW8 . . . . .1B **32**
   SE16 . . . . .3E **121**
   W6 . . . . .2A **130**
Abbey Ho. E15 . . . . .5F **27**
   NW8 . . . . .2C **32**
Abbey La. E15 . . . . .5C **26**
   (not continuous)

Abbey La. Commercial Est.
  E15 . . . . .5F **27**
Abbey Life Ct. E16 . . . . . .1A **74**
Abbey Lodge NW8 . . . . . .3A **34**
Abbey Orchard St. SW1 . .1D **115**
Abbey Orchard St. Est.
  SW1 . . . . .1E **115**
          (not continuous)
Abbey Rd. E15 . . . . .4F **27**
  NW6 . . . . .2F **9**
  NW8 . . . . .3A **10**
Abbey Rd. Apartments
  NW8 . . . . .1C **32**
Abbey St. SE1 . . . . .1A **120**
Abbot Ct. SW8 . . . . .5F **137**
Abbot Ho. E14 . . . . .5A **70**
Abbotsbury NW1 . . . . . . .2D **15**
Abbotsbury Cl. E15 . . . . . .5C **26**
  W14 . . . . .5A **80**
Abbotsbury Ho. W14 . . . . .4A **80**
Abbotsbury Rd. W14 . . . . .4A **80**
Abbots Ct. W8 . . . . .5A **82**
Abbotshade Rd. SE16 . . . . .2E **95**
Abbot's Ho. W14 . . . . .2C **108**
Abbots Mnr. SW1 . . . . . . .5F **113**
          (not continuous)
Abbot's Pl. NW6 . . . . .3F **9**
Abbots Wlk. W8 . . . . .2F **109**
Abbott Rd. E14 . . . . .2C **70**
          (not continuous)
Abbotts Cl. N1 . . . . .1B **18**
Abbotts Ho. SW1 . . . . . . .1D **137**
Abbott's Wharf E14 . . . . . .3D **69**
Abbotts Wharf Moorings
  E14 . . . . .3D **69**
          (off Stainsby Rd.)
Abchurch La. EC4 . . . . . . .5E **63**
          (not continuous)
Abchurch Yd. EC4 . . . . . . .5D **63**
Abdale Rd. W12 . . . . .2A **78**
Abel Ho. SE11 . . . . .2E **139**
Aberavon Rd. E3 . . . . .3A **46**
Abercorn Cl. NW8 . . . . . . .1B **32**
Abercorn Cotts. NW8 . . . . .2B **32**
Abercorn Mans. NW8 . . . . .1C **32**
Abercorn Pl. NW8 . . . . . . .2B **32**
Abercorn Wlk. NW8 . . . . . .2B **32**
Abercorn Way SE1 . . . . . .5D **121**
Abercrombie Rd. E20 . . . . .2A **6**
Aberdale Ct. SE16 . . . . . . .5D **95**
Aberdare Gdns. NW6 . . . . .2A **10**
Aberdeen Ct. W9 . . . . .5D **33**
Aberdeen Mans. WC1 . . . . .4F **37**
Aberdeen Pl. NW8 . . . . . . .5D **33**
Aberdeen Sq. E14 . . . . . . .1C **96**
Aberdeen Wharf E1 . . . . . .3A **94**
Aberdour St. SE1 . . . . .2F **119**
Aberfeldy Ho. SE5 . . . . . . .4F **139**
          (not continuous)
Aberfeldy St. E14 . . . . . . .2C **70**
          (not continuous)
Ability Pl. E14 . . . . .5F **97**
Ability Towers EC1 . . . . . . .2B **40**
Abingdon W14 . . . . .4C **108**
Abingdon Cl. SE1 . . . . . . .4C **120**
Abingdon Ct. W8 . . . . .2E **109**
Abingdon Gdns. W8 . . . . . .2E **109**
Abingdon Ho. E2 . . . . .4B **42**
Abingdon Lodge W8 . . . . . .2F **109**
Abingdon Mans. W8 . . . . . .1D **109**
Abingdon Rd. W8 . . . . .1D **109**
Abingdon St. SW1 . . . . . . .1F **115**
Abingdon Vs. W8 . . . . .2D **109**
Abinger Gro. SE8 . . . . .3B **146**

Abinger Ho. SE1 . . . . .5D **91**
Abinger M. W9 . . . . .4D **31**
Ablett St. SE16 . . . . .1B **144**
Acacia Cl. SE8 . . . . .4F **123**
Acacia Gdns. NW8 . . . . . . .5E **11**
Acacia Pl. NW8 . . . . .5E **11**
Acacia Rd. NW8 . . . . .5E **11**
Acacia Wlk. SW10 . . . . .5C **132**
Academy, The SW8 . . . . . . .2B **138**
Academy Bldgs. N1 . . . . . . .2F **41**
Academy Ct. E2 . . . . .2C **44**
  NW6 . . . . .3D **9**
Academy Gdns. W8 . . . . . . .4D **81**
Academy Ho. E3 . . . . .1F **69**
Acanthus Dr. SE1 . . . . .5E **121**
Acer Rd. E8 . . . . .1C **20**
Achilles Cl. SE1 . . . . .5E **121**
Achilles Ho. E2 . . . . .1A **44**
Achilles Statue 3E **85**
Achilles St. SE14 . . . . .5A **146**
Achilles Way W1 . . . . .3E **85**
Acklam Rd. W10 . . . . .2A **52**
          (not continuous)
Ackroyd Dr. E3 . . . . .1C **68**
Acme Studios E14 . . . . .2C **70**
          (Leven Rd,)
  E14 . . . . .1B **70**
          (Gillender St.)
Acol Ct. NW6 . . . . .2E **9**
Acol Rd. NW6 . . . . .2E **9**
Acorn Ct. E3 . . . . .5D **25**
Acorn Pde. SE15 . . . . .5F **143**
Acorn Production Cen. N7 . . .1A **16**
Acorn Wlk. SE16 . . . . .2A **96**
Acton Ho. E8 . . . . .3B **20**
Acton M. E8 . . . . .3B **20**
Acton St. WC1 . . . . .3B **38**
Ada Ct. N1 . . . . .4B **18**
  W9 . . . . .3C **32**
Ada Gdns. E14 . . . . .3D **71**
Adagio Point SE8 . . . . .3F **147**
Ada Ho. E2 . . . . .4E **21**
Adair Ho. SW3 . . . . .3A **134**
Adair Rd. W10 . . . . .5A **30**
Adair Twr. W10 . . . . .5A **30**
Ada Kennedy Ct. SE10 . . . . . .5B **148**
Adam & Eve Ct. W1 . . . . .3C **58**
Adam & Eve M. W8 . . . . .1E **109**
Ada Maria Ct. E1 . . . . .4A **66**
          (off James Voller Way)
Adam Ct. SE11 . . . . .4F **117**
  SW7 . . . . .3C **110**
Adams Ct. EC2 . . . . .3E **63**
Adams Gdns. Est. SE16 . . . . .4B **94**
Adams Ho. E14 . . . . .4D **71**
Adamson Rd. E16 . . . . .4E **73**
  NW3 . . . . .1E **11**
Adams Pl. E14 . . . . .2F **97**
Adam's Row W1 . . . . .1E **85**
Adams Ter. E3 . . . . .3E **47**
Adam St. WC2 . . . . .1A **88**
Ada Pl. E2 . . . . .4E **21**
Ada Rd. SE5 . . . . .5F **141**
Adastral Ho. WC1 . . . . .1B **60**
Ada St. E8 . . . . .4F **21**
Ada Workshops E8 . . . . .4F **21**
Adderley St. E14 . . . . .4B **70**
Addey Ho. SE8 . . . . .4C **146**
Addington Lofts SE5 . . . . . . .4C **140**
Addington Rd. E3 . . . . .2D **47**
  E16 . . . . .5F **49**
Addington Sq. SE5 . . . . .4C **140**
          (not continuous)
Addington St. SE1 . . . . .5C **88**

Addis Ho. E1 . . . . .1B **66**
Addisland Ct. W14 . . . . . . .4F **79**
Addison Av. W11 . . . . .2F **79**
Addison Bri. Pl. W14 . . . . . .3B **108**
Addison Ct. NW6 . . . . .4E **9**
Addison Cres. W14 . . . . . . .1A **108**
          (not continuous)
Addison Gdns. W14 . . . . . . .1D **107**
Addison Ho. NW8 . . . . .2D **33**
Addison Pk. Mans. W14 . . . .1E **107**
Addison Pl. W11 . . . . .3F **79**
Addison Rd. W14 . . . . .4F **79**
Addle Hill EC4 . . . . .4A **62**
Addlestone Ho. W10 . . . . . .1B **50**
Addle St. EC2 . . . . .2C **62**
Addy Ho. SE16 . . . . .4C **122**
Adela Ho. W6 . . . . .5B **106**
Adelaide Ct. E9 . . . . .3A **4**
  NW8 . . . . .1C **32**
Adelaide Ho. W11 . . . . .4B **52**
Adelaide Rd. NW3 . . . . .2D **11**
Adelaide St. WC2 . . . . .1F **87**
          (not continuous)
Adela St. W10 . . . . .4F **29**
Adelina Gro. E1 . . . . .1E **66**
Adelina Yd. E1 . . . . .1E **66**
Adeline Pl. WC1 . . . . .2E **59**
Adelphi Ct. E8 . . . . .2C **20**
  SE16 . . . . .5D **95**
Adelphi Ter. WC2 . . . . .1A **88**
Adelphi Theatre 1A **88**
Adeyfield Ho. EC1 . . . . .3E **41**
Adie Rd. W6 . . . . .2B **106**
Adler St. E1 . . . . .3D **65**
Adley St. E5 . . . . .1A **4**
Admiral Ct. SE5 . . . . .5F **141**
  W1 . . . . .2D **57**
Admiral Ho. SW1 . . . . .3C **114**
Admiral Hyson Ind. Est.
  SE16 . . . . .4F **121**
Admiral M. W10 . . . . .5E **29**
Admiral Pl. SE16 . . . . .2A **96**
Admirals Ct. E6 . . . . .4F **77**
  SE1 . . . . .3B **92**
Admiral's Twr. SE10 . . . . . . .2F **147**
Admirals Way E14 . . . . .4E **97**
Admiralty Arch 2E **87**
Admiralty Cl. SE8 . . . . .5D **147**
Admiral Wlk. W9 . . . . .1E **53**
Adolphus St. SE8 . . . . .4C **146**
Adpar St. W2 . . . . .1D **55**
Adrian Boult Ho. E2 . . . . . . .2F **43**
Adrian Ho. E15 . . . . .2D **27**
  N1 . . . . .4C **16**
  SW8 . . . . .4F **137**
Adrian M. SW10 . . . . .2A **132**
Adriatic Apartments E16 . . . .5D **73**
Adriatic Bldg. E14 . . . . .5F **67**
Adriatic Ho. E1 . . . . .5E **45**
Adron Ho. SE16 . . . . .4C **122**
Adstock Ho. N1 . . . . .2F **17**
Adventurers Ct. E14 . . . . . . .1E **99**
Aegean Apartments E16 . . . .1E **101**
Aegon Ho. E14 . . . . .1A **126**
Affleck St. N1 . . . . .1C **38**
Afsil Ho. EC1 . . . . .2E **61**
Aftab Ter. E1 . . . . .4F **43**
Agar Gro. NW1 . . . . .2C **14**
Agar Gro. Est. NW1 . . . . . . .2D **15**
Agar Pl. NW1 . . . . .2C **14**
Agar St. WC2 . . . . .1F **87**
Agate Cl. E16 . . . . .4E **75**
Agate Rd. W6 . . . . .1B **106**
Agatha Cl. E1 . . . . .2B **94**

Agdon St. EC1 . . . . .4F 39
Agnes Cl. E6 . . . . .5E 77
Agnes George Wlk. E16 . .3D 103
Agnes Ho. W11 . . . . .1E 79
Agnes St. E14 . . . . .3C 68
Agricola Ct. E3 . . . . .4C 24
Ahoy Sailing Cen. 1E 147
Aigburth Mans. SW9 . . . . .5D 139
Ailsa Ho. E16 . . . . .1E 105
Ailsa St. E14 . . . . .1C 70
Ailsa Wlk. E14 . . . . .5E 97
Ainger M. NW3 . . . . .2C 12
(not continuous)
Ainger Rd. NW3 . . . . .2B 12
Ainsdale NW1 . . . . .1B 36
Ainsdale Dr. SE1 . . . . .1D 143
Ainsley St. E2 . . . . .3A 44
Ainsty Est. SE16 . . . . .4C 94
Ainsty St. SE16 . . . . .4C 94
Ainsworth Ct. NW10 . . . . . .2A 28
Ainsworth Ho. NW8 . . . . . .4A 10
W10 . . . . .2F 29
Ainsworth Rd. E9 . . . . .2C 22
Ainsworth Way NW8 . . . . . .3B 10
Aintree Est. SW6 . . . . .4A 130
Aintree St. SW6 . . . . .5A 130
Aird Ho. SE1 . . . . .2B 118
Airdrie Cl. N1 . . . . .2B 16
Airedale Wlk. E15 . . . . .5F 7
Airlie Gdns. W8 . . . . .3D 81
Air St. W1 . . . . .1C 86
Aisgill Av. W14 . . . . .1C 130
(not continuous)
Aithan Ho. E14 . . . . .4B 68
Aitken Cl. E8 . . . . .3D 21
Ajax Ho. E2 . . . . .1A 44
Akbar Ho. E14 . . . . .4F 125
Akintaro Ho. SE8 . . . . .2B 146
Alamoro Lodge SE10 . . . . .1C 128
Aland Ct. SE16 . . . . .2A 124
Alan Hocken Way E15 . . . . .1F 49
Alaska Apartments E16 . . . .5D 73
Alaska Bldgs. SE1 . . . . . . .2B 120
Alaska St. SE1 . . . . .3D 89
Alastor Ho. E14 . . . . .1B 126
Alban Highwalk EC2 . . . . . .2C 62
(not continuous)
Albany, The **4D 147**
Albany W1 . . . . .1B 86
Albany Ct. E1 . . . . .3D 65
NW8 . . . . .1D 33
NW10 . . . . .2A 28
Albany Courtyard W1 . . . . . .1C 86
Albany Mans. SW11 . . . . . .5A 134
Albany M. N1 . . . . .1E 17
SE5 . . . . .3C 140
Albany Rd. SE5 . . . . .3C 140
Albany St. NW1 . . . . .5F 13
Albany Ter. NW1 . . . . .5A 36
Albany Works E3 . . . . .4A 24
Alba Pl. W11 . . . . .3B 52
Albatross Cl. E6 . . . . .1C 76
Albatross Way SE16 . . . . . .5D 95
Albemarle Ho. SE8 . . . . . . .4C 124
Albemarle St. W1 . . . . .1A 86
Albemarle Way EC1 . . . . . . .5F 39
Alberta Est. SE17 . . . . .5A 118
Alberta St. SE17 . . . . .5F 117
Albert Av. SW8 . . . . .5B 138
Albert Barnes Ho. SE1 . . . . .2B 118
Albert Bigg Point E15 . . . . .4C 26
Albert Bri. SW3 . . . . .3A 134
Albert Bri. Rd. SW11 . . . . .4A 134
Albert Cl. E9 . . . . .4A 22

Albert Cotts. E1 . . . . .1D 65
Albert Ct. SW7 . . . . .5D 83
Albert Ct. Ga. SW1 . . . . . . .5B 84
Albert Emb. SE1 . . . . .2B 116
(Lambeth Pal. Rd.)
SE1 . . . . .1A 138
(Vauxhall Bri.)
Albert Gdns. E1 . . . . .4D 67
Albert Ga. SW1 . . . . .4C 84
Albert Gray Ho. SW10 . . . .4D 133
Albert Hall Mans. SW7 . . . .5D 83
Albert Memorial
Knightsbridge 5D 83
Albert M. E14 . . . . .5A 68
W8 . . . . .1B 110
Albert Pal. Mans. SW11 . . .5F 135
Albert Pl. W8 . . . . .5A 82
Albert Rd. E16 . . . . .3F 103
NW6 . . . . .1B 30
Alberts Ct. NW1 . . . . .4A 34
Albert Sq. E15 . . . . .2F 7
SW8 . . . . .5B 138
Albert Starr Ho. SE8 . . . . . .4D 123
Albert St. NW1 . . . . .4A 14
Albert Ter. NW1 . . . . .3D 13
Albert Ter. M. NW1 . . . . . . .4D 13
Albert Wlk. E16 . . . . .4E 105
Albert Way SE15 . . . . .4F 143
Albert Westcott Ho.
SE17 . . . . .5A 118
Albery Ct. E8 . . . . .2B 20
Albion Bldgs. N1 . . . . .1A 38
Albion Cl. W2 . . . . .5A 56
Albion Ct. SE10 . . . . .4B 128
W6 . . . . .4A 106
Albion Dr. E8 . . . . .2B 20
Albion Est. SE16 . . . . .5C 94
Albion Gdns. W6 . . . . .3A 106
Albion Ga. W2 . . . . .5A 56
(not continuous)
Albion Ho. E16 . . . . .3F 105
SE8 . . . . .5D 147
Albion M. N1 . . . . .2D 17
NW6 . . . . .1C 8
W2 . . . . .4A 56
W6 . . . . .4A 106
Albion Pl. EC1 . . . . .1F 61
EC2 . . . . .2E 63
W6 . . . . .4A 106
Albion Riverside Bldg.
SW11 . . . . .4F 133
Albion Sq. E8 . . . . .2B 20
(not continuous)
Albion St. SE16 . . . . .5B 94
W2 . . . . .4A 56
Albion Ter. E8 . . . . .2B 20
Albion Wlk. N1 . . . . .1A 38
Albion Way EC1 . . . . .2B 62
Albion Yd. E1 . . . . .1A 66
N1 . . . . .1A 38
Albury Ct. SE8 . . . . .3E 147
Albury Ho. SE1 . . . . .5A 90
Albury St. SE8 . . . . .3D 147
Aldbridge St. SE17 . . . . . . .5A 120
Aldburgh M. W1 . . . . .3E 57
Aldeburgh Pl. SE10 . . . . . . .4E 129
Aldeburgh St. SE10 . . . . . . .5D 129
Aldenham Ho. NW1 . . . . . . .1C 36
Aldenham St. NW1 . . . . . . .1C 36
Alden Ho. E8 . . . . .3F 21
Aldensley Rd. W6 . . . . .2A 106
Alder Cl. SE15 . . . . .3C 142

Alder Ho. E3 . . . . .3B 24
SE15 . . . . .3C 142
Aldermanbury EC2 . . . . .3C 62
Aldermanbury Sq. EC2 . . . . .2C 62
Aldermans Ho. E9 . . . . .3A 4
Aldermans Wlk. EC2 . . . . . .2F 63
Alderney Ct. SE10 . . . . .2E 149
Alderney Ho. N1 . . . . .1C 18
Alderney M. SE1 . . . . .1D 119
Alderney Rd. E1 . . . . .4D 45
Alderney St. SW1 . . . . .4A 114
Aldersgate Ct. EC1 . . . . . . .2B 62
Aldersgate St. EC1 . . . . . . .1B 62
Aldershot Rd. NW6 . . . . .3C 8
Alderson St. W10 . . . . .4A 30
Alderwick Ct. N7 . . . . .1C 16
Aldford Ho. W1 . . . . .2D 85
Aldford St. W1 . . . . .2D 85
ALDGATE 4C 64
Aldgate EC3 . . . . .4B 64
Aldgate Av. E1 . . . . .3B 64
Aldgate Barrs E1 . . . . .3C 64
Aldgate High St. EC3 . . . . . .4B 64
Aldgate Twr. E1 . . . . .3C 64
Aldine Ct. W12 . . . . .3C 78
Aldine Pl. W12 . . . . .4C 78
Aldine St. W12 . . . . .4C 78
Aldington Ct. E8 . . . . .2E 21
Aldrick Ho. N1 . . . . .4C 16
Aldridge Ct. W11 . . . . .2C 52
Aldridge Rd. Vs. W11 . . . . . .2C 52
Aldsworth Cl. W9 . . . . .5F 31
Aldworth Rd. E15 . . . . .2F 27
Aldwych WC2 . . . . .5B 60
Aldwych Bldgs. WC2 . . . . . .3A 60
Aldwych Ct. E8 . . . . .2C 20
Aldwych Theatre 4B 60
Aldwyn Ho. SW8 . . . . .4F 137
Alestan Beck Rd. E16 . . . . . .3E 75
Alexa Ct. W8 . . . . .3E 109
Alexander Fleming Laboratory
Mus. 3E 55
Alexander Ho. E14 . . . . . . .1E 125
Alexander M. W2 . . . . .3F 53
Alexander Pl. SW7 . . . . .3F 111
Alexander Sq. SW3 . . . . . . .3F 111
Alexander St. W2 . . . . .3E 53
Alexandra Cl. SE8 . . . . .2B 146
Alexandra Ct. SE5 . . . . .3C 140
SW7 . . . . .1C 110
W2 . . . . .5A 54
W9 . . . . .4C 32
Alexandra Ho. E16 . . . . . . .2F 101
(off Wesley Av.)
W6 . . . . .5B 106
Alexandra Mans. SW3 . . . .3D 133
W12 . . . . .3B 78
Alexandra Pl. NW8 . . . . .3C 10
Alexandra Rd. NW8 . . . . . . .2C 10
Alexandra St. E16 . . . . .1D 73
SE14 . . . . .4A 146
Alexandra Ter. E14 . . . . . . .5A 126
Alexandra Wharf E2 . . . . . . .4F 21
Alexandra Yd. E9 . . . . .3D 23
Alexandria Apartments
SE17 . . . . .3F 119
Alexia Sq. E14 . . . . .1A 126
Alexis St. SE16 . . . . .3E 121
Alford Ct. N1 . . . . .1C 40
(not continuous)
Alford Pl. N1 . . . . .1C 40
Alfred Ct. SE16 . . . . .3F 121
Alfred Dickens Ho. E16 . . . .3B 72
Alfred Ho. E9 . . . . .2A 4

Alfred M. W1 . . . . .1D **59**
Alfred Pl. WC1 . . . . .1D **59**
Alfred Rd. W2 . . . . .1E **53**
Alfred Salter Ho. SE1 . . . . .4C **120**
Alfred St. E3 . . . . .1C **46**
Algar Ho. SE1 . . . . .5F **89**
Algernon Rd. NW6 . . . . .4D **9**
Alice Gilliatt Ct. W14 . . .2B **130**
Alice La. E3 . . . . .4B **24**
Alice Owen Technology Cen.
 EC1 . . . . .2F **39**
Alice Shepherd Ho. E14 . . . .5C **98**
Alice St. SE1 . . . . .2F **119**
 (not continuous)
Alie St. E1 . . . . .4C **64**
Alison Cl. E6 . . . . .4E **77**
Allen Edwards Dr. SW8 . . .5F **137**
Allen Ho. W8 . . . . .1E **109**
Allen Mans. W8 . . . . .1E **109**
Allen Rd. E3 . . . . .5B **24**
Allensbury Pl. NW1 . . . . . . .2E **15**
Allen St. W8 . . . . .1E **109**
Allerton Ho. N1 . . . . .2D **41**
Allerton St. N1 . . . . .2E **41**
Allestree Rd. SW6 . . . . . .5A **130**
Alleyn Ho. SE1 . . . . .2E **119**
Allgood St. E2 . . . . .1C **42**
Allhallows La. EC4 . . . . .1D **91**
Allhallows Rd. E6 . . . . .2F **75**
Alliance Rd. E13 . . . . .1B **74**
Allied Ct. N1 . . . . .2A **20**
Allingham M. N1 . . . . .5B **18**
Allingham St. N1 . . . . .5B **18**
Allington Ct. SW1 . . . . . . .2A **114**
Allington Rd. W10 . . . . .1F **29**
Allington St. SW1 . . . . . . .2A **114**
Alliston Ho. E2 . . . . .3C **42**
Allitsen Rd. NW8 . . . . .1F **33**
 (not continuous)
All Nations Ho. E8 . . . . .2F **21**
Alloa Rd. SE8 . . . . .5E **123**
Allom Ho. W11 . . . . .5F **51**
Allonby Ho. E14 . . . . .2F **67**
Alloway Rd. E3 . . . . .2A **46**
Allport M. E1 . . . . .5C **44**
All Saints Ct. E1 . . . . .5C **66**
 SW11 . . . . .5F **135**
All Saints Ho. W11 . . . . . . .2B **52**
All Saints Rd. W11 . . . . . . .2B **52**
All Saints St. N1 . . . . .5B **16**
Allsop Pl. NW1 . . . . .5C **34**
All Souls Av. NW10 . . . . . . .1A **28**
All Souls' Pl. W1 . . . . .2A **58**
Alluvium Ct. *SE1* *1F* **59**
 (off Long La.)
Alma Birk Ho. NW6 . . . . . . .1A **8**
Alma Gro. SE1 . . . . .4C **120**
Alma Pl. NW10 . . . . .3A **28**
Alma Sq. NW8 . . . . .1C **32**
Alma St. E15 . . . . .4D **7**
Alma Ter. E3 . . . . .4B **24**
 W8 . . . . .2E **109**
Almeida St. N1 . . . . .3F **17**
Almeida Theatre 3F **17**
Almond Ho. E15 . . . . .2F **49**
Almond Rd. SE16 . . . . .3A **122**
Almorah Rd. N1 . . . . .2D **19**
Alnwick Rd. E16 . . . . .4B **74**
Alperton St. W10 . . . . .4A **30**
Alphabet Sq. E3 . . . . .2E **69**
Alpha Cl. NW1 . . . . .3A **34**
Alpha Gro. E14 . . . . .5E **97**
Alpha Ho. NW6 . . . . .5E **9**
 NW8 . . . . .5F **33**

Alpha Pl. NW6 . . . . .5E **9**
 SW3 . . . . .2A **134**
Alpha Rd. SE14 . . . . .5C **106**
Alpine Bus. Cen. E6 . . . . . . .1E **77**
Alpine Gro. E9 . . . . .2C **22**
Alpine Rd. SE16 . . . . .4C **122**
Alpine Way E6 . . . . .1D **77**
Alsace Rd. SE17 . . . . .5F **119**
Alscot Rd. SE1 . . . . .3B **120**
Alscot Rd. Ind. Est.
 SE1 . . . . .2C **120**
Alscot Way SE1 . . . . .3B **120**
Altius Apartments E3 . . . . . .5E **25**
Altius Wlk. E20 . . . . .4C **6**
Alton Ho. E3 . . . . .2A **48**
Alton St. E14 . . . . .2F **69**
Alverstone Ho. SE11 . . . .3D **139**
Alverton St. SE8 . . . . .1B **146**
 (not continuous)
Alvey St. SE17 . . . . .5F **119**
Alwyne La. N1 . . . . .1A **18**
Alwyne Pl. N1 . . . . .1B **18**
Alwyne Rd. N1 . . . . .1B **18**
Alwyne Vs. N1 . . . . .1A **18**
Alzette Ho. E2 . . . . .1D **45**
Amazon St. E1 . . . . .4F **65**
Ambassador Gdns. E6 . . . . .2B **76**
Ambassador Ho. NW8 . . . . .4C **10**
Ambassadors Ct. E8 . . . . . .2C **20**
 SW1 . . . . .3C **86**
Ambassador Sq. E14 . . . . .4F **125**
Ambassadors Theatre 4E **59**
Amber Ct. E15 . . . . .4C **26**
Ambergate St. SE17 . . . . .5A **118**
Amber Ho. E1 . . . . .3D **67**
Amberley Rd. W9 . . . . .1E **53**
Amber Wharf E2 . . . . .4B **20**
Ambleside NW1 . . . . .1A **36**
Ambleside Point SE15 . . . .4B **144**
Ambrosden Av. SW1 . . . . .2C **114**
Ambrose Cl. E6 . . . . .2B **76**
Ambrose Ho. E14 . . . . .2D **69**
Ambrose St. SE16 . . . . .3F **121**
Ambrose Wlk. E3 . . . . .1D **47**
Amelia Ho. W6 . . . . .5B **106**
Amelia Mans. E20 . . . . .4A **6**
Amelia St. SE17 . . . . .5A **118**
Amen Corner EC4 . . . . .4A **62**
Amen Ct. EC4 . . . . .4A **62**
American International
 University in London, The
 Kensington Campus,
 Ansdell Street 1A **110**
 Kensington Campus,
 St Albans Grove 1A **110**
 Kensington Campus,
 Young Street 5F **81**
America Sq. EC3 . . . . .5B **64**
America St. SE1 . . . . .3B **90**
Amersham Gro. SE14 . . . .4B **146**
Amersham Rd. SE14 . . . . .5B **146**
Amersham Va. SE14 . . . . .4B **146**
Amery Ho. SE17 . . . . .5A **120**
Ames Cotts. E14 . . . . .2F **67**
Ames Ho. E2 . . . . .1D **45**
Amethyst Ho. E15 . . . . .1E **7**
Amherst Ho. SE16 . . . . .5E **95**
Amias Ho. EC1 . . . . .4B **40**
Amiel St. E1 . . . . .4C **44**
Amigo Ho. SE1 . . . . .1E **117**
Amina Way SE16 . . . . .2D **121**
Amisha Ct. SE1 . . . . .2B **120**
Amor Rd. W6 . . . . .2B **106**
Amory Ho. N1 . . . . .4C **16**

Amoy Pl. E14 . . . . .4C **68**
 (not continuous)
Ampthill Est. NW1 . . . . .1C **36**
Ampthill Sq. NW1 . . . . .1C **36**
Ampton Pl. WC1 . . . . .3B **38**
Ampton St. WC1 . . . . .3B **38**
Amstel Ct. SE15 . . . . .4B **142**
Amsterdam Rd. E14 . . . . . .2C **126**
Amundsen Ct. E14 . . . . . . .5E **125**
Amwell St. EC1 . . . . .2D **39**
Amy Warne Cl. E6 . . . . .1A **76**
Anchorage Ho. E14 . . . . .5D **71**
Anchorage Point E14 . . . . . .4C **96**
Anchor Brewhouse SE1 . . . . .3B **92**
Anchor Ct. SW1 . . . . .4D **115**
Anchor Ho. E16 . . . . .2B **72**
 (Barking Rd.)
 E16 . . . . .4B **74**
 (Prince Regent La.)
 EC1 . . . . .4B **40**
 SW10 . . . . .3E **133**
Anchor Retail Pk. E1 . . . . . .5C **44**
Anchor St. SE16 . . . . .3F **121**
Anchor Ter. E1 . . . . .5C **44**
 SE1 . . . . .2C **90**
Anchor Wharf E3 . . . . .1F **69**
Anchor Yd. EC1 . . . . .4C **40**
Anderson Ho. E14 . . . . .5C **70**
Anderson Sq. N1 . . . . .4F **17**
Anderson St. SW3 . . . . . . .5B **112**
Anderson St. SW3 . . . . . . .5B **112**
Andover Av. E16 . . . . .4D **75**
Andover Pl. NW6 . . . . .5F **9**
Andoversford Ct. SE15 . . .3A **142**
Andover Ter. W6 . . . . .3A **106**
Andrewes Gdns. E6 . . . . . . .3F **75**
Andrewes Highwalk EC2 . . .2C **62**
Andrewes Ho. EC2 . . . . .2C **62**
Andrew Pl. SW8 . . . . .5E **137**
Andrews Crosse WC2 . . . . .4D **61**
Andrews Ho. NW3 . . . . .1B **12**
Andrew's Rd. E8 . . . . .4F **21**
Andrew St. E14 . . . . .3B **70**
Andrews Wlk. SE17 . . . . . .3A **140**
ANGEL 1E **39**
Angel All. E1 . . . . .3C **64**
Angel Centre, The N1 . . . . . .1E **39**
Angel Ct. EC2 . . . . .3E **63**
 SW1 . . . . .3C **86**
Angel Ga. EC1 . . . . .2A **40**
 (not continuous)
Angel Ho. E3 . . . . .3F **47**
Angelica Dr. E6 . . . . .2E **77**
Angelica Ho. E3 . . . . .3C **24**
Angelina Ho. SE15 . . . . . .5E **143**
Angelis Apartments N1 . . . . .1A **40**
Angel La. E15 . . . . .4E **7**
 EC4 . . . . .1D **91**
Angel M. E1 . . . . .5A **66**
 N1 . . . . .1E **39**
Angel Pl. SE1 . . . . .4D **91**
Angel Sq. EC1 . . . . .1F **39**
Angel St. EC1 . . . . .3B **62**
Angel Wlk. W6 . . . . .4B **106**
Angel Wharf E3 . . . . .5C **18**
Angerstein Bus. Pk.
 SE10 . . . . .4D **129**
Anglebury W2 . . . . .3D **53**
Anglesea Ter. *W6* *2A* **106**
 (off Wellesley Av.)
Anglesey Ho. E14 . . . . .3D **69**
Anglia Ho. E14 . . . . .3A **68**
Anglo Rd. E3 . . . . .5C **24**
Angrave Ct. E8 . . . . .3C **20**
Angrave Pas. E8 . . . . .3C **20**

Angus St. SE14 . . . . .4A 146
Anhalt Rd. SW11 . . . . .4A 134
Anley Rd. W14 . . . . .5D 79
Annabel Cl. E14 . . . . .4F 69
Anna Cl. E8 . . . . .3C 20
Annandale Rd. SE10 . . . . . .5C 128
Anne Goodman Ho. E1 . . . .3B 66
Anne Matthews Ct.
    E14 . . . . .2D 69
Annes Ct. NW1 . . . . .4A 34
Annesley Ho. SW9 . . . . . . .5E 139
Annette Cres. N1 . . . . .2C 18
Annexe Mkt. E1 . . . . .1B 64
Annie Besant Cl. E3 . . . . . . .4C 24
Anning St. EC2 . . . . .4A 42
Annis Rd. E9 . . . . .5A 4
    E9 . . . . .1F 23
Ann La. SW10 . . . . .4D 133
Ann Moss Way SE16 . . . . . .1B 122
Ann's Cl. SW1 . . . . .5C 84
Ann's Pl. E1 . . . . .2B 64
Ansdell St. W8 . . . . .1A 110
Ansdell Ter. W8 . . . . .1A 110
Ansell Ho. E1 . . . . .1B 66
Anselm Rd. SW6 . . . . .3D 131
Ansleigh Pl. W11 . . . . .1E 79
Anson Ho. E1 . . . . .5F 45
    SW1 . . . . .2B 136
Anstey Ho. E9 . . . . .3B 22
Antenor Ho. E2 . . . . .1F 43
Anthems Way E20 . . . . .4A 6
Anthony Cope Ct. N1 . . . . . .2E 41
Anthony Ho. NW8 . . . . .5F 33
Anthony St. E1 . . . . .3A 66
Antila Ct. E1 . . . . .4C 42
Antilles Bay E14 . . . . .4B 98
Antill Rd. E3 . . . . .2A 46
Antill Ter. E1 . . . . .3D 67
Antonine Hgts. SE1 . . . .5F 91
Antony Ho. SE16 . . . . .3B 122
Antwerp Way E16 . . . . .4D 105
Apex Ho. E1 . . . . .4C 42
Aphrodite Ct. E14 . . . . .3D 125
    E15 . . . . .3C 26
Apollo Bldg. E14 . . . . .3D 125
Apollo Bus. Cen. SE8 . . . . . .1E 145
Apollo Ct. E1 . . . . .1D 93
    E15 . . . . .3C 26
    SW9 . . . . .5D 139
Apollo Ho. E2 . . . . .1A 44
    E3 . . . . .5D 25
    SW10 . . . . .3D 133
Apollo Pl. SW10 . . . . .4D 133
Apollo Theatre
    Soho **5D 59**
Apollo Victoria Theatre **2B 114**
Apothecary St. EC4 . . . . . . .4F 61
Appian Ct. E3 . . . . .5C 24
Apple Blossom Ct.
    SW8 . . . . .4E 137
Appleby Rd. E8 . . . . .1E 21
    E16 . . . . .4C 72
Appleby St. E2 . . . . .5B 20
Appleford Ho. W10 . . . . . . .5A 30
Appleford Rd. W10 . . . . . . .5A 30
Applegarth Ho. SE1 . . . . . . .4A 90
    SE15 . . . . .4D 143
Applegarth Rd. W14 . . . . . .2D 107
Applegate Ho. E20 . . . . .3B 6
Apple Tree Yd. E1 . . . . .3E 45
    SW1 . . . . .2C 86
Appold St. EC2 . . . . .1F 63
Approach Rd. E2 . . . . .1B 44
April Ct. E2 . . . . .5E 21

Apsley Ho. E1 . . . . .2C 66
    NW8 . . . . .5D 11
Apsley House (Wellington Mus.)
    . . . .**4E 85**
Apsley Way W1 . . . . .4E 85
                    (not continuous)
Aquarelle Ho. EC1 . . . . .2B 40
Aquatics Centre
    Queen Elizabeth Olympic Pk.
    . . . .**2B 26**
Aqua Vista Sq. E3 . . . . .2E 69
Aquila St. NW8 . . . . .5E 11
Aquinas St. SE1 . . . . .3E 89
Arabella Ct. NW8 . . . . .5C 10
Arabian Ho. E1 . . . . .5F 45
Aragon Ct. SE11 . . . . .5D 117
Aragon Ho. E16 . . . . .2E 101
Aragon Twr. SE8 . . . . .4C 124
Aral Ho. E1 . . . . .5E 45
Aran Lodge NW6 . . . . .1F 9
Aran M. N7 . . . . .1D 17
Arapiles Ho. E14 . . . . .4D 71
Arbery Rd. E3 . . . . .2F 45
Arbon Ct. N1 . . . . .4C 18
Arborfield Ho. E14 . . . . .5E 69
Arbour Ho. E1 . . . . .3D 67
Arbour Sq. E1 . . . . .3D 67
Arbutus St. E8 . . . . .3B 20
Arcade, The E20 . . . . .5C 6
    EC2 . . . . .2F 63
Arcadia Ct. E1 . . . . .3B 64
Arcadia St. E14 . . . . .3E 69
Archangel St. SE16 . . . . .5E 95
Archdale Ct. W12 . . . . .3A 78
Archdale Ho. SE1 . . . . .1F 119
Archel Rd. W14 . . . . .2B 130
Archer Apartments N1 . . . . .5F 19
Archer Ho. N1 . . . . .4A 20
    W1 . . . . .5C 52
Archers Lodge SE16 . . . . . . .1F 143
Archer Sq. SE14 . . . . .3F 145
Archer St. W1 . . . . .5D 59
Archery Cl. W2 . . . . .4A 56
Archery Flds. Ho. WC1 . . . . .2C 38
Archery Steps W2 . . . . .5A 56
Arches SW8 . . . . .3A 138
Arches, The E16 . . . . .4F 49
    NW1 . . . . .1F 13
    SE8 . . . . .2A 146
    SW8 . . . . .4D 137
    WC2 . . . . .2A 88
Arches Leisure Cen. **2F 149**
Archibald M. W1 . . . . .1E 85
Archibald St. E3 . . . . .3D 47
Archie St. SE1 . . . . .5A 92
Arc Ho. SE1 . . . . .5B 92
Arch St. SE1 . . . . .2B 118
Archway Cl. W10 . . . . .2D 51
Arden Cres. E14 . . . . .3E 125
Arden Est. N1 . . . . .1F 41
Arden Ho. N1 . . . . .1F 41
    SE11 . . . . .4B 116
Ardent Ho. E3 . . . . .1F 45
Ardleigh Rd. N1 . . . . .1F 19
Arena Ho. E3 . . . . .5D 25
Ares Ct. E14 . . . . .3D 125
Arethusa Ho. E14 . . . . .4E 125
Argent Ct. E14 . . . . .2E 69
Argo Bus. Cen. NW6 . . . . . . .3E 31
Argon M. SW6 . . . . .5E 131
Argos Ct. SW9 . . . . .5D 139
Argos Ho. E2 . . . . .1F 43
Argosy Ho. SE8 . . . . .4A 124
Argyle Ho. E14 . . . . .1C 126

Argyle Pl. W6 . . . . .4A 106
Argyle Rd. E1 . . . . .4D 45
    E15 . . . . .1F 7
    E16 . . . . .4A 74
Argyle Sq. WC1 . . . . .2A 38
                    (not continuous)
Argyle St. WC1 . . . . .2F 37
Argyle Wlk. WC1 . . . . .3F 37
Argyle Way SE16 . . . . .1E 143
Argyll Mans. SW3 . . . . .2E 133
    W14 . . . . .3A 108
Argyll Rd. W8 . . . . .5D 81
Argyll St. W1 . . . . .4B 58
Arica Ho. SE16 . . . . .1A 122
Ariel Apartments E16 . . . . . .3E 73
Ariel Ct. SE11 . . . . .4F 117
Ariel Way W12 . . . . .2C 78
Ark, The W6 . . . . .5D 107
Arklow Ho. SE17 . . . . .3D 141
Arklow Rd. SE14 . . . . .3B 146
Arklow Rd. Trad. Est.
    SE14 . . . . .3A 146
Arlidge Ho. EC1 . . . . .1E 61
Arlington Av. N1 . . . . .5C 18
Arlington Bldg. E3 . . . . .1E 47
Arlington Ho. EC1 . . . . .2E 39
    SE8 . . . . .2C 146
    SW1 . . . . .2B 86
    W12 . . . . .3A 78
Arlington Pl. SE10 . . . . .5B 148
Arlington Rd. NW1 . . . . .3F 13
Arlington Sq. N1 . . . . .4C 18
Arlington St. SW1 . . . . .2B 86
Arlington Way EC1 . . . . .2E 39
Armada Ct. SE8 . . . . .3D 147
Armadale Rd. SW6 . . . . .4D 131
Armada St. SE8 . . . . .3E 147
Armada Way E6 . . . . .2F 77
Armagh Rd. E3 . . . . .4C 24
Arminger Rd. W12 . . . . .3A 78
Armitage Ho. NW1 . . . . .1A 56
Armitage Rd. SE10 . . . . .4B 128
Armoury Ho. E3 . . . . .4A 24
Armsby Ho. E1 . . . . .2B 66
Armstrong Cl. E6 . . . . .3B 76
Armstrong Rd. SW7 . . . . . . .2D 111
Arncliffe NW6 . . . . .5A 10
Arne Ho. SE11 . . . . .5B 116
Arne St. WC2 . . . . .4A 60
Arneway St. SW1 . . . . .2E 115
Arnhem Pl. E14 . . . . .2D 125
Arnhem Wharf E14 . . . . .2C 124
Arnold Cir. E2 . . . . .3B 42
Arnold Est. SE1 . . . . .5C 92
                    (not continuous)
Arnold Ho. SE17 . . . . .1A 140
Arnold Mans. W14 . . . . .2A 130
Arnold Rd. E3 . . . . .2D 47
Arnot Ho. SE5 . . . . .5C 140
Arnside Ho. SE17 . . . . .2D 141
Arnside St. SE17 . . . . .2C 140
Arran Ho. E14 . . . . .3C 98
Arran Wlk. N1 . . . . .1B 18
Arrol Ho. SE1 . . . . .2C 118
Arrow Ct. SW5 . . . . .4D 109
Arrow Ho. N1 . . . . .4A 20
Arrow Rd. E3 . . . . .2F 47
Arrows Ho. SE15 . . . . .5C 144
Arrowsmith Ho. SE11 . . . . . .5B 116
Arta Ho. E1 . . . . .4C 66
Artbrand Ho. SE1 . . . . .5F 91
Artemis Ct. E14 . . . . .4D 125
Artesian Ho. SE1 . . . . .2C 120
Artesian Rd. W2 . . . . .4D 53

Arthingworth St. E15 . . . . . . .3F 27
Arthur Ct. W2 . . . . .3F 53
W10 . . . . .4E 51
Arthur Deakin Ho. E1 . . . . . .1D 65
Arthur Ho. *N1* *4F 19*
(off Halcomb St.)
Arthur St. EC4 . . . . .5E 63
Arthur Wade Ho. E2 . . . . . . .2C 42
Artichoke Hill E1 . . . . .1F 93
Artillery Building, The *E1* . . .*2A 64*
(off Artillery La.)
Artillery Ho. E3 . . . . .3A 24
Artillery La. E1 . . . . .2A 64
Artillery Mans. SW1 . . . . . .2D 115
Artillery Pas. E1 . . . . .2A 64
Artillery Pl. SW1 . . . . .2D 115
Artillery Row SW1 . . . . .2D 115
Artisan Cl. E6 . . . . .5F 77
Artisan M. NW10 . . . . .3D 29
Artisan Quarter NW10 . . . . . .3D 29
Artizan St. E1 . . . . .3A 64
Arts Sq. E1 . . . . .4F 45
Arts Theatre 5F 59
Arundel Bldgs. SE1 . . . . . . .2A 120
Arundel Cl. E15 . . . . .1F 7
Arundel Ct. SE16 . . . . .1A 144
SW3 . . . . .5A 112
W11 . . . . .5B 52
Arundel Gdns. W11 . . . . .5B 52
Arundel Gt. Ct. WC2 . . . . . . .5C 60
Arundel Mans. SW6 . . . . . . .5C 130
Arundel Pl. N1 . . . . .1D 17
Arundel St. WC2 . . . . .5C 60
Asbridge Ct. W6 . . . . .2A 106
Ascalon Ho. SW8 . . . . .5B 136
Ascalon St. SW8 . . . . .5B 136
Ascot Ct. NW8 . . . . .3D 33
Ascot Ho. NW1 . . . . .2A 36
W9 . . . . .5D 31
Ascot Lodge NW6 . . . . .4A 10
Ashbee Ho. E2 . . . . .3C 44
Ashbourne Ct. E5 . . . . .1A 4
Ashbridge St. NW8 . . . . .5F 33
Ashburn Gdns. SW7 . . . . . . .3B 110
Ashburnham Gro. SE10 . . .5A 148
Ashburnham Mans.
SW10 . . . . .4C 132
Ashburnham Pl. SE10 . . . . .5A 148
Ashburnham Retreat
SE10 . . . . .5A 148
Ashburnham Rd. NW10 . . . .2B 28
SW10 . . . . .4C 132
Ashburnham Twr. SW10 . . . .4D 133
Ashburn Pl. SW7 . . . . .3B 110
Ashburton Ho. W9 . . . . .4C 30
Ashburton Rd. E16 . . . . .3E 73
Ashby Ct. NW8 . . . . .4E 33
Ashby Gro. N1 . . . . .1C 18
(not continuous)
Ashby Ho. N1 . . . . .1C 18
Ashbys Ct. E3 . . . . .5C 24
Ashby St. EC1 . . . . .3A 40
Ashcombe Ho. E3 . . . . .3A 48
Ashcroft Sq. W6 . . . . .4B 106
Ashdene SE15 . . . . .5F 143
Ashdown Wlk. E14 . . . . .3E 125
Ashen E6 . . . . .3D 77
Ashenden Rd. E5 . . . . .2A 4
Ashentree Ct. EC4 . . . . .4E 61
Asher Way E1 . . . . .1E 93
Ashfield Ho. W14 . . . . .5C 108
Ashfield St. E1 . . . . .2F 65
(not continuous)

Ashfield Yd. E1 . . . . .2B 66
Ashford Ho. SE8 . . . . .2C 146
Ashford St. N1 . . . . .2F 41
Ash Gro. E8 . . . . .4A 22
(not continuous)
Ashgrove Ct. W9 . . . . .1D 53
Ashgrove Ho. SW1 . . . . .5E 115
Ash Ho. E14 . . . . .5B 98
SE1 . . . . .4C 120
W10 . . . . .4A 30
Ashington Ho. E1 . . . . .4A 44
Ashland Pl. W1 . . . . .1D 57
Ashley Ct. SW1 . . . . .2B 114
Ashley Gdns. SW1 . . . . .2C 114
(not continuous)
Ashley Pl. SW1 . . . . .2B 114
(not continuous)
Ashlin Rd. E15 . . . . .1E 7
Ashmead Bus. Cen. E16 . . .4E 49
Ashmead Ho. E9 . . . . .2A 4
Ashmill St. NW1 . . . . .1F 55
Ashmole Pl. SW8 . . . . .3D 139
Ashmole St. SW8 . . . . .3C 138
Ashmore NW1 . . . . .1D 15
Ashmore Ct. SE15 . . . . .5C 142
Ashmore Ho. W14 . . . . .2A 108
Ashmore Rd. W9 . . . . .2B 30
Ashpark Ho. E14 . . . . .3B 68
Ashton Ho. SE11 . . . . .5F 117
SW9 . . . . .5E 139
Ashton Rd. E15 . . . . .3D 7
Ashton St. E14 . . . . .5C 70
Ash Tree Ho. SE5 . . . . .4B 140
Ashvale Ct. E3 . . . . .5D 25
Ashwell Cl. E6 . . . . .3A 76
Ashworth Mans. W9 . . . . . . .3A 32
Ashworth Rd. W9 . . . . .2A 32
Aske Ho. N1 . . . . .2F 41
Aske St. N1 . . . . .2F 41
Asland Rd. E15 . . . . .4E 27
Asman Ho. N1 . . . . .5F 17
Asolando Dr. SE17 . . . . .4C 118
Aspect Ct. E14 . . . . .5B 98
Aspen Gdns. W6 . . . . .5A 106
Aspen Ho. E15 . . . . .2F 49
SE15 . . . . .3C 144
Aspen Lodge W8 . . . . .2F 109
Aspen Way E14 . . . . .1E 97
Aspinden Rd. SE16 . . . . .3A 122
Asquith Ho. SW1 . . . . .2E 115
Assam St. E1 . . . . .3D 65
Assembly Pas. E1 . . . . .1C 66
Astbury Bus. Pk. SE15 . . . . .5B 144
Astbury Ho. SE11 . . . . .2D 117
Astbury Rd. SE15 . . . . .5B 144
Astell Ho. SW3 . . . . .5A 112
Astell St. SW3 . . . . .5A 112
Asterid Hgts. E20 . . . . .3C 6
Aste St. E14 . . . . .5B 98
Astey's Row N1 . . . . .3A 18
Astley Ho. SE1 . . . . .5C 120
W2 . . . . .1D 53
Aston Ho. EC4 . . . . .2D 61
W11 . . . . .5C 52
Aston M. W10 . . . . .2E 29
Aston St. E14 . . . . .2F 67
Aston Webb Ho. SE1 . . . . . . .3F 91
Astor Ct. E16 . . . . .3B 74
SW6 . . . . .5B 132
Astoria Ct. E8 . . . . .2C 20
Astra Ho. E3 . . . . .2C 46
SE14 . . . . .3B 146
Astral Ho. E1 . . . . .2A 64
Astrop M. W6 . . . . .1B 106

Astrop Ter. W6 . . . . .1B 106
Astwood M. SW7 . . . . .3A 110
Asylum Rd. SE15 . . . . .3A 144
Atelier Ct. Central E14 . . . . .2C 70
Atelier Ct. Nth. E14 . . . . .2C 70
Atelier Ct. Sth. E14 . . . . .2C 70
Athelstane Gro. E3 . . . . .1B 46
Athelstan Gdns. NW6 . . . . . . .2A 8
Athelstan Ho. E9 . . . . .2B 4
Athena Bldgs. E15 . . . . .3C 26
Athena Ct. SE1 . . . . .5F 91
Athene Pl. EC4 . . . . .3E 61
Athenia Ho. E14 . . . . .4D 71
Athens Gdns. W9 . . . . .5D 31
Atherstone Ct. W2 . . . . .1A 54
Atherstone M. SW7 . . . . .3C 110
Athlone Ho. E1 . . . . .3B 66
Atholl Ho. W9 . . . . .3B 32
Athol Sq. E14 . . . . .4C 70
Atkin Bldg. WC1 . . . . .1C 60
Atkins Ct. E3 . . . . .4B 24
Atkins Lodge W8 . . . . .4D 81
Atkinson Ho. E2 . . . . .5E 21
SE17 . . . . .4E 119
Atkinson Rd. E16 . . . . .2C 74
Atlanta Ho. SE16 . . . . .2F 123
Atlantic Apartments E16 . . . .5D 73
Atlantic Ct. E14 . . . . .1E 99
SW3 . . . . .5B 112
Atlantic Wharf E1 . . . . .5E 67
Atlas Wharf E9 . . . . .4D 5
Atrium Apartments N1 . . . . . .4E 19
Atrium Hgts. SE8 . . . . .3F 147
Atrium Ho. SE8 . . . . .5D 147
Atterbury St. SW1 . . . . .4F 115
Attilburgh Ho. SE1 . . . . .1B 120
Attneave St. WC1 . . . . .3D 39
Atunbi Ct. NW1 . . . . .1A 14
Atwood Ho. W14 . . . . .4C 108
Atwood Rd. W6 . . . . .3A 106
Aubrey Beardsley Ho.
SW1 . . . . .4C 114
Aubrey Mans. NW1 . . . . .1F 55
Aubrey Moore Point E15 . . . .5C 26
Aubrey Pl. NW8 . . . . .1B 32
Aubrey Rd. W8 . . . . .2C 80
Aubrey Wlk. W8 . . . . .3C 80
Auburn Cl. SE14 . . . . .5F 145
Auckland St. SE11 . . . . .1B 138
Auden Pl. NW1 . . . . .3D 13
Audley Dr. E16 . . . . .2F 101
Audley Sq. W1 . . . . .2E 85
Audrey St. E2 . . . . .5D 21
Augustas La. N1 . . . . .1D 17
Augusta St. E14 . . . . .3F 69
Augustine Bell Twr. E3 . . . . . .5D 25
Augustine Rd. W14 . . . . .2D 107
Augustus Bldg. E1 . . . . .4A 66
Augustus Cl. W12 . . . . .5A 78
Augustus Ct. SE1 . . . . .3F 119
Augustus Ho. NW1 . . . . .1B 36
Augustus St. NW1 . . . . .1A 36
Aulay Ho. SE16 . . . . .2C 120
Aulton Pl. SE11 . . . . .1E 139
Aurelia Ho. E20 . . . . .3B 6
Auriol Ho. W12 . . . . .2A 78
Auriol Mans. W14 . . . . .4F 107
Auriol Rd. W14 . . . . .4F 107
Aurora Bldg. E14 . . . . .2C 98
Aurora Ho. E14 . . . . .3A 70
Austen Ho. NW6 . . . . .2D 31
Austin Friars EC2 . . . . .3E 63
Austin Friars Pas. EC2 . . . . . .3E 63
Austin Friars Sq. EC2 . . . . . . .3E 63

Austin Ho. SE14 . . . . .5B 146
Austin St. E2 . . . . .3B 42
Austin Ter. SE1 . . . . .1E 117
Australian War Memorial . . .4E 85
Australia Rd. W12 . . . . .5A 50
Austral St. SE11 . . . . .3F 117
Autumn St. E3 . . . . .4E 25
Avantgarde Pl. E1 . . . . .4C 42
Avantgarde Twr. E1 . . . . . . .4B 42
Avebury Ct. N1 . . . . .4D 19
Avebury St. N1 . . . . .4D 19
Aveline St. SE11 . . . . .5D 117
Ave Maria La. EC4 . . . . .4A 62
Avenfield Ho. W1 . . . . .5C 56
Avenons Rd. E13 . . . . .1D 73
Avenue, The EC2 . . . . .3A 64
　NW6 . . . . .3A 8
　SE10 . . . . .4D 149
Avenue Cl. NW8 . . . . .4A 12
　(not continuous)
Avenue Ct. SW3 . . . . .4B 112
Avenue Ho. NW6 . . . . .2A 8
　NW8 . . . . .1F 33
　NW10 . . . . .1A 28
Avenue Lodge NW8 . . . . .2E 11
Avenue Rd. NW3 . . . . .2D 11
　NW8 . . . . .3F 11
Avenue Studios SW3 . . . . . . .4E 111
Avery Farm Row SW1 . . . . . .4F 113
Avery Row W1 . . . . .5F 57
Aviary Cl. E16 . . . . .2C 72
Avington Ct. SE1 . . . . .4A 120
Avis Sq. E1 . . . . .3E 67
Avocet Cl. SE1 . . . . .5D 121
Avon Ct. W9 . . . . .1D 53
Avondale Ct. E16 . . . . .1A 72
Avondale Ho. SE1 . . . . .1D 143
Avondale Pk. Gdns. W11 . . . .1F 79
Avondale Pk. Rd. W11 . . . . . .5F 51
Avondale Pavement SE1 . . . .1D 143
Avondale Rd. E16 . . . . .1A 72
Avondale Sq. SE1 . . . . .1D 143
Avon Ho. W8 . . . . .1E 109
　W14 . . . . .4C 108
Avonley Rd. SE14 . . . . .5C 144
Avonmore Gdns. W14 . . . . . .4C 108
Avonmore Mans. W14 . . . . . .3A 108
Avonmore Pl. W14 . . . . .3A 108
Avonmore Rd. W14 . . . . .3A 108
Avonmouth St. SE1 . . . . .1B 118
Avon Pl. SE1 . . . . .5C 90
Avro Ct. E9 . . . . .3A 4
Avro Ho. SW8 . . . . .5B 136
Axis Apartments E1 . . . . . . .4C 42
　(off Sclater St.)
Axis Ct. SE10 . . . . .2F 149
　SE16 . . . . .4E 93
Aybrook St. W1 . . . . .2D 57
Aycliffe Ho. SE17 . . . . .2E 141
Aylesbury Ho. SE15 . . . . . . .3E 143
Aylesbury Rd. SE17 . . . . . . .1E 141
Aylesbury St. EC1 . . . . .5F 39
Aylesford Ho. SE1 . . . . .5E 91
Aylesford St. SW1 . . . . .5D 115
Aylmer Ho. SE10 . . . . .1E 149
Aylton Est. SE16 . . . . .5C 94
Aylward St. E1 . . . . .3C 66
　(Jamaica St.)
　E1 . . . . .3B 66
　(Jubilee St.)
Aylwin Est. SE1 . . . . .1A 120
Aynhoe Mans. W14 . . . . .3E 107
Aynhoe Rd. W14 . . . . .3E 107
Ayres St. SE1 . . . . .4C 90

Ayrton Gould Ho. E2 . . . . . . .2E 45
Ayrton Rd. SW7 . . . . .1D 111
Ayston Ho. SE16 . . . . .3E 123
Azalea Ho. SE14 . . . . .5B 146
Azof St. SE10 . . . . .4A 128
Azov Ho. E1 . . . . .5F 45
Azura Ct. E15 . . . . .3B 26
Azure Ho. E2 . . . . .3D 43

B

Babington Ct. WC1 . . . . .1B 60
Babington Ho. SE1 . . . . .4C 90
Babmaes St. SW1 . . . . .1D 87
Bacchus Wlk. N1 . . . . .1F 41
Bache's St. N1 . . . . .2E 41
Back All. EC3 . . . . .4A 64
Bk. Church La. E1 . . . . .4D 65
Backhouse Pl. SE17 . . . . . . .4A 120
Back Pas. EC1 . . . . .1A 62
Bacon Gro. SE1 . . . . .2B 120
Bacon's College Sports Cen.
　. .3F 95
Bacon St. E1 . . . . .4C 42
　E2 . . . . .4C 42
Bacton St. E2 . . . . .2C 44
Baddesley Ho. SE11 . . . . . . .5C 116
Baddow Wlk. N1 . . . . .3C 18
Baden Pl. SE1 . . . . .4D 91
Baden Powell Ho. SW7 . . . . .2C 110
Badminton M. E16 . . . . .2E 101
Badsworth Rd. SE5 . . . . .5B 140
Baffin Way E14 . . . . .1C 98
Bagnigge Ho. WC1 . . . . .3D 39
Bagshot Ho. NW1 . . . . .2A 36
Bagshot St. SE17 . . . . .1A 142
Baildon E2 . . . . .1C 44
Baildon St. SE8 . . . . .5C 146
Bailey Cotts. E14 . . . . .2A 68
Bailey Ho. E3 . . . . .3A 48
　SW10 . . . . .4A 132
Bailey Twr. E1 . . . . .5F 65
Bainbridge St. WC1 . . . . .3E 59
Baird Ho. W12 . . . . .1A 78
Baird St. EC1 . . . . .4C 40
Baker Ho. E3 . . . . .2F 47
　WC1 . . . . .5A 38
Bakers Hall Ct. EC3 . . . . .1A 92
Baker's M. W1 . . . . .3D 57
Baker's Rents E2 . . . . .3B 42
Baker's Row E15 . . . . .5F 27
　EC1 . . . . .5D 39
BAKER STREET 1C 56
Baker St. NW1 . . . . .5C 34
　W1 . . . . .5C 34
Baker's Yd. EC1 . . . . .5D 39
Bakery Cl. SW9 . . . . .5C 138
Balaclava Rd. SE1 . . . . .4C 120
Balcombe Ho. NW1 . . . . .4A 34
Balcombe St. NW1 . . . . .4B 34
Balcorne St. E9 . . . . .2C 22
Balderton Flats W1 . . . . .4E 57
Balderton St. W1 . . . . .4E 57
Baldock St. E3 . . . . .1F 47
Baldrey Ho. SE10 . . . . .5B 128
Baldwins Gdns. EC1 . . . . . . .1D 61
Baldwin St. EC1 . . . . .3D 41
Baldwin Ter. N1 . . . . .5B 18
Balearic Apartments E16 . . . .1E 101
Bale Rd. E1 . . . . .1F 67
Balfe St. N1 . . . . .5A 16
Balfour Ho. W10 . . . . .1E 51

Balfour M. W1 . . . . .2E 85
Balfour Pl. W1 . . . . .1E 85
Balfour St. SE17 . . . . .3D 119
Balfron Twr. E14 . . . . .3B 70
Balin Ho. SE1 . . . . .4D 91
Balkan Wlk. E1 . . . . .1F 93
Balladier Wlk. E14 . . . . .1F 69
Ballance Rd. E9 . . . . .4A 4
Ballard Ho. SE10 . . . . .2A 148
Ballast Quay SE10 . . . . .5E 127
Ball Ct. EC3 . . . . .4E 63
Balletica Apartments WC2 . . .4A 60
Ballin Ct. E14 . . . . .5C 98
Ballinger Point E3 . . . . .2A 48
Balliol Rd. W10 . . . . .3C 50
Ballow Cl. SE5 . . . . .5F 141
Balman Ho. SE16 . . . . .4D 123
Balmer Rd. E3 . . . . .1B 46
Balmes Rd. N1 . . . . .3E 19
Balmoral Apartments W2 . . . .2F 55
Balmoral Ct. NW8 . . . . .5D 11
　SE16 . . . . .2E 95
　SE17 . . . . .1D 141
Balmoral Ho. E14 . . . . .1A 126
　E16 . . . . .2F 101
　W14 . . . . .3F 107
Balmore Cl. E14 . . . . .3C 70
Balniel Ga. SW1 . . . . .5E 115
Balsam Ho. E14 . . . . .5A 70
Baltic Apartments E16 . . . . . .1E 101
Baltic Ct. E1 . . . . .3A 94
　SE16 . . . . .4E 95
Baltic Pl. N1 . . . . .4A 20
Baltic St. E. EC1 . . . . .5B 40
Baltic St. W. EC1 . . . . .5B 40
Baltimore Ct. SW1 . . . . .4D 115
Baltimore Ho. SE11 . . . . .4D 117
Baltimore Wharf E14 . . . . . . .1A 126
Balvaird Pl. SW1 . . . . .1E 137
Bamber Rd. SE15 . . . . .5B 142
Bamborough Gdns. W12 . . . .5C 78
Banbury Ct. WC2 . . . . .5F 59
Banbury Ho. E9 . . . . .2E 23
Banbury Rd. E9 . . . . .2D 23
Bancroft Ct. SW8 . . . . .5F 137
Bancroft Ho. E1 . . . . .4B 44
Bancroft Rd. E1 . . . . .3C 44
Bangla Ho. E8 . . . . .3B 20
Banim St. W6 . . . . .2A 106
Banister Ho. SW8 . . . . .5B 136
　W10 . . . . .3A 30
Banister M. NW6 . . . . .1F 9
Banister Rd. W10 . . . . .2E 29
Bank End SE1 . . . . .2C 90
Bank of England 4D 63
Bank of England Mus. 4E 63
Banks Ho. SE1 . . . . .2B 118
Bankside SE1 . . . . .1B 90
　(not continuous)
Bankside Gallery 1A 90
Bankside Lofts SE1 . . . . .2A 90
Bankside Mix SE1 . . . . .2B 90
Bank St. E14 . . . . .3F 97
Bannatyne's Health Club
　Maida Vale 5F 9
　Russell Square 4E 37
Banner Ct. SE16 . . . . .4B 122
Banner Ho. EC1 . . . . .5C 40
Bannerman Ho. SW8 . . . . . . .3B 138
Banner St. EC1 . . . . .5C 40
Banning St. SE10 . . . . .1F 149
Bannister Ho. SE14 . . . . .3E 145
Bannon Ct. SW6 . . . . .5A 132
Banqueting House 3F 87

Bantock Ho. W10	3A **30**
Bantry Ho. E1	5E **45**
Bantry St. SE5	5E **141**
Banyard Rd. SE16	2A **122**
Barandon Rd. W11	5E **51**
Barandon Wlk. W11	5E **51**
Barbanel Ho. E1	4C **44**
Barbara Brosnan Ct. NW8	1D **33**
Barbara Castle Cl. SW6	3C **130**
Barber Beaumont Ho. E1	3D **45**
Barberry Ct. E15	4F **7**
Barbers Rd. E15	5F **25**
Barbican Arts Cen.	**1C 62**
Barbican Cinema	
Beech St.	**1C 62**
Whitecross St.	**1C 62**
Barbican Theatre	
Silk St.	**1C 62**
Barb M. W6	2C **106**
Barbon All. EC2	3A **64**
Barbon Cl. WC1	1A **60**
Barchester St. E14	2F **69**
Barclay Cl. SW6	5D **131**
Barclay Ho. E9	2B **22**
Barclay Rd. E13	1B **74**
SW6	5D **131**
Bardell Ho. SE1	5D **93**
Bard Rd. W10	5D **51**
Bardsey Pl. E1	5B **44**
Bardsley Ho. SE10	3B **148**
Bardsley La. SE10	3B **148**
Barents Ho. E1	5D **45**
Barfett St. W10	4B **30**
Barfleur La. SE8	4B **124**
Barford Ho. E3	1C **46**
Barford St. N1	4E **17**
Barge Ho. Rd. E16	3F **105**
Barge Ho. St. SE1	2E **89**
Barge La. E3	4A **24**
Barge Wlk. SE10	1C **128**
Barham Ho. SE17	5A **120**
Baring Ct. N1	4D **19**
Baring Ho. E14	4D **69**
Baring St. N1	4D **19**
Barker Dr. NW1	2C **14**
Barker Ho. SE17	4F **119**
Barker St. SW10	2B **132**
Barkham Ter. SE1	1E **117**
Barking Rd. E13	3A **72**
E16	3A **72**
Barkis Ho. W11	2F **79**
Bark Pl. W2	5F **53**
Barkston Gdns. SW5	4F **109**
Barkwith Ho. SE14	3D **145**
Barkworth Rd. SE16	1A **144**
Barlborough St SE14	4D **145**
Barlby Gdns. W10	5D **29**
Barlby Rd. W10	2C **50**
Barleycorn Way E14	5B **68**
(not continuous)	
Barley Mow Pas. EC1	2A **62**
Barley Shotts Bus. Pk.	
W10	1B **52**
Barling NW1	1A **14**
Barlow Ho. N1	2D **41**
SE16	4A **122**
W11	5F **51**
Barlow Pl. W1	1A **86**
Barlow St. SE17	4E **119**
Barnabas Ho. EC1	3B **40**
Barnaby Ct. SE16	5E **93**
Barnaby Ho. SE15	3B **144**
Barnaby Pl. SW7	4D **111**
Barnard Ho. E2	2F **43**
Barnard Lodge *W9*	*1E 53*
(off Admiral Wlk.)	
Barnardo Gdns. E1	5D **67**
Barnardo St. E1	4D **67**
Barnards Ho. SE16	5B **96**
Barnard's Inn EC1	3E **61**
Barnbrough NW1	4B **14**
Barnby Sq. E15	3F **27**
Barnby St. E15	3F **27**
NW1	1C **36**
Barnes Ct. E16	1C **74**
N1	2D **17**
Barnes Ho. E2	5B **22**
SE14	3D **145**
Barnes St. E14	3F **67**
Barnes Ter. SE8	1C **146**
Barnet Gro. E2	2D **43**
Barnett St. E1	3F **65**
Barnfield Pl. E14	4E **125**
Barnham St. SE1	4A **92**
BARNSBURY	**2B 16**
Barnsbury Est. N1	4C **16**
(not continuous)	
Barnsbury Gro. N7	1C **16**
Barnsbury Pk. N1	1D **17**
Barnsbury Rd. N1	5D **17**
Barnsbury Sq. N1	2D **17**
Barnsbury St. N1	2E **17**
Barnsbury Ter. N1	2C **16**
Barnsdale Av. E14	3E **125**
Barnsdale Rd. W9	4C **30**
Barnsley St. E1	4A **44**
Barnstaple Ho. SE10	5F **147**
Barnston Wlk. N1	3B **18**
Barnwell Ho. SE5	5F **141**
Barnwood Cl. W9	5F **31**
Baron Cl. N1	5D **17**
Baroness Rd. E2	2C **42**
BARONS COURT	**1A 130**
Baron's Ct. Rd. W14	5F **107**
Barons Court Theatre	**1A 130**
(off Comeragh Rd.)	
Barons Keep W14	5F **107**
Barons Lodge E14	4C **126**
Baron's Pl. SE1	5E **89**
Baron St. N1	5D **17**
Baron Wlk. E16	1B **72**
Barque M. SE8	2D **147**
Barratt Ho. N1	1A **18**
Barratt Ind. Pk. E3	5B **48**
Barret Ho. NW6	4D **9**
Barrett Ho. SE17	5C **118**
Barrett St. W1	4E **57**
Barrie Est. W2	5D **55**
Barrie Ho. NW8	4B **12**
W2	1C **82**
Barrier Point Rd. E16	3B **102**
Barrow Hill Est. NW8	1F **33**
Barrow Hill Rd. NW8	1F **33**
Barrow Store Ct. SE1	1F **119**
Barry Ho. SE16	4A **122**
Barry Rd. E6	3A **76**
Barter St. WC1	2A **60**
Bartholomew Cl. EC1	2A **62**
(not continuous)	
Bartholomew Ct. E14	1E **99**
EC1	4C **40**
Bartholomew Ho. W10	5F **29**
Bartholomew La. EC2	4E **63**
Bartholomew Pl. EC1	2B **62**
Bartholomew Sq. E1	4A **44**
EC1	3C **40**
Bartholomew St. SE1	2E **119**
Bartle Rd. W11	4E **51**
Bartlett Cl. E14	3E **69**
Bartlett Ct. EC4	3E **61**
Bartlett M. E14	5A **126**
Bartletts Pas. EC4	3E **61**
Bartok Ho. W11	2B **80**
Barton Cl. E6	3C **76**
Barton Ct. W14	1A **130**
Barton Ho. E3	2F **47**
N1	1A **18**
Barton Rd. W14	5F **107**
W14	1A **130**
Barton St. SW1	1F **115**
Bartonway NW8	5D **11**
Bartrip St. E9	4B **4**
Barwell Ho. E2	4E **43**
Baseing Cl. E6	5E **77**
Baseline Bus. Studios	
W11	5E **51**
Basevi Way SE8	2F **147**
Basildon Ct. W1	1E **57**
Basil Ho. E1	3E **65**
SW8	4F **137**
Basil Mans. SW3	5B **84**
Basil St. SW3	1B **112**
Basin App. E14	4A **68**
E16	1F **105**
Basinghall Av. EC2	2D **63**
Basinghall St. EC2	2C **62**
Basing Ho. Yd. E2	2A **42**
Basing Pl. E2	2A **42**
Basing St. W11	3B **52**
Basin Mill Apartments E2	4C **20**
Basire St. N1	3B **18**
Basque Ct. SE16	5D **95**
Bassett Rd. W10	3E **51**
Bassingbourn Ho. N1	1E **17**
Bassishaw Highwalk EC2	2D **63**
Basterfield Ho. EC1	5B **40**
Bastion Highwalk EC2	2C **62**
Bastion Ho. EC2	2B **62**
Bastwick St. EC1	4A **40**
Batavia Ho. SE14	5A **146**
Batavia M. SE14	5A **146**
Batavia Rd. SE14	5A **146**
Batchelor St. N1	5E **17**
Bateman Ho. SE17	3F **139**
Bateman's Bldgs. W1	4D **59**
Bateman's Row EC2	4A **42**
Bateman St. W1	4D **59**
Bate St. E14	5C **68**
Bath Cl. SE15	5A **144**
Bath Ct. EC1	3D **41**
(St Luke's Est.)	
EC1	5D **39**
(Warner St.)	
Bath Gro. E2	1D **43**
Bath Ho. E2	4E **43**
SE1	1B **118**
Bath Pl. EC2	3F **41**
W6	5C **106**
Baths Ct. W12	4A **78**
Bath St. EC1	3C **40**
Bath Ter. SE1	2B **118**
Bathurst Gdns. NW10	1A **28**
Bathurst Ho. W12	5A **50**
Bathurst M. W2	5E **55**
Bathurst St. W2	5E **55**
Batman Cl. W12	1A **78**
Batoum Gdns. W6	1C **106**
Batson Ho. E1	4E **65**
Batten Cl. E6	4C **76**
Batten Cotts. E14	2A **68**
Batten Ho. W10	3A **30**

BATTERSEA 5A 134
Battersea Bri. SW3 . . . . . . .4E 133
Battersea Bri. Rd. SW11 . . . .4F 133
Battersea Church Rd.
　SW11 . . . . .5E 133
Battersea Park 4C 134
Battersea Park Children's Zoo
　. . . . . .4D 135
Battersea Pk. Rd. SW8 . . . .5A 136
Battishill St. N1 . . . . .2F 17
Battlebridge Ct. N1 . . . . . . .5A 16
Battle Bri. La. SE1 . . . . .3F 91
Battle Ho. SE15 . . . . .3D 143
Batty St. E1 . . . . .3E 65
Batwa Ho. SE16 . . . . .1A 144
Bawley Ter. E15 . . . . .4D 27
Bawtree Rd. SE14 . . . . . . .4F 145
Baxendale St. E2 . . . . .2D 43
Baxter Ho. E3 . . . . .2F 47
Baxter Rd. E16 . . . . .3C 74
Bay Ct. E1 . . . . .5D 45
Bayer Ho. EC1 . . . . .5B 40
Bayes Ct. NW3 . . . . .1B 12
Bayes Ho. N1 . . . . .1D 17
Bayford M. E8 . . . . .2A 22
Bayford Rd. NW10 . . . . . . .3D 29
Bayford St. E8 . . . . .2A 22
Bayford St. Bus. Cen. E8 . . .2A 22
Bayham Pl. NW1 . . . . .4B 14
Bayham St. NW1 . . . . .3A 14
Bayley St. WC1 . . . . .2D 59
Baylis Rd. SE1 . . . . .1D 117
Bayne Ct. E6 . . . . .4C 76
Baynes St. NW1 . . . . .2C 14
Bayonne Rd. W6 . . . . .3A 130
BAYSWATER 5B 54
Bayswater Rd. W2 . . . . .1F 81
Baythorne Ho. E16 . . . . .4C 72
　(off Turner St.)
Baythorne St. E3 . . . . .1C 68
Bayton Ct. E8 . . . . .2E 21
Bay Tree Ho. EC1 . . . . .5D 39
Baytree M. SE17 . . . . .3D 119
Bazalgette Ho. NW8 . . . . . .4E 33
Bazeley Ho. SE1 . . . . .5F 89
Bazely St. E14 . . . . .5B 70
BBC Broadcasting House . . .2A 58
BBC Maida Vale Studios . . .4F 31
BDA Dental Mus. 2F 57
Beach Ho. SW5 . . . . .5D 109
Beachy Rd. E3 . . . . .2D 25
Beacon Ho. E14 . . . . .5F 125
　SE5 . . . . .5F 141
Beacon Point SE10 . . . . . .2A 148
Beacons Cl. E6 . . . . .2A 76
Beaconsfield WC1 . . . . .2B 60
Beaconsfield Rd. SE17 . . . .1E 141
Beaconsfield St. N1 . . . . . . .3F 15
Beaconsfield Ter. Rd.
　W14 . . . . .2F 107
Beaconsfield Wlk. E6 . . . . . .4E 77
Beadnell Ct. E1 . . . . .5E 65
Beadon Rd. W6 . . . . .4B 106
Beak St. W1 . . . . .5B 58
Beale Pl. E3 . . . . .5B 24
Beale Rd. E3 . . . . .4B 24
Beaminster Ho. SW8 . . . . .4B 138
Beamish Ho. SE16 . . . . . . .4B 122
Beanacre Cl. E9 . . . . .4C 4
Bear All. EC4 . . . . .3F 61
Bear Gdns. SE1 . . . . .2B 90
Bear La. SE1 . . . . .2A 90
Bear Pit Apartments SE1 . . .2B 90
Bear St. WC2 . . . . .5E 59

Beatrice Ho. W6 . . . . .5B 106
Beatrice Pl. W8 . . . . .2F 109
Beatrice Rd. SE1 . . . . .4E 121
Beatrice Webb Ho. E3 . . . . .5F 23
Beatrix Apartments E3 . . . . .5B 46
Beatrix Ho. SW5 . . . . .5A 110
Beatson Wlk. SE16 . . . . . . .2F 95
　(not continuous)
Beatty Ho. E14 . . . . .4E 97
　SW1 . . . . .1C 136
Beatty St. NW1 . . . . .5B 14
Beauchamp Pl. SW3 . . . . . .1A 112
Beauchamp St. EC1 . . . . . .2D 61
Beauclerc Rd. W6 . . . . . . .1A 106
Beaufort E6 . . . . .2E 77
Beaufort Ct. E14 . . . . .4E 97
　SW6 . . . . .2D 131
Beaufort Gdns. SW3 . . . . . .1A 112
Beaufort Ho. E16 . . . . .2F 101
　SW1 . . . . .1D 137
　SW3 . . . . .3E 133
Beaufort Mans. SW3 . . . . . .3E 133
Beaufort M. SW6 . . . . .2C 130
Beaufort St. SW3 . . . . .1D 133
Beaufort Ter. E14 . . . . .5B 126
Beaufoy Ho. SW8 . . . . .4B 138
Beaufoy Wlk. SE11 . . . . . . .4C 116
Beaulieu Av. E16 . . . . .2F 101
Beaulieu Lodge E14 . . . . . .2D 127
Beaumanor Mans. W2 . . . . .5A 54
Beaumont W14 . . . . .4C 108
Beaumont Av. W14 . . . . . . .5B 108
Beaumont Bldgs. WC2 . . . . .4A 60
Beaumont Ct. E1 . . . . .3F 45
　NW1 . . . . .3C 14
　W1 . . . . .1E 57
Beaumont Cres. W14 . . . . . .5B 108
Beaumont Gro. E1 . . . . .5D 45
Beaumont Ho. W9 . . . . .2C 30
Beaumont Lodge E8 . . . . . . .1E 21
Beaumont M. W1 . . . . .1E 57
Beaumont Pl. W1 . . . . .4C 36
Beaumont Sq. E1 . . . . .5D 45
Beaumont St. W1 . . . . .1E 57
Beaumont Wlk. NW3 . . . . . .1C 12
Beauvale NW1 . . . . .1E 13
Beccles St. E14 . . . . .4C 68
Bechtel Ho. W6 . . . . .4D 107
Becket Ho. E16 . . . . .2F 101
　SE1 . . . . .5D 91
Becket St. SE1 . . . . .1D 119
Beckett Ho. E1 . . . . .2B 66
Beckfoot NW1 . . . . .1C 36
Beckford Cl. W14 . . . . .3C 108
Beckford Pl. SE17 . . . . . . .1C 140
Beckham Ho. SE11 . . . . . . .4C 116
Beckhaven Ho. SE11 . . . . . .3E 117
Beckley Ho. E3 . . . . .4B 46
Beck Rd. E8 . . . . .3F 21
BECKTON 2E 77
BECKTON PARK 4C 76
Beckton Retail Pk. E6 . . . . .1D 77
Beckton Rd. E16 . . . . .1C 72
Beckway St. SE17 . . . . .4E 119
　(not continuous)
Beckwith Ho. E2 . . . . .2A 22
Becquerel Ct. SE10 . . . . . .2C 128
Bedale St. SE1 . . . . .3D 91
Beddalls Farm Ct. E6 . . . . . .1F 75
Bedefield WC1 . . . . .3A 38
Bede Sq. E3 . . . . .5C 46
Bedford Av. WC1 . . . . .2E 59
Bedfordbury WC2 . . . . .5F 59
　(not continuous)

Bedford Ct. WC2 . . . . .1F 87
Bedford Ct. Mans. WC1 . . . .2E 59
Bedford Gdns. W8 . . . . .3D 81
Bedford Gdns. Ho. W8 . . . . .3E 81
Bedford Pas. SW6 . . . . . . .4A 130
　W1 . . . . .1C 58
Bedford Pl. WC1 . . . . .1C 60
Bedford Row SE1 . . . . .1C 118
　WC1 . . . . .1C 60
Bedford Sq. WC1 . . . . .2E 59
Bedford St. WC2 . . . . .5F 59
Bedford Way WC1 . . . . .5E 37
Bedlam M. SE11 . . . . .3D 117
Bedmond Ho. SW3 . . . . . . .5F 111
Bedser Cl. SE11 . . . . .2C 138
Beeby Rd. E16 . . . . .2F 73
Beech Cl. SE8 . . . . .3C 146
Beech Ct. W9 . . . . .1D 53
Beechdene SE15 . . . . .5F 143
Beechey Ho. E1 . . . . .3A 94
Beech Gdns. EC2 . . . . .1B 62
Beech Ho. SE16 . . . . .4D 95
Beech St. EC2 . . . . .1B 62
Beech Tree Cl. N1 . . . . .1D 17
Beechwood Ho. E2 . . . . . . .5E 21
Beehive Cl. E8 . . . . .1B 20
Beehive Pas. EC3 . . . . .4F 63
Beeston Ho. SE1 . . . . .2D 119
Beeston Pl. SW1 . . . . .2A 114
Beethoven St. W10 . . . . . . .2A 30
Begonia Cl. E6 . . . . .1A 76
Bekesbourne St. E14 . . . . . .4F 67
Belford Ho. E8 . . . . .3C 20
Belfry Cl. SE16 . . . . .5A 122
Belgrave Ct. E2 . . . . .1F 43
　E14 . . . . .1C 96
　SW8 . . . . .5B 136
Belgrave Gdns. NW8 . . . . . .4A 10
Belgrave Ho. SW9 . . . . . . .4D 139
Belgrave M. Nth. SW1 . . . . .1D 113
Belgrave M. Sth. SW1 . . . . .1E 113
Belgrave M. W. SW1 . . . . . .1D 113
Belgrave Pl. SW1 . . . . .1E 113
Belgrave Rd. SW1 . . . . .3A 114
Belgrave Sq. SW1 . . . . .1D 113
Belgrave St. E1 . . . . .2E 67
Belgrave Yd. SW1 . . . . .2F 113
BELGRAVIA 2E 113
Belgravia Ct. SW1 . . . . .2F 113
Belgravia Ho. SW1 . . . . . . .1D 113
Belgrove St. WC1 . . . . .2A 38
Belitha Vs. N1 . . . . .1C 16
Bella Best Ho. SW1 . . . . . . .5A 114
　(off Westmoreland Ter.)
Bellamy Cl. E14 . . . . .4D 97
　W14 . . . . .1C 130
Bellamy's Ct. SE16 . . . . . . .2D 95
Bellevue Pl. E1 . . . . .5B 44
Bellflower Cl. E6 . . . . .1F 75
Bellhaven E15 . . . . .4E 7
Bell Ho. SE10 . . . . .3B 148
Bell Inn Yd. EC3 . . . . .4E 63
Bell La. E1 . . . . .2B 64
　E16 . . . . .3C 100
Bellmaker Ct. E3 . . . . .1D 69
Bellot Gdns. SE10 . . . . . . .5A 128
Bellot St. SE10 . . . . .5A 128
Bell St. NW1 . . . . .1F 55
Bell Wharf La. EC4 . . . . . . .1C 90
Bell Yd. WC2 . . . . .4D 61
Bell Yd. M. SE1 . . . . .5A 92
Belmont St. NW1 . . . . .1E 13
Belsize Pk. NW3 . . . . .1D 11

Belsize Rd. NW6 . . . . .4E **9**
Belton Rd. E11 . . . . .1F **7**
Belton Way E3 . . . . .1D **69**
Belvedere Bldgs. SE1 . . . . . .5A **90**
Belvedere Ct. N1 . . . . .3F **19**
Belvedere Pl. SE1 . . . . .5A **90**
Belvedere Rd. SE1 . . . . .5B **88**
Belvoir Ho. SW1 . . . . .4C **114**
Bembridge Ho. SE8 . . . . . . .4B **124**
Bemerton Est. N1 . . . . .2B **16**
Bemerton St. N1 . . . . .3B **16**
Benbow Ct. W6 . . . . .1B **106**
Benbow Ho. SE8 . . . . .2E **147**
Benbow Rd. W6 . . . . .1A **106**
Benbow St. SE8 . . . . .2E **147**
Bence Ho. SE8 . . . . .4F **123**
Bendall Ho. NW1 . . . . .1A **56**
Bendall M. NW1 . . . . .1A **56**
Benenden Ho. SE17 . . . . .5A **120**
Ben Ezra Ct. SE17 . . . . .4C **118**
Benfleet Ct. E8 . . . . .3C **20**
Bengal Ct. EC3 . . . . .4E **63**
Benham Ho. SW10 . . . . .4A **132**
Benhill Rd. SE5 . . . . .5E **141**
Benin Ho. WC1 . . . . .2B **60**
Benjamin Cl. E8 . . . . .3E **21**
Benjamin Franklin House . . .*2F* **87**
(off Craven St.)
Benjamin St. EC1 . . . . .1F **61**
Ben Jonson Ct. N1 . . . . .5A **20**
Ben Jonson Ho. EC2 . . . . . . .1C **62**
Ben Jonson Pl. EC2 . . . . .1C **62**
Ben Jonson Rd. E1 . . . . .2E **67**
Benledi Rd. E14 . . . . .3D **71**
Bennelong Cl. W12 . . . . .4A **50**
Bennet's Hill EC4 . . . . .5A **62**
Bennet St. SW1 . . . . .2B **86**
Bennett Ho. SW1 . . . . .3E **115**
Bennett Rd. E13 . . . . .1B **74**
Bennett's Yd. SW1 . . . . .2E **115**
Benn St. E9 . . . . .4A **4**
Ben Smith Way SE16 . . . . . . .1E **121**
Benson Ho. E2 . . . . .4B **42**
SE1 .3E **89**
Benson Quay E1 . . . . .1B **94**
Bentham Ct. N1 . . . . .2B **18**
Bentham Ho. SE1 . . . . .1D **119**
Ben Tillet Cl. E16 . . . . .3B **104**
Bentinck Cl. NW8 . . . . .1A **34**
Bentinck Ho. SW1 . . . . .2E **115**
W12 . . . . .5A **50**
Bentinck Mans. W1 . . . . .3E **57**
Bentinck M. W1 . . . . .3E **57**
Bentinck St. W1 . . . . .3E **57**
Bentley Ho. E3 . . . . .4D **47**
Bentworth Ct. E2 . . . . .4D **43**
Bentworth Rd. W12 . . . . .4A **50**
Ben Uri Gallery **4A 10**
Benville Ho. SW8 . . . . .5C **138**
Benwick Cl. SE16 . . . . .3A **122**
Benworth St. E3 . . . . .2C **46**
Benyon Ct. N1 . . . . .3F **19**
Benyon Ho. EC1 . . . . .2E **39**
Benyon Rd. N1 . . . . .3E **19**
Benyon Wharf N1 . . . . .3A **20**
Berberis Ho. E3 . . . . .1E **69**
Berber Pl. E14 . . . . .5D **69**
Berebinder Ho. E3 . . . . .1B **46**
Beregaria Ct. SE11 . . . . .2E **139**
Berenger Twr. SW10 . . . . . . .4D **133**
Berenger Wlk. SW10 . . . . . . .4D **133**
Berens Rd. NW10 . . . . .3D **29**
Beresford Ct. E9 . . . . .3A **4**
Bere St. E1 . . . . .5E **67**

Bergen Sq. SE16 . . . . .1A **124**
Berghem M. W14 . . . . .2E **107**
Bergholt M. NW1 . . . . .2C **14**
Berglen Ct. E14 . . . . .4F **67**
Bering Sq. E14 . . . . .5E **125**
Bering Wlk. E16 . . . . .4D **75**
Berkeley Ct. NW1 . . . . .5C **34**
Berkeley Gdns. W8 . . . . .3E **81**
Berkeley Ho. E3 . . . . .3D **47**
SE8 .1B **146**
Berkeley M. W1 . . . . .4C **56**
Berkeley Sq. W1 . . . . .1F **85**
Berkeley St. W1 . . . . .1A **86**
Berkeley Twr. E14 . . . . .2C **96**
Berkley Gro. NW1 . . . . .2D **13**
Berkley Rd. NW1 . . . . .2C **12**
Berkshire Rd. E9 . . . . .4C **4**
BERMONDSEY **5D 93**
Bermondsey Exchange
SE1 .5A **92**
Bermondsey Sq. SE1 . . . . . . .1A **120**
Bermondsey St. SE1 . . . . .3F **91**
Bermondsey Trad. Est.
SE16 . . . . .5B **122**
Bermondsey Wall E. SE16 . . .5E **93**
Bermondsey Wall W. SE16 . . .4D **93**
Bernard Angell Ho. SE10 . . . .2E **149**
Bernard Cassidy St. E16 . . . . .1C **72**
Bernard Hegarty Lodge E8 . . .2E **21**
Bernard Ho. E1 . . . . .2B **64**
Bernard Mans. WC1 . . . . .5F **37**
Bernard Myers Ho. SE5 . . . . .5F **141**
Bernard Shaw Ct. NW1 . . . . . .1B **14**
Bernard St. WC1 . . . . .5F **37**
Bernard Sunley Ho. SW9 . . . .5D **139**
Berners Ho. N1 . . . . .5D **17**
Berners M. W1 . . . . .2C **58**
Berners Pl. W1 . . . . .3C **58**
Berners Rd. N1 . . . . .4F **17**
Berners St. W1 . . . . .2C **58**
Berner Ter. E1 . . . . .4E **65**
Bernhard Baron Ho. E1 . . . . . .4E **65**
Bernhardt Cres. NW8 . . . . . . .4F **33**
Berrington Ho. W2 . . . . .5E **53**
Berry Cotts. E14 . . . . .3A **68**
Berryfield Rd. SE17 . . . . .5A **118**
Berry Ho. E1 . . . . .5A **44**
Berry Pl. EC1 . . . . .3A **40**
Berry St. EC1 . . . . .4A **40**
Bertrand Ho. E16 . . . . .3F **73**
Berwick Ct. SE1 . . . . .5C **90**
Berwick Rd. E16 . . . . .4A **74**
Berwick St. W1 . . . . .3C **58**
Beryl Av. E6 . . . . .1A **76**
Besant Ho. NW8 . . . . .3B **10**
Besford Ho. E2 . . . . .5E **21**
Bessborough Gdns. SW1 . . . .5E **115**
Bessborough Pl. SW1 . . . . . . .5D **115**
Bessborough St. SW1 . . . . . . .5D **115**
Bessemer Ct. NW1 . . . . .1C **14**
Bessemer Pl. SE10 . . . . .1C **128**
Bessie Lansbury Cl. E6 . . . . . .4D **77**
Besson St. SE14 . . . . .5D **145**
Bessy St. E2 . . . . .2C **44**
Bestwood St. SE8 . . . . .4E **123**
Bethersden Ho. SE17 . . . . . . .5A **120**
Bethlehem Ho. E14 . . . . .5C **68**
BETHNAL GREEN **3F 43**
**Bethnal Green Centre for Sports
& Performing Arts** **3C 42**
Bethnal Grn. Rd. E1 . . . . .4B **42**
E2 . . . . .3E **43**
Bethwin Rd. SE5 . . . . .4A **140**
Betsham Ho. SE1 . . . . .4D **91**

Betterton Ho. WC2 . . . . .4A **60**
Betterton St. WC2 . . . . .4F **59**
Betts Ho. E1 . . . . .5F **65**
Betts Rd. E16 . . . . .5A **74**
Betts St. E1 . . . . .5F **65**
Betty May Gray Ho. E14 . . .3C **126**
Bevan Ct. E3 . . . . .5D **25**
Bevan Ho. N1 . . . .*4F* **19**
(off Halcomb St.)
WC1 . . . . .1A **60**
Bevan St. N1 . . . . .4C **18**
Bevenden St. N1 . . . . .2E **41**
Beverley Ct. NW6 . . . . .2C **10**
Beverston M. W1 . . . . .2B **56**
Bevin Cl. SE16 . . . . .2F **95**
Bevin Ct. WC1 . . . . .2C **38**
Bevington Path SE1 . . . . .5B **92**
Bevington Rd. W10 . . . . .1A **52**
Bevington St. SE16 . . . . .1E **121**
Bevin Ho. E2 . . . . .2C **44**
E3 . . . . .2D **47**
Bevin Way WC1 . . . . .2D **39**
Bevis Marks EC3 . . . . .3A **64**
Bewdley St. N1 . . . . .1D **17**
Bewick M. SE15 . . . . .5F **143**
Bewley Ho. E1 . . . . .5A **66**
Bewley St. E1 . . . . .5A **66**
Bexhill Wlk. E15 . . . . .4F **27**
Bezier Apartments EC2 . . . . . .4E **41**
BFI IMAX **3D 89**
BFI Southbank **2C 88**
Bianca Ho. N1 . . . . .1F **41**
Bianca Rd. SE15 . . . . .3C **142**
Bibury Cl. SE15 . . . . .3A **142**
(not continuous)
Bickels Yd. SE1 . . . . .5A **92**
Bickenhall Mans. W1 . . . . .1C **56**
(not continuous)
Bickenhall St. W1 . . . . .1C **56**
Bicknell Ho. E1 . . . . .4E **65**
Bidborough St. WC1 . . . . .3F **37**
Biddenham Ho. SE16 . . . . . . .3E **123**
Bidder St. E16 . . . . .1F **71**
(not continuous)
Biddesden Ho. SW3 . . . . .4B **112**
Biddulph Mans. W9 . . . . .3F **31**
Biddulph Rd. W9 . . . . .3F **31**
Big Ben **5A 88**
Biggerstaff Rd. E15 . . . . .3C **26**
Biggs Sq. E9 . . . . .5C **4**
Bigland St. E1 . . . . .4F **65**
Bilberry Ho. E3 . . . . .1E **69**
Billing Ho. E1 . . . . .4D **67**
Billingley NW1 . . . . .4B **14**
Billing Pl. SW10 . . . . .4A **132**
Billing Rd. SW10 . . . . .4A **132**
Billingsgate Market **2A 98**
Billing St. SW10 . . . . .4A **132**
Billington Rd. SE14 . . . . .5D **145**
Billiter Sq. EC3 . . . . .4A **64**
Billiter St. EC3 . . . . .4A **64**
Billson St. E14 . . . . .4C **126**
Bilton Towers W1 . . . . .4C **56**
Bina Gdns. SW5 . . . . .4B **110**
Binbrook Ho. W10 . . . . .1B **50**
Bingfield St. N1 . . . . .3A **16**
(not continuous)
Bingham Ct. N1 . . . . .1A **18**
Bingham Pl. W1 . . . . .1D **57**
Bingley Rd. E16 . . . . .3B **74**
Binnacle Ho. E1 . . . . .2A **94**
Binney St. W1 . . . . .4E **57**
Binnie Ho. SE1 . . . . .2B **118**
Bioko Ct. E1 . . . . .1F **67**

Birch Cl. E16 . . . . .1A 72
Birchdown Ho. E3 . . . . .3F 47
Birchfield Ho. E14 . . . . .5D 69
Birchfield St. E14 . . . . .5D 69
Birch Ho. W10 . . . . .4A 30
Birchington Ct. NW6 . . . . .3F 9
Birchington Rd. NW6 . . . . .3E 9
Birchin La. EC3 . . . . .4E 63
Birchmere Lodge SE16 . . . .1F 143
Birch Va. Ct. NW8 . . . . .4E 33
Birdbrook Ho. N1 . . . . .2B 18
Birdcage Wlk. SW1 . . . . .5B 86
Bird in Bush BMX Track 4F 143
Bird in Bush Rd. SE15 . . . .4D 143
Birdsfield La. E3 . . . . .3B 24
Bird St. W1 . . . . .4E 57
Birkbeck St. E2 . . . . .3A 44
Birkdale Cl. SE16 . . . . .1F 143
Birkenhead St. WC1 . . . . . . .2A 38
Birley Lodge NW8 . . . . .5E 11
Birtwhistle Ho. E3 . . . . .3C 24
Biscay Ho. E1 . . . . .5E 45
Biscayne Av. E14 . . . . .1C 98
Biscay Rd. W6 . . . . .5D 107
Biscott Ho. E3 . . . . .4A 48
Bishop King's Rd. W14 . . . .3A 108
Bishop's Bri. Rd. W2 . . . . . .4A 54
Bishops Ct. EC4 . . . . .3F 61
  W2 . . . . .3A 54
  WC2 . . . . .3D 61
Bishopsdale Ho. NW6 . . . . . .3E 9
Bishopsgate EC2 . . . . .4F 63
Bishopsgate Arc. EC2 . . . . . .2A 64
Bishopsgate Chyd. EC2 . . . . .3F 63
Bishopsgate Institute & Libraries
. . . . .2A 64
Bishops Ho. SW8 . . . . .5A 138
Bishops Mead SE5 . . . . . . .5C 140
Bishops Rd. SW6 . . . . .5B 130
  SW11 . . . . .5A 134
Bishops Sq. E1 . . . . .1A 64
Bishop's Ter. SE11 . . . . .3E 117
Bishop St. N1 . . . . .3B 18
Bishop's Way E2 . . . . .5A 22
Bishops Wharf Ho. SW11 . . .5A 134
Bissagos Ct. E1 . . . . .1F 67
Bisson Rd. E15 . . . . .5C 26
Bittern Ct. SE8 . . . . .3D 147
Bittern Ho. SE1 . . . . .5B 90
Bittern St. SE1 . . . . .5B 90
Blackall St. EC2 . . . . .4F 41
Blackbird Yd. E2 . . . . .2C 42
Black Bull Yd. EC1 . . . . .1D 61
Blackburne's M. W1 . . . . . . .5D 57
Blackfriars Bri. EC4 . . . . . . .5F 61
Blackfriars Ct. EC4 . . . . .5F 61
Black Friars La. EC4 . . . . . . .5F 61
  (not continuous)
Blackfriars Pas. EC4 . . . . . . .5F 61
Blackfriars Rd. SE1 . . . . . . .1D 119
Blackfriars Underpass EC4 . .5F 61
Blackheath Av. SE10 . . . . . .4E 149
Black Horse Ct. SE1 . . . . . .1E 119
Blackhorse Rd. SE8 . . . . . . .2A 146
Blacklands Ter. SW3 . . . . . .4B 112
Blackmans Yd. E2 . . . . .4D 43
Blackmore Ho. N1 . . . . .4C 16
Black Prince Rd. SE1 . . . . . .4B 116
  SE11 . . . . .4B 116
Blacks Rd. W6 . . . . .4B 106
Blackstone Est. E8 . . . . .2E 21
Blackstone Ho. SW1 . . . . . .1B 136
Black Swan Yd. SE1 . . . . . . .4F 91
Blackthorn Av. N7 . . . . .1D 17

Blackthorn Ct. E15 . . . . .1E 7
Blackthorne Ct. SE15 . . . .4C 142
Blackthorn St. E3 . . . . .5E 47
BLACKWALL 2C 98
Blackwall La. SE10 . . . . . . .3A 128
Blackwall Trad. Est. E14 . . .2E 71
Blackwall Tunnel E14 . . . . . .2D 99
  (not continuous)
Blackwall Tunnel App.
  E14 . . . . .5C 70
Blackwall Tunnel Northern App.
  E3 . . . . .1A 48
  E14 . . . . .1B 70
Blackwall Tunnel Southern App.
  SE10 . . . . .1F 127
Blackwall Way E14 . . . . .1C 98
Blackwater Ho. NW8 . . . . . .1E 55
Blackwood Ho. E1 . . . . .5A 44
Blackwood St. SE17 . . . . . .5D 119
Bladen Ho. E1 . . . . .3D 67
Blades Ct. W6 . . . . .5A 106
Blades Ho. SE11 . . . . .3D 139
Blagrove Rd. W10 . . . . .2A 52
Blair Ct. NW8 . . . . .3D 11
Blairgowrie Ct. E14 . . . . . . .3E 71
Blair St. E14 . . . . .4C 70
Blake Cl. W10 . . . . .1C 50
Blake Ct. NW6 . . . . .2D 31
  SE16 . . . . .5A 122
Blake Gdns. SW6 . . . . .5F 131
Blake Ho. E14 . . . . .4F 97
  SE1 . . . . .1D 117
  SE8 . . . . .2D 147
Blakeney Cl. NW1 . . . . .2D 15
Blaker Rd. E15 . . . . .4B 26
Blake's Rd. SE15 . . . . .4A 142
Blanchard Way E8 . . . . .1E 21
Blanch Cl. SE15 . . . . .5B 144
Blandford Ct. N1 . . . . .2A 20
Blandford Ho. SW8 . . . . . . .4B 138
Blandford Sq. NW1 . . . . . . .5A 34
Blandford St. W1 . . . . .3C 56
Bland Ho. SE11 . . . . .5C 116
Blantyre St. SW10 . . . . . . .4D 133
Blantyre Twr. SW10 . . . . . .4D 133
Blantyre Wlk. SW10 . . . . . .4D 133
Blashford NW3 . . . . .1B 12
Blasker Wlk. E14 . . . . .5F 125
Blaxland Ho. W12 . . . . .5A 50
Blazer Ct. NW8 . . . . .3E 33
Blechynden Ho. W10 . . . . . .4E 51
Blechynden St. W10 . . . . . . .5E 51
Bledlow Cl. NW8 . . . . .5E 33
Bleeding Heart Yd. EC1 . . . .2E 61
Blemundsbury WC1 . . . . . . .1B 60
Blendon Row SE17 . . . . . . .4D 119
Blenheim Ct. SE10 . . . . . . .5D 129
  SE16 . . . . .2E 95
Blenheim Cres. W11 . . . . . .5F 51
Blenheim Ho. E16 . . . . .2F 101
  SW3 . . . . .1A 134
Blenheim Pas. NW8 . . . . . . .5B 10
Blenheim Rd. E15 . . . . .1F 7
  NW8 . . . . .5C 10
Blenheim St. W1 . . . . .4F 57
Blenheim Ter. NW8 . . . . .5B 10
Bletchley Ct. N1 . . . . .1D 41
Bletchley St. N1 . . . . .1C 40
Bletsoe Wlk. N1 . . . . .5C 18
Blick Ho. SE16 . . . . .1B 122
Blissett St. SE10 . . . . .5B 148
Bliss M. W10 . . . . .2A 30
Blisworth Ho. E2 . . . . .4E 21
Blithehale Ct. E2 . . . . .3A 44

Blithfield St. W8 . . . . .2F 109
Block Wharf E14 . . . . .4D 97
Bloemfontein Av. W12 . . . . .3A 78
Bloemfontein Rd. W12 . . . . .2A 78
Blomfield Ct. W9 . . . . .4C 32
Blomfield Mans. W12 . . . . . .3B 78
Blomfield Rd. W9 . . . . .1A 54
Blomfield St. EC2 . . . . .2E 63
Blomfield Vs. W2 . . . . .2A 54
Blondin St. E3 . . . . .5D 25
Bloomberg Arc. EC4 . . . . . . .4C 62
Bloomberg Ct. SW1 . . . . . .4D 115
Bloomburg St. SW1 . . . . . . .4C 114
Bloomfield Ho. E1 . . . . .2D 65
Bloomfield Pl. W1 . . . . .5A 58
Bloomfield Ter. SW1 . . . . . . .5E 113
Bloom Pk. Rd. SW6 . . . . . . .5B 130
BLOOMSBURY 1A 60
Bloomsbury Ct. WC1 . . . . . . .2A 60
Bloomsbury Pl. WC1 . . . . . . .1A 60
Bloomsbury Sq. WC1 . . . . . .2A 60
Bloomsbury St. WC1 . . . . . . .2E 59
Bloomsbury Theatre 4D 37
Bloomsbury Way WC1 . . . . .3F 59
Blore Ct. W1 . . . . .5D 59
Blore Ho. SW10 . . . . .4B 132
Blossom St. E1 . . . . .5A 42
Blount St. E14 . . . . .3A 68
Blucher Rd. SE5 . . . . .5C 140
Blue Anchor La. SE16 . . . . .3E 121
Blue Anchor Yd. E1 . . . . .5D 65
Blue Ball Yd. SW1 . . . . .3B 86
Bluebell Cl. E9 . . . . .3B 22
Blue Bldg. SE10 . . . . .5C 128
Blue Ct. N1 . . . . .3D 19
Blue Elephant Theatre 4B 140
Blue Fin Bldg. SE1 . . . . .2A 90
Bluegate M. E1 . . . . .5A 66
Blue Lion Pl. SE1 . . . . .1F 119
Blundell St. N7 . . . . .1A 10
Blunden Ct. SW6 . . . . .4E 131
Blyth Cl. E14 . . . . .3D 127
Blythe Ho. SE11 . . . . .2E 139
Blythe M. W14 . . . . .1D 107
Blythendale Ho. E2 . . . . .1E 43
Blythe Rd. W14 . . . . .1D 107
Blythe St. E2 . . . . .2F 43
Blyth's Wharf E14 . . . . .1A 96
Boadicea St. N1 . . . . .4B 16
Boardwalk Pl. E14 . . . . .2B 98
Boarley Ho. SE17 . . . . .4F 119
Boathouse Centre, The
  W10 . . . . .4E 29
Boathouse Wlk. SE15 . . . . .4C 142
  (not continuous)
Boat Lifter Way SE16 . . . . .3A 124
Boat Quay E16 . . . . .1C 102
Boatyard Apartments E14 . .1B 148
Bocking St. E8 . . . . .3F 21
Boden Ho. E1 . . . . .1D 65
Bodington Ct. W12 . . . . .4D 79
Bogart Ct. E14 . . . . .1D 97
Bohn Rd. E1 . . . . .1F 67
Boisseau Ho. E1 . . . . .2C 66
Bolanachi Bldg. SE16 . . . . .2D 121
Boldero Pl. NW8 . . . . .5F 33
Boleyn Ho. E16 . . . . .2E 101
Bolina Rd. SE16 . . . . .5C 122
Bolingbroke Rd. W14 . . . . .1D 107
Bolingbroke Wlk. SW11 . . . .5E 133
Bolney Ga. SW7 . . . . .5F 83
Bolney St. SW8 . . . . .5B 138
Bolsover St. W1 . . . . .5A 36
Bolt Ct. EC4 . . . . .4E 61

Bolt Ho. N1 . . . . .4A **20**
Bolton Cres. SE5 . . . . .4F **139**
Bolton Gdns. NW10 . . . . . . .1D **29**
SW5 . . . . .5F **109**
Bolton Gdns. M. SW10 . . . . .5A **110**
Bolton Ho. SE10 . . . . .1F **149**
SE11 . . . . .3F **117**
Bolton Pl. NW8 . . . . .4A **10**
Bolton Rd. NW8 . . . . .4A **10**
Boltons, The SW10 . . . . .5B **110**
Boltons Ct. SW5 . . . . .5A **110**
Boltons Pl. SW5 . . . . .5B **110**
Bolton St. W1 . . . . .2A **86**
Bolton Studios SW10 . . . . .1C **132**
Bombay Ct. SE16 . . . . .4B **94**
Bombay St. SE16 . . . . .3F **121**
Bomore Rd. W11 . . . . .5E **51**
Bonar Rd. SE15 . . . . .5D **143**
Bonchurch Rd. W10 . . . . . . .1F **51**
Bond Ct. EC4 . . . . .4D **63**
Bondfield Rd. E6 . . . . .2B **76**
Bond Ho. NW6 . . . . .1C **30**
SE14 . . . . .5A **146**
Bonding Yd. Wlk. SE16 . . . .1A **124**
Bond St. E15 . . . . .2F **7**
Bondway SW8 . . . . .3A **138**
Bonham Ho. W11 . . . . .2B **80**
Bonhill St. EC2 . . . . .5E **41**
Bonner Rd. E2 . . . . .5B **22**
Bonner St. E2 . . . . .1C **44**
Bonnington Ho. N1 . . . . .1B **38**
Bonnington Sq. SW8 . . . . . .2B **138**
Bonny St. NW1 . . . . .2B **14**
Bonsor St. SE5 . . . . .5F **141**
Bookbinders Ct. E1 . . . . .4A **44**
Booker Cl. E14 . . . . .2C **68**
Boord St. SE10 . . . . .2A **128**
Booth Cl. E9 . . . . .4A **22**
Booth La. EC4 . . . . .5B **62**
Booth Rd. E16 . . . . .4C **102**
Booth's Pl. W1 . . . . .2C **58**
Boot St. N1 . . . . .3F **41**
Bordeaux Ho. E15 . . . . .3F **7**
Boreas Wlk. N1 . . . . .1A **40**
Boreham Av. E16 . . . . .4D **73**
Boreman Ho. SE10 . . . . .2B **148**
BOROUGH, THE 5C **90**
Borough High St. SE1 . . . . . .5C **90**
Borough Mkt. SE1 . . . . .3D **91**
Borough Rd. SE1 . . . . .1F **117**
Borough Sq. SE1 . . . . .5B **90**
Borrett Cl. SE17 . . . . .1B **140**
Borrowdale NW1 . . . . .3B **36**
Borthwick M. E15 . . . . .1F **7**
Borthwick Rd. E15 . . . . .1F **7**
Borthwick St. SE8 . . . . .1D **147**
Boscobel Pl. SW1 . . . . .3E **113**
Boscobel St. NW8 . . . . .5E **33**
Boscombe Cl. E5 . . . . .2A **4**
Boss Ho. SE1 . . . . .4B **92**
Boss St. SE1 . . . . .4B **92**
Boston Ho. SW5 . . . . .4A **110**
Boston Pl. NW1 . . . . .5B **34**
Bosun Cl. E14 . . . . .4E **97**
Boswell Ct. W14 . . . . .2E **107**
WC1 .1A **60**
Boswell Ho. WC1 . . . . .1A **60**
Boswell St. WC1 . . . . .1A **60**
Bosworth Ho. W10 . . . . .5A **30**
Bosworth Rd. W10 . . . . .5A **30**
Botha Rd. E13 . . . . .1A **74**
Bothwell Cl. E16 . . . . .2C **72**
Botolph All. EC3 . . . . .5F **63**
Botolph La. EC3 . . . . .1F **91**

Botts M. W2 . . . . .4E **53**
Boughton Ho. SE1 . . . . .4D **91**
Boulcott St. E1 . . . . .4E **67**
Boulogne Ho. SE1 . . . . .1B **120**
Boultwood Rd. E6 . . . . .4B **76**
Boundary Ho. SE5 . . . . .4B **140**
W11 .2E **79**
Boundary La. SE17 . . . . .3C **140**
Boundary Pas. E2 . . . . .4B **42**
Boundary Rd. NW8 . . . . .4A **10**
Boundary Row SE1 . . . . .4F **89**
Boundary St. E2 . . . . .3B **42**
Bourbon La. W12 . . . . .3D **79**
Bourchier St. W1 . . . . .5D **59**
Bourdon Pl. W1 . . . . .5A **58**
Bourdon St. W1 . . . . .5A **58**
Bourlet Cl. W1 . . . . .2B **58**
Bourne Est. EC1 . . . . .1D **61**
Bourne M. W1 . . . . .3E **57**
Bourne St. SW1 . . . . .4D **113**
Bourne Ter. W2 . . . . .1F **53**
Bouton Pl. N1 . . . . .2F **17**
Bouverie Pl. W2 . . . . .3E **55**
Bouverie St. EC4 . . . . .4E **61**
Bovet Ct. E1 . . . . .1F **67**
Bovril Ct. SW6 . . . . .4F **131**
BOW 2D **47**
Bowater Ho. EC1 . . . . .5B **40**
Bow Bell Twr. E3 . . . . .4D **25**
Bow Brook, The E2 . . . . .1E **45**
Bow Chyd. EC4 . . . . .4C **62**
BOW COMMON 1E **69**
Bow Comn. La. E3 . . . . .5B **46**
Bow Creek Ecology Pk. 4F **71**
Bowden Ho. E3 . . . . .3F **47**
Bowden St. SE11 . . . . .1E **139**
Bowditch SE8 . . . . .4B **124**
Bowen St. E14 . . . . .3A **70**
Bower Av. SE10 . . . . .5F **149**
Bowerman Av. SE14 . . . . . . .3A **146**
Bower St. E1 . . . . .4D **67**
Bowers Wlk. E6 . . . . .3A **76**
Bowes-Lyon Hall E16 . . . . . .2E **101**
Bow Exchange E3 . . . . .1F **69**
Bow Fair E3 . . . . .1E **47**
Bowhill Cl. SW9 . . . . .4E **139**
Bow Ho. N1 . . . . .4F **19**
BOW INTERCHANGE 1A **48**
Bowland Yd. SW1 . . . . .5C **84**
Bow La. EC4 . . . . .4C **62**
Bowl Ct. EC2 . . . . .5A **42**
Bowles Rd. SE1 . . . . .2D **143**
Bowley Ho. SE16 . . . . .1D **121**
Bowling Grn. Ho. SW10 . . . .4D **133**
Bowling Grn. La. EC1 . . . . . .4E **39**
Bowling Grn. Pl. SE1 . . . . . .4D **91**
Bowling Grn. St. SE11 . . . . .2D **139**
Bowling Grn. Wlk. N1 . . . . . .2F **41**
Bow Locks E3 . . . . .4C **48**
Bowman Av. E16 . . . . .5C **72**
Bowman Ho. N1 . . . . .4A **20**
Bowman's Bldgs. NW1 . . . . .1F **55**
Bowman's M. E1 . . . . .5D **65**
Bowmore Wlk. NW1 . . . . . . .1E **15**
Bowness Ho. SE15 . . . . .4B **144**
Bow Rd. E3 . . . . .3C **46**
Bowry Ho. E14 . . . . .2C **68**
Bowsprit Point E14 . . . . .1D **125**
Bow St. E15 . . . . .3F **7**
WC2 .4A **60**
Bow Triangle Bus. Cen. E3 . . .4E **47**
(not continuous)
Bowyer Cl. E6 . . . . .1C **76**
Bowyer Ho. N1 . . . . .4A **20**

Bowyer Pl. SE5 . . . . .4C **140**
Bowyer St. SE5 . . . . .4C **140**
Boxley St. E16 . . . . .3F **101**
Boxmoor Ho. E2 . . . . .4E **21**
W11 .3E **79**
Box Tree Ho. SE8 . . . . .1A **146**
Boxworth Gro. N1 . . . . .3C **16**
Boyce Ho. W10 . . . . .3B **30**
Boydell Ct. NW8 . . . . .2D **11**
(not continuous)
Boyd St. E1 . . . . .4E **65**
Boyfield St. SE1 . . . . .5A **90**
Boyle St. W1 . . . . .5B **58**
Boyne Ter. M. W11 . . . . .2B **80**
Boyson Rd. SE17 . . . . .2C **140**
(not continuous)
Boyson Wlk. SE17 . . . . .2D **141**
Boyton Cl. E1 . . . . .4C **44**
Boyton Ho. NW8 . . . . .5E **11**
Brabant Ct. EC3 . . . . .5F **63**
Brabazon St. SW1 . . . . .5D **115**
Brabazon St. E14 . . . . .3F **69**
Brabner Ho. E2 . . . . .2D **43**
Bracer Ho. N1 . . . . .4A **20**
Bracewell Rd. W10 . . . . .2B **50**
Brackenbury Gdns. W6 . . . . .1A **106**
Brackenbury Rd. W6 . . . . . .1A **106**
Bracken Cl. E6 . . . . .1B **76**
Bracken Ho. E3 . . . . .1E **69**
Brackley Ct. NW8 . . . . .4D **33**
Brackley St. EC1 . . . . .1C **62**
Bracklyn Ct. N1 . . . . .5D **19**
(not continuous)
Bracklyn St. N1 . . . . .5D **19**
Bradbeer Ho. E2 . . . . .3B **44**
Bradby Ho. NW8 . . . . .1A **32**
Braddyll St. SE10 . . . . .1F **149**
Bradenham SE17 . . . . .2D **141**
Bradenham Cl. SE17 . . . . . .2D **141**
Braden St. W9 . . . . .5F **31**
Bradfield Ct. NW1 . . . . .1A **14**
Bradfield Rd. E16 . . . . .4E **101**
Bradford Ho. W14 . . . . .2E **107**
Bradiston Rd. W9 . . . . .2C **30**
Bradley Cl. N7 . . . . .1B **16**
Bradley Ho. E3 . . . . .1A **48**
SE16 . . . . .3A **122**
Bradley's Cl. N1 . . . . .5E **17**
Bradley Stone Rd. E6 . . . . . .2B **76**
Bradman Ho. NW8 . . . . .2B **32**
Bradmead SW8 . . . . .5A **136**
Bradmore Pk. Rd. W6 . . . . . .2A **106**
Bradshaw Cotts. E14 . . . . . .3A **68**
Bradstock Ho. E9 . . . . .1F **23**
Bradstock Rd. E9 . . . . .1E **23**
Brad St. SE1 . . . . .3E **89**
Bradwell Ho. NW6 . . . . .4F **9**
Brady Ho. SW8 . . . . .5C **136**
Bradymead E6 . . . . .3E **77**
Brady St. E1 . . . . .4F **43**
Braemar Cl. SE16 . . . . .1F **143**
Braemar Ho. W9 . . . . .3B **32**
Braemar Mans. SW7 . . . . . .2A **110**
Braemar Rd. E13 . . . . .1C **72**
Braes St. N1 . . . . .1A **18**
Braganza St. SE17 . . . . .5F **117**
Braham Ho. SE11 . . . . .1C **138**
Braham St. E1 . . . . .3C **64**
Braidwood Pas. EC1 . . . . . . .1B **62**
Braidwood St. SE1 . . . . .3F **91**
Braintree Ho. E1 . . . . .4B **44**
Braintree St. E2 . . . . .4B **44**
Braithwaite Ho. EC1 . . . . . . .4D **41**
Braithwaite St. E1 . . . . .5B **42**

Braithwaite Twr. W2	1D 55	
Bramah Ho. SW1	1F 135	
Bramber WC1	3F 37	
Bramber Ct. W14	2C 130	
Bramber Rd. W14	2B 130	
Bramble Ho. E3	1E 69	
Brambling Ct. SE8	3B 146	
Bramcote Gro. SE16	5B 122	
Bramerton St. SW3	2F 133	
Bramham Gdns. SW5	5F 109	
Bramley Cres. SW8	4E 137	
Bramley Ho. W10	4E 51	
Bramley Rd. W10	1E 79	
Brampton WC1	2B 60	
Bramshaw Rd. E9	1E 23	
Bramshurst NW8	4A 10	
Bramwell Ho. SE1	2C 118	
SW1	1B 136	
Bramwell M. N1	3C 16	
Bramwell Way E16	3C 102	
Brancaster Ho. E1	3E 45	
Branch Pl. N1	3E 19	
Branch Rd. E14	5F 67	
Branch St. SE15	5A 142	
Brandon Est. SE17	3F 139	
Brandon Mans. W14	2A 130	
Brandon M. EC2	2D 63	
SE17	4C 118	
Brandon Rd. N7	1F 15	
Brandon St. SE17	4C 118	
(not continuous)		
Brandrams Wharf SE16	4B 94	
Brandreth Rd. E6	3C 76	
Brands Ho. NW6	3B 8	
Brangton Rd. SE11	1C 138	
Brangwyn Ct. W14	2F 107	
Branksome Ho. SW8	4B 138	
Bransoombe NW1	4C 14	
Bransdale Cl. NW6	3E 9	
Brantwood Ho. SE5	4B 140	
Brassett Point E15	4F 27	
Brassey Ho. E14	4F 125	
Brass Talley All. SE16	5E 95	
Brathay NW1	1C 36	
Bratley St. E1	5D 43	
Bravington Pl. W9	4B 30	
Bravington Rd. W9	1B 30	
Bravingtons Wlk. N1	1A 38	
Brawne Ho. SE17	3A 140	
Bray NW3	1F 11	
Bray Ct. E2	2E 45	
Bray Cres. SE16	4D 95	
Bray Dr. E16	5C 72	
Brayfield Ter. N1	2D 17	
Brayford Sq. E1	3C 66	
Bray Pas. E16	5D 73	
Bray Pl. SW3	4B 112	
Bread St. EC4	5C 62	
(not continuous)		
Breakwell Ct. W10	5F 29	
Breamore Ho. SE15	4E 143	
Bream's Bldgs. EC4	3D 61	
Bream St. E3	2E 25	
Brechin Pl. SW7	5C 110	
Brecon Ho. E3	1C 46	
W2	3B 54	
Brecon Rd. W6	3A 130	
Bredel Ho. E14	2D 69	
Bredin Ho. SW10	4A 132	
Breezers Ct. E1	1E 93	
Breezer's Hill E1	1E 93	
Bremner Rd. SW7	1C 110	
Brendon St. W1	3A 56	
Brenley Ho. SE1	4D 91	
Brent Ho. E9	1B 22	
Brenthouse Rd. E9	1A 22	
Brenton Ct. E9	3A 4	
Brenton St. E14	3A 68	
Brent Rd. E16	3E 73	
Bressenden Pl. SW1	1A 114	
Bresslaw Ct. E3	1B 68	
Breton Highwalk EC2	1C 62	
Breton Ho. EC2	1C 62	
SE1	1B 120	
Brettell St. SE17	1E 141	
Brettinghurst SE1	1D 143	
Brewers Bldgs. EC1	2F 39	
Brewers Ct. W2	3C 54	
Brewer's Grn. SW1	1D 115	
Brewer's Hall Gdn. EC2	2C 62	
Brewer St. W1	1C 86	
Brewery, The EC2	1D 63	
Brewery Ind. Estate, The		
N1	1C 40	
Brewery Rd. N7	1F 15	
Brewery Sq. EC1	4A 40	
SE1	3B 92	
Brewhouse La. E1	3A 94	
Brewhouse Wlk. SE16	3F 95	
Brewhouse Yd. EC1	4F 39	
Brewster Gdns. W10	1B 50	
Brewster Ho. E14	5B 68	
SE1	3C 120	
Briant Ho. SE1	2D 117	
Briant St. SE14	5D 145	
Briar Cl. E3	1D 47	
Briar Wlk. W10	4A 30	
Briary Cl. NW3	1F 11	
Briary Ct. E16	4C 72	
Brickbarn Cl. SW10	4C 132	
Brick Ct. EC4	4D 61	
Brickfield Cl. E9	1B 22	
Brickfield Ho. N1	3A 20	
Brick La. E1	4C 42	
E2	3C 42	
Brick Lane Music Hall	**3E 103**	
BRICKLAYER'S ARMS	**2E 119**	
Bricklayers Arms Distribution Cen.		
SE1	3A 120	
(not continuous)		
Brick St. W1	3F 85	
Brideale Cl. SE15	3C 142	
Bride Ct. EC4	4F 61	
Bride La. EC4	4F 61	
Bridel M. N1	4F 17	
Brides Pl. N1	2F 19	
Bridewain St. SE1	1B 120	
Bridewell Pl. E1	3A 94	
EC4	4F 61	
Bridford M. W1	4E 35	
Bridge, The SW8	5F 135	
Bridge App. NW1	1D 13	
Bridge Av. W6	4B 106	
Bridge Av. Mans. W6	5B 106	
Bridge Cl. W10	4E 51	
Bridge Ct. E14	5E 71	
Bridgefield Ho. W2	3F 53	
Bridgefoot SE1	1A 138	
Bridge Ho. NW3	1D 13	
NW10	1D 29	
SW1	5F 113	
W2	2D 55	
Bridgehouse Ct. SE1	4F 89	
Bridge Ho. Quay E14	2C 98	
Bridgeland Rd. E16	5E 73	
Bridgeman Ho. E9	1B 22	
W14	3B 108	
Bridgeman Rd. N1	2B 16	
Bridgeman St. NW8	1F 33	
Bridge Mdws. SE14	2D 145	
Bridgen Ho. E1	3A 66	
Bridge Pl. SW1	3A 114	
Bridgeport Pl. E1	2E 93	
Bridge Rd. E15	2D 27	
Bridge Rd. Depot E15	4F 27	
Bridges Ho. SE5	5D 141	
Bridgeside Lodge N1	5B 18	
Bridge St. SW1	5F 87	
Bridge Ter. E15	2E 27	
Bridge Vw. W6	5B 106	
Bridge Vw. Ct. SE1	2A 120	
Bridge Wlk. SE8	3F 147	
Bridgewalk Hgts. SE1	4E 91	
Bridgewater Highwalk EC2	1B 62	
Bridgewater Ho. E15	3B 26	
Bridgewater Sq. EC2	1B 62	
Bridgewater St. EC2	1B 62	
Bridgeway St. NW1	1C 36	
Bridge Wharf E2	1D 45	
N1	5B 16	
Bridge Yd. SE1	2E 91	
Bridgnorth Ho. SE15	3E 143	
Bridgwater Ho. W2	3B 54	
Bridle La. W1	5C 58	
Bridport SE17	1D 141	
Bridport Ho. N1	4E 19	
Bridport Pl. N1	3E 19	
(not continuous)		
Bridstow Pl. W2	3E 53	
Brierfield NW1	4B 14	
Brierly Gdns. E2	1C 44	
Briggs Ho. E2	2C 42	
Brightlingsea Pl. E14	5B 68	
Brighton Bldgs. SE1	2F 119	
Brighton Gro. SE14	5F 145	
Bright St. E14	2A 70	
Brightwell Ho. E3	3D 147	
Brill Pl. NW1	1F 37	
Brimsdown Ho. E3	4B 48	
Brimstone Ho. E15	1F 27	
Brindley Ho. W2	1E 53	
Brine Ho. E3	5A 24	
Brinklow Ho. W2	2F 53	
Brinkworth Way E9	4C 4	
Brinsley Ho. E1	4B 66	
Brinton Wlk. SE1	3F 89	
Brion Pl. E14	2B 70	
Brisbane Ho. W12	5A 56	
Brisbane St. SE5	5D 141	
Briset St. EC1	1F 61	
Bristol Gdns. W9	5A 32	
Bristol Ho. SE11	2D 117	
SW1	5D 113	
WC1	2A 60	
Bristol M. W9	5A 32	
Bristow Ct. E8	3A 22	
Britannia Bldg. N1	2D 41	
Britannia Ga. E16	2E 101	
BRITANNIA JUNC.	**3A 14**	
Britannia Leisure Cen.	**4E 19**	
Britannia Rd. E14	4E 125	
SW6	5F 131	
Britannia Row N1	3A 18	
Britannia St. WC1	2B 38	
Britannia Wlk. N1	1D 41	
(not continuous)		
Britannia Way SW6	5A 132	
Britannic Highwalk EC2	2D 63	
British Genius Site	**4D 135**	
British Library	**2E 37**	
British Mus.	**2F 59**	

British Music Experience 3F 99
British Postal Museum and
   Archive, The 4D 39
British St. E3 . . . . .3C 46
British Telecom Cen. EC1 . .3B 62
British Wharf Ind. Est.
   SE14 . . . . .1E 145
Britley Ho. E14 . . . . .4B 68
Brittany Point SE11 . . . . . .4D 117
Britten Ct. E15 . . . . .5D 27
Britten Ho. SW3 . . . . .5F 111
Britten St. SW3 . . . . .1F 133
Britten Theatre 1D 111
Britton St. EC1 . . . . .5F 39
Brixham St. E16 . . . . .3C 104
Brixton Rd. SE11 . . . . .3D 139
   SW9 . . . . .5D 139
Broadbent St. W1 . . . . .5F 57
Broad Ct. WC2 . . . . .4A 60
Broadfield La. NW1 . . . . .2F 15
Broadford Ho. E1 . . . . .5A 46
Broadgate EC2 . . . . .2F 63
Broadgate Arena 2F 63
Broadgate Circ. EC2 . . . . . .1F 63
Broadgate Ice Rink 2F 63
Broadgate Plaza EC2 . . . . . .1A 64
Broadgate Rd. E16 . . . . .3D 75
Broadgates Ct. SE11 . . . . . .1E 139
Broadgate Twr. EC2 . . . . . . .5A 42
Broad La. EC2 . . . . .1F 63
Broadley St. NW8 . . . . .1E 55
Broadley Ter. NW1 . . . . .5A 34
Broadmayne SE17 . . . . .5D 119
Broadmead W14 . . . . .4F 107
Broadoak Ho. NW6 . . . . .4F 9
Broad Sanctuary SW1 . . . . .5E 87
Broadstone NW1 . . . . .2D 15
Broadstone Ho. SW8 . . . . . .5B 138
Broadstone Pl. W1 . . . . .2D 57
Broad St. Av. EC2 . . . . .2F 63
Broad St. Pl. EC2 . . . . .2E 63
Broad Wlk. NW1 . . . . .4E 13
   W1 . . . . .1C 84
Broad Walk, The W8 . . . . . . .1A 82
Broadwalk Ct. W8 . . . . .2E 81
Broadwalk Ho. EC2 . . . . .1F 63
   SW7 . . . . .5B 82
Broadwall SE1 . . . . .2E 89
Broadway E15 . . . . .1E 27
   SW1 . . . . .1D 115
Broadway Arc. W6 . . . . .4C 106
Broadway Centre, The
   W6 . . . . .4C 106
Broadway Chambers W6 . . .4C 106
Broadway Ho. E8 . . . . .4F 21
Broadway Mans. SW6 . . . . .5E 131
Broadway Mkt. E8 . . . . .4F 21
    (not continuous)
Broadway Mkt. M. E8 . . . . . .4E 21
Broadway Shop. Mall
   SW1 . . . . .1D 115
Broadway Wlk. E14 . . . . . . .1E 125
Broadwick St. W1 . . . . .5C 58
Broadwood Ter. W8 . . . . . . .3C 108
Broad Yd. EC1 . . . . .5F 39
Brocas Cl. NW3 . . . . .1A 12
Brockham Ho. NW1 . . . . . . .4C 14
Brockham St. SE1 . . . . .1C 118
Brocklebank Ho. E16 . . . . . .3E 105
Brocklebank Ind. Est.
   SE7 . . . . .3E 129
Brocklebank Rd. SE7 . . . . . .3F 129
Brocklehurst St. SE14 . . . . .4E 145
Brockmer Ho. E1 . . . . .5F 65

Brock Pl. E3 . . . . .5F 47
Brock Rd. E13 . . . . .1A 74
Brockweir E2 . . . . .1C 44
Brockwell Ho. SE11 . . . . . . .2C 138
Brodick Ho. E3 . . . . .5B 24
Brodie Ho. SE1 . . . . .5C 120
Brodie St. SE1 . . . . .5C 120
Brodlove La. E1 . . . . .5D 67
Brody Ho. E1 . . . . .2B 64
Broken Wharf EC4 . . . . .5B 62
Brokesley St. E3 . . . . .3B 46
Broke Wlk. E8 . . . . .3C 20
Bromehead St. E1 . . . . .3B 66
Bromfield Ct. SE16 . . . . . . .1E 121
Bromfield St. N1 . . . . .5E 17
Bromhead Rd. E1 . . . . .3B 66
Bromleigh Ho. SE1 . . . . .1B 120
BROMLEY 2F 47
Bromley Hall Rd. E14 . . . . . .1B 70
Bromley High St. E3 . . . . . . .2F 47
Bromley Pl. W1 . . . . .1B 58
Bromley St. E1 . . . . .2E 67
BROMPTON 2A 112
Brompton Arc. SW3 . . . . . . .5C 84
Brompton Cemetery 2F 131
Brompton Cotts. SW10 . . . .2C 132
Brompton Oratory 2F 111
Brompton Pk. Cres. SW6 . . .3E 131
Brompton Pl. SW3 . . . . .1A 112
Brompton Rd. SW1 . . . . .3F 111
   SW3 . . . . .3F 111
Brompton Sq. SW3 . . . . .1F 111
Brompton Vs. SW6 . . . . .2D 131
Bromyard Ho. SE15 . . . . . . .4F 143
Bron Ct. NW6 . . . . .4E 9
BRONDESBURY 1C 8
Brondesbury M. NW6 . . . . . .2D 9
Brondesbury Pk. NW6 . . . . . .2A 8
Brondesbury Pk. Mans. NW6 . .3A 8
Brondesbury Rd. NW6 . . . . . .5B 8
Brondesbury Vs. NW6 . . . . . .5B 8
Bronsart Rd. SW6 . . . . .4A 130
Bronte Ct. W14 . . . . .2E 107
Bronte Ho. NW6 . . . . .2E 31
Bronti Cl. SE17 . . . . .1C 140
Bronwen Ct. NW8 . . . . .3D 33
Bronze St. SE8 . . . . .4E 147
Brook Dr. SE11 . . . . .2E 117
Brooke Ct. W10 . . . . .1B 30
Brooke's Ct. EC1 . . . . .2D 61
Brooke's Mkt. EC1 . . . . .1D 61
Brooke St. EC1 . . . . .2D 61
Brookfield Rd. E9 . . . . .5A 4
Brook Ga. W1 . . . . .1C 84
BROOK GREEN 3E 107
Brook Grn. W6 . . . . .2D 107
Brook Grn. Flats W14 . . . . . .2D 107
Brook Ho. E1 . . . . .5E 65
   W6 . . . . .4C 106
Brook Ho's. NW1 . . . . .1C 36
Brooklands Ct. NW6 . . . . . . .1B 8
Brooklyn Ct. W12 . . . . .2B 78
Brooklyn Pas. W12 . . . . .5B 78
Brookman Ho. E3 . . . . .1D 47
Brookmarsh Ind. Est.
   SE10 . . . . .4F 147
Brook M. WC2 . . . . .4E 59
Brook M. Nth. W2 . . . . .5C 54
Brooks Apartments E3 . . . . .1D 69
Brooksby Ho. N1 . . . . .2E 17
Brooksby M. N1 . . . . .1E 17
Brooksby St. N1 . . . . .2D 17
Brooks Ct. SW8 . . . . .4C 136
Brooks Lodge N1 . . . . .5A 20

Brook's M. W1 . . . . .5F 57
Brook St. W1 . . . . .5E 57
   W2 . . . . .5E 55
Brooksville Av. NW6 . . . . . . .4A 8
Brookville Rd. SW6 . . . . .5B 130
Brookwood Ho. SE1 . . . . . . .5A 90
Broome Way SE5 . . . . .5D 141
Broomfield NW1 . . . . .1E 13
Broomfield Ho. SE17 . . . . . .4F 119
Broomfield St. E14 . . . . .2E 69
Brougham Rd. E8 . . . . .3E 21
Brough Cl. SW8 . . . . .5A 138
Browne Ho. SE8 . . . . .4E 147
Brownfield Area E14 . . . . . . .4B 70
Brownfield St. E14 . . . . .4A 70
Brown Hart Gdns. W1 . . . . . .5E 57
Browning Apartments E3 . . .4B 46
Browning Cl. W9 . . . . .5C 32
Browning Ct. W14 . . . . .2B 130
Browning Ho. W12 . . . . .4B 50
Browning M. W1 . . . . .2E 57
Browning St. SE17 . . . . .5C 118
Brownlow Ho. SE16 . . . . . . .5D 93
Brownlow M. WC1 . . . . .4C 60
Brownlow Rd. E8 . . . . .3C 20
Brownlow St. WC1 . . . . .2C 60
Brown's Bldgs. EC3 . . . . . . .4A 64
Brown St. W1 . . . . .3B 56
Broxbourne Ho. E3 . . . . .4A 48
Broxwood Way NW8 . . . . . . .4A 12
Bruce Cl. W10 . . . . .1E 51
Bruce Ho. W10 . . . . .1E 51
Bruce Rd. E3 . . . . .3F 47
Bruckner St. W10 . . . . .2B 30
Bruford Ct. SE8 . . . . .3E 147
Bruges Pl. NW1 . . . . .2C 14
Brune Ho. E1 . . . . .2B 64
Brunei Gallery 1E 59
Brunel Ct. SE16 . . . . .4C 94
Brunel Est. W2 . . . . .2D 53
Brunel Ho. E14 . . . . .5F 125
Brunel M. W10 . . . . .2E 29
Brunel Mus. 4B 94
Brunel Rd. SE16 . . . . .3C 94
Brunel St. E16 . . . . .4B 72
Brunel Wlk. SW10 . . . . .4E 133
Brune St. E1 . . . . .2B 64
Brunlees Ho. SE1 . . . . .2B 118
Brunswick Cen. WC1 . . . . . .4F 37
Brunswick Cl. Est. EC1 . . . . .3F 39
Brunswick Ct. EC1 . . . . .3F 39
   SE1 . . . . .5A 92
   SW1 . . . . .4E 115
Brunswick Flats W11 . . . . . .4D 53
Brunswick Gdns. W8 . . . . . .3E 81
Brunswick Ho. E2 . . . . .5C 20
   SE16 . . . . .1F 123
Brunswick Mans. WC1 . . . . .4A 38
Brunswick M. W1 . . . . .3C 56
Brunswick Pl. N1 . . . . .3E 41
   NW1 . . . . .5E 35
    (not continuous)
Brunswick Quay SE16 . . . . .2E 123
Brunswick Rd. E14 . . . . .4C 70
Brunswick Sq. WC1 . . . . . . .4A 38
Brunswick Vs. SE5 . . . . .5F 141
Brunton Pl. E14 . . . . .4A 68
Brushfield St. E1 . . . . .1A 64
Brushwood Cl. E14 . . . . .1A 70
Bruton La. W1 . . . . .1A 86
Bruton Pl. W1 . . . . .1A 86
Bruton St. W1 . . . . .1A 86
Brutus Ct. SE11 . . . . .4F 117
Bryan Ho. SE16 . . . . .4B 96

Bryan Rd. SE16 . . . . .4B 96
Bryanston Ct. W1 . . . . .3B 56
(not continuous)
Bryanston Mans. W1 . . . . .1B 56
Bryanston M. E. W1 . . . . .2B 56
Bryanston M. W. W1 . . . . .2B 56
Bryanston Pl. W1 . . . . .2B 56
Bryanston Sq. W1 . . . . .2B 56
Bryanston St. W1 . . . . .4B 56
Bryan St. N1 . . . . .4B 16
Bryant Ct. E2 . . . . .5B 20
(not continuous)
Bryant Ho. E3 . . . . .1E 47
Bryant St. E15 . . . . .2E 27
Bryce Ho. SE14 . . . . .3D 145
Brydale Ho. SE16 . . . . .3D 123
Brydges Pl. WC2 . . . . .1F 87
Brydges Rd. E15 . . . . .2E 7
Brydon Wlk. N1 . . . . .3A 16
Bryer Ct. EC2 . . . . .1B 62
Bryher Ct. SE11 . . . . .5D 117
Brymay Cl. E3 . . . . .1E 47
Buchanan Ct. SE16 . . . . .3E 123
Buchanan Gdns. NW10 . . . . .1A 28
Buckfast St. E2 . . . . .3E 43
Buck Hill Wlk. W2 . . . . .1E 83
Buckhurst St. E1 . . . . .5A 44
Buckingham Arc. WC2 . . . . .1A 88
Buckingham Chambers
SW1 . . . . .3C 114
Buckingham Ct. W11 . . . . .1D 81
Buckingham Ga. SW1 . . . . .1B 114
Buckingham M. SW1 . . . . .1B 114
Buckingham Palace **5A 86**
Buckingham Pal. Rd.
SW1 . . . . .4F 113
Buckingham Pl. SW1 . . . . .1B 114
Buckingham St. WC2 . . . . .1A 88
Buckland Ct. N1 . . . . .5F 19
Buckland Cres. NW3 . . . . .1D 11
Buckland Ho. SW1 . . . . .5F 113
Buckland St. N1 . . . . .1E 41
Bucklebury NW1 . . . . .4B 36
Bucklers All. SW6 . . . . .4C 130
Bucklersbury EC4 . . . . .4D 63
Bucklersbury Pas. EC4 . . . . .4D 63
Buckle St. E1 . . . . .3C 64
Buckley Ct. NW6 . . . . .2C 8
Buckley Ho. W14 . . . . .4F 79
Buckley Rd. NW6 . . . . .2C 8
Bucknall St. WC2 . . . . .3E 59
Bucknill Ho. SW1 . . . . .5F 113
Buckridge Ho. EC1 . . . . .1D 61
Buckshead Ho. W2 . . . . .2D 53
Buck St. NW1 . . . . .2A 14
Buckters Rents SE16 . . . . .3F 95
Buckthorn Ho. E15 . . . . .2F 49
Budge Row EC4 . . . . .4D 63
Budge's Wlk. W2 . . . . .3B 82
Budleigh Ho. SE15 . . . . .4E 143
Bugsby's Way SE7 . . . . .3B 128
SE10 . . . . .3B 128
Buick Ho. E3 . . . . .4D 47
Bulbarrow NW8 . . . . .4A 10
Bulinga St. SW1 . . . . .4F 115
Bullace Row SE5 . . . . .5D 141
Bullard's Pl. E2 . . . . .2D 45
Bulleid Way SW1 . . . . .4A 114
Bullen Ho. E1 . . . . .5A 44
Buller Cl. SE15 . . . . .5D 143
Buller Rd. NW10 . . . . .3E 29
Bullingham Mans. W8 . . . . .4E 81
Bull Inn Ct. WC2 . . . . .1A 88
Bullivant St. E14 . . . . .5B 70

Bulls Gdns. SW3 . . . . .3A 112
Bulls Head Pas. EC3 . . . . .4F 63
Bulmer M. W11 . . . . .2D 81
Bulmer Pl. W11 . . . . .2D 81
Bulwer St. W12 . . . . .3C 78
Bunbury Ho. SE15 . . . . .5D 143
Bunhill Row EC1 . . . . .4D 41
Bunhouse Pl. SW1 . . . . .5D 113
Bunning Way N7 . . . . .1B 16
Bunsen Ho. E3 . . . . .5F 23
Bunsen St. E3 . . . . .5F 23
Bunwell Ho. E3 . . . . .5C 46
Bunyan Ct. EC2 . . . . .1B 62
Buonaparte M. SW1 . . . . .5D 115
Burbage Cl. SE1 . . . . .2D 119
Burbage Ho. N1 . . . . .4E 19
SE14 . . . . .3D 145
Burcham St. E14 . . . . .3A 70
Burchell Ho. SE11 . . . . .5C 116
Burcher Gale Gro. SE15 . . . . .4A 142
Burden Ho. SW8 . . . . .5F 137
Burdett M. W2 . . . . .3F 53
Burdett Rd. E3 . . . . .4A 46
E14 . . . . .2C 68
Burford Rd. E15 . . . . .2D 27
Burford Wlk. SW6 . . . . .5A 132
Burford Wharf Apartments
E15 . . . . .3D 27
Burgess Bus. Pk. SE5 . . . . .4E 141
Burgess Ho. SE5 . . . . .4B 140
Burgess Lofts SE5 . . . . .4C 140
Burgess Pk. **3D 141**
Burgess Pk. Kart Track **3E 141**
Burgess Rd. E15 . . . . .1F 7
Burgess St. E14 . . . . .2D 69
Burge St. SE1 . . . . .2E 119
Burgh St. N1 . . . . .5A 18
Burgon St. EC4 . . . . .4A 62
Burgos Gro. SE10 . . . . .5F 147
Burgundy Ho. E20 . . . . .3C 6
Burgundy Pl. W12 . . . . .3D 79
Burke St. E16 . . . . .2B 72
(not continuous)
Burleigh Ho. SW3 . . . . .3E 133
W10 . . . . .1F 51
Burleigh St. WC2 . . . . .5A 60
Burley Ho. E1 . . . . .3E 67
Burley Rd. E16 . . . . .3B 74
Burlington Arc. W1 . . . . .1B 86
Burlington Cl. E6 . . . . .3A 76
W9 . . . . .4D 31
Burlington Cnr. NW1 . . . . .2B 14
Burlington Ct. E1 . . . . .5E 65
(off Cable St.)
Burlington Gdns. W1 . . . . .1B 86
Burlington Ho. SE16 . . . . .5C 94
Burnaby St. SW10 . . . . .5B 132
Burnand Ho. W14 . . . . .1E 107
Burne Jones Ho. W14 . . . . .4A 108
Burnelli Bldg. SW8 . . . . .4F 135
Burnell Wlk. SE1 . . . . .5C 120
Burne St. NW1 . . . . .1F 55
Burney St. SE10 . . . . .4C 148
Burnham NW3 . . . . .1F 11
Burnham Cl. SE1 . . . . .4C 120
Burnham Ct. NW6 . . . . .2C 10
W2 . . . . .5F 53
Burnham Est. E2 . . . . .2B 44
Burnham St. E2 . . . . .2B 44
Burnhill Cl. SE15 . . . . .4A 144
Burnhill Ho. EC1 . . . . .3B 40
Burnsall St. SW3 . . . . .5A 112

Burns Ho. E2 . . . . .3B 44
SE17 . . . . .1A 140
Burnside Cl. SE16 . . . . .2E 95
Burnthwaite Rd. SW6 . . . . .5C 130
Burnt Oak Apartments E16 . . . . .3D 73
Buross St. E1 . . . . .3A 66
Burrage Ct. SE16 . . . . .3E 123
Burrard Ho. E2 . . . . .5B 22
Burrard Rd. E16 . . . . .3F 73
Burr Cl. E1 . . . . .2D 93
Burrell St. SE1 . . . . .2F 89
Burrells Wharf Sq. E14 . . . . .5F 125
Burrhill Ct. SE16 . . . . .2E 123
Burroughs Cotts. E14 . . . . .2A 68
Burrows M. SE1 . . . . .4F 89
Burrows Rd. NW10 . . . . .2B 28
Bursar St. SE1 . . . . .3F 91
Burslem St. E1 . . . . .4F 65
Burton Bank N1 . . . . .2D 19
Burton Ct. SW3 . . . . .5C 112
(not continuous)
Burton Gro. SE17 . . . . .1D 141
Burton Ho. SE16 . . . . .5F 93
Burton M. SW1 . . . . .4E 113
Burton Pl. WC1 . . . . .4E 37
Burton Rd. NW6 . . . . .2C 8
Burtons Ct. E15 . . . . .1E 27
Burton St. WC1 . . . . .3E 37
Burt Rd. E16 . . . . .3C 102
Burtt Ho. N1 . . . . .2F 41
Burwash Ho. SE1 . . . . .5E 91
Burwell Cl. E1 . . . . .4A 66
Burwell Wlk. E3 . . . . .4E 47
Burwood Pl. W2 . . . . .3A 56
Bury Cl. SE16 . . . . .2E 95
Bury Ct. EC3 . . . . .3A 64
Buryfield Ct. SE8 . . . . .4E 123
Bury Pl. WC1 . . . . .2F 59
Bury St. EC3 . . . . .4A 64
SW1 . . . . .2B 86
Bury Wlk. SW3 . . . . .4F 111
Busbridge Ho. E14 . . . . .2E 69
Bushbaby Cl. SE1 . . . . .2F 119
Bushberry Rd. E9 . . . . .4A 4
Bush Ct. W12 . . . . .4E 79
Bushell St. E1 . . . . .3E 93
Bush La. EC4 . . . . .5D 63
Bush Rd. E8 . . . . .4F 21
SE8 . . . . .4E 123
Bush Theatre **4B 78**
Bushwood Dr. SE1 . . . . .4C 120
Business Design Cen. N1 . . . . .4E 17
Buspace Studios W10 . . . . .5F 29
Butcher Row E14 . . . . .5E 67
Butchers Rd. E16 . . . . .4D 73
Bute Gdns. W6 . . . . .4D 107
Bute St. SW7 . . . . .3D 111
Butler Ho. E2 . . . . .2C 44
E3 . . . . .1C 68
E14 . . . . .3C 68
SW9 . . . . .5A 140
Butler Pl. SW1 . . . . .1D 115
Butlers & Colonial Wharf
SE1 . . . . .4C 92
Butler St. E2 . . . . .2C 44
Butlers Wharf SE1 . . . . .3C 92
Butlers Wharf W. SE1 . . . . .3B 92
Butley Ct. E3 . . . . .5A 24
Butterfield Cl. SE16 . . . . .5E 93
Butterfield Sq. E6 . . . . .4B 76
Buttermere NW1 . . . . .2A 36
Buttermere Cl. E15 . . . . .1E 7
SE1 . . . . .4B 120
Buttermere Ct. NW8 . . . . .3D 11

Buttermere Ho. E3 . . . . .3B 46
Butterwick W6 . . . . .4D 107
Butterworth Ter. SE17 . . . .1C 140
Buttesland St. N1 . . . . .2E 41
Buxhall Cres. E9 . . . . .4B 4
Buxted Rd. E8 . . . . .1B 20
Buxton Ct. N1 . . . . .2C 40
            (not continuous)
Buxton Rd. E15 . . . . .2F 7
Buxton St. E1 . . . . .5C 42
Byards Ct. SE16 . . . . .2E 123
Byas Ho. E3 . . . . .2C 46
Byelands Cl. SE16 . . . . .2E 95
Byfield Cl. SE16 . . . . .3A 96
Bygrove St. E14 . . . . .3F 69
            (not continuous)
Byng Pl. WC1 . . . . .5E 37
Byng St. E14 . . . . .4D 97
Byron Cl. E8 . . . . .3D 21
Byron Ct. NW6 . . . . .2C 10
   SW3 . . . . .4A 112
   W9 . . . . .4E 31
   WC1 . . . . .4B 38
Byron M. W9 . . . . .4E 31
Byron St. E14 . . . . .3B 70
Byward St. EC3 . . . . .1A 92
Bywater Pl. SE16 . . . . .2A 96
Bywater St. SW3 . . . . .5B 112
Bywell Pl. W1 . . . . .2B 58

C

Cabbell St. NW1 . . . . .2F 55
Cable Car
   Emirates Air Line 4B 100
Cable St. SE16 . . . . .3F 123
Cable Ho. WC1 . . . . .2D 39
Cable Pl. SE10 . . . . .5C 148
Cable St. E1 . . . . .5D 65
Cabot Ct. SE16 . . . . .2E 123
Cabot Sq. E14 . . . . .2E 97
Cab Rd. SE1 . . . . .3D 89
Caci Ho. W14 . . . . .4B 108
Cadbury Way SE16 . . . . . .2C 120
Cadell Cl. E2 . . . . .1C 42
Cade Rd. SE10 . . . . .5D 149
Cadet Dr. SE1 . . . . .5C 120
Cadet Pl. SE10 . . . . .5F 127
Cadiz St. SE17 . . . . .1C 140
Cadman Cl. SW9 . . . . .5F 139
Cadmore Ho. N1 . . . . .2F 17
Cadmus Ct. SW9 . . . . .5D 139
Cadnam Lodge E14 . . . . . .2C 126
Cadogan Cl. E9 . . . . .1C 24
Cadogan Ct. E9 . . . . .1C 24
   SW3 . . . . .4B 112
Cadogan Ct. Gdns. SW1 . .3D 113
Cadogan Gdns. SW3 . . . . .3C 112
Cadogan Ga. SW1 . . . . . . .3C 112
Cadogan Hall 3C 112
Cadogan Ho. SW3 . . . . . . .3E 133
Cadogan La. SW1 . . . . . . .1D 113
Cadogan Mans. SW3 . . . . .4C 112
Cadogan Pl. SW1 . . . . . . .1C 112
Cadogan Sq. SW1 . . . . . . .2B 112
Cadogan St. SW3 . . . . . . .4B 112
Cadogan Ter. E9 . . . . .5B 4
Caernarvon Ho. E16 . . . . .2F 101
   W2 . . . . .3B 54
Caesar Ct. E2 . . . . .1E 45
Café Gallery 2B 122
Cahill St. EC1 . . . . .5C 40
Cahir St. E14 . . . . .4F 125

Caird St. W10 . . . . .3A 30
Caister Ho. N7 . . . . .1C 16
Caithness Ho. N1 . . . . .3B 16
Caithness Rd. W14 . . . . . . .3D 107
Calcott Ct. W14 . . . . .2F 107
Calcraft Ho. E2 . . . . .5B 22
Calder Ct. SE16 . . . . .2B 96
Calderon Ho. NW8 . . . . . . .5F 11
Calderon Pl. W10 . . . . .2B 50
Caldew St. SE5 . . . . .4D 141
Caldwell St. SW9 . . . . .5C 138
Caldy Wlk. N1 . . . . .1C 18
Caleb St. SE1 . . . . .4C 90
Caledonia Ho. E14 . . . . .4A 68
Caledonian Rd. N1 . . . . .1A 38
   N7 . . . . .1B 16
Caledonian Wharf E14 . . . .4D 127
Caledonia St. N1 . . . . .1A 38
Cale St. SW3 . . . . .5F 111
Caletock Way SE10 . . . . . . .5B 128
Calgarth NW1 . . . . .1C 36
Calgary Ct. SE16 . . . . .5C 94
Calia Ho. E20 . . . . .4B 6
Caliban Twr. N1 . . . . .1F 41
Calico Ho. E20 . . . . .4C 6
   EC4 . . . . .4C 62
   SE1 . . . . .5F 91
Callahan Cotts. E1 . . . . .1B 66
Callcott Ct. NW6 . . . . .2B 8
Callcott Rd. NW6 . . . . .2B 8
Callcott St. W8 . . . . .2D 81
Callendar Rd. SW7 . . . . . . .1D 111
Callingham Cl. E14 . . . . .2C 68
Callisons Pl. SE10 . . . . .5A 128
Calliston Ct. E16 . . . . .2E 73
Callow St. SW3 . . . . .2C 132
Cally Swimming Pool 3B 16
Calshot Ho. N1 . . . . .5B 16
Calshot St. N1 . . . . .5B 16
Calstock NW1 . . . . .4D 15
Calstock Ho. SE11 . . . . .5E 117
Calthorpe St. WC1 . . . . . . .4C 38
Calvert Av. E2 . . . . .3A 42
Calvert Ho. W12 . . . . .5A 50
Calverton SE5 . . . . .2F 141
Calvert Rd. SE10 . . . . .5B 128
Calvert's Bldgs. SE1 . . . . . . .3D 91
Calvert St. NW1 . . . . .3D 13
Calvin St. E1 . . . . .5B 42
Calypso Cres. SE15 . . . . . . .4A 142
Calypso Way SE16 . . . . . . .2B 124
Cambay Ho. E1 . . . . .5F 45
Camber Ho. SE15 . . . . .2C 144
Camberley Ho. NW1 . . . . . . .1A 36
CAMBERWELL 5D 141
Camberwell Bus. Cen.
   SE5 . . . . .5D 141
Camberwell New Rd.
   SE5 . . . . .3D 139
Camberwell Rd. SE5 . . . . . .2C 140
Camborne M. W11 . . . . .4F 51
Cambria Ho. E14 . . . . .3A 68
Cambria St. SW6 . . . . .5A 132
Cambridge Arc. E9 . . . . .1C 22
Cambridge Av. NW6 . . . . . . .5E 9
Cambridge Cir. WC2 . . . . . .4E 59
Cambridge Ct. E2 . . . . .1A 44
   NW6 . . . . .5E 9
            (not continuous)
   W2 . . . . .2F 55
   W6 . . . . .3C 106
Cambridge Cres. E2 . . . . . . .1F 43
Cambridge Gdns. NW6 . . . . .5E 9
   W10 . . . . .3E 51

Cambridge Ga. NW1 . . . . . . .4F 35
Cambridge Ga. M. NW1 . . . .4A 36
Cambridge Gro. W6 . . . . . .3A 106
Cambridge Heath Rd. E1 . . .1A 66
   E2 . . . . .5A 22
Cambridge Ho. W6 . . . . . . .3A 106
Cambridge Pl. W8 . . . . .5A 82
Cambridge Rd. NW6 . . . . . . .2E 31
            (not continuous)
Cambridge Sq. W2 . . . . .3F 55
Cambridge St. SW1 . . . . . . .4A 114
Cambridge Ter. NW1 . . . . . .3F 35
Cambridge Ter. M. NW1 . . . .3A 36
Cambridge Theatre 4F 59
Cambus Rd. E16 . . . . .1E 73
Cam Ct. SE15 . . . . .3B 142
Camden Ct. NW1 . . . . .2C 14
Camden Gdns. NW1 . . . . . . .2A 14
Camden High St. NW1 . . . . .2A 14
Camden Ho. SE8 . . . . .1B 146
Camdenhurst St. E14 . . . . . .3A 68
Camden Lock Market 2F 13
Camden Lock Pl. NW1 . . . . .2F 13
Camden Markets 2F 13
Camden M. NW1 . . . . .1C 14
Camden Pas. N1 . . . . .5F 17
Camden Peoples Theatre . . .4B 36
Camden Rd. NW1 . . . . .2B 14
Camden Sq. NW1 . . . . .1D 15
            (not continuous)
Camden St. NW1 . . . . .2B 14
Camden Studios NW1 . . . . .4C 14
CAMDEN TOWN 3A 14
Camden Wlk. N1 . . . . .4F 17
Camelford NW1 . . . . .4C 14
Camelford Ct. W11 . . . . .5F 51
Camelford Ho. SE1 . . . . . . .1A 138
Camelford Wlk. W11 . . . . . . .4F 51
Camellia Ho. SE8 . . . . .4C 146
Camellia St. SW8 . . . . .5F 137
            (not continuous)
Camel Rd. E16 . . . . .2E 103
Camera Pl. SW10 . . . . .2D 133
Camera Press Gallery, The
   . . . . .4B 92
   (off Queen Elizabeth St.)
Cameret Ct. W11 . . . . .4E 79
Cameron Ho. NW8 . . . . .5F 11
   SE5 . . . . .5B 140
Cameron Pl. E1 . . . . .3A 66
Camgate Mans. SE5 . . . . . .2C 140
Camilla Rd. SE16 . . . . .4F 121
Camlet St. E2 . . . . .4B 42
Camley St. N1 . . . . .2D 15
Camley Street Natural Pk. . .5F 15
Camley Street Natural Pk. Vis. Cen.
   . . . . .4E 15
Camomile St. EC3 . . . . .3F 63
Campaign Ct. W9 . . . . .5C 30
Campania Bldg. E1 . . . . .5E 67
Campbell Ct. SW7 . . . . .2B 110
Campbell Ho. SW1 . . . . . . .1B 136
   W2 . . . . .1D 56
   W12 . . . . .1A 78
Campbell Rd. E3 . . . . .2E 47
Campbell Wlk. N1 . . . . .3A 16
Campden Gro. W8 . . . . .4E 81
Campden Hill W8 . . . . .4C 80
Campden Hill Ct. W8 . . . . . .4E 81
Campden Hill Gdns. W8 . . . .2D 81
Campden Hill Ga. W8 . . . . . .4D 81
Campden Hill Mans. W8 . . . .2E 81
Campden Hill Pl. W11 . . . . .2C 80
Campden Hill Rd. W8 . . . . . .2D 81

Campden Hill Sq. W8 . . . . . . .2C 80
Campden Hill Towers
  W11 . . . . .2D 81
Campden Ho. NW6 . . . . .1D 11
  W8 . . . . .3E 81
Campden Ho. Cl. W8 . . . . .4D 81
Campden Ho's. W8 . . . . .3D 81
Campden Ho. Ter. W8 . . . . . . .3E 81
Campden Mans. W8 . . . . .2E 81
Campden St. W8 . . . . .3D 81
Camperdown St. E1 . . . . .4C 64
Campion Cl. E6 . . . . .5C 76
Campion Ho. E14 . . . . .3C 68
Camplin St. SE14 . . . . .4E 145
Cam Rd. E15 . . . . .3D 27
Canada Est. SE16 . . . . .1C 122
Canada House 2E 87
Canada Ho. SE16 . . . . .2F 123
Canada Memorial 4A 86
Canada Pl. E14 . . . . .2A 98
Canada Sq. E14 . . . . .2F 97
Canada St. SE16 . . . . .5D 95
Canada Way W12 . . . . .5A 50
Canada Wharf SE16 . . . . .2B 96
Canal App. SE8 . . . . .2F 145
CANAL BRIDGE 2E 143
Canal Bldg. N1 . . . . .5B 18
Canal Cl. E1 . . . . .4F 45
  W10 . . . . .4E 29
Canal Cotts. E3 . . . . .3B 24
Canal Gro. SE15 . . . . .2E 143
Canal Market 2F 13
Canal Path E2 . . . . .4B 20
Canal Reach N1 . . . . .3F 15
Canalside Activity Cen. 4E 29
Canalside Sq. N1 . . . . .5C 18
Canal Side Studios NW1 . . . . .3D 15
Canalside Studios N1 . . . . . . .4A 20
Canal St. SE5 . . . . .3D 141
Canal Wlk. N1 . . . . .3E 19
Canal Way W10 . . . . .4D 29
Canal Wharf E8 . . . . .3A 20
Canary Vw. SE10 . . . . .2A 148
Cancell Rd. SW9 . . . . .5E 139
Candida Ct. NW1 . . . . .1A 14
Candid Ho. NW10 . . . . .3A 28
Candle St. E1 . . . . .1F 67
Candover St. W1 . . . . .2B 58
Candy St. E3 . . . . .3C 24
Candy Wharf E3 . . . . .1A 68
Canfield Gdns. NW6 . . . . .1F 9
Cann Hall Rd. E11 . . . . .1F 7
Cann Ho. W14 . . . . .2A 108
Canning Ho. W12 . . . . .1A 78
Canning Pas. W8 . . . . .1B 110
Canning Pl. W8 . . . . .1B 110
Canning Pl. M. W8 . . . . .1B 110
Canning Rd. E15 . . . . .5F 27
CANNING TOWN 4C 72
CANNING TOWN 2A 72
Cannon Ct. EC1 . . . . .4A 40
Cannon Dr. E14 . . . . .1D 97
Cannon Ho. SE11 . . . . .4C 116
Cannon St. EC4 . . . . .4B 62
Cannon St. Rd. E1 . . . . .3F 65
Cannon Wharf Bus. Cen.
  SE8 . . . . .4F 123
Cannon Workshops E14 . . .1D 97
Canon All. EC4 . . . . .4B 62
Canon Beck Rd. SE16 . . . . . . .4C 94
Canonbury Bus. Cen. N1 . . .3C 18
Canonbury Ct. N1 . . . . .2A 18
Canonbury Cres. N1 . . . . .1C 18
Canonbury Gro. N1 . . . . .1B 18

Canonbury La. N1 . . . . .1F 17
Canonbury Pl. N1 . . . . .1A 18
  (not continuous)
Canonbury Rd. N1 . . . . .1A 18
Canonbury Sq. N1 . . . . .1A 18
Canonbury St. N1 . . . . .1B 18
Canonbury Vs. N1 . . . . .2A 18
Canon Row SW1 . . . . .5F 87
  (not continuous)
Canons Ct. E15 . . . . .1F 7
Canon St. N1 . . . . .4B 18
Canrobert St. E2 . . . . .1F 43
Cantelowes Rd. NW1 . . . . . . .1E 15
Canterbury Cl. E6 . . . . .3B 76
Canterbury Ct. NW6 . . . . .5D 9
  SE5 . . . . .4E 139
Canterbury Ho. E3 . . . . .2F 47
  SE1 . . . . .1C 116
  SE8 . . . . .1E 147
Canterbury Ind. Pk. SE15 . . .3C 144
Canterbury Pl. SE17 . . . . .4A 118
Canterbury Rd. NW6 . . . . .1C 30
  (Carlton Va.)
  NW6 . . . . .1D 31
  (Princess Rd.)
Canterbury Ter. NW6 . . . . .5D 9
Cantium Retail Pk. SE1 . . . .2D 143
Canto Ct. EC1 . . . . .4C 40
Canton St. E14 . . . . .4D 69
Cantrell Rd. E3 . . . . .5C 46
Canute Gdns. SE16 . . . . .3D 123
Canvey St. SE1 . . . . .2B 90
Cape Henry Ct. E14 . . . . .1E 99
Capel Ct. EC2 . . . . .4E 63
Capel Ho. E9 . . . . .1B 22
Capener's Cl. SW1 . . . . .5C 84
Cape Yd. E1 . . . . .2E 93
Capital E. Apartments
  E16 . . . . .1E 101
Capital Wharf E1 . . . . .3F 93
Capland Ho. NW8 . . . . .4E 33
Capland St. NW8 . . . . .4E 33
Caple Ho. SW10 . . . . .4C 132
Capper St. WC1 . . . . .5C 36
Capstan Ct. E1 . . . . .1C 94
Capstan Ho. E14 . . . . .5D 71
  (Clove Cres.)
  E14 . . . . .4C 126
  (Stebondale St.)
Capstan Rd. SE8 . . . . .3B 124
Capstan Sq. E14 . . . . .5C 98
Capstan Way SE16 . . . . .3A 96
Captain Cook Statue 2E 87
Capulet M. E16 . . . . .2D 101
Capulet Sq. E3 . . . . .3A 48
Caradoc Cl. W2 . . . . .3D 53
Caradoc St. SE10 . . . . .5F 127
Cara Ho. N1 . . . . .2E 17
Caramel Ct. E3 . . . . .1F 47
Caranday Vs. W11 . . . . .3E 79
Carat Ho. E14 . . . . .2E 69
Caravel Cl. E14 . . . . .1D 125
Caravel M. SE8 . . . . .2D 147
Caraway Apartments SE1 . . . .4C 92
Caraway Cl. E13 . . . . .1F 73
Caraway Hgts. E14 . . . . .1B 98
Carbis Rd. E14 . . . . .3B 68
Carbrooke Ho. E9 . . . . .3B 22
Carburton St. W1 . . . . .1A 58
Cardale St. E14 . . . . .1B 126
Cardamom Bldg. SE1 . . . . . . .3C 92
Cardiff Ho. SE15 . . . . .3E 143
Cardigan Rd. E3 . . . . .5C 24
Cardigan St. SE11 . . . . .5D 117

Cardigan Wlk. N1 . . . . .1C 18
Cardinal Bourne St.
  SE1 . . . . .2E 119
Cardinal Cap All. SE1 . . . . . . .1B 90
Cardinal Ct. E1 . . . . .1D 93
Cardinal Mans. SW1 . . . . .3B 114
Cardinal Pl. SW1 . . . . .1B 114
  (not continuous)
Cardinal Wlk. SW1 . . . . .2B 114
Cardine M. SE15 . . . . .4F 143
Cardington St. NW1 . . . . .2C 36
Cardross Ho. W6 . . . . .1A 106
Cardross St. W6 . . . . .1A 106
Career Ct. SE16 . . . . .4D 95
Carew Ct. SE14 . . . . .3D 145
Carey Ct. SE5 . . . . .5B 140
Carey La. EC2 . . . . .3B 62
Carey Mans. SW1 . . . . .3D 115
Carey Pl. SW1 . . . . .4D 115
Carey St. WC2 . . . . .4C 60
Carfree Cl. N1 . . . . .1E 17
Carillon Ct. E1 . . . . .2D 65
Carina Ho. E20 . . . . .3C 6
Carinthia Ct. SE16 . . . . .3F 123
Carisbrooke Ct. W1 . . . . .2E 57
Carisbrooke Gdns. SE15 . . . .4C 142
Carlile Cl. E3 . . . . .1C 46
Carlile Ho. SE1 . . . . .2E 119
Carlisle Av. EC3 . . . . .4A 64
Carlisle La. SE1 . . . . .2C 116
Carlisle Mans. SW1 . . . . .3B 114
Carlisle Pl. SW1 . . . . .2B 114
Carlisle Rd. NW6 . . . . .3A 8
Carlisle St. W1 . . . . .4D 59
Carlos Pl. W1 . . . . .1E 85
Carlow St. NW1 . . . . .5B 14
Carlton Ct. W9 . . . . .5A 10
Carlton Gdns. SW1 . . . . .2D 87
Carlton Gro. SE15 . . . . .5A 144
Carlton Hill NW8 . . . . .1A 32
Carlton Ho. NW6 . . . . .5D 9
  (not continuous)
  SE16 . . . . .5D 95
Carlton Ho. Ter. SW1 . . . . . . .3D 87
Carlton Mans. NW6 . . . . .2E 9
  W9 . . . . .2F 31
  W14 . . . . .4A 80
Carlton Sq. E1 . . . . .4D 45
  (not continuous)
Carlton St. SW1 . . . . .1D 87
Carlton Twr. Pl. SW1 . . . . .1C 112
Carlton Va. NW6 . . . . .1C 30
Carlton Works, The SE15 . . .4F 143
Carlyle Ho. SE5 . . . . .4B 140
  SW3 . . . . .2E 133
Carlyle Mans. SW3 . . . . .3F 133
  W8 . . . . .2E 81
  (off Kensington Mall)
Carlyle M. E1 . . . . .4E 45
Carlyle's House 3F 133
Carlyle Sq. SW3 . . . . .1E 133
Carly M. E2 . . . . .3D 43
Carmarthen Pl. SE1 . . . . .4F 91
Carmel Ct. W8 . . . . .4F 81
Carmelite St. EC4 . . . . .5E 61
Carmel Lodge SW6 . . . . .2D 131
Carmen St. E14 . . . . .3F 69
Carmichael Ho. E14 . . . . .5B 70
Carmine St. W1 . . . . .2E 55
Carmine Wharf E14 . . . . .3C 68
Carnaby St. W1 . . . . .4B 58
Carnegie St. N1 . . . . .4B 16
Carnell Apartments E14 . . . . .4C 68
Carnival Ho. SE1 . . . . .4C 92

Carnoustie Dr. N1 . . . . .2B 16
(not continuous)
Carole Ho. NW1 . . . . .3C 12
Carolina Cl. E15 . . . . .3F 7
Caroline Cl. W2 . . . . .1A 82
Caroline Gdns. E2 . . . . .2A 42
SE15 . . . . .4F 143
(not continuous)
Caroline Ho. W2 . . . . .1A 82
Caroline Pl. W2 . . . . .5A 54
Caroline Pl. M. W2 . . . . .1A 82
Caroline St. E1 . . . . .4E 67
Caroline Ter. SW1 . . . . .4D 113
Caroline Wlk. W6 . . . . .3A 130
Carol St. NW1 . . . . .3B 14
Caronia Ct. SE16 . . . . .3F 123
Carpenter Ho. E1 . . . . .1E 67
E14 . . . . .2D 69
Carpenters Arms Apartments
SE1 . . . . .4D 121
Carpenters Ct. NW1 . . . . .3B 14
Carpenters Rd. E15 . . . . .2C 66
E20 . . . . .5E 5
Carpenter St. W1 . . . . .1F 85
Carp Ho. E3 . . . . .4B 24
Carradale Ho. E14 . . . . .3B 70
Carriage Dr. E. SW11 . . . . . . .4E 135
Carriage Dr. Nth. SW11 . . . .3D 135
(Carriage Dr. E.)
SW11 . . . . .5B 134
(The Parade)
Carriage Dr. Sth. SW11 . . . .5E 135
(not continuous)
Carriage Dr. W.
SW11 . . . . .5B 134
Carrick Ho. SE11 . . . . .5F 117
Carrick M. SE8 . . . . .2D 147
Carrington Ho. W1 . . . . .3F 85
Carrington St. W1 . . . . .3F 85
Carroll Ho. W2 . . . . .5D 55
Carron Cl. E14 . . . . .3A 70
Carroun Rd. SW8 . . . . .4B 138
Carr St. E14 . . . . .2A 68
Carson Rd. E16 . . . . .1E 73
Carson Ter. W11 . . . . .2F 79
Carter Ct. EC4 . . . . .4A 62
Carteret Ho. W12 . . . . .5A 50
Carteret St. SW1 . . . . .5D 87
Carteret Way SE8 . . . . .4A 124
Carter Ho. E1 . . . . .2B 64
Carter La. EC4 . . . . .4A 62
Carter Pl. SE17 . . . . .1C 140
Carter St. SE17 . . . . .2B 140
Carthew Rd. W6 . . . . .2A 106
Carthew Vs. W6 . . . . .1A 106
Carthusian St. EC1 . . . . .1B 62
Cartier Circ. E14 . . . . .2B 98
Carting La. WC2 . . . . .1A 88
Cartmel NW1 . . . . .2B 36
Carton Ho. W11 . . . . .1E 79
Cartoon Mus. **2F 59**
Cartwright Gdns. WC1 . . . . . .3F 37
Cartwright Ho. SE1 . . . . .2C 118
Cartwright St. E1 . . . . .5C 64
Carvel Ho. E14 . . . . .5C 126
Casby Ho. SE16 . . . . .1D 121
Cascades Twr. E14 . . . . .3D 97
Casella Rd. SE14 . . . . .5D 145
Casey Cl. NW8 . . . . .3F 33
Casey Ct. SE14 . . . . .5D 145
Caspian St. SE5 . . . . .4D 141
Caspian Wlk. E16 . . . . .4D 75
Caspian Wharf E3 . . . . .1F 69
Cass Ho. E9 . . . . .1E 23

Cassidy Rd. SW6 . . . . .5D 131
(not continuous)
Cassilis Rd. E14 . . . . .5E 97
Cassini Apartments E16 . . . .3D 73
Cassland Rd. E9 . . . . .5A 4
Casson Apartments E14 . . . .4E 69
Casson Ho. E1 . . . . .1D 65
Casson St. E1 . . . . .2D 65
Castalia Sq. E14 . . . . .5B 98
Castellain Mans. W9 . . . . .4F 31
(not continuous)
Castellain Rd. W9 . . . . .4F 31
Castell Ho. SE8 . . . . .4E 147
Casterbridge NW6 . . . . .3A 10
W11 . . . . .3C 52
Castleacre W2 . . . . .4F 55
Castle Baynard St. EC4 . . . . .5A 62
Castlebrook Cl. SE11 . . . . . . .3F 117
Castle Cl. E9 . . . . .3A 4
Castle Ct. EC3 . . . . .4E 63
Castleden Ho. NW3 . . . . .2D 11
Castleford St. NW8 . . . . .4E 33
Castlehaven Rd. NW1 . . . . . . .2F 13
Castle Ho. SW8 . . . . .4A 138
Castle Ind. Est. SE17 . . . . . . .3B 118
Castle La. SW1 . . . . .1B 114
Castlemain St. E1 . . . . .1F 65
Castle Mead SE5 . . . . .5C 140
Castle Pl. NW1 . . . . .1A 14
Castlereagh St. W1 . . . . .3B 56
Castle Rd. NW1 . . . . .1F 13
Castleton Ho. E14 . . . . .3C 126
Castletown Rd. W14 . . . . .1A 130
Castle Wharf E14 . . . . .5A 72
Castle Yd. SE1 . . . . .2A 90
Castor La. E14 . . . . .1F 97
Catesby Ho. E9 . . . . .1C 22
Catesby St. SE17 . . . . .4E 119
Cathay Ho. SE16 . . . . .5A 94
Cathay St. SE16 . . . . .5A 94
Cathcart Ho. W10 . . . . .1B 132
Cathcart Rd. SW10 . . . . .2A 132
Cathedral Lodge EC1 . . . . . . .1B 62
Cathedral Mans. SW1 . . . . . . .3B 114
Cathedral Piazza SW1 . . . . . .2B 114
Cathedral St. SE1 . . . . .2D 91
Cathedral Wlk. SW1 . . . . .1B 114
Catherine Ct. SW3 . . . . .2C 132
Catherine Griffiths Ct. EC1 . . .4E 39
Catherine Gro. SE10 . . . . .5F 147
Catherine Ho. E3 . . . . .1E 47
N1 . . . . .4A 20
Catherine Pl. SW1 . . . . .1B 114
Catherine St. WC2 . . . . .5B 60
Catherine Wheel All. E1 . . . . .2A 64
Catherine Wheel Yd.
SW1 . . . . .3B 86
Catherwood Ct. N1 . . . . .1D 41
Cathnor Rd. W12 . . . . .5A 78
Catlin St. SE16 . . . . .1E 143
Cator St. SE15 . . . . .4C 142
(Commercial Way)
SE15 . . . . .3B 142
(Ebley Cl.)
Cato St. W1 . . . . .2A 56
Catton St. WC1 . . . . .2B 60
Caughley Ho. SE11 . . . . .2D 117
Caulfield Ct. NW1 . . . . .2C 14
(off Baynes St.)
Causton Cotts. E14 . . . . .3A 68
Causton Ho. SE5 . . . . .4C 140
Causton St. SW1 . . . . .4E 115
Cavalry Memorial **3D 85**
Cavalry Sq. SW3 . . . . .4C 112

Cavatina Point SE8 . . . . .3F 147
Cavaye Ho. SW10 . . . . .2C 132
Cavaye Pl. SW10 . . . . .1C 132
Cavell Ho. N1 . . . . .4F 19
Cavell St. E1 . . . . .1A 66
Cavendish Av. NW8 . . . . .1E 33
Cavendish Cl. NW6 . . . . .1B 8
NW8 . . . . .2E 33
Cavendish Ct. EC3 . . . . .3A 64
Cavendish Ho. NW8 . . . . .1E 33
SW1 . . . . .2E 115
W1 . . . . .2B 58
Cavendish Mans. EC1 . . . . . . .5D 39
Cavendish M. Nth. W1 . . . . . .1A 58
Cavendish M. Sth. W1 . . . . . .2A 58
Cavendish Pl. W1 . . . . .3A 58
Cavendish Rd. NW6 . . . . .2A 8
Cavendish Sq. W1 . . . . .3A 58
Cavendish St. N1 . . . . .1D 41
Cavendish Ter. E3 . . . . .3B 46
Caversham Ho. SE15 . . . . .3D 143
Caversham M. SW3 . . . . .2B 134
Caversham St. SW3 . . . . .2B 134
Caverswall St. W12 . . . . .3B 50
Cavesson Ho. E20 . . . . .3C 6
Cavour Ho. SE17 . . . . .5A 118
Caxton Gro. E3 . . . . .2D 47
Caxton Hall SW1 . . . . .1D 115
Caxton Rd. W12 . . . . .3D 79
Caxtons, The SW9 . . . . .5A 140
Caxton St. SW1 . . . . .1C 114
Caxton St. Nth. E16 . . . . .4B 72
Caxton Wlk. WC2 . . . . .4E 59
Cayenne Ct. SE1 . . . . .3C 92
Cayton Pl. EC1 . . . . .3D 41
Cayton St. EC1 . . . . .3D 41
Cecil Ct. NW6 . . . . .2F 9
SW10 . . . . .2B 132
WC2 . . . . .5F 59
Cecil Rhodes Ho. NW1 . . . . . .5D 15
Cecil Sharp House **3E 13**
Cedar Cl. E3 . . . . .3C 24
Cedar Ct. N1 . . . . .1C 18
SE1 . . . . .5A 92
Cedar Ho. E2 . . . . .5B 22
E14 . . . . .5B 98
SE16 . . . . .5D 95
W8 . . . . .1F 109
Cedarne Rd. SW6 . . . . .5F 131
Cedars, The E9 . . . . .2D 23
Cedars Rd. E15 . . . . .4F 7
Cedar Way N1 . . . . .2D 15
Cedar Way Ind. Est. N1 . . . . . .2D 15
Cedric Chambers NW8 . . . . . .4D 33
Celandine Cl. E14 . . . . .2D 69
Celandine Dr. E8 . . . . .1C 20
Celandine Way E15 . . . . .2F 49
Celbridge M. W2 . . . . .3A 54
Celebration Av. E20 . . . . .2B 6
Celia Ho. N1 . . . . .1F 41
Celtic St. E14 . . . . .1A 70
Cenotaph **4F 87**
Centaur St. SE1 . . . . .1C 116
Central Av. SW11 . . . . .5B 134
Central Courtyard EC2 . . . . .2A 64
Central Criminal Court
Old Bailey **3A 62**
Central Ho. E15 . . . . .5B 26
Central Markets (Smithfield)
. . . .**2F 61**
Central St Giles Piazza
WC2 . . . . .3E 59
Central St. EC1 . . . . .2B 40
Central Wharf E14 . . . . .3D 69

Centre for the Magic Arts, The	Chambord St. E2 . . . . .2C 42	Charing Cross Rd. WC2 . . . . .4E 59
. . . . .4C 36	Champions Wlk. E20 . . . . .3C 6	Charing Cross Theatre 2A 88
Centre Hgts. NW3 . . . . .1D 11	Champlain Ho. W12 . . . . .1A 78	Charing Cross Underground
Centre of Cell 2F 65	Chancel Ct. W1 . . . . .5D 59	Shop. Cen. WC2 . . . . .1F 87
Centre Point SE1 . . . . .5D 121	Chancellor Ho. E1 . . . . .3A 94	Charing Ho. SE1 . . . . .4E 89
Centrepoint WC2 . . . . .3E 59	SW7 . . . . .1C 110	Chariot Cl. E3 . . . . .4D 25
Centre St. E2 . . . . .1F 43	Chancellor Pas. E14 . . . . . . .3E 97	Charis Ho. E3 . . . . .3A 48
Centric Cl. NW1 . . . . .3F 13	Chancellors Ct. WC1 . . . . . . .1B 60	Charlbert Ct. NW8 . . . . .5F 11
Centurion Bldg. SW8 . . . . . .3F 135	Chancel St. SE1 . . . . .3F 89	Charlbert St. NW8 . . . . .5F 11
Centurion Cl. N7 . . . . .1B 16	Chancery Bldgs. E1 . . . . .5A 66	Charles II Pl. SW3 . . . . .1A 134
Centurion La. E3 . . . . .5C 24	Chancery La. WC2 . . . . .2C 60	Charles II St. SW1 . . . . .2D 87
Century Ct. NW8 . . . . .3E 33	Chance St. E1 . . . . .4B 42	Charles Auffray Ho. E1 . . . . .2C 66
Cephas Av. E1 . . . . .4C 44	E2 . . . . .4B 42	Charles Burton Ct. E5 . . . . . .2A 4
Cephas Ho. E1 . . . . .5B 44	Chandler Av. E16 . . . . .1D 73	Charles Darwin Ho. E2 . . . . . .2F 43
Cephas St. E1 . . . . .5B 44	Chandler Ho. NW6 . . . . .3C 8	(off Canrobert St.)
Cerney M. W2 . . . . .5D 55	WC1 . . . . .5A 38	Charles Dickens Ho. E2 . . . . .2E 43
Cervantes Ct. W2 . . . . .4A 54	Chandlers Av. SE10 . . . . . . .1C 128	Charles Dickens Museum, The
W11 . . . . .4F 51	Chandlers M. E14 . . . . .4D 97	. . . . .5C 38
Cester St. E2 . . . . .4D 21	Chandler St. E1 . . . . .2A 94	Charles Flemwell M. E16 . . .2E 101
Ceylon Rd. W14 . . . . .2E 107	Chandler Way SE15 . . . . .3A 142	Charles Gardner Ct. N1 . . . . .2E 41
Ceylon Wharf Apartments	Chandlery, The SE1 . . . . . . .1E 117	Charles Ho. W14 . . . . .3B 108
SE16 . . . . .4B 94	Chandlery Ho. E1 . . . . .4D 65	Charles Lamb Ct. N1 . . . . . . .5A 18
CFGS Community Performing Arts	Chandos Pl. WC2 . . . . .1F 87	Charles La. NW8 . . . . .1E 33
& Sports Cen. 2C 46	Chandos Rd. E15 . . . . .2D 7	Charles Mackenzie Ho.
Chadbourn St. E14 . . . . .2A 70	Chandos St. W1 . . . . .2A 58	SE16 . . . . .3E 121
Chadston Ho. N1 . . . . .1A 18	Change All. EC3 . . . . .4E 63	Charles Pl. NW1 . . . . .3C 36
Chadswell WC1 . . . . .3A 38	Channel 4 TV 2D 115	Charles Rowan Ho. WC1 . . . .3D 39
Chadwell Ho. SE17 . . . . . . .1E 141	Channel Ho. E14 . . . . .2F 67	Charles Simmons Ho.
Chadwell St. EC1 . . . . .2E 39	SE16 . . . . .5D 95	WC1 . . . . .3C 38
Chadwick St. SW1 . . . . .2E 115	Channelsea Bus. Cen. E15 . . .1E 49	Charles Sq. N1 . . . . .3E 41
Chadwin Rd. E13 . . . . .1F 73	Channelsea Path E15 . . . . . . .3D 27	Charles Sq. Est. N1 . . . . .3E 41
Chadworth Ho. EC1 . . . . .3B 40	Channelsea Rd. E15 . . . . .3D 27	Charles St. E16 . . . . .3C 102
Chagford Ho. E3 . . . . .3A 48	Chantrey Ho. SW1 . . . . .3F 113	W1 . . . . .2F 85
Chagford St. NW1 . . . . .5B 34	Chantry Cl. W9 . . . . .5C 30	Charleston St. SE17 . . . . . . .4C 118
Chalbury Wlk. NW1 . . . . .5C 16	Chantry Sq. W8 . . . . .2F 109	Charles Townsend Ho. EC1 . . .3F 39
Chalcot Cres. NW1 . . . . .2C 12	Chantry St. N1 . . . . .4A 18	Charles Whincup Rd. E16 . . .2F 101
Chalcot Rd. NW1 . . . . .2D 13	Chant Sq. E15 . . . . .2E 27	Charlesworth Ho. E14 . . . . . .4C 68
Chalcot Sq. NW1 . . . . .2C 12	Chant St. E15 . . . . .2E 27	Charleville Ct. W14 . . . . .1B 130
(not continuous)	(not continuous)	Charleville Mans. W14 . . . . .1A 130
Chaldon Rd. SW6 . . . . .4A 130	Chapel Ct. SE1 . . . . .4D 01	(not continuous)
Chalfont Ct. NW1 . . . . .5C 34	Chapel Ho. St. E14 . . . . .5A 126	Charleville Rd. W14 . . . . . . .1A 130
Chalfont Ho. SE16 . . . . .1F 121	Chapel Mkt. N1 . . . . .5D 17	Charlie Chaplin Wlk. SE1 . . . .3C 88
Chalford NW6 . . . . .1C 10	Chapel of St John the Evangelist	Charlotte Ct. SE1 . . . . .3F 119
CHALK FARM 1E 13	. . . . .1B 92	Charlotte Ho. E16 . . . . .2F 101
Chalk Farm Pde. NW3 . . . . . .1D 13	(within The Tower of London)	Charlotte M. W1 . . . . .1C 58
(off Adelaide Rd.)	Chapel of St Peter & St Paul	W10 . . . . .4D 51
Chalk Farm Rd. NW1 . . . . . . .1D 13	. . . . .2D 149	W14 . . . . .3F 107
Chalk Hill Rd. W6 . . . . .4D 107	Chapel Pl. EC2 . . . . .3F 41	Charlotte Pl. SW1 . . . . .4B 114
Chalk Rd. E13 . . . . .1A 74	N1 . . . . .5E 17	W1 . . . . .2C 58
Chalkwell Ho. E1 . . . . .4E 67	W1 . . . . .4F 57	Charlotte Rd. EC2 . . . . .3F 41
Challenger Ho. E14 . . . . .5A 68	Chapel Side W2 . . . . .5F 53	Charlotte St. W1 . . . . .1C 58
Challoner Ct. W14 . . . . .1B 130	Chapel St. NW1 . . . . .2F 55	Charlotte Ter. N1 . . . . .4C 16
Challoner Cres. W14 . . . . . .1B 130	SW1 . . . . .1E 113	Charlton Ct. E2 . . . . .4C 20
Challoner Mans. W14 . . . . . .1B 130	Chaplin Cl. SE1 . . . . .4E 89	Charlton Pl. N1 . . . . .5F 17
Challoner St. W14 . . . . .5B 108	Chaplin Ct. E3 . . . . .5C 46	Charlwood Ho. SW1 . . . . . . .4D 115
Chalmers Wlk. SE17 . . . . . . .3A 140	Chaplin Ho. N1 . . . . .3D 19	Charlwood Ho's. WC1 . . . . . .3A 38
Chaloner Ct. SE1 . . . . .4D 91	Chapman Ho. E1 . . . . .4A 66	(off Midhope St.)
Chalton Ho. NW1 . . . . .2D 37	Chapman Rd. E9 . . . . .5B 4	Charlwood Pl. SW1 . . . . .4C 114
Chalton St. NW1 . . . . .5C 14	Chapman St. E1 . . . . .5F 65	Charlwood St. SW1 . . . . .1B 136
(not continuous)	Chapone Pl. W1 . . . . .4D 59	(not continuous)
Chamberlain Ho. E1 . . . . .5B 66	Chapter Chambers SW1 . . . .4D 115	Charmans Ho. SW8 . . . . .4F 137
NW1 . . . . .1D 37	Chapter House 4B 62	Charmeuse Ct. E2 . . . . .5A 22
SE1 . . . . .5D 89	Chapter Ho. E2 . . . . .4E 43	Charmian Ho. N1 . . . . .1F 41
Chamberlain St. NW1 . . . . . . .2C 12	Chapter Rd. SE17 . . . . .1A 140	Charmouth Ho. SW8 . . . . . . .4B 138
Chamberlayne Mans.	Chapter St. SW1 . . . . .4D 115	Charnock Ho. W12 . . . . .1A 78
NW10 . . . . .2E 29	Charcroft Ct. W14 . . . . .5D 79	Charnwood Gdns. E14 . . . . . .3E 125
Chamberlayne Rd. NW10 . . . .1D 29	Chardin Ho. SW9 . . . . .5E 139	Charrington St. NW1 . . . . . . .5D 15
Chamberlens Garages	Chardwell Cl. E6 . . . . .3B 76	(not continuous)
W6 . . . . .4A 106	Charecroft Way W12 . . . . . . .5D 79	Charterhouse 5A 40
Chambers St. SE16 . . . . .4D 93	W14 . . . . .5D 79	Charter Ho. WC2 . . . . .4A 60
Chamber St. E1 . . . . .5C 64	Charfield Ct. W9 . . . . .5A 32	Charterhouse Bldgs. EC1 . . . .5B 40
Chambers Wharf SE16 . . . . . .5E 93	Charford Rd. E16 . . . . .2E 73	Charterhouse M. EC1 . . . . . . .1A 62
Chambord Ho. E2 . . . . .3C 42	Chargrove Cl. SE16 . . . . .4E 95	Charterhouse Sq. EC1 . . . . . .1A 62
	Charing Cross SW1 . . . . .2F 87	Charterhouse St. EC1 . . . . . . .2E 61

Charteris Community Sports Cen.
. . . .**4D 9**
Charteris Rd. NW6 . . . . .4C 8
Chartes Ho. SE1 . . . . .1A 120
Chartham Ho. SE1 . . . . .1E 119
Chart Ho. E14 . . . . .5F 125
Chartridge SE17 . . . . .2D 141
Chart St. N1 . . . . .2E 41
Chartwell Ho. W11 . . . . .2C 80
Charville Ct. SE10 . . . . .2E 149
Chase Ct. SW3 . . . . .2B 112
Chase Ho. NW6 . . . . .2E 31
Chaseley St. E14 . . . . .4F 67
Chasemore Ho. SW6 . . . . . . .4A 130
Chaseway Lodge E16 . . . . . .4E 73
Chater Ho. E2 . . . . .2D 45
Chatham St. SE17 . . . . .3D 119
Chatsworth Ct. W8 . . . . .3D 109
Chatsworth Ho. E16 . . . . . . .2F 101
Chatsworth Rd. NW2 . . . . . . .1A 8
Chaucer Dr. SE1 . . . . .4C 120
Chaucer Ho. SW1 . . . . .1B 136
Chaucer Mans. W14 . . . . . . .2A 130
Chaulden Ho. EC1 . . . . .3E 41
Chauntler Cl. E16 . . . . .5A 74
Cheadle Ct. NW8 . . . . .4E 33
Cheadle Ho. E14 . . . . .4B 68
Cheapside EC2 . . . . .4B 62
Cheapside Pas. EC2 . . . . . . .4B 62
Cheddington Ho. E2 . . . . . . .4D 21
Chedworth Cl. E16 . . . . .3B 72
Cheering La. E20 . . . . .3C 6
Cheesegrater, The **4F 63**
Cheesemans Ter. W14 . . . . .1B 130
   (not continuous)
Chelmsford Cl. E6 . . . . .3B 76
CHELSEA **1A 134**
Chelsea Bri. SW1 . . . . .2F 135
Chelsea Bri. Rd. SW1 . . . . . .5D 113
Chelsea Bri. Wharf SW8 . . . .3F 135
Chelsea Cinema **1A 134**
Chelsea Cloisters SW3 . . . .4A 112
Chelsea Ct. SW3 . . . . .2D 135
Chelsea Emb. SW3 . . . . .3F 133
Chelsea Farm Ho. Studios
  SW10 . . . . .3D 133
Chelsea FC **4F 131**
Chelsea Gdns. SW1 . . . . . . .1E 135
Chelsea Ga. SW1 . . . . .1E 135
Chelsea Lodge SW3 . . . . . . .2C 134
Chelsea Mnr. Ct. SW3 . . . . .2A 134
Chelsea Mnr. Gdns. SW3 . . .2A 134
Chelsea Mnr. St. SW3 . . . . .1F 133
Chelsea Mnr. Studios
  SW3 . . . . .1A 134
Chelsea Pk. Gdns. SW3 . . . .2D 133
Chelsea Physic Garden **2B 134**
Chelsea Reach Twr.
  SW10 . . . . .4D 133
Chelsea Sports Cen. **1A 134**
Chelsea Sq. SW3 . . . . .5E 111
Chelsea Studios SW6 . . . . .4A 132
Chelsea Theatre, The **4D 133**
Chelsea Towers SW3 . . . . . .1A 134
Chelsea Village SW6 . . . . . .4A 132
Chelsea Wharf SW10 . . . . . .5D 133
Chelsfield Ho. SE17 . . . . . . .4F 119
Chelsfield Point E9 . . . . . . .2D 23
Cheltenham Ter. SW3 . . . . . .5C 112
Chelwood Ho. W2 . . . . .4E 55
Chenies, The NW1 . . . . .5E 15
Chenies Ho. W2 . . . . .5F 53
Chenies M. WC1 . . . . .5D 37
Chenies Pl. NW1 . . . . .5E 15

Chenies St. WC1 . . . . .1D 59
Cheniston Gdns. W8 . . . . . .1F 109
Chepstow Cnr. W2 . . . . .4E 53
Chepstow Ct. W11 . . . . .5D 53
Chepstow Cres. W11 . . . . . .5D 53
Chepstow Pl. W2 . . . . .4E 53
Chepstow Rd. W2 . . . . .2D 53
Chepstow Vs. W11 . . . . .5C 52
Chequers Ct. EC1 . . . . .5D 41
Chequers Ho. NW8 . . . . .4F 33
Chequer St. EC1 . . . . .5C 40
   (not continuous)
Cherbury Ct. N1 . . . . .1E 41
Cherbury St. N1 . . . . .1E 41
Cherry Gdn. Ho. SE16 . . . . .5F 93
Cherry Gdn. St. SE16 . . . . . .5F 93
Cherry Tree Cl. E9 . . . . .3C 22
Cherry Tree Ct. NW1 . . . . . .1C 14
Cherry Tree Rd. E15 . . . . . . .2F 7
Cherry Tree Ter. SE1 . . . . . .5A 92
Cherry Tree Wlk. EC1 . . . . . .5C 40
Cherrywood Cl. E3 . . . . .2A 46
Chertsey Ho. *E2* *3B 42*
   (off Arnold Cir.)
Cherwell Ho. NW8 . . . . .5E 33
Chesham Cl. SW1 . . . . .2D 113
Chesham Flats W1 . . . . .5E 57
Chesham M. SW1 . . . . .1D 113
Chesham Pl. SW1 . . . . .2D 113
   (not continuous)
Chesham St. SW1 . . . . .2D 113
Cheshire Ct. EC4 . . . . .4E 61
Cheshire St. E2 . . . . .4C 42
Cheshunt Ho. NW6 . . . . .4F 9
Chesil Ct. E2 . . . . .5B 22
  SW3 . . . . .2A 134
Chesilton Rd. SW6 . . . . .5B 130
Chesney St. SW9 . . . . .4E 31
Chesson Rd. W14 . . . . .2B 130
Chester Cl. SW1 . . . . .5F 85
Chester Cl. Nth. NW1 . . . . . .2A 36
Chester Cl. Sth. NW1 . . . . . .3A 36
Chester Cotts. SW1 . . . . . . .4D 113
Chester Ct. NW1 . . . . .2A 36
   (not continuous)
  SE5 . . . . .5D 141
  SE8 . . . . .5E 123
  W6 . . . . .4D 107
Chesterfield Gdns. SE10 . . .5D 149
  W1 . . . . .2F 85
Chesterfield Hill W1 . . . . . . .2F 85
Chesterfield Ho. W1 . . . . . . .2E 85
Chesterfield St. W1 . . . . .2F 85
Chesterfield Wlk. SE10 . . . . .5D 149
Chesterfield Way SE15 . . . .5B 144
Chester Ga. NW1 . . . . .3F 35
Chester Ho. SE8 . . . . .2C 146
  SW1 . . . . .3F 113
  SW9 . . . . .4E 139
Chester M. SW1 . . . . .1F 113
Chester Pl. NW1 . . . . .2F 35
Chester Rd. E16 . . . . .5F 49
  NW1 . . . . .3E 35
Chester Row SW1 . . . . .4D 113
Chester Sq. SW1 . . . . .3E 113
Chester Sq. M. SW1 . . . . . . .2F 113
Chester St. E2 . . . . .4E 43
  SW1 . . . . .1E 113
Chester Ter. NW1 . . . . .2F 35
   (not continuous)
Chesterton Ho. W10 . . . . . . .1F 51
Chesterton Rd. W10 . . . . . . .2E 51
Chesterton Sq. W8 . . . . .3C 108
Chester Way SE11 . . . . .4E 117

Chestnut All. SW6 . . . . .2C 130
Chestnut Ct. SW6 . . . . .2C 130
  W8 . . . . .2F 109
Chestnut Ho. E3 . . . . .3B 24
Chestnut Plaza E20 . . . . . . .1B 26
Chettle Cl. SE1 . . . . .1D 119
Chetwode Ho. NW8 . . . . . . .4F 33
Chetwood Wlk. E6 . . . . .3A 76
Cheval Pl. SW7 . . . . .1A 112
Cheval St. E14 . . . . .1D 125
Chevening Rd. NW6 . . . . . . .4A 8
  SE10 . . . . .5C 128
Cheverell Ho. E2 . . . . .5E 21
Chevet St. E9 . . . . .3A 4
Cheviot Ct. SE14 . . . . .3C 144
Cheviot Ho. E1 . . . . .3A 66
Chevron Cl. E16 . . . . .3E 73
Cheylesmore Ho. SW1 . . . . .1F 135
Cheyne Ct. SW3 . . . . .2B 134
Cheyne Gdns. SW3 . . . . .2A 134
Cheyne Ho. SW3 . . . . .3B 134
Cheyne M. SW3 . . . . .3A 134
Cheyne Pl. SW3 . . . . .2B 134
Cheyne Row SW3 . . . . .3F 133
Cheyne Wlk. SW3 . . . . .4D 133
   (not continuous)
  SW10 . . . . .4D 133
Chicheley St. SE1 . . . . .4C 88
Chichester Cl. E6 . . . . .4A 76
Chichester Ct. NW1 . . . . . . .1B 14
Chichester Ho. NW6 . . . . . . .1D 31
  SW9 . . . . .4D 139
Chichester Rents WC2 . . . . .3D 61
Chichester Rd. NW6 . . . . . . .1D 31
  W2 . . . . .1A 54
Chichester St. SW1 . . . . . . .1C 136
Chichester Way E14 . . . . . . .3D 127
Chicksand Ho. E1 . . . . .1D 65
Chicksand St. E1 . . . . .2C 64
   (not continuous)
Chigwell Ct. E9 . . . . .4A 4
Chigwell Hill E1 . . . . .1F 93
Chilcot Cl. E14 . . . . .4F 69
Childeric Rd. SE14 . . . . .4A 146
Childers St. SE8 . . . . .2A 146
Child La. SE10 . . . . .2C 128
Child's M. SW5 . . . . .4E 109
Child's Pl. SW5 . . . . .4E 109
Child's St. SW5 . . . . .4E 109
Child's Wlk. SW5 . . . . .4E 109
Chilham Ho. SE1 . . . . .1E 119
  SE15 . . . . .2C 144
Chilianwalla Memorial . . .**2D 135**
Chiltern Ct. NW1 . . . . .5C 34
  SE14 . . . . .4C 144
Chiltern Ho. SE17 . . . . .2E 141
  W10 . . . . .1F 51
Chiltern Rd. E3 . . . . .5E 47
Chiltern St. W1 . . . . .1D 57
Chilton Gro. SE8 . . . . .4E 123
Chilton St. E2 . . . . .4C 42
Chilver St. SE10 . . . . .5C 128
Chilworth M. W2 . . . . .4C 54
Chilworth St. W2 . . . . .4C 54
Chimney Ct. E1 . . . . .3A 94
China Ct. E1 . . . . .2F 93
China Hall M. SE16 . . . . .2C 122
China Town **5E 59**
China Wharf SE1 . . . . .4D 93
Ching Ct. WC2 . . . . .4F 59
Chinnock's Wharf E14 . . . . . .5F 67
Chipka St. E14 . . . . .5B 98
   (not continuous)
Chipley St. SE14 . . . . .3F 145

Chippendale Ho. SW1 .....1A **136**
Chippenham Gdns.
  NW6 ....3D **31**
Chippenham M. W9 ....5D **31**
Chippenham Rd. W9 ......5D **31**
Chipperfield Ho. SW3 .....5F **111**
Chisenhale Rd. E3 ....5F **23**
Chisledon Wlk. E9 ....4C **4**
Chiswell St. EC1 ....1C **62**
  SE5 ....4E **141**
Chitty St. W1 ....1C **58**
Chobham Rd. E15 ....2D **7**
Chocolate Studios N1 .....2D **41**
Choppin's Ct. E1 ....2A **94**
Chopwell Cl. E15 ....2E **27**
Choudhury Mans. N1 ......2A **16**
Chrisp Ho. SE10 ....2F **149**
Chrisp St. E14 ....2F **69**
  (not continuous)
Christabel Pankhurst Ct.
  SE5 ....5D **141**
Christchurch Av. NW6 .....2A **8**
Christchurch Ct. EC4 .....3A **62**
  NW6 ....1A **8**
Christchurch Sq. E9 ......4B **22**
Christchurch St. SW3 .....2B **134**
Christchurch Ter. SW3 ....2B **134**
Christchurch Way SE10 ....5A **128**
  SE10 ....1F **149**
Christian Ct. SE16 ....3B **96**
Christian Pl. E1 ....4E **65**
Christian St. E1 ....3E **65**
Christie Ho. SE10 ....5B **128**
  W12 ....4A **50**
Christie Rd. E9 ....5A **4**
  E9 ....1F **23**
Christina St. EC2 ....4F **41**
Christopher Bell Twr.
  E3 ....5D **25**
Christopher Cl. SE16 .....5D **95**
Christopher Ct. E1 ....4D **65**
Christopher Pl. NW1 ......3E **37**
Christophers M. W11 .....2F **79**
Christopher St. EC2 ......5E **41**
Chroma Mans. E20 ....4C **6**
Chryssell Rd. SW9 ....5E **139**
Chubworthy St. SE14 .....3F **145**
Chudleigh St. E1 ....3D **67**
Chumleigh Gdns.
  SE5 ....2F **141**
Chumleigh St. SE5 ....2F **141**
Church Cloisters EC3 .....1F **91**
Church Cl. W8 ....4F **81**
Church Ct. EC4 ....4D **61**
  SE16 ....4B **96**
Church Cres. E9 ....1D **23**
Church Entry EC4 ....4A **62**
Churchfield Ho. W2 ....5D **33**
Churchfields SE10 ....3B **148**
Church Ho. EC1 ....4A **40**
  SW1 ....1E **115**
Churchill Gdns. SW1 ......1B **136**
  (not continuous)
Churchill Gdns. Rd.
  SW1 ....1A **136**
Churchill Pl. E14 ....3A **98**
Churchill Rd. E16 ....4B **74**
Churchill War Rooms 4E 87
Church Mead SE5 ....5C **140**
Church Pas. *EC2* *3C 62*
  (off Gresham St.)
Church Pl. SW1 ....1C **86**
Church Rd. N1 ....1C **18**
Church Row SW6 ....5F **131**

Church St. E15 ....3F **27**
  E16 ....3F **105**
  NW8 ....1E **55**
  (not continuous)
  W2 ....1E **55**
  (not continuous)
Church St. Est. NW8 ......5E **33**
Church St. Nth. E15 ......3F **27**
Churchward Ho. SE17 .....2A **140**
  W14 ....1C **130**
Churchway NW1 ....2E **37**
  (not continuous)
Churchyard Row SE11 .....3A **118**
Church Yd. Wlk. W2 ......1D **55**
Churston Mans. WC1 ......5C **38**
Churton Pl. SW1 ....4C **114**
Churton St. SW1 ....4C **114**
Chusan Pl. E14 ....4C **68**
Chuter Ede Ho. SW6 ......3C **130**
Cicely Ho. NW8 ....1E **33**
Cine Lumiere 3D 111
Cineworld Cinema
  Chelsea, Fulham Rd.
  ....1C 132
  Chelsea, King's Rd. ..2E 133
  Hammersmith 4A 106
  Haymarket 1D 87
  Shaftesbury Av. 1D 87
  The O2 ....3F 99
  West India Quay ...1E 97
Cinnabar Wharf Central E1 ...3E **93**
Cinnabar Wharf E. E1 .....3E **93**
Cinnabar Wharf W. E1 .....3E **93**
Cinnamon Cl. SE15 ....4B **142**
Cinnamon St. E1 ....3A **94**
Cinnamon Wharf SE1 .....4C **92**
Circa Apartments NW1 ....1D **13**
Circle, The SE1 ....4C **92**
Circus Lodge NW8 ....2D **33**
Cirque M W1 ....1B **56**
Circus Pl. EC2 ....2E **03**
Circus Rd. NW8 ....2D **33**
Circus St. SE10 ....5B **148**
Cirencester St. W2 ....1F **53**
Cirrus Apartments E1 .....4C **42**
Citadel Pl. SE11 ....5B **116**
Citius Apartments E3 .....5D **25**
Citius Wlk. E20 ....4C **6**
Citrus Ho. SE8 ....1B **146**
City Apartments *E1* *3D 65*
  (off White Church La.)
City Bus. Cen. SE16 ......5B **94**
City Cross Bus. Pk.
  SE10 ....3A **128**
City Forum EC1 ....2B **40**
City Gdn. Row N1 ....1A **40**
City Gateway E1 ....1D **93**
City Hall 3A 92
City Harbour E14 ....2A **126**
City Hgts. E8 ....3A **20**
City Lights Ct. SE11 ......5E **117**
City Mill River Path E15 ....4B **26**
CITY OF LONDON 3E 63
City of London Distillery 4F 61
City of London Police Mus.
  ....3C 62
City of Westminster College
  Paddington Green Campus
  ....1D 55
City Pav. EC1 ....1F **61**
City Pl. Ho. EC2 ....2C **62**
Citypoint EC2 ....1D **63**
City Rd. EC1 ....1F **39**
City Tower EC2 ....2D **63**

City University London
  Goswell Pl. 3A 40
  Northampton Square Campus
  ....3F 39
City University London
  Saddlers Sports Centre, The
  ....4A 40
City Vw. Apartments N1 ....2B **18**
City Wlk. SE1 ....1F **119**
City Wlk. Apartments
  EC1 ....3A **40**
Civil Justice Cen.
  Central London 5F 35
Clabon M. SW1 ....2B **112**
Clack St. SE16 ....5C **94**
Claire Pl. E14 ....1E **125**
Clandon Ho. SE1 ....5A **90**
Clanricarde Gdns. W2 .....1E **81**
Clapham Rd. SW9 ....5C **138**
CLAPTON PARK 1A 4
Clara Grant Ho. E14 ......1E **125**
Clare Ct. W11 ....1A **80**
  WC1 ....3A **38**
Claredale Ho. E2 ....1F **43**
Claredale St. E2 ....1E **43**
Clare Gdns. W11 ....4A **52**
Clare Ho. E3 ....3B **24**
  E16 ....1E **105**
  SE1 ....5C **120**
Clare La. N1 ....2C **18**
Clare Mkt. WC2 ....4C **60**
Clare M. SW6 ....5F **131**
Claremont Cl. E16 ....3E **105**
  N1 ....1E **39**
Claremont Ct. *E2* *1E 43*
  (off Claredale St.)
  E2 ....5A **22**
  (Cambridge Heath Rd.)
  W2 ....3A **54**
  W9 ....1B **30**
Olaromont Rd. W9 ....1A **30**
Claremont Sq. N1 ....1D **39**
Claremont St. E16 ....3E **105**
  SE10 ....4A **148**
Claremont Vs. SE5 ....4E **141**
Clarence Ct. W6 ....4A **106**
Clarence Gdns. NW1 ......3A **36**
Clarence Ga. Gdns. NW1 ...5C **34**
Clarence House 4C 86
Clarence Ho. SE17 ....2C **140**
Clarence M. SE16 ....3D **95**
Clarence Rd. E16 ....5F **49**
  E16 ....1A **72**
  NW6 ....2B **8**
  SE8 ....3F **147**
Clarence Ter. NW1 ....4C **34**
Clarence Way NW1 ....1F **13**
Clarendon Cl. E9 ....2C **22**
  W2 ....5F **55**
Clarendon Ct. W9 ....4C **32**
Clarendon Cross W11 .....1A **80**
Clarendon Flats W1 ......4E **57**
Clarendon Gdns. W9 ......5C **32**
Clarendon Gro. NW1 ......2D **37**
Clarendon Ho. NW1 ......1C **36**
  W2 ....5F **55**
Clarendon Lodge W11 .....1A **80**
Clarendon M. W2 ....5F **55**
Clarendon Pl. W2 ....5F **55**
Clarendon Rd. W11 ....5F **51**
Clarendon St. SW1 ....1A **136**
Clarendon Ter. W9 ....4C **32**
Clarendon Wlk. W11 ......4F **51**
Clare St. E2 ....5A **22**

Clareville Ct. SW7 . . . . . . .4C 110
Clareville Gro. SW7 . . . . . . .4C 110
Clareville Gro. M. SW7 . . . .4C 110
Clareville St. SW7 . . . . . .4C 110
Clarewood Ct. W1 . . . . .2B 56
Clarges M. W1 . . . . .2F 85
Clarges St. W1 . . . . .2A 86
Clarion Ho. E3 . . . . .1F 45
          (off Roman Rd.)
SW1 . . . . .5C 114
W1 . . . . .4D 59
Clarissa Ho. E14 . . . . .3A 70
Clarissa St. E8 . . . . .3B 20
Clarke's M. W1 . . . . .1E 57
Clark Ho. SW10 . . . . .4B 132
Clarkson Rd. E16 . . . . .3B 72
Clarkson Row NW1 . . . . . .5A 14
Clarkson St. E2 . . . . .2F 43
Clark St. E1 . . . . .2A 66
          (not continuous)
Clarson Ho. SE5 . . . . .4F 139
SE8 . . . . .2A 146
Classic Mans. E9 . . . . .2B 22
Claude St. E14 . . . . .3D 105
Clavell St. SE10 . . . . .3B 148
Claverton St. SW1 . . . . . .1C 136
Clave St. E1 . . . . .3B 94
Clay Ct. SE1 . . . . .1F 119
          (off Long La.)
Clayhall Ct. E3 . . . . .1B 46
Claylands Pl. SW8 . . . . . . .4D 139
Claylands Rd. SW8 . . . . . .3C 138
Claypole Rd. E15 . . . . .5C 26
Clay St. W1 . . . . .2C 56
Clayton Cl. E6 . . . . .3C 76
Clayton Cres. N1 . . . . .4A 16
Clayton Dr. SE8 . . . . .5F 123
Clayton Ho. E9 . . . . .1B 22
Clayton St. SE11 . . . . .2D 139
Clearbrook Way E1 . . . . . .3C 66
Clearwater Ter. W11 . . . . . .4E 79
Clearwater Yd. NW1 . . . . . .3A 14
Clearwell Dr. W9 . . . . .5F 31
Cleaver Ho. NW3 . . . . .1B 12
Cleaver Sq. SE11 . . . . .1E 139
Cleaver St. SE11 . . . . .5E 117
Cleeve Ho. E2 . . . . .3A 42
Cleeve Workshops E2 . . . . .3A 42
Clegg Ho. SE16 . . . . .1C 122
Clegg St. E1 . . . . .2A 94
Cleland Ho. E2 . . . . .5C 22
Clematis Apartments E3 . . .3C 46
Clem Attlee Ct. SW6 . . . . . .3C 130
Clem Attlee Pde. SW6 . . . .3C 130
Clemence St. E14 . . . . .2B 68
Clement Danes Ho. W12 . . .4A 50
Clement Ho. SE8 . . . . .4A 124
W10 . . . . .1C 50
Clementina Ct. E3 . . . . .5A 46
Clement's Av. E16 . . . . . . .5D 73
Clement's Inn WC2 . . . . . . .4C 60
Clement's Inn Pas. WC2 . . .4C 60
Clements La. EC4 . . . . .5E 63
Clements Rd. SE16 . . . . . . .2E 121
Clemson Ho. E8 . . . . .4C 20
Clennam St. SE1 . . . . .4C 90
Clenston M. W1 . . . . .3B 56
Cleopatra's Needle 2B 88
Clere Pl. EC2 . . . . .4E 41
Clere St. EC2 . . . . .4E 41
CLERKENWELL 5E 39
Clerkenwell Cl. EC1 . . . . . .4E 39
          (not continuous)
Clerkenwell Ct. N1 . . . . . . .5F 17

Clerkenwell Grn. EC1 . . . . . .5E 39
Clerkenwell Rd. EC1 . . . . . . .1D 61
Clerk's Pl. EC2 . . . . .3F 63
Clermont Rd. E9 . . . . .3B 22
Cleve Ho. NW6 . . . . .1F 9
Cleveland Gdns. W2 . . . . . .4B 54
Cleveland Gro. E1 . . . . .5B 44
Cleveland Mans. NW6 . . . . .2C 8
SW9 . . . . .5D 139
W9 . . . . .4E 31
Cleveland M. W1 . . . . .1B 58
Cleveland Pl. SW1 . . . . .2C 86
Cleveland Rd. N1 . . . . .2E 19
Cleveland Row SW1 . . . . . . .3B 86
Cleveland Sq. W2 . . . . .4B 54
Cleveland St. W1 . . . . .5A 36
Cleveland Ter. W2 . . . . .4B 54
Cleveland Way E1 . . . . .5B 44
Cleve Rd. NW6 . . . . .1E 9
Cleves Ho. E16 . . . . .2F 101
Clichy Est. E1 . . . . .2C 66
Clichy Ho. E1 . . . . .2C 66
Cliffe Ho. SE10 . . . . .5B 128
Clifford Ct. W2 . . . . .2F 53
Clifford Gdns. NW10 . . . . . .1B 28
Clifford Ho. W14 . . . . .4B 108
Clifford Rd. N1 . . . . .3F 19
Clifford's Inn EC4 . . . . .4D 61
Clifford's Inn Pas. EC4 . . . .4D 61
Clifford St. W1 . . . . .1B 86
Cliff Wlk. E16 . . . . .1B 72
Clifton Ct. NW8 . . . . .4D 33
SE15 . . . . .4A 144
Clifton Cres. SE15 . . . . .5A 144
Clifton Gdns. W9 . . . . .5B 32
Clifton Ga. SW10 . . . . .2B 132
Clifton Hill NW8 . . . . .5A 10
Clifton Hill Studios NW8 . . .5B 10
Clifton Ho. E2 . . . . .4B 42
Clifton Pl. SE16 . . . . .4C 94
SW10 . . . . .2B 132
W2 . . . . .4E 55
Clifton Ri. SE14 . . . . .4A 146
          (not continuous)
Clifton Rd. E16 . . . . .1A 72
W9 . . . . .4C 32
Clifton St. EC2 . . . . .5F 41
Clifton Vs. W9 . . . . .1A 54
Clifton Wlk. W6 . . . . .4A 106
Clifton Way SE15 . . . . .5A 144
Climsland Ho. SE1 . . . . .2E 89
Clinger Ct. N1 . . . . .4F 19
Clink Prison Mus. 2D 91
Clink St. SE1 . . . . .2C 90
Clink Wharf SE1 . . . . .2D 91
Clinton Rd. E3 . . . . .3F 45
Clinton Ter. SE8 . . . . .2D 147
Clipper Apartments SE10 . .2B 148
Clipper Cl. SE16 . . . . .4D 95
Clipper Ho. E14 . . . . .5C 126
Clipstone M. W1 . . . . .1B 58
Clipstone St. W1 . . . . .1A 58
Clive Ct. W9 . . . . .4C 32
Cliveden Ho. E16 . . . . .2D 101
SW1 . . . . .3D 113
Cliveden Pl. SW1 . . . . .3D 113
Clive Ho. SE10 . . . . .3B 148
Cloak La. EC4 . . . . .5C 62
Clock Ho. E3 . . . . .3B 48
Clockmaker's Museum, The
          . . . . .3C 62
Clock Pl. SE1 . . . . .3A 118
Clock Twr. M. N1 . . . . .4C 18
Cloisters, The 1F 115

Cloisters, The E1 . . . . .1B 64
Cloisters Bus. Cen. SW8 . . .5A 136
Clonmel Rd. SW6 . . . . .5C 130
Cloth Ct. EC1 . . . . .2A 62
Cloth Fair EC1 . . . . .2A 62
Clothier St. E1 . . . . .3A 64
Cloth St. EC1 . . . . .1B 62
Cloudesley Mans. N1 . . . . . .4D 17
Cloudesley Pl. N1 . . . . .4D 17
Cloudesley Rd. N1 . . . . .3D 17
          (not continuous)
Cloudesley Sq. N1 . . . . .4D 17
Cloudesley St. N1 . . . . .4E 17
Clove Cres. E14 . . . . .5D 71
Clovelly Ho. W2 . . . . .3B 54
Clovelly Way E1 . . . . .3C 66
Clover M. SW3 . . . . .2C 134
Cloysters Grn. E1 . . . . .2D 93
Club Row E1 . . . . .4B 42
E2 . . . . .4B 42
Clunbury St. N1 . . . . .1E 41
Clunie Ho. SW1 . . . . .1C 112
Cluny Est. SE1 . . . . .1F 119
Cluny M. SW5 . . . . .4D 109
Cluny Pl. SE1 . . . . .1F 119
Cluse Ct. N1 . . . . .5B 18
          (not continuous)
Clutton St. E14 . . . . .2A 70
Clyde Ct. NW1 . . . . .5E 15
Clyde Flats SW6 . . . . .4B 130
Clydesdale Ho. W11 . . . . . . .3C 52
Clydesdale Rd. W11 . . . . . . .3B 52
Clyde St. SE8 . . . . .3C 146
Clyde Wharf E16 . . . . .3C 100
Clynes Ho. E2 . . . . .2D 45
Coach & Horses Yd. W1 . . . .5A 58
Coach Ho. M. SE1 . . . . .1F 119
Coalbrookdale Gates 5D 83
Coal Drops N1 . . . . .4F 15
Coalport Ho. SE11 . . . . .3D 117
Coalstore Ct. E1 . . . . .1A 68
Coatbridge Ho. N1 . . . . .2B 16
Coate St. E2 . . . . .1E 43
Cobalt Building, The EC2 . . .5B 40
Cobalt Sq. SW8 . . . . .2B 138
Cobbett St. SW8 . . . . .5C 138
Cobble La. N1 . . . . .1E 17
Cobblestone Sq. E1 . . . . . . .2A 94
Cobbold Ct. SW1 . . . . .3D 115
Cobb's Ct. EC4 . . . . .4A 62
Cobb St. E1 . . . . .2B 64
Cobden Bldgs. WC1 . . . . . . .2B 38
Cobden Ho. E2 . . . . .2E 43
NW1 . . . . .5B 14
Cobham M. NW1 . . . . .1D 15
Coborn M. E3 . . . . .3C 46
Coborn Rd. E3 . . . . .1B 46
Coborn St. E3 . . . . .2B 46
Cobourg Rd. SE5 . . . . .2B 142
Cobourg St. NW1 . . . . .3C 36
Coburg Cl. SW1 . . . . .3C 114
Coburg Dwellings E1 . . . . . .4C 66
Cochrane Cl. NW8 . . . . .1E 33
Cochrane Ho. E14 . . . . .4E 97
Cochrane M. NW8 . . . . .1E 33
Cochrane St. NW8 . . . . .1E 33
Cockburn Ho. SW1 . . . . .1E 137
Cock Hill E1 . . . . .2A 64
Cock La. EC1 . . . . .2F 61
Cockpit Steps SW1 . . . . . . .5E 87
Cockpit Theatre 5F 33
Cockpit Yd. WC1 . . . . .1C 60
Cockspur Ct. SW1 . . . . .2E 87
Cockspur St. SW1 . . . . .2E 87

Coda Centre, The
  SW6 . . . . .5A 130
Code St. E1 . . . . .5C 42
Codicote Ho. SE8 . . . . .4E 123
Codling Cl. E1 . . . . .2E 93
Codrington Ct. E1 . . . . .5F 43
  SE16 . . . . .2A 96
Codrington M. W11 . . . . . . .4A 52
Cody Rd. E16 . . . . .5E 49
Coffey St. SE8 . . . . .4E 147
Coin St. SE1 . . . . .2D 89
  (not continuous)
Coke St. E1 . . . . .3D 65
Colas M. NW6 . . . . .3E 9
Colbeck M. SW7 . . . . .4A 110
Colborne Ho. E14 . . . . .5E 69
Colchester Ho. E3 . . . . .4C 24
Coldbath Sq. EC1 . . . . .4D 39
Cold Blow La. SE14 . . . . . . .4D 145
  (not continuous)
Coldharbour E14 . . . . .4C 98
Colebeck M. N1 . . . . .1A 18
Colebert Av. E1 . . . . .4B 44
Colebert Ho. E1 . . . . .4C 44
Colebrook Ct. SW3 . . . . . . .4A 112
Colebrooke Pl. N1 . . . . .4A 18
Colebrooke Row N1 . . . . . . .1F 39
Colebrook Ho. E14 . . . . .3F 69
Coleby Path SE5 . . . . .5E 141
Colechurch Ho. SE1 . . . . . .1D 143
Colefax Bldgs. E1 . . . . .3E 65
Colegrave Rd. E15 . . . . .2D 7
Colegrove Rd. SE15 . . . . . . .3C 142
Coleherne Ct. SW5 . . . . . . .1A 132
Coleherne Mans. SW5 . . . . .5A 110
Coleherne M. SW10 . . . . . . .1F 131
Coleherne Rd. SW10 . . . . . .1F 131
Cole Ho. SE1 . . . . .5E 89
Coleman Flds. N1 . . . . .3C 18
Coleman Rd. SE5 . . . . .4F 141
Coleman St. EC2 . . . . .3D 63
Coleman St. Bldgs.
  EC2 . . . . .3D 63
Coleridge Ct. N1 . . . . .3B 18
  SW1 . . . . .3D 115
  W14 . . . . .2E 107
Coleridge Gdns. NW6 . . . . . .2B 10
  SW10 . . . . .4A 132
Coleridge Ho. SE17 . . . . . . .5C 118
  SW1 . . . . .1B 136
Coleridge Sq. SW10 . . . . . . .4B 132
Coleshill Flats SW1 . . . . . . .4E 113
Cole St. SE1 . . . . .5C 90
Colet Ct. W6 . . . . .4E 107
Colet Flats E1 . . . . .3F 67
Colet Gdns. W14 . . . . .4E 107
Colet Ho. SE17 . . . . .1A 140
Colette Ct. SE16 . . . . .4D 95
Coley St. WC1 . . . . .5C 38
Colinsdale N1 . . . . .4F 17
Colin Winter Ho. E1 . . . . . . .4C 44
Coliseum Theatre 1F 87
Collard Pl. NW1 . . . . .1F 13
Collection Pl. NW8 . . . . .4A 10
College App. SE10 . . . . .2C 148
College Ct. NW3 . . . . .1D 11
  SW3 . . . . .1C 134
  W6 . . . . .5C 106
College Cres. NW3 . . . . .1C 10
College Cross N1 . . . . .1E 17
College East E1 . . . . .2C 64
College Gro. NW1 . . . . .3D 15
College Hill EC4 . . . . .5C 62
College Mans. NW6 . . . . . . .3A 8

College M. N1 . . . . .1E 17
  (not continuous)
  SW1 . . . . .1F 115
College of Arms 5B 62
College Pde. NW6 . . . . .3A 8
College Pl. NW1 . . . . .3C 14
  SW10 . . . . .4B 132
College Rd. NW10 . . . . .1B 28
College St. EC4 . . . . .5C 62
College Ter. E3 . . . . .2B 46
College Yd. NW6 . . . . .3A 8
Collerston Ho. SE10 . . . . . . .5B 128
Collett Rd. SE16 . . . . .2E 121
Collier Cl. E6 . . . . .5F 77
Collier St. N1 . . . . .1B 38
Collingham Gdns. SW5 . . . .4A 110
Collingham Pl. SW5 . . . . . . .4F 109
Collingham Rd. SW5 . . . . . . .3A 110
Collington St. SE10 . . . . . . .1E 149
Collingwood Ho. E1 . . . . . . .5A 44
  SE16 . . . . .5F 93
  (off Cherry Gdn. St.)
  SW1 . . . . .1D 137
  W1 . . . . .1B 58
Collingwood St. E1 . . . . .4A 44
Collins Ct. E8 . . . . .1D 21
Collins Ho. E14 . . . . .5B 70
  SE10 . . . . .5B 128
Collinson Ct. SE1 . . . . .5B 90
Collinson Ho. SE15 . . . . . . .4D 143
Collinson St. SE1 . . . . .5B 90
Collinson Wlk. SE1 . . . . .5B 90
Collin's Yd. N1 . . . . .4F 17
Coll's Rd. SE15 . . . . .5B 144
Colman Rd. E16 . . . . .2B 74
Colmans Wharf E14 . . . . . . .1F 69
Colmar Cl. E1 . . . . .4D 45
Colnbrook St. SE1 . . . . .2F 117
Colne Ho. NW8 . . . . .5F 33
Colne Rd. E5 . . . . .1A 4
Colnmore Ct. E2 . . . . .3D 45
Colombo St. SE1 . . . . .3F 89
**Colombo Street Sports
& Community Cen. 3F 89**
Colomb St. SE10 . . . . .5A 128
Colonnade WC1 . . . . .5F 37
Colonnade, The SE1 . . . . . . .4D 89
  SE8 . . . . .4B 124
Colonnades, The W2 . . . . . . .3A 54
Colonnade Wlk. SW1 . . . . . .4F 113
Colony Mans. SW5 . . . . . . .5F 109
  (off Earl's Ct. Rd.)
Colosseum Apartments E2 . .1E 45
Colosseum Ter. NW1 . . . . . . .3A 36
Colour Ct. SW1 . . . . .3C 86
Colour Ho. SE1 . . . . .5A 92
Colstead Ho. E1 . . . . .4A 66
Coltash Ct. EC1 . . . . .4C 40
Coltman Ho. SE10 . . . . .2B 148
Coltman St. E14 . . . . .2F 67
Columbia Ho. E3 . . . . .3C 46
Columbia Point SE16 . . . . . .1C 122
Columbia Rd. E2 . . . . .2B 42
**Columbia Road Flower Market
. . . . .2C 42
(off Columbia Rd.)**
Columbine Av. E6 . . . . .2F 75
Columbus Ct. SE16 . . . . .3C 94
Columbus Courtyard E14 . . .2D 97
Colverson Ho. E1 . . . . .2B 66
Colville Est. N1 . . . . .4F 19
Colville Est. W. E2 . . . . .3C 42
Colville Gdns. W11 . . . . .4C 52
  (not continuous)

Colville Ho. E2 . . . . .5B 22
Colville Ho's. W11 . . . . .3B 52
Colville Mans. E20 . . . . .3A 6
Colville M. W11 . . . . .4C 52
Colville Pl. W1 . . . . .2C 58
Colville Rd. W11 . . . . .4C 52
Colville Sq. W11 . . . . .4B 52
Colville Ter. W11 . . . . .4B 52
Colvin Ho. W10 . . . . .4E 51
Colworth Gro. SE17 . . . . . . .4C 118
Colwyn Ho. SE1 . . . . .2D 117
Combe, The NW1 . . . . .3A 36
Combedale Rd. SE10 . . . . . . .5D 129
Combe Ho. W2 . . . . .2D 53
Comber Gro. SE5 . . . . .5C 140
Comber Ho. SE5 . . . . .5C 140
Comedy Store 1D 87
Comeragh M. W14 . . . . .1A 130
Comeragh Rd. W14 . . . . .1A 130
Comerell Pl. SE10 . . . . .5B 128
Comet Pl. SE8 . . . . .5D 147
  (not continuous)
Comet St. SE8 . . . . .5D 147
Comfort St. SE15 . . . . .3F 141
Commercial Dock Path
  SE16 . . . . .1B 124
Commercial Rd. E1 . . . . .3D 65
  E14 . . . . .4A 68
Commercial St. E1 . . . . .5A 42
Commercial Way SE10 . . . . .4C 128
  SE15 . . . . .5B 142
Commercial Wharf E8 . . . . . .3A 20
Commerell St. SE10 . . . . . . .5A 128
Commodity Quay E1 . . . . . . .1C 92
Commodore Ho. E14 . . . . . . .5B 70
Commodore St. E1 . . . . .5F 45
Commonwealth Av. W12 . . . .1A 78
  (not continuous)
**Commonwealth Conference Cen.
. . . . .3C 86**
Community Rd. E15 . . . . .3E 7
Compass Ct. SE1 . . . . .3B 92
Compass Ho. E1 . . . . .2A 94
Compass Point E14 . . . . .5C 68
Compayne Gdns. NW6 . . . . .1F 9
Compayne Mans. NW6 . . . . .1A 10
Compter Pas. EC2 . . . . .4C 62
Compton Av. N1 . . . . .1F 17
Compton Cl. E3 . . . . .1E 69
  NW1 . . . . .3A 36
  SE15 . . . . .5D 143
Compton Pas. EC1 . . . . .4A 40
Compton Pl. WC1 . . . . .4F 37
Compton Rd. N1 . . . . .1A 18
  NW10 . . . . .3D 29
Compton St. EC1 . . . . .4F 39
Compton Ter. N1 . . . . .1F 17
Comus Ho. SE17 . . . . .4F 119
Comus Pl. SE17 . . . . .4F 119
Comyns Cl. E16 . . . . .1B 72
Conant Ho. SE11 . . . . .2F 139
Conant M. E1 . . . . .5D 65
Concert Hall App. SE1 . . . . . .3C 88
Concorde Dr. E6 . . . . .1B 76
Concorde Way SE16 . . . . . . .4D 123
Concordia Wharf E14 . . . . . .3C 98
Conder St. E14 . . . . .3F 67
Condray Pl. SW11 . . . . .5F 133
Conduit Av. SE10 . . . . .5E 149
Conduit Ct. WC2 . . . . .5F 59
Conduit M. W2 . . . . .4D 55
Conduit Pas. W2 . . . . .4D 55
Conduit Pl. W2 . . . . .4D 55
Conduit St. W1 . . . . .5A 58

Coney Way SW8	3C **138**	
Congers Ho. SE8	4E **147**	
Congreve St. SE17	3F **119**	
Congreve Wlk. E16	2E **75**	
Coningham Ct. SW10	4C **132**	
Coningham Rd. W12	4A **78**	
Conisbrough NW1	4B **14**	
Coniston NW1	2B **36**	
Coniston Ct. SE16	4D **95**	
W2	4A **56**	
Conistone Way N7	1A **16**	
Coniston Ho. E3	4B **46**	
SE5	4B **140**	
Conlan St. W10	4F **29**	
Conley St. SE10	5A **128**	
Connaught Bri. E16	3D **103**	
Connaught Cl. W2	4A **56**	
Connaught Ct. W2	4A **56**	
Connaught Hgts. E16	3D **103**	
Connaught Ho. NW10	2A **28**	
W1	1F **85**	
Connaught Pl. W2	5B **56**	
Connaught Rd. E16	2E **103**	
Connaught Rdbt. E16	5D **75**	
Connaught Sq. W2	4B **56**	
Connaught St. W2	4F **55**	
Connaught Works E3	4B **24**	
Connell Ct. SE14	2D **145**	
Connor St. E9	3D **23**	
Conrad Ho. E14	5A **68**	
E16	*2F **101***	
(off Wesley Av.)		
SW8	4F **137**	
Consort Ct. W8	1F **109**	
Consort Ho. E14	1A **148**	
W2	1A **82**	
Consort Lodge NW8	4B **12**	
Cons St. SE1	4E **89**	
Constable Av. E16	2F **101**	
Constable Ct. SE16	5A **122**	
Constable Ho. NW3	1C **12**	
Constable Ho's. E14	1E **97**	
Constance Allen Ho.		
W10	4E **51**	
Constance St. E16	3F **103**	
Constant Ho. E14	1A **98**	
Constantine Ct. E1	4E **65**	
Constitution Hill SW1	4F **85**	
Consul Ho. E3	4D **47**	
Content St. SE17	4D **119**	
Convent Gdns. W11	4B **52**	
Conway Ho. E14	4E **125**	
SW3	1C **134**	
Conway M. W1	5B **36**	
Conway St. W1	5B **36**	
(not continuous)		
Conybeare NW3	1A **12**	
Conyer St. E3	1F **45**	
Cook Ct. SE8	5F **123**	
SE16	3C **94**	
Cookham Cres. SE16	4D **95**	
Cookham Ho. E2	4B **42**	
Cooks Cl. E14	2E **97**	
Cooks Rd. E15	5F **25**	
SE17	2F **139**	
Coolfin Rd. E16	4E **73**	
Coomassie Rd. W9	4B **30**	
Coombrook Ct. SE16	5A **96**	
Coombs St. N1	1A **40**	
Coomer M. SW6	3C **130**	
Coomer Pl. SW6	3C **130**	
Coomer Rd. SW6	3C **130**	
Cooperage, The SE1	3B **92**	
SW8	4A **138**	

Cooper Cl. SE1	5E **89**	
Cooper Ho. NW8	5D **33**	
Coopers Cl. E1	5C **44**	
Coopers Ct. E3	4B **46**	
Coopers La. NW1	5E **15**	
Coopers Lodge SE1	4B **92**	
Cooper's Rd. SE1	1C **142**	
Coopers Row EC3	5B **64**	
Cooper St. E16	2C **72**	
Coopers Wlk. E15	3F **7**	
Coopers Yd. N1	1F **17**	
Copeland Dr. E14	3E **125**	
Copeland Ho. SE11	2C **116**	
Copenhagen Ho. N1	4C **16**	
Copenhagen Pl. E14	3C **68**	
(not continuous)		
Copenhagen St. N1	4A **16**	
Cope Pl. W8	2D **109**	
Cope St. SE16	3D **123**	
Copford Wlk. N1	3B **18**	
Copley Cl. SE17	3A **140**	
Copley St. E1	2D **67**	
Copperas St. SE8	3F **147**	
Copper Box Arena	**5E 5**	
Copperfield Ho. SE1	5D **93**	
W1	1E **57**	
W11	2E **79**	
Copperfield M. E2	1E **43**	
Copperfield Rd. E3	5A **46**	
Copperfield St. SE1	4A **90**	
Copper Row SE1	3B **92**	
Copperworks, The N1	1A **38**	
Copthall Av. EC2	3E **63**	
(not continuous)		
Copthall Bldgs. EC2	3D **63**	
Copthall Cl. EC2	3D **63**	
Coptic St. WC1	2F **59**	
Coral Apartments E16	1E **101**	
Coral Ho. E1	5F **45**	
Coral Mans. NW6	3D **9**	
Coral St. SE1	5E **89**	
Coram Ho. WC1	4F **37**	
Coram Mans. *WC1*	*5B **38***	
(off Millman St.)		
Coram St. WC1	5F **37**	
Corbet Ct. EC3	4E **63**	
Corbet Ho. N1	5D **17**	
SE5	5B **140**	
Corbet Pl. E1	1B **64**	
Corbett Ho. SW10	2B **132**	
Corbetts La. SE16	4B **122**	
(not continuous)		
Corbetts Pas. SE16	4B **122**	
Corbetts Wharf SE16	4F **93**	
Corbidge Ct. SE8	2F **147**	
Corbiere Ho. N1	3E **19**	
Corbin Ho. E3	2A **48**	
Corbridge Cres. E2	5F **21**	
Corby Way E3	5D **47**	
Cordage Ho. E1	2A **94**	
Cordelia Ho. N1	5A **20**	
Cordelia St. E14	3F **69**	
Cording St. E14	2A **70**	
Cordwainer Ho. E8	4A **22**	
Cordwainers Ct. E9	1A **22**	
Cord Way E14	1E **125**	
Corelli Ct. SE1	4A **122**	
SW5	4D **109**	
Corfe Ho. SW8	4B **138**	
Corfield St. E2	3A **44**	
Coriander Av. E14	4D **71**	
Coriander Ct. SE1	4C **92**	
Cork Sq. E1	2F **93**	

Cork St. W1	1B **86**	
Cork St. M. W1	1B **86**	
Corlett St. NW1	1F **55**	
Cormorant Ct. SE8	2B **146**	
Cormorant Lodge *E1*	*2D **93***	
(off Thomas More St.)		
Cornbury Ho. SE8	2D **147**	
Cornelia St. N7	1C **16**	
Cornell Bldg. E1	3D **65**	
Corner Ct. E2	4A **44**	
Corner Ho. St. WC2	2F **87**	
Cornhill EC3	4E **63**	
Cornick Ho. SE16	2A **122**	
Cornish Ho. SE17	3F **139**	
Cornmill Ho. SE8	1E **147**	
Cornwall Av. E2	3B **44**	
Cornwall Cres. W11	5F **51**	
Cornwall Gdns. SW7	2A **110**	
Cornwall Gdns. Wlk.		
SW7	2A **110**	
Cornwallis Ho. SW7	2A **110**	
Cornwallis Ho. SE16	5F **93**	
W12	1A **78**	
Cornwall Mans. SW10	4C **132**	
W8	5A **82**	
W14	1D **107**	
Cornwall M. Sth. SW7	2B **110**	
Cornwall M. W. SW7	2A **110**	
Cornwall Rd. SE1	2D **89**	
Cornwall Sq. SE11	5F **117**	
Cornwall St. E1	5A **66**	
Cornwall Ter. NW1	5C **34**	
Cornwall Ter. M. NW1	5C **34**	
Cornwood Dr. E1	3B **66**	
Corona Bldg. E14	2C **98**	
Coronation Ct. W10	2B **50**	
Coroners Court		
City of London	**5D 63**	
Poplar	**5A 70**	
St Pancras	**4E 15**	
Southwark	**4D 91**	
Westminster	**3E 115**	
Coronet Cinema	**2D 81**	
Coronet Theatre	**2B 118**	
Coronet St. N1	3F **41**	
Corporation Row EC1	4E **39**	
Corporation St. E15	1F **49**	
Corringham Ho. E1	4E **67**	
Corry Ho. E14	5F **69**	
Corsham St. N1	3E **41**	
Corsley Way E9	4C **4**	
Corunna Rd. SW8	5C **136**	
Corvette Sq. SE10	2E **149**	
Coryton Path W9	4C **30**	
Cosgrove Ho. E2	4E **21**	
Cosmo Pl. WC1	1A **60**	
Cosser St. SE1	1D **117**	
Cosway Mans. NW1	1A **56**	
Cosway St. NW1	1A **56**	
Cotall St. E14	3E **69**	
Cotes Ho. NW8	5F **33**	
Cotham St. SE17	4C **118**	
Cotleigh Rd. NW6	1D **9**	
Cotman Ho. NW8	5F **11**	
Cotswold Ct. EC1	4B **40**	
Cottage Cl. E1	5C **44**	
Cottage Grn. SE5	4E **141**	
Cottage Pl. SW3	1F **111**	
Cottage St. E14	5A **70**	
Cottesbrook St. SE14	4F **145**	
Cottesloe Ho. NW8	4F **33**	
Cottesloe M. SE1	1E **117**	
Cottesmore Ct. W8	1A **110**	
Cottesmore Gdns. W8	1A **110**	

Cottingham Rd. SW8 . . . . .4C 138
Cottington St. SE11 . . . . . . .5E 117
Cottle Way SE16 . . . . .5A 94
Cottons Cen. SE1 . . . . .2F 91
Cotton's Gdns. E2 . . . . .2A 42
Cottons La. SE1 . . . . .2E 91
Cotton St. E14 . . . . .5B 70
Cottrell Ct. SE10 . . . . .3C 128
Coulson St. SW3 . . . . .5B 112
Coulter Rd. W6 . . . . .2A 106
Councillor St. SE5 . . . . .5B 140
Counter Ct. SE1 . . . . .3D 91
Counters Ct. W14 . . . . .1A 108
Counter St. SE1 . . . . .3F 91
County Court
    Central London 5F 35
    Clerkenwell and Shoreditch
    .4B 40
    Lambeth 5E 117
    West London 5D 107
County Gro. SE5 . . . . .5B 140
County Hall Apartments
    SE1 . . . . .5B 88
County Hall (Former) 4B 88
County Rd. E6 . . . . .2F 77
County St. SE1 . . . . .2C 118
Court Annexe 5C 90
Courtauld Gallery 5B 60
Courtauld Ho. E2 . . . . .4E 21
Court Cl. NW8 . . . . .2D 11
    (not continuous)
Courtenay Sq. SE11 . . . . . . .1D 139
Courtenay St. SE11 . . . . . . .5C 116
Courtfield Gdns. SW5 . . . . . .3A 110
Courtfield Ho. EC1 . . . . .1D 61
Courtfield M. SW5 . . . . .4A 110
Courtfield Rd. SW7 . . . . .4B 110
Courthope Ho. SE16 . . . . . . .2C 122
    SW8 . . . . .5F 137
Court Lodge SW1 . . . . .4D 113
    (off Sloane Sq.)
Courtnell St. W2 . . . . .3D 53
Courtney Ho. W14 . . . . .1A 108
Court St. E1 . . . . .1F 65
Courtville Ho. W10 . . . . .3A 30
Courtyard SW3 . . . . .5B 112
Courtyard, The E2 . . . . .2C 42
    EC3 . . . . .4E 63
    (within Royal Exchange)
    N1 . . . . .1C 16
    NW1 . . . . .2E 13
    SW3 . . . . .2E 133
Courtyard Apartments
    E1 . . . . .4C 42
Courtyard Theatre
    Shoreditch 3F 41
Cousin La. EC4 . . . . .1D 91
Couzens Ho. E3 . . . . .1C 68
Covelees Wall E6 . . . . .3D 77
Covell Ct. SE8 . . . . .5E 147
COVENT GARDEN 5A 60
Covent Garden 5A 60
Covent Gdn. WC2 . . . . .5A 60
Coventry Cl. E6 . . . . .4B 76
    NW6 . . . . .5E 9
Coventry Rd. E1 . . . . .5A 44
    E2 . . . . .4A 44
Coventry St. W1 . . . . .1D 87
Coverdale Rd. W12 . . . . .3A 78
Coverley Cl. E1 . . . . .1E 65
Coverley Point SE11 . . . . . .4B 116
Cowan Ct. E6 . . . . .3A 76
Cowcross St. EC1 . . . . .1F 61
Cowdenbeath Path N1 . . . . .3B 16

Cow Leaze E6 . . . . .3E 77
Cowley Rd. SW9 . . . . .5E 139
    (not continuous)
Cowley St. SW1 . . . . .2F 115
Cowling Cl. W11 . . . . .2F 79
Cowper Ho. SE17 . . . . .5C 118
    SW1 . . . . .1E 137
Cowper's Ct. EC3 . . . . .4E 63
Cowper St. EC2 . . . . .4E 41
Cowper Ter. W10 . . . . .2D 51
Cowthorpe Rd. SW8 . . . . . . .5E 137
Cox Ho. W6 . . . . .2A 130
Coxson Way SE1 . . . . .5B 92
Crabtree Cl. E2 . . . . .1B 42
Crabtree Pl. W1 . . . . .2D 59
Crace St. NW1 . . . . .2D 37
Crafts Council & Gallery 1E 39
Cragie Ho. SE1 . . . . .4C 120
Craig's Ct. SW1 . . . . .2F 87
Craik Ct. NW6 . . . . .1C 30
Crail Row SE17 . . . . .4E 119
Cramer St. W1 . . . . .2E 57
Crampton St. SE17 . . . . .4B 118
Cranberry La. E16 . . . . .5F 49
Cranbourn All. WC2 . . . . .5E 59
Cranbourne NW1 . . . . .1D 15
Cranbourne Ct. SW11 . . . . . .4A 134
Cranbourne Pas. SE16 . . . . . .5F 93
Cranbourne Rd. E15 . . . . . . .1C 6
Cranbourn Ho. SE16 . . . . . . .5F 93
Cranbourn St. WC2 . . . . .5E 59
Cranbrook NW1 . . . . .4C 14
Cranbrook Est. E2 . . . . .1D 45
Cranbrook St. E2 . . . . .1E 45
Crandley Ct. SE8 . . . . .4A 124
    (not continuous)
Crane Ct. EC4 . . . . .4E 61
Crane Ho. E3 . . . . .1F 45
Crane Mead SE16 . . . . .5C 122
Crane St. SE10 . . . . .1D 140
Cranfield Ct. W1 . . . . .2A 56
Cranfield Ho. WC1 . . . . .1F 59
Cranfield Row SE1 . . . . .1E 117
Cranford Cotts. E1 . . . . .5E 67
Cranford St. E1 . . . . .5E 67
Cranleigh W11 . . . . .2B 80
Cranleigh Ho's. NW1 . . . . . . .1C 36
Cranleigh St. NW1 . . . . .1C 36
Cranley Gdns. SW7 . . . . .5C 110
Cranley M. SW7 . . . . .5C 110
Cranley Pl. SW7 . . . . .4D 111
Cranley Rd. E13 . . . . .1F 73
Cranmer Ct. SW3 . . . . .4A 112
Cranmer Ho. SW9 . . . . .4D 139
Cranmer Rd. SW9 . . . . .4E 139
Cranston St. NW1 . . . . .5E 19
Cranswick Rd. SE16 . . . . . . .5A 122
Cranwell Cl. E3 . . . . .5F 47
Cranwood Ct. EC1 . . . . .3E 41
Cranwood St. EC1 . . . . .3E 41
Craven Hill W2 . . . . .5C 54
Craven Hill Gdns. W2 . . . . . . .5B 54
    (not continuous)
Craven Hill M. W2 . . . . .5C 54
Craven Lodge W2 . . . . .5C 54
Craven Pas. WC2 . . . . .2F 87
Craven Rd. W2 . . . . .5C 54
Craven St. WC2 . . . . .2F 87
Craven Ter. W2 . . . . .5C 54
Crawford Bldgs. W1 . . . . . . .2A 56
Crawford Mans. W1 . . . . .2A 56
Crawford M. W1 . . . . .2B 56
Crawford Pas. EC1 . . . . .5D 39
Crawford Pl. W1 . . . . .3A 56

Crawford St. W1 . . . . .2A 56
Crayford Cl. E6 . . . . .3F 75
Crayford Ho. SE1 . . . . .5E 91
Cray Ho. NW8 . . . . .1E 55
Crayle Ho. EC1 . . . . .4F 39
Creasy Est. SE1 . . . . .2F 119
Creative Ho. SW8 . . . . .5A 136
Crecy Ct. SE11 . . . . .5D 117
Credenhill Ho. SE15 . . . . . . .4F 143
Crediton Rd. E16 . . . . .3E 73
Credon Rd. SE16 . . . . .5A 122
Creechurch La. EC3 . . . . .4A 64
    (not continuous)
Creechurch Pl. EC3 . . . . .4A 64
Creed Ct. E1 . . . . .3F 45
    EC4 . . . . .4A 62
Creed La. EC4 . . . . .4A 62
Creek Ho. W14 . . . . .1A 108
Creek Rd. SE8 . . . . .3D 147
    SE10 . . . . .3D 147
Creekside SE8 . . . . .3F 147
Creekside Discovery Cen.
    .4F 147
Creekside Foyer SE8 . . . . . . .3F 147
Creighton Rd. NW6 . . . . .1E 29
Cremer Bus. Cen. E2 . . . . . . .1B 42
Cremer Ho. SE8 . . . . .5E 147
Cremer St. E2 . . . . .1B 42
Cremorne Est. SW10 . . . . . .3D 133
    (not continuous)
Cremorne Riverside Cen.
    .4D 133
Cremorne Rd. SW10 . . . . . . .4C 132
Creon Ct. SW9 . . . . .5D 139
Crescent EC3 . . . . .5B 64
Crescent Arc. SE10 . . . . .3B 148
Crescent Ct. Bus. Cen.
    E16 . . . . .4E 49
Crescent Ho. EC1 . . . . .5B 40
Crescent Mans. SW3 . . . . . . .4F 111
    W11 . . . . .5A 52
Crescent Pl. SW3 . . . . .3A 112
Crescent Row EC1 . . . . .5B 40
Crescent St. N1 . . . . .1C 16
Crescent Wharf E16 . . . . .3A 102
    (not continuous)
Cressal Ho. E14 . . . . .1E 125
Cresswell Gdns. SW5 . . . . . .5B 110
Cresswell Pl. SW10 . . . . .5B 110
Cressy Ct. E1 . . . . .1C 66
    W6 . . . . .1A 106
Cressy Ho's. E1 . . . . .1C 66
Cressy Pl. E1 . . . . .1C 66
Cresta Ho. E3 . . . . .4D 47
    NW3 . . . . .1D 11
Crestfield St. WC1 . . . . .2A 38
Creswick Wlk. E3 . . . . .2D 47
Crewdson Rd. SW9 . . . . .4D 139
Crewkerne Ct. SW11 . . . . . .5E 133
Crews St. E14 . . . . .3D 125
Cricketers Ct. SE11 . . . . .4F 117
Crimscott St. SE1 . . . . .2A 120
Crimsworth Rd. SW8 . . . . . . .5E 137
Crinan St. N1 . . . . .5A 16
Cringle St. SW8 . . . . .3B 136
Cripplegate St. EC2 . . . . .1C 62
Crispe Ho. N1 . . . . .4C 16
Crispin Ct. SE17 . . . . .4A 120
Crispin Pl. E1 . . . . .1B 64
Crispin St. E1 . . . . .2B 64
Criterion Ct. E8 . . . . .2C 20
Criterion Theatre 1D 87
Crofters Ct. SE8 . . . . .4F 123
Crofters Way NW1 . . . . .3D 15

Croft Ho. W10 . . . . .3A 30
Crofton Ho. SW3 . . . . . .3F 133
Crofton Ter. E5 . . . . .2A 4
Crofts Ho. E2 . . . . .5E 21
Crofts St. E1 . . . . .1D 93
Croft St. SE8 . . . . .4F 123
Crogsland Rd. NW1 . . . . .1D 13
Cromarty Ho. E1 . . . . . . .2F 67
Cromer St. WC1 . . . . .3F 37
Crompton Ct. SW3 . . . . . .3F 111
Crompton Ho. SE1 . . . . .2C 118
  W2 . . . . .5D 33
Crompton St. W2 . . . . . . .5D 33
Cromwell Av. W6 . . . . . .5A 106
Cromwell Cl. E1 . . . . .2E 93
Cromwell Cres. SW5 . . . .3D 109
Cromwell Gdns. SW7 . . . .2E 111
Cromwell Gro. W6 . . . . . .1C 106
Cromwell Highwalk
  EC2 . . . . .1C 62
Cromwell Lodge E1 . . . . .5B 44
Cromwell Mans. SW5 . . .3E 109
Cromwell M. SW7 . . . . . .3E 111
Cromwell Pl. EC2 . . . . . .1C 62
  SW7 . . . . .3E 111
Cromwell Rd. SW5 . . . . .3E 109
  SW7 . . . . .3B 110
Cromwell Twr. EC2 . . . . .1C 62
Crondall Ct. N1 . . . . .1F 41
Crondall St. N1 . . . . .1E 41
Crone Ct. NW6 . . . . .1C 30
Cronin St. SE15 . . . . . . .5B 142
Crooked Billet Yd. E2 . . . .2A 42
Crooke Rd. SE8 . . . . .5F 123
Croombs Rd. E16 . . . . . . .2B 74
Croom's Hill SE10 . . . . . .4C 148
Croom's Hill Gro. SE10 . .4C 148
Cropley Ct. N1 . . . . .5D 19
  (not continuous)
Cropley St. N1 . . . . .5D 19
Cropthorne Ct. W9 . . . . . .3C 32
Crosby Cl. SE1 . . . . .4D 91
Crosby Ho. E14 . . . . .2C 126
Crosby Row SE1 . . . . . . .5D 91
Crosby Sq. EC3 . . . . .3F 63
Cross Av. SE10 . . . . .3E 149
Crossbones Graveyard 3C 90
Crossbow Ho. N1 . . . . . . .4F 19
Crossfield Ct. W10 . . . . . .3E 51
Crossfield Ho. W11 . . . . .1F 79
Crossfield Rd. NW3 . . . . .1E 11
Crossfield St. SE8 . . . . . .4D 147
  (not continuous)
Cross Keys Cl. W1 . . . . . .2E 57
Cross Keys Sq. EC1 . . . . .2B 62
Cross La. EC3 . . . . .1F 91
  (not continuous)
Crossleigh Ct. SE14 . . . . .5B 146
Crosslet St. SE17 . . . . . . .3E 119
Crossmount Ho. SE5 . . . .4B 140
Cross St. N1 . . . . .3F 17
Crosstrees Ho. E14 . . . . . .1E 125
Crosswall EC3 . . . . .5B 64
Croston St. E8 . . . . .3E 21
Crowder St. E1 . . . . .5F 65
Crowfoot Cl. E9 . . . . .3C 4
Crowland Ho. NW8 . . . . . .4B 10
Crowland Ter. N1 . . . . . . .1D 19
Crown Cl. E3 . . . . .3D 25
Crown Cl. Bus. Cen. E3 . .4D 25
Crown Court
  Blackfriars 4A 90
  Inner London 1B 118
  Southwark 2F 91

Crown Ct. EC2 . . . . .4C 62
  NW8 . . . . .3A 34
  WC2 . . . . .4A 60
Crowndale Ct. NW1 . . . . .5D 15
Crowndale Rd. NW1 . . . . .5C 14
Crownfield Rd. E15 . . . . . .2D 7
Crowngate Ho. E3 . . . . . .1C 46
Crown Lodge SW3 . . . . . .4A 112
Crown M. E1 . . . . .1E 67
Crown Office Row EC4 . . .5D 61
Crown Pas. SW1 . . . . . . .3C 86
Crown Pl. EC2 . . . . .1F 63
  SE16 . . . . .1A 144
Crown Reach SW1 . . . . . .1E 137
Crown St. SE5 . . . . .4C 140
Crown Wharf E14 . . . . . . .3C 98
  SE8 . . . . .5A 124
Crows Rd. E3 . . . . .3E 49
  E15 . . . . .3E 49
Crowther Cl. SW6 . . . . . . .3C 130
Crowthorne Rd. W10 . . . .4D 51
Croxley Rd. W9 . . . . .3C 30
Croydon Ho. SE1 . . . . . . .4E 89
Crozier Ho. SW8 . . . . . . .5B 138
Crozier Ter. E9 . . . . .3A 4
  (not continuous)
Crucifix La. SE1 . . . . .4F 91
Cruden Ho. E3 . . . . .5C 24
  SE17 . . . . .3A 140
Cruden St. N1 . . . . .4A 18
Cruikshank Ho. NW8 . . . .5F 11
Cruikshank St. WC1 . . . . .2D 39
Crutched Friars EC3 . . . . .5A 64
Crystal, The 1D 101
Crystal Ct. E8 . . . . .4F 21
Crystal Wharf N1 . . . . . . .1A 40
Cuba St. E14 . . . . .4D 97
Cube Ho. SE16 . . . . .2B 120
Cubitt Bldg. SW1 . . . . . . .1F 135
Cubitt Ct. NW1 . . . . .1B 36
Cubitt Steps E14 . . . . . . .2E 97
Cubitt St. WC1 . . . . .3C 38
Cubitt's Yd. WC2 . . . . . . .5A 60
CUBITT TOWN 3B 126
Cudworth St. E1 . . . . .4A 44
Cuffley Ho. W10 . . . . .1B 50
Cuff Point E2 . . . . .2B 42
Culand Ho. SE17 . . . . . . .4F 119
Culford Gdns. SW3 . . . . .4C 112
Culford Gro. N1 . . . . .1F 19
Culford Mans. SW3 . . . . .4C 112
Culford Rd. N1 . . . . .1F 19
Culham Ho. E2 . . . . .3B 42
  W2 . . . . .2D 53
Culling Rd. SE16 . . . . . . .1B 122
Culloden Cl. SE16 . . . . . . .1E 143
Cullum St. EC3 . . . . .5F 63
Cullum Welch Ct. N1 . . . .2E 41
Cullum Welch Ho.
  EC1 . . . . .5B 40
Culmore Rd. SE15 . . . . . .5A 144
Culpepper Ct. SE11 . . . . .3D 117
Culross Ho. W10 . . . . . . .4E 51
Culross St. W1 . . . . .1D 85
Culverhouse WC1 . . . . . . .2B 60
Culworth Ho. NW8 . . . . . .5F 11
Culworth St. NW8 . . . . . .1F 33
Cumberland Ct. SW1 . . . .5A 114
  W1 . . . . .4C 56
Cumberland Cres. W14 . . .3A 108
  (not continuous)
Cumberland Gdns.
  WC1 . . . . .2D 39
Cumberland Ga. W1 . . . . .5B 56

Cumberland Ho. E16 . . . . . .2E 101
  (off Wesley Av.)
  W8 . . . . .5A 82
Cumberland Mans. W1 . . .3B 56
Cumberland Mkt. NW1 . . . .2A 36
Cumberland M. SE11 . . . .1E 139
Cumberland Mills Sq.
  E14 . . . . .5D 127
Cumberland Pl. NW1 . . . . .2F 35
Cumberland Rd. E13 . . . . .1F 73
Cumberland St. SW1 . . . .5A 114
Cumberland Ter. NW1 . . . .1F 35
Cumberland Ter. M. NW1 . .1F 35
  (not continuous)
Cumberland Wharf
  SE16 . . . . .4C 94
Cuming Mus. 4B 118
Cumming St. N1 . . . . .1C 38
Cunard Pl. EC3 . . . . .4A 64
Cunard Wlk. SE16 . . . . . . .3E 123
Cundy Rd. E16 . . . . .4B 74
Cundy St. SW1 . . . . .4E 113
Cunningham Ct. W9 . . . . .5C 32
Cunningham Ho. SE5 . . . .5D 141
Cunningham Pl. NW8 . . . .4D 33
Cureton St. SW1 . . . . . . .4E 115
Curlew St. SE1 . . . . .4B 92
Curran Ho. SW3 . . . . .4F 111
Cursitor St. EC4 . . . . .3D 61
Curtain Pl. EC2 . . . . .4A 42
Curtain Rd. EC2 . . . . .3A 42
Curtis Ho. SE17 . . . . .5D 119
Curtis St. SE1 . . . . .3B 120
Curtis Way SE1 . . . . .3B 120
Curzon Cinema
  Mayfair 3F 85
  Soho 5E 59
Curzon Ga. W1 . . . . .3E 85
Curzon Sq. W1 . . . . .3E 85
Curzon St. W1 . . . . .3E 85
Custance Ho. N1 . . . . . . .1D 41
Custance St. N1 . . . . .2D 41
CUSTOM HOUSE 4B 74
Custom Ho. EC3 . . . . .1F 91
Custom Ho. Reach SE16 . . .5B 96
Custom Ho. Wlk. EC3 . . . .1F 91
Cut, The SE1 . . . . .4E 89
Cuthbert Bell Twr. E3 . . . .4D 25
Cuthbert Harrowing Ho.
  EC1 . . . . .5B 40
Cuthbert Ho. W2 . . . . . . .1D 55
Cuthbert St. W2 . . . . .5D 33
Cutlers Gdns. EC2 . . . . . .2A 64
Cutlers Gdns. Arc. EC2 . . .3A 64
Cutlers Sq. E14 . . . . .4E 125
Cutler St. E1 . . . . .3A 64
Cutter La. SE10 . . . . .3A 100
Cutty Sark 2C 148
Cutty Sark Gdns. SE10 . . .2C 148
Cutty Sark Hall SE10 . . . . .2B 148
Cuxton Ho. SE17 . . . . . . .5A 120
Cyclops M. E14 . . . . .3D 125
Cygnet Ho. SE15 . . . . . . .3E 143
  SW3 . . . . .1A 134
Cygnet Ho. Nth. E14 . . . . .4A 70
Cygnet Ho. Sth. E14 . . . . .4A 70
Cygnet St. E1 . . . . .4C 42
Cynthia St. N1 . . . . .1C 38
Cyntra Pl. E8 . . . . .1A 22
Cypress Ct. E15 . . . . .1E 7
Cypress Ho. SE16 . . . . . . .5D 95
  (off Woodland Cres.)
Cypress Pl. W1 . . . . .5C 36
CYPRUS 5E 77

Cyprus Pl. E2 . . . . .1C **44**	Daniel Gdns. SE15 . . . . .4B **142**	Davidge St. SE1 . . . . .5F **89**
E6 . . . . .5E **77**	Daniell Ho. N1 . . . . .5E **19**	David Hewitt Ho. E3 . . . . . . .1F **69**
Cyprus St. E2 . . . . .1B **44**	Dan Leno Wlk. SW6 . . . . . . .5F **131**	David Ho. SW8 . . . . .4F **137**
(not continuous)	Dansey Pl. W1 . . . . .5D **59**	David Lee Point E15 . . . . .4F **27**
Cyrus Ho. EC1 . . . . .4A **40**	Danson Rd. SE17 . . . . .1A **140**	**David Lloyd Leisure**
Cyrus St. EC1 . . . . .4A **40**	Dante Pl. SE11 . . . . .4A **118**	**Fulham** **4E 131**
Czar St. SE8 . . . . .2D **147**	Dante Rd. SE11 . . . . .3F **117**	**South Kensington** **3A 110**
	Danube Ct. SE15 . . . . .4C **142**	David M. SE10 . . . . .4B **148**
	Danube St. SW3 . . . . .5A **112**	W1 . . . . .1D **57**
	Danvers Ho. E1 . . . . .4E **65**	Davidson Gdns. SW8 . . . . . .5F **137**
D	Danvers St. SW3 . . . . .3E **133**	David St. E15 . . . . .4E **7**
	Da Palma Ct. SW6 . . . . .3D **131**	Davies M. W1 . . . . .5F **57**
Dabbs La. EC1 . . . . .5E **39**	Daplyn St. E1 . . . . .1D **65**	Davies St. W1 . . . . .4F **57**
Dacca St. SE8 . . . . .2C **146**	D'Arblay St. W1 . . . . .4C **58**	Da Vinci Ct. SE16 . . . . .5F **121**
Dace Rd. E3 . . . . .2D **25**	Darcy Ho. E8 . . . . .3F **21**	Da Vinci Lodge SE10 . . . . . .2C **128**
Dacre Ho. SW3 . . . . .3E **133**	Darent Ho. NW8 . . . . .1E **55**	Davis Ho. W12 . . . . .1A **78**
Dacre St. SW1 . . . . .1D **115**	Darfield NW1 . . . . .4B **14**	Dawes Ho. SE17 . . . . .4D **119**
Da Gama Pl. E14 . . . . .5E **125**	Darfield Way W10 . . . . .4D **51**	Dawes Rd. SW6 . . . . .4A **130**
Dagmar Ct. E14 . . . . .1C **126**	Daring Ho. E3 . . . . .1F **45**	Dawes St. SE17 . . . . .5E **119**
Dagmar Gdns. NW10 . . . . . . .1D **29**	Dark Ho. Wlk. EC3 . . . . .1E **91**	Dawn Cres. E15 . . . . .3E **27**
Dagmar Pas. N1 . . . . .3A **18**	Darlan Rd. SW6 . . . . .5C **130**	Dawson Ho. E2 . . . . .3B **44**
Dagmar Ter. N1 . . . . .3A **18**	Darley Ho. SE11 . . . . .1B **138**	Dawson Pl. W2 . . . . .5D **53**
Dagobert Ho. E1 . . . . .2C **66**	Darley Rd. E14 . . . . .3A **68**	Dawson St. E2 . . . . .1C **42**
Daimler Ho. E3 . . . . .4D **47**	Darling Row E1 . . . . .5A **44**	Day Ho. SE5 . . . . .4B **140**
Dain Ct. W8 . . . . .3E **109**	Darlington Ho. SW8 . . . . . . .5E **137**	Daynor Ho. NW6 . . . . .3E **9**
Dainton Ho. W2 . . . . .2D **53**	Darnall Ho. SE10 . . . . .5B **148**	Deacon Ho. SE11 . . . . .4C **116**
Daintry Way E9 . . . . .4C **4**	Darnaway Pl. E14 . . . . .2C **70**	Deacon M. N1 . . . . .2E **19**
Daisy Rd. E16 . . . . .4F **49**	Darnay Apartments E15 . . . . . .4E **7**	Deacon Way SE17 . . . . .3B **118**
Dakin Pl. E1 . . . . .2F **67**	Darnley Ho. E14 . . . . .3A **68**	Deal Ho. SE15 . . . . .2D **145**
Dakota Gdns. E6 . . . . .1F **75**	Darnley Ter. W11 . . . . .2E **79**	SE17 . . . . .5A **120**
Dalehead NW1 . . . . .1B **36**	Darsley Dr. SW8 . . . . .5F **137**	Deal Porters Wlk. SE16 . . . . .3D **95**
Dale Ho. *N1* *4F 19*	Dartford Ho. SE1 . . . . .4C **120**	Deal Porters Way SE16 . . . . .1C **122**
(off Halcomb St.)	Dartford St. SE17 . . . . .2C **140**	Deal St. E1 . . . . .1D **65**
NW8 . . . . .4B **10**	Dartington NW1 . . . . .4C **14**	Deal Wlk. SW9 . . . . .5D **139**
Dalemain M. E16 . . . . .2E **101**	Dartington Ho. W2 . . . . .1F **53**	Dean Abbott Ho. SW1 . . . . . .3D **115**
Dale Rd. SE17 . . . . .3A **140**	Dartle Ct. SE16 . . . . .5E **93**	Dean Bradley St. SW1 . . . . . .2F **115**
Dale Row W11 . . . . .4A **52**	Dartmoor Wlk. E14 . . . . .3E **125**	Dean Cl. SE16 . . . . .3E **95**
Daley Ho. W12 . . . . .4A **50**	Dartmouth Cl. W11 . . . . .3C **52**	Dean Ct. SW8 . . . . .5F **137**
Dalgarno Gdns. W10 . . . . . . .1B **50**	Dartmouth Ho. SE10 . . . . . . .5F **147**	Deancross St. E1 . . . . .4E **66**
Dalgarno Way W10 . . . . .5B **28**	Dartmouth St. SW1 . . . . .5D **87**	Deanery M. W1 . . . . .2E **85**
Dalgleish St. E14 . . . . .4A **68**	Dartrey Twr. SW10 . . . . .4C **132**	Deanery Rd. E15 . . . . .5F **7**
Daling Way E3 . . . . .4A **24**	Dartrey Wlk. SW10 . . . . .4C **132**	Deanery St. W1 . . . . .2E **85**
Dalkeith Ct. SW1 . . . . .4E **115**	Dart St. W10 . . . . .2A **30**	Dean Farrar St. SW1 . . . . . . .1E **115**
Dalkeith Ho. SW9 . . . . .5A **140**	Darvell Ho. SE17 . . . . .1E **141**	Dean Ho. E1 . . . . .4B **66**
Dalling Rd. W6 . . . . .2A **106**	Darwen Pl. E2 . . . . .4F **21**	SE14 . . . . .5A **146**
Dallington Sq. *EC1* *4A 40*	Darwin Ct. NW1 . . . . .3E **13**	Dean Ryle St. SW1 . . . . .3F **115**
(off Dallington St.)	(not continuous)	Dean's Bldgs. SE17 . . . . . . .4D **119**
Dallington St. EC1 . . . . .4A **40**	SE17 . . . . .4E **119**	Dean's Ct. EC4 . . . . .4A **62**
Dalo Lodge E3 . . . . .1E **69**	Darwin Ho. SW1 . . . . .2B **136**	Deanshanger Ho. SE8 . . . . . .3E **123**
DALSTON **1C 20**	Darwin St. SE17 . . . . .3E **119**	Dean's M. W1 . . . . .3A **58**
Dalton Ho. E3 . . . . .5A **24**	(not continuous)	Dean Stanley St. SW1 . . . . . .2F **115**
SE14 . . . . .3D **145**	Darwood Ct. NW6 . . . . .1C **10**	Deanston Wharf E16 . . . . . . .4F **101**
SW1 . . . . .5F **113**	Daryngton Ho. SE1 . . . . .5D **91**	(not continuous)
Dalwood St. SE5 . . . . .5A **142**	SW8 . . . . .5F **137**	Dean St. W1 . . . . .3D **59**
Damask Cres. E16 . . . . .4F **49**	Dashwood Studios SE17 . . . .4B **118**	Dean's Yd. SW1 . . . . .1E **115**
Damer Ter. SW10 . . . . .5C **132**	Data Point Bus. Cen. E16 . . . .5E **49**	Dean Trench St. SW1 . . . . . . .2F **115**
Dame St. N1 . . . . .5B **18**	Datchet Ho. E2 . . . . .3B **42**	**Death Trap, London's** **5B 88**
Damien Ct. E1 . . . . .3A **66**	NW1 . . . . .2A **36**	Deauville Ct. SE16 . . . . .4D **95**
Damien St. E1 . . . . .3A **66**	Datchworth Ho. N1 . . . . .2F **17**	Debdale Ho. E2 . . . . .4E **21**
Damory Ho. SE16 . . . . .3A **122**	Date St. SE17 . . . . .1C **140**	De Beauvoir Ct. N1 . . . . .1E **19**
Danbury St. N1 . . . . .5A **18**	Daubeney Rd. E5 . . . . .1A **4**	De Beauvoir Cres. N1 . . . . . .3F **19**
Danby Ho. E9 . . . . .2B **22**	Daubeney Twr. SE8 . . . . .5B **124**	De Beauvoir Est. N1 . . . . . . .3F **19**
W10 . . . . .3A **30**	Dauncey Ho. SE1 . . . . .5F **89**	De Beauvoir Rd. N1 . . . . .3F **19**
Dancers Way SE8 . . . . .3F **147**	Dave Adams Ho. E3 . . . . .1A **46**	De Beauvoir Sq. N1 . . . . .1A **20**
Dance Sq. EC1 . . . . .3B **40**	Davenant Ho. E1 . . . . .1E **65**	**DE BEAUVOIR TOWN** **3F 19**
Dandridge Cl. SE10 . . . . .5C **128**	Davenant St. E1 . . . . .2E **65**	De Beauvoir Wharf N1 . . . . . .3A **20**
Dandridge Ho. E1 . . . . .1B **64**	Davenport Ho. SE11 . . . . . . .2D **117**	Debenham Ct. E8 . . . . .4D **21**
Danehurst St. SW6 . . . . .5A **130**	Daventry St. NW1 . . . . .1F **55**	Debnams Rd. SE16 . . . . .4B **122**
Dane Pl. E3 . . . . .5A **24**	Daver Ct. SW3 . . . . .1A **134**	De Bruin Ct. E14 . . . . .5B **126**
Danes Ct. NW8 . . . . .4B **12**	Davern Cl. SE10 . . . . .4B **128**	Decima St. SE1 . . . . .1F **119**
Danesdale Rd. E9 . . . . .5A **4**	Davey Rd. E9 . . . . .1D **25**	Decima Studios SE1 . . . . . . .1F **119**
Danesfield SE5 . . . . .2F **141**	Davey's Ct. WC2 . . . . .5F **59**	Deck Cl. SE16 . . . . .4E **95**
Danes Ho. W10 . . . . .4E **31**	Davey St. SE15 . . . . .3C **142**	De Coubertin St. E20 . . . . . . .3C **6**
Dane St. WC1 . . . . .2B **60**	David Ct. E14 . . . . .1A **70**	Deepdene Rd. SE5
Daniel Bolt Cl. E14 . . . . .1A **70**	Davidge Ho. SE1 . . . . .5E **89**	Deerhurst Ho. SE15 . . . . . . .3D **143**

Dee St. E14 . . . . .3C 70
Defoe Cl. SE16 . . . . .5B 96
Defoe Ho. EC2 . . . . .1B 62
Defoe Pl. EC2 . . . . .1B 62
Dekker Ho. SE5 . . . . .5E 141
Delafield Ho. E1 . . . . .4E 65
Delaford Rd. SE16 . . . . .5A 122
Delaford St. SW6 . . . . .4A 130
Delahay Ho. SW3 . . . . .3B 134
Delamere St. W2 . . . . .1B 54
Delamere Ter. W2 . . . . .1A 54
Delancey Pas. NW1 . . . . . . .4A 14
Delancey St. NW1 . . . . .4F 13
Delancey Studios NW1 . . . . .4A 14
Delany Ho. SE10 . . . . .2B 148
Delarch Ho. SE1 . . . . .5F 89
De Laune St. SE17 . . . . .1F 139
Delaware Mans. W9 . . . . . . .4F 31
Delaware Rd. W9 . . . . .4F 31
Delhi St. N1 . . . . .4A 16
Delius Gro. E15 . . . . .5C 26
Dell Cl. E15 . . . . .3E 27
Dellow Ho. E1 . . . . .5A 66
Dellow St. E1 . . . . .5A 66
Dell's M. SW1 . . . . .4C 114
Delmerend Ho. SW3 . . . . . . .5F 111
Delta Bldg. E14 . . . . .4C 70
Delta Ct. SE8 . . . . .2F 145
Delta Ho. N1 . . . . .2D 41
Delta Point E2 . . . . .2D 43
Delta St. E2 . . . . .2D 43
Delverton Ho. SE17 . . . . . . .5A 118
Delverton Rd. SE17 . . . . . . .1A 140
Den, The 1C 144
Denbigh Cl. W11 . . . . .5C 52
Denbigh Ho. SW1 . . . . .1C 112
    W11 . . . . .4C 52
Denbigh M. SW1 . . . . .4B 114
Denbigh Pl. SW1 . . . . .5B 114
Denbigh Rd. W11 . . . . .5C 52
Denbigh St. SW1 . . . . .4B 114
    (not continuous)
Denbigh Ter. W11 . . . . .5C 52
Denbury Ho. E3 . . . . .3A 48
Denby Ct. SE11 . . . . .3C 116
Dence Ho. E2 . . . . .3D 43
Denford St. SE10 . . . . .5C 128
Dengie Wlk. N1 . . . . .3B 18
Denham Ct. NW6 . . . . .2C 10
Denham Ho. W12 . . . . .1A 78
Denham St. SE10 . . . . .5D 129
Denholme Rd. W9 . . . . .2C 30
Denison Ho. E14 . . . . .5E 97
Denland Ho. SW8 . . . . .5C 138
Denman St. W1 . . . . .1D 87
Denmark Gro. N1 . . . . .5D 17
Denmark Pl. E3 . . . . .2E 47
    WC2 . . . . .3E 59
Denmark Rd. NW6 . . . . .1C 30
Denmark St. E13 . . . . .1F 73
    WC2 . . . . .4E 59
Denne Ter. E8 . . . . .4C 20
Denning Cl. NW8 . . . . .2C 32
Denning Point E1 . . . . .3C 64
Dennis Ho. E3 . . . . .5B 24
Dennison Point E15 . . . . . . .2C 26
Denny Cres. SE11 . . . . .5E 117
Denny St. SE11 . . . . .5E 117
Densham Ho. NW8 . . . . .1E 33
Densham Rd. E15 . . . . .3F 27
Denstone Ho. SE15 . . . . . . .3D 143
Dent Ho. SE17 . . . . .4F 119
Denton NW1 . . . . .1E 13

Denton Ho. N1 . . . . .1A 18
Denyer St. SW3 . . . . .4A 112
Denys Ho. EC1 . . . . .1D 61
Department for Communities
    .1B 114
Depot Rd. W12 . . . . .5C 50
Depot St. SE5 . . . . .3D 141
DEPTFORD 5D 147
Deptford B'way. SE8 . . . . . . .5D 147
Deptford Bus. Pk. SE15 . . . . .2C 144
Deptford Chu. St. SE8 . . . . . .3E 147
Deptford Creek Bri. SE8 . . . . .3A 148
Deptford Ferry Rd. E14 . . . . .4E 125
Deptford Grn. SE8 . . . . .3E 147
Deptford High St. SE8 . . . . . .3D 147
Deptford Pk. Bus. Cen.
    SE8 . . . . .1A 146
Deptford Strand SE8 . . . . . . .4C 124
Deptford Trad. Est. SE8 . . . . .1A 146
Deptford Wharf SE8 . . . . . . .3B 124
De Quincey Ho. SW1 . . . . . . .1B 136
De Quincey M. E16 . . . . .2E 101
Derby Ga. SW1 . . . . .4F 87
    (not continuous)
Derby Ho. SE11 . . . . .3D 117
Derby Lodge WC1 . . . . .2B 38
Derby Rd. E9 . . . . .3D 23
Derbyshire St. E2 . . . . .3E 43
    (not continuous)
Derby St. W1 . . . . .3E 85
Dere Cl. SW6 . . . . .5A 130
Dereham Pl. EC2 . . . . .3A 42
Dericote St. E8 . . . . .3F 21
Derifall Cl. E6 . . . . .1C 76
Dering St. W1 . . . . .4F 57
Dering Yd. W1 . . . . .4A 58
Derrycombe Ho. W2 . . . . . . .2D 53
Derry Ho. NW8 . . . . .5E 33
Derry St. W8 . . . . .5F 81
Derwent NW1 . . . . .3B 36
Derwent Ct. SE16 . . . . .4D 95
Derwent Ho. E3 . . . . .4B 46
    SW7 . . . . .3C 110
Derwent Point EC1 . . . . .2F 39
    (off Goswell Rd.)
Derwent St. SE10 . . . . .5F 127
Desborough Cl. W2 . . . . .1A 54
Desborough Ho. W14 . . . . . . .2C 130
Desborough St. W2 . . . . .1F 53
Design Mus. 4C 92
Desmond St. SE14 . . . . .3A 146
Dethick Ct. E3 . . . . .4A 24
Detling Ho. SE17 . . . . .4F 119
Devalls Cl. E6 . . . . .5E 77
Devas St. E3 . . . . .4A 48
De Vere Cotts. W8 . . . . .1B 110
De Vere Gdns. W8 . . . . .5B 82
Deverell St. SE1 . . . . .2D 119
De Vere M. W8 . . . . .1B 110
Devereux Ct. WC2 . . . . .4D 61
Devitt Ho. E14 . . . . .5F 69
Devizes St. N1 . . . . .4E 19
Devon Ho. N1 . . . . .5F 17
Devonia Rd. N1 . . . . .5A 18
Devon Mans. SE1 . . . . .5B 92
Devonport W2 . . . . .4F 55
Devonport Ho. W2 . . . . .2D 53
Devonport M. W12 . . . . .3A 78
Devonport Rd. W12 . . . . .3A 78
    (not continuous)
Devonport St. E1 . . . . .4C 66
Devonshire Cl. W1 . . . . .1F 57
Devonshire Ct. E1 . . . . .3C 44
    WC1 . . . . .1A 60

Devonshire Dr. SE10 . . . . . . .5F 147
Devonshire Gro. SE15 . . . . . .3A 144
Devonshire Hall E9 . . . . .1B 22
Devonshire Ho. E14 . . . . .4E 125
    NW6 . . . . .1B 8
    SE1 . . . . .1B 118
    SW1 . . . . .5E 115
    W2 . . . . .1E 55
Devonshire M. SW10 . . . . . . .3D 133
Devonshire M. Nth. W1 . . . . .1F 57
Devonshire M. Sth. W1 . . . . .1F 57
Devonshire M. W. W1 . . . . . .5E 35
Devonshire Pl. W1 . . . . .5E 35
    W8 . . . . .2F 109
Devonshire Pl. M. W1 . . . . . .5E 35
Devonshire Rd. E16 . . . . .3A 74
Devonshire Row EC2 . . . . . . .2A 64
Devonshire Row M. W1 . . . . .5A 36
Devonshire Sq. EC2 . . . . .3A 64
Devonshire St. W1 . . . . .1E 57
Devonshire Ter. W2 . . . . .4C 54
Devons Rd. E3 . . . . .1E 69
Devon St. SE15 . . . . .3F 143
Devon Wharf E14 . . . . .2C 70
De Walden Ho. NW8 . . . . . . .5F 11
De Walden St. W1 . . . . .2E 57
Dewberry Gdns. E6 . . . . .1F 75
Dewberry St. E14 . . . . .2B 70
Dewey Rd. N1 . . . . .5D 17
Dewhurst Rd. W14 . . . . .1D 107
Dewsbury Ter. NW1 . . . . .3A 14
Dhonau Ho. SE1 . . . . .3C 120
Diadem Ct. W1 . . . . .4D 59
Dial Walk, The W8 . . . . .4A 82
Diamond Gdns. E3 . . . . .1C 68
Diamond Ho. E3 . . . . .1A 46
Diamond St. SE15 . . . . .5A 142
Diamond Ter. SE10 . . . . .5C 148
Diamond Way SE8 . . . . .3D 147
Diana Cl. SE8 . . . . .3C 146
Diana, Princess of Wales
    Memorial Playground . . .2A 82
Diana, Princess of Wales
    Memorial Walk 2A 82
Dibden Ho. SE5 . . . . .5A 142
Dibden St. N1 . . . . .3A 18
Dibdin Ho. W9 . . . . .5F 9
Dibdin Row SE1 . . . . .1E 117
Dickens Est. SE1 . . . . .5D 93
    SE16 . . . . .1D 121
Dickens Ho. NW6 . . . . .2D 31
    NW8 . . . . .4E 33
    SE17 . . . . .1A 140
    WC1 . . . . .4F 37
Dickens M. EC1 . . . . .1F 61
Dickens Sq. SE1 . . . . .1C 118
Dickinson Ct. EC1 . . . . .5A 40
Dicksee Ho. NW8 . . . . .5D 33
Dickson Ho. E1 . . . . .3F 65
    N1 . . . . .1D 17
Dieppe Cl. W14 . . . . .5C 108
Digby Mans. W6 . . . . .5A 106
Digby St. E2 . . . . .3C 44
Diggon St. E1 . . . . .2D 67
Dighton Ct. SE5 . . . . .3B 140
Dignum St. N1 . . . . .5D 17
Dilke St. SW3 . . . . .2C 134
Dilston Gro. SE16 . . . . .3B 122
Dimes Pl. W6 . . . . .4A 106
Dimsdale Hgts. E1 . . . . .4B 66
Dimson Cres. E3 . . . . .4D 47
Dinerman St. NW8 . . . . .3C 10
Dingle Gdns. E14 . . . . .5E 69
Dingley Pl. EC1 . . . . .3C 40

Dingley Rd. EC1 . . . . .2C **40**
Dinmont Est. E2 . . . . .5E **21**
Dinmont Ho. E2 . . . . .5F **21**
Dinmont St. E2 . . . . .5F **21**
Dinmore Ho. E9 . . . . .3B **22**
Dinnington Ho. E1 . . . . .4A **44**
Dinton Ho. NW8 . . . . .4F **33**
Disbrowe Rd. W6 . . . . .3A **130**
Discover
   Stratford **2E 27**
Discover Greenwich Vis. Cen.
   . . . .**2C 148**
Discovery Bus. Pk. SE16 . . .2D **121**
Discovery Dock Apartments E.
   E14 . . . . .4F **97**
Discovery Dock Apartments W.
   E14 . . . . .4F **97**
Discovery Ho. E14 . . . . .5B **70**
Dickens Est. E1 . . . . .2F **93**
Disney Pl. SE1 . . . . .4C **90**
Disney St. SE1 . . . . .4C **90**
Diss St. E2 . . . . .1B **42**
Distaff La. EC4 . . . . .5B **62**
Distin St. SE11 . . . . .4D **117**
Ditchburn St. E14 . . . . .1C **98**
Dixon Cl. E6 . . . . .3C **76**
Dixon Ho. W10 . . . . .4D **51**
Dixon's All. SE16 . . . . .5F **93**
Dobson Cl. NW6 . . . . .2D **11**
Dobson Ho. SE14 . . . . .3D **145**
Doby Ct. EC4 . . . . .5C **62**
Dock Cotts. E1 . . . . .1C **94**
Dockers Tanner Rd. E14 . . . .3D **125**
Dockhead SE1 . . . . .5C **92**
Dockhead Wharf SE1 . . . . . .4C **92**
Dock Hill Av. SE16 . . . . .3E **95**
Docklands Ct. E14 . . . . .4B **68**
Docklands Sailing
   & Watersports Cen . . .**2F 125**
Dockland St. E16 . . . . .3D **105**
   (not continuous)
Dockley Rd. SE16 . . . . .2D **121**
Dockley Rd. Ind. Est.
   SE16 . . . . .2D **121**
Dock Offices SE16 . . . . .1C **122**
Dock Rd. E16 . . . . .1C **100**
Dockside Rd. E16 . . . . .1D **103**
Dock St. E1 . . . . .5D **65**
Dodd Ho. SE16 . . . . .4A **122**
Doddington Gro. SE17 . . . . . .2F **139**
Doddington Pl. SE17 . . . . . . .2F **139**
Dodson St. SE1 . . . . .5E **89**
Dod St. E14 . . . . .4C **68**
Dog & Duck Yd. WC1 . . . . . .1B **60**
Dolben Ct. SW1 . . . . .4E **115**
Dolben St. SE1 . . . . .3F **89**
   (not continuous)
Dolland Ho. SE11 . . . . .1C **138**
Dolland St. SE11 . . . . .1C **138**
Dollar Bay Ct. E14 . . . . .4B **98**
Dolphin Ct. SE16 . . . . .4D **95**
Dolphin La. E14 . . . . .1F **97**
Dolphin Sq. SW1 . . . . .1C **136**
Dolphin Twr. SE8 . . . . .3C **146**
Dombey Ho. SE1 . . . . .5D **93**
   W11 . . . . .2E **79**
Dombey St. WC1 . . . . .1B **60**
   (not continuous)
Domecq Ho. EC1 . . . . .4A **40**
Domingo St. EC1 . . . . .4B **40**
Dominion Ct. E8 . . . . .2C **20**
Dominion Dr. SE16 . . . . .5D **95**
Dominion Ho. E14 . . . . .5A **126**
Dominion St. EC2 . . . . .1E **63**

Dominion Theatre **3E 59**
Domville Ct. SE17 . . . . .1A **142**
Donaldson Rd. NW6 . . . . . . .4C **8**
Donato Dr. SE15 . . . . .3F **141**
Donegal Ho. E1 . . . . .4A **44**
Donegal St. N1 . . . . .1C **38**
Doneraile Ho. SW1 . . . . . . .1F **135**
Dongola Rd. E1 . . . . .1F **67**
Don Gratton Ho. E1 . . . . .2E **65**
Donkin Ho. SE16 . . . . .4A **122**
Donmar Warehouse Theatre
   . . . .**4F 59**
Donne Ho. E14 . . . . .3D **69**
   SE14 . . . . .3D **145**
Donnelly Ct. SW6 . . . . .4A **130**
Donnelly Ho. SE1 . . . . .1D **117**
Donne Pl. SW3 . . . . .3A **112**
Donnington Ct. NW1 . . . . . . .1A **14**
Donnybrook Ct. E3 . . . . .4C **24**
Donoghue Cotts. E14 . . . . . .2A **68**
Donovan Ct. SW10 . . . . . . .1D **133**
Donovan Ho. E1 . . . . .5B **66**
Don Phelan Cl. SE5 . . . . . . .5D **141**
Doon St. SE1 . . . . .3D **89**
Dora Ho. E14 . . . . .3B **68**
   W11 . . . . .1E **79**
Dorando Cl. W12 . . . . .5A **50**
Doran Wlk. E15 . . . . .2C **26**
Dora St. E14 . . . . .3B **68**
Dorchester Ct. N1 . . . . .1A **20**
   SW1 . . . . .2C **112**
Dorfman Theatre **2C 88**
   (within National Theatre)
Doric Ho. E2 . . . . .1D **45**
Doric Way NW1 . . . . .2D **37**
Dorking Cl. SE8 . . . . .2B **146**
Dorking Ho. SE1 . . . . .1E **119**
Dorman Way NW8 . . . . .3D **11**
Dormstone Ho. SE17 . . . . . .4F **119**
Dorney NW3 . . . . .1A **12**
Dornoch Ho. E3 . . . . .5C **24**
Dorrington Point E3 . . . . .2F **47**
Dorrington St. EC1 . . . . .1D **61**
Dorrit Ho. W11 . . . . .2E **79**
Dorrit St. SE1 . . . . .4C **90**
Dorset Bldgs. EC4 . . . . .4F **61**
Dorset Cl. NW1 . . . . .1B **56**
Dorset Ct. N1 . . . . .1A **20**
Dorset Ho. NW1 . . . . .5C **34**
Dorset M. SW1 . . . . .1F **113**
Dorset Pl. E15 . . . . .4D **7**
Dorset Ri. EC4 . . . . .4F **61**
Dorset Rd. SW8 . . . . .4A **138**
Dorset Sq. NW1 . . . . .5B **34**
Dorset St. W1 . . . . .2C **56**
Dorton Cl. SE15 . . . . .5A **142**
Doughty Ct. E1 . . . . .2A **94**
Doughty Ho. SW10 . . . . . . .3C **132**
Doughty M. WC1 . . . . .5B **38**
Doughty St. WC1 . . . . .4B **38**
Douglas Ct. NW6 . . . . .2E **9**
Douglas Johnstone Ho.
   SW6 . . . . .3B **130**
Douglas Path E14 . . . . .5C **126**
Douglas Rd. E16 . . . . .1E **73**
   N1 . . . . .1B **18**
   NW6 . . . . .3C **8**
Douglas Rd. Sth. N1 . . . . . . .1C **18**
Douglas St. SW1 . . . . .4D **115**
Douglas Waite Ho. NW6 . . . .1F **9**
Douglas Way SE8 . . . . .5C **146**
   (Stanley St.)
   SE8 . . . . .5D **147**
   (Watsons St.)

Doulton Ho. SE11 . . . . .3C **116**
Douro Pl. W8 . . . . .1A **110**
Douro St. E3 . . . . .5D **25**
Douthwaite Sq. E1 . . . . .2E **93**
Dove App. E6 . . . . .2F **75**
Dovecote Ho. SE16 . . . . .5D **95**
Dovehouse St. SW3 . . . . . . .5E **111**
Dove M. SW5 . . . . .4B **110**
Dover Ct. EC1 . . . . .4F **39**
   N1 . . . . .1E **19**
Dover Flats SE1 . . . . .4A **120**
Dover Ho. SE15 . . . . .2C **144**
Dover Row E2 . . . . .4D **21**
Dover St. W1 . . . . .1A **86**
Dover Yd. W1 . . . . .2B **86**
Doves Yd. N1 . . . . .4E **17**
Doveton Ho. E1 . . . . .4B **44**
Doveton St. E1 . . . . .4B **44**
Dove Wlk. SW1 . . . . .5D **113**
Dovey Lodge N1 . . . . .1E **17**
Dovoll Ct. SE16 . . . . .1D **121**
Dowells St. SE10 . . . . .2A **148**
Dowgate Hill EC4 . . . . .5D **63**
Dowland St. W10 . . . . .2A **30**
Dowlas St. SE5 . . . . .4F **141**
Dowler Ho. E1 . . . . .4E **65**
Downend Ct. SE15 . . . . .3B **142**
Downesbury NW3 . . . . .1B **12**
Downey Ho. E1 . . . . .5D **45**
Downfield Cl. W9 . . . . .5F **31**
Downham Ct. N1 . . . . .2E **19**
Downham Rd. N1 . . . . .2D **19**
Downham Wharf N1 . . . . . . .3A **20**
Downing Ct. WC1 . . . . .5A **38**
Downing Ho. W10 . . . . .3E **51**
Downings E6 . . . . .3E **77**
Downing St. SW1 . . . . .4F **87**
Down Pl. W6 . . . . .4A **106**
Downsell Rd. E15 . . . . .1C **6**
Down St. W1 . . . . .0F **06**
Down St. M. W1 . . . . .3F **85**
Downtown Rd. SE16 . . . . . . .4A **96**
Dowrey St. N1 . . . . .3D **17**
Dowson Ho. E1 . . . . .4D **67**
Doyce St. SE1 . . . . .4B **90**
D'Oyley St. SW1 . . . . .3D **113**
Draco St. SE17 . . . . .2B **140**
Dragon Rd. SE15 . . . . .3F **141**
Dragon Yd. WC1 . . . . .3A **60**
Dragoon Rd. SE8 . . . . .1B **146**
Drake Cl. SE16 . . . . .4E **95**
Drake Ct. SE1 . . . . .5C **90**
   W12 . . . . .5B **78**
Drake Hall E16 . . . . .2F **101**
Drake Ho. E1 . . . . .2B **66**
   E14 . . . . .5A **68**
   SW1 . . . . .2D **137**
Drakeland Ho. W9 . . . . .4C **30**
Drakes, The SE8 . . . . .3D **147**
Drakes Courtyard NW6 . . . . .1C **8**
Drake St. WC1 . . . . .2B **60**
Draper Ho. SE1 . . . . .3A **118**
Draper Pl. N1 . . . . .3A **18**
Drapers Almshouses E3 . . . .2E **47**
Drapers Gdns. EC2 . . . . .3E **63**
Drapers Rd. E15 . . . . .1D **7**
Drappers Way SE16 . . . . . . .3E **121**
Drawdock Rd. SE10 . . . . . . .4E **99**
Draycott Av. SW3 . . . . .3A **112**
Draycott Cl. SE5 . . . . .5D **141**
   (not continuous)
Draycott Pl. SW3 . . . . .4B **112**
Draycott Ter. SW3 . . . . .4C **112**
Drayford Cl. W9 . . . . .4C **30**

Drayson M. W8	.5E **81**
Drayton Gdns. SW10	.5C **110**
Drayton Ho. SE5	.5D **141**
Dray Wlk. E1	.5C **42**
Dreadnought St. SE10	.2A **128**
Dresden Ho. SE11	.3C **116**
Drewett Ho. E1	.4E **65**
Drew Ho. SE8	.1D **147**
Drew Rd. E16	.3E **103**
(not continuous)	
Driffield Rd. E3	.5F **23**
Driftway Ho. E3	.1B **46**
Drinkwater Ho. SE5	.5D **141**
Dr Johnson's House	.3E **61**
Dron Ho. E1	.1B **66**
Droop St. W10	.3E **29**
Drovers Pl. SE15	.4A **144**
Druid St. SE1	.4A **92**
(not continuous)	
Drummond Cres. NW1	.2D **37**
Drummond Ga. SW1	.5E **115**
Drummond Ho. E2	.5E **21**
Drummond Rd. SE16	.1F **121**
Drummond St. NW1	.4B **36**
Drummond Way N1	.1D **17**
Drury La. WC2	.3A **60**
Drury Lane Theatre Royal	.4B **60**
Dryburgh Ho. SW1	.5F **113**
Dryden Bldg. E1	.3D **65**
Dryden Ct. SE11	.4E **117**
Dryden Mans. W14	.2A **130**
Dryden St. WC2	.4A **60**
Dryfield Wlk. SE8	.2D **147**
Drysdale Pl. N1	.2A **42**
Drysdale St. N1	.2A **42**
Dublin Av. E8	.3E **21**
Ducaine Apartments E3	.3C **46**
Ducal St. E2	.3C **42**
Du Cane Cl. W12	.4B **50**
Du Cane Rd. W12	.4A **50**
Duchess M. W1	.2A **58**
Duchess of Bedford Ho.	
W8	.4D **81**
Duchess of Bedford's Wlk.	
W8	.5D **81**
Duchess St. W1	.2A **58**
Duchess Theatre	.5B **60**
Duchy St. SE1	.2E **89**
(not continuous)	
Duckett's Apartments E3	.2C **24**
Duckett St. E1	.5E **45**
Duck La. W1	.4D **59**
Dudley Ct. W1	.4B **56**
WC2	.3F **59**
Dudley Ho. W2	.2D **55**
Dudley Rd. NW6	.5A **8**
Dudley St. W2	.2D **55**
Dudmaston M. SW3	.5E **111**
Duffell Ho. SE11	.1C **138**
Dufferin Av. EC1	.5D **41**
Dufferin Ct. EC1	.5D **41**
Dufferin St. EC1	.5C **40**
Duff St. E14	.4F **69**
Dufour's Pl. W1	.4C **58**
Dufton Dwellings E15	.1F **7**
Dugard Way SE11	.3F **117**
Dugdale Ct. NW10	.2A **28**
Duke of Clarence Ct.	
SE17	.5B **118**
Duke of Wellington Pl.	
SW1	.5E **85**
Duke of York Column (Memorial)	
	.3D **87**
Duke of York Sq. SW3	.4C **112**

Duke of York's Theatre	.1F **87**
Duke of York St. SW1	.2C **86**
Dukes Ct. W2	.5A **54**
Duke Shore Wharf E14	.1B **96**
Duke's Ho. SW1	.3E **115**
Dukes La. W8	.4F **81**
Duke's La. Chambers W8	.4F **81**
(off Dukes La.)	
Duke's La. Mans. W8	.4F **81**
(off Dukes La.)	
Dukes Lodge W8	.3C **80**
Duke's M. W1	.3E **57**
Duke's Pl. EC3	.4A **64**
Duke's Rd. WC1	.3E **37**
Duke St. W1	.3E **57**
Duke St. Hill SE1	.2E **91**
Duke St. Mans. W1	.4E **57**
Duke St. St James's SW1	.2C **86**
Duke's Yd. W1	.5E **57**
Dulford St. W11	.5F **51**
Dulverton Ho. NW1	.4C **14**
Dulverton Mans. WC1	.5C **38**
Dumain Ct. SE11	.4F **117**
Dumpton Pl. NW1	.2D **13**
Dunbar Wharf E14	.1B **96**
Dunbridge St. E2	.4E **43**
Duncan Ct. E14	.1B **70**
Duncan Ho. NW3	.1B **12**
SW1	.1C **136**
Duncannon Ho. SW1	.1E **137**
Duncannon St. WC2	.1F **87**
Duncan Rd. E8	.4F **21**
Duncan St. N1	.5F **17**
Duncan Ter. N1	.1F **39**
(not continuous)	
Dunch St. E1	.4A **66**
Dundalk Ho. E1	.3B **66**
Dundas Ct. SE10	.2A **148**
Dundas Ho. E2	.5B **22**
Dundee Ct. E1	.3F **93**
SE1	.1F **119**
(off Long La.)	
Dundee Ho. W9	.2B **32**
Dundee St. E1	.3F **93**
Dundee Wharf E14	.1C **96**
Dundonald Cl. E6	.3A **76**
Dunedin Ho. E16	.3C **104**
Dunelm St. E1	.3D **67**
Dunkirk Ho. SE1	.5E **91**
Dunlin Ho. SE16	.3E **123**
Dunloe Ct. E2	.1C **42**
Dunloe Pas. E2	.1C **42**
Dunloe St. E2	.1B **42**
Dunlop Pl. SE16	.2C **120**
Dunmore Point E2	.3B **42**
Dunmore Rd. NW6	.4A **8**
Dunmow Ho. SE11	.5C **116**
Dunmow Rd. E15	.1E **7**
Dunmow Wlk. N1	.3B **18**
Dunnage Cres. SE16	.3A **124**
(not continuous)	
Dunnett Ho. E3	.5C **24**
Dunnico Ho. SE17	.5F **119**
Dunnock Rd. E6	.3A **76**
Dunn's Pas. WC1	.3A **60**
Dunoon Ho. N1	.4B **16**
Dunraven St. W1	.5C **56**
Dunsany Rd. W14	.2D **107**
Dunstable M. W1	.1E **57**
Dunstan Ho's. E1	.1C **66**
Dunster Ct. EC3	.5A **64**
Dunster Gdns. NW6	.1C **8**
Dunsterville Way SE1	.5E **91**
Dunston Rd. E8	.4B **20**

Dunston St. E8	.3B **20**
Dunton Rd. SE1	.5B **120**
Dunworth M. W11	.3B **52**
Duplex Ride SW1	.5C **84**
Dupree Rd. SE7	.5F **129**
Durands Wlk. SE16	.4A **96**
Durant St. E2	.2D **43**
Durban Ho. W12	.1A **78**
Durban Rd. E15	.2F **49**
Durdans Ho. NW1	.1B **14**
Durell Ho. SE16	.5D **95**
Durfey Pl. SE5	.4E **141**
Durham Ct. NW6	.1E **31**
Durham Ho. NW8	.3F **33**
Durham Ho. St. WC2	.1A **88**
Durham Pl. SW3	.1B **134**
Durham Rd. E16	.1A **72**
Durham Row E1	.2E **67**
Durham St. SE11	.1B **138**
Durham Ter. W2	.3F **53**
Durham Yd. E2	.2F **43**
Durnford St. SE10	.3C **148**
Durrant Ho. EC1	.1D **63**
Durrels Ho. W14	.3C **108**
Durward Ho. W8	.5A **82**
Durward St. E1	.1F **65**
Durweston M. W1	.1C **56**
Durweston St. W1	.2C **56**
Dye Ho. La. E3	.4E **25**
Dyer's Bldgs. EC1	.2D **61**
Dyne Rd. NW6	.2A **8**
Dynham Rd. NW6	.1D **9**
Dyott St. WC1	.3E **59**
Dysart St. EC2	.5F **41**
Dyson Ho. SE10	.5B **128**

E

Eagle Cl. SE16	.1B **144**
Eagle Ct. EC1	.1F **61**
Eagle Dwellings EC1	.2C **40**
Eagle Ho. E1	.5A **44**
N1	.5D **19**
Eagle Pl. SW1	.1C **86**
SW7	.5C **110**
Eagle St. WC1	.2B **60**
Eagle Wharf Ct. SE1	.3B **92**
Eagle Wharf E. E14	.5F **67**
(off Narrow St.)	
Eagle Wharf Rd. N1	.5C **18**
Eagle Wharf W. E14	.5F **67**
(off Narrow St.)	
Eagle Works E. E1	.5C **42**
Eagle Works W. E1	.5B **42**
Eagling Cl. E3	.3E **47**
Eamont Ct. NW8	.5A **12**
Eamont St. NW8	.5F **11**
Eardley Cres. SW5	.5E **109**
Earle Ho. SW1	.4E **115**
Earlham St. WC2	.4E **59**
Earl Ho. NW1	.5A **34**
Earlom Ho. WC1	.3D **39**
EARL'S COURT	.5E **109**
Earl's Ct. Gdns. SW5	.4F **109**
Earl's Ct. Rd. SW5	.3E **109**
W8	.1D **109**
Earl's Ct. Sq. SW5	.5E **109**
Earlsferry Way N1	.2A **16**
(not continuous)	
Earlsmead Rd. NW10	.2B **28**
Earls Ter. W8	.2C **108**
Earlstoke St. EC1	.2F **39**
Earlston Gro. E9	.4A **22**

Earl St. EC2 . . . . .1E **63**
Earls Wlk. W8 . . . . .2D **109**
Earlswood St. SE10 . . . . .1F **149**
Early M. NW1 . . . . .3A **14**
Early Rivers Ho. E20 . . . . . . .3C **6**
Earnshaw Ho. EC1 . . . . .3A **40**
Earnshaw St. WC2 . . . . .3E **59**
Earsby St. W14 . . . . .3A **108**
(not continuous)
Easleys M. W1 . . . . .3E **57**
E. Arbour St. E1 . . . . .3D **67**
E. Beckton District Cen.
E6 . . . . .2C **76**
East Block SE1 . . . . .4C **88**
Eastbourne M. W2 . . . . .3C **54**
Eastbourne Rd. E15 . . . . .4F **27**
Eastbourne Ter. W2 . . . . .3C **54**
Eastbury Rd. E6 . . . . .1D **77**
Eastbury Ter. E1 . . . . .5D **45**
Eastcastle St. W1 . . . . .3B **58**
Eastcheap EC3 . . . . .5E **63**
E. Cross Route E3 . . . . .1C **24**
E9 . . . . .3C **4**
(Crowfoot Cl.)
E9 . . . . .1C **24**
(Wansbeck Rd.)
E10 . . . . .3C **4**
Eastern Ct. E15 . . . . .5E **7**
Eastern Gateway E16 . . . . . .5C **74**
Eastern Ho. E2 . . . . .3F **43**
Eastern Quay Apartments
E16 . . . . .2A **102**
E. Ferry Rd. E14 . . . . .3A **126**
Eastfield St. E14 . . . . .2A **68**
East Ham Ind. Est. E6 . . . . . .1F **75**
East Ham Mnr. Way E6 . . . . .4D **77**
E. Handyside Canopy N1 . . . .4A **16**
E. Harding St. EC4 . . . . .3E **61**
E. India Bldgs. F14 . . . . .5E **69**
E. India Ct. SE16 . . . . .4B **94**
**East India Dock Basin Nature
Reserve** 5F **71**
E. India Dock Ho. E14 . . . . . .4C **70**
E. India Dock Rd. E14 . . . . . .4D **69**
Eastlake Ho. NW8 . . . . .5E **33**
East La. SE16 . . . . .4D **93**
(Chambers St.)
SE16 . . . . .5D **93**
(Scott Lidgett Cres.)
East Lodge E16 . . . . .2E **101**
(off Wesley Av.)
East London Gymnastic Cen.
. . . . .3B **76**
East Mt. St. E1 . . . . .1A **66**
(not continuous)
Eastney St. SE10 . . . . .1D **149**
Eastone Apartments E1 . . . .2C **64**
Easton St. WC1 . . . . .4D **39**
East Parkside SE10 . . . . . . .5A **100**
East Pas. EC1 . . . . .1A **62**
East Point SE1 . . . . .5D **121**
E. Poultry Av. EC1 . . . . .2F **61**
East Rd. N1 . . . . .3D **41**
SW3 . . . . .1D **135**
East Row W10 . . . . .5F **29**
Eastry Ho. SW8 . . . . .5F **137**
W11 .5F **51**
East Side W12 . . . . .4B **78**
Eastside Halls SW7 . . . . . . .1E **111**
Eastside M. E3 . . . . .1D **47**
East Smithfield E1 . . . . .1C **92**
East St. SE17 . . . . .5C **118**
(not continuous)
E. Surrey Gro. SE15 . . . . . .5B **142**

E. Tenter St. E1 . . . . .4C **64**
East Twr. E14 . . . . .4F **97**
Eastway E9 . . . . .4B **4**
(not continuous)
Eastwell Ho. SE1 . . . . .1E **119**
East Wintergarden 3F **97**
Eastwood Ho. E3 . . . . .1E **69**
Eaton Cl. SW1 . . . . .4D **113**
Eaton Ga. SW1 . . . . .3D **113**
Eaton Ho. E14 . . . . .1C **96**
Eaton La. SW1 . . . . .2A **114**
Eaton Mans. SW1 . . . . .4D **113**
Eaton M. Nth. SW1 . . . . .3D **113**
Eaton M. Sth. SW1 . . . . .3E **113**
Eaton M. W. SW1 . . . . .3E **113**
Eaton Pl. SW1 . . . . .2D **113**
Eaton Row SW1 . . . . .2F **113**
Eaton Sq. SW1 . . . . .3D **113**
Eaton Ter. E3 . . . . .3A **46**
SW1 . . . . .3D **113**
Eaton Ter. M. SW1 . . . . .3D **113**
Ebbisham Dr. SW8 . . . . .2B **138**
Ebenezer Ho. SE11 . . . . . . .4E **117**
Ebenezer Mussel Ho. E2 . . .1B **44**
Ebenezer St. N1 . . . . .2D **41**
Ebley Cl. SE15 . . . . .3B **142**
Ebony Ho. E2 . . . . .3D **43**
Ebor St. E1 . . . . .4B **42**
Ebury Bri. SW1 . . . . .5F **113**
Ebury Bri. Est. SW1 . . . . . . .5F **113**
Ebury Bri. Rd. SW1 . . . . . . .1E **135**
Ebury M. SW1 . . . . .3E **113**
Ebury M. E. SW1 . . . . .3F **113**
Ebury Sq. SW1 . . . . .4E **113**
Ebury St. SW1 . . . . .4E **113**
Ecclesbourne Apartments
N1 . . . . .1D **19**
Ecclesbourne Rd. N1 . . . . . .2C **18**
Eccleston Bri. SW1 . . . . .0A **114**
Eccleston M. SW1 . . . . .2E **113**
Eccleston Pl. SW1 . . . . .4F **113**
Eccleston Sq. SW1 . . . . .4A **114**
(not continuous)
Eccleston Sq. M. SW1 . . . . .4A **114**
Eccleston St. SW1 . . . . .2E **113**
Eckford St. N1 . . . . .5D **17**
Eclipse Bldg. N1 . . . . .1E **17**
Eclipse Rd. E13 . . . . .1F **73**
Ecology Centre and Arts Pavilion
. . . . .3F **45**
Edbrooke Rd. W9 . . . . .5D **31**
Eddington Ct. E16 . . . . .2B **72**
Eddystone Twr. SE8 . . . . . . .5A **124**
Edenbridge Cl. SE16 . . . . . .1F **143**
Edenbridge Rd. E9 . . . . .2E **23**
Eden Cl. W8 . . . . .1E **109**
Edenham Way W10 . . . . .1B **52**
Eden Ho. NW8 . . . . .5F **33**
SE8 .5D **147**
SE16 . . . . .5D **95**
Eden Way E3 . . . . .3C **24**
Edgar Ho. E9 . . . . .2A **4**
SW8 .4F **137**
Edgar Myles Ho. E16 . . . . . .2B **72**
Edgar Rd. E3 . . . . .2A **48**
Edgar Wallace Cl. SE15 . . . .4A **142**
Edgar Wright Ct. SW6 . . . . .4B **130**
Edgcott Ho. W10 . . . . .1B **50**
Edge, The SE8 . . . . .5C **146**
Edge Apartments E15 . . . . . .2D **27**
Edge St. W8 . . . . .2E **81**
Edgeworth Ho. NW8 . . . . . . .3B **10**
Edgson Ho. SW1 . . . . .5F **113**
Edgware Rd. W2 . . . . .5D **33**

Edinburgh Cl. E2 . . . . .1B **44**
Edinburgh Ct. SE16 . . . . .2E **95**
Edinburgh Ga. SW1 . . . . .4B **84**
Edinburgh Ho. W9 . . . . .2A **32**
Edison Bldg. E14 . . . . .4D **97**
Edison Ct. SE10 . . . . .2C **128**
Edison Hgts. E1 . . . . .4C **42**
Edison Ho. SE1 . . . . .3D **119**
Edis St. NW1 . . . . .3D **13**
Editha Mans. SW10 . . . . .3B **132**
Edith Brinson Ho. E14 . . . . . .3E **71**
Edith Cavell Ho. E14 . . . . . . .4A **70**
(off Sturry St.)
Edith Gro. SW10 . . . . .3B **132**
Edith Ho. W6 . . . . .5B **106**
Edith Neville Cotts.
NW1 . . . . .2D **37**
Edith Ramsay Ho. E1 . . . . . . .1F **67**
Edith Rd. E15 . . . . .1D **7**
W14 .4F **107**
Edith Row SW6 . . . . .5A **132**
Edith St. E2 . . . . .5C **20**
Edith Summerskill Ho.
SW6 . . . . .4C **130**
Edith Ter. SW10 . . . . .4B **132**
Edith Vs. W14 . . . . .4B **108**
Edith Yd. SW10 . . . . .4C **132**
Edmeston Cl. E9 . . . . .4A **4**
Edmonton Ct. SE16 . . . . .1C **122**
Edmund Halley Way SE10 . . .5F **99**
Edmund Ho. SE17 . . . . .1A **140**
Edmund Hurst Dr. E6 . . . . . .2F **77**
Edmund St. SE5 . . . . .4D **141**
Ednam Ho. SE15 . . . . .3D **143**
Edred Ho. E9 . . . . .1A **4**
Edric Ho. SW1 . . . . .3E **115**
Edric Rd. SE14 . . . . .4D **145**
Edward VII Mans. NW10 . . . .2D **29**
Edward Bond Ho. WC1 . . . . .3A **38**
(off Cromer St.)
Edward Clifford Ho. SE17 . . .4E **119**
(off Elsted St.)
Edward Ct. E16 . . . . .1D **73**
Edward Dodd Ct. N1 . . . . . . .2E **41**
Edward Edward's Ho. SE1 . . .3F **89**
Edwardes Pl. W8 . . . . .2C **108**
Edwardes Sq. W8 . . . . .2C **108**
Edward Heylin Ct. E15 . . . . . .1A **48**
Edward Heylyn Ho. E3 . . . . . .1E **47**
Edward Ho. SE11 . . . . .5C **116**
W2 . . . . .5D **33**
W14 .3B **108**
Edward Kennedy Ho. W10 . . .5A **30**
Edward Mann Cl. E1 . . . . .4E **67**
Edward M. NW1 . . . . .1A **36**
Edward Mills Way E14 . . . . . .4E **69**
Edward Pl. SE8 . . . . .3C **146**
Edward's Cotts. N1 . . . . .1F **17**
Edwards M. N1 . . . . .1E **17**
W1 . . . . .4D **57**
Edward Sq. N1 . . . . .4B **16**
SE16 . . . . .2A **96**
Edward St. E16 . . . . .1D **73**
(not continuous)
SE8 .3C **146**
SE14 . . . . .4A **146**
Edwin Ho. SE15 . . . . .5D **143**
Edwin's Mead E9 . . . . .1A **4**
Edwin St. E1 . . . . .4C **44**
E16 .2D **73**
Edwy Ho. E9 . . . . .1B **4**
Effie Pl. SW6 . . . . .5E **131**
Effie Rd. SW6 . . . . .5E **131**
Egbert Ho. E9 . . . . .2A **4**

Egbert St. NW1 . . . . .3D **13**
Egerton Cres. SW3 . . . . .3A **112**
Egerton Dr. SE10 . . . . .5A **148**
Egerton Gdns. SW3 . . . . .2F **111**
Egerton Gdns. M. SW3 . . . . .2A **112**
Egerton Pl. SW3 . . . . .2A **112**
Egerton Ter. SW3 . . . . .2A **112**
Egham Rd. E13 . . . . .1A **74**
Eglington Ct. SE17 . . . . . . .2B **140**
Eglon M. NW1 . . . . .2C **12**
Egmont St. SE14 . . . . .5E **145**
Egremont Ho. E20 . . . . .3C **6**
Egret Ho. SE16 . . . . .3E **123**
Eider Ct. SE8 . . . . .2B **146**
Eisenhower Dr. E6 . . . . .1A **76**
Elan Ct. E1 . . . . .2F **65**
Elba Pl. SE17 . . . . .3C **118**
Elbourne Ct. SE16 . . . . .2E **123**
Elbourn Ho. SW3 . . . . .5F **111**
Elbury Dr. E16 . . . . .4E **73**
Elcho St. SW11 . . . . .5F **133**
Elcot Av. SE15 . . . . .4F **143**
Elden Ho. SW3 . . . . .3F **111**
Elderfield Ho. E14 . . . . .5D **69**
Elderflower Way E15 . . . . . .1F **27**
Elder Ho. E15 . . . . .2F **49**
Elder St. E1 . . . . .1B **64**
(not continuous)
Elder Wlk. N1 . . . . .3A **18**
Eldon Ct. NW6 . . . . .4D **9**
Eldon Rd. W8 . . . . .2A **110**
Eldons Pas. E1 . . . . .5E **65**
Eldon St. EC2 . . . . .2E **63**
Eldridge Ct. SE16 . . . . .2D **121**
Eleanor Cl. SE16 . . . . .4D **95**
Eleanor Ct. E2 . . . . .4D **21**
Eleanor Ho. W6 . . . . .5B **106**
Eleanor Rd. E8 . . . . .1F **21**
Eleanor St. E3 . . . . .3D **47**
Electra Bus. Pk. E16 . . . . . . .1E **71**
Electric Cinema **4B 52**
Electric Ho. E3 . . . . .2D **47**
Elektron Twr. E14 . . . . .5E **71**
ELEPHANT & CASTLE 2A **118**
Elephant & Castle SE1 . . . . .3A **118**
Elephant & Castle Leisure Cen.
. . . .**3A 118**
Elephant & Castle Shop. Cen.
SE1 . . . . .3B **118**
Elephant La. SE16 . . . . .4B **94**
Elephant Rd. SE17 . . . . .3B **118**
Elfin Oak **2A 82**
Elf Row E1 . . . . .5C **66**
Elgar Cl. SE8 . . . . .5D **147**
Elgar Ct. NW6 . . . . .2C **30**
W14 . . . . .2F **107**
Elgar Ho. NW6 . . . . .1C **10**
SW1 . . . . .1A **136**
Elgar St. SE16 . . . . .5A **96**
Elgin Av. W9 . . . . .2D **31**
Elgin Ct. W9 . . . . .4F **31**
Elgin Cres. W11 . . . . .5A **52**
Elgin Est. W9 . . . . .5D **31**
Elgin Ho. E14 . . . . .4F **69**
Elgin Mans. W9 . . . . .3F **31**
Elgin M. W11 . . . . .4A **52**
Elgin M. Nth. W9 . . . . .2A **32**
Elgin M. Sth. W9 . . . . .2A **32**
Elgood Cl. W11 . . . . .1F **79**
Elgood Ho. NW8 . . . . .1E **33**
SE1 . . . . .5D **91**
Elia M. N1 . . . . .1F **39**
Elias Pl. SW8 . . . . .3D **139**
Elia St. N1 . . . . .1F **39**

Elim Est. SE1 . . . . .1F **119**
Elim St. SE1 . . . . .1E **119**
(not continuous)
Eliot M. NW8 . . . . .1B **32**
Elis Way E20 . . . . .3C **6**
Elizabeth Av. N1 . . . . .3C **18**
Elizabeth Blount Ct. E14 . . . .3A **68**
Elizabeth Bri. SW1 . . . . . . .4F **113**
Elizabeth Cl. E14 . . . . .4F **69**
W9 . . . . .5C **32**
Elizabeth Ct. NW1 . . . . .4A **34**
SW1 . . . . .2E **115**
SW10 . . . . .3E **133**
Elizabeth Croll Ho. WC1 . . . .2C **38**
Elizabeth Fry M. E8 . . . . . . .2A **22**
Elizabeth Ho. E3 . . . . .3B **48**
SE11 . . . . .4E **117**
W6 . . . . .5C **106**
Elizabeth Ind. Est. SE14 . . . .2E **145**
Elizabeth M. E2 . . . . .1E **43**
Elizabeth Newcomen Ho.
SE1 . . . . .4D **91**
Elizabeth Sq. SE16 . . . . . . .1F **95**
Elizabeth St. SW1 . . . . .3E **113**
Elkington Point SE11 . . . . . .4D **117**
Elkstone Rd. W10 . . . . .1B **52**
Elland Ho. E14 . . . . .4B **68**
Ellenborough Ho. W12 . . . . .5A **50**
Ellen Julia Ct. E1 . . . . .4B **66**
Ellen St. E1 . . . . .4E **65**
Ellen Terry Ct. NW1 . . . . . . .1A **14**
Ellen Wilkinson Ho. E2 . . . . .2D **45**
SW6 . . . . .3B **130**
Ellerslie Rd. W12 . . . . .2A **78**
Ellery Ho. SE17 . . . . .4E **119**
Ellesmere Ho. SW10 . . . . . .2C **132**
Ellesmere Mans. NW6 . . . . .1B **10**
Ellesmere Rd. E3 . . . . .5F **23**
Ellesmere St. E14 . . . . .3F **69**
Ellingfort Rd. E8 . . . . .1A **22**
Ellingham Rd. E15 . . . . .1D **7**
Ellington Ho. SE1 . . . . .2C **118**
Elliot Cl. E15 . . . . .2F **27**
Elliot Ho. W1 . . . . .2A **56**
Elliott Rd. SW9 . . . . .5F **139**
Elliott's Pl. N1 . . . . .4A **18**
Elliott Sq. NW3 . . . . .1A **12**
Elliotts Row SE11 . . . . .3A **118**
Ellis Ct. E1 . . . . .4B **66**
Ellis Franklin Ct. NW8 . . . . .5B **10**
Ellis Ho. SE17 . . . . .5D **119**
Ellison Apartments E3 . . . . . .3D **47**
Ellis St. SW1 . . . . .3C **112**
Ellsworth St. E2 . . . . .2A **44**
Ellwood Ct. W9 . . . . .5F **31**
Elmbridge Wlk. E8 . . . . .1E **21**
Elm Ct. EC4 . . . . .4D **61**
SE1 . . . . .5F **91**
W9 . . . . .1E **53**
Elmer Ho. NW8 . . . . .1F **55**
Elmfield Ho. NW8 . . . . .5A **10**
W9 . . . . .5E **31**
Elmfield Way W9 . . . . .1D **53**
Elm Friars Wlk. NW1 . . . . . . .2E **15**
Elmgreen Cl. E15 . . . . .3F **27**
Elm Ho. E3 . . . . .3B **24**
E14 . . . . .5B **98**
W10 . . . . .4A **30**
Elmington Est. SE5 . . . . . . .4D **141**
Elmington Rd. SE5 . . . . . . .5D **141**
Elmley Cl. E6 . . . . .2A **76**
Elmore Ho. N1 . . . . .1D **19**
Elmore St. N1 . . . . .1C **18**
Elm Pk. Chambers SW10 . . .1D **133**

Elm Pk. Gdns. SW10 . . . . . .1D **133**
Elm Pk. Ho. SW10 . . . . .1D **133**
Elm Pk. La. SW3 . . . . .1D **133**
Elm Pk. Mans. SW10 . . . . . .2C **132**
Elm Pk. Rd. SW3 . . . . .2D **133**
Elm Pl. SW7 . . . . .5D **111**
Elm Quay Ct. SW8 . . . . .3D **137**
Elmslie Point E3 . . . . .1C **68**
Elms M. W2 . . . . .5D **55**
Elm St. WC1 . . . . .5C **38**
Elmton Ct. NW8 . . . . .4D **33**
Elm Tree Cl. NW8 . . . . .2D **33**
Elm Tree Ct. NW8 . . . . .2D **33**
Elm Tree Rd. NW8 . . . . .2D **33**
Elmwood Ho. NW10 . . . . . . .1A **28**
Elnathan M. W9 . . . . .5A **32**
Elsa Cotts. E14 . . . . .2A **68**
Elsa St. E1 . . . . .2F **67**
Elsdale St. E9 . . . . .1C **22**
Elsden M. E2 . . . . .1C **44**
Elsham Rd. W14 . . . . .5F **79**
Elsham Ter. W14 . . . . .1F **107**
Elsie La. Ct. W2 . . . . .2E **53**
Elsinore Ho. N1 . . . . .4D **17**
W6 . . . . .5C **106**
Elsted St. SE17 . . . . .4E **119**
Elsworthy Ct. NW3 . . . . .2B **12**
Elsworthy Ri. NW3 . . . . .1A **12**
Elsworthy Rd. NW3 . . . . .3F **11**
Elsworthy Ter. NW3 . . . . . . .2A **12**
Elton Ho. E3 . . . . .3C **24**
Eluna Apartments E1 . . . . . . .1A **94**
Elvaston M. SW7 . . . . .1C **110**
Elvaston Pl. SW7 . . . . .2B **110**
Elver Gdns. E2 . . . . .1E **43**
Elverton St. SW1 . . . . .3D **115**
Elwin St. E2 . . . . .2D **43**
Elworth Ho. SW8 . . . . .5C **138**
Ely Cotts. SW8 . . . . .5B **138**
Ely Ct. EC1 . . . . .2E **61**
NW6 . . . . .5D **9**
Ely Ho. SE15 . . . . .4E **143**
Ely Pl. EC1 . . . . .2E **61**
Elysium Apartments E1 . . . . .4C **44**
Elystan Ho. SW3 . . . . .4F **111**
Elystan Pl. SW3 . . . . .5A **112**
Elystan St. SW3 . . . . .4F **111**
Elystan Wlk. N1 . . . . .4D **17**
Ely's Yd. E1 . . . . .1C **64**
Emanuel Ho. SW1 . . . . .2D **115**
Embankment Galleries **1B 88**
Embankment Gdns.
SW3 . . . . .2C **134**
Embankment Pl. WC2 . . . . . .2A **88**
Embassy Ct. E2 . . . . .4F **43**
NW8 . . . . .1E **33**
Embassy Ho. NW6 . . . . .1F **9**
Embassy Theatre
Central School of Speech
& Drama **1D 11**
Emba St. SE16 . . . . .5E **93**
Emberton SE5 . . . . .2F **141**
Emberton Ct. EC1 . . . . .3F **39**
Emerald Cl. E16 . . . . .4F **75**
Emerald St. WC1 . . . . .1B **60**
Emerson St. SE1 . . . . .2B **90**
Emery Hill St. SW1 . . . . . . .2C **114**
Emery St. SE1 . . . . .1E **117**
Emery Theatre **4F 69**
Emily Ct. SE1 . . . . .5B **90**
Emily Ho. W10 . . . . .4A **30**
Emily St. E16 . . . . .4B **72**
Emirates Air Line
Cable Car **4B 100**

Emmanuel Ho. SE11 . . . . . .4D 117
Emma St. E2 . . . . .5F 21
Emminster NW6 . . . . .3F 9
Emmott Cl. E1 . . . . .5A 46
Emperor Ho. E20 . . . . .3B 6
Emperor's Ga. SW7 . . . . . .2A 110
Empingham Ho. SE8 . . . . . .3E 123

Empire Cinema
   Leicester Square 5E 59
Empire Ho. SW7 . . . . .2F 111
Empire Reach SE10 . . . . . .2A 148
Empire Sq. SE1 . . . . .5D 91
Empire Sq. E. SE1 . . . . . . .5D 91
Empire Sq. Sth. SE1 . . . . . .5D 91
Empire Sq. W. SE1 . . . . . . .5D 91
Empire Wharf E3 . . . . .4A 24
Empire Wharf Rd. E14 . . . . .4D 127
Empress App. SW6 . . . . . . .2D 131
Empress Pl. SW6 . . . . .1D 131
Empress State Bldg.
   SW6 . . . . .1D 131
Empress St. SE17 . . . . .2C 146
Empson St. E3 . . . . .4A 48
EMT House E6 . . . . .1E 77
Enard Ho. E3 . . . . .5C 24
Enbrook St. W10 . . . . .3A 30
Enclave Ct. EC1 . . . . .4A 40
Endeavour Ho. E14 . . . . . . .4D 97
Endell St. WC2 . . . . .3F 59
Enderby St. SE10 . . . . .5F 127
Endsleigh Ct. WC1 . . . . . . .4E 37
Endsleigh Gdns. WC1 . . . . .4D 37
Endsleigh Pl. WC1 . . . . . . .4E 37
Endsleigh St. WC1 . . . . . . .4D 37

Energize Fitness Club
   Hammersmith 5F 107
Energy Centre, The N1 . . . . .3F 41
Enfield Cloisters N1 . . . . . . .2F 41
Enfield Rd. N1 . . . . .2A 20
Enford St. W1 . . . . .1B 56
Engine Ct. SW1 . . . . .3C 86
Englefield NW1 . . . . .3B 36
Englefield Rd. N1 . . . . .1D 19
English Grounds SE1 . . . . . . .3F 91
English St. E3 . . . . .4B 46
Enid St. SE16 . . . . .1C 120
Ennerdale NW1 . . . . .2B 36
Ennerdale Ho. E3 . . . . .4B 46
Ennis Ho. E14 . . . . .4A 70
Ennismore Gdns. SW7 . . . . .5F 83
Ennismore Gdns. M. SW7 . . .1F 111
Ennismore M. SW7 . . . . . . .5F 83
Ennismore St. SW7 . . . . . . .1F 111
Ensbury Ho. SW8 . . . . .4B 138
Ensign Ho. E14 . . . . .4E 97
Ensign St. E1 . . . . .5D 65
Ensor M. SW7 . . . . .5D 111
Enterprise Bus. Pk. E14 . . . . .4F 97
Enterprise Ho. E9 . . . . .2B 22
   E14 . . . . .5A 126
Enterprise Ind. Est. SE16 . . . .1C 144
Enterprize Way SE8 . . . . . . .3B 124
Entertainment Av. SE10 . . . . .3F 99
Epcot M. NW10 . . . . .3E 29
Epirus M. SW6 . . . . .4D 131
Epirus Rd. SW6 . . . . .4C 130
Epping Cl. E14 . . . . .3E 125
Epstein Ct. N1 . . . . .4A 18
Epworth St. EC2 . . . . .5E 41
Equana Apartments SE8 . . . .5A 124
Equiano Ho. SW9 . . . . .5C 138
Equinox Sq. E14 . . . . .3A 70
Equity Sq. E2 . . . . .3C 42
Erasmus St. SW1 . . . . .4E 115

Eresby Ho. SW7 . . . . .5A 84
Eresby Pl. NW6 . . . . .2D 9
Eric Fletcher Ct. N1 . . . . . . .1C 18
Eric St. E3 . . . . .3A 46
   (not continuous)
Eric Wilkins Ho. SE1 . . . . . .1D 143
Erin Cl. SW6 . . . . .5E 131
Erlich Cotts. E1 . . . . .1B 66
Ermine Ho. E3 . . . . .4C 24
Ermine M. E2 . . . . .4B 20
Ernest Harriss Ho. W9 . . . . .4D 31
Ernest Shackleton Lodge
   SE10 . . . . .4F 127
Ernest St. E1 . . . . .5E 45
Eros 1D 87
Errington Rd. W9 . . . . .4C 30
Errol St. EC1 . . . . .5C 40
Erskine Ho. SW1 . . . . .1B 136
Erskine M. NW3 . . . . .2C 12
Erskine Rd. NW3 . . . . .2C 12
Eskdale NW1 . . . . .1B 36
Esk Ho. E3 . . . . .4C 46
Esmeralda Rd. SE1 . . . . . . .4E 121
Esmond Ct. W8 . . . . .1A 110
Esmond Rd. NW6 . . . . .4C 8
Esprit Ct. E1 . . . . .2B 64
Essendine Mans. W9 . . . . . .3E 31
Essendine Rd. W9 . . . . .4E 31
Essex Ct. EC4 . . . . .4D 61
   W6 . . . . .1B 106
Essex Ho. E14 . . . . .3F 69
Essex Rd. N1 . . . . .4A 18
Essex St. WC2 . . . . .4D 61
Essex Vs. W8 . . . . .5D 81
Essian St. E1 . . . . .1F 67
Estcourt Rd. SW6 . . . . .4B 130
Estella Apartments E15 . . . . .5E 7
Estella Ho. W11 . . . . .1E 79
Esterbrooke St. SW1 . . . . . .4D 115
Esther Randall Ct. NW1 . . . . .4A 36

Estorick Collection of Modern
   Italian Art 1A 18
Estuary Ho. E16 . . . . .3D 103
Etal Ho. N1 . . . . .1F 17

Etcetera Theatre 2A 14
Etchingham Rd. E15 . . . . . . .1C 6
Ethelbert Ho. E9 . . . . .1A 4
Ethelburga St. SW11 . . . . . .5A 134
Ethelburga Twr. SW11 . . . . .5A 134
Ethelden Rd. W12 . . . . .2A 78
Ethel Rd. E16 . . . . .4F 73
Ethel St. SE17 . . . . .4C 118
Ethnard Rd. SE15 . . . . .3F 143

Ethos Sport Imperial 1E 111
Eton Av. NW3 . . . . .1D 11
Eton Coll. Rd. NW3 . . . . . . .1C 12
Eton Ct. NW3 . . . . .1E 11
Eton Garages NW3 . . . . . . .1A 12
Eton Hall NW3 . . . . .1C 12
Eton Pl. NW3 . . . . .1D 13
Eton Ri. NW3 . . . . .1C 12
Eton Rd. NW3 . . . . .1B 12
Eton Vs. NW3 . . . . .1C 12
Etta St. SE8 . . . . .2A 146
Ettrick St. E14 . . . . .3C 70
   (not continuous)
Eugene Cotter Ho. SE17 . . . .4E 119
Eugenia Rd. SE16 . . . . .4C 122
Europa Ho. E16 . . . . .4C 72
Europa Pl. EC1 . . . . .3B 40
Europa Trade Pk. E16 . . . . . .5F 49
Eustace Bldg. SW8 . . . . . . .3F 135
Eustace Ho. SE11 . . . . .3B 116
Eustace Rd. SW6 . . . . .4D 131

Euston Gro. NW1 . . . . .3D 37
Euston Rd. N1 . . . . .2F 37
   NW1 . . . . .5A 36
Euston Sq. NW1 . . . . .3D 37
   (not continuous)
Euston Sta. Colonnade
   NW1 . . . . .3D 37
Euston St. NW1 . . . . .4C 36
Euston Twr. NW1 . . . . .4B 36
EUSTON UNDERPASS 4C 36
Evangelist Ho. EC4 . . . . . . .4F 61
   (off Black Friars La.)
Evan Ho. E16 . . . . .2E 73
Evans Ho. SW8 . . . . .5E 137
   W12 . . . . .1A 78
Evedon Ho. N1 . . . . .4F 19
   (off Halcomb St.)
Evelina Mans. SE5 . . . . . . .4D 141
Eveline Lowe Est. SE16 . . . . .2D 121
Evelyn Ct. E3 . . . . .1B 68
   N1 . . . . .1D 41
Evelyn Denington Ct. N1 . . . .1F 17
Evelyn Denington Rd. E6 . . . .1A 76
Evelyn Fox Ct. W10 . . . . . . .2C 50
Evelyn Gdns. SW7 . . . . . . .1C 132
Evelyn Ho. W8 . . . . .5F 81
Evelyn Mans. SW1 . . . . . . .2B 114
   W14 . . . . .2A 130
Evelyn Rd. E16 . . . . .2E 101
Evelyn St. SE8 . . . . .4F 123
Evelyn Wlk. N1 . . . . .1D 41
Evelyn Yd. W1 . . . . .3D 59
Everard Ho. E1 . . . . .4E 65
Everest Pl. E14 . . . . .1B 70
Everett Ho. SE17 . . . . .5E 119
Evergreen Sq. E8 . . . . .1B 20
Everilda St. N1 . . . . .4C 16
Eve Rd. E11 . . . . .1F 7
   E15 . . . . .1F 49
Evershed Ho. E1 . . . . .3C 64
Eversholt St. NW1 . . . . .5C 14
Eversley Ho. E2 . . . . .3D 43
Everton Bldgs. NW1 . . . . . . .3B 36
Evesham Ho. E2 . . . . .1B 44
   NW8 . . . . .4B 10
   SW1 . . . . .5A 114
Evesham St. W11 . . . . .1D 79
Ewart Pl. E3 . . . . .5B 24
Ewen Henderson Ct.
   SE14 . . . . .5F 145
Ewen Ho. N1 . . . . .4B 16
Ewer St. SE1 . . . . .3B 90
Ewhurst Cl. E1 . . . . .2C 66
Exbury Ho. E9 . . . . .1B 22
   SW1 . . . . .5D 115
ExCeL 1A 102
Excel Ct. WC2 . . . . .1E 87
Excel Marina E16 . . . . .1E 101
Excelsior Ind. Est. SE15 . . . .2C 144
Excel Waterfront E16 . . . . . .1F 101
Exchange Arc. EC2 . . . . . . .1A 64
Exchange Bldg. E1 . . . . .5B 42
Exchange Ct. WC2 . . . . .1A 88
Exchange Ho. EC2 . . . . .1A 64
   SW1 . . . . .4D 115
Exchange Pl. EC2 . . . . .1F 63
Exchange Sq. EC2 . . . . .1F 63
Exchange St. EC1 . . . . .3B 40
Exeter Cl. E6 . . . . .3B 76
Exeter Ct. NW6 . . . . .1E 31
Exeter Ho. N1 . . . . .4F 19
   (off New Era Est.)
   SE15 . . . . .3E 143
   W2 . . . . .3B 54

Exeter M. NW6 . . . . .1F **9**
  SW6 . . . . .4D **131**
Exeter Rd. E16 . . . . .2E **73**
Exeter St. WC2 . . . . .5A **60**
Exeter Way SE14 . . . . . .5B **146**
Exhibition Cl. W12 . . . . . .1B **78**
Exhibition Rd. SW7 . . . . .5E **83**
Exmoor Ho. E3 . . . . .1F **45**
Exmoor St. W10 . . . . . . .5E **29**
Exmouth Ho. E14 . . . . . .4F **125**
  EC1 . . . . .4E **39**
Exmouth Mkt. EC1 . . . . . .4D **39**
Exmouth M. NW1 . . . . . .3C **36**
Exmouth Pl. E8 . . . . .2F **21**
Exmouth St. E1 . . . . .3C **66**
Exning Rd. E16 . . . . .1B **72**
Exonbury NW8 . . . . .4A **10**
Exon St. SE17 . . . . .4F **119**
Explorers Ct. E14 . . . . . . .5E **71**
Export Ho. SE1 . . . . .5A **92**
Express Newspapers SE1 . . .2F **89**
Express Wharf E14 . . . . . .5D **97**
Exton St. SE1 . . . . .3D **89**
Eynham Rd. W12 . . . . . . .3B **50**
Eynsford Ho. SE1 . . . . . . .5D **91**
  SE15 . . . . .2C **144**
  SE17 . . . . .4F **119**
Eyot Ho. SE16 . . . . .1D **121**
Eyre Ct. NW8 . . . . .5D **11**
Eyre St. Hill EC1 . . . . . . .5D **39**
Ezra St. E2 . . . . .2C **42**

F

Fabian Bell Twr. E3 . . . . . .5D **25**
Fabian Rd. SW6 . . . . . . .4C **130**
Factory Rd. E16 . . . . . . .3E **103**
Fairbank Est. N1 . . . . .1E **41**
Fairbriar Residence SW7 . . .3C **110**
Fairburn Ho. W14 . . . . . .1C **130**
Fairby Ho. SE1 . . . . .3C **120**
Faircharm Trad. Est. SE8 . . .4F **147**
Fairchild Ho. E2 . . . . .5F **21**
  E9 . . . . .1C **22**
  N1 . . . . .2F **41**
Fairchild Pl. EC2 . . . . . . .5A **42**
Fairchild St. EC2 . . . . . . .5A **42**
Fairclough St. E1 . . . . . . .4E **65**
Fairfax Ct. NW6 . . . . . . .2C **10**
Fairfax Mans. NW6 . . . . . .1C **10**
Fairfax M. E16 . . . . .2F **101**
Fairfax Pl. NW6 . . . . . . .2C **10**
  W14 . . . . .2A **108**
Fairfax Rd. NW6 . . . . . . .2C **10**
Fairfield E1 . . . . .1C **66**
  NW1 . . . . .4B **14**
Fairfield Rd. E3 . . . . .5D **25**
Fairfoot Rd. E3 . . . . .5D **47**
Fairford Ho. SE11 . . . . . .4E **117**
Fairhazel Gdns. NW6 . . . . .1A **10**
Fairhazel Mans. NW6 . . . . .1B **10**
Fairholme Rd. W14 . . . . .1A **130**
Fairholt St. SW7 . . . . . . .1A **112**
Fairlead Ho. E14 . . . . . . .1E **125**
Fairlie Ct. E3 . . . . .2F **47**
Fairmead Ho. E9 . . . . .1A **4**
Fairmont Av. E14 . . . . . . .2D **99**
Fairmont Ho. E3 . . . . .4D **47**
  SE16 . . . . .5D **95**
Fairstead Wlk. N1 . . . . . . .3B **18**
Fair St. SE1 . . . . .4A **92**
Fairthorne Vs. SE7 . . . . . .5E **129**
Fairthorn Rd. SE7 . . . . . .5E **129**

Fairway Ct. SE16 . . . . . . .5D **95**
Faith Ct. E3 . . . . .5D **25**
  SE1 . . . . .5C **120**
Fakruddin St. E1 . . . . .5E **43**
Falcon WC1 . . . . .1A **60**
Falconberg M. W1 . . . . . .3D **59**
Falcon Ct. EC4 . . . . .4D **61**
  N1 . . . . .1A **40**
Falconet Ct. E1 . . . . .3A **94**
Falcon Highwalk EC2 . . . . .2B **62**
Falcon Ho. E14 . . . . .1A **148**
  NW6 . . . . .4F **9**
  SW5 . . . . .5A **110**
Falcon Lodge W9 . . . . . . .1E **53**
Falcon Point SE1 . . . . . . .1A **90**
Falcon Way E14 . . . . . . .3A **126**
Falkirk Ct. SE16 . . . . .2E **95**
Falkirk Ho. W9 . . . . .2A **32**
Falkirk St. N1 . . . . .1A **42**
Falkland Ho. W8 . . . . . . .2F **109**
  W14 . . . . .5B **108**
Fallodon Ho. W11 . . . . . .2C **52**
Fallow Ct. SE16 . . . . .1E **143**
Falmouth Ho. SE11 . . . . . .5E **117**
  W2 . . . . .5F **55**
Falmouth Rd. SE1 . . . . . .2C **118**
Falmouth St. E15 . . . . .3E **7**
Falstaff Bldg. E1 . . . . .5F **65**
Falstaff Ct. SE11 . . . . . . .4F **117**
Falstaff Ho. N1 . . . . .1F **41**
Fane St. W14 . . . . .2C **130**
Fan Museum, The 4C **148**
Fann St. EC1 . . . . .5B **40**
  EC2 . . . . .5B **40**
  (not continuous)
Fanshaw St. N1 . . . . .2F **41**
Faraday Ho. E14 . . . . . . .5B **68**
  SE1 . . . . .5D **91**
  W10 . . . . .1A **52**
Faraday Lodge SE10 . . . . .1C **128**
Faraday Mans. W14 . . . . .2A **130**
Faraday Rd. W10 . . . . . . .1F **51**
Faringford Rd. E15 . . . . . .2F **27**
Farjeon Ho. NW6 . . . . . . .2D **11**
Farleigh Ho. N1 . . . . .2A **18**
Farley Ct. NW1 . . . . .5D **35**
  W14 . . . . .1B **108**
Farm Cl. SW6 . . . . .4E **131**
Farmdale Rd. SE10 . . . . . .5E **129**
Farmer's Rd. SE5 . . . . . . .5A **140**
Farmer St. W8 . . . . .2D **81**
Farm La. SW6 . . . . .3E **131**
Farm La. Trad. Est.
  SW6 . . . . .3D **131**
Farm Pl. W8 . . . . .2D **81**
Farm St. W1 . . . . .1F **85**
Farnaby Ho. W10 . . . . . . .3B **30**
Farncombe St. SE16 . . . . .5E **93**
Farndale Ho. NW6 . . . . . . .2F **9**
Farnell M. SW5 . . . . .5F **109**
Farnham Ho. NW1 . . . . . .5A **34**
  SE1 . . . . .3B **90**
Farnham Pl. SE1 . . . . . . .3A **90**
Farnham Royal SE11 . . . . .1C **138**
Farnsworth Ct. SE10 . . . . .2C **128**
Farnworth Ho. E14 . . . . . .3D **127**
Faroe Rd. W14 . . . . .2E **107**
Farrance St. E14 . . . . . . .4C **68**
Farrell Ho. E1 . . . . .4C **66**
Farrer Ho. SE8 . . . . .4E **147**
Farrier Ho. EC1 . . . . .5C **40**
Farrier St. NW1 . . . . .1A **14**
Farrier Wlk. SW10 . . . . . .2B **132**

Farringdon La. EC1 . . . . . .5E **39**
Farringdon Rd. EC1 . . . . . .4D **39**
Farringdon St. EC4 . . . . . .2F **61**
Farrins Rents SE16 . . . . . .3F **95**
Farrow La. SE14 . . . . . . .4C **144**
Farrow Pl. SE16 . . . . .1F **123**
Farthingale Wlk. E15 . . . . .2D **27**
Farthing All. SE1 . . . . . . .5D **93**
Farthing Flds. E1 . . . . . . .2A **94**
Fashion & Textile Mus. 4A **92**
Fashion St. E1 . . . . .2B **64**
Fathom Ct. E16 . . . . .1F **105**
Faulkners All. EC1 . . . . . . .1F **61**
Faulkner St. SE14 . . . . . . .5C **144**
Faunce Ho. SE17 . . . . . . .2A **140**
Faunce St. SE17 . . . . .1F **139**
Faversham Ho. NW1 . . . . .4C **14**
  SE17 . . . . .1F **141**
Fawcett Ct. SW10 . . . . . .2B **132**
Fawcett St. SW10 . . . . . .3A **132**
Fawe St. E14 . . . . .2A **70**
Fawkham Ho. SE1 . . . . . .4C **120**
Fawley Lodge E14 . . . . . .3D **127**
Fazeley Ct. W9 . . . . .1D **53**
Fearon St. SE10 . . . . .5D **129**
Feather M. E1 . . . . .2E **65**
Feathers Pl. SE10 . . . . . . .2E **149**
Featherstone St. EC1 . . . . .4D **41**
Felgate M. W6 . . . . .4A **106**
Felix Ho. E16 . . . . .1E **105**
Felixstowe Ct. E16 . . . . . .3F **105**
Felixstowe Rd. NW10 . . . .2A **28**
Felix St. E2 . . . . .1A **44**
Fellbrigg St. E1 . . . . .5A **44**
Fellmongers Path SE1 . . . .5B **92**
Fellows Ct. E2 . . . . .5B **20**
  (not continuous)
Fellows Rd. NW3 . . . . . . .1E **11**
Felltram M. SE7 . . . . .5E **129**
Felltram Way SE7 . . . . . .5E **129**
Felstead Gdns. E14 . . . . . .1B **148**
Felstead Rd. E9 . . . . .5D **5**
Felstead St. E9 . . . . .5C **4**
Felstead Wharf E14 . . . . . .1B **148**
Felsted Rd. E16 . . . . .4D **75**
Felton Hall Ho. SE16 . . . . .5D **93**
Felton Ho. N1 . . . . .4E **19**
Felton St. N1 . . . . .4E **19**
Fenchurch Av. EC3 . . . . . .4F **63**
Fenchurch Bldgs. EC3 . . . .4A **64**
Fenchurch Ho. EC3 . . . . . .4B **64**
Fenchurch Pl. EC3 . . . . . .5A **64**
Fenchurch St. EC3 . . . . . .5F **63**
Fen Ct. EC3 . . . . .4F **63**
Fendall St. SE1 . . . . .2A **120**
  (not continuous)
Fendt Cl. E16 . . . . .5C **72**
Fenelon Pl. W14 . . . . . . .4C **108**
Fenham Rd. SE15 . . . . . . .5E **143**
Fennel Apartments SE1 . . . .4B **92**
Fenner Cl. SE16 . . . . .3A **122**
Fenner Ho. E1 . . . . .2A **94**
Fenning St. SE1 . . . . .4F **91**
Fen St. E16 . . . . .5C **72**
Fentiman Rd. SW8 . . . . . .3A **138**
Fenton Ho. SE14 . . . . . . .5B **146**
Fenton St. E1 . . . . .3A **66**
Ferdinand Dr. SE15 . . . . . .5A **142**
Ferdinand Ho. NW1 . . . . . .1E **13**
Ferdinand Pl. NW1 . . . . . . .1E **13**
Ferdinand St. NW1 . . . . . .1E **13**
Ferguson Cl. E14 . . . . . . .4D **125**
Ferial Ct. SE15 . . . . .5E **143**
Fermain Ct. E. N1 . . . . . . .3A **20**

Fermain Ct. Nth. N1 . . . . .3A 20
Fermain Ct. W. N1 . . . . .3F 19
Fermoy Ho. W9 . . . . .5C 30
Fermoy Rd. W9 . . . . .5B 30
    (not continuous)
Fern Cl. N1 . . . . .5F 19
Ferndale St. E6 . . . . .5F 77
Ferndown NW1 . . . . .2D 15
Ferndown Lodge E14 . . . . . .2C 126
Fernhead Rd. W9 . . . . .1C 30
Fernhill St. E16 . . . . .3C 104
Fernhurst Rd. SW6 . . . . .5A 130
Fernleigh Cl. W9 . . . . .2C 30
Fernsbury St. WC1 . . . . .3D 39
Fernshaw Cl. SW10 . . . . . . .3B 132
Fernshaw Mans. SW10 . . . . .3B 132
Fernshaw Rd. SW10 . . . . . . .3B 132
Fern St. E3 . . . . .5E 47
Fern Wlk. SE16 . . . . .1E 143
Ferriby Cl. N1 . . . . .1D 17
Ferrier Point E16 . . . . .2D 73
Ferrybridge Ho. SE11 . . . . . .2C 116
Ferry St. E14 . . . . .5B 126
Festival Ct. E8 . . . . .2C 20
Festival Way E14 . . . . .4E 69
Festive Mans. E20 . . . . .3B 6
Festoon Way E16 . . . . .5D 75
Festuca Ho. E20 . . . . .3C 6
Fetter La. EC4 . . . . .4E 61
Fetter La. Apartments
    EC4 . . . . .4D 61
    (off Fetter La.)
Fettes Ho. NW8 . . . . .1E 33
Ffinch St. SE8 . . . . .4D 147
Fidelis Ho. E1 . . . . .2B 64
Field Ct. WC1 . . . . .2C 60
Fieldgate Mans. E1 . . . . .2E 65
    (not continuous)
Fieldgate St. E1 . . . . .2E 65
Field Ho. NW6 . . . . .2E 29
Fielding Ct. WC2 . . . . .4F 59
Fielding Ho. NW6 . . . . .2E 31
    NW8 . . . . .3B 10
Fielding Rd. W14 . . . . .1E 107
Fielding St. SE17 . . . . .2B 140
Field Rd. W6 . . . . .1A 130
Fields Est. E8 . . . . .2E 21
Field St. WC1 . . . . .2B 38
Fife Rd. E16 . . . . .2D 73
Fife Ter. N1 . . . . .5C 16
Fifth Av. W10 . . . . .4F 29
Fight for Peace Academy
    .3E 105
Figure Ct. SW3 . . . . .1C 134
Filigree Ct. SE16 . . . . .3B 96
Filmer Chambers SW6 . . . . .5A 130
Filmer Rd. SW6 . . . . .5B 130
Filton Ct. SE14 . . . . .4C 144
Finborough Ho. SW10 . . . . .2B 132
Finborough Rd. SW10 . . . . .1F 131
Finborough Theatre, The
    .2A 132
Finch Ho. E3 . . . . .4B 24
    SE8 . . . . .4F 147
Finch La. EC3 . . . . .4E 63
Finchley Pl. NW8 . . . . .5D 11
Finchley Rd. NW3 . . . . .1C 10
    NW8 . . . . .4D 11
Finch Lodge W9 . . . . .1E 53
Finch M. SE15 . . . . .5B 142
Finch's Ct. E14 . . . . .5A 70
Findhorn St. E14 . . . . .3C 70
Findlay Ho. E3 . . . . .3E 47
Fingal St. SE10 . . . . .5C 128

Fingest Ho. NW8 . . . . .4F 33
Finland St. SE16 . . . . .1A 124
Finley Ct. SE5 . . . . .5B 140
Finnemore Ho. N1 . . . . .3B 18
Finn Ho. N1 . . . . .2E 41
Finnis St. E2 . . . . .3A 44
FINSBURY **3E 39**
Finsbury Av. EC2 . . . . .2E 63
Finsbury Av. Sq. EC2 . . . . . .1F 63
Finsbury Cir. EC2 . . . . .2E 63
Finsbury Est. EC1 . . . . .3F 39
Finsbury Leisure Cen. **4B 40**
Finsbury Mkt. EC2 . . . . .5F 41
    (not continuous)
Finsbury Pavement EC2 . . . .1E 63
Finsbury Sq. EC2 . . . . .5E 41
Finsbury St. EC2 . . . . .1D 63
Finstock Rd. W10 . . . . .3D 51
Finwhale Ho. E14 . . . . .1A 126
Fiona Ct. NW6 . . . . .5C 8
Firbank Cl. E16 . . . . .1D 75
Firefly Gdns. E6 . . . . .1F 75
Firehorn Ho. E15 . . . . .2F 49
Firewatch Ct. E1 . . . . .1F 67
Fir Ho. W10 . . . . .4F 29
Firle Ho. W10 . . . . .1B 50
First Av. W10 . . . . .4B 30
First St. SW3 . . . . .3A 112
Firth Ho. E2 . . . . .3D 43
Fir Trees Cl. SE16 . . . . .3A 96
Fisher Ho. E1 . . . . .5C 66
    N1 . . . . .4D 17
Fishermans Dr. SE16 . . . . . . .4E 95
Fisherman's Wlk. E14 . . . . . .2D 97
Fishers Ct. SE14 . . . . .5D 145
Fisher St. E16 . . . . .1D 73
    WC1 . . . . .2B 60
Fisherton St. NW8 . . . . .5D 33
Fishguard Way E16 . . . . .3F 105
    E16 . . . . .4F 105
Fishmongers Hall Wharf
    EC4 . . . . .1E 91
Fish St. Hill EC3 . . . . .1E 91
Fish Wharf EC3 . . . . .1E 91
Fit4less
    Aldgate **5C 64**
Fitness First
    America Square **5B 64**
    Baker Street **2C 56**
    Berkeley Square **1A 86**
    Bloomsbury **5F 37**
    Camden **4A 14**
    Chancery Lane **3E 61**
    Covent Garden **1A 88**
    Embankment *2A 88*
    (off Embankment Pl.)
    Fetter Lane **3E 61**
    Gracechurch Street . . .**5F 63**
    Great Marlborough Street
    . . . .**4B 58**
    Hammersmith **3C 106**
    High Holborn **3B 60**
    Islington **1F 39**
    Kilburn **4B 8**
    Kingly Street **5B 58**
    London Bridge *3E 91*
    (off London Bri. St.)
    Old Street **4D 41**
    Paternoster Square **3A 62**
    Queen Victoria Street . .**5B 62**
    South Kensington **3D 111**
    Thomas More Square . .**1D 93**
    Victoria **1B 114**
    Walworth Road **1C 140**

Fitrooms **3C 130**
    (off North End Rd.)
Fitzalan St. SE11 . . . . .3C 116
Fitzclarence Ho. W11 . . . . . .4F 79
Fitzgeorge Av. W14 . . . . .4F 107
Fitzgerald Ho. E14 . . . . .4A 70
Fitzhardinge Ho. W1 . . . . . . .3D 57
Fitzhardinge St. W1 . . . . .3D 57
Fitzjames Av. W14 . . . . .4A 108
Fitzmaurice Ho. SE16 . . . . . .4A 122
Fitzmaurice Pl. W1 . . . . .2A 86
FITZROVIA **1A 58**
Fitzrovia Apartments W1 . . . .5A 36
Fitzroy Bri. NW1 . . . . .3E 13
Fitzroy Ct. W1 . . . . .5C 36
Fitzroy Ho. E14 . . . . .3C 68
    SE1 . . . . .5C 120
Fitzroy House Mus. **5B 36**
Fitzroy M. W1 . . . . .5B 36
Fitzroy Rd. NW1 . . . . .3D 13
Fitzroy Sq. W1 . . . . .5B 36
Fitzroy St. W1 . . . . .5B 36
    (not continuous)
Fitzroy Yd. NW1 . . . . .3D 13
Fitzwilliam M. E16 . . . . .2D 101
Five Bell All. E14 . . . . .4C 68
Fives Ct. SE11 . . . . .2F 117
Flamborough St. E14 . . . . . . .4F 67
Flamborough Wlk. E14 . . . . .4F 67
Flamingo Ct. SE8 . . . . .4D 147
    SE17 . . . . .5B 118
Flamstead Ho. *SW3* *5F 111*
    (off Cale St.)
Flanagan Apartments E3 . . . .5B 46
Flank St. E1 . . . . .5D 65
Flannery Ct. SE16 . . . . .1F 121
Flansham Ho. E14 . . . . .3B 68
Flat Iron Sq. SE1 . . . . .3C 90
Flatiron Yd. SE1 . . . . .3C 90
Flavell M. SE10 . . . . .5A 128
Flaxley Ho. SW1 . . . . .5F 113
Flaxman Ct. W1 . . . . .4D 59
    WC1 . . . . .3E 37
Flaxman Ho. SE1 . . . . .1F 117
Flaxman Ter. WC1 . . . . .3E 37
Flecker Ho. SE5 . . . . .5D 141
Fleetbank Ho. EC4 . . . . .4E 61
Fleet Bldg. EC4 . . . . .3F 61
Fleetfield WC1 . . . . .2A 38
Fleet Ho. E14 . . . . .5A 68
Fleet Pl. EC4 . . . . .3F 61
Fleet Sq. WC1 . . . . .3C 38
Fleet St. EC4 . . . . .4D 61
Fleetway WC1 . . . . .2A 38
Fleetwood Cl. E16 . . . . .1E 75
Fleetwood Ct. E6 . . . . .1B 76
Fleming Cl. SW10 . . . . .2C 132
    W9 . . . . .5D 31
Fleming Collection, The . .**2A 86**
Fleming Ct. W2 . . . . .1D 55
Fleming Ho. SE16 . . . . .5D 93
Fleming Lodge W9 . . . . .1E 53
Fleming Rd. SE17 . . . . .2A 140
Fletcher Bldgs. WC2 . . . . . . .4A 60
Fletcher Cl. E6 . . . . .5F 77
Fletcher Ho. N1 . . . . .4A 20
    SE15 . . . . .5C 144
Fletcher Path SE8 . . . . .5E 147
Fletcher St. E1 . . . . .5E 65
Fleur de Lis St. E1 . . . . .5A 42
Flight Ho. N1 . . . . .4F 19
Flinders Ho. E1 . . . . .3A 94
Flinton St. SE17 . . . . .5A 120
Flint St. SE17 . . . . .4E 119

Flitcroft St. WC2	Forset St. W1	Foxfield NW1
Flitcroft St. WC2 .... .4E **59**	Forset St. W1 .... .3A **56**	Foxfield NW1 .... .4A **14**
Flitton Ho. N1 .... .2F **17**	(not continuous)	Foxglove Ct. E3 .... .5D **25**
Flockton St. SE16 .... .5D **93**	Forston St. N1 .... .5C **18**	(off Four Seasons Cl.)
Flodden Rd. SE5 .... .5B **140**	Forsyte Ho. SW3 .... .1A **134**	Foxley Ho. E3 .... .2A **48**
Flood St. SW3 .... .1A **134**	Forsyth Gdns. SE17 ..... .2A **140**	Foxley Rd. SW9 .... .4E **139**
Flood Wlk. SW3 .... .2A **134**	Forsyth Ho. E9 .... .1C **22**	Foxley Sq. SW9 .... .5F **139**
Flora Cl. E14 .... .4F **69**	SW1 .... .5C **114**	Fox Rd. E16 .... .2B **72**
Flora Gdns. W6 .... .3A **106**	Fortescue Av. E8 .... .2A **22**	Fox's Yd. E2 .... .4C **42**
Flora Ho. E3 .... .4D **25**	Forth Ho. E3 .... .1C **46**	Foxton Ho. E16 .... .4E **105**
Floral St. WC2 .... .5F **59**	Fortis Cl. E16 .... .4B **74**	Frampton NW1 .... .2D **15**
Florence Ct. N1 .... .2F **17**	Fortius Apartments E3 ... .5D **25**	Frampton Ho. NW8 .... .5E **33**
W9 .... .3C **32**	Fortius Wlk. E20 .... .4C **6**	Frampton Pk. Est. E9 .... .1C **22**
Florence Ho. SE16 .... .1F **143**	Fort Rd. SE1 .... .4C **120**	Frampton Pk. Rd. E9 ..... .1B **22**
W11 .... .1E **79**	Fortrose Cl. E14 .... .3E **71**	Frampton St. NW8 .... .5E **33**
Florence Nightingale Mus.	Fort St. E1 .... .2A **64**	Frances Wharf E14 .... .3C **68**
.... .5B **88**	E16 .... .3A **102**	Francis Bacon Ct.
Florence Rd. SE14 .... .5C **146**	Fortuna Ho. E20 .... .3A **6**	SE16 .... .4A **122**
Florence Sq. E3 .... .4A **48**	Fortune Ct. E8 .... .2C **20**	Francis Cl. E14 .... .3D **127**
Florence St. N1 .... .2F **17**	Fortune Ho. EC1 .... .5C **40**	Francis Ct. EC1 .... .1F **61**
Florey Lodge *W9* .... *.1E* **53**	SE11 .... .4D **117**	SE14 .... .3D **145**
(off Admiral Wlk.)	Fortune Pl. SE1 .... .1C **142**	Francis Ho. N1 .... .4F **19**
Florian Ct. E16 .... .2E **73**	Fortune St. EC1 .... .5C **40**	SW10 .... .4A **132**
Florida St. E2 .... .3D **43**	Fortunes Wlk. E20 .... .3B **6**	Francis St. E15 .... .3F **7**
Florin Ct. EC1 .... .1B **62**	**Fortune Theatre** .... **.4A 60**	SW1 .... .3B **114**
SE1 .... .5B **92**	Forty Acre La. E16 .... .2D **73**	Francis Wlk. N1 .... .3B **16**
Flower & Dean Wlk. E1 ... .2C **64**	Forum Cl. E3 .... .4D **25**	Frank Beswick Ho. SW6 ... .3C **130**
Flower Walk, The SW7 .... .5B **82**	Forum Magnum Sq. SE1 ... .4B **88**	Frankham Ho. SE8 .... .5E **147**
Flying Angel Ho. E16 ..... .4A **74**	Forward Bus. Centre, The	Frankham St. SE8 .... .5D **147**
Flynn Ct. E14 .... .1D **97**	E16 .... .4E **49**	Frank Ho. SW8 .... .4F **137**
Foley Ho. E1 .... .4B **66**	Fosbrooke Ho. SW8 ...... .5F **137**	Frankland Cl. SE16 ...... .2A **122**
Foley St. W1 .... .2B **58**	Fosbury M. W2 .... .1A **82**	Frankland Rd. SW7 ...... .2D **111**
Folgate St. E1 .... .1A **64**	Foscote Ct. W9 .... .1E **53**	Franklin Bldg. E14 ...... .4D **97**
(not continuous)	Foscote M. W9 .... .5E **31**	Franklin Ho. E1 .... .3A **94**
Foliot Ho. N1 .... .5B **16**	Foss Ho. NW8 .... .5A **10**	E14 .... .4D **71**
Folkestone Ho. SE17 ..... .5A **120**	Fossil Ct. *SE1* .... *.1F* **119**	NW6 .... .2E **31**
Follett Ho. SW10 .... .4D **133**	(off Long La.)	Franklin Sq. W14 .... .1C **130**
Follett St. E14 .... .4B **70**	Foster Ct. E16 .... .5C **72**	Franklin's Row SW3 ..... .5C **112**
Follingham Ct. N1 .... .2A **42**	NW1 .... .1B **14**	Franklin St. E3 .... .2A **48**
Folly M. W11 .... .3B **52**	Foster La. EC2 .... .3B **62**	Frank M. SE1 .... .4F **121**
Folly Wall E14 .... .5C **98**	Foubert's Pl. W1 .... .4B **58**	Frank Soskice Ho. SW6 ... .3C **130**
Fonda Ct. E14 .... .1D **97**	Foulis Ter. SW7 .... .5E **111**	Frank Whymark Ho.
Fondant Ct. E3 .... .1F **47**	Founder Cl. E6 .... .4F **77**	SE16 .... .5B **94**
Fontenoy Ho. SE11 ...... .4F **117**	Founders Ct. EC2 .... .3D **63**	Frans Hals Ct. E14 ...... .1C **126**
Fonthill Ho. SW1 .... .5A **114**	Founders Ho. SW1 ...... .5D **115**	Fraserburgh Ho. E3 ...... .1C **46**
W14 .... .1A **108**	Foundling Ct. WC1 ...... .4F **37**	Fraser Cl. E6 .... .3F **75**
Forber Ho. E2 .... .3B **44**	**Foundling Museum, The** ... **.4A 38**	Fraser Ct. E14 .... .5B **126**
Forbes St. E1 .... .4E **65**	Foundry, The EC2 .... .3A **42**	SE1 .... .1C **118**
Ford Cl. E3 .... .5A **24**	Foundry Cl. SE16 .... .2F **95**	Frazier St. SE1 .... .5D **89**
Fordham Ho. SE14 .... .4A **146**	Foundry Ho. E14 .... .1A **70**	Frean St. SE16 .... .1D **121**
Fordham St. E1 .... .3E **65**	Foundry M. NW1 .... .4C **36**	Frearson Ho. WC1 ...... .2C **38**
Fordie Ho. SW1 .... .2C **112**	Foundry Pl. E1 .... .1B **66**	Freda Corbett Cl. SE15 ... .4D **143**
Fordingley Rd. W9 .... .3C **30**	Fountain Ct. EC4 .... .5D **61**	Frederica St. N7 .... .1B **16**
Ford Rd. E3 .... .5B **24**	SW1 .... .4F **113**	Frederick Charrington Ho.
Fords Pk. Rd. E16 .... .2D **73**	W11 .... .4E **79**	E1 .... .4B **44**
Ford Sq. E1 .... .2A **66**	Fountain Grn. Sq. SE16 ... .5E **93**	Frederick Cl. W2 .... .5B **56**
Ford St. E3 .... .4A **24**	Fountain Ho. E2 .... .4B **42**	Frederick Ct. SW3 ...... .4C **112**
E16 .... .3B **72**	NW6 .... .2A **8**	Frederick Cres. SW9 .... .5F **139**
Foreland Ho. W11 .... .5F **51**	SE16 .... .5E **93**	Frederick Dobson Ho.
Foreshore SE8 .... .4C **124**	W1 .... .2D **85**	W11 .... .1F **79**
Forest Cl. NW6 .... .1A **8**	Fountain Sq. SW1 .... .3F **113**	Frederick Rd. SE17 ..... .2A **140**
Forester Ho. *E14* .... *.5A* **68**	Fount St. SW8 .... .5E **137**	Frederick's Pl. EC2 ..... .4D **63**
(off Victory Pl.)	Four Dials E20 .... .5B **6**	Frederick Sq. SE16 ..... .1F **95**
Forest Gro. E8 .... .1C **20**	Fournier St. E1 .... .1B **64**	Frederick's Row EC1 .... .2F **39**
Forest La. E15 .... .4F **7**	Fourscore Mans. E8 ..... .2E **21**	Frederick St. WC1 ...... .3B **38**
Forest St. EC2 .... .2C **62**	Four Seasons Cl. E3 ..... .5D **25**	Frederick Ter. E8 .... .2B **20**
Fore St. Av. EC2 .... .2D **63**	Fourth Av. W10 .... .4F **29**	Frederic M. SW1 .... .5C **84**
Forest Rd. E8 .... .1B **20**	Fowey Cl. E1 .... .2F **93**	Freeling Ho. NW8 ...... .3D **11**
Forge Pl. NW1 .... .1E **13**	Fowey Ho. SE11 .... .5E **117**	Freeling St. N1 .... .2B **16**
Forge Sq. E14 .... .4F **125**	Fowler Rd. N1 .... .3A **18**	(Carnoustie Dr.)
Formation, The E16 ...... .4F **105**	Fox & Knot St. EC1 ..... .1A **62**	N1 .... .2A **16**
Formosa Ho. E1 .... .5F **45**	Fox Cl. E1 .... .4C **44**	(Pembroke St.)
Formosa St. W9 .... .1A **54**	E16 .... .2D **73**	Freeman Ho. SE11 ...... .3F **117**
Formunt Cl. E16 .... .2C **72**	Foxcote SE5 .... .1A **142**	Freemantle St. SE17 .... .5F **119**
Forset Ct. W2 .... .3A **56**	Foxcroft WC1 .... .1C **38**	**Freemasons' Hall** ...... **.4A 60**

Freemasons Rd. E16 . . . . .2F 73
Free Trade Wharf E1 . . . . . . .5D 67
Freight La. N1 . . . . .2E 15
Fremantle Ho. E1 . . . . .5F 43
Fremont St. E9 . . . . .3B 22
(not continuous)
French Horn Yd. WC1 . . . . . . .2B 60
French Ordinary Ct. EC3 . . . .5A 64
French Pl. E1 . . . . .4A 42
Frensham St. SE15 . . . . .3E 143
Freshfield Av. E8 . . . . .1B 20
Freshwater Ct. *W1* *2A 56*
(off Crawford St.)
Freston Rd. W10 . . . . .5D 51
W11 . . . . .1E 79
Freswick Ho. SE8 . . . . .3E 123
Frewell Ho. EC1 . . . . .1D 61
Friars Cl. SE1 . . . . .2A 90
Friars Mead E14 . . . . .2C 126
Friar St. EC4 . . . . .4A 62
Friary Ct. SW1 . . . . .3C 86
Friary Est. SE15 . . . . .3E 143
(not continuous)
Friary Rd. SE15 . . . . .3E 143
Friday St. EC4 . . . . .5B 62
Friendship Ho. SE1 . . . . .5A 90
Friendship Way E15 . . . . .3C 26
Friend St. EC1 . . . . .2F 39
Frigate Ho. E14 . . . . .4C 126
Frigate M. SE8 . . . . .2D 147
Frimley St. E1 . . . . .5D 45
Frimley Way E1 . . . . .5D 45
Frinstead Ho. W10 . . . . .5D 51
Frith Ho. NW8 . . . . .5E 33
Frith St. W1 . . . . .4D 59
Frithville Ct. W12 . . . . .3B 78
Frithville Gdns. W12 . . . . .2B 78
Frobisher Ct. SE8 . . . . .5F 123
SE10 . . . . .2E 149
W12 . . . . .5B 78
Frobisher Cres. EC2 . . . . .1C 62
Frobisher Ho. E1 . . . . .2A 94
SW1 . . . . .2D 137
Frobisher Pas. E14 . . . . .2E 97
Frobisher Rd. E6 . . . . .3C 76
Frobisher St. SE10 . . . . .2F 149
Frome St. N1 . . . . .5B 18
Frostic Wlk. E1 . . . . .2C 64
Fruiterers Pas. *EC4* *1C 90*
(off Queen St. Pl.)
Frye Ct. E3 . . . . .2C 46
Frye Ho. E20 . . . . .4C 6
Frying Pan Alley E1 . . . . .2B 64
Fulbeck Ho. N7 . . . . .1B 16
Fulbourne St. E1 . . . . .1F 65
Fulcher Ho. N1 . . . . .4F 19
SE8 . . . . .1B 146
Fulford St. SE16 . . . . .5A 94
FULHAM **5D 131**
FULHAM BROADWAY **4E 131**
Fulham B'way. SW6 . . . . .5E 131
Fulham Broadway Shop. Cen.
SW6 . . . . .4E 131
Fulham Ct. SW6 . . . . .5D 131
Fulham Island SW6 . . . . .4D 131
Fulham Pal. Rd. W6 . . . . .5C 106
Fulham Pools
Virgin Active **3A 130**
Fulham Rd. SW3 . . . . .2C 132
SW6 . . . . .5E 131
(Fulham B'way.)
SW6 . . . . .5D 131
(Fulham High St.)
SW10 . . . . .2C 132

Fuller Cl. E2 . . . . .4D 43
Fullwood's M. N1 . . . . .2E 41
Fulmar Ho. SE16 . . . . .3E 123
Fulmer Ho. NW8 . . . . .5A 34
Fulmer Rd. E16 . . . . .2D 75
Fulneck E1 . . . . .1C 66
Fulton M. W2 . . . . .5B 54
Fulwood Pl. WC1 . . . . .2C 60
Furber St. W6 . . . . .2A 106
Furley Ho. SE15 . . . . .4E 143
Furley Rd. SE15 . . . . .5E 143
Furness Ho. SW1 . . . . .5A 114
Furnival Ct. *E3* *5D 25*
(off Four Seasons Cl.)
Furnival Mans. W1 . . . . .2B 58
Furnival St. EC4 . . . . .3D 61
Fursecroft W1 . . . . .3B 56
Furze St. E3 . . . . .1E 69
Fye Foot La. EC4 . . . . .5B 62
Fynes St. SW1 . . . . .3D 115

G

Gables Cl. SE5 . . . . .5F 141
Gabriel Ho. N1 . . . . .4F 17
SE11 . . . . .3B 116
SE16 . . . . .1B 124
Gabriels Wharf SE1 . . . . .2E 89
Gaddesden Ho. EC1 . . . . .3E 41
Gadebridge Ho. *SW3* *5F 111*
(off Cale St.)
Gadsden Ho. W10 . . . . .5A 30
Gadwall Cl. E16 . . . . .3F 73
Gage Brown Ho. *W10* *4E 51*
(off Bridge Cl.)
Gage Rd. E16 . . . . .1A 72
Gage St. WC1 . . . . .1A 60
Gainford Ho. E2 . . . . .2F 43
Gainford St. N1 . . . . .3D 17
Gainsborough Ct. SE16 . . . . .5A 122
W12 . . . . .4B 78
Gainsborough Ho. E14 . . . . . .5E 97
(Cassilis Rd.)
E14 . . . . .3A 68
(Victory Pl.)
SW1 . . . . .4E 115
Gainsborough Mans.
W14 . . . . .2A 130
Gainsborough Rd. E15 . . . . . .3F 49
Gainsborough St. E9 . . . . .5C 4
Gainsborough Studios E.
N1 . . . . .4D 19
Gainsborough Studios Nth.
N1 . . . . .4D 19
Gainsborough Studios Sth.
N1 . . . . .4D 19
Gainsborough Studios W.
N1 . . . . .4D 19
Gainsford St. SE1 . . . . .3B 92
Gairloch Ho. NW1 . . . . .1D 15
Gaitskell Ho. SE17 . . . . .2F 141
Gaitskell Way SE1 . . . . .4B 90
Gala Bingo
Camberwell **5C 140**
Stratford **3D 27**
Surrey Quays **1E 123**
Galaxy Bldg. E14 . . . . .3D 125
Galaxy Ho. EC2 . . . . .4E 41
Galbraith St. E14 . . . . .1B 126
Galena Arches W6 . . . . .4A 106
Galena Hgts. E20 . . . . .4C 6
Galena Rd. W6 . . . . .4A 106
Galen Pl. WC1 . . . . .2A 60

Gales Gdns. E2 . . . . .3A 44
Gale St. E3 . . . . .1E 69
Galleon Cl. SE16 . . . . .4C 94
Galleon Ho. E14 . . . . .4C 126
Galleons Vw. E14 . . . . .5C 98
Galleria Ct. SE15 . . . . .3C 142
Galleries, The NW8 . . . . .1C 32
Gallery, The E20 . . . . .5C 6
SE14 . . . . .5C 146
Gallery Apartments E1 . . . . . .3B 66
SE1 . . . . .5F 91
Gallery at London
Glassblowing, The **4F 91**
Gallery Ct. SE1 . . . . .5D 91
SW10 . . . . .3B 132
Galleywall Rd. SE16 . . . . .3F 121
Galleywall Rd. Trad. Est.
SE16 . . . . .4A 122
Galleywood Ho. W10 . . . . . . .1B 50
Gallions Rd. E16 . . . . .1F 105
SE7 . . . . .4F 129
(not continuous)
Gallions Rdbt. E16 . . . . .5F 77
Galsworthy Av. E14 . . . . .3A 68
Galsworthy Ho. W11 . . . . .4A 52
Galton St. W10 . . . . .3F 29
Galveston Ho. E1 . . . . .5F 45
Galway Cl. SE16 . . . . .1A 144
Galway Ho. E1 . . . . .1E 67
EC1 . . . . .3C 40
Galway St. EC1 . . . . .3C 40
Gambia St. SE1 . . . . .3A 90
Gambier Ho. EC1 . . . . .3C 40
Gandolfi St. SE15 . . . . .3F 141
Ganton St. W1 . . . . .5B 58
Garbett Ho. SE17 . . . . .2F 139
Garbutt Pl. W1 . . . . .2E 57
Garden Ct. EC4 . . . . .5D 61
NW8 . . . . .2D 33
W11 . . . . .1A 80
Garden Ho. SW7 . . . . .2A 110
Garden M. W2 . . . . .1E 81
Garden Museum, The **2B 116**
Garden Pl. E8 . . . . .4C 20
Garden Rd. NW8 . . . . .2C 32
Garden Row SE1 . . . . .2F 117
Garden St. E1 . . . . .2E 67
Garden Ter. SW1 . . . . .5D 115
SW7 . . . . .5A 84
Garden Wlk. EC2 . . . . .4F 41
Gardner Ct. EC1 . . . . .4F 39
Gardners La. EC4 . . . . .5B 62
Gard St. EC1 . . . . .2A 40
Garford St. E14 . . . . .1D 97
Garland Ct. E14 . . . . .1D 97
SE17 . . . . .4C 118
Garlands Ho. NW8 . . . . .5B 10
Garlick Hill EC4 . . . . .5C 62
Garnault M. EC1 . . . . .3E 39
Garnault Pl. EC1 . . . . .3E 39
Garner St. E2 . . . . .1E 43
Garnet Ho. E1 . . . . .2B 94
Garnet St. E1 . . . . .1B 94
Garnet Wlk. E6 . . . . .1A 76
Garnies Cl. SE15 . . . . .4B 142
Garrett Ho. SE1 . . . . .4F 89
Garrett St. EC1 . . . . .4C 40
Garrick Ct. *E8* *2C 20*
(off Jacaranda Gro.)
Garrick Ho. W1 . . . . .3F 85
SW1 . . . . .5F 59
Garrick Theatre **1F 87**
Garrick Yd. WC2 . . . . .5F 59
Garrison Rd. E3 . . . . .4D 25

Garsdale Ter. W14 . . . . .5C **108**
Garson Ho. W2 . . . . .5D **55**
Garston Ho. N1 . . . . .2F **17**
Garter Way SE16 . . . . .5D **95**
Garvary Rd. E16 . . . . .4A **74**
Garway Ct. E3 . . . . .1D **47**
Garway Rd. W2 . . . . .4F **53**
Gascoigne Pl. E2 . . . . .2B **42**
 (not continuous)
Gascony Av. NW6 . . . . .2D **9**
Gascony Pl. W12 . . . . .3D **79**
Gascoyne Ho. E9 . . . . .1F **23**
Gascoyne Rd. E9 . . . . .1E **23**
Gaselee St. E14 . . . . .2C **98**
Gaskin St. N1 . . . . .3F **17**
Gaspar Cl. SW5 . . . . .3A **110**
Gaspar M. SW5 . . . . .3A **110**
Gasson Ho. SE14 . . . . .3D **145**
Gastigny Ho. EC1 . . . . .3C **40**
Gataker Ho. SE16 . . . . .1A **122**
Gataker St. SE16 . . . . .1A **122**
Gatcombe Rd. E16 . . . . .2E **101**
Gate Cinema **2D 81**
Gateforth St. NW8 . . . . .5F **33**
Gate Hill Ct. W11 . . . . .2C **80**
Gate Ho. E3 . . . . .4A **24**
 N1 . . . . .2E **19**
Gatehouse Sq. SE1 . . . . .2C **90**
Gate Lodge W9 . . . . .1E **53**
Gately Ct. SE15 . . . . .4B **142**
Gate M. SW7 . . . . .5A **84**
Gatesborough St. EC2 . . . . . .4F **41**
Gates Ct. SE17 . . . . .1B **140**
Gatesden WC1 . . . . .3A **38**
Gate St. WC2 . . . . .3B **60**
Gate Theatre, The
 London **2D 81**
Gateway SE17 . . . . .2C **140**
Gateway Arc. N1 . . . . .5F **17**
Gateways, The SW3 . . . . .4A **112**
Gathorne St. E2 . . . . .1E **45**
Gatliff Cl. SW1 . . . . .1F **135**
Gatliff Rd. SW1 . . . . .1F **135**
Gattis Wharf N1 . . . . .5A **16**
Gatwick Ho. E14 . . . . .3B **68**
Gaugin Ct. SE16 . . . . .5F **121**
Gaumont Ter. W12 . . . . .4B **78**
Gaunt St. SE1 . . . . .1B **118**
Gautrey Sq. E6 . . . . .4C **76**
Gavel St. SE17 . . . . .3E **119**
Gaverick M. E14 . . . . .3D **125**
Gawber St. E2 . . . . .2B **44**
Gawthorne Ct. E3 . . . . .1D **47**
Gaydon Ho. W2 . . . . .1F **53**
Gayfere St. SW1 . . . . .2F **115**
Gayhurst SE17 . . . . .2E **141**
Gayhurst Ho. NW8 . . . . .4F **33**
Gayhurst Rd. E8 . . . . .1D **21**
Gaymead NW8 . . . . .4A **10**
Gay Rd. E15 . . . . .5D **27**
Gaysley Ho. SE11 . . . . .4D **117**
Gayton Ho. E3 . . . . .5E **47**
Gaywood St. SE1 . . . . .2F **117**
Gaza St. SE17 . . . . .1F **139**
Gaze Ho. E14 . . . . .4D **71**
Gazelle Ho. E15 . . . . .4F **7**
Gean Ct. E11 . . . . .1E **7**
Gedling Ct. SE1 . . . . .5C **92**
Gedling Pl. SE1 . . . . .1C **120**
Gees Ct. W1 . . . . .4E **57**
Gee St. EC1 . . . . .4B **40**
Geffrye Ct. N1 . . . . .1A **42**
Geffrye Est. N1 . . . . .1A **42**
Geffrye Mus. **1B 42**

Geffrye St. E2 . . . . .5B **20**
Geldart Rd. SE15 . . . . .5F **143**
Gem Ct. SE10 . . . . .5F **147**
Gemini Apartments E1 . . . . . .4C **42**
Gemini Bus. Cen. E16 . . . . . . .5E **49**
Gemini Bus. Est. SE14 . . .1E **145**
Gemini Ct. E1 . . . . .1D **93**
Gemini Ho. E3 . . . . .4D **25**
Genoa Ho. E1 . . . . .5E **45**
Geoff Cade Way E3 . . . . .1D **69**
Geoffrey Chaucer Way
 E3 . . . . .1C **68**
Geoffrey Ho. SE1 . . . . .1E **119**
George Beard Rd. SE8 . . . .4B **124**
George Belt Ho. E2 . . . . .2D **45**
George Ct. WC2 . . . . .1A **88**
George Eliot Ho. SE17 . . . .5B **118**
 SW1 . . . . .4C **114**
George Elliston Ho. SE1 . . .1D **143**
George Eyre Ho. NW8 . . . . . .1E **33**
George Gillett Ct. EC1 . . . . . . .4C **40**
George Ho. NW6 . . . . .1C **30**
George Hudson Twr.
 E15 . . . . .5A **26**
George Inn Yd. SE1 . . . . .3D **91**
George Lansbury Ho. E3 . . .3C **46**
George Leybourne Ho. E1 . . .5E **65**
 (off Fletcher St.)
George Lindgren Ho.
 SW6 . . . . .4C **130**
George Loveless Ho. E2 . . .2C **42**
George Lowe Ct. W2 . . . . . . .1F **53**
George Mathers Rd.
 SE11 . . . . .3F **117**
George M. NW1 . . . . .3B **36**
George Padmore Ho. E8 . . .3E **21**
George Peabody Ct.
 NW1 . . . . .1F **55**
George Row SE16 . . . . .5D **93**
George Scott Ho. E1 . . . . .3D **67**
George's Sq. SW6 . . . . .2C **130**
George St. E16 . . . . .4B **72**
 W1 . . . . .3B **56**
Georgette Pl. SE10 . . . . .5C **148**
George Vale Ho. E2 . . . . .1E **43**
George Walter Ct. SE16 . . .4C **122**
George Yd. EC3 . . . . .4E **63**
 W1 . . . . .5E **57**
Georgia Ct. SE16 . . . . .2E **121**
Georgiana St. NW1 . . . . .3B **14**
Georgian Ct. E9 . . . . .3C **22**
Georgian Ho. E16 . . . . .2D **101**
 N1 . . . . .3A **20**
Georgina Gdns. E2 . . . . .2C **42**
Geraldine St. SE11 . . . . .2F **117**
Gerald M. SW1 . . . . .3E **113**
Gerald Rd. SW1 . . . . .3E **113**
Gerard Pl. E9 . . . . .1D **23**
Gerards Cl. SE16 . . . . .1B **144**
Germander Way E15 . . . . .3F **49**
Gernon Rd. E3 . . . . .1F **45**
Gerrard Ho. SE14 . . . . .5C **144**
Gerrard Pl. W1 . . . . .5E **59**
Gerrard Rd. N1 . . . . .5F **17**
Gerrard St. W1 . . . . .5D **59**
Gerridge Ct. SE1 . . . . .1E **117**
 (off Gerridge St.)
Gerridge St. SE1 . . . . .1E **117**
Gerry Raffles Sq. E15 . . . . . . .5E **7**
Gertrude St. SW10 . . . . .3C **132**
Gervase St. SE15 . . . . .4A **144**
Gherkin, The **3A 64**
Gibbings Ho. SE1 . . . . .5A **90**
Gibbins Rd. E15 . . . . .2C **26**

Gibbon Ho. NW8 . . . . .5E **33**
Gibbon's Rents SE1 . . . . .3F **91**
Gibbs Grn. W14 . . . . .5B **108**
 (not continuous)
Gibraltar Wlk. E2 . . . . .3C **42**
Gibson Cl. E1 . . . . .4C **44**
Gibson Rd. SE11 . . . . .4C **116**
Gibson Sq. N1 . . . . .3E **17**
Gibson Sq. Gdns. N1 . . . . .3E **17**
Gibson St. SE10 . . . . .1F **149**
Gielgud Theatre **5D 59**
Giffin Sq. Mkt. SE8 . . . . .4D **147**
Giffin St. SE8 . . . . .4D **147**
Gifford Ho. SE10 . . . . .1E **149**
 SW1 . . . . .1B **136**
Gifford St. N1 . . . . .2A **16**
Gilbert Bri. EC2 . . . . .2C **62**
 (off Wood St.)
Gilbert Ho. E2 . . . . .2D **45**
 (off Usk St.)
 EC2 . . . . .2C **62**
 SE8 . . . . .2E **147**
 SW1 . . . . .1A **136**
 SW8 . . . . .4F **137**
Gilbert Pl. WC1 . . . . .2F **59**
Gilbert Rd. SE11 . . . . .4E **117**
Gilbert Sheldon Ho. W2 . . .1E **55**
Gilbertson Ho. E14 . . . . .1E **125**
Gilbert St. E15 . . . . .1F **7**
 W1 . . . . .4E **57**
Gilbey Ho. NW1 . . . . .2F **13**
Gilbeys Yd. NW1 . . . . .2E **13**
Gildea St. W1 . . . . .2A **58**
Giles Ho. W11 . . . . .4D **53**
Gillam Ho. SE16 . . . . .4B **122**
Gill Av. E16 . . . . .5C **70**
Gillender St. E3 . . . . .4B **48**
 E14 . . . . .4B **48**
Gillfoot NW1 . . . . .1B **36**
Gillies Ho. NW6 . . . . .2D **11**
Gillingham M. SW1 . . . . .3B **114**
Gillingham Row SW1 . . . . .3B **114**
Gillingham St. SW1 . . . . .3A **114**
Gillison Wlk. SE16 . . . . .1E **121**
Gillman Ho. E2 . . . . .5E **21**
Gillray Ho. SW10 . . . . .3D **133**
Gill St. E14 . . . . .4C **68**
Gilman Ho. N1 . . . . .1D **17**
Gilpin Cl. W2 . . . . .1D **55**
Gilray Ho. W2 . . . . .5D **55**
Gilston Rd. SW10 . . . . .1C **132**
Giltspur St. EC1 . . . . .3A **62**
Ginger Apartments SE1 . . . .4C **92**
Giralda Cl. E16 . . . . .2D **75**
Giraud St. E14 . . . . .3F **69**
Girdler's Rd. W14 . . . . .3E **107**
Girling Ho. N1 . . . . .4F **19**
Gironde Rd. SW6 . . . . .5C **130**
Girton Vs. W10 . . . . .3E **51**
Gisburn Ho. SE15 . . . . .3E **143**
Gissing Wlk. N1 . . . . .2E **17**
Giverny Ho. SE16 . . . . .5D **95**
Glade, The E8 . . . . .1D **21**
Glade Wlk. E20 . . . . .4A **6**
Gladstone Ct. NW6 . . . . .1C **10**
 SW1 . . . . .4E **115**
Gladstone Ct. Bus. Cen.
 SW8 . . . . .5A **136**
Gladstone Ho. E14 . . . . .4D **69**
Gladstone M. NW6 . . . . .1B **8**
Gladstone Pl. E3 . . . . .5C **24**
Gladstone St. SE1 . . . . .2F **117**
Gladwin Ho. NW1 . . . . .1C **36**
Gladys Rd. NW6 . . . . .1E **9**

Glaisher St. SE8 . . . . .2E 147
Glamis Pl. E1 . . . . .5C 66
Glamis Rd. E1 . . . . .5C 66
Glasgow Ho. W9 . . . . .1A 32
Glasgow Ter. SW1 . . . . .1B 136
Glasier Ct. E15 . . . . .1F 27
Glaskin M. E9 . . . . .5A 4
Glass Building, The NW1 . . . .2F 13
Glass Foundry Yd. E13 . . . . .1F 73
Glasshill St. SE1 . . . . .4A 90
Glass Ho. WC2 . . . . .4F 59
Glass House, The SE1 . . . . . .5F 91
Glasshouse Flds. E1 . . . . . . .5D 67
      (not continuous)
Glasshouse St. W1 . . . . .1C 86
Glasshouse Wlk. SE11 . . . . .5A 116
Glasshouse Yd. EC1 . . . . . . .5B 40
Glass St. E2 . . . . .4A 44
Glassworks Studios E2 . . . . .2A 42
Glastonbury Ct. SE14 . . . . . .4C 144
Glastonbury Ho. SW1 . . . . . .5F 113
Glastonbury Pl. E1 . . . . .4B 66
Glaucus St. E3 . . . . .1F 69
Glazbury Rd. W14 . . . . .4A 108
Glebe Ct. E3 . . . . .2F 47
Glebe Ho. SE16 . . . . .2A 122
Glebe Pl. SW3 . . . . .2F 133
Glebe Rd. E8 . . . . .2B 20
Gledhow Gdns. SW5 . . . . . .4B 110
Gledstanes Rd. W14 . . . . . .1A 130
Glenaffric Av. E14 . . . . .4D 127
Glenallan Ho. W14 . . . . .4B 108
Glenavon Rd. E15 . . . . .1F 27
Glencairne Cl. E16 . . . . .1D 75
Glencoe Mans. SW9 . . . . . . .5D 139
Glendower Pl. SW7 . . . . .3D 111
Gleneagles Cl. SE16 . . . . . . .1F 143
Glenfinlas Way SE5 . . . . . .4A 140
Glenforth St. SE10 . . . . .1C 128
Glengall Bus. Cen.
      SE15 . . . . .2C 142
Glengall Gro. E14 . . . . .1A 126
Glengall Pas. NW6 . . . . .3D 9
Glengall Rd. NW6 . . . . .4C 8
      SE15 . . . . .2C 142
Glengall Ter. SE15 . . . . .2C 142
Glengariff Mans. SW9 . . . . .5D 139
Glengarnock Av. E14 . . . . . .4C 126
Glen Ho. E16 . . . . .4E 105
Glenister Rd. SE10 . . . . . . .5B 128
Glenister St. E16 . . . . .3E 105
Glenkerry Ho. E14 . . . . .3B 70
Glenridding NW1 . . . . .1C 36
Glenrose Ct. SE1 . . . . .1F 119
      (off Long La.)
Glenroy St. W12 . . . . .3B 50
Glenshaw Mans. SW9 . . . . .5D 139
Glen Ter. E14 . . . . .4C 98
Glenthorne M. W6 . . . . .4A 106
Glenthorne Rd. W6 . . . . . . .3A 106
Glentworth St. NW1 . . . . . . .5C 34
Glenville Gro. SE8 . . . . .5C 146
Glenworth Av. E14 . . . . .4D 127
Gliddon Rd. W14 . . . . .4F 107
Global App. E3 . . . . .1A 48
Globe Pond Rd. SE16 . . . . . .3F 95
Globe Rd. E1 . . . . .3C 44
      E2 . . . . .1B 44
Globe Rope Wlk. E14 . . . . . .4A 126
Globe St. SE1 . . . . .1D 119
Globe Ter. E2 . . . . .2C 44
GLOBE TOWN 2D 45
Globe Town Mkt. E2 . . . . . . .2D 45
Globe Vw. EC4 . . . . .5B 62

Globe Wharf SE16 . . . . .1E 95
Globe Yd. W1 . . . . .4F 57
Gloster Ridley Ct. E14 . . . . .4C 68
Gloucester W14 . . . . .3B 108
Gloucester Arc. SW7 . . . . . .3B 110
Gloucester Av. NW1 . . . . . . .2D 13
Gloucester Cir. SE10 . . . . . .4C 148
Gloucester Ct. EC3 . . . . . . .1A 92
      SE1 . . . . .5C 120
            (Rolls Rd.)
      SE1 . . . . .1C 118
            (Swan St.)
Gloucester Cres. NW1 . . . . .3F 13
Gloucester Gdns. W2 . . . . . .3B 54
Gloucester Ga. NW1 . . . . . . .5F 13
      (not continuous)
Gloucester Ga. Bri. NW1 . . . .5F 13
Gloucester Ga. M. NW1 . . . . .5F 13
Gloucester Ho. E16 . . . . .2E 101
      (off Gatcombe Rd.)
      NW6 . . . . .1E 31
      SW9 . . . . .4E 139
Gloucester M. W2 . . . . .4C 54
Gloucester M. W. W2 . . . . . .4B 54
Gloucester Pk. Apartments
      SW7 . . . . .3B 110
Gloucester Pl. NW1 . . . . .4B 34
      W1 . . . . .1C 56
Gloucester Pl. M. W1 . . . . . .2C 56
Gloucester Rd. SW7 . . . . . . .1B 110
Gloucester Sq. E2 . . . . .4D 21
      W2 . . . . .4E 55
      (not continuous)
Gloucester St. SW1 . . . . . . .1B 136
Gloucester Ter. W2 . . . . .3A 54
Gloucester Wlk. W8 . . . . . . .4E 81
Gloucester Way EC1 . . . . . . .3E 39
Glover Ho. NW6 . . . . .1C 10
Glynde M. SW3 . . . . .2A 112
Glynde Reach WC1 . . . . . . .3A 38
Glyn Mans. W14 . . . . .3A 108
Glyn St. SE11 . . . . .1B 138
Goater's All. SW6 . . . . .5C 130
Godalming Rd. E14 . . . . .2F 69
Godbold Rd. E15 . . . . .3F 49
Goddard Ho. SE11 . . . . .4F 117
Godfree Ct. SE1 . . . . .4D 91
Godfrey Ho. EC1 . . . . .3D 41
Godfrey Pl. E2 . . . . .3B 42
Godfrey St. E15 . . . . .5C 26
      SW3 . . . . .5A 112
Goding St. SE11 . . . . .5A 116
Godliman St. EC4 . . . . .4B 62
Godolphin Ho. NW3 . . . . . . .1F 11
Godolphin Rd. W12 . . . . . . .3A 78
      (not continuous)
Godson St. N1 . . . . .5D 17
Godson Yd. NW6 . . . . .3D 31
Godstone Ho. SE1 . . . . .1E 119
Godwin Cl. N1 . . . . .5C 18
Godwin Ct. NW1 . . . . .5C 14
Godwin Ho. E2 . . . . .5C 20
      NW6 . . . . .5F 9
      (not continuous)
Golborne Gdns. W10 . . . . . .5A 30
      (not continuous)
Golborne M. W10 . . . . .1A 52
Golborne Rd. W10 . . . . .1A 52
Goldbeaters Ho. W1 . . . . . . .4E 59
      (off Manette St.)
Goldcrest Cl. E16 . . . . .1D 75
Golden Cross M. W11 . . . . . .3B 52
Golden Hinde 2D 91
Golden Hind Pl. SE8 . . . . . . .4A 124

Golden Jubilee Bridges 3B 88
Golden La. EC1 . . . . .4B 40
Golden La. Campus EC1 . . . .5C 40
Golden La. Est. EC1 . . . . . . .5B 40
Golden Lane Leisure Cen.
      . . . . .5B 40
Golden Plover Cl. E16 . . . . . .3E 73
Golden Sq. W1 . . . . .5C 58
Goldfinch Ct. E3 . . . . .5D 25
      (off Four Seasons Cl.)
Goldhawk Ind. Est. W6 . . . . .1A 106
Goldhawk M. W12 . . . . .5A 78
Goldhawk Rd. W12 . . . . .1A 106
Goldhurst Mans. NW6 . . . . . .1C 10
Goldhurst Ter. NW6 . . . . .2F 9
Golding St. E1 . . . . .4E 65
      (not continuous)
Golding Ter. E1 . . . . .3E 65
Goldington Bldgs. NW1 . . . . .4D 15
Goldington Cres. NW1 . . . . . .5D 15
Goldington St. NW1 . . . . . . .5D 15
Goldman Cl. E2 . . . . .4D 43
Goldney Rd. W9 . . . . .5D 31
Goldsboro' Rd. SW8 . . . . . . .5E 137
Goldsborough Ho. E14 . . . . .1A 148
Goldsmith Ct. WC2 . . . . .3A 60
Goldsmith Rd. SE15 . . . . . . .5E 143
Goldsmiths College 5A 146
Goldsmith's Pl. NW6 . . . . . . .4F 9
Goldsmith's Row E2 . . . . . . .1D 43
Goldsmith's Sq. E2 . . . . .5E 21
Goldsmith St. EC2 . . . . .3C 62
Goldsworthy Gdns. SE16 . . . .4C 122
Goldthorpe NW1 . . . . .4B 14
Goldwing Cl. E16 . . . . .4E 73
Gomm Rd. SE16 . . . . .2B 122
Gonson St. SE8 . . . . .3F 147
Gooch Ho. EC1 . . . . .1D 61
Goodfaith Ho. E14 . . . . .1A 98
Goodge Pl. W1 . . . . .2C 58
Goodge St. W1 . . . . .2C 58
Goodhart Pl. E14 . . . . .5A 68
Goodhope Ho. E14 . . . . .1A 98
Goodman's Ct. E1 . . . . .5B 64
Goodman's Stile E1 . . . . . . .3D 65
Goodmans Yd. E1 . . . . .5B 64
Goodrich Ct. W10 . . . . .4D 51
Goodrich Ho. E2 . . . . .5C 22
Goodspeed Ho. E14 . . . . . . .1A 98
Goods Way N1 . . . . .5F 15
Goodway Gdns. E14 . . . . . . .3D 71
Goodwill Ho. E14 . . . . .1A 98
Goodwin Cl. SE16 . . . . .2C 120
Goodwins Ct. WC2 . . . . .5F 59
Goodwood Ct. W1 . . . . .1A 58
Goodwood Ho. SE14 . . . . . . .5F 145
Goodwood Rd. SE14 . . . . . . .5F 145
Goodyear Pl. SE5 . . . . .3C 140
Goodyer Ho. SW1 . . . . .5D 115
Goose Sq. E6 . . . . .4B 76
Gophir La. EC4 . . . . .5D 63
Gopsall St. N1 . . . . .4E 19
Gordon Cotts. W8 . . . . .4E 81
Gordon Ho. E1 . . . . .5C 66
      SW1 . . . . .2C 114
Gordon Mans. W14 . . . . .1D 107
      WC1 . . . . .5D 37
Gordon Pl. W8 . . . . .4E 81
Gordon Rd. E15 . . . . .1C 6
Gordon Sq. WC1 . . . . .4C 37
Gordon St. WC1 . . . . .4D 37
Gorefield Ho. NW6 . . . . .5E 9
Gorefield Pl. NW6 . . . . .5D 9
Gore Ho. N1 . . . . .1D 17

Gore Rd. E9 . . . . .3C 22
Gore St. SW7 . . . . .1C 110
Gorham Ho. SE16 . . . . . . .5E 95
Gorham Pl. W11 . . . . .1F 79
Goring St. EC3 . . . . .3A 64
Gorleston St. W14 . . . . . . .3A 108
(not continuous)
Gorse Cl. E16 . . . . .4D 73
Gorsefield Ho. E14 . . . . . . .5D 69
Gorsuch Pl. E2 . . . . .2B 42
Gorsuch St. E2 . . . . .2B 42
Gosfield St. W1 . . . . .1B 58
Gosford Ho. E3 . . . . .1C 46
Goslett Yd. WC2 . . . . .4E 59
Gosling Ho. E1 . . . . .5B 66
Gosling Way SW9 . . . . . . .5E 139
Gosse Ct. N1 . . . . .3A 20
Gosset St. E2 . . . . .2C 42
Gosterwood St. SE8 . . . . . .2A 146
Goston Ga. SW8 . . . . .5B 138
Goswell Pl. EC1 . . . . .3A 40
Goswell Rd. EC1 . . . . .1F 39
Gothic Ct. SE5 . . . . .4B 140
Gough Ho. N1 . . . . .3A 18
Gough Sq. EC4 . . . . .3E 61
Gough St. WC1 . . . . .4C 38
Gough Wlk. E14 . . . . .4D 69
Gouldman Ho. E1 . . . . .5B 44
Goulston St. E1 . . . . .3B 64
Govan St. E2 . . . . .4E 21
Gowan Ho. E2 . . . . .3C 42
Gower Ct. WC1 . . . . .4C 36
Gower Ho. SE17 . . . . .5C 118
Gower M. WC1 . . . . .2E 59
Gower M. Mans. WC1 . . . . . .1E 59
Gower Pl. WC1 . . . . .4C 36
Gower St. WC1 . . . . .4C 36
Gower's Wlk. E1 . . . . .3D 65
Gracechurch St. EC3 . . . . . .5E 63
Gracehill E1 . . . . .1C 66
Grace Ho. SE11 . . . . .2C 138
Grace Jones Cl. E8 . . . . . . .1D 21
Grace Pl. E3 . . . . .3A 48
Graces All. E1 . . . . .5D 65
Graces M. NW8 . . . . .1C 32
Grace St. E3 . . . . .3A 48
Graduate Pl. SE1 . . . . .1F 119
Grafton Chambers NW1 . . . .3E 37
Grafton Ho. E3 . . . . .3D 47
SE8 . . . . .1B 146
Grafton M. W1 . . . . .5B 36
Grafton Pl. NW1 . . . . .3D 37
Grafton St. W1 . . . . .1A 86
Grafton Way W1 . . . . .5B 36
(not continuous)
WC1 . . . . .5B 36
Graham Ct. SE14 . . . . .2D 145
Graham St. N1 . . . . .1A 40
Graham Ter. SW1 . . . . .4D 113
Grainger Ct. SE5 . . . . .5B 140
Grainstore, The E16 . . . . . .5F 73
Grampians, The W6 . . . . . .5D 79
Granary Ct. E15 . . . . .4E 7
Granary Rd. E1 . . . . .5F 43
Granary Sq. N1 . . . . .4F 15
Granary St. NW1 . . . . .4D 15
Granby Pl. SE1 . . . . .5D 89
Granby St. E2 . . . . .4C 42
(not continuous)
Granby Ter. NW1 . . . . .1B 36
Grand Av. EC1 . . . . .1A 62
(not continuous)
Grand Connaught Rooms . . .3B 60
Grand Junc. Wharf N1 . . . . .1B 40

Grand Union Canal Wlk.
W10 . . . . .4B 28
Grand Union Cen. W10 . . . .4E 29
Grand Union Cl. W9 . . . . . .1C 52
Grand Union Cres. E8 . . . . .3E 21
Grand Union Ho. N1 . . . . . .3A 20
Grand Union Wlk. NW1 . . . .2A 14
Grand Vitesse Ind. Cen.
SE1 . . . . .3A 90
Grand Wlk. E1 . . . . .4A 46
Grange, The SE1 . . . . .1B 120
W14 . . . . .4B 108
Grange Ct. WC2 . . . . .4C 60
Grangefield NW1 . . . . .1E 15
Grange Ho. SE1 . . . . .2B 120
Grange Pl. NW6 . . . . .2D 9
Grange Rd. SE1 . . . . .2A 120
Grange St. N1 . . . . .4E 19
Grange Wlk. SE1 . . . . .1A 120
Grange Wlk. M. SE1 . . . . . .2A 120
Grange Way NW6 . . . . .2D 9
Grange Yd. SE1 . . . . .2B 120
Granite Apartments E15 . . . .4E 7
Gransden Av. E8 . . . . .2A 22
Gransden Ho. SE8 . . . . . . .5B 124
Grantbridge St. N1 . . . . . . .5A 18
Grantham Ct. SE16 . . . . . . .4D 95
Grantham Ho. SE15 . . . . . .3E 143
Grantham Pl. W1 . . . . .3F 85
Grantley Ho. SE14 . . . . . . .2D 145
Grantley St. E1 . . . . .3D 45
Grant Museum of Zoology . . .5D 37
Grants Quay Wharf EC3 . . . .1E 91
Grant St. N1 . . . . .5D 17
Grantully Rd. W9 . . . . .3F 31
Granville Ct. N1 . . . . .3E 19
SE14 . . . . .4F 145
Granville Ho. E14 . . . . .4D 69
Granville Mans. W12 . . . . . .4C 78
Granville Pl. SW6 . . . . .5F 131
W1 . . . . .4D 57
Granville Rd. NW6 . . . . .1D 31
(not continuous)
Granville Sq. SE15 . . . . . . .4A 142
WC1 . . . . .3C 38
Granville St. WC1 . . . . .3C 38
Grape St. WC2 . . . . .3F 59
Graphite Apartments, The
N1 . . . . .1D 41
Graphite Sq. SE11 . . . . . . .5B 116
Grasmere NW1 . . . . .3A 36
Grasmere Point SE15 . . . . .4B 144
Graspan Royal Marines Memorial
. . .2E 87
Gratton Rd. W14 . . . . .2F 107
Gravel La. E1 . . . . .3B 64
Gravely Ho. SE8 . . . . .3F 123
Gray Ct. E1 . . . . .1A 68
Gray Ho. SE17 . . . . .5C 118
Grayling Cl. E16 . . . . .4F 49
Grayling Sq. E2 . . . . .2E 43
Gray's Inn 1C 60
Gray's Inn Bldgs. EC1 . . . . .5D 39
(off Rosebery Av.)
Gray's Inn Pl. WC1 . . . . . . .2C 60
Gray's Inn Rd. WC1 . . . . . . .2A 38
Gray's Inn Sq. WC1 . . . . . . .1D 61
Grayson Ho. EC1 . . . . .3C 40
Gray St. SE1 . . . . .5E 89
Gray's Yd. W1 . . . . .4E 57
Gt. Arthur Ho. EC1 . . . . .5B 40
Gt. Bell All. EC2 . . . . .3D 63
Gt. Castle St. W1 . . . . .3A 58
Gt. Central St. NW1 . . . . . . .1B 56

Gt. Chapel St. W1 . . . . .3D 59
Gt. Church La. W6 . . . . .5E 107
Gt. College St. SW1 . . . . . . .1F 115
Great Cft. WC1 . . . . .3A 38
Gt. Cross Av. SE10 . . . . . . .5E 149
Gt. Cumberland M. W1 . . . . .4B 56
Gt. Cumberland Pl. W1 . . . . .3B 56
Gt. Dover St. SE1 . . . . .5C 90
Gt. Eastern Ent. Cen. E14 . . .5F 97
Gt. Eastern Rd. E15 . . . . . . .1D 27
Gt. Eastern St. EC2 . . . . . . .3F 41
Gt. Eastern Wlk. EC2 . . . . . .2A 64
Gt. Eastern Wharf SW11 . . . .4A 134
Greater London Ho. NW1 . . .5B 14
Gt. George St. SW1 . . . . . . .5E 87
Gt. Guildford Bus. Sq. SE1 . .3B 90
Gt. Guildford St. SE1 . . . . . .2B 90
Great Hall 1C 134
Gt. James St. WC1 . . . . .1B 60
Gt. Marlborough St. W1 . . . . .4B 58
Gt. Maze Pond SE1 . . . . . . .4E 91
Gt. Newport St. WC2 . . . . . .5F 59
Gt. New St. EC4 . . . . .3E 61
Greatorex Ho. E1 . . . . .1D 65
Greatorex St. E1 . . . . .1D 65
Gt. Ormond St. WC1 . . . . . . .1A 60
Gt. Percy St. WC1 . . . . .2C 38
Gt. Peter St. SW1 . . . . .2D 115
Gt. Portland St. W1 . . . . .5A 36
Gt. Pulteney St. W1 . . . . . . .5C 58
Gt. Queen St. WC2 . . . . . . .4A 60
Gt. Russell Mans. WC1 . . . . .2F 59
Gt. Russell St. WC1 . . . . . . .1B 60
Great St Helen's EC3 . . . . . .3F 63
Great St Thomas Apostle
EC4 . . . . .5C 62
Gt. Scotland Yd. SW1 . . . . . .3F 87
Gt. Smith St. SW1 . . . . .1E 115
Gt. Suffolk St. SE1 . . . . .3A 90
Gt. Sutton St. EC1 . . . . .5A 40
Gt. Swan All. EC2 . . . . .3D 63
Gt. Titchfield St. W1 . . . . . . .5A 36
Gt. Tower St. EC3 . . . . .5F 63
Gt. Trinity La. EC4 . . . . .5C 62
Great Turnstile WC1 . . . . . . .2C 60
Gt. Turnstile Ho. WC1 . . . . . .2C 60
Gt. Western Rd. W9 . . . . . . .5C 30
W11 . . . . .5C 30
Gt. West Rd. W6 . . . . .5A 106
Gt. Winchester St. EC2 . . . . .3E 63
Gt. Windmill St. W1 . . . . . . .5D 59
Great Yd. SE1 . . . . .4A 92
Greaves Cotts. E14 . . . . . . .2A 68
Greaves Twr. SW10 . . . . . . .4C 132
Grebe Ct. E14 . . . . .5C 98
SE8 . . . . .2B 146
Greek Ct. W1 . . . . .4E 59
Greek St. W1 . . . . .4E 59
Greenacre Sq. SE16 . . . . . .4E 95
Greenan Ct. E2 . . . . .3D 45
Green Arbour Ct. EC1 . . . . . .3F 61
Greenaway Ho. NW8 . . . . . .3B 10
WC1 . . . . .3D 39
Green Bank E1 . . . . .3F 93
Greenberry St. NW8 . . . . . . .1F 33
Greencoat Mans. SW1 . . . . .2C 114
Greencoat Pl. SW1 . . . . . . .3C 114
Greencoat Row SW1 . . . . . .2C 114
Greencourt Ho. E1 . . . . .5D 45
Greencroft Cl. E6 . . . . .2F 75
Greencroft Gdns. NW6 . . . . .2F 9
Green Dragon Ct. SE1 . . . . .3D 91
Green Dragon Ho. WC2 . . . .3A 60
Green Dragon Yd. E1 . . . . . .2D 65

Greene Ct. SE14 . . . . .3D 145
Greene Ho. SE1 . . . . .1D 119
Greenfell Mans. SE8 . . . . . .2F 147
Greenfield Rd. E1 . . . . .2E 65
Greenham Cl. SE1 . . . . .5D 89
Greenham Ho. E9 . . . . .3B 22
Greenheath Bus. Cen. E2 . .4A 44
Greenhill's Rents EC1 . . . . . .1F 61
Green Hundred Rd.
  SE15 . . . . .3E 143
Greenland Ho. E1 . . . . .5F 45
Greenland M. SE8 . . . . .1E 145
Greenland Pl. NW1 . . . . .3A 14
Greenland Quay SE16 . . . . .3E 123
Greenland Rd. NW1 . . . . .3A 14
Greenland St. NW1 . . . . .3A 14
Greenman St. N1 . . . . .2B 18
Green M. N1 . . . . .2E 41
Green Park
  London 3A 86
Green Pl. SE10 . . . . .4A 100
Greenroof Way SE10 . . . . . .2C 128
Green's Ct. W1 . . . . .5D 59
  W11 . . . . .3B 80
Greenshields Ind. Est.
  E16 . . . . .3F 101
Green St. W1 . . . . .5C 56
Green Ter. EC1 . . . . .3E 39
Green Wlk. SE1 . . . . .2F 119
Greenway E15 . . . . .4C 26
  E20 . . . . .3F 25
Greenwell St. W1 . . . . .5A 36
Greenwich 4B 148
Greenwich Bus. Pk. SE10 . .4A 148
Greenwich Centre, The 5B 128
Greenwich Chu. St.
  SE10 . . . . .2C 148
Greenwich Ct. E1 . . . . .3A 66
Greenwich Cres. E6 . . . . .2F 75
Greenwich High Rd. SE10 . .5F 147
Greenwich Mkt. SE10 . . . . .3C 148
GREENWICH MILLENNIUM VILLAGE
  . . . . .2C 128
Greenwich Park 4E 149
Greenwich Pk. St. SE10 . . .1E 149
Greenwich Peninsula Ecology Pk.
  . . . . .1D 129
Greenwich Picturehouse . . .4C 148
Greenwich Quay SE8 . . . . . .3F 147
Greenwich Shop. Pk. SE7 . .4F 129
Greenwich Sth. St. SE10 . . .5B 148
Greenwich Theatre 4C 148
Greenwich Vw. Pl. E14 . . . .2F 125
Greenwich Yacht Club 1D 129
Greenwood Ho. EC1 . . . . . . .3D 39
Greenwood Rd. E8 . . . . .1E 21
Greenwood Theatre 4E 91
Green Yd. WC1 . . . . .4C 38
Green Yard, The EC3 . . . . . .4F 63
Greet Ho. SE1 . . . . .5E 89
Greet St. SE1 . . . . .3E 89
Gregory Pl. W8 . . . . .4F 81
Greig Ter. SE17 . . . . .2A 140
Grenada Ho. E14 . . . . .5C 68
Grenade St. E14 . . . . .5C 68
Grenadier St. E16 . . . . .3D 105
Grenard Cl. SE15 . . . . .5D 143
Grendon Ho. E9 . . . . .2B 22
  N1 . . . . .1B 38
Grendon St. NW8 . . . . .4F 33
Grenfell Ho. SE5 . . . . .5B 140
Grenfell Rd. W11 . . . . .5E 51
Grenfell Twr. W11 . . . . .5E 51
Grenfell Wlk. W11 . . . . .5E 51

Grenier Apartments SE15 . . .4A 144
Grenville Ho. E3 . . . . .1F 45
  SE8 . . . . .2D 147
  SW1 . . . . .2D 137
Grenville M. SW7 . . . . .3C 110
Grenville Pl. SW7 . . . . .2B 110
Grenville St. WC1 . . . . .5A 38
Gresham Rd. E16 . . . . .4A 74
Gresham St. EC2 . . . . .3B 62
Gresse St. W1 . . . . .2D 59
Gretton Ho. E2 . . . . .2B 44
Greville Hall NW6 . . . . .5A 10
Greville Ho. SW1 . . . . .1C 112
Greville M. NW6 . . . . .4F 9
Greville Pl. NW6 . . . . .5A 10
Greville Rd. NW6 . . . . .5F 9
Greville St. EC1 . . . . .2D 61
  (not continuous)
Greycoat Gdns. SW1 . . . . . .2D 115
Greycoat Pl. SW1 . . . . .2D 115
Greycoat St. SW1 . . . . .2D 115
Grey Eagle St. E1 . . . . .5C 42
Greyfriars Pas. EC1 . . . . .3A 62
Greyhound Ct. WC2 . . . . . . .5C 60
Greyhound Mans. W6 . . . . . .2A 130
Greyhound Rd. NW10 . . . . . .2A 28
  W6 . . . . .2A 130
  W14 . . . . .2A 130
Grey Ho. W12 . . . . .1A 78
Greystoke Ho. SE15 . . . . . . .3E 143
Greystoke Pl. EC4 . . . . .3D 61
Griffin Ho. E14 . . . . .4F 69
  N1 . . . . .4F 19
  (off Halcomb St.)
  W6 . . . . .4E 107
Griggs Ct. SE1 . . . . .2A 120
Grigg's Pl. SE1 . . . . .1A 120
Grimaldi Ho. N1 . . . . .5B 16
Grimsby Gro. E16 . . . . .4F 105
Grimsby St. E2 . . . . .3C 42
Grimsel Path SE5 . . . . .4A 140
Grimthorpe Ho. EC1 . . . . . . .4F 39
Grindall Ho. E1 . . . . .5A 44
Grindal St. SE1 . . . . .5D 89
Grindley Ho. E3 . . . . .1C 68
Grinling Pl. SE8 . . . . .3D 147
Grinstead Rd. SE8 . . . . .1F 145
Grisedale NW1 . . . . .2B 36
Grittleton Rd. W9 . . . . .4D 31
Grocer's Hall Ct. EC2 . . . . . .4D 63
Grocer's Hall Gdns. EC2 . . . .4D 63
Groombridge Ho. SE17 . . . .5A 120
Groombridge Rd. E9 . . . . . . .2D 23
Groome Ho. SE11 . . . . .4C 116
Groom Pl. SW1 . . . . .1E 113
Grosvenor Cotts. SW1 . . . . .3D 113
Grosvenor Ct. E14 . . . . .4B 68
  SE5 . . . . .3C 140
  W14 . . . . .1E 107
Grosvenor Ct. Mans. W2 . . .4B 56
Grosvenor Cres. SW1 . . . . . .5E 85
Grosvenor Cres. M. SW1 . . .5D 85
Grosvenor Est. SW1 . . . . . . .3E 115
Grosvenor Gdns. SW1 . . . . .1F 113
Grosvenor Gdns. M. E.
  SW1 . . . . .1A 114
Grosvenor Gdns. M. Nth.
  SW1 . . . . .2F 113
Grosvenor Gdns. M. Sth.
  SW1 . . . . .2A 114
Grosvenor Ga. W1 . . . . .1D 85
Grosvenor Hill W1 . . . . .5F 57
Grosvenor Hill Ct. W1 . . . . . .5F 57
Grosvenor Pk. SE5 . . . . .3B 140

Grosvenor Pl. SW1 . . . . .4E 85
Grosvenor Rd. SW1 . . . . . . .2F 135
Grosvenor Sq. W1 . . . . .5E 57
Grosvenor St. W1 . . . . .5F 57
Grosvenor Studios SW1 . . . .3D 113
Grosvenor Ter. SE5 . . . . .4A 140
Grosvenor Wharf Rd. E14 . . .4D 127
Grotto Ct. SE1 . . . . .4B 90
Grotto Pas. W1 . . . . .1E 57
Grove, The E15 . . . . .5F 7
Grove Cotts. SW3 . . . . .2A 134
Grove Ct. NW8 . . . . .2D 33
  SE15 . . . . .5A 142
  SW10 . . . . .1C 132
Grove Cres. Rd. E15 . . . . .5E 7
Grove Dwellings E1 . . . . .1B 66
Grove End Gdns. NW8 . . . . . .1D 33
Grove End Ho. NW8 . . . . .3D 33
Grove End Rd. NW8 . . . . .1D 33
Grove Gdns. NW8 . . . . .3A 34
Grove Hall Ct. E3 . . . . .1E 47
  NW8 . . . . .2C 32
Grove Ho. SW3 . . . . .2A 134
Groveland Ct. EC4 . . . . .4C 62
Grove Mans. W6 . . . . .5B 78
Grove M. W6 . . . . .1B 106
Grove Pas. E2 . . . . .5F 21
Grover Ho. SE11 . . . . .1C 138
Grove Rd. E3 . . . . .4E 23
Grove St. SE8 . . . . .3B 124
Grove Vs. E14 . . . . .5A 70
Grundy St. E14 . . . . .4F 69
Gtec Ho. E15 . . . . .1E 49
Guards Memorial 3E 87
Guards' Museum, The 5C 86
Guerin Sq. E3 . . . . .2B 46
Guildford Ct. SW8 . . . . .5A 138
Guildford Rd. E6 . . . . .4A 76
  SW8 . . . . .5A 138
Guildhall
  City 3D 63
Guildhall Art Gallery 3D 63
Guildhall Bldgs. EC2 . . . . . . .3D 63
Guildhall Library 3C 62
Guildhall Offices EC2 . . . . . .3C 62
Guildhall Yd. EC2 . . . . .3C 62
Guildhouse St. SW1 . . . . . . .3B 114
Guilford Pl. WC1 . . . . .5B 38
Guilford St. WC1 . . . . .5F 37
Guillemot Ct. SE8 . . . . .2B 146
Guinea Ct. E1 . . . . .5D 65
Guinea Point E14 . . . . .3A 68
Guinness Cl. E9 . . . . .2F 23
Guinness Ct. E1 . . . . .4B 64
  EC1 . . . . .3C 40
  NW8 . . . . .4A 12
  SE1 . . . . .4F 91
  SW3 . . . . .4B 112
Guinness Sq. SE1 . . . . .2F 119
Guinness Trust SW3 . . . . . . .4B 112
Guinness Trust Bldgs.
  SE11 . . . . .5F 117
  W6 . . . . .5C 106
Gulland Wlk. N1 . . . . .1C 18
Gullane Ho. E3 . . . . .1C 46
Gulliver's Ho. EC1 . . . . .5B 40
Gulliver St. SE16 . . . . .1B 124
Gulston Wlk. SW3 . . . . .4C 112
Gun Ho. E1 . . . . .3B 94
Gunmakers La. E3 . . . . .4A 24
Gunpowder Sq. EC4 . . . . . . .3E 61
  (not continuous)
Gun St. E1 . . . . .2B 64
Gunter Gro. SW10 . . . . .3B 132

Gunter Hall Studios
  SW10 . . . . .3B 132
Gunterstone Rd. W14 . . . .4F 107
Gunthorpe St. E1 . . . . .2C 64
Gunwhale Cl. SE16 . . . . . . .3E 95
Gun Wharf E1 . . . . .3B 94
Gun Wharf Bus. Cen. E3 . . . .4A 24
Gurdon Ho. E14 . . . . .3D 69
Gurdon Rd. SE7 . . . . .5E 129
Gurney Cl. E15 . . . . .2F 7
Gurney Ho. E2 . . . . .5E 21
Gurney Rd. E15 . . . . .2F 7
Guthrie Ct. SE1 . . . . .5E 89
Guthrie St. SW3 . . . . .5F 111
Gutter La. EC2 . . . . .3B 62
Guy St. SE1 . . . . .4E 91
Gwendwr Rd. W14 . . . . . . .5A 108
Gwen Morris Ho. SE5 . . . .5C 140
Gwent Cl. SE16 . . . . .2E 95
Gwilym Maries Ho. E2 . . . . .2F 43
Gwyn Cl. SW6 . . . . .5B 132
Gwynne Ho. E1 . . . . .2F 65
  SW1 . . . . .5D 113
  WC1 . . . . .3D 39
Gwynne Pl. WC1 . . . . .3C 38

H

Haarlem Rd. W14 . . . . .2D 107
Haberdasher Est. N1 . . . . . .2E 41
Haberdasher Pl. N1 . . . . . . .2E 41
Haberdasher St. N1 . . . . . . .2E 41
Habitat Sq. SE10 . . . . .1C 128
Hackford Rd. SW9 . . . . . . .5D 139
HACKNEY 1A 22
Hackney City Farm 1D 43
Hackney Rd. E2 . . . . .3A 42
HACKNEY WICK 4C 4
HACKNEY WICK 4B 4
Hackworth Point E3 . . . . . . .3F 47
Hacon Sq. E8 . . . . .1A 22
Haddo Ho. SE10 . . . . .3A 148
Haddonfield SE8 . . . . .4E 123
Haddon Hall St. SE1 . . . . . .2E 119
Haddo St. SE10 . . . . .3A 148
Hadfield Ho. E1 . . . . .4E 65
Hadleigh Cl. E1 . . . . .4B 44
Hadleigh Ho. E1 . . . . .4B 44
Hadleigh St. E2 . . . . .4C 44
Hadleigh Wlk. E6 . . . . .3A 76
Hadley St. NW1 . . . . .1F 13
  (not continuous)
Hadlow Ho. SE17 . . . . .5A 120
Hadrian Cl. E3 . . . . .4D 25
Hadrian Est. E2 . . . . .1E 43
Hadrian M. N7 . . . . .1C 16
Hadrian St. SE10 . . . . .5F 127
Hadstock Ho. NW1 . . . . . . .2E 37
HAGGERSTON 1B 20
Haggerston Rd. E8 . . . . . . .2B 20
Haggerston Studios E8 . . . . .3A 20
Hague St. E2 . . . . .3E 43
Haig Ho. E2 . . . . .1D 43
Hailsham Ho. NW8 . . . . . . .5F 33
Haines Cl. N1 . . . . .2F 19
Haines St. SW8 . . . . .4C 136
Hainton Cl. E1 . . . . .4A 66
Halcomb St. N1 . . . . .4F 19
Halcrow St. E1 . . . . .2A 66
Halcyon Wharf E1 . . . . .3E 93
Haldane Rd. SW6 . . . . .4C 130
Hale Ho. SW1 . . . . .5E 115
Hales Prior N1 . . . . .1B 38

Hales St. SE8 . . . . .5D 147
Hale St. E14 . . . . .5F 69
Half Moon Ct. EC1 . . . . . . .2B 62
Half Moon Cres. N1 . . . . . . .5C 16
  (not continuous)
Half Moon Pas. E1 . . . . . . .4C 64
  (not continuous)
Half Moon St. W1 . . . . .2A 86
Halford Rd. SW6 . . . . .3D 131
Haliwell Ho. NW6 . . . . .4F 9
Halkett Ho. E2 . . . . .4B 22
Halkin Arc. SW1 . . . . .1C 112
Halkin M. SW1 . . . . .1D 113
Halkin Pl. SW1 . . . . .1D 113
Halkin St. SW1 . . . . .5E 85
Hallam Ct. W1 . . . . .1A 58
Hallam Ho. SW1 . . . . .1C 136
Hallam M. W1 . . . . .1A 58
Hallam St. W1 . . . . .5A 36
Hall Apartments E3 . . . . . . .1C 68
Halley Ho. E2 . . . . .5E 21
  SE10 . . . . .5B 128
Halley St. E14 . . . . .2F 67
Hallfield Est. W2 . . . . .3B 54
  (not continuous)
Hall Ga. NW8 . . . . .2C 32
Halliday Ho. E1 . . . . .4E 65
Halliford St. N1 . . . . .1C 18
Halling Ho. SE1 . . . . .5E 91
Hallings Wharf Studios
  E15 . . . . .3D 27
Hallmark Ho. E14 . . . . .2E 69
Hall Pl. W2 . . . . .5D 33
  (not continuous)
Hall Rd. E15 . . . . .1E 7
  NW8 . . . . .3C 32
Hall St. EC1 . . . . .2A 40
Hallsville Rd. E16 . . . . .4B 72
Hall Twr. W2 . . . . .1E 55
Hallywell Cres. E6 . . . . .1C 76
Halo E15 . . . . .4C 26
Halpin Pl. SE17 . . . . .4E 119
Halsey Ho. WC1 . . . . .2B 60
Halsey M. SW3 . . . . .3B 112
Halsey St. SW3 . . . . .3B 112
Halstead Ct. N1 . . . . .1E 41
Halstow Rd. NW10 . . . . . . .3D 29
  SE10 . . . . .5D 129
Halton Cross St. N1 . . . . . . .3A 18
Halton Ho. N1 . . . . .2A 18
Halton Mans. N1 . . . . .2A 18
Halton Pl. N1 . . . . .3B 18
Halton Rd. N1 . . . . .1A 18
Halyard Ho. E14 . . . . .1C 126
Hambledon SE17 . . . . .2E 141
Hambley Ho. SE16 . . . . . . .4F 121
Hamella Ho. E9 . . . . .3A 4
Hamilton Cl. NW8 . . . . .3D 33
  SE16 . . . . .5A 96
Hamilton Ct. W9 . . . . .2B 32
Hamilton Gdns. NW8 . . . . . .2C 32
Hamilton Hall NW8 . . . . . . .1B 32
Hamilton Ho. E3 . . . . .3C 46
  E14 . . . . .5A 126
  (St Davids Sq.)
  E14 . . . . .5B 68
  (Victory Pl.)
  NW8 . . . . .2D 33
  W8 . . . . .4F 81
Hamilton Lodge E1 . . . . . . .5B 44
Hamilton M. W1 . . . . .4F 85
Hamilton Pl. W1 . . . . .3E 85
Hamilton Rd. E15 . . . . .3F 49
Hamilton Sq. SE1 . . . . .4E 91

Hamilton St. SE8 . . . . .4D 147
Hamilton Ter. NW8 . . . . . . .1A 32
Hamlet Ct. E3 . . . . .2E 47
  SE11 . . . . .5F 117
Hamlet Ind. Est. E9 . . . . . . .1E 25
Hamlets Way E3 . . . . .4B 46
Hamlet Way SE1 . . . . .4E 91
Hammerfield Ho. SW3 . . . . .5A 112
Hammersley Ho. SE14 . . . . .5C 144
Hammersley Rd. E16 . . . . . .2D 73
HAMMERSMITH 4C 106
Hammersmith Apollo 5C 106
Hammersmith Bri. Rd.
  W6 . . . . .5B 106
HAMMERSMITH BROADWAY
  . . . . .4C 106
Hammersmith B'way.
  W6 . . . . .4C 106
Hammersmith Fitness
  & Squash Cen. 5D 107
HAMMERSMITH FLYOVER
  . . . . .5B 106
Hammersmith Flyover
  W6 . . . . .5B 106
Hammersmith Gro. W6 . . . . .5B 78
Hammersmith Rd. W6 . . . . .4D 107
  W14 . . . . .4D 107
Hammett St. EC3 . . . . .5B 64
Hammond Ct. SE11 . . . . . . .5D 117
Hammond Ho. E14 . . . . . . .1E 125
  SE14 . . . . .5C 144
Hammond Lodge W9 . . . . . .1E 53
  (off Admiral Wlk.)
Hamond Sq. N1 . . . . .5F 19
Hampden Cl. NW1 . . . . .1E 37
Hampden Gurney St. W1 . . . .4B 56
Hampson Way SW8 . . . . . . .5B 138
Hampstead Ho. NW1 . . . . . .3B 36
Hampstead Lodge NW1 . . . .1F 55
Hampstead Rd. NW1 . . . . . .1B 36
Hampstead Theatre 1D 11
Hampstead Wlk. E3 . . . . . . .3C 24
Hampton Cl. NW6 . . . . .3D 31
Hampton Ct. SE16 . . . . . . .1E 95
Hampton St. SE1 . . . . .4A 118
  SE17 . . . . .4A 118
Hamston Ho. W8 . . . . .1A 110
Ham Yd. W1 . . . . .5D 59
Hanameel St. E16 . . . . .2E 101
Hanbury Ho. E1 . . . . .1D 65
  SW8 . . . . .3A 138
Hanbury M. N1 . . . . .4C 18
Hanbury St. E1 . . . . .1B 64
Hancock Nunn Ho. NW3 . . . .1B 12
Hancock Rd. E3 . . . . .2B 48
Hand Ct. WC1 . . . . .2C 60
Handel Bus. Cen. SW8 . . . . .2F 137
Handel House Mus. 5F 57
Handel Mans. WC1 . . . . . . .4A 38
Handel St. WC1 . . . . .4F 37
Handforth Rd. SW9 . . . . . . .4D 139
Handley Rd. E9 . . . . .2C 22
Hands Wlk. E16 . . . . .3E 73
Handyside St. N1 . . . . .4F 15
Hanging Sword All. EC4 . . . . .4E 61
Hankey Ho. SE1 . . . . .5E 91
Hankey Pl. SE1 . . . . .5E 91
Hannaford Wlk. E3 . . . . .4A 48
Hannah Bldg. E1 . . . . .4A 66
Hannah Mary Way SE1 . . . . .4E 121
Hannell Rd. SW6 . . . . .4A 130
Hannibal Rd. E1 . . . . .1C 66
Hanover Av. E16 . . . . .2D 101
Hanover Ct. E8 . . . . .4B 20

Hanover Flats W1	.5E 57
Hanover Gdns. SE11	.3D 139
Hanover Ga. NW1	.3A 34
Hanover Ga. Mans. NW1	.4A 34
Hanover Ho. E14	.2C 96
NW8	.1F 33
SE16	.5D 95
Hanover Pl. E3	.3B 46
WC2	.4A 60
Hanover Sq. W1	.4A 58
Hanover Steps W2	.4A 56
Hanover St. W1	.4A 58
Hanover Ter. NW1	.3B 34
Hanover Ter. M. NW1	.3A 34
Hanover Yd. N1	.5A 18
Hansard M. W14	.4E 79
Hans Ct. SW3	.1B 112
Hans Cres. SW1	.1B 112
Hanseatic Wlk. EC4	.1D 91
Hansel Rd. NW6	.2E 31
Hanson Ho. E1	.4E 65
Hanson St. W1	.1B 58
Hans Pl. SW1	.1B 112
Hans Rd. SW3	.1B 112
Hans St. SW1	.2C 112
Hanway Pl. W1	.3D 59
Hanway St. W1	.3D 59
Hanwell Ho. W2	.2D 53
Hanworth Ho. SE5	.4F 139
Harad's Pl. E1	.1E 93
Harben Pde. NW3	.1C 10
Harben Rd. NW6	.1C 10
Harbet Rd. W2	.2E 55
Harbinger Rd. E14	.4F 125
Harbledown Ho. SE1	.5D 91
Harbord Ho. SE16	.3D 123
Harbour Club Notting Hill	**.1E 53**
Harbour Exchange Sq.	
E14	.5A 98
Harbour Quay E14	.3B 98
Harcourt Bldgs. EC4	.5D 61
Harcourt Ho. W1	.3F 57
Harcourt St. W1	.2A 56
Harcourt Ter. SW10	.1A 132
Harding Cl. SE17	.2B 140
Hardinge La. E1	.4C 66
(not continuous)	
Hardinge St. E1	.4C 66
(Johnson St.)	
E1	.4C 66
(Steel's La.)	
Hardington NW1	.1E 13
Hardman Rd. SE7	.5F 129
Hardwicke M. WC1	.3C 38
Hardwick Ho. NW8	.4A 34
Hardwick St. EC1	.3E 39
Hardwidge St. SE1	.4F 91
Hardy Av. E16	.2E 101
Hardy Cl. SE16	.5E 95
Hardy Cotts. SE10	.2E 149
Harebell Dr. E6	.2E 77
Hare Ct. EC4	.4D 61
Haredale Ho. SE16	.5D 93
Hare Marsh E2	.4D 43
Hare Pl. EC4	.4E 61
Hare Row E2	.5A 22
Hare Wlk. N1	.1A 42
(not continuous)	
Harewood Av. NW1	.5A 34
Harewood Pl. W1	.4A 58
Harewood Row NW1	.1A 56
Harfleur St. SE11	.4F 117
Harford Ho. SE5	.3C 140
W11	.2C 52

Harford St. E1	.5F 45
Hargraves Ho. W12	.5A 50
Harkness Ho. E1	.4E 65
Harlequin Ct. E1	.1D 93
Harleyford Ct. SE11	.2B 138
Harleyford Rd. SE11	.2B 138
Harleyford St. SE11	.3D 139
Harley Gdns. SW10	.1C 132
Harley Gro. E3	.2C 46
Harley Ho. E14	.3C 68
NW1	.5E 35
Harley Pl. W1	.2F 57
Harley Rd. NW3	.2E 11
Harley St. W1	.5F 35
Harlynwood SE5	.5B 140
Harman Cl. SE1	.1D 143
Harmon Ho. SE8	.4B 124
Harmont Ho. W1	.2F 57
Harmony Pl. SE1	.5C 120
SE8	.3F 147
Harmood Gro. NW1	.1F 13
Harmood Ho. NW1	.1F 13
Harmood Pl. NW1	.1E 13
Harmood St. NW1	.1F 13
Harmsworth M. SE11	.2F 117
Harmsworth St. SE17	.1F 139
Harold Cl. SE16	.5D 95
Harold Est. SE1	.2A 120
Harold Ho. E2	.1D 45
Harold Laski Ho. EC1	.3A 40
Harold Maddison Ho.	
SE17	.5A 118
Harold Pinter Theatre	**.1D 87**
Harold Pl. SE11	.1D 139
Harold Wilson Ho.	
SW6	.3C 130
Harp All. EC4	.3F 61
Harper Rd. E6	.4B 76
SE1	.1B 118
Harp La. EC3	.1F 91
Harpley Sq. E1	.3D 45
Harpur M. WC1	.1B 60
Harpur St. WC1	.1B 60
Harrier Way E6	.1B 76
Harriet Cl. E8	.3D 21
Harriet Ho. SW6	.5A 132
Harriet St. SW1	.5C 84
Harriet Wlk. SW1	.5C 84
Harrington Ct. SW7	.3E 111
W10	.2B 30
Harrington Gdns. SW7	.4A 110
Harrington Ho. NW1	.2B 36
Harrington Rd. SW7	.3D 111
Harrington Sq. NW1	.5B 14
Harrington St. NW1	.1B 36
(not continuous)	
Harriott Cl. SE10	.4B 128
Harriott Ho. E1	.2C 66
Harris Bldgs. E1	.4E 65
Harris Ho. E3	.2D 47
Harrison Ho. E1	.4F 65
SE17	.5D 119
Harrisons Ct. SE14	.2D 145
Harrison St. WC1	.3A 38
Harris St. SE5	.5E 141
Harrods	**.1B 112**
Harrold Ho. NW3	.1C 10
Harrowby Ho. W1	.3B 56
Harrowby St. W1	.3A 56
Harrowgate Ho. E9	.1E 23
Harrowgate Rd. E9	.1F 23
Harrow La. E14	.1B 98
Harrow Lodge NW8	.4D 33

Harrow Pl. E1	.3A 64
Harrow Rd. NW10	.2A 28
W2	.2A 54
(not continuous)	
W9	.5C 30
W10	.4E 29
Harrow Rd. Bri. W2	.1C 54
Harrow St. NW1	.1A 56
Harry Hinkins Ho. SE17	.1C 140
Harry Lambourn Ho.	
SE15	.4A 144
Harston Wlk. E3	.4B 48
Hartfield Ter. E3	.1E 47
Hartington Ho. SW1	.5E 115
Hartington Rd. E16	.4F 73
SW8	.5F 137
Hartismere Rd. SW6	.4C 130
Hartlake Rd. E9	.5A 4
Hartland NW1	.4C 14
Hartland Rd. NW1	.1F 13
NW6	.5B 8
Hartley Ho. SE1	.3C 120
Hartley St. E2	.2C 44
(not continuous)	
Hartmann Rd. E16	.2E 103
Hartop Point SW6	.4A 130
Hartshorn All. EC3	.4A 64
Hart's La. SE14	.5F 145
Hart St. EC3	.5A 64
Hartwell Ho. SE7	.5F 129
Harvard Ho. SE17	.2F 139
Harvey Ho. E1	.5F 43
N1	.4E 19
SW1	.1E 137
Harvey Lodge W9	.1E 53
Harvey's Bldgs. WC2	.1A 88
Harvey St. N1	.4E 19
Harvington Wlk. E8	.1E 21
Harvist Rd. NW6	.2E 29
Harwicke Ho. E3	**.2F 47**
Harwood Ct. N1	.4E 19
Harwood M. SW6	.5E 131
Harwood Point SE16	.4B 96
Harwood Rd. SW6	.5E 131
Hasker St. SW3	.3A 112
Haslam Cl. N1	.1E 17
Haslam Ho. N1	.2B 18
Haslam St. SE15	.5C 142
Haslers Wharf E3	.4F 23
Hassard St. E2	.1C 42
Hassett Rd. E9	.4A 4
Hastings Cl. SE15	.5D 143
Hastings Ho. W12	.5A 50
WC1	.3F 37
Hastings Rd. E16	.2E 73
Hastings St. WC1	.3F 37
Hat & Mitre Ct. EC1	.5A 40
Hatcham Mews Bus. Cen.	
SE14	.5E 145
Hatcham Pk. M. SE14	.5E 145
Hatcham Pk. Rd. SE14	.5E 145
Hatcham Rd. SE15	.3B 144
Hatchers M. SE1	.5A 92
Hatcliffe Almshouses	
SE10	.1F 149
Hatcliffe St. SE10	.5B 128
Hatfield Cl. SE14	.5D 145
Hatfield Ho. EC1	.5B 40
SE10	.5F 147
Hatfields SE1	.2E 89
Hathaway Ho. N1	.2F 41
Hatherley Ct. W2	.4F 53
Hatherley Gro. W2	.3F 53
Hatherley St. SW1	.4C 114

Hatteraick St. SE16 . . . . . .4C 94
Hatton Gdn. EC1 . . . . .5E 39
Hatton Ho. E1 . . . . .5E 65
Hatton Pl. EC1 . . . . .1E 61
Hatton Row NW8 . . . . .5E 33
Hatton St. NW8 . . . . .5E 33
Hatton Wall EC1 . . . . .1E 61
Haunch of Venison Yd.
   W1 . . . . .4F 57
Havannah St. E14 . . . . .5E 97
Havelock Cl. W12 . . . . .5A 50
Havelock Ho. SE1 . . . . . . .4C 120
Havelock St. N1 . . . . .3A 16
Havelock Ter. SW8 . . . . . . .5A 136
Havelock Ter. Arches
   SW8 . . . . .5A 136
Haven M. E3 . . . . .2B 68
   N1 . . . . .2E 17
Havenpool NW8 . . . . .4A 10
Haven St. NW1 . . . . .2F 13
Haven Way SE1 . . . . .1B 120
Haverfield Rd. E3 . . . . .2F 45
Havering NW1 . . . . .1A 14
Havering St. E1 . . . . .4D 67
Haverstock Hill NW3 . . . . . .1D 13
Haverstock Pl. N1 . . . . .1A 40
Haverstock St. N1 . . . . .1A 40
Havilland M. W12 . . . . .4A 78
Havil St. SE5 . . . . .5F 141
Havisham Apartments
   E15 . . . . .5E 7
Havisham Ho. SE16 . . . . . . .5D 93
Hawes St. N1 . . . . .2A 18
Hawgood St. E3 . . . . .2E 69
Hawke Ho. E1 . . . . .5E 45
Hawke Pl. SE16 . . . . .4E 95
Hawke Twr. SE14 . . . . .3A 146
   SW1 . . . . .2C 136
Hawkins Ho. SE8 . . . . .2D 147
   SW1 . . . . .2C 136
Hawkshead NW1 . . . . .2B 36
Hawks M. SE10 . . . . .5C 148
Hawksmoor Cl. E6 . . . . . . .3F 75
Hawksmoor M. E1 . . . . .5F 65
Hawksmoor Pl. E2 . . . . . . .4D 43
Hawkstone Rd. SE16 . . . . . .3C 122
Hawkwell Wlk. N1 . . . . .3C 18
Hawley Cres. NW1 . . . . . . .2A 14
Hawley M. NW1 . . . . .1F 13
Hawley Rd. NW1 . . . . .1F 13
   (not continuous)
Hawley St. NW1 . . . . .2F 13
Hawthorn Av. E3 . . . . .3B 24
Hawthorne Ho. SW1 . . . . . .1C 136
Hawthorn Wlk. W10 . . . . . . .4F 29
Hawtrey Rd. NW3 . . . . .2F 11
Hay Currie St. E14 . . . . .3A 70
Hayday Rd. E16 . . . . .1D 73
   (not continuous)
Hayden Piper Ho. SW3 . . . .2B 134
Hayden's Pl. W11 . . . . .3B 52
Haydon St. E1 . . . . .5B 64
   EC3 . . . . .5B 64
Haydon Wlk. E1 . . . . .5C 64
Hayes Ct. SE5 . . . . .5B 140
Hayes Pl. NW1 . . . . .5A 34
Hayfield Pas. E1 . . . . .5C 44
Hayfield Yd. E1 . . . . .5C 44
Hay Hill W1 . . . . .1A 86
Hayhurst Ct. N1 . . . . .3A 18
Hayles Bldgs. SE11 . . . . . . .3A 118
Hayles St. SE11 . . . . .3F 117
Haymans Point SE11 . . . . . .5B 116
Hayman St. N1 . . . . .2A 18
Haymarket SW1 . . . . .1D 87

Haymarket Arc. SW1 . . . . . .1D 87
Haymarket Ct. E8 . . . . .2C 20
   (off Jacaranda Gro.)
Haymarket Theatre Royal
   . . . . .1E 87
Haymerle Ho. SE15 . . . . . . .3D 143
Haymerle Rd. SE15 . . . . . . .3D 143
Hayne Ho. W11 . . . . .2F 79
Hayne St. EC1 . . . . .1A 62
Hay's Ct. SE16 . . . . .4C 94
Hay's Galleria SE1 . . . . .2F 91
Hays La. SE1 . . . . .2F 91
Hay's M. W1 . . . . .1F 85
Hay St. E2 . . . . .4E 21
Hayward Gallery 2C 88
Hayward Ho. N1 . . . . .5D 17
Hayward's Pl. EC1 . . . . .5F 39
Hazel Ho. E3 . . . . .3B 24
Hazelmere Rd. NW6 . . . . . . .3C 8
Hazel Rd. E15 . . . . .2F 7
   NW10 . . . . .2B 28
   (not continuous)
Hazel Way SE1 . . . . .3B 120
Hazelwood Ho. SE8 . . . . . . .4F 123
Hazelwood Cres. W10 . . . . .5A 30
Hazelwood Twr. W10 . . . . . .5A 30
Hazlitt M. W14 . . . . .2F 107
Hazlitt Rd. W14 . . . . .2F 107
Headbourne Ho. SE1 . . . . . .1E 119
Headfort Pl. SW1 . . . . .5E 85
Headlam St. E1 . . . . .5A 44
Head's M. W11 . . . . .4D 53
Head St. E1 . . . . .3D 67
   (not continuous)
Healey Ho. E3 . . . . .4D 47
   SW9 . . . . .5E 139
Hearn's Bldgs. SE17 . . . . . .4E 119
Hearnshaw St. E14 . . . . . . .3F 67
Hearn St. EC2 . . . . .5A 42
Heathcock Ct. WC2 . . . . . . .1A 88
   (off Exchange Ct.)
Heathcote St. WC1 . . . . . . .4B 38
Heather Cl. E6 . . . . .4F 77
Heather Ho. E14 . . . . .3C 70
Heather Wlk. W10 . . . . .4A 30
Heathfield Cl. E16 . . . . .1D 75
Heathfield Ct. E3 . . . . .5D 25
   SE14 . . . . .4C 144
Heathpool Ct. E1 . . . . .5F 43
Heaton Ho. SW10 . . . . .2C 132
Hebden Ct. E2 . . . . .4B 20
Heber Mans. W14 . . . . .2A 130
Hebrides Ct. E1 . . . . .2F 67
Hebron Rd. W6 . . . . .2A 106
Heckfield Pl. SW6 . . . . .5D 131
Heckford Ho. E14 . . . . .4F 69
Heckford St. E1 . . . . .5E 67
Hector Ct. SW9 . . . . .5D 139
Hector Ho. E2 . . . . .1F 43
Heddon St. W1 . . . . .5B 58
Hedgegate Ct. W11 . . . . . . .3C 52
Hedgers Gro. E9 . . . . .5A 4
Hedger St. SE11 . . . . .3F 117
Hedingham Cl. N1 . . . . .2B 18
Hedley Ho. E14 . . . . .1C 126
Hedsor Ho. E2 . . . . .4B 42
Heer M. E2 . . . . .1E 43
Hega Ho. E14 . . . . .2B 70
Helby St. SE17 . . . . .3A 140
Heldar Ct. SE1 . . . . .5E 91
Helena Pl. E9 . . . . .4A 22
Helena Sq. SE16 . . . . .1F 95
Helen Gladstone Ho. SE1 . . .4F 89
Helen Ho. E2 . . . . .1F 43

Helen Mackay Ho. E14 . . . . .3D 71
Helen Peele Cotts.
   SE16 . . . . .1B 122
Helen's Pl. E2 . . . . .2B 44
Helen Taylor Ho. SE16 . . . . .2D 121
Heligan Ho. SE16 . . . . .5D 95
Helix Ct. W11 . . . . .3E 79
Hellings St. E1 . . . . .3E 93
Helmet Row EC1 . . . . .3C 40
Helmsdale Ho. NW6 . . . . . . .1F 31
Helmsley Pl. E8 . . . . .2F 21
Helmsley St. E8 . . . . .2A 22
Helsby Ct. NW8 . . . . .4D 33
Helsinki Sq. SE16 . . . . .1A 124
Helston NW1 . . . . .5C 14
Helston Ho. SE11 . . . . .5E 117
Hemans St. SW8 . . . . .4E 137
Hemans St. Est. SW8 . . . . . .5F 137
Hemingford Rd. N1 . . . . . . .4C 16
Hemming St. E1 . . . . .5E 43
Hemp Wlk. SE17 . . . . .3E 119
Hemstal Rd. NW6 . . . . .1D 9
Hemsworth Ct. N1 . . . . .5F 19
Hemsworth St. N1 . . . . .5F 19
Hemus Pl. SW3 . . . . .1A 134
Hen & Chicken Ct. EC4 . . . .4D 61
Henderson Ct. SE14 . . . . . .2D 145
Henderson Dr. NW8 . . . . . . .4D 33
Hendre Ho. SE1 . . . . .4A 120
Hendre Rd. SE1 . . . . .4A 120
Heneage La. EC3 . . . . .4A 64
Heneage Pl. EC3 . . . . .4A 64
Heneage St. E1 . . . . .1C 64
Henley Cl. SE16 . . . . .4B 94
Henley Dr. SE1 . . . . .3C 120
Henley Ho. E2 . . . . .4C 42
Henley Prior N1 . . . . .1B 38
Henley Rd. E16 . . . . .4C 104
Henniker M. SW3 . . . . .2D 133
Henniker Point E15 . . . . .3F 7
Henniker Rd. E15 . . . . .3D 7
Henrietta Cl. SE8 . . . . .2E 147
Henrietta Ho. W6 . . . . .5B 106
Henrietta M. WC1 . . . . .4A 38
Henrietta Pl. W1 . . . . .4F 57
Henrietta St. WC2 . . . . .5A 60
Henriques St. E1 . . . . .3E 65
Henry Addlington Cl. E6 . . . .2F 77
Henry Dickens Ct. W11 . . . . .1E 79
Henry Ho. SE1 . . . . .3E 89
   SW8 . . . . .4A 138
Henry Moore Ct. SW3 . . . . .1F 133
Henry Purcell Ho. E16 . . . . .2A 102
   (off Evelyn Rd.)
Henry Wise Ho. SW1 . . . . . .4C 114
Henshall Point E3 . . . . .2F 47
Henshaw St. SE17 . . . . .3D 119
Henslow Ho. SE15 . . . . . . .4D 143
Henstridge Pl. NW8 . . . . . . .5F 11
Henty Cl. SW11 . . . . .5A 134
Hepscott Rd. E9 . . . . .5D 5
Hepworth Ct. N1 . . . . .3F 17
   SW1 . . . . .1F 135
Hera Ct. E14 . . . . .3D 125
Herald's Pl. SE11 . . . . .3F 117
Herald St. E2 . . . . .4A 44
Herbal Hill EC1 . . . . .5E 39
Herbal Hill Gdns. EC1 . . . . . .5E 39
Herbal Pl. EC1 . . . . .5E 39
Herbert Cres. SW1 . . . . .1C 112
Herbert Gdns. NW10 . . . . . .1A 28
Herbert Ho. E1 . . . . .3B 64
Herbert Morrison Ho.
   SW6 . . . . .3B 130

Herbrand Est. WC1 . . . . .4F 37
Herbrand St. WC1 . . . . .4F 37
Hercules Ct. SE14 . . . . .3A 146
Hercules Rd. SE1 . . . . .2C 116
Hercules Wharf E14 . . . . . . .5A 72
Hereford Bldgs. SW3 . . . . . .2E 133
Hereford Ho. NW6 . . . . .1E 31
   SW3 . . . . .1A 112
   SW10 . . . . .4A 132
Hereford Mans. W2 . . . . .4E 53
Hereford M. W2 . . . . .4E 53
Hereford Pl. SE14 . . . . .4B 146
Hereford Retreat SE15 . . . . .3D 143
Hereford Rd. E3 . . . . .1C 46
   W2 . . . . .3E 53
Hereford Sq. SW7 . . . . .4C 110
Hereford St. E2 . . . . .4D 43
Heritage Ct. SE8 . . . . .1E 145
Her Majesty's Theatre 2D 87
Hermes Cl. W9 . . . . .5D 31
Hermes Ct. SW9 . . . . .5D 139
Hermes St. N1 . . . . .1D 39
Hermitage Ct. E1 . . . . .3E 93
Hermitage Ho. N1 . . . . .5F 17
Hermitage Moorings E1 . . . . .3D 93
Hermitage St. W2 . . . . .2D 55
Hermitage Vs. SW6 . . . . .2D 131
Hermitage Wall E1 . . . . .3E 93
Hermitage Waterside
   E1 . . . . .2D 93
Hermit Pl. NW6 . . . . .4F 9
Hermit Rd. E16 . . . . .1B 72
Hermit St. EC1 . . . . .2F 39
Heron Ct. E14 . . . . .1C 126
Herongate N1 . . . . .3C 18
Heron Ho. E3 . . . . .3B 24
   NW8 . . . . .1F 33
   SW11 . . . . .5A 134
Horon Pl. E16 . . . . .3C 102
   SE16 . . . . .2A 96
   W1 . . . . .3E 57
Heron Quay E14 . . . . .3D 97
Heron Tower 3F 63
Herrick Ho. SE5 . . . . .5E 141
Herrick St. SW1 . . . . .4E 115
Herries St. W10 . . . . .1A 30
Hertford Lock Ho. E3 . . . . . . .3B 24
Hertford Pl. W1 . . . . .5C 36
Hertford Rd. N1 . . . . .3A 20
   (not continuous)
Hertford St. W1 . . . . .3F 85
Hertford Wharf N1 . . . . .3A 20
Hertsmere Ho. E14 . . . . .1D 97
Hertsmere Rd. E14 . . . . .2D 97
Hesketh Pl. W11 . . . . .1F 79
Hesper M. SW5 . . . . .5F 109
Hesperus Cres. E14 . . . . . . .4F 125
Hessel St. E1 . . . . .4F 65
Hester Rd. SW11 . . . . .5F 133
Hestia Ho. SE1 . . . . .5F 91
Hethpool Ho. W2 . . . . .5D 33
Hetley Rd. W12 . . . . .3A 78
Hevelius Cl. SE10 . . . . .5B 128
Hever Ho. SE15 . . . . .2D 145
Heversham Ho. SE15 . . . . . .4B 144
Hewer St. W10 . . . . .1E 51
Hewett St. EC2 . . . . .5A 42
Hewison St. E3 . . . . .5C 24
Hewlett Ho. SW8 . . . . .5A 136
Hewlett Rd. E3 . . . . .5A 24
Heybridge NW1 . . . . .1F 13
Heyford Av. SW8 . . . . .4A 138
Heyford Ter. SW8 . . . . .4A 138
Heygate St. SE17 . . . . .4B 118

Heylyn Sq. E3 . . . . .2C 46
Heywood Ho. SE14 . . . . .2D 145
Hibbert Ho. E14 . . . . .1E 125
Hibiscus Lodge E15 . . . . .5F 7
Hickes Ho. NW6 . . . . .1D 11
Hickin St. E14 . . . . .1B 126
Hickleton NW1 . . . . .4C 14
Hickling Ho. SE16 . . . . .2A 122
Hickman Cl. E16 . . . . .2D 75
Hicks Bolton Ho. NW6 . . . . . .1C 30
Hicks Ho. SE16 . . . . .1D 121
Hicks St. SE8 . . . . .5F 123
Hide E6 . . . . .3E 77
Hide Pl. SW1 . . . . .4D 115
Hide Twr. SW1 . . . . .4D 115
Hierro Ct. E1 . . . . .1F 67
Higgins Ho. N1 . . . . .4F 19
Higginson Ho. NW3 . . . . .1B 12
High Bri. SE10 . . . . .1E 149
Highbridge Ct. SE14 . . . . . . .4C 144
High Bri. Wharf SE10 . . . . . . .1E 149
Highbury Mans. N1 . . . . .2F 17
Highfield M. NW6 . . . . .1F 9
High Holborn WC1 . . . . .3F 59
Highlever Rd. W10 . . . . .1B 50
High Meads Rd. E16 . . . . . . .3D 75
High Rd. Leyton E15 . . . . . . .1C 6
High Rd. Leytonstone
   E11 . . . . .1F 7
   E15 . . . . .1F 7
Highstone Mans. NW1 . . . . . .2B 14
High St. E15 . . . . .1A 48
High Timber St. EC4 . . . . . . .5B 62
Highway, The E1 . . . . .1D 93
Highway Bus. Park, The
   E1 . . . . .5E 67
Highway Trad. Centre, The
   E1 . . . . .5D 67
Highworth St. NW1 . . . . .1A 56
Hi-Gloss Con. SE8 . . . . .1A 146
Hilary Cl. SW6 . . . . .4F 131
Hilborough Ct. E8 . . . . .2C 20
Hilda Rd. E16 . . . . .4F 49
Hildyard Rd. SW6 . . . . .2E 131
Hiley Rd. NW10 . . . . .2B 28
Hilgrove Rd. NW6 . . . . .2C 10
Hillary Ct. W12 . . . . .5B 78
Hillary M. E14 . . . . .1A 70
Hillbeck Cl. SE15 . . . . .3B 144
   (not continuous)
Hillcrest W11 . . . . .1B 80
Hillcroft Rd. E6 . . . . .1F 77
Hillersden Ho. SW1 . . . . .5F 113
Hillery Cl. SE17 . . . . .4E 119
Hill Farm Rd. W10 . . . . .1C 50
Hillgate Pl. W8 . . . . .2D 81
Hillgate St. W8 . . . . .2D 81
Hill Ho. Apartments N1 . . . . .1C 38
Hilliard Ho. E1 . . . . .2A 94
Hilliards Ct. E1 . . . . .2A 94
Hillier Ho. NW1 . . . . .1D 15
Hillingdon St. SE17 . . . . .3F 139
Hillman Dr. W10 . . . . .5C 28
Hill Rd. NW8 . . . . .2C 32
Hillsborough Ct. NW6 . . . . . .4F 9
Hillside SE10 . . . . .5D 149
Hillside Cl. NW8 . . . . .5A 10
Hillsleigh Rd. W8 . . . . .2C 80
Hills Pl. W1 . . . . .4B 58
Hillstone Ct. E3 . . . . .3A 48
Hill St. W1 . . . . .2E 85
Hilltop Cl. NW8 . . . . .2C 10
Hilltop Rd. NW6 . . . . .1E 9
Hill Vw. NW3 . . . . .3B 12

Hill-Wood Ho. NW1 . . . . .1C 36
Hillyfield Cl. E9 . . . . .4A 4
Hilton's Wharf SE10 . . . . . . .3A 148
Hinchinbrook Ho. NW6 . . . . . .4F 9
Hind Ct. EC4 . . . . .4E 61
Hinde Ho. W1 . . . . .3E 57
Hinde M. W1 . . . . .3E 57
Hinde St. W1 . . . . .3E 57
Hind Gro. E14 . . . . .4D 69
Hind Ho. SE14 . . . . .3D 145
Hindmarsh Cl. E1 . . . . .5E 65
Hindon Ct. SW1 . . . . .3B 114
Hinstock NW6 . . . . .3F 9
Hippodrome M. W11 . . . . . . .1F 79
Hippodrome Pl. W11 . . . . . . .1F 79
Hirst Ct. SW1 . . . . .1F 135
Hitchcock La. E20 . . . . .5B 6
Hitchin Sq. E3 . . . . .5A 24
Hithe Gro. SE16 . . . . .2C 122
Hittard Ct. SE17 . . . . .2D 141
HMP Pentonville N7 . . . . . . .1B 16
HMS Belfast 2F 91
Hoadly Ho. SE1 . . . . .3B 90
Hobart Pl. SW1 . . . . .1F 113
Hobbs Ct. SE1 . . . . .4C 92
Hobbs Pl. N1 . . . . .4F 19
Hobbs Pl. Est. N1 . . . . .4F 19
Hobby Ho. SE1 . . . . .4F 121
Hobday St. E14 . . . . .3F 69
Hobhouse Ct. SW1 . . . . .1E 87
   (off Suffolk St.)
Hobson's Pl. E1 . . . . .1D 65
Hobury St. SW10 . . . . .3C 132
Hocker St. E2 . . . . .3B 42
Hockett Cl. SE8 . . . . .3A 124
Hockliffe Ho. W10 . . . . .1B 50
Hockney Ct. SE16 . . . . .5A 122
Hodister Cl. SE5 . . . . .5B 140
Hodnet Gro. SE16 . . . . .3D 123
Hoffman Sq. N1 . . . . .2E 41
Holland Rd. W14 . . . . .1F 107
Hogan M. W2 . . . . .1D 55
Hogarth Cl. E16 . . . . .1D 75
Hogarth Ct. E1 . . . . .3E 65
   EC3 . . . . .4A 64
   NW1 . . . . .1C 14
Hogarth Ho. SW1 . . . . .4E 115
Hogarth Pl. SW5 . . . . .4F 109
Hogarth Rd. SW5 . . . . .4F 109
Hogshead Pas. E1 . . . . .1A 94
Holbeck Row SE15 . . . . .5E 143
Holbein Ho. SW1 . . . . .5D 113
Holbein M. SW1 . . . . .5D 113
Holbein Pl. SW1 . . . . .4D 113
Holberton Gdns. NW10 . . . . .2A 28
HOLBORN 2B 60
Holborn EC1 . . . . .2D 61
Holborn Bars EC1 . . . . .2D 61
Holborn Cir. EC1 . . . . .2E 61
Holborn Ho. W12 . . . . .3A 50
Holborn Pl. WC1 . . . . .2B 60
Holborn Rd. E13 . . . . .1F 73
Holborn Viaduct EC1 . . . . . . .2E 61
Holcombe St. W6 . . . . .5A 106
Holcombe Ct. W1 . . . . .1B 58
Holcroft Rd. E9 . . . . .1C 22
Holden Ho. N1 . . . . .4B 18
   SE8 . . . . .4E 147
Holden Point E15 . . . . .4E 7
Holford Ho. SE16 . . . . .4F 121
   WC1 . . . . .2C 38
Holford M. WC1 . . . . .2D 39
Holford Pl. WC1 . . . . .2C 38
Holford St. WC1 . . . . .2D 39

Holford Yd. WC1 . . . . .1C 38
Holland Dwellings
    WC2 . . . . .3A 60
Holland Gdns. W14 . . . . .1A 108
Holland Gro. SW9 . . . . . . .5E 139
Holland Ho. NW10 . . . . . . .1A 28
HOLLAND PARK **3B 80**
Holland Park **4B 80**
Holland Pk. W11 . . . . .3A 80
Holland Pk. Av. W11 . . . . . .4E 79
Holland Pk. Ct. W14 . . . . . .4A 80
Holland Pk. Gdns. W14 . . . .3F 79
Holland Pk. Mans. W14 . . . .3A 80
Holland Pk. M. W11 . . . . . .3A 80
Holland Pk. Rd. W14 . . . . .2B 108
HOLLAND PARK RDBT. 4E 79
Holland Pk. Ter. W11 . . . . .3A 80
Holland Park Theatre (Open Air)
  . . . .**5C 80**
Holland Pas. N1 . . . . .3B 18
Holland Pl. W8 . . . . .4F 81
Holland Pl. Chambers W8 . .4F 81
Holland Ri. Ho. SW9 . . . . .5C 138
Holland Rd. E15 . . . . .2F 49
    NW10 . . . . .1A 28
    W14 . . . . .4E 79
Holland St. SE1 . . . . .2A 90
    W8 . . . . .5E 81
Holland Vs. Rd. W14 . . . . . .4F 79
Holland Wlk. W8 . . . . .3C 80
Hollen St. W1 . . . . .3D 59
Holles St. W1 . . . . .3A 58
Hollisfield WC1 . . . . .3A 38
Hollister Ho. NW6 . . . . .2E 31
Hollybush Gdns. E2 . . . . . .2A 44
Hollybush Ho. E2 . . . . .2A 44
Hollybush Pl. E2 . . . . .2A 44
Holly Ct. SE10 . . . . .2C 128
Hollydene SE15 . . . . .5F 143
Holly Ho. W10 . . . . .4F 29
Holly Lodge W8 . . . . .4D 81
Holly M. SW10 . . . . .1C 132
Holly St. E8 . . . . .1C 60
Holly Vs. *W6* *2A 106*
    (off Wellesley Av.)
Hollywood Bowl
  Surrey Quays **1E 123**
Hollywood Ct. SW10 . . . . . .2B 132
Hollywood M. SW10 . . . . . .2B 132
Hollywood Rd. SW10 . . . . . .2B 132
Holman Ho. E2 . . . . .2D 45
Holman Hunt Ho. W6 . . . . .1A 130
Holmbrook NW1 . . . . .1C 36
Holmead Rd. SW6 . . . . . . .5A 132
Holmefield Ho. W10 . . . . . . .5A 30
Holme Ho. SE15 . . . . .5F 143
Holmesdale Ho. NW6 . . . . . .3E 9
Holmes Pl. SW10 . . . . .2C 132
Holmes Ter. SE1 . . . . .4D 89
Holmsdale Ho. E14 . . . . . . .1A 98
Holmwood Vs. SE7 . . . . . . .5E 129
Holocaust Memorial **4C 84**
Holocaust Memorial Garden, The
  . . . .**4C 84**
Holst Ct. SE1 . . . . .1D 117
Holst Ho. W12 . . . . .4A 50
Holsworthy Ho. E3 . . . . .3A 48
Holsworthy Sq. WC1 . . . . . .5C 38
Holt Ct. SE10 . . . . .2B 148
Holton St. E1 . . . . .4D 45
Holt Rd. E16 . . . . .3A 104
Holyhead Cl. E6 . . . . .1B 76
Holyoake Ct. SE16 . . . . . . .4A 96
Holyoak Rd. SE11 . . . . .4F 117

Holyrood Ct. NW1 . . . . .4F 13
Holyrood M. E16 . . . . .2E 101
Holyrood St. SE1 . . . . .3F 91
Holywell Cl. SE16 . . . . .5A 122
Holywell La. EC2 . . . . .4A 42
Holywell Row EC2 . . . . .5F 41
Homefield St. N1 . . . . .1F 41
Homer Dr. E14 . . . . .3D 125
Homer Rd. E9 . . . . .5A 4
Homer Row W1 . . . . .2A 56
Homer St. W1 . . . . .2A 56
HOMERTON **3A 4**
Homerton Rd. E9 . . . . .2A 4
Homestead Rd. SW6 . . . . . .5B 130
Honduras St. EC1 . . . . .4B 40
Honey La. EC2 . . . . .4C 62
Honey La. Ho. SW10 . . . . .2A 132
Honiton Rd. NW6 . . . . .5B 8
Honour Lea Av. E20 . . . . . . .3A 6
Hood Ct. EC4 . . . . .4E 61
Hood Ho. SE5 . . . . .5D 141
    SW1 . . . . .1D 137
Hood Point SE16 . . . . .4B 96
Hooke Ho. E3 . . . . .1F 45
Hooper Rd. E16 . . . . .4E 73
Hooper's Ct. SW3 . . . . .5B 84
Hooper Sq. E1 . . . . .4D 65
Hooper St. E1 . . . . .4D 65
Hoopers Yd. E1 . . . . .4D 65
    NW6 . . . . .3B 8
Hope Cl. NW10 . . . . .2E 29
    SE1 . . . . .5D 121
Hopefield Av. NW6 . . . . .5A 8
Hope Sq. EC2 . . . . .2F 63
Hopetown St. E1 . . . . .2C 64
Hopewell St. SE5 . . . . .5E 141
Hopewell Yd. SE5 . . . . .5E 141
Hope Wharf SE16 . . . . .4B 94
Hop Gdns. WC2 . . . . .1F 87
Hopgood St. W12 . . . . .3C 78
Hopground Ho. E20 . . . . . . .4C 6
Hopkins Ho. E14 . . . . .4D 69
Hopkinsons Pl. NW1 . . . . . .3D 13
Hopkins St. W1 . . . . .4C 58
Hop St. SE10 . . . . .3C 128
Hopton's Gdns. SE1 . . . . . .2A 90
Hopton St. SE1 . . . . .1F 89
Hopwood Rd. SE17 . . . . . . .2E 141
Hopwood Wlk. E8 . . . . .1E 21
Horace Bldg. SW8 . . . . .4F 135
Horatio Ct. SE16 . . . . .3C 94
Horatio Ho. E2 . . . . .1C 42
    W6 . . . . .5D 107
Horatio Pl. E14 . . . . .3C 98
Horatio St. E2 . . . . .1C 42
Horbury Cres. W11 . . . . .1D 81
Horbury M. W11 . . . . .1C 80
Hordle Prom. E. SE15 . . . . .4C 142
Hordle Prom. Sth.
    SE15 . . . . .3B 142
Horizon Bldg. E14 . . . . .1E 97
Horizon Ind. Est. SE15 . . . .3D 143
Horizon Way SE7 . . . . .4F 129
Hormead Rd. W9 . . . . .5B 30
Hornbeam Cl. SE11 . . . . . . .3D 117
Hornbeam Sq. E3 . . . . .3B 24
Hornbean Ho. E15 . . . . .2F 49
Hornblower Cl. SE16 . . . . . .3F 123
Hornby Cl. NW3 . . . . .1E 11
Hornby Ho. SE11 . . . . .2D 139
Horner Ho. N1 . . . . .4A 20
Horner Sq. E1 . . . . .1F 19
Horn La. SE10 . . . . .5D 129
    (not continuous)

Horn Link Way SE10 . . . . . .3E 129
Hornshay St. SE15 . . . . . . .3C 144
Hornton Ct. W8 . . . . .5E 81
Hornton Pl. W8 . . . . .5E 81
Hornton St. W8 . . . . .4E 81
Horse & Dolphin Yd.
    W1 . . . . .5E 59
Horseferry Pl. SE10 . . . . . . .3B 148
Horseferry Rd. E14 . . . . .5F 67
    SW1 . . . . .2D 115
Horseferry Rd. Est.
    SW1 . . . . .2D 115
Horse Guards Av. SW1 . . . .3F 87
Horse Guards Parade **3E 87**
Horse Guards Rd. SW1 . . . .3E 87
Horse Leaze E6 . . . . .3B 77
Horseley Ct. E1 . . . . .1F 67
Horselydown La. SE1 . . . . . .4B 92
Horselydown Mans. SE1 . . . .4B 92
Horsemongers M. SE1 . . . . .5C 90
Horse Ride SW1 . . . . .4C 86
Horseshoe Cl. E14 . . . . . . .5B 126
Horseshoe Ct. EC1 . . . . . . .4A 40
Horseshoe Wharf SE1 . . . . .2D 91
Horse Yd. N1 . . . . .3A 18
Horsfield Ho. N1 . . . . .2B 18
Horsley Ct. SW1 . . . . .4E 115
Horsley St. SE17 . . . . .2D 141
Horsman Ho. SE5 . . . . .3B 140
Horsman St. SE5 . . . . .3C 140
Hortensia Ho. SW10 . . . . . .4B 132
Hortensia Rd. SW10 . . . . . .3B 132
Horton Ho. SE15 . . . . .3C 144
    SW8 . . . . .4B 138
Horwood Ho. E2 . . . . .3A 44
    NW8 . . . . .4A 34
Hosier La. EC1 . . . . .2F 61
Hoskins Cl. E16 . . . . .3C 74
Hoskins St. SE10 . . . . .1E 149
Hotham St. E15 . . . . .3F 27
Hothfield Pl. SE16 . . . . .2C 122
Hotspur St. SE11 . . . . .5D 117
Houghton Ct. EC1 . . . . .5B 40
Houghton St. WC2 . . . . .4C 60
    (not continuous)
Houlton Ho. SW3 . . . . .5B 112
Houndsditch EC3 . . . . .3A 64
Household Cavalry Museum, The
  Whitehall **3E 87**
Houseman Way SE5 . . . . . .5E 141
House Mill, The **2C 48**
Houses of Parliament **1A 116**
Hove St. SE15 . . . . .5B 144
Howard Bldg. SW8 . . . . . . .3F 135
Howard Ho. E16 . . . . .2F 101
    SE8 . . . . .2C 146
    SW1 . . . . .1C 136
    W1 . . . . .5A 36
Howcroft Ho. E3 . . . . .2C 46
Howell Wlk. SE1 . . . . .4A 118
Howick Pl. SW1 . . . . .2C 114
Howie St. SW11 . . . . .5F 133
Howland Est. SE16 . . . . . . .1B 122
Howland Mews E. W1 . . . . .1C 58
Howland St. W1 . . . . .1B 58
Howland Way SE16 . . . . . . .5A 96
Howley Pl. W2 . . . . .1C 54
How's St. E2 . . . . .5B 20
HOXTON **1E 41**
Hoxton Hall Theatre **1A 42**
Hoxton Mkt. N1 . . . . .3F 41
Hoxton Sq. N1 . . . . .3F 41
Hoxton St. N1 . . . . .4F 19
Hoyland Cl. SE15 . . . . .4F 143

Hoy St. E16 . . . . .4C **72**
HQS Wellington 1D **89**
Hub, The
  Westminster 1C **34**
Hubbard Ho. *SW10* 4D **133**
  (off World's End Pas.)
Hubbard St. E15 . . . . .4F **27**
Huberd Ho. SE1 . . . . .1E **119**
Hubert Ho. NW8 . . . . .5F **33**
Hucknall Ct. NW8 . . . . . .4D **33**
Huddart St. E3 . . . . .1C **68**
  (not continuous)
Huddleston Cl. E2 . . . . . .1A **44**
Hudson Bldg. E1 . . . . . . .2D **65**
Hudson Cl. W12 . . . . .5A **50**
Hudson Ct. E14 . . . . .5E **125**
Hudson Ho. SW10 . . . . . .4B **132**
  W11 . . . . .4A **52**
Hudson's Pl. SW1 . . . . . . .3B **114**
Huggin Ct. EC4 . . . . .5C **62**
Huggin Hill EC4 . . . . .5C **62**
Huggins Ho. E3 . . . . .2D **47**
Hughan Rd. E15 . . . . .2E **7**
Hugh Astor Ct. SE1 . . . . . .1A **118**
Hugh Cubitt Ho. N1 . . . . . .1C **38**
Hugh Dalton Av. SW6 . . . . .3B **130**
Hughenden Ho. NW8 . . . . .4F **33**
Hughes Ho. E2 . . . . .3B **44**
  E3 . . . . .3E **47**
  SE8 . . . . .2E **147**
  SE17 . . . . .4A **118**
Hughes Mans. E1 . . . . . . .5E **43**
Hugh Gaitskell Cl. SW6 . . . .3B **130**
Hugh M. SW1 . . . . .4A **114**
Hugh Platt Ho. E2 . . . . . . .1A **44**
Hugh St. SW1 . . . . .4A **114**
Hugo Ho. SW1 . . . . .1C **112**
Huguenot Pl. E1 . . . . .1C **64**
Hullbridge M. N1 . . . . . . .3D **19**
Hull Cl. SE16 . . . . .3E **95**
Hull St. EC1 . . . . .3B **40**
Hulme Pl. SE1 . . . . .5C **90**
Humber Dr. W10 . . . . . . .5D **29**
Humberton Cl. E9 . . . . . . .3A **4**
Humbolt Rd. W6 . . . . . . .3A **130**
Hume Ct. N1 . . . . .2A **18**
Hume Ho. W11 . . . . .3E **79**
Hume Ter. E16 . . . . .3A **74**
Humphrey St. SE1 . . . . . .5B **120**
Hungerford Ho. SW1 . . . . .2C **136**
Hungerford La. WC2 . . . . .2F **87**
  (not continuous)
Hungerford St. E1 . . . . . . .4A **66**
Hunsdon Rd. SE14 . . . . . .3D **145**
Hunslett St. E2 . . . . .1C **44**
Hunstanton Ho. NW1 . . . . .1A **56**
Hunt Cl. W11 . . . . .2E **79**
Hunter Cl. SE1 . . . . .2E **119**
Hunter Ho. SE1 . . . . .5A **90**
  SW5 . . . . .1E **131**
  SW8 . . . . .5E **137**
  WC1 . . . . .4F **37**
Hunterian Museum, The . . .4C **60**
Hunter Lodge W9 . . . . . . .1E **53**
Hunter St. WC1 . . . . .4A **38**
Huntingdon St. E16 . . . . . .4C **72**
  N1 . . . . .2B **16**
Huntley St. WC1 . . . . . . .5C **36**
Hunton St. E1 . . . . .5D **43**
Hunt's Ct. WC2 . . . . .1E **87**
Huntshaw Ho. E3 . . . . . . .3F **47**
Hunts La. E15 . . . . .4D **71**
Huntsman St. SE17 . . . . . .4F **119**
Huntsworth M. NW1 . . . . . .4B **34**

Hurdwick Ho. NW1 . . . . . .1B **36**
Hurdwick Pl. *NW1* 5B **14**
  (off Hampstead Rd.)
Hurleston Ho. SE8 . . . . . . .1B **146**
Hurley Cres. SE16 . . . . . .4E **95**
Hurley Ho. SE11 . . . . .4E **117**
Hurst Ct. E6 . . . . .1E **75**
Hurst Ho. WC1 . . . . .1C **38**
Hurstway Rd. W11 . . . . . .5E **51**
Hurstway Wlk. W11 . . . . . .5E **51**
Husborne Ho. SE8 . . . . . . .3F **123**
Huson Cl. NW3 . . . . .1F **11**
Hutchings St. E14 . . . . . . .5D **97**
Hutchings Wharf E14 . . . . .5D **97**
Hutchins Cl. E15 . . . . .2C **26**
Hutchinson Ho. NW3 . . . . .1B **12**
  SE14 . . . . .5C **144**
Hutton St. EC4 . . . . .4F **61**
Huxley Ho. NW8 . . . . .5E **33**
Huxley St. W10 . . . . .3F **29**
Hyde Park 1A **84**
HYDE PARK CORNER 4E **85**
Hyde Pk. Cnr. W1 . . . . . . .4E **85**
Hyde Pk. Cres. W2 . . . . . .4F **55**
Hyde Pk. Gdns. W2 . . . . . .5E **55**
  (not continuous)
Hyde Pk. Gdns. M. W2 . . . .5E **55**
Hyde Pk. Ga. SW7 . . . . . .5B **82**
  (not continuous)
Hyde Pk. Ga. M. SW7 . . . . .5C **82**
Hyde Pk. Mans. NW1 . . . . .2F **55**
  (not continuous)
Hyde Pk. Pl. W2 . . . . .5A **56**
Hyde Pk. Sq. W2 . . . . . . .4F **55**
Hyde Pk. Sq. M. W2 . . . . .4F **55**
Hyde Pk. St. W2 . . . . .4F **55**
Hyde Pk. Towers W2 . . . . . .1B **82**
Hyderabad Way E15 . . . . . .1F **27**
Hyde Rd. N1 . . . . .4F **19**
Hyde's Pl. N1 . . . . .1F **17**
Hyde St. SE8 . . . . .3D **147**
Hyde Va. SE10 . . . . .5C **148**
Hydra Building, The EC1 . . . .3E **39**
Hyndman St. SE15 . . . . . . .3F **143**
Hyperion Ct. E16 . . . . . . .2E **73**
Hyperion Ho. E3 . . . . .1F **45**
Hyson Rd. SE16 . . . . .5A **122**
Hythe Ho. SE16 . . . . .4C **94**
  W6 . . . . .3C **106**

I

Ian Bowater Ct. N1 . . . . . . .2E **39**
Ibberton Ho. SW8 . . . . . . .4B **138**
  W14 . . . . .2A **108**
Ibbotson Av. E16 . . . . .3C **72**
Ibbott St. E1 . . . . .4C **44**
Ibex Ho. E15 . . . . .4F **7**
Ibis Ct. SE8 . . . . .3D **147**
ICA Cinema 3E **87**
Icarus Ho. E3 . . . . .3C **46**
ICA Theatre 3E **87**
Iceland Rd. E3 . . . . .4E **25**
Iceland Wharf SE16 . . . . . .3F **123**
Iceni Ct. E3 . . . . .4C **24**
Ice Wharf N1 . . . . .5B **16**
Ice Wharf Marina N1 . . . . . .5A **16**
Ice Works, The NW1 . . . . . .2F **13**
Icknield Ho. SW3 . . . . . . .5A **112**
Icon Apartments SE1 . . . . .1F **119**
Icona Point E15 . . . . .3B **26**
Ida St. E14 . . . . .3B **70**
  (not continuous)

Ide Mans. E1 . . . . .5D **67**
Idol La. EC3 . . . . .1F **91**
Idonia St. SE8 . . . . .4D **147**
Iffley Rd. W6 . . . . .1A **106**
Ifield Ho. SE17 . . . . .5A **120**
Ifield Rd. SW10 . . . . .2A **132**
Ifor Evans Pl. E1 . . . . .5E **45**
Ightham Ho. SE17 . . . . . . .4F **119**
Ikon Ho. E1 . . . . .5C **66**
Ilbert St. W10 . . . . .3E **29**
Ilchester Gdns. W2 . . . . . .5F **53**
Ilchester Mans. W8 . . . . . .1D **109**
Ilchester Pl. W14 . . . . .1B **108**
Ilderton Rd. SE15 . . . . . . .4B **144**
  SE16 . . . . .5A **122**
Ilderton Wharf SE15 . . . . . .2C **144**
Ilfracombe Flats *SE1* 4C **90**
  (off Marshalsea Rd.)
Iliffe St. SE17 . . . . .5A **118**
Iliffe Yd. SE17 . . . . .5A **118**
Ilkley Rd. E16 . . . . .2B **74**
Imber St. N1 . . . . .4D **19**
Imperial College London
  Chelsea & Westminster
  Campus 3C **132**
  (within Chelsea
    & Westminster Hospital)
  Royal Brompton Campus
  . . . . .1F **133**
  St Mary's 3E **55**
  Sth. Kensington Campus
  . . . . .1D **111**
Imperial Coll. Rd. SW7 . . . .2C **110**
Imperial Ct. NW8 . . . . . . .5A **12**
  SE11 . . . . .1D **139**
Imperial Ho. E3 . . . . .2F **45**
  E14 . . . . .5B **68**
Imperial St. E3 . . . . .3B **48**
Imperial War Mus.
  All Saints Annexe 2E **117**
  Lambeth Rd. 2E **117**
Imperial Wharf E2 . . . . . . .5F **21**
Imperium Ho. E1 . . . . .4F **65**
Imre Cl. W12 . . . . .2A **78**
Indescon Ct. E14 . . . . . . .5F **97**
Indescon Sq. E14 . . . . . . .5E **97**
India Ho. WC2 . . . . .5B **60**
India Pl. WC2 . . . . .5B **60**
India St. EC3 . . . . .4B **64**
India Way W12 . . . . .5A **50**
IndigO2 . . . . .3F **99**
Indigo M. E14 . . . . .4C **70**
Indus Ct. SE15 . . . . .4C **142**
Infirmary St. SW3 . . . . . . .2C **134**
Inforum M. SE15 . . . . .4E **143**
Ingal Rd. E13 . . . . .1E **73**
Ingelow Ho. W8 . . . . .4F **81**
Ingersoll Rd. W12 . . . . . . .3A **78**
Ingestre Pl. W1 . . . . .4C **58**
Inglebert St. EC1 . . . . . . .2D **39**
Inglefield Sq. E1 . . . . .2A **94**
Ingle M. EC1 . . . . .2D **39**
Inglesham Wlk. E9 . . . . . . .4C **4**
Inglewood Cl. E14 . . . . . . .3E **125**
Ingoldisthorpe Gro. SE15 . . .2C **142**
Ingot Twr. E14 . . . . .2E **69**
Ingram Cl. SE11 . . . . .3C **116**
Ingram Ho. E3 . . . . .5A **24**
Ingrebourne Ho. NW8 . . . . .1E **55**
Inigo Pl. WC2 . . . . .5F **59**
Ink Bldg. W10 . . . . .1D **51**
Inkerman Ter. NW8 . . . . . .2E **109**
Ink Works Ct. SE1 . . . . . . .5A **92**
Inner Circ. NW1 . . . . .3D **35**

Inner Ct. SW3 . . . . .3F **133**
Inner London Family
  Proceedings Court
  Magistrates' Court **3B 58**
Inner Temple La. EC4 . . . . . .4D **61**
Innes St. SE15 . . . . .4A **142**
Innis Ho. SE17 . . . . .5F **119**
Innova Pas. E1 . . . . .4B **42**
Innovation Centre, The E14 . .4B **98**
Inns of Court & City Yeomanry Mus.
  . . . .**2C 60**
Insley Ho. E3 . . . . .2F **47**
Institute of Archaeology Collections
  . . . .**4D 37**
Institute of Contemporary Arts
  . . . .**3E 87**
Interchange, The NW1 . . . . . .2F **13**
International Bus. Pk. E15 . . .4D **27**
International Ho. E1 . . . . . . .1C **92**
International Sq. E20 . . . . . . .5B **6**
International Way E20 . . . . . . .5B **6**
Inver Ct. W2 . . . . .4A **54**
Invergarry Ho. NW6 . . . . . . .1F **31**
Inverine Rd. SE7 . . . . .5F **129**
Inverness Gdns. W8 . . . . . . .3F **81**
Inverness M. W2 . . . . .5A **54**
Inverness Pl. W2 . . . . .5A **54**
Inverness St. NW1 . . . . .3F **13**
Inverness Ter. W2 . . . . .4A **54**
Invicta Cl. E3 . . . . .2E **69**
Invicta Plaza SE1 . . . . .2F **89**
Inville Rd. SE17 . . . . .1E **141**
  (not continuous)
Inville Wlk. SE17 . . . . .1E **141**
Inwen Ct. SE8 . . . . .1F **145**
  (not continuous)
Inwood Ct. NW1 . . . . .1C **14**
Inwood Ho. N1 . . . . .4A **18**
Inworth Wlk. N1 . . . . .3B **18**
Ion Ct. E2 . . . . .1D **43**
Ionian Bldg. E14 . . . . .5F **67**
Ionian Ho. E1 . . . . .5E **45**
Ion Sq. E2 . . . . .1D **43**
Ipsden Bldgs. SE1 . . . . .4E **89**
Ireland Cl. E6 . . . . .2B **76**
Ireland Yd. EC4 . . . . .4A **62**
Ireton St. E3 . . . . .4D **47**
Iris Cl. E6 . . . . .1A **76**
Iris Ct. SE14 . . . . .5C **144**
Iron Bri. Ho. NW1 . . . . .1C **12**
Ironmonger La. EC2 . . . . . . .4C **62**
Ironmonger Pas. EC1 . . . . . .3C **40**
Ironmonger Row EC1 . . . . . .3C **40**
Ironmonger Row Baths **3B 40**
Ironmongers Pl. E14 . . . . . .4E **125**
Ironside Cl. SE16 . . . . .4D **95**
Ironside Ho. E9 . . . . .1A **4**
Iron Works E3 . . . . .3E **25**
Ironworks, The N1 . . . . .1A **38**
Irvine Cl. E14 . . . . .1A **70**
Irvine Ct. W1 . . . . .5C **36**
Irving Ho. SE17 . . . . .1F **139**
Irving Mans. W14 . . . . .2A **130**
Irving Rd. W14 . . . . .1E **107**
Irving St. WC2 . . . . .1E **87**
Irwell Est. SE16 . . . . .5B **94**
Isaac Way SE1 . . . . .4C **90**
Isabella Ho. SE11 . . . . .5F **117**
  W6 . . . . .5B **106**
Isabella St. SE1 . . . . .3F **89**
Isambard M. E14 . . . . .2C **126**
Isambard Pl. SE16 . . . . .3C **94**
Isis Ho. NW8 . . . . .5E **33**
Island Apartments N1 . . . . . .3C **18**

Island Ho. E3 . . . . .2B **48**
Island Rd. SE16 . . . . .4D **123**
Island Row E14 . . . . .4B **68**
Isleden Ho. N1 . . . . .3B **18**
ISLE OF DOGS **5F 97**
ISLINGTON **4F 17**
Islington Bus. Cen. N1 . . . . .3C **18**
Islington Grn. N1 . . . . .4F **17**
  (not continuous)
Islington High St. N1 . . . . . .1E **39**
  (not continuous)
Islington Mus. **3F 39**
Islington Pk. M. N1 . . . . . . .1F **17**
Islington Pk. St. N1 . . . . . . .1E **17**
Islington Pl. N1 . . . . .4D **17**
Isola Ct. N1 . . . . .3B **18**
Istra Ho. E20 . . . . .3B **6**
Ivanhoe Ho. E3 . . . . .1F **45**
Ivatt Pl. W14 . . . . .1C **130**
Iveagh Cl. E9 . . . . .3E **23**
Iveagh Ct. E1 . . . . .4B **64**
Iveagh Ho. SW10 . . . . .4C **132**
Iver Ho. N1 . . . . .4F **19**
  (off Halcomb St.)
Iverna Ct. W8 . . . . .1E **109**
Iverna Gdns. W8 . . . . .1E **109**
Iverson Rd. NW6 . . . . .1C **8**
Ives Rd. E16 . . . . .2F **71**
Ives St. SW3 . . . . .3A **112**
Ivimey St. E2 . . . . .2E **43**
Ivor Ct. NW1 . . . . .4B **34**
Ivories, The N1 . . . . .1B **18**
Ivor Pl. NW1 . . . . .5B **34**
Ivor St. NW1 . . . . .2B **14**
Ivory Ho. E1 . . . . .2C **92**
Ivory Pl. W11 . . . . .5F **51**
Ivybridge Ct. NW1 . . . . .1A **14**
Ivybridge La. WC2 . . . . .1A **88**
Ivychurch La. SE17 . . . . . . .5B **120**
Ivy Cotts. E14 . . . . .5A **70**
Ivy Ct. SE16 . . . . .1E **143**
Ivy Lodge W11 . . . . .2D **81**
Ivy Rd. E16 . . . . .3D **73**
Ivy St. N1 . . . . .5F **19**
Ixworth Pl. SW3 . . . . .5F **111**

J

Jacana Ct. E1 . . . . .1C **92**
Jacaranda Gro. E8 . . . . .2C **20**
Jack Clow Rd. E15 . . . . .1F **49**
Jackman Ho. E1 . . . . .3A **94**
Jackman St. E8 . . . . .4F **21**
Jackson & Joseph Bldg.
  E1 . . . . .1C **64**
Jackson Cl. E9 . . . . .2D **23**
Jacks Pl. E1 . . . . .1B **64**
Jacob Mans. E1 . . . . .3F **65**
Jacobs Ct. E1 . . . . .3E **65**
Jacobs Island Ho. SE16 . . . .2C **120**
Jacobs Island Pier SE16 . . . .4D **93**
Jacob St. SE1 . . . . .4C **92**
Jacob's Well M. W1 . . . . . . .3E **57**
Jacotts Ho. W10 . . . . .5B **28**
Jacqueline Ho. NW1 . . . . . . .3C **12**
Jade Cl. E16 . . . . .4E **75**
Jade Ter. NW6 . . . . .1C **10**
Jagger Ho. SW11 . . . . .5B **134**
Jago Wlk. SE5 . . . . .5D **141**
Jake Russell Wlk. E16 . . . . . .5C **74**
Jamaica Rd. SE1 . . . . .5C **92**
  SE16 . . . . .1D **121**
Jamaica St. E1 . . . . .3C **66**

James Anderson Ct. E2 . . . . .5A **20**
James Brine Ho. E2 . . . . . . .2C **42**
James Campbell Ho. E2 . . . .1B **44**
James Collins Cl. W9 . . . . . .5B **30**
James Ct. N1 . . . . .3C **18**
James Docherty Ho. E2 . . . . .1A **44**
James Hammett Ho. E2 . . . . .2C **42**
James Hill Ho. W10 . . . . . . .4A **30**
James Ho. E1 . . . . .5F **45**
  SE16 . . . . .5D **95**
  SW8 . . . . .4F **137**
  W10 . . . . .5A **30**
James Lighthill Ho. WC1 . . . .1C **38**
James Lind Ho. SE8 . . . . . .4B **124**
James Middleton Ho. E2 . . . .2A **44**
Jameson Ct. E2 . . . . .1B **44**
Jameson Ho. SE11 . . . . . . .5B **116**
Jameson St. W8 . . . . .2E **81**
James Riley Point E15 . . . . . .3C **26**
James Stewart Ho. NW6 . . . . .1B **8**
James St. W1 . . . . .3E **57**
  WC2 . . . . .4A **60**
James Stroud Ho. SE17 . . . .1C **140**
Jamestown Rd. NW1 . . . . . . .3F **13**
Jamestown Way E14 . . . . . . .1E **99**
James Voller Way E1 . . . . . . .4B **66**
Jam Factory, The SE1 . . . . .2F **119**
Jamilah Ho. E16 . . . . .1E **105**
Jamuna Cl. E14 . . . . .2A **68**
Jane Austen Hall E16 . . . . .2A **102**
Jane Austen Ho. SW1 . . . . .1B **136**
Jane St. E1 . . . . .3F **65**
Janet St. E14 . . . . .1D **125**
Janeway Pl. SE16 . . . . .5F **93**
Janeway St. SE16 . . . . .5E **93**
Janson Cl. E15 . . . . .2F **7**
Janson Rd. E15 . . . . .2F **7**
Jaquard Ct. E2 . . . . .5B **22**
Jardine Rd. E1 . . . . .5E **67**
Jarman Ho. E1 . . . . .2B **66**
  SE16 . . . . .3D **123**
Jarret Ho. E3 . . . . .2E **47**
Jarrow Rd. SE16 . . . . .4B **122**
Jarrow Way E9 . . . . .1A **4**
Jasmine Sq. E3 . . . . .4B **24**
Jasmin Lodge SE16 . . . . . . .1F **143**
Jason Ct. SW9 . . . . .5D **139**
  W1 . . . . .3E **57**
Jasper Rd. E16 . . . . .4E **75**
Jasper Wlk. N1 . . . . .2D **41**
Java Wharf SE1 . . . . .4C **92**
Jay Ho. E3 . . . . .4B **24**
Jay M. SW7 . . . . .5C **82**
Jays St. N1 . . . . .4C **16**
Jean Darling Ho. SW10 . . . .3D **133**
Jean Pardies Ho. E1 . . . . . . .2B **66**
Jebb St. E3 . . . . .1E **47**
Jefferson Bldg. E14 . . . . . . .4D **97**
Jeffrey's Pl. NW1 . . . . .1B **14**
Jeffrey's St. NW1 . . . . .1A **14**
Jeger Av. E2 . . . . .4B **20**
Jelico Point SE16 . . . . .4B **96**
Jellicoe Ho. E2 . . . . .1D **43**
Jemotts Ct. SE14 . . . . .2D **145**
Jenkinson Ho. E2 . . . . .2D **45**
Jenner Ho. WC1 . . . . .4A **38**
Jennifer Ho. SE11 . . . . .4E **117**
Jenningsbury Ho. SW3 . . . .5A **112**
  (off Cale St.)
Jennings Ho. SE10 . . . . . . .1E **149**
Jensen Ho. E3 . . . . .4D **47**
Jephson Ho. SE17 . . . . .2F **139**
Jerdan Ho. SW6 . . . . .4D **131**
Jerdan Pl. SW6 . . . . .4D **131**

Jeremiah St. E14 . . . . .4F 69
Jeremy Bentham Ho. E2 . . . . .2E 43
Jermyn St. SW1 . . . . .2B 86
Jermyn Street Theatre 1D 87
Jerome Cres. NW8 . . . . .4F 33
Jerome Ho. NW1 . . . . .1A 56
   SW7 . . . . .3D 111
Jerome St. E1 . . . . .1B 64
Jerrold St. N1 . . . . .1A 42
Jersey Rd. E16 . . . . .3B 74
Jersey St. E2 . . . . .3A 44
Jerusalem Pas. EC1 . . . . .5F 39
Jervis Bay Ho. E14 . . . . .4D 71
Jervis Ct. SE10 . . . . .5B 148
   W1 . . . . .4A 58
Jervis Rd. SW6 . . . . .3C 130

Jerwood Space Art Gallery
   . . . . .4A 90
Jessel Ho. SW1 . . . . .3E 115
   WC1 . . . . .3F 37
Jessel Mans. W14 . . . . .2A 130
Jessie Duffett Ho. SE5 . . . . . .4B 140
Jessie Wood Ct. SW9 . . . . . .5D 139
Jesson Ho. SE17 . . . . .4D 119
Jessop Ct. N1 . . . . .1A 40
Jessop Sq. E14 . . . . .3E 97
Jevons Ho. NW8 . . . . .2D 11
Jewel Tower 1F 115
Jewish Mus.
   Camden Town 4A 14
Jewry St. EC3 . . . . .4B 64
Jim Griffiths Ho. SW6 . . . . . .3B 130
Joanna Ho. W6 . . . . .5B 106
Joan St. SE1 . . . . .3F 89
Jocelin Ho. N1 . . . . .4C 16
Jocelyn St. SE15 . . . . .5D 143
Jockey's Flds. WC1 . . . . .1C 60
Jodane St. SE8 . . . . .4B 124
Jodrell Rd. E3 . . . . .3C 24
Johanna St. SE1 . . . . .5D 09
John Adam St. WC2 . . . . .1A 88
John Aird Ct. W2 . . . . .1A 56
   (not continuous)
John Bell Twr. E. E3 . . . . .5D 25
John Bell Twr. W. E3 . . . . . . .5D 25
John Bond Ho. E3 . . . . .5B 24
John Bowles Ct. E1 . . . . .5D 67
John Brent Ho. SE8 . . . . .4E 123
John Carpenter St. EC4 . . . . . .5F 61
John Cartwright Ho. E2 . . . . . .2F 43
John Fearon Wlk. W10 . . . . . .2A 30
   (off Dart St.)
John Felton Rd. SE16 . . . . . .5D 93
John Fielden Ho. E2 . . . . .2F 43
John Fisher St. E1 . . . . .5D 65
John Harrison Way SE10 . . . .2B 128
John Horner M. N1 . . . . .5B 18
John Islip St. SW1 . . . . .5E 115
John Kennedy Ho. SE16 . . . . .3D 123
John Kirk Ho. E6 . . . . .3D 77
John Knight Lodge SW6 . . . . .4E 131
John McDonald Ho. E14 . . . . .1B 126
John McKenna Wlk. SE16 . . . .1E 121
John Maurice Cl. SE17 . . . . . .3D 119
John Milton Pas. EC4 . . . . . . .4C 62
Johnny Andrews Ho. E1 . . . . . .4E 67
John Orwell Sports Cen. 3F 93
John Parry Ct. N1 . . . . .5A 20
John Penn Ho. SE14 . . . . . . .4C 146
John Penry Ho. SE1 . . . . .1D 143
John Prince's St. W1 . . . . . . .3A 58
John Pritchard Ho. E1 . . . . . . .5E 43
John Ratcliffe Ho. NW6 . . . . . .3D 31
John Rennie Wlk. E1 . . . . .2A 94

John Riley Ho. E3 . . . . .1B 68
John Roll Way SE16 . . . . . . .1E 121
John Ruskin St. SE5 . . . . . . .4F 139
John Scurr Ho. E14 . . . . .4F 67
John Silkin La. SE8 . . . . .4E 123
John's M. WC1 . . . . .5C 38
John Smith Av. SW6 . . . . .4B 130
John Smith M. E14 . . . . .5D 71
Johnson Cl. E8 . . . . .3D 21
Johnson Ho. E2 . . . . .3E 43
   NW1 . . . . .1C 36
   NW3 . . . . .1B 12
   SW1 . . . . .4E 113
   SW8 . . . . .5E 137
   W8 . . . . .4C 80
Johnson Lock Ct. E1 . . . . .1A 68
Johnson Lodge W9 . . . . .1E 53
Johnson Mans. W14 . . . . . . .2A 130
Johnson's Ct. EC4 . . . . .4E 61
Johnson's Pl. SW1 . . . . .1B 136
Johnston St. SE1 . . . . .5C 66
John's Pl. E1 . . . . .3A 66
John Strachey Ho. SW6 . . . . .3C 130
John St. WC1 . . . . .5C 38
John Trundle Ct. EC2 . . . . . . .1B 62
John Trundle Highwalk
   EC2 . . . . .1B 62
John Tucker Ho. E14 . . . . . . .1E 125
John Wesley Highwalk
   EC2 . . . . .2B 62
John Wetherby Ct. E15 . . . . . .1A 48
John Wetherby Ct. E. E15 . . . .1A 48
John Wetherby Ct. W. E15 . . . .1A 48
John Wheatley Ho. SW6 . . . . .3C 130
John Williams Cl. SE14 . . . . . .3D 145
Joiner St. SE1 . . . . .3E 91
Joiners Yd. N1 . . . . .1A 38
Jolles Ho. E3 . . . . .2F 47
Jonathan St. SE11 . . . . .5B 116
Jonoo Ho. E14 . . . . .4D 71
Jones Rd. E13 . . . . .1A 74
Jones St. W1 . . . . .1F 85
Jonson Ho. SE1 . . . . .2E 119
Jordan Ho. N1 . . . . .3E 19
Jordans Ho. NW8 . . . . .4E 33
Joscoyne Ho. E1 . . . . .3A 66
Joseph Conrad Ho. SW1 . . . .4C 114
Joseph Hardcastle Cl.
   SE14 . . . . .4E 145
Joseph Irwin Ho. E14 . . . . . . .5C 68
Joseph M. N7 . . . . .1D 17
Joseph Priestley Ho. E2 . . . . .2F 43
   (off Canrobert St.)
Joseph St. E3 . . . . .5C 46
Joseph Trotter Cl. EC1 . . . . . .3E 39
Joshua St. E14 . . . . .2B 70
Joubert Mans. SW3 . . . . .5A 112
Jowett St. SE15 . . . . .5C 142
Jowitt Ho. E2 . . . . .2D 45
Joy of Life Fountain 2D 85
Jubilee, The SE10 . . . . .5A 148
Jubilee Bldgs. NW8 . . . . .4D 11
Jubilee Ct. E16 . . . . .2B 72
   SE10 . . . . .2A 148
Jubilee Cres. E14 . . . . .2C 126
Jubilee Hall Gym 5A 60
Jubilee Ho. SE11 . . . . .4E 117
   WC1 . . . . .4B 38
Jubilee Mans. E1 . . . . .3B 66
Jubilee Mkt. WC2 . . . . .5A 60
   (off Covent Gdn.)
Jubilee Pl. SW3 . . . . .5A 112
Jubilee Pl. Shop. Mall E14 . . .3F 97

Jubilee Sports Cen.
   London 3B 30
Jubilee St. E1 . . . . .3B 66
Jubilee Walkway SE1 . . . . . . .1A 90
Jubilee Yd. SE1 . . . . .4B 92
Judd St. WC1 . . . . .2F 37
Jude St. E16 . . . . .4B 72
Juer St. SW11 . . . . .5A 134
Julia Garfield M. E16 . . . . . .2A 102
   (not continuous)
Julian Ct. NW1 . . . . .1C 14
Julian Pl. E14 . . . . .5A 126
Juliet Ho. N1 . . . . .1F 41
Julius Ho. E14 . . . . .4D 71
Julius Nyerere Cl. N1 . . . . . . .4B 16
Junction M. W2 . . . . .3F 55
Junction Pl. W2 . . . . .3E 55
Juniper Ct. W8 . . . . .2F 109
Juniper Cres. NW1 . . . . .2E 13
Juniper Ho. E16 . . . . .4C 72
   SE14 . . . . .5C 144
   W10 . . . . .4F 29
Juniper La. E6 . . . . .2A 76
Juniper St. E1 . . . . .5E 66
Juno Ct. SW9 . . . . .5D 139
Juno Enterprise Cen.
   SE14 . . . . .2D 145
Juno Ho. E3 . . . . .4D 25
Juno Way SE14 . . . . .2E 145
Juno Way Ind. Est. SE14 . . . . .2E 145
Jupiter Ct. E3 . . . . .5D 25
   (off Four Seasons Cl.)
   SW9 . . . . .5D 139
Jupiter Ho. E14 . . . . .5A 126
Jupp Rd. E15 . . . . .2D 27
Jupp Rd. W. E15 . . . . .3C 26
Jura Ho. SE16 . . . . .3E 123
Jurston Ct. SE1 . . . . .5E 89
Justice Apartments E1 . . . . . .3D 67
Justice Wlk. SW3 . . . . .3F 133
Justines Pl. E2 . . . . .1E 45
Juxon Ho. EC4 . . . . .4A 62
Juxon St. SE11 . . . . .3C 116

K

Kaleidoscope Ho. E20 . . . . . . .3C 6
Kamen Ho. SE1 . . . . .3F 91
Karachi Ho. E15 . . . . .4F 7
Karner Ho. E20 . . . . .3A 6
Katherine Bell Twr. E3 . . . . . .5D 25
Katherine Cl. SE16 . . . . .3D 95
Katherine Ho. W10 . . . . .5F 29
Katherine Sq. W11 . . . . .2F 79
Kayani Ho. E16 . . . . .3F 73
Kay St. E2 . . . . .5E 21
   E15 . . . . .2E 27
Kean Ho. SE17 . . . . .2F 139
Kean St. WC2 . . . . .4B 60
Keats Av. E16 . . . . .2F 101
Keats Cl. SE1 . . . . .4B 120
Keats Ho. E2 . . . . .2B 44
   SE5 . . . . .5C 140
   SW1 . . . . .2C 136
Keats Pl. EC2 . . . . .2D 63
Kedge Ho. E14 . . . . .1E 125
Kedleston Wlk. E2 . . . . .2A 44
Keel Cl. SE16 . . . . .3E 95
Keel Ct. E14 . . . . .5E 71
Keeley St. WC2 . . . . .4B 60
Keeling Ho. E2 . . . . .1F 43
Keelson Ho. E14 . . . . .1E 125
Keepier Wharf E14 . . . . .5E 67

Keeton's Rd. SE16 . . . . .1F **121**
(not continuous)
Keiller Ho. E16 . . . . .3B **104**
Keith Ho. NW6 . . . . .2F **31**
SW8 . . . . .4F **137**
Kelby Ho. N7 . . . . .1B **16**
Kelday Hgts. E1 . . . . .4A **66**
Kelfield Ct. W10 . . . . .3E **51**
Kelfield Gdns. W10 . . . . .3C **50**
Kelfield M. W10 . . . . .3D **51**
Kellet Ho's. *WC1* *3A 38*
(off Tankerton St.)
Kellett Ho. N1 . . . . .4F **19**
Kellow Ho. SE1 . . . . .4D **91**
Kell St. SE1 . . . . .1A **118**
Kelly Av. SE15 . . . . .5B **142**
Kelly Ct. E14 . . . . .1D **97**
Kelly M. W9 . . . . .5C **30**
Kelmscott House **5A 106**
Kelsey St. E2 . . . . .4F **43**
Kelson Ho. E14 . . . . .1C **126**
Kelso Pl. W8 . . . . .1F **109**
Kelvedon Ho. SW8 . . . . .5A **138**
Kelvedon Rd. SW6 . . . . .5C **130**
Kelvin Ct. W11 . . . . .1D **81**
Kelway Ho. W14 . . . . .1C **130**
Kember St. N1 . . . . .2B **16**
Kemble St. WC2 . . . . .4B **60**
Kemey's St. E9 . . . . .3A **4**
Kemp Ct. SW8 . . . . .5F **137**
Kempe Ho. SE1 . . . . .2E **119**
Kempe Rd. NW6 . . . . .1D **29**
Kemp Ho. E2 . . . . .5D **23**
W1 . . . . .5D **59**
Kemps Ct. W1 . . . . .4D **59**
Kemps Dr. E14 . . . . .5E **69**
Kempsford Gdns.
SW5 . . . . .1E **131**
Kempsford Rd. SE11 . . . . . . .4E **117**
(not continuous)
Kempson Rd. SW6 . . . . .5E **131**
Kempthorne Rd. SE8 . . . . . . .3A **124**
Kempton Ct. E1 . . . . .1F **65**
Kempton Ho. N1 . . . . .4F **19**
Kemsing Ho. SE1 . . . . .5E **91**
Kemsing Rd. SE10 . . . . .5D **129**
Kenbrook Ho. W14 . . . . .1C **108**
Kenchester Cl. SW8 . . . . . . .5A **138**
Kendal NW1 . . . . .2A **36**
Kendal Cl. SW9 . . . . .4F **139**
Kendal Ho. E9 . . . . .2B **22**
N1 . . . . .1C **38**
Kendal Pl. W1 . . . . .2D **57**
Kendal Steps W2 . . . . .4A **56**
Kendal St. W2 . . . . .4A **56**
Kender St. SE14 . . . . .5C **144**
Kendon Ho. E15 . . . . .2E **27**
Kendrick M. SW7 . . . . .3D **111**
Kendrick Pl. SW7 . . . . .4D **111**
Kenilworth Rd. E3 . . . . .5F **23**
NW6 . . . . .3C **8**
Kenley Wlk. W11 . . . . .2F **79**
Kenmore Ct. NW6 . . . . .2F **9**
Kennacraig Cl. E16 . . . . .3E **101**
Kennard Rd. E15 . . . . .2D **27**
Kennard St. E16 . . . . .3B **104**
Kennedy Cox Ho. E16 . . . . . .2B **72**
Kennedy Ho. SE11 . . . . .5B **116**
Kennedy Wlk. SE17 . . . . .4E **119**
Kennet Ct. W9 . . . . .1D **53**
Kenneth Campbell Ho.
NW8 . . . . .4E **33**
Kenneth Ct. SE11 . . . . .3E **117**
Kennet Ho. NW8 . . . . .5E **33**

Kenneth Younger Ho.
SW6 . . . . .3C **130**
Kennet Rd. W9 . . . . .4C **30**
Kennet St. E1 . . . . .2E **93**
Kenning Ho. N1 . . . . .3F **19**
Kenning St. SE16 . . . . .4C **94**
Kennings Way SE11 . . . . . . .5E **117**
KENNINGTON **2E 139**
Kennington Grn. SE11 . . . . . .1D **139**
Kennington La. SE11 . . . . . . .1B **138**
KENNINGTON OVAL **3D 139**
Kennington Oval SE11 . . . . . .2C **138**
Kennington Pal. Ct. SE11 . . . .5D **117**
Kennington Pk. Gdns.
SE11 . . . . .2F **139**
Kennington Pk. Ho. SE11 . . . .1E **139**
Kennington Pk. Pl. SE11 . . . . .1E **139**
Kennington Pk. Rd. SE11 . . . .3D **139**
Kennington Rd. SE1 . . . . .1D **117**
SE11 . . . . .1D **117**
Kenrick Pl. W1 . . . . .1D **57**
KENSAL GREEN **2B 28**
Kensal Ho. W10 . . . . .5E **29**
KENSAL RISE **1D 29**
Kensal Rd. W10 . . . . .4E **29**
KENSAL TOWN **5A 30**
Kensal Wharf W10 . . . . .4E **29**
KENSINGTON **5F 81**
Kensington Arc. W8 . . . . .5F **81**
Kensington Cen. W14 . . . . . . .3F **107**
(not continuous)
Kensington Chu. Ct. W8 . . . . .5F **81**
Kensington Chu. St. W8 . . . . .2E **81**
Kensington Chu. Wlk. W8 . . . .4F **81**
(not continuous)
Kensington Ct. SE16 . . . . . . .2E **95**
W8 . . . . .5A **82**
Kensington Ct. Gdns. W8 . . . .1A **110**
Kensington Ct. Mans. W8 . . . .5A **82**
Kensington Ct. M. W8 . . . . . .1A **110**
Kensington Ct. Pl. W8 . . . . . .1A **110**
Kensington Gdns. **2B 82**
Kensington Gdns. Sq. W2 . . . .4F **53**
Kensington Ga. W8 . . . . .1B **110**
Kensington Gore SW7 . . . . . .5C **82**
Kensington Hall Gdns.
W14 . . . . .5B **108**
Kensington Hgts. W8 . . . . . . .3D **81**
Kensington High St. W8 . . . . .3B **108**
W14 . . . . .3B **108**
Kensington Ho. W8 . . . . .5A **82**
W14 . . . . .5E **79**
Kensington Leisure Cen. **5E 51**
Kensington Mall W8 . . . . .2E **81**
Kensington Mans. SW5 . . . . .5E **109**
(not continuous)
Kensington Palace **3A 82**
Kensington Pal. Gdns. W8 . . . .2F **81**
Kensington Pk. Gdns. W11 . . . .1B **80**
Kensington Pk. M. W11 . . . . . .4B **52**
Kensington Pk. Rd. W11 . . . . .4B **52**
Kensington Pl. W8 . . . . .3D **81**
Kensington Rd. SW7 . . . . .5E **83**
W8 . . . . .5A **82**
Kensington Sq. W8 . . . . .5F **81**
Kensington Village W14 . . . . .4C **108**
Kensington W. W14 . . . . .3F **107**
Kensworth Ho. EC1 . . . . .3E **41**
Kent Ct. E2 . . . . .5C **20**
Kent Ho. SE1 . . . . .1C **142**
SW1 . . . . .1D **137**
W8 . . . . .5A **82**
W11 . . . . .2B **80**

Kentish Bldgs. SE1 . . . . .3D **91**
Kentish Town Rd. NW1 . . . . . .3A **14**
Kentmere Ho. SE15 . . . . .3B **144**
Kenton Ct. W14 . . . . .2B **108**
Kenton Ho. E1 . . . . .4C **44**
Kenton Rd. E9 . . . . .1E **23**
Kenton St. WC1 . . . . .4F **37**
Kent Pk. Ind. Est. SE15 . . . . .2F **143**
Kent Pas. NW1 . . . . .4B **34**
Kent St. E2 . . . . .5C **20**
Kent Ter. NW1 . . . . .3A **34**
Kent Wharf SE8 . . . . .4F **147**
Kent Yd. SW7 . . . . .5A **84**
Kenway Rd. SW5 . . . . .4F **109**
Ken Wilson Ho. E2 . . . . .5E **21**
Kenworthy Rd. E9 . . . . .3A **4**
Kenwrick Ho. N1 . . . . .4C **16**
Kenyon Ho. SE5 . . . . .4C **140**
Kenyon Mans. W14 . . . . .2A **130**
Keogh Rd. E15 . . . . .4F **7**
Kepler Ho. SE10 . . . . .5B **128**
Keppel Ho. SE8 . . . . .1B **146**
SW3 . . . . .4F **111**
Keppel Row SE1 . . . . .3B **90**
Keppel St. WC1 . . . . .1E **59**
Kerbela St. E2 . . . . .4D **43**
Kerbey St. E14 . . . . .3A **70**
Kerrier Ho. SW10 . . . . .5C **132**
Kerrington Ct. W10 . . . . .5F **29**
W12 . . . . .4C **78**
Kerris Ho. SE11 . . . . .5E **117**
Kerrison Rd. E15 . . . . .3D **27**
Kerry Cl. E16 . . . . .4F **73**
Kerry Ho. E1 . . . . .3B **66**
Kerry Path SE14 . . . . .3B **146**
Kerry Rd. SE14 . . . . .3B **146**
Kerscott Ho. E3 . . . . .3F **47**
Kerwick Cl. N7 . . . . .1B **16**
Keslake Mans. NW10 . . . . . . .1D **29**
Keslake Rd. NW6 . . . . .1D **29**
Keston Ho. SE17 . . . . .5A **120**
Kestrel Av. E6 . . . . .2F **75**
Kestrel Ct. *E3* *5D 25*
(off Four Seasons Cl.)
Kestrel Ho. EC1 . . . . .2B **40**
Kestrel Pl. SE14 . . . . .3A **146**
Ketton Ho. W10 . . . . .5B **28**
Kevan Ho. SE5 . . . . .5B **140**
Keybridge Ho. SW8 . . . . .3A **138**
Key Cl. E1 . . . . .5A **44**
Keyes Ho. SW1 . . . . .1D **137**
Keyham Ho. W2 . . . . .2D **53**
Key Ho. SE11 . . . . .2D **139**
Keyse Rd. SE1 . . . . .2B **120**
Keystone Cres. N1 . . . . .1A **38**
Keyworth Pl. SE1 . . . . .1A **118**
Keyworth St. SE1 . . . . .1A **118**
Kezia M. SE8 . . . . .1F **145**
Kezia St. SE8 . . . . .1F **145**
Kia Oval **2C 138**
Kibworth St. SW8 . . . . .5B **138**
Kierbeck Bus. Complex
E16 . . . . .3F **101**
(not continuous)
Kiffen St. EC2 . . . . .4E **41**
Kilbrennan Ho. E14 . . . . .3C **70**
KILBURN **5B 8**
Kilburn Bri. NW6 . . . . .4E **9**
Kilburn Ga. NW6 . . . . .5F **9**
Kilburn High Rd. NW6 . . . . . . .1B **8**
Kilburn Ho. NW6 . . . . .1C **30**
Kilburn La. W9 . . . . .2E **29**
W10 . . . . .2E **29**
Kilburn Pk. Rd. NW6 . . . . .3D **31**

Kilburn Pl. NW6 . . . . .4E **9**
Kilburn Priory NW6 . . . . .4F **9**
Kilburn Sq. NW6 . . . . .3D **9**
Kilburn Va. NW6 . . . . .4F **9**
Kilburn Va. Est. NW6 . . . . . . .3E **9**
Kilby Ct. SE10 . . . . .2C **128**
Kildare Ct. W2 . . . . .3E **53**
Kildare Gdns. W2 . . . . .3E **53**
Kildare Rd. E16 . . . . .1D **73**
Kildare Ter. W2 . . . . .3E **53**
Kildare Wlk. E14 . . . . .4D **69**
Killick St. N1 . . . . .5B **16**
Killip Cl. E16 . . . . .3C **72**
Killoran Ho. E14 . . . . .1B **126**
Killowen Rd. E9 . . . . .1D **23**
Kilmaine Rd. SW6 . . . . .5A **130**
Kilmarsh Rd. W6 . . . . .3B **106**
Kilmore Ho. E14 . . . . .4A **70**
Kilmuir Ho. SW1 . . . . .4E **113**
Kiln Ct. E14 . . . . .5B **68**
Kilner Ho. E16 . . . . .2F **73**
  SE11 . . . . .2D **139**
Kilner St. E14 . . . . .2D **69**
Kiln Ho. E1 . . . . .1E **67**
Kilravock St. W10 . . . . .3F **29**
Kimber Ct. SE1 . . . . .1F **119**
  (off Long La.)
Kimberley Ct. NW6 . . . . .3A **8**
Kimberley Ho. E14 . . . . .1B **126**
Kimberley Rd. NW6 . . . . .3A **8**
Kimble Ho. NW8 . . . . .4A **34**
Kimbolton Ct. SW3 . . . . .4F **111**
Kimbolton Row SW3 . . . . . . .4F **111**
Kimmins Ct. SE16 . . . . .1D **121**
Kimpton Rd. SE5 . . . . .5D **141**
Kinburn St. SE16 . . . . .4D **95**
Kincaid Rd. SE15 . . . . .5F **143**
Kincardine Gdns. W9 . . . . . . .5D **31**
Kinder Ho. N1 . . . . .5E **19**
Kindersley Ho. SE1 . . . . .4E **65**
Kinder St. E1 . . . . .4F **65**
King & Queen St. SE17 . . . . .4C **118**
King & Queen Wharf
  SE16 . . . . .1E **95**
King Arthur Cl. SE15 . . . . . . .5B **144**
King Charles I Island
  WC2 . . . . .2F **87**
King Charles Ct. SE17 . . . . . .2F **139**
King Charles Ho. SW6 . . . . . .4A **132**
King Charles's Ct. SE10 . . . . .2C **148**
King Charles St. SW1 . . . . . . .4E **87**
King Charles Ter. E1 . . . . . . .1A **94**
King David La. E1 . . . . .5B **66**
Kingdom St. W2 . . . . .2B **54**
Kingdon Ho. E14 . . . . .1B **126**
King Edward III M. SE16 . . . . .5A **94**
King Edward Bldg. EC1 . . . . . .3A **62**
King Edward Mans. E8 . . . . . .4A **22**
King Edwards Mans.
  SW6 . . . . .5D **131**
King Edward's Rd. E9 . . . . . . .3A **22**
King Edward St. EC1 . . . . . . .3B **62**
King Edward Wlk. SE1 . . . . . .1E **117**
Kingfield St. E14 . . . . .3C **126**
Kingfisher Ct. E14 . . . . .5C **98**
  SE1 . . . . .5C **90**
Kingfisher Hgts. E16 . . . . . . .3C **102**
Kingfisher Ho. W14 . . . . .1B **108**
Kingfisher Sq. SE8 . . . . .3C **146**
Kingfisher St. E6 . . . . .2A **76**
King Frederick IX Twr.
  SE16 . . . . .1B **124**
King George IV Ct. SE17 . . . . .5D **119**
  (off Dawes St.)

King George VI Memorial . . .3D **87**
King George Av. E16 . . . . . . .3C **74**
King George St. SE10 . . . . . .5C **148**
Kingham Cl. W11 . . . . .4E **79**
King Henry's Rd. NW3 . . . . . .2E **11**
King Henry's Stairs E1 . . . . . .3A **94**
King Henry Ter. E1 . . . . .1A **94**
Kinghorn St. EC1 . . . . .1A **62**
King Ho. W12 . . . . .4A **50**
Kingisholt Ct. NW10 . . . . . . .3E **29**
King James Ct. SE1 . . . . .5A **90**
King James St. SE1 . . . . .5A **90**
King John Ct. EC2 . . . . .4A **42**
King John St. E1 . . . . .2E **67**
Kinglake Est. SE17 . . . . .5A **120**
Kinglake St. SE17 . . . . .1F **141**
  (not continuous)
Kingly Ct. W1 . . . . .5C **58**
Kingly St. W1 . . . . .4B **58**
Kings Arms Ct. E1 . . . . .2D **65**
Kings Arms Yd. EC2 . . . . .3D **63**
King's Bench St. SE1 . . . . . . .4A **90**
King's Bench Wlk. EC4 . . . . . .4E **61**
King's Blvd. N1 . . . . .1F **37**
Kingsbridge Ct. E14 . . . . .2E **125**
  NW1 . . . . .1A **14**
Kingsbridge Rd. W10 . . . . . . .3C **50**
Kings Coll. Ct. NW3 . . . . . . .1A **12**
King's College London
  Guy's Campus 4D **91**
  St Thomas' Campus - Lambeth
  Pal. Rd. 2A **116**
  St Thomas' Campus -
  St Thomas' House . . .1B **116**
  Strand Campus 5C **60**
  Waterloo Campus 3D **89**
King's Coll. Rd. NW3 . . . . . . .1F **11**
Kingscote St. EC4 . . . . .5F **61**
Kings Ct. N7 . . . . .1B **16**
  NW0 . . . . .4B **12**
  SE1 . . . . .4B **90**
Kings Ct. Nth. SW3 . . . . .1F **133**
Kings Ct. Sth. SW3 . . . . .2F **133**
KING'S CROSS 5F **15**
King's Cross Bri. N1 . . . . .2A **38**
King's Cross Rd. WC1 . . . . . . .2B **38**
Kingsdale Gdns. W11 . . . . . . .3E **79**
Kingsdown Cl. SE16 . . . . .1A **144**
  W10 . . . . .4E **51**
Kingsford Way E6 . . . . .2C **76**
King's Gdns. NW6 . . . . .2E **9**
Kingsgate Mans. WC1 . . . . . .1B **60**
Kingsgate Pde. SW1 . . . . . . .2C **114**
Kingsgate Pl. NW6 . . . . .2D **9**
Kingsgate Rd. NW6 . . . . .1D **9**
King's Gro. SE15 . . . . .5A **144**
  (not continuous)
Kings Head Theatre 3F **17**
King's Head Yd. SE1 . . . . . . .3D **91**
Kingshold Rd. E9 . . . . .2C **22**
Kings Ho. SW8 . . . . .4A **138**
  SW10 . . . . .3D **133**
King's Ho. Studios SW10 . . . .3D **133**
KINGSLAND 1F **19**
Kingsland NW8 . . . . .4A **12**
Kingsland Rd. E2 . . . . .2A **42**
  E8 . . . . .3A **20**
Kingsley Flats SE1 . . . . .3F **119**
Kingsley Ho. SW3 . . . . .3E **133**
  W14 . . . . .3A **108**
Kingsley Mans. W14 . . . . .2A **130**
Kingsley M. E1 . . . . .1A **94**
  W8 . . . . .2A **110**
Kingsley Rd. NW6 . . . . .3C **8**

Kings Mall W6 . . . . .4B **106**
Kings Mans. SW3 . . . . .3F **133**
Kingsmead Ho. E9 . . . . .2A **4**
Kingsmead Way E9 . . . . .1A **4**
King's M. WC1 . . . . .5C **38**
Kingsmill NW8 . . . . .5E **11**
Kingsmill Ho. SW3 . . . . .5A **112**
  (off Cale St.)
Kingsmill Ter. NW8 . . . . .5E **11**
Kingsnorth Ho. W10 . . . . .4E **51**
Kings Place 5A **16**
King's Pl. SE1 . . . . .5B **90**
Kings Sq. EC1 . . . . .3B **40**
Kings Quarter Apartments
  N1 . . . . .4A **16**
King's Reach Twr. SE1 . . . . . .2E **89**
King's Rd. SW3 . . . . .2E **133**
  SW6 . . . . .5A **132**
  SW10 . . . . .4C **132**
King's Scholars' Pas.
  SW1 . . . . .2B **114**
King Stairs Cl. SE16 . . . . .4A **94**
King's Ter. NW1 . . . . .4B **14**
Kingston Ho. NW1 . . . . .4C **14**
  (off Camden St.)
  NW6 . . . . .2A **8**
Kingston Ho. E. SW7 . . . . . . .5F **83**
Kingston Ho. Nth. SW7 . . . . . .5F **83**
Kingston Ho. Sth. SW7 . . . . . .5F **83**
Kingstown St. NW1 . . . . .3D **13**
  (not continuous)
King St. EC2 . . . . .4C **62**
  SW1 . . . . .3C **86**
  W6 . . . . .4A **106**
  WC2 . . . . .5F **59**
King St. Cloisters W6 . . . . . . .4A **106**
  (off King St.)
Kings Wlk. Shop. Cen.
  SW3 . . . . .5B **112**
Kingswater Pl. SW11 . . . . . . .5F **133**
Kingsway WC2 . . . . .3B **60**
Kingsway Mans. WC1 . . . . . . .1B **60**
Kingsway Pl. EC1 . . . . .4E **39**
Kings Wharf E8 . . . . .3A **20**
  SE10 . . . . .2A **148**
Kingswood E2 . . . . .1B **44**
Kingswood Av. NW6 . . . . .4A **8**
Kingswood Cl. SW8 . . . . .5A **138**
Kingswood Ct. NW6 . . . . .2E **9**
Kington Ho. NW6 . . . . .4A **10**
Kingward Ho. E1 . . . . .1D **65**
King Wardrobe Apartments
  EC4 . . . . .4A **62**
  (off Carter La.)
King William La. SE10 . . . . . .1F **149**
King William's Ct. SE10 . . . . .2D **149**
King William St. EC4 . . . . . . .4E **63**
King William Wlk. SE10 . . . . .2C **148**
  (not continuous)
Kingwood Rd. SW6 . . . . .5A **130**
Kinnerton Pl. Nth. SW1 . . . . .5C **84**
Kinnerton Pl. Sth. SW1 . . . . .5C **84**
Kinnerton St. SW1 . . . . .5D **85**
Kinnerton Yd. SW1 . . . . .5C **84**
Kinnoul Rd. W6 . . . . .2A **130**
Kinross Ho. N1 . . . . .3B **16**
Kinsham Ho. E2 . . . . .4E **43**
Kintore Way SE1 . . . . .3B **120**
Kintyre Ho. E14 . . . . .3C **98**
Kipling Est. SE1 . . . . .5E **91**
Kipling Ho. SE5 . . . . .5C **140**
Kipling St. SE1 . . . . .5E **91**
Kira Bldg. E3 . . . . .3C **46**
Kiran Apartments E1 . . . . . . .2C **64**

Kirby Est. SE16 . . . . .1A **122**
Kirby Gro. SE1 . . . . .4F **91**
Kirby St. EC1 . . . . .1E **61**
Kirkby Apartments E3 . . . . . .1C **68**
Kirkeby Ho. EC1 . . . . .1D **61**
Kirkham Rd. E6 . . . . .3A **76**
Kirkland Ho. E14 . . . . .1A **148**
    (St Davids Sq.)
E14 . . . . .5A **126**
    (Westferry Rd.)
Kirkman Pl. W1 . . . . .2D **59**
Kirkmichael Rd. E14 . . . . . . .3C **70**
Kirk's Place 2B **68**
Kirkstall Ho. SW1 . . . . .5F **113**
Kirkstone NW1 . . . . .2B **36**
Kirk St. WC1 . . . . .5C **38**
Kirkwall Pl. E2 . . . . .2C **44**
Kirkwood Pl. NW1 . . . . .1D **13**
Kirtling St. SW8 . . . . .4B **136**
Kirton Gdns. E2 . . . . .3C **42**
    (not continuous)
Kirwyn Way SE5 . . . . .4A **140**
Kitcat Ter. E3 . . . . .2E **47**
Kite Ho. SE1 . . . . .5F **121**
Kite Pl. E2 . . . . .2E **43**
Kitson Rd. SE5 . . . . .4C **140**
Kittiwake Ct. *SE1* *5C 90*
    (off Gt. Dover St.)
SE8 . . . . .2C **146**
Kleine Wharf N1 . . . . .4A **20**
Klein's Wharf E14 . . . . .2D **125**
Knapp Rd. E3 . . . . .5D **47**
Knaresborough Pl. SW5 . . .3F **109**
Knighten St. E1 . . . . .3F **93**
Knighthead Point E14 . . . . . .5D **97**
Knight Ho. SE17 . . . . .4F **119**
Knightrider Ct. EC4 . . . . .5B **62**
Knightrider St. EC4 . . . . .5A **62**
Knights Arc. SW1 . . . . .5B **84**
KNIGHTSBRIDGE **5A 84**
Knightsbridge SW1 . . . . . . .5A **84**
SW7 . . . . .5A **84**
Knightsbridge Apartments, The
SW7 . . . . .5B **84**
Knightsbridge Ct. SW1 . . . . .5C **84**
Knightsbridge Grn. SW1 . . . .5B **84**
    (not continuous)
Knights Ho. SW8 . . . . .5A **138**
SW10 . . . . .4B **132**
W14 . . . . .5B **108**
Knight's Rd. E16 . . . . .4E **101**
Knights Twr. SE8 . . . . .1E **147**
Knight's Wlk. SE11 . . . . .4F **117**
    (not continuous)
Knivet Rd. SW6 . . . . .3D **131**
Knoll Ho. NW8 . . . . .5B **10**
Knolly's Ho. WC1 . . . . .4F **37**
Knot Ho. SE1 . . . . .3B **92**
Knottisford St. E2 . . . . .2C **44**
Knowlden Ho. E1 . . . . .5B **66**
Knowles Wharf NW1 . . . . . . .3C **14**
Knowlton Ho. SW9 . . . . .5E **139**
Knox St. W1 . . . . .1B **56**
Knoyle Ho. W14 . . . . .1F **107**
Knoyle St. SE14 . . . . .3F **145**
Kossuth St. SE10 . . . . .5F **127**
Kotata Ho. E20 . . . . .4B **6**
Kotree Way SE1 . . . . .4E **121**
Kramer M. SW5 . . . . .1E **131**
Krupnik Pl. EC2 . . . . .4A **42**
Kwame Ho. E16 . . . . .1F **105**
Kyle Ho. NW6 . . . . .3D **9**
Kylemore Rd. NW6 . . . . .1D **9**
Kylestrome Ho. SW1 . . . . . . .4E **113**

Kynance M. SW7 . . . . .2A **110**
Kynance Pl. SW7 . . . . .2B **110**

L

Laban Cen. **3F 147**
Laban Wlk. SE8 . . . . .3F **147**
Laburnum Cl. SE15 . . . . .5B **144**
Laburnum Ct. E2 . . . . .4B **20**
SE16 . . . . .5C **94**
Laburnum St. E2 . . . . .4B **20**
Lacey M. E3 . . . . .5D **25**
Lacine Ct. SE16 . . . . .4D **95**
Lackington St. EC2 . . . . .1E **63**
Lackland Ho. SE1 . . . . .5C **120**
Lacland Ho. SW10 . . . . .4D **133**
Lacon Ho. WC1 . . . . .1D **61**
Ladbroke Cres. W11 . . . . . . .4A **52**
Ladbroke Gdns. W11 . . . . . . .5B **52**
Ladbroke Gro. W10 . . . . .4E **29**
W11 . . . . .3A **52**
Ladbroke Gro. Ho. W11 . . . . .1B **80**
Ladbroke Grove Memorial . .**5E 29**
Ladbroke M. W11 . . . . .3A **80**
Ladbroke Rd. W11 . . . . .2A **80**
Ladbroke Sq. W11 . . . . .1B **80**
Ladbroke Ter. W11 . . . . .1C **80**
Ladbroke Wlk. W11 . . . . .2C **80**
Lady Dock Path SE16 . . . . . .5F **95**
Ladyfern Ho. E3 . . . . .1E **69**
Lady Florence Courtyard
SE8 . . . . .5E **147**
Lady Margaret Ho. SE17 . . . .2D **141**
Lady May Ho. SE5 . . . . .5B **140**
Lady Micos Almshouses
E1 . . . . .3C **66**
LA Fitness
  Bayswater **5F 53**
  Bloomsbury **1B 60**
  Leadenhall **4A 64**
  London Wall **2D 63**
  Marylebone, Balcombe St.
  . . . .**1B 56**
  Marylebone, Hallam St. .**1A 58**
  Novello **4B 60**
  Piccadilly **2D 87**
  St Pauls **2B 62**
  South Kensington **3F 111**
  West India Quay **1E 97**
Lafone St. SE1 . . . . .4B **92**
Lagado M. SE16 . . . . .3E **95**
Lagare Apartments SE1 . . . . .4A **90**
Lagonda Ho. E3 . . . . .4D **47**
Lagonier Ho. EC1 . . . . .3C **40**
Laing Ho. SE5 . . . . .5B **140**
Laird Ho. SE5 . . . . .5B **140**
Lake Ho. SE1 . . . . .5B **90**
Lakenham Pl. E3 . . . . .5B **46**
Lakeside Rd. W14 . . . . .1D **107**
Lakeside Ter. EC2 . . . . .1C **62**
Lake Vw. Ct. SW1 . . . . .1A **114**
Lake Vw. Est. E3 . . . . .5F **23**
Laleham Ho. E2 . . . . .4B **42**
Lambard Ho. SE10 . . . . .5B **148**
Lamb Ct. E14 . . . . .5A **68**
Lamberhurst Ho. SE15 . . . . . .3C **144**
Lambert Jones M. EC2 . . . . .1B **62**
Lambert Rd. E16 . . . . .3F **73**
Lambert St. N1 . . . . .2D **17**
LAMBETH **2B 116**
Lambeth Bri. SW1 . . . . .3A **116**
Lambeth High St. SE1 . . . . . .4B **116**
Lambeth Hill EC4 . . . . .5B **62**

Lambeth Palace **2B 116**
Lambeth Pal. Rd. SE1 . . . . .2B **116**
Lambeth Rd. SE1 . . . . .3B **116**
SE11 . . . . .3B **116**
Lambeth Towers SE11 . . . . . .2D **117**
Lambeth Wlk. SE11 . . . . .2D **117**
    (not continuous)
Lamb Ho. SE5 . . . . .5C **140**
SE10 . . . . .3B **148**
Lamb La. E8 . . . . .2F **21**
Lambourne Gro. SE16 . . . . . .4D **123**
Lambourne Ho. NW8 . . . . . . .1F **55**
Lamb's Bldgs. EC1 . . . . .5D **41**
Lamb's Conduit Pas. WC1 . . .1B **60**
Lamb's Conduit St. WC1 . . . .5B **38**
    (not continuous)
Lamb's M. N1 . . . . .4F **17**
Lambs Pas. EC1 . . . . .1D **63**
Lamb St. E1 . . . . .1B **64**
Lambton Pl. W11 . . . . .5C **52**
Lamb Wlk. SE1 . . . . .5F **91**
LAMDA **5E 107**
Lamerton St. SE8 . . . . .3D **147**
Lamington St. W6 . . . . .3A **106**
Lamlash St. SE11 . . . . .3F **117**
Lamley Ho. SE10 . . . . .5A **148**
Lammas Rd. E9 . . . . .2E **23**
Lamont Rd. SW10 . . . . .3C **132**
Lamont Rd. Pas. SW10 . . . . .3D **133**
Lampern Sq. E2 . . . . .2E **43**
Lampeter Sq. W6 . . . . .3A **130**
Lamplighter Cl. E1 . . . . .5B **44**
Lamp Office Ct. WC1 . . . . . . .5B **38**
Lanark Ho. SE1 . . . . .1D **143**
Lanark Mans. W9 . . . . .4C **32**
W12 . . . . .5C **78**
Lanark M. W9 . . . . .3B **32**
Lanark Pl. W9 . . . . .4C **32**
Lanark Rd. W9 . . . . .1A **32**
Lanark Sq. E14 . . . . .1A **126**
Lancashire Ct. W1 . . . . .5F **57**
Lancaster Cl. N1 . . . . .2A **20**
W2 . . . . .1F **81**
Lancaster Ct. SW6 . . . . .5C **130**
W2 . . . . .5C **54**
Lancaster Dr. E14 . . . . .3C **98**
Lancaster Ga. W2 . . . . .1B **82**
Lancaster Gro. NW3 . . . . . . .1A **12**
Lancaster Hall E16 . . . . .2E **101**
Lancaster House **4C 86**
Lancaster Lodge W11 . . . . . .3A **52**
Lancaster M. W2 . . . . .5C **54**
Lancaster Pl. WC2 . . . . .5B **60**
Lancaster Rd. W11 . . . . .4F **51**
Lancaster St. SE1 . . . . .5F **89**
Lancaster Ter. W2 . . . . .5D **55**
Lancaster Wlk. W2 . . . . .1C **82**
Lancefield St. W10 . . . . .2B **30**
Lancelot Pl. SW7 . . . . .5B **84**
Lancer Sq. W8 . . . . .4F **81**
Lanchester Ct. W2 . . . . .4B **56**
Lancing St. NW1 . . . . .3D **37**
Lancresse Ct. N1 . . . . .3F **19**
Landale Ho. SE16 . . . . .1C **122**
Landin Ho. E14 . . . . .3D **69**
Landmann Ho. SE16 . . . . . . .4A **122**
Landmann Way SE14 . . . . . . .2E **145**
Landmark East Twr. E14 . . . .4D **97**
Landmark Hgts. E5 . . . . .1A **4**
Landmark Ho. W6 . . . . .5B **106**
Landmark Sq. E14 . . . . .4D **97**
Landmark West Twr. E14 . . . .4D **97**
Landon Pl. SW1 . . . . .1B **112**
Landon's Cl. E14 . . . . .2C **98**

Landon Wlk. E14 . . . . .5A **70**
Landor Ho. SE5 . . . . .5D **141**
  W2 . . . . .2D **53**
Landrake NW1 . . . . .4C **14**
Landseer Ho. NW8 . . . . . . .4E **33**
  SW1 . . . . .4E **115**
Landulph Ho. SE11 . . . . . . .5E **117**
Landward Ct. W1 . . . . .3A **56**
Lane, The NW8 . . . . .1B **32**
Lanesborough Ct. N1 . . . . . .2F **41**
Lanesborough Pl. SW1 . . . .4E **85**
Laney Ho. EC1 . . . . .1D **61**
Lanfranc Rd. E3 . . . . .1F **45**
Lanfrey Pl. W14 . . . . .1B **130**
Langbourne Pl. E14 . . . . . .5F **125**
Langdale NW1 . . . . .2B **36**
Langdale Cl. SE17 . . . . . . .2B **140**
Langdale Ho. SW1 . . . . . . .1B **136**
Langdale Rd. SE10 . . . . . . .5B **148**
Langdale St. E1 . . . . .4F **65**
Langdon Ct. EC1 . . . . .1A **40**
Langdon Ho. E14 . . . . .4B **70**
Langdon Way SE1 . . . . . . .4E **121**
Langford Cl. NW8 . . . . .5C **10**
Langford Cl. NW8 . . . . .1C **32**
Langford Ho. SE8 . . . . .2D **147**
Langford M. N1 . . . . .1E **17**
Langford Pl. NW8 . . . . .5C **10**
Langham Mans. SW5 . . . . .1F **131**
Langham Pl. W1 . . . . .2A **58**
Langham St. W1 . . . . .2A **58**
Langhorne Ct. NW8 . . . . . .2D **11**
Lang Ho. SW8 . . . . .5F **137**
Langland Ho. SE5 . . . . .4E **141**
Langler Rd. NW10 . . . . . . .1C **28**
Langley Ct. WC2 . . . . .5F **59**
Langley Ho. W2 . . . . .1E **53**
Langley La. SW8 . . . . .2A **138**
Langley Mans. SW8 . . . . . .2B **138**
Langley St. WC2 . . . . .4F **59**
Langmead Ho. E3 . . . . .3A **48**
Langmore Ho. E1 . . . . .4E **65**
Lang St. E1 . . . . .4B **44**
Langthorn Ct. EC2 . . . . . . .3E **63**
Langthorne Ho. E3 . . . . . . .3C **46**
Langton Cl. WC1 . . . . .4C **38**
Langton Ho. SE11 . . . . . . .3C **116**
Langton Rd. SW9 . . . . .5A **140**
Langton St. SW10 . . . . . . .3C **132**
Langtry Pl. SW6 . . . . .2E **131**
Langtry Rd. NW8 . . . . .4F **9**
Langtry Wlk. NW8 . . . . . . .3A **10**
Lanhill Rd. W9 . . . . .4D **31**
Lannoy Point SW6 . . . . . . .4A **130**
Lanrick Rd. E14 . . . . .3E **71**
Lansbury Est. E14 . . . . . . .3F **69**
Lansbury Gdns. E14 . . . . . .3D **71**
Lanscombe Wlk. SW8 . . . . .5F **137**
Lansdowne Ct. W11 . . . . . .1A **80**
Lansdowne Cres. W11 . . . . .5A **52**
Lansdowne Dr. E8 . . . . . . .1E **21**
Lansdowne Gdns. SW8 . . . .5F **137**
Lansdowne Grn. SW8 . . . . .5F **137**
Lansdowne Ho. W11 . . . . . .2B **80**
Lansdowne M. W11 . . . . . .3B **80**
Lansdowne Pl. SE1 . . . . . . .1E **119**
Lansdowne Ri. W11 . . . . . .1A **80**
Lansdowne Rd. W11 . . . . . .5A **52**
Lansdowne Row W1 . . . . . .2A **86**
Lansdowne Ter. WC1 . . . . .5A **38**
Lansdowne Wlk. W11 . . . . .2A **80**
Lanson Apartments SW8 . . .4F **135**
Lantern SE1 . . . . .4B **90**
Lanterns Way E14 . . . . . . .5E **97**

Lant Ho. SE1 . . . . .5B **90**
Lant St. SE1 . . . . .4B **90**
Lanyard Ho. SE8 . . . . .4A **124**
Lapford Cl. W9 . . . . .4C **30**
Lapis M. E15 . . . . .3C **26**
Lapwing Ct. SE1 . . . . .5C **90**
              (off Swan St.)
Lapwing Twr. SE8 . . . . . . .2B **146**
Lapworth Ct. W2 . . . . .1A **54**
Larch Cl. SE8 . . . . .3C **146**
Larch Ct. SE1 . . . . .5F **91**
  W9 . . . . .1E **53**
Larch Ho. SE16 . . . . .4C **94**
  W10 . . . . .4F **29**
Larcom St. SE17 . . . . .4B **118**
Larissa St. SE17 . . . . .5E **119**
Lark Row E2 . . . . .4B **22**
Larkspur Cl. E6 . . . . .1F **75**
Larson Wlk. E14 . . . . .1E **125**
Lascar Wharf Bldg. E14 . . .3A **68**
Lascelles Ho. NW1 . . . . . . .5A **34**
Lassell St. SE10 . . . . .1E **149**
Latham Cl. E6 . . . . .3A **76**
Latham Ct. SW5 . . . . .5D **109**
Latham Ho. E1 . . . . .3E **67**
Latimer Ho. W11 . . . . .1C **80**
Latimer Ind. Est. W10 . . . . .3C **50**
Latimer Pl. W10 . . . . .3C **50**
Latimer Rd. W10 . . . . .2B **50**
            (not continuous)
Latitude Ho. NW1 . . . . . . .4F **13**
Latona Ct. SW9 . . . . .5D **139**
Latona Rd. SE15 . . . . .3D **143**
Latvia Ct. SE17 . . . . .1C **140**
Latymer Ct. W6 . . . . .4E **107**
Lauderdale Ho. SW9 . . . . . .5D **139**
Lauderdale Mans. W9 . . . . .3F **31**
Lauderdale Pde. W9 . . . . . .3F **31**
Lauderdale Pl. EC2 . . . . . . .1B **62**
Lauderdale Rd. W9 . . . . . . .3F **31**
Lauderdale Twr. EC2 . . . . . .1D **62**
Laud St. SE11 . . . . .5B **116**
Laugan Wlk. SE17 . . . . . . .5C **118**
Launcelot St. SE1 . . . . .5D **89**
Launceston Pl. W8 . . . . . . .1B **110**
Launch St. E14 . . . . .1B **126**
Laundry La. N1 . . . . .2B **18**
Laundry Rd. W6 . . . . .3A **130**
Laurel Apartments SE17 . . .3F **119**
Laurel Ho. E3 . . . . .3B **24**
  SE8 . . . . .2B **146**
Laurels, The SW9 . . . . .5A **140**
Laurence Ct. W11 . . . . .1B **80**
Laurence Pountney Hill
  EC4 . . . . .5D **63**
Laurence Pountney La.
  EC4 . . . . .5D **63**
Laurie Gro. SE14 . . . . .5A **146**
Laurie Ho. SE1 . . . . .2A **118**
  W8 . . . . .3D **81**
Lauriston Ho. E9 . . . . .2C **22**
Lauriston Rd. E9 . . . . .1C **22**
Lavender Cl. SW3 . . . . .3E **133**
Lavender Gro. E8 . . . . .2C **20**
Lavender Ho. SE16 . . . . . . .2E **95**
Lavender Pond Nature Pk.
                  . . .2A 96
Lavender Rd. SE16 . . . . . . .2F **95**
Lavender St. E15 . . . . .4F **7**
Lavendon Ho. NW8 . . . . . . .4A **34**
Laverton M. SW5 . . . . .4A **110**
Laverton Pl. SW5 . . . . .4A **110**
Lavette Ho. E3 . . . . .2E **47**
Lavina Gro. N1 . . . . .5B **16**

Lavington Cl. E9 . . . . .4B **4**
Lavington St. SE1 . . . . .3A **90**
Lawes Ho. W10 . . . . .2B **30**
Lawford Rd. N1 . . . . .2F **19**
Lawfords Wharf NW1 . . . . .2B **14**
Lawless Ho. E14 . . . . .5B **70**
Lawless St. E14 . . . . .5A **70**
Lawn Ho. Cl. E14 . . . . .4B **98**
Lawn La. SW8 . . . . .2A **138**
Lawrence Cl. E3 . . . . .1D **47**
  W12 . . . . .5A **50**
Lawrence Ho. NW1 . . . . . . .2A **14**
  SW1 . . . . .4E **115**
Lawrence La. EC2 . . . . .4C **62**
Lawrence Mans. SW3 . . . . .3F **133**
Lawrence Pl. N1 . . . . .3A **16**
Lawrence St. E16 . . . . .2C **72**
  SW3 . . . . .3F **133**
Lawrence Trad. Est. SE10 . .4A **128**
Lawson Cl. E16 . . . . .2C **74**
Lawson Ho. W12 . . . . .5A **50**
Law St. SE1 . . . . .1E **119**
Lawton Rd. E3 . . . . .3A **46**
            (not continuous)
Laxfield Ct. E8 . . . . .4E **21**
Laxford Ho. SW1 . . . . .4E **113**
Laxley Cl. SE5 . . . . .4A **140**
Laxton Pl. NW1 . . . . .4A **36**
Layard Rd. SE16 . . . . .3A **122**
Layard Sq. SE16 . . . . .3A **122**
Laybourne Ho. E14 . . . . . . .4F **97**
Laycock St. N1 . . . . .1E **17**
Layfield Ho. SE10 . . . . .5D **129**
Laystall Ct. WC1 . . . . .5D **39**
Laystall St. EC1 . . . . .5D **39**
Lazenby Ct. WC2 . . . . .5F **59**
Leabank Sq. E9 . . . . .4D **5**
Leadenhall Mkt. EC3 . . . . . .4F **63**
Leadenhall Pl. EC3 . . . . . . .4F **63**
Leadenhall St. EC3 . . . . . . .4F **63**
Loadenham Ct. E3 . . . . . . .5E **47**
Lea Ho. NW8 . . . . .3F **33**
LEA INTERCHANGE 1E **5**
Leake Ct. SE1 . . . . .5C **88**
Leake St. SE1 . . . . .4C **88**
            (not continuous)
Leamington Ho. W11 . . . . . .2C **52**
Leamington Rd. Vs. W11 . . .2C **52**
Leamore Ct. E2 . . . . .2E **45**
Leamore St. W6 . . . . .4A **106**
LEAMOUTH 5F **71**
Leamouth Rd. E6 . . . . .3F **75**
  E14 . . . . .4E **71**
Leander Ct. E9 . . . . .2C **22**
Learoyd Gdns. E6 . . . . .5D **77**
Leary Ho. SE11 . . . . .1C **138**
Lea Sq. E3 . . . . .4C **24**
Leatherdale St. E1 . . . . . . .3D **45**
Leather Gdns. E15 . . . . . . .4F **27**
Leather La. EC1 . . . . .1D **61**
            (not continuous)
Leathermarket, The SE1 . . .5F **91**
Leathermarket Ct. SE1 . . . .5F **91**
Leathermarket St. SE1 . . . .5F **91**
Leather Rd. SE16 . . . . .4D **123**
Leather St. E1 . . . . .5D **67**
Lebus Ho. NW8 . . . . .1F **33**
Lecky St. SW7 . . . . .5D **111**
Le Cordon
  Bleu London Culinary Arts
  Institute **2E 57**
           (off Marylebone La.)
Le Cordon Bleu
  London **2A 60**

Leda Ct. SW9 .....5D 139
Ledam Ho. EC1 .....1D 61
Ledbury Ho. W11 .....4C 52
Ledbury M. Nth. W11 .....4D 53
Ledbury M. W. W11 .....5D 53
Ledbury Rd. W11 .....3C 52
Ledbury St. SE15 .....4E 143
Lee Conservancy Rd.
  E9 .....2B 4
Leeds Ct. EC1 .....4F 39
Leeke St. WC1 .....2B 38
Leerdam Dr. E14 .....2C 126
Lees Ct. W1 .....5D 57
Lees Ho. SE17 .....1E 141
Leeside Ct. SE16 .....2D 95
Lees Pl. W1 .....5D 57
Lee St. E8 .....3B 20
Lee Valley Hockey & Tennis Cen.
  .....1F 5
Lee Valley Velopark 2A 6
Leeve Ho. W10 .....3B 30
Leeward Ct. E1 .....2E 93
Leeward Ho. N1 .....4F 19
  (off Halcomb St.)
Leeway SE8 .....5B 124
Lefevre Wlk. E3 .....5D 25
Leff Ho. NW6 .....2A 8
Lefroy Ho. SE1 .....5B 90
Leggatt Rd. E15 .....5C 26
Legion Cl. N1 .....1E 17
Legion Ter. E3 .....4C 24
Leicester Ct. W9 .....1D 53
  WC2 .....5E 59
Leicester Flds. WC2 .....1E 87
Leicester Pl. WC2 .....5E 59
Leicester Sq. WC2 .....1E 87
Leicester Square Theatre ...5E 59
Leicester St. WC2 .....5E 59
Leigh Ct. W14 .....3A 108
Leigh Gdns. NW10 .....1B 28
Leigh Pl. EC1 .....1D 61
Leigh St. WC1 .....4F 37
Leighton Ho. SW1 .....4E 115
Leighton House Mus. 1C 108
Leighton Mans. W14 .....2A 130
Leinster Gdns. W2 .....4B 54
Leinster M. W2 .....5B 54
Leinster Pl. W2 .....4B 54
Leinster Sq. W2 .....5E 53
  (not continuous)
Leinster Ter. W2 .....5B 54
Leirum St. N1 .....4C 16
Leitch Ho. NW8 .....2D 11
Leith Mans. W9 .....3F 31
Leith Yd. NW6 .....3E 9
Lelitia Cl. E8 .....4D 21
Leman Pas. E1 .....4D 65
Leman St. E1 .....3C 64
Lemmon Rd. SE10 .....2F 149
Le Moal Ho. E1 .....2C 66
Lemon Tree Ho. E3 .....2C 46
Lena Gdns. W6 .....2C 106
Lenanton Steps E14 .....4E 97
Len Bishop Ct. E1 .....5D 67
Len Freeman Pl. SW6 .....3B 130
Lenham Ho. SE1 .....5E 91
Lennox Gdns. SW1 .....2B 112
Lennox Gdns. M. SW1 .....2B 112
Lenthall Ho. SW1 .....1C 136
Lenthall Rd. E8 .....1C 20
Lenthorp Rd. SE10 .....4B 128
Len Williams Ct. NW6 .....1E 31
Leonard Ct. W8 .....1D 109
  WC1 .....4E 37

Leonard St. E16 .....3A 104
  EC2 .....4E 41
Leonora Ho. W9 .....4B 32
Leontine Cl. SE15 .....5E 143
Leopards Ct. EC1 .....1D 61
Leopold Bldgs. E2 .....2B 42
Leopold M. E9 .....3B 22
Leopold St. E3 .....1C 68
Leopold Wlk. SE11 .....1B 138
Leo St. SE15 .....4A 144
Leo Yd. EC1 .....5A 40
Leroy St. SE1 .....2F 119
Lerry Cl. W14 .....2C 130
Lesley Ct. SW1 .....2D 115
Leslie Ho. SW8 .....4F 137
Leslie Prince Ct. SE5 .....4D 141
Leslie Rd. E11 .....1C 6
  E16 .....4F 73
Lester Av. E15 .....4F 49
Lester Ct. E3 .....3A 48
Letchmore Ho. W10 .....5B 28
Letterstone Rd. SW6 .....5B 130
Lett Rd. E15 .....2D 27
  SW9 .....5C 138
Levant Ho. E1 .....5E 45
Leven Rd. E14 .....2C 70
Leverett St. SW3 .....3A 112
Leverington Pl. N1 .....3F 41
Leverstock Ho. SW3 .....5A 112
Lever St. EC1 .....3A 40
Levita Ho. NW1 .....2E 37
  (not continuous)
Levyne Ct. EC1 .....4D 39
Lewes Ho. SE1 .....4A 92
  SE15 .....3E 143
Lewey Ho. E3 .....5C 46
Lewington Apartments
  SE16 .....4C 122
Lewington Cen. SE16 .....4C 122
Lewis Ct. SE16 .....5A 122
Lewisham Lions Cen. 5C 122
Lewisham St. SW1 .....5E 87
Lewisham Way SE14 .....5B 146
Lewis Ho. E14 .....3C 98
Lewis Silkin Ho. SE15 .....2C 144
Lewis St. NW1 .....1F 13
  (not continuous)
Lexham Gdns. W8 .....3E 109
Lexham Gdns. M. W8 .....2A 110
Lexham Ho. W8 .....3F 109
Lexham M. W8 .....3E 109
Lexham Wlk. W8 .....2A 110
Lexington Apartments EC1 .....4D 41
Lexington Bldg. E3 .....1E 47
Lexington St. W1 .....4C 58
Leybourne Ho. E14 .....4C 68
  SE15 .....3C 144
Leybourne Rd. NW1 .....2A 14
Leybourne St. NW1 .....2F 13
Leyden St. E1 .....2B 64
Leydon Cl. SE16 .....3E 95
Leyes Rd. E16 .....4D 75
Ley Ho. SE1 .....5B 90
Leyland Ho. E14 .....5F 69
Leylang Rd. SE14 .....4E 145
Leysdown Ho. SE17 .....5A 120
Leyton Ho. E2 .....3B 42
  (off Calvert Av.)
Leyton Rd. E15 .....2C 6
Leytonstone Rd. E15 .....2F 7
Leywick St. E15 .....5F 27
Liardet St. SE14 .....3A 146
Libari Mans. E20 .....3B 6

Liberty Bri. Rd. E15 .....3C 6
  E20 .....3B 6
Liberty Ho. E1 .....5D 65
Liberty St. SW9 .....5C 138
Libra Mans. E3 .....5C 24
  (off Libra Rd.)
Libra Rd. E3 .....4C 24
Library Mans. W12 .....4B 78
Library Pl. E1 .....5A 66
Library Sq. E1 .....4F 45
Library St. SE1 .....1F 117
Lichfield Rd. E3 .....2A 46
Lickey Ho. W14 .....2C 130
Liddiard Ho. W11 .....5A 52
Lidgate Rd. SE15 .....5B 142
Lidlington Pl. NW1 .....1C 36
Lighter Cl. SE16 .....3A 124
Lighterman Ho. E14 .....5C 70
Lighterman M. E1 .....3E 67
Lightermans Rd. E14 .....5E 97
Lightfoot Vs. N1 .....1D 17
Light Horse Ct. SW3 .....1D 135
Lighthouse Apartments
  E1 .....3B 66
Ligonier St. E2 .....4B 42
Lilac Pl. SE11 .....4B 116
Lilestone Ho. NW8 .....4E 33
Lilestone St. NW8 .....4F 33
Lilian Knowles Ho. E1 .....2B 64
Lilley Cl. E1 .....3E 93
Lillie Bri. Dpt. W14 .....5C 108
Lillie Mans. SW6 .....3B 130
Lillie Rd. SW6 .....4A 130
Lillie Yd. SW6 .....2E 131
Lillington Gdns. Est.
  SW1 .....4C 114
Lily Cl. W14 .....4E 107
Lily Nichols Ho. E16 .....3E 103
Lily Pl. EC1 .....1E 61
Lilyville Rd. SW6 .....5B 130
Limborough Ho. E14 .....2D 69
Limeburner La. EC4 .....4F 61
Lime Cl. E1 .....2E 93
Lime Gro. W12 .....4B 78
Limeharbour E14 .....1A 126
LIMEHOUSE 3B 68
Limehouse C'way. E14 .....5C 68
Lime Ho. Ct. E14 .....4B 68
Limehouse Ct. E14 .....3C 68
Limehouse Cut E14 .....1A 70
Limehouse Flds. Est. E14 .....2A 68
Limehouse Link E14 .....4A 68
Limekiln Wharf E14 .....1C 96
Limelight Ho. SE11 .....4F 117
Limerston St. SW10 .....2C 132
Limes, The W2 .....1E 81
Lime St. EC3 .....5F 63
Lime St. Pas. EC3 .....4F 63
Lime Tree Ct. E3 .....1D 69
  SE17 .....1C 140
Lime Wlk. E15 .....3F 27
Limscott Ho. E3 .....3A 48
Linacre Ct. W6 .....5E 107
Linale Ho. N1 .....1D 41
Linberry Wlk. SE8 .....4B 124
Lincoln Ho. SE5 .....4E 139
  SW3 .....5B 84
Lincoln M. NW6 .....3B 8
Lincoln's Inn Flds. WC2 .....3B 60
Lincoln's Inn Hall 3C 60
Lincoln St. SW3 .....4B 112
Linden Av. NW10 .....1D 29
Linden Ct. W12 .....3B 78
Linden Gdns. W2 .....1E 81

Linden Ho. SE8 . . . . .2C 146
Linden M. W2 . . . . .1E 81
Lindfield St. E14 . . . . .3D 69
Lindisfarne Way E9 . . . . .1A 4
Lindley Est. SE15 . . . . .4E 143
Lindley Ho. E1 . . . . .1B 66
   SE15 . . . . .4D 143
Lindley St. E1 . . . . .1B 66
Lindop Ho. E1 . . . . .4F 45
Lindsay Ho. SW7 . . . . .1B 110
Lindsay Sq. SW1 . . . . .5E 115
Lindsey M. N1 . . . . .1C 18
Lindsey St. EC1 . . . . .1A 62
Lindwood Cl. E6 . . . . .2A 76
Linen House, The W10 . . . .1A 30
Linfield WC1 . . . . .3B 38
Linford Ho. E2 . . . . .4E 21
Lingard Ho. E14 . . . . .1B 126
Lingfield Ho. SE1 . . . . .5A 90
Ling Rd. E16 . . . . .1D 73
Linhope St. NW1 . . . . .4B 34
Link Ho. E3 . . . . .1F 47
   W10 . . . . .4E 51
Link Rd. E1 . . . . .5D 65
Links Yd. E1 . . . . .1C 64
Linkwood Wlk. NW1 . . . . . .1E 15
Linnell Ho. E1 . . . . .1B 64
   NW8 . . . . .3B 10
Linsey St. SE16 . . . . .3D 121
   (not continuous)
Linslade Ho. E2 . . . . .4E 21
   NW8 . . . . .4A 34
Linstead St. NW6 . . . . .1D 9
Lintaine Cl. W6 . . . . .3A 130
Linton Ct. NW1 . . . . .2C 14
Linton Gdns. E6 . . . . .3F 75
Linton Ho. E3 . . . . .2D 69
Linton St. N1 . . . . .4C 18
   (not continuous)
Lion Apartments SE16 . . . . .5A 122
Lion Ct. E1 . . . . .5D 67
   N1 . . . . .4B 16
   SE1 . . . . .3A 92
Lionel Ho. W10 . . . . .1F 51
Lionel Mans. W14 . . . . .2D 107
Lionel M. W10 . . . . .1F 51
Lion Mills E2 . . . . .1E 43
Lion Rd. E6 . . . . .2C 76
Lipton Rd. E1 . . . . .4D 67
Lisford St. SE15 . . . . .5D 143
Lisgar Ter. W14 . . . . .3B 108
Liskeard Ho. SE11 . . . . .5E 117
Lisle St. WC2 . . . . .5E 59
Lisson Gdn. Est. NW8 . . . . .4F 33
LISSON GROVE 1F 55
Lisson Gro. NW1 . . . . .1A 56
   NW8 . . . . .3E 33
Lisson Ho. NW1 . . . . .1F 55
Lisson St. NW1 . . . . .1F 55
Lister Ho. E1 . . . . .1E 65
Lister Lodge W9 . . . . .1E 53
Listowel Cl. SW9 . . . . .4E 139
Litcham Ho. E1 . . . . .3E 45
Litchfield Av. E15 . . . . .5F 7
Litchfield St. WC2 . . . . .5E 59
Lit. Albany St. NW1 . . . . .4A 36
Little Angel Theatre 3A 18
Lit. Argyll St. W1 . . . . .4B 58
Lit. Boltons, The SW5 . . . .5A 110
   SW10 . . . . .5A 110
Littlebourne Ho. SE17 . . . . .5A 120
Little Britain EC1 . . . . .2A 62
Lit. Chelsea SW10 . . . . . . .3C 132
Lit. Chester St. SW1 . . . . . .1F 113

Little Cloisters SW1 . . . . . . .1F 115
Lit. College La. EC4 . . . . . . .5C 62
Lit. College St. SW1 . . . . . . .1F 115
Lit. Cottage Pl. SE10 . . . . . .4A 148
Lit. Dean's Yd. SW1 . . . . . . .1F 115
Lit. Dorrit Ct. SE1 . . . . .4C 90
Lit. Edward St. NW1 . . . . . . .2A 36
Lit. Essex St. WC2 . . . . .5D 61
Lit. George St. SW1 . . . . . . .5F 87
Lit. London Ct. SE1 . . . . . . .5C 92
Lit. Marlborough St. W1 . . . .4B 58
Lit. Newport St. WC2 . . . . . .5E 59
Little New St. EC4 . . . . .3E 61
Lit. Portland St. W1 . . . . . . .3A 58
Lit. Russell St. WC1 . . . . . . .2F 59
Little St James's St. SW1 . . .3B 86
Little Sanctuary SW1 . . . . . .5F 87
Lit. Smith St. SW1 . . . . .1E 115
Lit. Somerset St. E1 . . . . . . .4B 64
Lit. South St. SE5 . . . . .5A 142
Lit. Thames Wlk. SE8 . . . . .3F 147
Lit. Titchfield St. W1 . . . . . . .2B 58
Littleton Ho. SW1 . . . . .1B 136
Lit. Trinity La. EC4 . . . . .5C 62
Little Turnstile WC1 . . . . . . .2B 60
Little Venice **1B 54**
Little Venice Sports Cen. . . .**1D 55**
Livermere Ct. E8 . . . . .3C 20
Livermere Rd. E8 . . . . .3B 20
Liverpool Gro. SE17 . . . . . . .1C 140
Liverpool Rd. E16 . . . . .1A 72
   N1 . . . . .1E 17
Liverpool St. EC2 . . . . .2F 63
Livesey Pl. SE15 . . . . .2E 143
Livingstone Ho. SE5 . . . . . .4B 140
Livingstone Lodge W9 . . . . .1E 53
Livingstone Mans. W14 . . . .2A 130
Livingstone Pl. E14 . . . . . . .5B 126
Livonia St. W1 . . . . .4C 58
Lizard Ct. EC1 . . . . .3C 40
Lizmans Ter. W8 . . . . .2E 109
Llandovery Ho. E14 . . . . . . .5B 98
Llewellyn Mans. W14 . . . . . .3F 107
Llewellyn St. SE16 . . . . .5E 93
Lloyd Baker St. WC1 . . . . . . .3C 38
   (not continuous)
Lloyd's Av. EC3 . . . . .4A 64
Lloyd's Building **4F 63**
Lloyd Sq. WC1 . . . . .2D 39
Lloyd's Row EC1 . . . . .3E 39
Lloyd St. WC1 . . . . .2D 39
Lloyds Wharf SE1 . . . . .4C 92
Loanda Cl. E8 . . . . .3B 20
Lobelia Cl. E6 . . . . .1F 75
Lochmore Ho. SW1 . . . . . . .4E 113
Lochnagar St. E14 . . . . .2B 70
Lockbridge Ct. W9 . . . . .1D 53
Lock Building, The E15 . . . . .5B 26
Locke Ho. SW8 . . . . .5B 136
Lockesfield Pl. E14 . . . . . . .5A 126
Lockgate Cl. E9 . . . . .2B 4
Lockhart St. E3 . . . . .5C 46
Lockhouse, The NW1 . . . . . .3E 13
Lockington Rd. SW8 . . . . . .5A 136
Lock Keepers Hgts.
   SE16 . . . . .2E 123
Locksfields SE17 . . . . .4E 119
Lockside E14 . . . . .5A 68
Locksley Est. E14 . . . . .3B 68
Locksley St. E14 . . . . .2B 68
Locksons Cl. E14 . . . . .2F 69
Lockton St. W10 . . . . .5D 51
Lock Vw. Ct. E14 . . . . .5A 68
Lockwood Ho. SE11 . . . . . . .3D 139

Lockwood Sq. SE16 . . . . . . .1F 121
Lockyer Est. SE1 . . . . .4E 91
   (not continuous)
Lockyer Ho. SE10 . . . . .5B 128
   SW8 . . . . .4E 137
Lockyer St. SE1 . . . . .5E 91
Locton Grn. E3 . . . . .3C 24
Loddiges Ho. E9 . . . . .1B 22
Loddiges Rd. E9 . . . . .1B 22
Loddon Ho. NW8 . . . . .5E 33
Loder St. SE15 . . . . .5B 144
Lodge, The W12 . . . . .4E 79
Lodge Rd. NW8 . . . . .3E 33
Lodore St. E14 . . . . .4B 70
Loft Ho. E1 . . . . .3B 64
Loftie St. SE16 . . . . .5E 93
Lofting Ho. N1 . . . . .2E 17
Lofting Rd. N1 . . . . .2C 16
Loftus Road **2A 78**
Loftus Rd. W12 . . . . .3A 78
Loftus Vs. W12 . . . . .3A 78
Logan Cl. E20 . . . . .3A 6
Logan M. W8 . . . . .3D 109
Logan Pl. W8 . . . . .3D 109
Lohmann Ho. SE11 . . . . . . .2D 139
Lolesworth Cl. E1 . . . . .2C 64
Lollard St. SE11 . . . . .3C 116
   (not continuous)
Loman St. SE1 . . . . .4A 90
Lomas Dr. E8 . . . . .1C 20
Lomas St. E1 . . . . .1E 65
Lombard Ct. EC3 . . . . .5E 63
Lombard La. EC4 . . . . .4E 61
Lombard St. EC3 . . . . .4E 63
Lombard Trad. Est. SE7 . . . .3F 129
Lombard Wall SE7 . . . . .2F 129
Lombardy Pl. W2 . . . . .1A 82
Lomond Gro. SE5 . . . . .4D 141
Lomond Ho. SE5 . . . . .5D 141
Loncroft Rd. SE5 . . . . .2B 142
Londinium Twr. E1 . . . . .5C 64
London Bri. SE1 . . . . .2E 91
London Bridge Experience . . .**2E 91**
   (off Tooley St.)
London Bri. St. SE1 . . . . .3E 91
London Bri. Wlk. SE1 . . . . . .2E 91
London Business School . .**4B 34**
London Canal Mus. **5A 16**
LONDON CITY AIRPORT . . .**2A 104**
London City College **3D 89**
London Coliseum **1F 87**
   (off St Martin's La.)
**London College of Fashion, The
   Hackney** **1A 22**
London Dungeon **4B 88**
London Eye **4B 88**
London Flds. East Side
   E8 . . . . .2F 21
London Fields Lido **1F 21**
London Flds. West Side
   E8 . . . . .1E 21
London Film Mus. **5A 60**
London Fire Brigade Mus.
   . . . .**4B 90**
London Fruit Exchange
   E1 . . . . .2B 64
London Ho. EC1 . . . . .2B 62
   NW8 . . . . .5A 12
   WC1 . . . . .4B 38
London Ind. Park, The E6 . . . .1F 77
   (not continuous)
London La. E8 . . . . .1A 22
London Metropolitan Archives
   . . . .**4E 39**

London Metropolitan University
  London City Campus, Calcutta House & Goulston St.
    . . . . .3B 64
  London City Campus, Central House 3D 65
  London City Campus, Commercial Rd. 3E 65
  London City Campus, Jewry St.
    . . . . .4B 64
  London City Campus, Moorgate
    . . . . .2E 63
  London City Campus, Tower Hill
    . . . . .5B 64
London M. W2 . . . . .4E 55
London Mill Apartments
  E2 . . . . .4C 20
London Palladium 4B 58
London Pavilion 1D 87
London Plane Ho. E15 . . . .3F 49
London Regatta Cen. 1E 103
London Rd. SE1 . . . . .1F 117
London School of Economics & Political Science, The
  . . . . .4C 60
London's Death Trap 5B 88
London Soccerdome 5B 100
London South Bank University
  Keyworth St. 1A 118
  Southwark Campus . . .1A 118
London South Bank University
  Sports Cen. 1A 118
London South Bank University
  Technopark 1A 118
London's Pleasure Gdns.
  . . . . .2A 102
London's Roman Amphitheatre
  . . . . .3D 63
London Stock Exchange . . .3A 62
London St. EC3 . . . . .5A 64
  W2 . . . . .3D 55
London Telecom Tower, The
  . . . . .1B 58
London Television Centre, The
  . . . . .2D 89
London Ter. E2 . . . . .1D 43
London Transport Mus. 5A 60
London Trocadero 1D 87
London Underwriting Cen.
  . . . . .5A 64
London Wall EC2 . . . . .2C 62
London Wall Bldgs. EC2 . . . .2E 63
London Wharf E2 . . . . .4F 21
London Zoo 5D 13
Long Acre WC2 . . . . .5F 59
Longbow Ho. EC1 . . . . .1D 63
Longbridge Ho. E16 . . . . . . .1F 105
Longfellow Way SE1 . . . . . .4C 120
Longfield Est. SE1 . . . . . . .3C 120
Longford Ho. E1 . . . . .3B 66
Longford St. NW1 . . . . .4A 36
Longhope Cl. SE15 . . . . . . .3A 142
Longhurst Ho. W10 . . . . . . .2B 30
Longland Ct. E9 . . . . .3A 4
  SE1 . . . . .5D 121
Longlands Ct. W11 . . . . .5C 52
Long La. EC1 . . . . .2A 62
  SE1 . . . . .5D 91
Longleat Ho. SW1 . . . . .5D 115
Longley St. SE1 . . . . .4D 121
Longman Ho. E2 . . . . .1D 45
  E8 . . . . .4C 20
Long Mark Rd. E16 . . . . .2D 75
Long Mill SE10 . . . . .5F 147

Longmoore St. SW1 . . . . . .4B 114
Longmore Gdns. Est.
  SW1 . . . . .4C 114
Longnor Est. E1 . . . . .3E 45
Longnor Rd. E1 . . . . .3E 45
Longridge Ho. SE1 . . . . .2C 118
Longridge Rd. SW5 . . . . . . .4D 109
Long's Ct. WC2 . . . . .1E 87
Longshore SE8 . . . . .4B 124
Longshott Ct. SW5 . . . . .4D 109
Longstone Ct. SE1 . . . . .5D 91
Long St. E2 . . . . .2B 42
Longville Rd. SE11 . . . . .3F 117
Long Wlk. SE1 . . . . .1A 120
Long Wall E15 . . . . .2D 49
Long Yd. WC1 . . . . .5B 38
Lonsdale Ho. W11 . . . . .4C 52
Lonsdale M. W11 . . . . .4C 52
Lonsdale Pl. N1 . . . . .2E 17
Lonsdale Rd. NW6 . . . . .5B 8
  W11 . . . . .4B 52
Lonsdale Sq. N1 . . . . .2E 17
Lonsdale Yd. W11 . . . . .1D 81
Lookout Education Centre, The
  . . . . .2B 84
Lord Amory Way E14 . . . . . .4B 98
Lorden Wlk. E2 . . . . .3D 43
Lord Hills Bri. W2 . . . . .2A 54
Lord Hills Rd. W2 . . . . .1A 54
Lord Nth. St. SW1 . . . . .2F 115
Lord Roberts M. SW6 . . . . . .5F 131
Lord's 3E 33
Lordship Pl. SW3 . . . . .3F 133
Lord St. E16 . . . . .3A 104
Lords Vw. NW8 . . . . .3F 33
         (not continuous)
Lorenzo St. WC1 . . . . .2B 38
Loris Rd. W6 . . . . .1C 106
Lorne Cl. NW8 . . . . .3A 34
Lorne Gdns. W11 . . . . .4E 79
Lorne Ho. E1 . . . . .2F 67
Lorraine Ct. NW1 . . . . .1A 14
Lorrimore Rd. SE17 . . . . . . .3A 140
Lorrimore Sq. SE17 . . . . . . .2A 140
Lorton Ho. NW6 . . . . .4E 9
Lothbury EC2 . . . . .3D 63
Lothian Rd. SW9 . . . . .5A 140
Lothrop St. W10 . . . . .2F 29
Lots Rd. SW10 . . . . .5B 132
Loudoun Rd. NW8 . . . . .2C 10
Loughborough St.
  SE11 . . . . .5C 116
Louisa Cl. E9 . . . . .3E 23
Louisa Gdns. E1 . . . . .5D 45
Louisa St. E1 . . . . .5D 45
Louise De Marillac Ho.
  E1 . . . . .2B 66
Louise Rd. E15 . . . . .4F 7
Lovage App. E6 . . . . .2A 76
Lovat La. EC3 . . . . .5F 63
Lovegrove St. SE1 . . . . .1E 143
Lovegrove Wlk. E14 . . . . . . .3B 98
Love La. EC2 . . . . .3C 62
Lovelinch Cl. SE15 . . . . .3C 144
Lovell Ho. E8 . . . . .3D 21
Lovell Pl. SE16 . . . . .1A 124
Lovers Wlk. SE10 . . . . .3E 149
  W1 . . . . .2D 85
Lowder Ho. E1 . . . . .2A 94
Lowe Av. E16 . . . . .2E 73
Lowell Ho. SE5 . . . . .4C 140
Lowell St. E14 . . . . .3A 68
Lwr. Addison Gdns.
  W14 . . . . .5F 79

Lwr. Belgrave St. SW1 . . . .2F 113
Lwr. Clarendon Wlk.
  W11 . . . . .4F 51
Lwr. Grosvenor Pl. SW1 . . .1A 114
Lwr. James St. W1 . . . . .5C 58
Lwr. John St. W1 . . . . .5C 58
Lwr. Lea Crossing E14 . . . . .5F 71
  E16 . . . . .5F 71
Lower Mall W6 . . . . .5A 106
Lower Marsh SE1 . . . . .5D 89
Lwr. Merton Ri. NW3 . . . . . . .1F 11
Lwr. New Change Pas.
  EC4 . . . . .4C 62
      (off One New Change)
Lower Rd. SE1 . . . . .4D 89
  SE8 . . . . .1B 122
  SE16 . . . . .5B 94
         (not continuous)
Lwr. Robert St. WC2 . . . . . . .1A 88
Lwr. Sloane St. SW1 . . . . . . .4D 113
Lwr. Thames St. EC3 . . . . . . .1E 91
Lowerwood Ct. W11 . . . . . . .4A 52
Lowestoft M. E16 . . . . .4F 105
Loweswater Ho. E3 . . . . .4B 46
Lowfield Rd. NW6 . . . . .1D 9
Lowndes Cl. SW1 . . . . .2E 113
Lowndes Ct. SW1 . . . . .1C 112
  W1 . . . . .4B 58
Lowndes Lodge SW1 . . . . . .1C 112
Lowndes Pl. SW1 . . . . .2D 113
Lowndes Sq. SW1 . . . . .5C 84
Lowndes St. SW1 . . . . .1C 112
Lowood Ho. E1 . . . . .5B 66
Lowood St. E1 . . . . .5A 66
Lowry Ct. SE16 . . . . .5A 122
Lowry Ho. E14 . . . . .5E 97
Lowther Ho. SW1 . . . . .1C 136
Loxham St. WC1 . . . . .3A 38
LSO St Lukes 4C 40
Lubbock Ho. E14 . . . . .1A 98
Lubbock St. SE14 . . . . .5C 144
Lucan Ho. N1 . . . . .4E 19
Lucan Pl. SW3 . . . . .4F 111
Lucas Ho. SW10 . . . . .4A 132
  WC1 . . . . .3A 38
Lucerne M. W8 . . . . .2E 81
Lucey Rd. SE16 . . . . .2D 121
Lucey Way SE16 . . . . .2D 121
Lucia Hgts. E20 . . . . .3A 6
Lucy Brown Ho. SE1 . . . . . . .3C 90
Ludgate B'way. EC4 . . . . . . .4F 61
Ludgate Cir. EC4 . . . . .4F 61
Ludgate Hill EC4 . . . . .4F 61
Ludgate Sq. EC4 . . . . .4A 62
Ludlow St. EC1 . . . . .4B 40
Ludwell Ho. W14 . . . . .1F 107
Ludwick M. SE14 . . . . .4F 145
Lugard Ho. W12 . . . . .2A 78
Luke Ho. E1 . . . . .4F 65
Luke St. EC2 . . . . .4F 41
Lukin St. E1 . . . . .4C 66
Luli Ct. SE14 . . . . .3B 146
Lullingstone Ho.
  SE15 . . . . .3C 144
Lulsgate M. E3 . . . . .4A 46
Lulworth NW1 . . . . .2D 15
  SE17 . . . . .5D 119
Lulworth Ct. N1 . . . . .2A 20
Lulworth Ho. SW8 . . . . .5B 138
Lumina Bldgs. E14 . . . . .2C 98
Lumina Loft Apartments
  SE1 . . . . .5A 92
Lumley Ct. WC2 . . . . .1A 88
Lumley Flats SW1 . . . . .5D 113

Lumley St. W1 . . . . .4E 57
Lumsdon NW8 . . . . .4A 10
Luna Ho. SE16 . . . . .4E 93
Lunan Ho. E3 . . . . .5C 24
Lunaria Ho. E20 . . . . .3C 6
Lund Point E15 . . . . .3C 26
Luntley Pl. E1 . . . . .2D 65
Lupino Ct. SE11 . . . . .3C 116
Lupin Point SE1 . . . . .5C 92
Lupus St. SW1 . . . . .2A 136
Luralda Wharf E14 . . . . .5C 126
Lurline Gdns. SW11 . . . . .5F 135
Luscombe Way SW8 . . . . .4F 137
Lushington Rd. NW10 . . . . . . .1A 28
Luton Pl. SE10 . . . . .5C 148
Luton St. NW8 . . . . .5E 33
Lutyens Ho. SW1 . . . . .1B 136
Luxborough Ho. W1 . . . . .1D 57
Luxborough St. W1 . . . . .5D 35
Luxborough Twr. W1 . . . . .1D 57
Luxembourg M. E15 . . . . .3F 7
Luxemburg Gdns. W6 . . . . . . .3D 107
Luxford St. SE16 . . . . .4D 123
Lyall M. SW1 . . . . .2D 113
Lyall M. W. SW1 . . . . .2D 113
Lyall St. SW1 . . . . .2D 113
Lyal Rd. E3 . . . . .1A 46
Lyceum Theatre
  Covent Garden 5B 60
Lydford NW1 . . . . .4C 14
Lydford Rd. W9 . . . . .4C 30
Lygon Ho. E2 . . . . .2D 43
Lygon Pl. SW1 . . . . .2F 113
Lyly Ho. SE1 . . . . .2E 119
Lyme Gro. E9 . . . . .1B 22
Lyme Gro. Ho. E9 . . . . .1B 22
Lyme St. NW1 . . . . .2B 14
Lyme Ter. NW1 . . . . .2B 14
Lymington Cl. E6 . . . . .1B 76
Lymington Lodge E14 . . . . . . .2D 127
Lympstone Gdns. SE15 . . . . . .4E 143
Lynbrook Gro. SE15 . . . . .4A 142
Lynch Wlk. SE8 . . . . .2C 146
Lynden Ho. E1 . . . . .3E 45
Lyndhurst Ct. NW8 . . . . .4D 11
Lyndhurst Lodge E14 . . . . . . .3D 127
Lyneham Wlk. E5 . . . . .2A 4
Lynford French Ho.
  SE17 . . . . .5B 118
Lyn M. E3 . . . . .3B 46
Lynne Ct. NW6 . . . . .2F 9
Lynnett Ct. E9 . . . . .5A 4
  E9 . . . . .1F 23
Lynn Ho. SE15 . . . . .3F 143
Lynton Est. SE1 . . . . .4D 121
Lynton Ho. W2 . . . . .4B 54
Lynton Mans. SE1 . . . . .1D 117
Lynton Rd. NW6 . . . . .4C 8
  SE1 . . . . .4C 120
Lynx Way E16 . . . . .5D 75
Lyon Ho. NW8 . . . . .5F 33
Lyons Pl. NW8 . . . . .5D 33
Lyon St. N1 . . . . .2B 16
Lyons Wlk. W14 . . . . .3F 107
Lyric Ct. E8 . . . . .2C 20
  (off Holly St.)
Lyric Sq. W6 . . . . .4C 106
Lyric Theatre
  Hammersmith 4B 106
  Westminster 5D 59
Lysander Ho. E2 . . . . .1F 43
Lytham St. SE17 . . . . .1D 141
Lyttelton Cl. NW3 . . . . .2F 11
Lyttelton Ho. E9 . . . . .1C 22

Lyttelton Theatre 2D 89
  (within National Theatre)
Lytton Ct. WC1 . . . . .2A 60

M

Mabledon Pl. WC1 . . . . .3E 37
Mablethorpe Rd. SW6 . . . . . .5A 130
Mabley St. E9 . . . . .3A 4
Macartney Ho. SE10 . . . . .5E 149
Macaulay Wlk. SW9 . . . . .5C 138
McAuley Cl. SE1 . . . . .1D 117
Macauley Ho. W10 . . . . .1F 51
McAusland Ho. E3 . . . . .5B 24
Macbeth Ho. N1 . . . . .5F 19
Macbeth St. W6 . . . . .5A 106
McBride Ho. E3 . . . . .5C 24
McCabe Ct. E16 . . . . .2B 72
Macclesfield Ho. EC1 . . . . . . .3B 40
Macclesfield Rd. EC1 . . . . . . .2B 40
Macclesfield St. W1 . . . . .5E 59
McCoid Way SE1 . . . . .5B 90
McCullum Rd. E3 . . . . .4B 24
McDonald Ho. NW6 . . . . .3D 31
McDowall Cl. E16 . . . . .2C 72
Mace Cl. E1 . . . . .2F 93
Mace St. E2 . . . . .1D 45
McEwan Ho. E3 . . . . .5C 24
McEwen Way E15 . . . . .3E 27
Macey St. SE10 . . . . .2B 148
Macfarland Gro. SE15 . . . . . . .4A 142
Macfarlane Rd. W12 . . . . .3B 78
Macfarren Pl. NW1 . . . . .5E 35
Macfarron Ho. W10 . . . . .2A 30
McGlashon Ho. E1 . . . . .5D 43
McGregor Ct. N1 . . . . .2A 42
Macgregor Rd. E16 . . . . .1C 74
McGregor Rd. W11 . . . . .2B 52
McIndoe Cl. N1 . . . . .3D 19
Macintosh Ho. W1 . . . . .1E 57
McIntosh Ho. SE16 . . . . .4C 122
Mackay Ho. W12 . . . . .1A 78
McKenna Ho. E3 . . . . .5B 24
Mackennal St. NW8 . . . . .1A 34
Mackenzie Cl. W12 . . . . .5A 50
Mackenzie Wlk. E14 . . . . .2D 97
Macklin St. WC2 . . . . .3A 60
Mackonochie Ho. EC1 . . . . . . .1D 61
Mackrow Wlk. E14 . . . . .5C 70
Mack's Rd. SE16 . . . . .3E 121
Mackworth Ho. NW1 . . . . .2B 36
Mackworth St. NW1 . . . . .2B 36
McLaren Ho. SE1 . . . . .5F 89
McLeod's M. SW7 . . . . .2A 110
Macleod St. SE17 . . . . .1C 140
Maclise Ho. SW1 . . . . .4F 115
Maclise Rd. W14 . . . . .2F 107
Macmillan Ho. NW8 . . . . .3A 34
McMillan St. SE8 . . . . .3E 147
McMillan Student Village
  SE8 . . . . .3E 147
Macnamara Ho. SW10 . . . . . .4D 133
Maconochies Rd. E14 . . . . . . .5F 125
MacOwan Theatre 3D 109
Macquarie Way E14 . . . . .4A 126
Macready Ho. W1 . . . . .2A 56
Macrea Ho. E3 . . . . .3C 46
Macroom Ho. W9 . . . . .2C 30
Macroom Rd. W9 . . . . .2C 30
Mac's Pl. EC4 . . . . .3E 61
Madame Tussaud's 5D 35
Maddams St. E3 . . . . .5F 47
Maddison Ct. E16 . . . . .2E 73

Maddocks Ho. E1 . . . . .5A 66
Maddock Way SE17 . . . . .3A 140
Maddox St. W1 . . . . .5A 58
Madison, The SE1 . . . . .4D 91
Madison Ho. E14 . . . . .5B 68
Madrigal La. SE5 . . . . .5A 140
Madron St. SE17 . . . . .5A 120
Magazine Ga. W2 . . . . .2A 84
Magdalen Ho. E16 . . . . .2F 101
Magdalen Pas. E1 . . . . .5C 64
Magdalen St. SE1 . . . . .3F 91
Magee St. SE11 . . . . .2D 139
Magellan Ho. E1 . . . . .5E 45
Magellan Pl. E14 . . . . .4E 125
Magistrates' Court
  Camberwell Green 5D 141
  City of London 4D 63
  Clerkenwell 2C 38
  Hammersmith 5D 107
  Inner London Family
    Proceedings Court . . .3B 58
  Stratford 2E 27
  Thames 2D 47
  Westminster 1A 56
Magnin Cl. E8 . . . . .3E 21
Magnolia Ho. SE8 . . . . .2C 146
Magnolia Lodge W8 . . . . .2F 109
Magpie All. EC4 . . . . .4E 61
Magpie Ho. E3 . . . . .3B 24
Magpie Pl. SE14 . . . . .3A 146
Magri Wlk. E1 . . . . .2B 66
Maguire Apartments E3 . . . . .1C 68
Maguire St. SE1 . . . . .4C 92
Maha Bldg. E3 . . . . .3D 47
Mahogany Cl. SE16 . . . . .3A 96
Maida Av. W2 . . . . .1C 54
MAIDA HILL 5C 30
MAIDA VALE 3F 31
Maida Vale W9 . . . . .5F 9
Maiden La. NW1 . . . . .1E 15
  SE1 . . . . .0C 00
  WC2 . . . . .1A 88
Maiden Rd. E15 . . . . .1F 27
Maidstone Bldgs. M. SE1 . . . .3C 90
Maidstone Ho. E14 . . . . .3F 69
Mail Coach Yd. E2 . . . . .2A 42
Main Mill SE10 . . . . .5E 147
Maismore St. SE15 . . . . .3E 143
Maitland Cl. SE10 . . . . .5A 148
Maitland Ct. W2 . . . . .5D 55
Maitland Ho. E2 . . . . .5B 22
  SW1 . . . . .2B 136
Maize Row E14 . . . . .5B 68
Major Rd. E15 . . . . .2C 6
  SE16 . . . . .1E 121
Makins St. SW3 . . . . .4A 112
Malabar Ct. W12 . . . . .1A 78
Malabar St. E14 . . . . .5E 97
Malam Ct. SE11 . . . . .4D 117
Malam Gdns. E14 . . . . .5F 69
Malcolm Ho. N1 . . . . .1F 41
Malcolm Pl. E2 . . . . .4B 44
Malcolm Rd. E1 . . . . .4B 44
Malcolm Sargent Ho.
  E16 . . . . .2A 102
    (off Evelyn Rd.)
Malcolmson Ho. SW1 . . . . . . .1D 137
Malden Cres. NW1 . . . . .1E 13
Maldon Cl. E15 . . . . .3F 7
  N1 . . . . .3C 18
Malet Pl. WC1 . . . . .5D 37
Malet St. WC1 . . . . .5D 37
Mall, The E15 . . . . .1E 27
  SW1 . . . . .4C 86

Mallard Cl. E9 . . . . .4C 4
　NW6 .4E 9
Mallard Ho. NW8 . . . . .1F 33
Mallard Point E3 . . . . .3E 47
Mall Chambers W8 . . . . .2E 81
Mall Galleries 2E 87
Mallon Gdns. E1 . . . . .2C 64
Mallord St. SW3 . . . . .2E 133
Mallory Bldgs. EC1 . . . . .5F 39
Mallory Cl. E14 . . . . .1A 70
Mallory St. NW8 . . . . .4A 34
Mallow St. EC1 . . . . .4D 41
Mall Rd. W6 . . . . .5A 106
Mall Vs. W6 . . . . .5A 106
Malmesbury E2 . . . . .1B 44
Malmesbury Rd. E3 . . . . .2B 46
　E16 . . . . .2A 72
Malmesbury Ter. E16 . . . . . . .1B 72
Malmsey Ho. SE11 . . . . .5C 116
Malmsmead Ho. E9 . . . . .2A 4
Malswick Ct. SE15 . . . . .4F 141
Malta St. EC1 . . . . .4A 40
Maltby Ho. SE1 . . . . .1B 120
Maltby St. SE1 . . . . .5B 92
Malting Ho. E14 . . . . .5B 68
Maltings Cl. E3 . . . . .4B 48
Maltings Pl. SE1 . . . . .5A 92
Malton M. W10 . . . . .3F 51
Malton Rd. W10 . . . . .3F 51
Maltravers St. WC2 . . . . .5C 60
Malt St. SE1 . . . . .2D 143
Malvern Cl. W10 . . . . .2B 52
Malvern Ct. SW7 . . . . .3E 111
Malvern Ho. SE17 . . . . .1C 140
Malvern M. NW6 . . . . .2D 31
Malvern Pl. NW6 . . . . .2C 30
Malvern Rd. E8 . . . . .2D 21
　NW6 . . . . .1C 30
　　　　　　　(not continuous)
Malvern Ter. N1 . . . . .3D 17
Managers St. E14 . . . . .3C 98
Manbey Gro. E15 . . . . .4F 7
Manbey Pk. Rd. E15 . . . . .4F 7
Manbey Rd. E15 . . . . .4F 7
Manbey St. E15 . . . . .5F 7
Manchester Ct. E16 . . . . .4A 74
Manchester Dr. W10 . . . . .5F 29
Manchester Gro. E14 . . . . . .5B 126
Manchester Ho. SE17 . . . . . .5C 118
Manchester M. W1 . . . . .2D 57
Manchester Rd. E14 . . . . .5C 98
Manchester Sq. W1 . . . . .3E 57
Manchester St. W1 . . . . .2D 57
Manciple St. SE1 . . . . .5D 91
Mancroft Ct. NW8 . . . . .3E 11
Mandarin Ct. SE8 . . . . .3D 147
Mandarin St. E14 . . . . .5D 69
Mandarin Wharf N1 . . . . .3A 20
Mandela Cl. W12 . . . . .1A 78
Mandela Ho. E2 . . . . .2B 42
Mandela Rd. E16 . . . . .4E 73
Mandela St. NW1 . . . . .3C 14
　SW9 . . . . .5D 139
　　　　　　　(not continuous)
Mandela Way SE1 . . . . .3F 119
Manderley W14 . . . . .1B 108
Mandeville Ho. SE1 . . . . .5C 120
Mandeville Pl. W1 . . . . .3E 57
Mandrake Way E15 . . . . .1F 27
Manette St. W1 . . . . .4E 59
Manhattan Bldg. E3 . . . . .5E 25
Manhattan Loft Gdns. E20 . . . .4B 6
Manilla St. E14 . . . . .4D 97
Manitoba Ct. SE16 . . . . .5C 94

Manley Ho. SE11 . . . . .5D 117
Manley St. NW1 . . . . .3D 13
Manna Ho. E20 . . . . .4B 6
Mannan Ho. E3 . . . . .5B 24
Manneby Prior N1 . . . . .1C 38
Manningford Cl. EC1 . . . . .2F 39
Manning Ho. W11 . . . . .4A 52
Manningtree St. E1 . . . . .3D 65
Manny Shinwell Ho. SW6 . . .3C 130
Manor Ct. SW3 . . . . .1A 134
Manor Est. SE16 . . . . .4F 121
Manor Gro. SE15 . . . . .3B 144
Manor Ho. NW1 . . . . .1A 56
Manor Ho. Ct. W9 . . . . .5B 32
Manor M. NW6 . . . . .5E 9
Manor Pl. SE17 . . . . .1A 140
Manor Rd. E15 . . . . .1F 49
　E16 . . . . .4F 49
Manresa Rd. SW3 . . . . .1F 133
Mansell St. E1 . . . . .4C 64
　EC3 . . . . .1C 92
Mansfield Ct. E2 . . . . .4C 20
　SE15 . . . . .4C 142
Mansfield Ho. N1 . . . . .4F 19
　　　　　　　(off Halcomb St.)
Mansfield M. W1 . . . . .2F 57
Mansfield St. W1 . . . . .2F 57
Mansford St. E2 . . . . .1E 43
Mansion House 4D 63
Mansion Ho. Pl. EC4 . . . . .4D 63
Mansion Ho. St. EC4 . . . . .4D 63
Mansions, The SW5 . . . . . . .5F 109
　　　　　　　(Earl's Ct. Rd.)
　SW5 . . . . .5F 109
　　　　　　　(Old Brompton Rd.)
Mansion Vw. E15 . . . . .3D 27
Manson Ho. N1 . . . . .1D 17
Manson M. SW7 . . . . .4C 110
Manson Pl. SW7 . . . . .4D 111
Manston NW1 . . . . .2C 14
Manston Ho. W14 . . . . .2A 108
Mantle Way E15 . . . . .1F 27
Mantus Cl. E1 . . . . .4C 44
Mantus Rd. E1 . . . . .4B 44
Manuka Hgts. E20 . . . . .3B 6
Manwood St. E16 . . . . .3C 104
Mapesbury Rd. NW2 . . . . .1A 8
Mapes Ho. NW6 . . . . .2A 8
Mape St. E2 . . . . .4F 43
　　　　　　　(not continuous)
Maple Ct. E3 . . . . .5D 25
　　　　　　　(off Four Seasons Cl.)
　E6 .2E 77
Maplecroft Cl. E6 . . . . .3F 75
Mapledene Est. E8 . . . . .1D 21
Mapledene Rd. E8 . . . . .1C 20
Maple Ho. SE8 . . . . .4C 146
Maple Leaf Sq. SE16 . . . . . . .4E 95
Maple Lodge W8 . . . . .2F 109
Maple M. NW6 . . . . .5F 9
　SE16 . . . . .5D 95
Maple Pl. W1 . . . . .5C 36
Maples Pl. E1 . . . . .1A 66
Maple St. E2 . . . . .1E 43
　W1 . . . . .1B 58
Maple Wlk. W10 . . . . .4E 29
Maplin Rd. E16 . . . . .3E 73
Maplin St. E3 . . . . .3B 46
Mara Ho. E20 . . . . .3A 6
Marathon Ho. NW1 . . . . .1B 56
Marban Rd. W9 . . . . .2B 30
Marble Arch 5C 56
MARBLE ARCH 5B 56
Marble Arch W1 . . . . .5B 56

Marble Arch Apartments
　W1 . . . . .3B 56
Marble Ho. W9 . . . . .5D 31
Marble Quay E1 . . . . .2D 93
Marbles Ho. SE5 . . . . .2C 140
Marchant Ho. N1 . . . . .4F 19
　　　　　　　(off Halcomb St.)
Marchant St. SE14 . . . . .3F 145
Marchbank Rd. W14 . . . . .1D 131
Marchmont St. WC1 . . . . .4F 37
Marchwood Cl. SE5 . . . . .5A 142
Marcia Ct. SE1 . . . . .4A 120
Marcia Rd. SE1 . . . . .4A 120
Marco Polo Ho. SW8 . . . . . . .4F 135
Marco Rd. W6 . . . . .2A 106
Marden Sq. SE16 . . . . .2F 121
Mardyke Ho. SE17 . . . . .3E 119
Mare St. E8 . . . . .1A 22
Margaret Bondfield Ho. E3 . . .5F 23
Margaret Ct. W1 . . . . .3B 58
Margaret Herbison Ho.
　SW6 . . . . .3C 130
Margaret Ho. W6 . . . . .5B 106
Margaret Ingram Cl.
　SW6 . . . . .3B 130
Margaret McMillan Ho.
　E16 . . . . .4B 74
Margaret St. W1 . . . . .3A 58
Margaretta Ter. SW3 . . . . .2F 133
Margaret White Ho.
　NW1 . . . . .2D 37
Margery St. WC1 . . . . .3D 39
Margravine Gdns. W6 . . . . . .5E 107
Maria Cl. SE1 . . . . .3E 121
Marian Pl. E2 . . . . .5F 21
Marian St. E2 . . . . .5F 21
Maria Ter. E1 . . . . .1D 67
Maribor SE10 . . . . .4C 148
Marie Lloyd Ho. N1 . . . . .1D 41
Marie Lloyd Wlk. E8 . . . . .1D 21
Marigold All. SE1 . . . . .1F 89
Marigold St. SE16 . . . . .5F 93
Marina Ct. E3 . . . . .2C 46
Marina One N1 . . . . .5A 16
Marina Point E14 . . . . .1A 126
Marinel Ho. SE5 . . . . .5C 140
Mariners M. E14 . . . . .3D 127
Marine St. SE16 . . . . .1D 121
Marine Twr. SE8 . . . . .2B 146
Marion Ho. NW1 . . . . .3C 12
Maritime Ind. Est. SE7 . . . . . .4F 129
Maritime Quay E14 . . . . .5E 125
Maritime St. E3 . . . . .5C 46
Marjorie M. E1 . . . . .4D 67
Market App. W12 . . . . .4B 78
Market Ct. W1 . . . . .3B 58
Market Entrance SW8 . . . . . .4C 136
Market La. W1 . . . . .5B 78
Market M. W1 . . . . .3F 85
Market Pl. SE16 . . . . .3E 121
　　　　　　　(not continuous)
　W1 . . . . .3B 58
Market Sq. E14 . . . . .4A 70
Market St. E1 . . . . .1B 64
Market Way E14 . . . . .4A 70
Market Yd. M. SE1 . . . . .1F 119
Markham Pl. SW3 . . . . .5B 112
Markham Sq. SW3 . . . . .5B 112
Markham St. SW3 . . . . .5A 112
Mark Ho. E2 . . . . .1D 45
Markland Ho. W10 . . . . .5D 51
Mark La. EC3 . . . . .5A 64
Mark Sq. EC2 . . . . .4F 41
Markstone Ho. SE1 . . . . .5F 89

Mark St. E15 . . . . .2F **27**
   EC2 . . . . .4F **41**
Markyate Ho. W10 . . . . . . .5B **28**
Marland Ho. SW1 . . . . . . .1C **112**
Marlborough W9 . . . . .2B **32**
Marlborough Av. E8 . . . . . .4D **21**
   (not continuous)
Marlborough Cl. SE17 . . . .4A **118**
Marlborough Ct. W1 . . . . . .4B **58**
   W8 . . . . .3D **109**
Marlborough Flats SW3 . . .3A **112**
Marlborough Ga. Ho.
   W2 . . . . .5D **55**
Marlborough Gro. SE1 . . . .1D **143**
Marlborough Hill NW8 . . . .5C **10**
Marlborough House 3C **86**
Marlborough Ho. E16 . . . . .2E **101**
Marlborough Lodge NW8 . . .1B **32**
Marlborough Pl. NW8 . . . . .1B **32**
Marlborough Rd. E15 . . . . .1F **7**
   SW1 . . . . .3C **86**
Marlborough St. SW3 . . . . .4F **111**
Marlbury NW8 . . . . .4A **10**
Marley Ho. E16 . . . . .1F **105**
   W11 . . . . .1E **79**
Marley St. SE16 . . . . .4D **123**
Marloes Rd. W8 . . . . .2F **109**
Marlowe Bus. Cen. SE14 . .5A **146**
Marlowe Ct. SW3 . . . . .4A **112**
Marlowe Path SE8 . . . . . . .2F **147**
Marlowes, The NW8 . . . . . .4D **11**
Marlow Ho. E2 . . . . .3B **42**
   SE1 . . . . .1B **120**
   W2 . . . . .4A **54**
Marlow Way SE16 . . . . .4D **95**
Marlow Workshops E2 . . . .3B **42**
Marlton St. SE10 . . . . .5C **128**
Marlu Ct. SE14 . . . . .5E **145**
Marlu Ho. SE14 . . . . .5E **145**
Marmara Apartments
   E16 . . . . .1E **101**
Marmont Rd. SE15 . . . . . . .5E **143**
Marner Point E3 . . . . .4B **48**
Marne St. W10 . . . . .2F **29**
Marnock Ho. SE17 . . . . . .5D **119**
Maroon St. E14 . . . . .2F **67**
Marqueen Ct. *W8* 4F **81**
   (off Kensington Chu. St.)
Marquis Rd. NW1 . . . . .1E **15**
Marrick Ho. NW6 . . . . .4A **10**
Marriott Rd. E15 . . . . .3F **27**
Marryat Ho. SW1 . . . . .1B **136**
Marryat Sq. SW6 . . . . .5A **130**
Marsalis Ho. E3 . . . . .2E **47**
Marshall Bldg. W2 . . . . . . .2D **55**
Marshall Ho. N1 . . . . .5E **19**
   SE1 . . . . .2A **120**
   SE17 . . . . .5D **119**
Marshall's Pl. SE16 . . . . . .2C **120**
Marshall St. W1 . . . . .4C **58**
Marshall Street Leisure Cen.
   .4C **58**
Marshalsea Rd. SE1 . . . . . .4C **90**
Marsham Ct. SW1 . . . . . . .3E **115**
Marsham St. SW1 . . . . . . .2E **115**
Marsh Centre, The E1 . . . .3C **64**
Marsh Ct. E8 . . . . .1D **21**
Marshfield St. E14 . . . . . . .1B **126**
Marshgate La. E15 . . . . . . .4A **26**
   E20 . . . . .1E **25**
Marsh Hill E9 . . . . .3A **4**
Marsh Ho. SW1 . . . . .1E **137**
Marsh St. E14 . . . . .4F **125**
Marsh Wall E14 . . . . .3D **97**

Marshwood Ho. NW6 . . . . .4E **9**
Marsland Cl. SE17 . . . . . . .1A **140**
Marsom Ho. N1 . . . . .1D **41**
Marston Cl. NW6 . . . . .1C **10**
Marsworth Ho. E2 . . . . . . .4D **21**
Martara M. SE17 . . . . .1B **140**
Martello St. E8 . . . . .1F **21**
Martello Ter. E8 . . . . .2F **21**
Martha's Bldgs. EC1 . . . . . .4D **41**
Martha St. E1 . . . . .4A **66**
Martin Ct. E14 . . . . .5C **98**
Martindale Av. E16 . . . . . . .5E **73**
Martindale Ho. E14 . . . . . .1A **98**
Martineau Est. E1 . . . . .5B **66**
Martineau Ho. SW1 . . . . . .1B **136**
Martineau Sq. E1 . . . . .5E **65**
Martingale Ho. E1 . . . . .2A **94**
Martin Ho. E3 . . . . .4B **24**
   SE1 . . . . .2C **118**
   SW8 . . . . .4F **137**
Martin La. EC4 . . . . .5E **63**
   (not continuous)
Martlett Ct. WC2 . . . . .4A **60**
Marvell Ho. SE5 . . . . .5D **141**
Marville Rd. SW6 . . . . .5B **130**
Mary Ann Gdns. SE8 . . . . .3D **147**
Mary Bayly Ho. W11 . . . . . .2F **79**
Mary Datchelor Cl. SE5 . . .5E **141**
Mary Flux Ct. SW5 . . . . . . .5F **109**
Mary Grn. NW8 . . . . .3A **10**
Mary Ho. W6 . . . . .5B **106**
Mary Jones Ct. E14 . . . . . .1D **97**
Maryland Ind. Est. E15 . . . .3E **7**
Maryland Pk. E15 . . . . .3F **7**
   (not continuous)
Maryland Point E15 . . . . . . .4F **7**
Maryland Rd. E15 . . . . .3E **7**
Maryland Sq. E15 . . . . .3F **7**
Marylands Rd. W9 . . . . .5E **31**
   (not continuous)
Maryland St. E15 . . . . .3E **7**
Maryland Wlk. N1 . . . . .3B **18**
MARYLEBONE 1E **57**
Marylebone Cricket Club . .2E **33**
MARYLEBONE FLYOVER . . .2F **55**
Marylebone Fly-Over
   NW1 . . . . .2E **55**
   W2 . . . . .2E **55**
Marylebone High St. W1 . . .1E **57**
Marylebone La. W1 . . . . . . .2E **57**
Marylebone M. W1 . . . . . . .2F **57**
Marylebone Pas. W1 . . . . . .3C **58**
Marylebone Rd. NW1 . . . . .1A **56**
Marylebone St. W1 . . . . . . .2E **57**
Marylee Way SE11 . . . . . . .4C **116**
Mary Macarthur Ho. E2 . . .2D **45**
   W6 . . . . .2A **130**
Maryon Ho. NW6 . . . . .2C **10**
Mary Pl. W11 . . . . .1F **79**
Mary Rose Mall E6 . . . . . . .2C **76**
Marys Ct. NW1 . . . . .4A **34**
Mary Seacole Cl. E8 . . . . . .3B **20**
Mary Smith Ct. SW5 . . . . . .4E **109**
Marysmith Ho. SW1 . . . . . .5E **115**
Mary St. E16 . . . . .2B **72**
   N1 . . . . .4C **18**
Mary Ter. NW1 . . . . .4A **14**
Mary Wharrie Ho. NW3 . . . .1B **12**
Marzell Ho. W14 . . . . .1B **130**
Masbro' Rd. W14 . . . . .2E **107**
Masefield Ho. NW6 . . . . . . .2D **31**
Maskelyne Cl. SW11 . . . . . .5A **134**
Mason Cl. E16 . . . . .5D **73**
   SE16 . . . . .5E **121**

Mason Ho. E9 . . . . .1C **22**
   SE1 . . . . .4E **121**
Mason's Arms M. W1 . . . . .4A **58**
Mason's Av. EC2 . . . . .3D **63**
Masons Pl. EC1 . . . . .2A **40**
Mason St. SE17 . . . . .4E **119**
Masons Yd. EC1 . . . . .2A **40**
   SW1 . . . . .2C **86**
Massinger St. SE17 . . . . . . .4F **119**
Massingham St. E1 . . . . . . .4D **45**
Mast Ct. SE16 . . . . .3A **124**
Masterman Ho. SE5 . . . . . .4D **141**
Masters Dr. SE16 . . . . .1F **143**
Masters Lodge E1 . . . . .4C **66**
Masters St. E1 . . . . .1E **67**
Mast Ho. Ter. E14 . . . . .4E **125**
   (not continuous)
Mastmaker Ct. E14 . . . . . . .5E **97**
Mastmaker Rd. E14 . . . . . . .5E **97**
Match Ct. E3 . . . . .5E **25**
Matching Ct. E3 . . . . .3D **47**
Matheson Lang Ho. SE1 . . .5D **89**
Matheson Rd. W14 . . . . . . .4B **108**
Mathews Yd. WC2 . . . . .4F **59**
Mathieson Ct. SE1 . . . . . . .5A **90**
Mathison Ho. SW10 . . . . . .4B **132**
Matilda Gdns. E3 . . . . .1D **47**
Matilda Ho. E1 . . . . .2D **93**
Matilda St. N1 . . . . .4C **16**
Matisse Ct. EC1 . . . . .4D **41**
Matlock Ct. NW8 . . . . .5B **10**
   W11 . . . . .1D **81**
Matlock St. E14 . . . . .3F **67**
Maton Ho. SW6 . . . . .4B **130**
Matson Ho. SE16 . . . . .2A **122**
Matthew Cl. W10 . . . . .5D **29**
Matthew Parker St. SW1 . . .5E **87**
Matthews Ho. E14 . . . . . . .2D **69**
Matthias Apartments N1 . . .1D **19**
Maude Ho. E2 . . . . .1D **43**
Maudlins Grn. E1 . . . . .2D **90**
Maud St. E16 . . . . .2B **72**
Maunsel St. SW1 . . . . .3D **115**
Maurer Ct. SE10 . . . . .1C **128**
Mauretania Bldg. E1 . . . . . .5E **67**
Maurice Ct. E1 . . . . .3F **45**
Maurice Drummond Ho.
   SE10 . . . . .5F **147**
Maurice St. W12 . . . . .4A **50**
Mauritius Rd. SE10 . . . . . . .4A **128**
Maverton Rd. E3 . . . . .4D **25**
Mavis Wlk. E6 . . . . .2F **75**
Mavor Ho. N1 . . . . .4C **16**
Mawbey Ho. SE1 . . . . .1C **142**
Mawbey Pl. SE1 . . . . .1C **142**
Mawbey Rd. SE1 . . . . .1C **142**
Mawbey St. SW8 . . . . .5F **137**
Mawdley Ho. SE1 . . . . .5E **89**
Mawson Ct. N1 . . . . .4E **19**
Mawson Ho. EC1 . . . . .1D **61**
Maxilla Wlk. W10 . . . . .4E **51**
Maxwell Rd. SW6 . . . . .5F **131**
Maya Apartments E20 . . . . .3A **6**
Maybury Ct. W1 . . . . .2E **57**
Maydew Ho. SE16 . . . . .3B **122**
Maydwell Ho. E14 . . . . .2D **69**
MAYFAIR 1F **85**
Mayfair M. NW1 . . . . .2C **12**
Mayfair Pl. W1 . . . . .2A **86**
Mayfield Cl. E8 . . . . .1B **20**
Mayfield Ho. E2 . . . . .1A **44**
Mayfield Rd. E8 . . . . .2B **20**
   E13 . . . . .1C **72**
Mayflower Cl. SE16 . . . . . . .3E **123**

Mayflower Ho. E14 . . . . .4D **97**
Mayflower St. SE16 . . . . . . .5B **94**
Mayford NW1 . . . . .5C **14**
    (not continuous)
Maygood Ho. N1 . . . . .5D **17**
Maygood St. N1 . . . . .5D **17**
Mayhill Ct. SE15 . . . . .4F **141**
May Ho. E3 . . . . .1E **47**
Maylands Ho. SW3 . . . . . . .4A **112**
Maylie Ho. SE16 . . . . .5F **93**
Maynard Cl. SW6 . . . . .5A **132**
Maynards Quay E1 . . . . . . .1B **94**
Mayo Ho. E1 . . . . .2B **66**
Mayor's & City of London
   Court, The **3D 63**
May's Bldgs. M. SE10 . . . .5D **149**
Mays Ct. SE10 . . . . .5D **149**
   WC2 . . . . .1F **87**
May St. W14 . . . . .1C **130**
   (Kelway Ho.)
   W14 . . . . .1B **130**
   (Orchard Sq.)
May Wynne Ho. E16 . . . . . .5F **73**
Maze Hill SE3 . . . . .3F **149**
   SE10 . . . . .2F **149**
Maze Hill Lodge SE10 . . . . .2E **149**
Mazenod Av. NW6 . . . . .2E **9**
MCC Cricket Museum & Tours
   . . . .**3D 33**
Meadbank Studios SW11 . .5A **134**
Mead Cl. NW1 . . . . .1E **13**
Meadcroft Rd. SE11 . . . . . .3F **139**
   (not continuous)
   SE17 . . . . .3F **139**
Meader Ct. SE14 . . . . .4E **145**
Mead Ho. W11 . . . . .2B **80**
Meadowbank NW3 . . . . .2B **12**
Meadow Cl. E9 . . . . .3C **4**
Meadow Ct. E16 . . . . .3C **102**
   N1 . . . . .5F **19**
Meadowcroft M. E1 . . . . . . .5E **65**
Meadow M. SW8 . . . . .3B **138**
Meadow Pl. SW8 . . . . .4A **138**
Meadow Rd. SW8 . . . . .4B **138**
Meadow Row SE1 . . . . .2B **118**
Meadowsweet Cl. E16 . . . .2D **75**
Mead Row SE1 . . . . .1D **117**
Meakin Est. SE1 . . . . .1F **119**
Meander Ho. E20 . . . . .3A **6**
Meard St. W1 . . . . .4D **59**
   (not continuous)
Mears Cl. E1 . . . . .2E **65**
Meath Cres. E2 . . . . .3D **45**
Mecca Bingo
   Camden **3A 14**
   Hackney **1C 42**
Mecklenburgh Pl. WC1 . . . .4B **38**
Mecklenburgh Sq. WC1 . . .4B **38**
Mecklenburgh St. WC1 . . . .4B **38**
Medals Way E20 . . . . .3C **6**
Medburn St. NW1 . . . . .5D **15**
Medhurst Cl. E3 . . . . .1A **46**
   (not continuous)
Medland Ho. E14 . . . . .5F **67**
Medlar St. SE5 . . . . .5C **140**
Medway Bldgs. E3 . . . . .1A **46**
Medway Ct. WC1 . . . . .3F **37**
Medway Ho. NW8 . . . . .5F **33**
   SE1 . . . . .5E **91**
Medway M. E3 . . . . .1A **46**
Medway Rd. E3 . . . . .1A **46**
Medway St. SW1 . . . . .2D **115**
Meeson St. E5 . . . . .1A **4**
Meeson's Wharf E15 . . . . . .1B **48**

Meeting Ho. All. E1 . . . . .2A **94**
Meeting Ho. La. SE15 . . . .5F **143**
Melbourne Ct. E5 . . . . .1A **4**
   W9 . . . . .4C **32**
Melbourne Ho. W8 . . . . .3D **81**
Melbourne Mans. W14 . . . .2A **130**
Melbourne Pl. WC2 . . . . . . .5C **60**
Melbourne Ter. SW6 . . . . . .5F **131**
Melbury Ct. W8 . . . . .1C **108**
Melbury Dr. SE5 . . . . .5F **141**
Melbury Ho. SW8 . . . . .4B **138**
Melbury Rd. W14 . . . . .1B **108**
Melchester W11 . . . . .3C **52**
Melcombe Ct. NW1 . . . . . . .1B **56**
Melcombe Ho. SW8 . . . . . .5B **138**
Melcombe Pl. NW1 . . . . . . .1B **56**
Melcombe Regis Ct. W1 . . . .2E **57**
   (off Weymouth St.)
Melcombe St. NW1 . . . . . . .5C **34**
Melford Ct. SE1 . . . . .1A **120**
Melina Ct. NW8 . . . . .3D **33**
Melina Pl. NW8 . . . . .3D **33**
Melior Pl. SE1 . . . . .4F **91**
Melior St. SE1 . . . . .4F **91**
Meller Ho. E20 . . . . .4C **6**
Mellish Ho. E1 . . . . .3F **65**
Mellish St. E14 . . . . .1D **125**
Mell St. SE10 . . . . .1F **149**
Melon Pl. W8 . . . . .4E **81**
Melrose Gdns. W6 . . . . .1C **106**
Melrose Ho. NW6 . . . . .2E **31**
   SW1 . . . . .5F **113**
Melrose Ter. W6 . . . . .5C **78**
Melton Ct. SW7 . . . . .4E **111**
Melton St. NW1 . . . . .3C **36**
Melville Ct. SE8 . . . . .4F **123**
   W12 . . . . .1A **106**
Melville Pl. N1 . . . . .2B **18**
Melwood Ho. E1 . . . . .4A **66**
Memel Ct. EC1 . . . . .5B **40**
Memel St. EC1 . . . . .5B **40**
Memorial Av. E15 . . . . .2F **49**
Menai Pl. E3 . . . . .5D **25**
Menard Ct. EC1 . . . . .3C **40**
Mendham Ho. SE1 . . . . . .1F **119**
Mendip Ct. SE14 . . . . .3C **144**
Mendip Ho's. E2 . . . . .2C **44**
Mendora Rd. SW6 . . . . . . .4A **130**
Menier Chocolate Factory
  (Theatre and Art Gallery)
   . . . .**3C 90**
Menotti St. E2 . . . . .4E **43**
Menteath Ho. E14 . . . . .3D **69**
Mentmore Ter. E8 . . . . .2A **22**
Mentone Mans. SW10 . . . .4A **132**
Mepham St. SE1 . . . . .3C **88**
Mercator Pl. E14 . . . . .5E **125**
Mercer Bldg. EC2 . . . . .4A **42**
Mercer Ct. E1 . . . . .1F **67**
Mercer St. WC1 . . . . .5F **113**
Merceron Ho's. E2 . . . . .2B **44**
Merceron St. E1 . . . . .5A **44**
Mercers Cl. SE10 . . . . .4B **128**
Mercer's Cotts. E1 . . . . .3F **67**
Mercers Pl. W6 . . . . .3C **106**
Mercer St. WC2 . . . . .4F **59**
Merchant Ct. E1 . . . . .2C **94**
Merchant Ho. E14 . . . . .2A **126**
Merchants Ho. SE10 . . . . .1E **149**
Merchant Sq. W2 . . . . .2E **55**
Merchants Row SE10 . . . . . .1E **149**
   (off Hoskins St.)
Merchant St. E3 . . . . .3C **46**
Mercury Ct. E14 . . . . .3D **125**

Mercury Ho. E3 . . . . .4D **25**
   E16 . . . . .4C **72**
Mercury Way SE14 . . . . . . .2D **145**
Meredith St. EC1 . . . . .3F **39**
Mereworth Ho. SE15 . . . . .2C **144**
Merganser Ct. E1 . . . . .1D **93**
   SE8 . . . . .3C **146**
Meriden Ct. SW3 . . . . .1F **133**
Meriden Ho. N1 . . . . .4A **20**
Meridia Ct. E15 . . . . .3C **26**
Meridian Ct. SE15 . . . . . . .4A **144**
   SE16 . . . . .4D **93**
   (off East La.)
Meridian Ga. E14 . . . . .4B **98**
Meridian Ho. NW1 . . . . .2C **14**
   SE10 . . . . .4A **128**
   (Azof St.)
   SE10 . . . . .4B **148**
   (Royal Hill)
Meridian Pl. E14 . . . . .4B **98**
Meridian Point SE8 . . . . . .3F **147**
Meridian Sq. E15 . . . . .1D **27**
Meridian Trad. Est. SE7 . . .3F **129**
Merino Ct. EC1 . . . . .3C **40**
Merita Ho. E1 . . . . .2D **93**
Merle Mans. E20 . . . . .4B **6**
Merlins Ct. WC1 . . . . .3D **39**
Merlin St. WC1 . . . . .3D **39**
Mermaid Ct. E8 . . . . .2B **20**
   SE1 . . . . .4D **91**
   SE16 . . . . .3B **96**
Mermaid Ho. E14 . . . . .5B **70**
Mermaid Twr. SE8 . . . . .3B **146**
Merriam Av. E9 . . . . .5B **4**
Merrick Sq. SE1 . . . . .1D **119**
Merrington Rd. SW6 . . . . . .2E **131**
Merrivale NW1 . . . . .4C **14**
Merrow Bldgs. SE1 . . . . . . .4A **90**
Merrow St. SE17 . . . . .2C **140**
Merrow Wlk. SE17 . . . . . . .5E **119**
Merryweather Pl. SE10 . . . .5F **147**
Merton Ri. NW3 . . . . .1F **11**
Mertoun Ter. W1 . . . . .2B **56**
Messenger Ct. SE16 . . . . .2D **121**
Messina Av. NW6 . . . . .2D **9**
Messiter Ho. N1 . . . . .4C **16**
Metcalfe Ct. SE10 . . . . . . .1C **128**
Methley St. SE11 . . . . .1E **139**
Methwold Rd. W10 . . . . .1D **51**
Metro Central Hgts.
   SE1 . . . . .2B **118**
Metropolis SE11 . . . . .2A **118**
Metropolitan Bus. Cen.
   N1 . . . . .2A **20**
Metropolitan Cl. E14 . . . . . .2E **69**
Metropolitan Sta. Bldgs.
   W6 . . . . .4C **106**
   (off Beadon Rd.)
Metropolitan Wharf E1 . . . . .2C **94**
Mews, The N1 . . . . .3C **18**
Mews St. E1 . . . . .2D **93**
Mexborough NW1 . . . . .4B **14**
Meymott St. SE1 . . . . .3F **89**
Meynell Cres. E9 . . . . .1D **23**
Meynell Gdns. E9 . . . . .1D **23**
Meynell Rd. E9 . . . . .1D **23**
Meyrick Ho. E14 . . . . .2D **69**
Miah Ter. E1 . . . . .3E **93**
Mica Ho. N1 . . . . .2D **17**
Micawber Ct. N1 . . . . .2C **40**
Micawber Ho. SE16 . . . . . . .5E **93**
Micawber St. N1 . . . . .2C **40**
Michael Cliffe Ho. EC1 . . . .3E **39**
Michael Cl. E3 . . . . .5C **46**

Michael Edwards Studio Theatre, The 2C 148
Michael Faraday Ho.
  SE17 . . . . .1F 141
Michael Haines Ho.
  SW9 . . . . .5D 139
Michael Rd. SW6 . . . . .5A 132
Michael Stewart Ho.
  SW6 . . . . .3C 130
Michelangelo Ct.
  SE16 . . . . .5F 121
Michelson Ho. SE11 . . . . . . .4C 116
Michigan Bldg. E14 . . . . . . .2C 98
Michigan Ho. E14 . . . . .2D 125
Mickledore NW1 . . . . .1C 36
Micklethwaite Rd.
  SW6 . . . . .3E 131
Mickleton Ho. W2 . . . . .2D 53
MID BECKTON **3B 76**
Middle Dartrey Wlk.
  SW10 . . . . .4C *132*
    (off Dartrey Wlk.)
Middlefield NW8 . . . . .3D 11
Middle New St. EC4 . . . . . . .3E 61
Middle Row W10 . . . . .5F 29
Middlesex Building, The
  E1 . . . . .2A *64*
    (off Artillery La.)
Middlesex CCC **2E 33**
Middlesex Guildhall **5E 87**
Middlesex Pas. EC1 . . . . . . .2A 62
Middlesex St. E1 . . . . .2A 64
Middle St. EC1 . . . . .1B 62
Middle Temple La. EC4 . . . . .4D 61
Middleton Dr. SE16 . . . . . . .4E 95
Middleton Ho. E8 . . . . .2C 20
  SE1 . . . . .2D 119
  SW1 . . . . .4E 115
Middleton Pl. W1 . . . . .2B 58
Middleton Rd. E8 . . . . .2B 20
Middleton St. E2 . . . . .2A 44
Middle Yd. SE1 . . . . .2F 91
Midford Pl. W1 . . . . .5C 36
Midhope Ho. WC1 . . . . .3A 38
Midhope St. WC1 . . . . .3A 38
Midhurst Ho. E14 . . . . .3B 68
Midland Goods Shed
  N1 . . . . .4A 16
Midland Pl. E14 . . . . .5B 126
Midland Rd. NW1 . . . . .5E 15
Midlothian Rd. E3 . . . . .5B 46
Midnight Av. SE5 . . . . .4F 139
Midship Cl. SE16 . . . . .3E 95
Midship Point E14 . . . . .5D 97
Midway Ho. EC1 . . . . .2A 40
Mikardo Ct. E14 . . . . .1B 98
Milborne Gro. SW10 . . . . . . .1C 132
Milborne St. E9 . . . . .1C 22
Milcote St. SE1 . . . . .5F 89
Mildrose Ct. NW6 . . . . .3D 31
MILE END **4A 46**
Mile End Climbing Wall . . .**2F 45**
Mile End Park **4A 46**
Mile End Park Leisure Cen.
  . . . .**1B 68**
Mile End Pl. E1 . . . . .4D 45
Mile End Rd. E1 . . . . .1B 66
  E3 . . . . .3A 46
Mile End Stadium **1A 68**
Miles Bldgs. NW1 . . . . .1F 55
    (not continuous)
Miles Ct. E1 . . . . .4F 65
Miles Ho. SE10 . . . . .1F 149
Miles Lodge E15 . . . . .1E 7

Miles Pl. NW8 . . . . .1E 55
Miles St. SW8 . . . . .3F 137
    (not continuous)
Milford La. WC2 . . . . .5D 61
Milk St. E16 . . . . .3F 105
  EC2 . . . . .4C 62
Milk Yd. E1 . . . . .1B 94
Millais Ho. SW1 . . . . .4F 115
Millais Rd. E11 . . . . .1C 6
Millard Rd. SE8 . . . . .5B 124
Millbank SW1 . . . . .2F 115
Millbank Ct. SW1 . . . . .3F 115
Millbank Twr. SW1 . . . . .4F 115
Millbrook Ho. SE15 . . . . . . .3E 143
Millbrook Pl. *NW1* *5B 14*
    (off Hampstead Rd.)
Millender Wlk. SE16 . . . . . . .4C 122
Millennium Arena **4E 135**
Millennium Bridge **1A 90**
Millennium Bri. Ho.
  EC4 . . . . .5B 62
Millennium Cl. E16 . . . . .3F 73
Millennium Dr. E14 . . . . .2D 127
Millennium Pl. E2 . . . . .1A 44
Millennium Sq. SE1 . . . . . . .4C 92
Millennium Way SE10 . . . . . .4F 99
Miller Ho. E1 . . . . .1E 67
  W10 . . . . .4B 30
Miller St. NW1 . . . . .5B 14
    (not continuous)
Millers Way W6 . . . . .5C 78
Millers Wharf Ho. E1 . . . . . . .3D 93
Miller Wlk. SE1 . . . . .3E 89
Millharbour E14 . . . . .1F 125
Milligan St. E14 . . . . .1C 96
Milliner Ho. SW10 . . . . .4B 132
Milliners Ho. SE1 . . . . .5A 92
Millman Ct. WC1 . . . . .5B 38
Millman M. WC1 . . . . .5B 38
Millman Pl. WC1 . . . . .5B 38
Millman Rd. E16 . . . . .5B 76
Millman St. WC1 . . . . .5B 38
MILL MEADS **1D 49**
Mill Pl. E14 . . . . .4A 68
Mill Pond Cl. SW8 . . . . .5E 137
Millpond Est. SE16 . . . . .5F 93
Mill Rd. E16 . . . . .3A 102
Mill Row N1 . . . . .4A 20
Mills Ct. EC2 . . . . .4F 41
Mills Gro. E14 . . . . .2B 70
Mills Ho. SW8 . . . . .5C 136
Millstone Cl. E15 . . . . .4E 7
Millstream Ho. SE16 . . . . . . .5A 94
Millstream Rd. SE1 . . . . .5B 92
Mill St. SE1 . . . . .5C 92
  W1 . . . . .5A 58
MILLWALL **4E 125**
Millwall Dock Rd. E14 . . . . . .1D 125
Millwall FC **1C 144**
Millwall Park **4B 126**
Millwood St. W10 . . . . .2F 51
Mill Yd. E1 . . . . .5D 65
Milman Rd. NW6 . . . . .1F 29
Milman's Ho. SW10 . . . . . . .3D 133
Milman's St. SW10 . . . . .3D 133
Milner Ct. SE15 . . . . .4C 142
Milner Pl. N1 . . . . .5C 8
Milner Rd. E15 . . . . .3F 49
Milner Sq. N1 . . . . .4D 8
Milner St. SW3 . . . . .3B 112
Milrood Ho. E1 . . . . .1D 67
Milroy Wlk. SE1 . . . . .2F 89
Milson Rd. W14 . . . . .1E 107
Milton Cl. SE1 . . . . .4B 120

Milton Ct. EC2 . . . . .1D 63
  SE14 . . . . .3A 146
    (not continuous)
Milton Court Concert Hall . .**1D 63**
Milton Ct. Rd. SE14 . . . . . . .3A 146
Milton Ho. E2 . . . . .2B 44
  SE5 . . . . .5D 141
Milton Mans. W14 . . . . .2A 130
Milton St. EC2 . . . . .1D 63
Milverton St. SE11 . . . . .1E 139
Milward St. E1 . . . . .2A 66
Mimosa Ho. E20 . . . . .3C 6
Mina Rd. SE17 . . . . .1A 142
Minchin Ho. E14 . . . . .3D 69
Mincing La. EC3 . . . . .5F 63
Minera M. SW1 . . . . .3E 113
Minerva Cl. SW9 . . . . .5E 139
Minerva Ct. EC1 . . . . .5E 39
Minerva St. E2 . . . . .1F 43
Minerva Wlk. EC1 . . . . .3A 62
Minford Gdns. W14 . . . . .5D 79
Minford Ho. W14 . . . . .5D 79
Ming St. E14 . . . . .5E 69
Miniver Pl. EC4 . . . . .5C 62
Minnow St. SE17 . . . . .4A 120
Minnow Wlk. SE17 . . . . .4A 120
Minories EC3 . . . . .4B 64
Minson Rd. E9 . . . . .3E 23
Minster Ct. EC3 . . . . .5A 64
Minster Pavement EC3 . . . . . .5F 63
Mint Bus. Pk. E16 . . . . .2E 73
Mintern St. N1 . . . . .5E 19
Minton Ho. SE11 . . . . .3D 117
Mint St. SE1 . . . . .4B 90
Mirabelle Gdns. E20 . . . . . . .3C 6
Mirabel Rd. SW6 . . . . .4C 130
Mira Ho. E20 . . . . .3C 6
Miranda Cl. E1 . . . . .2B 66
Miranda Ho. N1 . . . . .1F 41
Missenden SE17 . . . . .1E 141
Missenden Ho. NW0 . . . . . . .1F 33
Mission, The E14 . . . . .4B 68
Mitali Pas. E1 . . . . .4D 65
Mitchell Ho. N1 . . . . .1F 17
  W12 . . . . .1A 78
Mitchell St. EC1 . . . . .4B 40
    (not continuous)
Mitchell Wlk. E6 . . . . .2E 75
    (Allhallows Rd.)
  E6 . . . . .2B 76
    (Elmley Cl.)
Mitford Bldgs. SW6 . . . . .4D 131
Mitre, The E14 . . . . .5B 68
Mitre Bri. Ind. Pk. W10 . . . . .5A 28
    (not continuous)
Mitre Ho. SW3 . . . . .5B 112
Mitre Pas. SE10 . . . . .4A 100
Mitre Rd. E15 . . . . .5F 27
  SE1 . . . . .4E 89
Mitre Sq. EC3 . . . . .4A 64
Mitre St. EC3 . . . . .4A 64
Mitre Way W10 . . . . .5A 28
Mitre Yd. SW3 . . . . .3A 112
Mizen Ct. E14 . . . . .5E 97
Moatlands Ho. WC1 . . . . . . .3A 38
Moberly Sports & Education Cen.
  . . . .**2E 29**
Mobil Ct. *WC2* 4C *60*
    (off Clement's Inn)
Mocatta Ho. E1 . . . . .5F 43
Mocha Ct. E3 . . . . .1F 47
Modern Ct. EC4 . . . . .3F 61
Modling Ho. E2 . . . . .1D 45
Moffat Ho. SE5 . . . . .5B 140

Mohawk Ho. E3	.1F 45	
Mole Ho. NW8	.5E 33	
Molesworth Ho. SE17	.3F 139	
Mollis Ho. E3	.1E 69	
Molton Ho. N1	.4C 16	
Molyneux St. W1	.2A 56	
Monarch Dr. E16	.2D 75	
Monarch Ho. W8	.1D 109	
Mona St. E16	.2C 72	
Monck Ho. SE1	.5C 90	
Monck St. SW1	.2E 115	
Monckton Ct. W14	.1B 108	
Moncorvo Cl. SW7	.5F 83	
Moncrieff Cl. E6	.3F 75	
Monet Ct. SE16	.5F 121	
Moneyer Ho. N1	.2D 41	
Mongers Almshouses		
E9	.1D 23	
Monica Shaw Ct. NW1	.1E 37	
(not continuous)		
Monier Rd. E3	.3D 25	
Monk Dr. E16	.4D 73	
Monk Pas. E16	.5D 73	
Monkton Ho. SE16	.5D 95	
Monkton St. SE11	.3E 117	
Monkwell Sq. EC2	.2C 62	
Monmouth Pl. W2	.4F 53	
Monmouth Rd. W2	.4E 53	
Monmouth St. WC2	.4F 59	
Monnow Rd. SE1	.5D 121	
Monroe Ho. NW8	.3A 34	
Monson Rd. SE14	.4D 145	
Montagu Ct. W1	.2C 56	
Montague Cl. SE1	.2D 91	
Montague Ct. N7	.1D 17	
Montague Ho. E16	.2F 101	
(off Wesley Av.)		
N1	.4F 19	
(off Halcomb St.)		
Montague M. E3	.2B 46	
Montague Pl. WC1	.1E 59	
Montague Sq. SE15	.5C 144	
Montague St. EC1	.2B 62	
WC1	.1F 59	
Montagu Mans. W1	.1C 56	
Montagu M. Nth. W1	.2C 56	
Montagu M. Sth. W1	.3C 56	
Montagu M. W. W1	.3C 56	
Montagu Pl. W1	.2B 56	
Montagu Row W1	.2C 56	
Montagu Sq. W1	.2C 56	
Montagu St. W1	.3C 56	
Montaigne Cl. SW1	.4E 115	
Montanaro Ct. N1	.3C 18	
Montcalm Ho. E14	.3D 125	
Montclare St. E2	.3B 42	
Monteagle Ct. N1	.5A 20	
Monterey Studios W10	.1A 30	
Montevetro SW11	.5E 133	
Montfichet Rd. E20	.4D 7	
Montford Pl. SE11	.1D 139	
Montfort Ho. E2	.2B 44	
E14	.1B 126	
Montgomery Ho. W2	.2D 55	
Montgomery Lodge E1	.5B 44	
Montgomery St. E14	.3A 98	
Monthope Rd. E1	.2C 64	
Montpelier M. SW7	.1A 112	
Montpelier Pl. E1	.4B 66	
SW7	.1A 112	
Montpelier Rd. SE15	.5A 144	
Montpelier Sq. SW7	.5A 84	
Montpelier St. SW7	.1A 112	
Montpelier Ter. SW7	.5A 84	
Montpelier Wlk. SW7	.5A 84	
Montreal Ho. SE16	.5D 95	
Montreal Pl. WC2	.5B 60	
Montrose Av. NW6	.5A 8	
Montrose Ct. SW7	.5E 83	
Montrose Ho. E14	.2D 125	
SW1	.5E 85	
Montrose Pl. SW1	.5E 85	
Monument, The	.5E 63	
Monument St. EC3	.5E 63	
Monza St. E1	.2B 94	
Moodkee St. SE16	.1B 122	
Moody Rd. SE15	.5B 142	
Moody St. E1	.3E 45	
Moon St. N1	.3F 17	
Moore Ct. N1	.4F 17	
Moore Ho. E1	.5C 66	
E2	.3B 44	
E14	.5E 97	
SE10	.5B 128	
SW1	.1F 135	
Moore Pk. Rd. SW6	.5E 131	
Moore St. SW3	.3B 112	
Moorfields EC2	.2D 63	
Moorfields Highwalk EC2	.2D 63	
(not continuous)		
Moorgate EC2	.3D 63	
Moorgate Pl. EC2	.3D 63	
Moorgreen Ho. EC1	.2F 39	
Moorhen Ho. E3	.4B 24	
Moorhouse Rd. W2	.3D 53	
Moorings, The E16	.2B 74	
Moor La. EC2	.2D 63	
(not continuous)		
Moor Pl. EC2	.2D 63	
Moor St. W1	.4E 59	
Moran Ho. E1	.3A 94	
Morant St. E14	.5E 69	
Mora St. EC1	.3C 40	
Morat St. SW9	.5C 138	
Moravian Cl. SW10	.3D 133	
Moravian Pl. SW10	.3E 133	
Moravian St. E2	.2B 44	
Moray Ho. E1	.5F 45	
Morden Wharf SE10	.2F 127	
Morden Wharf Rd.		
SE10	.2F 127	
Mordern Ho. NW1	.5A 34	
Morecambe Cl. E1	.1D 67	
Morecambe St. SE17	.4C 118	
More Cl. E16	.3C 72	
W14	.4E 107	
More Copper Ho. SE1	.3F 91	
(off Magdalen St.)		
Moreland Cotts. E3	.1E 47	
Moreland St. EC1	.2A 40	
More London Pl. SE1	.3F 91	
(not continuous)		
More London Riverside		
SE1	.3A 92	
(not continuous)		
More's Gdn. SW3	.3E 133	
Moreton Cl. SW1	.5C 114	
Moreton Ho. SE16	.1A 122	
Moreton Pl. SW1	.5C 114	
Moreton St. SW1	.5C 114	
Moreton Ter. SW1	.5C 114	
Moreton Ter. M. Nth.		
SW1	.5C 114	
Moreton Ter. M. Sth.		
SW1	.5C 114	
Morgan Ho. SW1	.4C 114	
SW8	.5C 136	
Morgan Rd. W10	.1B 52	
Morgans La. SE1	.3F 91	
(off Tooley St.)		
Morgan St. E3	.3A 46	
(not continuous)		
E16	.1C 72	
Morland Ct. W12	.5A 78	
Morland Est. E8	.1E 21	
Morland Ho. NW1	.1C 36	
NW6	.4D 9	
SW1	.3F 115	
W11	.4F 51	
Morland M. N1	.2E 17	
Morley Ho. SE15	.5C 142	
Morley St. SE1	.1E 117	
Mornington Av. W14	.4B 108	
Mornington Av. Mans.		
W14	.4C 108	
Mornington Ct. NW1	.5B 14	
Mornington Cres. NW1	.5B 14	
Mornington Gro. E3	.2D 47	
Mornington Pl. NW1	.5A 14	
SE8	.5C 146	
Mornington Rd. SE8	.5C 146	
Mornington Sports & Leisure Cen.	.4A 14	
Mornington St. NW1	.5A 14	
Mornington Ter. NW1	.4A 14	
Morocco St. SE1	.5F 91	
Morocco Wharf E1	.3F 93	
(off Wapping High St.)		
Morpeth Gro. E9	.3D 23	
Morpeth Mans. SW1	.2B 114	
Morpeth Rd. E9	.4C 22	
Morpeth St. E2	.2D 45	
Morpeth Ter. SW1	.2B 114	
Morrel Ct. E2	.5E 21	
Morrells Yd. SE11	.5E 117	
Morris Ho. E2	.3B 44	
NW8	.5F 33	
Morrison Bldgs. Nth.		
E1	.3D 65	
Morrison Ct. SW1	.1E 115	
Morris Rd. E14	.1F 69	
E15	.1F 7	
Morriss Ho. SE16	.5F 93	
Morris St. E1	.4A 66	
Morshead Mans. W9	.3E 31	
Morshead Rd. W9	.3E 31	
Mortain Ho. SE16	.4F 121	
Mortham St. E15	.4F 27	
Mortimer Ct. NW8	.1C 32	
Mortimer Cres. NW6	.4F 9	
Mortimer Est. NW6	.4F 9	
Mortimer Ho. W11	.2E 79	
W14	.4A 108	
Mortimer Mkt. WC1	.5C 36	
Mortimer Pl. NW6	.4F 9	
Mortimer Rd. N1	.2A 20	
(not continuous)		
NW10	.2B 28	
Mortimer Sq. W11	.1E 79	
Mortimer St. W1	.3A 58	
Mortlake Rd. E16	.3F 73	
Morton Cl. E1	.4B 66	
Morton Ho. SE17	.2A 140	
Morton M. SW5	.4F 109	
Morton Pl. SE1	.2D 117	
Morton Rd. N1	.2C 18	
Morville Ho. SW18	.5D 25	
Morville St. E3	.5D 25	
Morwell St. WC1	.2D 59	
Moscow Mans. SW5	.3E 109	
Moscow Pl. W2	.5F 53	
Moscow Rd. W2	.5E 53	
Mosedale NW1	.3B 36	

Moseley Row SE10 . . . . .3C **128**
Mosque Ter. *E1* 2E **65**
(off Whitechapel Rd.)
Mosque Twr. *E1* 2D **65**
(off Fieldgate St.)
Moss Cl. E1 . . . . .2E **65**
Mossford St. E3 . . . . .4B **46**
Mossington Gdns.
SE16 . . . . .4B **122**
Mossop St. SW3 . . . . .3A **112**
Mostyn Gdns. NW10 . . . . . . .2D **29**
Mostyn Gro. E3 . . . . .1C **46**
Motcomb St. SW1 . . . . .1D **113**
Motley Av. EC2 . . . . .4F **41**
Moules Ct. SE5 . . . . .5B **140**
Moulins Rd. E9 . . . . .2C **22**
Moulsford Ho. W2 . . . . .2E **53**
Mounsey Ho. W10 . . . . .2A **30**
Mount, The W8 . . . . .3D **81**
Mountague Pl. E14 . . . . .5B **70**
Mountain Ho. SE11 . . . . .5C **116**
Mountbatten Ct. SE16 . . . . . .3C **94**
Mt. Carmel Chambers
W8 . . . . .4F **81**
Mountfort Cres. N1 . . . . .1D **17**
Mountfort Ter. N1 . . . . .2D **17**
Mountjoy Cl. *EC2* 2C **62**
(off Monkwell Sq.)
Mountjoy Ho. EC2 . . . . .2B **62**
Mount Mills EC1 . . . . .3A **40**
Mt. Pleasant WC1 . . . . .5D **39**
Mount Row W1 . . . . .1F **85**
Mount St. W1 . . . . .1D **85**
Mount St. M. W1 . . . . .1F **85**
Mount Ter. E1 . . . . .2F **65**
Mowbray Rd. NW6 . . . . .1A **8**
Mowlem St. E2 . . . . .5A **22**
Mowll St. SW9 . . . . .5D **139**
Moxon St. W1 . . . . .2D **57**
Moye Cl. E2 . . . . .5E **21**
Moylan Rd. W6 . . . . .3A **130**
Moyle Ho. SW1 . . . . .1C **136**
Mozart St. W10 . . . . .3B **30**
Mozart Ter. SW1 . . . . .4E **113**
MTV Europe 2A **14**
Mudchute Farm 3B **126**
Mudlarks Blvd. SE10 . . . . . .1C **128**
Mudlarks Way SE10 . . . . . . .1D **129**
Muirfield Cl. SE16 . . . . .1A **144**
Muirfield Cres. E14 . . . . .1F **125**
Muir St. E16 . . . . .3A **104**
(not continuous)
Mulberry Cl. SW3 . . . . .3E **133**
Mulberry Ct. EC1 . . . . .3A **40**
SW3 . . . . .2E **133**
(not continuous)
W9 . . . . .3C **30**
Mulberry Ho. E2 . . . . .2B **44**
SE8 . . . . .2B **146**
Mulberry Housing Co-operative
SE1 . . . . .2E **89**
Mulberry Pl. E14 . . . . .5C **70**
Mulberry Rd. E8 . . . . .2B **20**
Mulberry St. E1 . . . . .3D **65**
Mulberry Wlk. SW3 . . . . .2E **133**
Mulgrave Rd. SW6 . . . . .2B **130**
Mullen Twr. WC1 . . . . .5D **39**
Mullet Gdns. E2 . . . . .2E **43**
Mulletsfield WC1 . . . . .3A **38**
Mull Ho. E3 . . . . .1B **46**
Mulligans Apartments
NW6 . . . . .2D **9**
Mulready Ho. SW1 . . . . .4F **115**
Mulready St. NW8 . . . . .5F **33**

Multon Ho. E9 . . . . .2B **22**
Mulvaney Way SE1 . . . . .5E **91**
(not continuous)
Mumford Mills SE10 . . . . . . .5F **147**
Munday Ho. SE1 . . . . .2D **119**
Munday Rd. E16 . . . . .4D **73**
Munden Ho. E3 . . . . .2A **48**
Munden St. W14 . . . . .3F **107**
Mund St. W14 . . . . .1C **130**
Mundy Ho. W10 . . . . .2A **30**
Mundy St. N1 . . . . .2F **41**
Munkenbeck Bldg. W2 . . . . .2D **55**
Munnings Ho. *E16* 2A **102**
(off Portsmouth M.)
Munro Ho. SE1 . . . . .5D **89**
Munro M. W10 . . . . .2A **52**
(not continuous)
Munro Ter. SW10 . . . . .4D **133**
Munster M. SW6 . . . . .4A **130**
Munster Rd. SW6 . . . . .4A **130**
Munster Sq. NW1 . . . . .3A **36**
Munton Rd. SE17 . . . . .3C **118**
Muratori Ho. WC1 . . . . .3D **39**
Murchison Ho. W10 . . . . .1F **51**
Murdoch Ho. SE16 . . . . .1C **122**
Murdock Cl. E16 . . . . .3C **72**
Murdock St. SE15 . . . . .3F **143**
Muriel St. N1 . . . . .5C **16**
(not continuous)
Muro Ct. SE1 . . . . .5A **90**
Murphy Ho. SE1 . . . . .1A **118**
Murphy St. SE1 . . . . .5D **89**
Murray Ct. E3 . . . . .1C **68**
Murray Gro. N1 . . . . .1C **40**
Murray M. NW1 . . . . .1D **15**
Murray Sq. E16 . . . . .4E **73**
Murray St. NW1 . . . . .1C **14**
Mursell Est. SW8 . . . . .5B **138**
Musard Rd. W6 . . . . .2A **130**
Musbury St. E1 . . . . .3D **00**
Muscal W6 . . . . .2A **130**
Muscatel Pl. SE5 . . . . .5A **142**
Muscott Ho. E2 . . . . .4D **21**
Muscovy St. EC3 . . . . .5A **64**
Museum Chambers
WC1 . . . . .2F **59**
Museum Ho. E2 . . . . .2B **44**
Museum La. SW7 . . . . .2E **111**
Museum Mans. WC1 . . . . . . .2F **59**
Museum of Brands, Packaging
and Advertising 4C **52**
(off Colville M.)
Museum of Childhood
Bethnal Green 2B **44**
Museum of Freemasonry . . .4A **60**
(off Gt. Queen St.)
Museum of London 2B **62**
Museum of London Docklands
. . . . .1D **97**
Museum of The Order of St John
. . . . .5F **39**
Museum Pas. E2 . . . . .2B **44**
Museum St. WC1 . . . . .2F **59**
Musgrave Ct. SW11 . . . . .5F **133**
Musgrave Cres. SW6 . . . . . . .5E **131**
Mutrix Rd. NW6 . . . . .3E **9**
Myatt Rd. SW9 . . . . .5F **139**
Myddelton Pas. EC1 . . . . .2E **39**
Myddelton Sq. EC1 . . . . .2E **39**
Myddelton St. EC1 . . . . .3E **39**
Myddleton Ho. N1 . . . . .1D **39**
Myers Ho. SE5 . . . . .4B **140**
Myers La. SE14 . . . . .2D **145**
Myles Ct. SE16 . . . . .5B **94**

Mylius Cl. SE14 . . . . .5C **144**
Mylne St. EC1 . . . . .2D **39**
Myrdle Ct. E1 . . . . .3E **65**
Myrdle St. E1 . . . . .2E **65**
Myrtle Wlk. N1 . . . . .1F **41**
Mytton Ho. SW8 . . . . .5B **138**

N

N1 Shop. Cen. N1 . . . . .5E **17**
Nags Head Ct. EC1 . . . . .5C **40**
Nainby Ho. SE11 . . . . .4D **117**
Nairn St. E14 . . . . .2C **70**
Nalton Ho. NW6 . . . . .2C **10**
Nankin St. E14 . . . . .4E **69**
Nantes Pas. E1 . . . . .1B **64**
Nant St. E2 . . . . .2A **44**
Naoroji St. WC1 . . . . .3D **39**
Napa Cl. E20 . . . . .3B **6**
Napier Av. E14 . . . . .5E **125**
Napier Cl. SE8 . . . . .4C **146**
W14 . . . . .1B **108**
Napier Ct. N1 . . . . .5D **19**
Napier Gro. N1 . . . . .1C **40**
Napier Ho. E3 . . . . .3E **47**
SE17 . . . . .3A **140**
Napier Pl. W14 . . . . .2B **108**
Napier Rd. NW10 . . . . .2A **28**
W14 . . . . .2B **108**
Napier St. SE8 . . . . .4C **146**
Napier Ter. N1 . . . . .2F **17**
Narrow St. E14 . . . . .5E **67**
Nascot St. W12 . . . . .3B **50**
Naseby Cl. NW6 . . . . .1C **10**
Nashe Ho. SE1 . . . . .2D **119**
Nash Ho. E14 . . . . .5E **97**
NW1 . . . . .5A **14**
SW1 . . . . .1A **136**
Nash Pl. E14 . . . . .3F **97**
Nash St. NW1 . . . . .2A **36**
Nasmyth St. W6 . . . . .2A **106**
Nassau St. W1 . . . . .2B **58**
Nathan Ho. SE11 . . . . .4E **117**
Nathaniel Cl. E1 . . . . .2C **64**
National Army Mus. 2C **134**
National Gallery 1E **87**
National Maritime Mus. . . .3D **149**
National Portrait Gallery 1E **87**
National Ter. SE16 . . . . .4F **93**
National Theatre 2C **88**
Natural History Mus.
Knightsbridge 2D **111**
Nautilus Building, The EC1 . .2E **39**
Naval Ho. E14 . . . . .5D **71**
Naval Row E14 . . . . .5C **70**
Navarino Rd. E8 . . . . .1F **21**
Navarre St. E2 . . . . .4B **42**
Naxos Bldg. E14 . . . . .5D **97**
Naylor Bldg. E. E1 . . . . .3D **65**
Naylor Bldg. W. E1 . . . . .3D **65**
Naylor Ho. SE17 . . . . .4E **119**
W10 . . . . .2A **30**
Naylor Rd. SE15 . . . . .4F **143**
Nazrul St. E2 . . . . .2B **42**
Neal St. WC2 . . . . .4F **59**
Neal's Yd. WC2 . . . . .4F **59**
Neate Ho. SW1 . . . . .1C **136**
Neate St. SE5 . . . . .3F **141**
Neathouse Pl. SW1 . . . . .3B **114**
Neatscourt Rd. E6 . . . . .2E **75**
Nebraska St. SE1 . . . . .5D **91**
Neckinger SE16 . . . . .1C **120**

Neckinger Est. SE16 . . . . . . .1C 120
Neckinger St. SE1 . . . . .5C 92
Needham Ho. SE11 . . . . . . .4D 117
Needham Rd. W11 . . . . .4D 53
Needleman St. SE16 . . . . . . .5D 95
Nelldale Rd. SE16 . . . . . . .3A 122
Nell Gwynn Ho. SW3 . . . . .4A 112
Nelson Cl. NW6 . . . . .2D 31
Nelson Ct. SE16 . . . . .3C 94
Nelson Gdns. E2 . . . . .2E 43
Nelson Ho. SW1 . . . . .2C 136
Nelson Pas. EC1 . . . . .2C 40
Nelson Pl. N1 . . . . .1A 40
Nelson Rd. SE10 . . . . .3C 148
Nelson's Column 2F 87
Nelson Sq. SE1 . . . . .4F 89
Nelson St. E1 . . . . .3F 65
  E16 . . . . .5C 72
Nelsons Yd. NW1 . . . . .5B 14
Nelson Ter. N1 . . . . .1A 40
Nelson Wlk. E3 . . . . .4A 48
  SE16 . . . . .3F 95
Nemus Apartments SE8 . . . .4E 123
Neptune Ct. E14 . . . . .3D 125
  E16 . . . . .2E 73
Neptune Ho. E3 . . . . .4D 25
  SE16 . . . . .1C 122
Neptune St. SE16 . . . . .1B 122
Nero Ho. E20 . . . . .4B 6
Nesham Ho. N1 . . . . .4F 19
Nesham St. E1 . . . . .2D 93
Ness St. SE16 . . . . .1D 121
Nestor Ho. E2 . . . . .1F 43
Nethercott Ho. E3 . . . . .3F 47
Netherton Gro. SW10 . . . . .3C 132
Netherwood Pl. W14 . . . . .1D 107
Netherwood Rd. W14 . . . . .1D 107
Netherwood St. NW6 . . . . . .1C 8
Netley SE5 . . . . .5A 142
Netley St. NW1 . . . . .3B 36
Nettlecombe NW1 . . . . .1D 15
Nettleden Ho. SW3 . . . . . .4A 112
Nettleton Ct. EC2 . . . . .2B 62
Nettleton Rd. SE14 . . . . . . .5E 145
Neutron Twr. E14 . . . . .5E 71
Nevada St. SE10 . . . . .3C 148
Nevern Mans. SW5 . . . . . . .5D 109
Nevern Pl. SW5 . . . . .4E 109
Nevern Rd. SW5 . . . . .4D 109
Nevern Sq. SW5 . . . . .4D 109
Nevill Ct. SW10 . . . . .4C 132
Neville Cl. NW1 . . . . .1E 37
  NW6 . . . . .1C 30
  SE15 . . . . .5D 143
Neville Ct. NW8 . . . . .1D 33
Neville Ho. NW6 . . . . .1C 30
Neville Rd. NW6 . . . . .1C 30
Neville St. SW7 . . . . .5D 111
Neville Ter. SW7 . . . . .5D 111
Nevill La. EC4 . . . . .3E 61
Nevitt Ho. N1 . . . . .1E 41
Newall Ho. SE1 . . . . .1C 118
Newark Knok E6 . . . . .3D 77
Newark St. E1 . . . . .2F 65
  (not continuous)
New Atlas Wharf E14 . . . . . .1D 125
New Baltic Wharf SE8 . . . . .5A 124
New Barn St. E13 . . . . .1E 73
New Bell Yd. EC4 . . . . .4A 62
New Bentham Ct. N1 . . . . . .2C 18
Newbery Ho. N1 . . . . .2B 18
Newbold Cotts. E1 . . . . .3B 66
Newbolt Ho. SE17 . . . . . . .5D 119
New Bond St. W1 . . . . .4F 57

New Bridge St. EC4 . . . . . . .4F 61
New Broad St. EC2 . . . . .2E 63
Newburgh St. W1 . . . . .4B 58
New Burlington M. W1 . . . . .5B 58
New Burlington Pl. W1 . . . . .5B 58
New Burlington St. W1 . . . . .5B 58
Newburn Ho. SE11 . . . . .5C 116
Newburn St. SE11 . . . . .1C 138
Newbury Ct. E5 . . . . .2A 4
Newbury Ho. W2 . . . . .4A 54
Newbury St. EC1 . . . . .1B 62
New Butt La. SE8 . . . . .5E 147
New Butt La. Nth. SE8 . . . . .5D 147
Newby NW1 . . . . .3B 36
Newby Ho. E14 . . . . .5B 70
Newby Pl. E14 . . . . .5B 70
New Caledonian Mkt.
  SE1 . . . . .1A 120
New Caledonian Wharf
  SE16 . . . . .1B 124
Newcastle Cl. EC4 . . . . .3F 61
Newcastle Ct. EC4 . . . . .5C 62
Newcastle Ho. W1 . . . . .1D 57
Newcastle Pl. W2 . . . . .1E 55
Newcastle Row EC1 . . . . . . .5E 39
New Cavendish St. W1 . . . . .2E 57
New Century Ho. E16 . . . . . .4C 72
  (off Jude St.)
New Change EC4 . . . . .4B 62
New Change Pas. EC4 . . . . .4B 62
New Charles St. EC1 . . . . . .2A 40
New Church Rd. SE5 . . . . . .4C 140
  (not continuous)
New Claremont Apartments
  SE1 . . . . .3B 120
New College Ct. NW3 . . . . . .1D 11
  (off College Cres.)
New College M. N1 . . . . .1E 17
New College Pde. NW3 . . . .1C 10
Newcombe St. W8 . . . . .2E 81
Newcomen St. SE1 . . . . .4D 91
New Compton St. WC2 . . . . .4E 59
New Concordia Wharf
  SE1 . . . . .4C 92
New Ct. EC4 . . . . .4D 61
Newcourt Ho. E2 . . . . .3A 44
Newcourt St. NW8 . . . . .1F 33
New Covent Garden Market
   .5D 137
New Crane Pl. E1 . . . . .2B 94
New Crane Wharf E1 . . . . . . .2B 94
NEW CROSS 5B 146
NEW CROSS GATE 5E 145
New Cross Rd. SE14 . . . . . . .4B 144
  SE14 . . . . .5F 145
New Diorama Theatre 4A 36
Newell St. E14 . . . . .4B 68
Newent Cl. SE15 . . . . .4F 141
New Era Est. N1 . . . . .4F 19
New Era Ho. N1 . . . . .4F 19
  (off Halcomb St.)
New Fetter La. EC4 . . . . .3E 61
Newgate St. EC1 . . . . .3A 62
New Globe Wlk. SE1 . . . . . .2B 90
New Goulston St. E1 . . . . . . .3B 64
Newhall Ct. N1 . . . . .3B 18
Newham City Farm 3E 75
Newham Dockside E16 . . . .1F 103
Newham Leisure Cen. 1C 74
Newham's Row SE1 . . . . . . .5A 92
Newham Way E16 . . . . .3F 71
Newhaven La. E16 . . . . .1C 72
New Hope Ct. NW10 . . . . . .2A 28

NEWINGTON 2B 118
Newington Butts SE1 . . . . . .4A 118
  SE11 . . . . .4A 118
Newington C'way. SE1 . . . . .2A 118
Newington Ct. Bus. Cen.
  SE1 . . . . .1B 118
Newington Ind. Est. SE17 . . .4B 118
New Inn B'way. EC2 . . . . . . .4A 42
New Inn Pas. WC2 . . . . .4C 60
New Inn Sq. EC2 . . . . .4A 42
New Inn St. EC2 . . . . .4A 42
New Inn Yd. EC2 . . . . .4A 42
New Jubilee Wharf E1 . . . . . .2B 94
New Kent Rd. SE1 . . . . .2B 118
New King St. SE8 . . . . .2D 147
Newland Apartments
  E16 . . . . .2D 73
Newland Ct. EC1 . . . . .4D 41
Newland Ho. SE14 . . . . .3D 145
Newlands NW1 . . . . .2B 36
Newlands Quay E1 . . . . .1B 94
Newland St. E16 . . . . .3A 104
Newling Cl. E6 . . . . .3C 76
New London St. EC3 . . . . . .5A 64
New London Theatre 3A 60
Newlyn NW1 . . . . .4C 14
Newman Ho. SE1 . . . . .2F 117
Newman Pas. W1 . . . . .2C 58
Newman's Ct. EC3 . . . . .4E 63
Newman's Row WC2 . . . . . .2C 60
Newman St. W1 . . . . .2C 58
Newman Yd. W1 . . . . .3D 59
Newmill Ho. E3 . . . . .4B 48
New Mount St. E15 . . . . .2E 27
Newnham Ter. SE1 . . . . .1D 117
New North Pl. EC2 . . . . .4F 41
New North Rd. N1 . . . . .2B 18
New North St. WC1 . . . . . . .1B 60
New Oxford St. WC1 . . . . . . .3E 59
New Pl. Sq. SE16 . . . . .1F 121
New Plaistow Rd. E15 . . . . .3F 27
Newport Av. E14 . . . . .5E 71
Newport Ct. WC2 . . . . .5E 59
Newport Ho. E3 . . . . .2F 45
Newport Pl. WC2 . . . . .5E 59
Newport St. SE11 . . . . .4B 116
New Priory Ct. NW6 . . . . . . .2E 9
New Providence Wharf
  E14 . . . . .2D 99
Newquay Ho. SE11 . . . . .5D 117
New Quebec St. W1 . . . . . . .4C 56
New Ride SW1 . . . . .5E 83
  SW7 . . . . .5E 83
New River Head EC1 . . . . . .2E 39
New River Wlk. N1 . . . . .3B 18
  (not continuous)
New Rd. E1 . . . . .2F 65
New Row WC2 . . . . .5F 59
New Spring Gdns. Wlk.
  SE11 . . . . .1A 138
New Sq. WC2 . . . . .3D 61
New Sq. Pas. WC2 . . . . .3D 61
Newstead Ho. N1 . . . . .5E 17
New St. EC2 . . . . .2A 64
New St. Sq. EC4 . . . . .3E 61
  (not continuous)
Newton Ct. E3 . . . . .2E 69
  NW6 . . . . .1C 10
  W8 . . . . .4E 81
Newton Ho. E1 . . . . .5F 65
  NW8 . . . . .3A 10
Newton Lodge SE10 . . . . . .2C 128
Newton Mans. W14 . . . . . . .2A 130
Newton Pl. E14 . . . . .3D 125

Newton Rd. E15 . . . . .2E 7
  W2 . . . . .4F 53
Newton St. WC2 . . . . .3A 60
New Tower Bldgs. E1 . . . . . . .3A 94
New Turnstile WC1 . . . . .2B 60
New Union Cl. E14 . . . . . . .1C 126
New Union St. EC2 . . . . .2D 63
New Wharf Rd. N1 . . . . .5A 16
New Zealand War Memorial
  . . . . .4E 85
New Zealand Way W12 . . . . . .1A 78
Nexus Cl. NW6 . . . . .2D 31
Niagara Cl. N1 . . . . .5C 18
Niagra Ct. SE16 . . . . .1C 122
Nice Bus. Pk. SE15 . . . . .3A 144
Nicholas La. EC4 . . . . .5E 63
  (not continuous)
Nicholas Pas. EC4 . . . . .5E 63
Nicholas Rd. E1 . . . . .4C 44
  W11 . . . . .1D 79
Nicholas Stacey Ho. SE7 . . . .5F 129
Nicholl St. E2 . . . . .4D 21
Nichols Ct. E2 . . . . .1B 42
Nicholson Ho. SE17 . . . . . . .5D 119
Nicholson St. SE1 . . . . .3F 89
Nickelby Apartments E15 . . . . .5E 7
Nickleby Ho. SE16 . . . . .5D 93
  W11 . . . . .2E 79
Nigel Ho. EC1 . . . . .1D 61
Nigel Playfair Av. W6 . . . . . .5A 106
Nightingale Ct. E14 . . . . .5C 98
Nightingale Ho. E1 . . . . .2D 93
  E2 . . . . .4A 20
  NW8 . . . . .5F 33
  W12 . . . . .3B 50
Nightingale Lodge W9 . . . . . .1E 53
  (off Admiral Wlk.)
Nightingale M. E3 . . . . .5E 23
  SE11 . . . . .3F 117
Nightingale Pl. SW10 . . . . . .3C 132
Nightingale Way E6 . . . . .1A 76
Nile Ho. N1 . . . . .2D 41
Nile St. N1 . . . . .2C 40
Nile Ter. SE15 . . . . .1B 142
Nimrod Ho. E16 . . . . .2F 73
Nina Mackay Cl. E15 . . . . . . .3F 27
NINE ELMS 4C 136
Nine Elms La. SW8 . . . . .4C 136
Nipponzan Myohoji Peace Pagoda
  . . . . .4C 134
Noble Ct. E1 . . . . .5F 65
Noble St. EC2 . . . . .3B 62
Noble Yd. N1 . . . . .4F 17
Noel Coward Ho. SW1 . . . . . .4C 114
Noel Coward Theatre 5F 59
Noel Ho. NW6 . . . . .1D 11
Noel Rd. N1 . . . . .5F 17
Noel St. W1 . . . . .4C 58
Noko W10 . . . . .2E 29
Nook Apartments E1 . . . . .4C 44
Nora Leverton Ct. NW1 . . . . .2C 14
  (off Randolph St.)
Norbiton Ho. NW1 . . . . .4C 14
  (off Camden St.)
Norbiton Rd. E14 . . . . .3B 68
Norburn St. W10 . . . . .2F 51
Norden Ho. E2 . . . . .3A 44
Norfolk Cres. W2 . . . . .3F 55
Norfolk Ho. EC4 . . . . .5B 62
  SW1 . . . . .3E 115
Norfolk M. W10 . . . . .2A 52
Norfolk Pl. W2 . . . . .3E 55
  (not continuous)
Norfolk Rd. NW8 . . . . .4E 11

Norfolk Row SE1 . . . . .3B 116
Norfolk Sq. W2 . . . . .4E 55
Norfolk Sq. M. W2 . . . . .4E 55
Norfolk Ter. W6 . . . . .1A 130
Norland Ho. W11 . . . . .3E 79
Norland Pl. W11 . . . . .3A 80
Norland Rd. W11 . . . . .3E 79
Norland Sq. W11 . . . . .3A 80
Norland Sq. Mans. W11 . . . . .3F 79
Norman Butler Ho. W10 . . . . .5F 29
Normand Gdns. W14 . . . . . . .2A 130
Normand Mans. W14 . . . . . . .2A 130
Normand M. W14 . . . . .2A 130
Normand Rd. W14 . . . . .2B 130
Normandy Ho. E14 . . . . .5B 98
Normandy Pl. W12 . . . . .3D 79
Normandy Ter. E16 . . . . .4F 73
Norman Gro. E3 . . . . .1A 46
Norman Ho. SE1 . . . . .1A 120
  SW8 . . . . .4F 137
Norman Rd. SE10 . . . . .4A 148
Norman St. EC1 . . . . .3B 40
Norris Ho. E9 . . . . .3C 22
  N1 . . . . .4F 19
  SE8 . . . . .1B 146
Norris St. SW1 . . . . .1D 87
Northampton Rd. EC1 . . . . . . .4E 39
Northampton Row EC1 . . . . . .3E 39
Northampton Sq. EC1 . . . . . . .3F 39
Northampton St. N1 . . . . .1B 18
Nth. Audley St. W1 . . . . .4D 57
Northaw Ho. W10 . . . . .5B 28
North Bank NW8 . . . . .3F 33
NORTH BECKTON 1B 76
North Block SE1 . . . . .4C 88
Northburgh St. EC1 . . . . .5A 40
Nth. Carriage Dr. W2 . . . . .5F 55
Northchurch SE17 . . . . .5E 119
  (not continuous)
Northchurch Ho. E2 . . . . .4E 21
Northchurch Rd. N1 . . . . .1D 19
  (not continuous)
Northchurch Ter. N1 . . . . .2F 19
Nth. Colonnade, The E14 . . . .2E 97
  (not continuous)
North Ct. SW1 . . . . .2F 115
  W1 . . . . .1C 58
North Cres. E16 . . . . .5E 49
  WC1 . . . . .1D 59
Northdown St. N1 . . . . .5A 16
North End Cres. W14 . . . . . . .4B 108
North End Ho. W14 . . . . .4A 108
North End Pde. W14 . . . . . . .4A 108
North End Rd. SW6 . . . . .3C 130
  W14 . . . . .3A 108
Northesk Ho. E1 . . . . .5F 43
Northey St. E14 . . . . .5A 68
Northfield Ho. SE15 . . . . .3E 143
Northfleet Ho. SE1 . . . . .4D 91
Northflock St. SE16 . . . . .4D 93
Nth. Flower Wlk. W2 . . . . .1C 82
North Gdn. E14 . . . . .2C 96
North Gate NW8 . . . . .1F 33
Northgate Ho. E14 . . . . .5E 69
Nth. Gower St. NW1 . . . . .3B 36
North Ho. SE8 . . . . .1B 146
Northiam WC1 . . . . .3A 38
Northiam St. E9 . . . . .4B 22
Northington St. WC1 . . . . .5C 38
NORTH KENSINGTON 2B 50
Northleigh Ho. E3 . . . . .3A 48
North Lodge E16 . . . . .2F 101
  (off Wesley Av.)
North M. WC1 . . . . .5C 38

Nth. Pole Rd. W10 . . . . .2B 50
Northport St. N1 . . . . .4E 19
North Quay Pl. E14 . . . . .1F 97
North Ride W2 . . . . .5E 55
North Ri. W2 . . . . .4A 56
North Row W1 . . . . .5C 56
Nth. Row Bldgs. W1 . . . . .5D 57
Northside Studios E8 . . . . . . .4F 21
Nth. Tenter St. E1 . . . . .4C 64
North Ter. SW3 . . . . .2F 111
  WC2 . . . . .2E 87
Northumberland All. EC3 . . . .4A 64
  (not continuous)
Northumberland Av. WC2 . . . .2F 87
Northumberland Ho. SW1 . . . .2F 87
Northumberland Pl. W2 . . . . . .3D 53
Northumberland Rd. E6 . . . . . .3A 76
Northumberland St. WC2 . . . .2F 87
Northumbria St. E14 . . . . .3E 69
North Wlk. W2 . . . . .1C 82
  W8 . . . . .1A 82
Northwall Rd. E20 . . . . .2E 5
Northways NW3 . . . . .1D 11
Northways Pde. NW3 . . . . . . .1D 11
  (not continuous)
Nth. Western Commercial Cen.
  NW1 . . . . .2F 15
Northwest Pl. N1 . . . . .5E 17
North Wharf E14 . . . . .3C 98
Nth. Wharf Rd. W2 . . . . .2D 55
Northwick Cl. NW8 . . . . .4D 33
Northwick Ho. NW8 . . . . .4C 32
Northwick Ter. NW8 . . . . .4D 33
NORTH WOOLWICH 3E 105
Nth. Woolwich Rd. E16 . . . . .2D 101
Norton Folgate E1 . . . . .1A 64
Norton Folgate Ho. E1 . . . . . .1B 64
Norton Ho. E1 . . . . .4F 65
  E2 . . . . .1D 45
  SW1 . . . . .2E 115
Norway Ga. SE16 . . . . .1A 124
Norway Ho. N1 . . . . .3A 20
Norway Pl. E14 . . . . .4B 68
Norway St. SE10 . . . . .3A 148
Norway Wharf E14 . . . . .4B 68
Norwegian War Memorial . . .3A 84
Norwich Ho. E14 . . . . .3F 69
Norwich St. EC4 . . . . .3D 61
Norwood Ho. E14 . . . . .1A 98
Notley St. SE5 . . . . .4D 141
Notting Barn Rd. W10 . . . . . . .5D 29
Nottingdale Sq. W11 . . . . .2F 79
Nottingham Av. E16 . . . . .2B 74
Nottingham Ct. WC2 . . . . .4F 59
Nottingham Ho. WC2 . . . . .4F 59
Nottingham Pl. W1 . . . . .5D 35
Nottingham St. W1 . . . . .1D 57
Nottingham Ter. NW1 . . . . . . .5D 35
NOTTING HILL 1B 80
Notting Hill Ga. W11 . . . . .2C 80
Nottingwood Ho. W11 . . . . . . .5F 51
Nova Bldg. E14 . . . . .3D 125
Nova Ct. E. E14 . . . . .2C 98
Nova Ct. W. E14 . . . . .2C 98
Novello Ct. N1 . . . . .3B 18
Novello Theatre
  Covent Garden 5B 60
Novem Ho. E1 . . . . .2C 64
Nuffield Health Club
  Bloomsbury 4B 38
  Cannon Street 5D 63
  Covent Garden 4A 60
  Paddington 2C 54
Nuffield Lodge W9 . . . . .1E 53

Nugent Ter. NW8 . . . . .1C 32
Number One EC1 . . . . .5D 41
Nun Ct. EC2 . . . . .3D 63
Nursery La. E2 . . . . .4B 20
　　W10 . . . . .2B 50
Nursery Row SE17 . . . . .4D 119
Nutbourne St. W10 . . . . .2F 29
Nutcroft Rd. SE15 . . . . .4F 143
Nutford Pl. W1 . . . . .3A 56
Nutmeg Cl. E16 . . . . .4F 49
Nutmeg La. E14 . . . . .4D 71
Nuttall St. N1 . . . . .5A 20
Nutt St. SE15 . . . . .4C 142
Nye Bevan Ho. SW6 . . . . .4B 130
Nynehead St. SE14 . . . . .4F 145

O

O2, The 3F 99
O2 Shepherd's Bush Empire
　Theatre 4B 78
Oak Ct. SE15 . . . . .4C 142
Oak Cres. E16 . . . . .2A 72
Oakdene SE15 . . . . .5F 143
Oakden St. SE11 . . . . .3E 117
Oakeford Ho. W14 . . . . .2A 108
Oakes Cl. E6 . . . . .4C 76
Oakes M. E14 . . . . .2C 70
Oakey La. SE1 . . . . .1D 117
Oakfield Ho. E3 . . . . .1E 69
Oakfield St. SW10 . . . . .2B 132
Oakham Ho. W10 . . . . .5B 28
Oak Ho. E14 . . . . .5C 98
　　W10 . . . . .4F 29
Oakington Rd. W9 . . . . .4E 31
Oakland Quay E14 . . . . .1A 126
Oakland Rd. E15 . . . . .1E 7
Oak La. E14 . . . . .5B 68
Oakleigh Ct. N1 . . . . .2D 41
Oakley Cl. E6 . . . . .3A 76
Oakley Cres. EC1 . . . . .1A 40
Oakley Gdns. SW3 . . . . .2A 134
Oakley Ho. SE11 . . . . .4D 117
　　SW1 . . . . .3C 112
Oakley Pl. SE1 . . . . .1B 142
Oakley Rd. N1 . . . . .1D 19
Oakley Sq. NW1 . . . . .5C 14
Oakley St. SW3 . . . . .2F 133
Oakley Studios SW3 . . . . .2F 133
Oakley Yd. E2 . . . . .4C 42
Oak Lodge W8 . . . . .2F 109
Oakshott Ct. NW1 . . . . .1D 37
　　(not continuous)
Oak Tree Ho. W9 . . . . .4E 31
Oak Tree Rd. NW8 . . . . .3E 33
Oakville Ho. SE16 . . . . .5D 95
Oakwood Ct. W14 . . . . .1B 108
Oakwood Ho. E9 . . . . .1B 22
Oakwood La. W14 . . . . .1B 108
Oakwood Mans. W14 . . . . . . .1B 108
Oakworth Rd. W10 . . . . .1C 50
Oasis Sports Cen. 3F 59
Oast Ct. E14 . . . . .5B 68
Oat La. EC2 . . . . .3B 62
Oatwell Ho. SW3 . . . . .5A 112
Oban Ho. E14 . . . . .3E 71
Oban St. E14 . . . . .3E 71
Oberon Ho. N1 . . . . .5F 19
O'Brien Ho. E2 . . . . .2E 45
Observatory Gdns. W8 . . . . . .4E 81
Observatory M. E14 . . . . .3D 127
Observatory Rd. SW7 . . . . . . .2D 111
Occupation Rd. SE17 . . . . . . .5B 118

Ocean Est. E1 . . . . .1F 67
　　(Ben Jonson Rd.)
E1 .5E 45
　　(Ernest St.)
Oceanis Apartments E16 . . . .5D 73
Ocean St. E1 . . . . .1E 67
Ocean Wharf E14 . . . . .5D 97
Ockbrook E1 . . . . .1C 66
Ockendon Rd. N1 . . . . .1D 19
Octagon, The SW10 . . . . .4B 132
Octagon Arc. EC2 . . . . .2F 63
Octagon Ct. SE16 . . . . .3D 95
Octavia Ho. SW1 . . . . .2D 115
　　W10 . . . . .5F 29
Octavia M. W9 . . . . .4B 30
Octavius St. SE8 . . . . .4D 147
Odelia Ct. E15 . . . . .3C 26
Odeon Cinema
　Camden Town 3A 14
　Covent Garden 4E 59
　Greenwich 3C 128
　Kensington 1D 109
　Leicester Square 1E 87
　Marble Arch 4C 56
　Panton Street 1E 87
　Surrey Quays 1E 123
　Swiss Cottage 2D 11
　Tottenham Court Road
　　. . . . . .2D 59
　West End 1E 87
　Whiteleys 4A 54
Odeon Ct. E16 . . . . .1D 73
Odessa St. SE16 . . . . .5B 96
Odessa Wharf SE16 . . . . .1B 124
Odette Duval Ho. E1 . . . . .2C 66
Odhams Wlk. WC2 . . . . .4A 60
O'Donnell Ho. WC1 . . . . .4A 38
Offa's Mead E9 . . . . .1B 4
Offenbach Ho. E2 . . . . .1D 45
Offham Ho. SE17 . . . . .4F 119
Offley Rd. SW9 . . . . .4D 139
Offord Rd. N1 . . . . .1C 16
Offord St. N1 . . . . .1C 16
Ogilvie Ho. E1 . . . . .4E 67
Ogle St. W1 . . . . .1B 58
O'Gorman Ho. SW10 . . . . .4C 132
Ohio Rd. E13 . . . . .1B 72
Olaf Ct. W8 . . . . .4E 81
Olaf St. W11 . . . . .1E 79
Old Aeroworks, The NW8 . . . .5E 33
Old Bailey
　Central Criminal Court
　　. . . . . .3A 62
Old Bailey EC4 . . . . .4A 62
Old Barge Ho. All. SE1 . . . . . .1E 89
Old Barracks W8 . . . . .4A 82
Old Barrack Yd. SW1 . . . . .5D 85
　　(not continuous)
Old Bellgate Pl. E14 . . . . .2D 125
Old Bethnal Grn. Rd. E2 . . . . .2E 43
Old Billingsgate Mkt. EC3 . . . .1F 91
Old Billingsgate Wlk.
　EC3 . . . . .1F 91
Old Bond St. W1 . . . . .1B 86
Old Brewer's Yd. WC2 . . . . . . .4F 59
Old Broad St. EC2 . . . . .4E 63
Old Brompton Rd. SW5 . . . . . .1E 131
　　SW7 . . . . .1E 131
Old Buildings WC2 . . . . .3D 61
Old Burlington St. W1 . . . . . . .5B 58
Oldbury Ct. E9 . . . . .3A 4
Oldbury Ho. W2 . . . . .1F 53
Oldbury Pl. W1 . . . . .5E 35
Old Canal M. SE15 . . . . .1C 142

Old Castle St. E1 . . . . .2B 64
Old Cavendish St. W1 . . . . . . .3F 57
Old Change Ct. EC4 . . . . .4B 62
Old Chelsea M. SW3 . . . . . . .3F 133
Old Church Rd. E1 . . . . .3D 67
Old Church St. SW3 . . . . .5E 111
Old Compton St. W1 . . . . .5D 59
Old Court Ho. W8 . . . . .5F 81
Old Court Pl. W8 . . . . .4F 81
Old Curiosity Shop 3C 60
Oldfield Gro. SE16 . . . . .4D 123
Old Fish St. Hill EC4 . . . . .5B 62
Old Fleet La. EC4 . . . . .3F 61
OLD FORD 3B 24
OLD FORD 5E 25
Old Ford Rd. E2 . . . . .2B 44
　E3 . . . . .4C 24
Old Ford Trading Cen. E3 . . . .4D 25
Old Gloucester St. WC1 . . . . . .1A 60
Old Goods Yard, The W2 . . . . .2B 54
Old Jamaica Bus. Est.
　SE16 . . . . .1C 120
Old Jamaica Rd. SE16 . . . . . . .1D 121
Old Jewry EC2 . . . . .4D 63
Old Kent Rd. SE1 . . . . .3F 119
　SE15 . . . . .2E 143
Old Library Ho. E3 . . . . .1F 45
Old Manor Ct. NW8 . . . . .5C 19
Old Manor Yd. SW5 . . . . .4F 109
Old Market Sq. E2 . . . . .2C 42
Old Marylebone Rd. NW1 . . . . .2A 56
Old Mitre Ct. EC4 . . . . .4E 61
Old Montague St. E1 . . . . .2D 65
Old Nichol St. E2 . . . . .4B 42
Old North St. WC1 . . . . .1B 60
Old Nursery Ct. E2 . . . . .1C 42
Old Operating Theatre Museum
　& Herb Garret 3E 91
Old Palace Yd. SW1 . . . . .1F 115
Old Paradise St. SE11 . . . . . . .3B 116
Old Park La. W1 . . . . .3E 85
Old Pearson St. SE10 . . . . . . .4A 148
Old Pye St. SW1 . . . . .1D 115
Old Pye St. Est. SW1 . . . . . . .2D 115
Old Quebec St. W1 . . . . .4C 56
　　(not continuous)
Old Queen St. SW1 . . . . .5E 87
Old Railway Wlk. SE16 . . . . . .4C 94
Old Red Lion Theatre 1E 39
Old Royal Free Pl. N1 . . . . . . .4E 17
Old Royal Free Sq. N1 . . . . . . .4E 17
Old Royal Naval College . . .1C 148
Old School, The WC1 . . . . .1C 60
Old School Cl. SE10 . . . . .2A 128
Old School Sq. E14 . . . . .4D 69
Old Seacoal La. EC4 . . . . .4F 61
Old Sth. Lambeth Rd.
　SW8 . . . . .4A 138
Old Spitalfields Market 1B 64
Old Square WC2 . . . . .3D 61
Old Station Ho. SE17 . . . . . . .1C 140
OLD STREET 3D 41
Old St. EC1 . . . . .3D 41
Old Sun Wharf E14 . . . . .5F 67
Old Theatre Ct. SE1 . . . . .2C 90
Old Vic Theatre, The 4E 89
Old Woolwich Rd. SE10 . . . . . .2D 149
O'Leary Sq. E1 . . . . .1B 66
Olga St. E3 . . . . .1A 46
Oliphant St. W10 . . . . .3E 29
Olive Blythe Ho. W10 . . . . . . .5F 29
Olive Ct. N1 . . . . .4E 17
Olive Ho. EC1 . . . . .4E 39
Oliver Gdns. E6 . . . . .2A 76

Oliver Ho. SE14 ....5C 146
  SE16 ....5D 93
  SW8 ....4F 137
Olivers Wharf E1 ....3F 93
Olivers Yd. EC1 ....4E 41
Olive Tree Ho. SE15 ....3C 144
Olive Waite Ho. NW6 ....1F 9
Olivier Theatre **2D 89**
  (within National Theatre)
Ollerton Grn. E3 ....3C 24
Olliffe St. E14 ....2C 126
Olmar St. E1 ....2D 143
Olney Ho. NW8 ....4A 34
Olney Rd. SE17 ....3A 140
  (not continuous)
Olympia **2A 108**
Olympia M. W2 ....1A 82
Olympian Ct. E3 ....5D 25
  E14 ....3D 125
Olympia Way W14 ....2A 108
Olympic Pk. Av. E20 ....3F 5
O'Meara St. SE1 ....3C 90
Omega Cl. E14 ....1F 125
Omega Ho. SW10 ....4C 132
Omega Pl. N1 ....1A 38
Omega Works E3 ....1E 25
Omnium Ct. WC1 ....1B 60
  (off Princeton St.)
Onedin Ct. E1 ....5D 65
Onega Ga. SE16 ....1F 123
One Hyde Pk. SW1 ....4B 84
O'Neill Ho. NW8 ....1F 33
One New Change EC4 ....4C 62
One Owen St. EC1 ....1F 39
One The Elephant SE1 ....3A 118
Ongar Ho. SW6 ....2D 131
Onslow Cl. W10 ....2B 30
Onslow Ct. SW10 ....1C 132
Onslow Cres. SW7 ....4E 111
Onslow Gdns. SW7 ....4D 111
Onslow M. E. SW7 ....4D 111
Onslow M. W. SW7 ....4D 111
Onslow Sq. SW7 ....3E 111
Onslow St. EC1 ....5E 39
Ontario St. SE1 ....2A 118
Ontario Twr. E14 ....1D 99
Ontario Way E14 ....1D 97
  (not continuous)
Opal Apartments W2 ....4E 53
Opal Cl. E16 ....4E 75
Opal Ct. E15 ....4C 26
Opal M. NW6 ....3C 8
Opal St. SE11 ....4F 117
Ophelia Ho. W6 ....5D 107
Opie Ho. NW8 ....5F 11
Oppidan Apartments
  NW6 ....1D 9
Oppidans Rd. NW3 ....2B 12
Orange Pl. SE16 ....2C 122
Orangery Gallery, The **5B 80**
Orange St. WC2 ....1E 87
Orange Tree Ct. SE5 ....5F 141
Orange Yd. W1 ....4E 59
Oransay Rd. N1 ....1C 18
Oratory La. SW3 ....5F 111
Orbain Rd. SW6 ....5A 130
Orbit, The **2A 26**
Orb St. SE17 ....4D 119
Orchard Cl. N1 ....2C 18
  W10 ....1A 52
Orchard Ct. W1 ....3D 57
Orchard Ho. SE5 ....5B 140
  SE16 ....1C 122
  SW6 ....5A 130

Orchard M. N1 ....2E 19
Orchard Pl. E14 ....5F 71
  (not continuous)
Orchardson Ho. NW8 ....5D 33
Orchardson St. NW8 ....5D 33
Orchard Sq. W14 ....1B 130
Orchard St. W1 ....4D 57
Orchard Studios W6 ....3D 107
Orchard Wharf E14 ....5F 71
Orchid Cl. E6 ....1F 75
Orde Hall St. WC1 ....5B 38
Ordell Ct. E3 ....1C 46
Ordell Rd. E3 ....1C 46
Ordnance Cres. SE10 ....5F 99
Ordnance Hill NW8 ....4E 11
Ordnance M. NW8 ....5E 11
Ordnance Rd. E16 ....1B 72
Oregano Dr. E14 ....4E 71
Oriana Ho. E14 ....5B 68
Oriel Ho. NW6 ....3D 9
Oriel Rd. E9 ....4A 4
Oriens M. E20 ....4C 6
Oriental Rd. E16 ....3E 103
Oriental St. E14 ....5E 69
Orient St. SE11 ....3F 117
Orient Wharf E1 ....3F 93
Orion E14 ....3D 125
Orion Bus. Cen. SE14 ....1D 145
Orion Ho. E1 ....5A 44
Orkney Ct. E1 ....1F 67
Orkney Ho. N1 ....4B 16
Orlop St. SE10 ....1F 149
Orme Ct. W2 ....1A 82
Orme Ct. M. W2 ....1A 82
Orme Ho. E8 ....3C 20
Orme La. W2 ....1F 81
Orme Sq. W2 ....1F 81
Ormond Cl. WC1 ....1A 60
Ormonde Ga. SW3 ....1C 134
  (not continuous)
Ormonde Mans. WC1 ....1A 60
Ormonde Pl. SW1 ....4E 113
Ormonde Ter. NW8 ....4B 12
Ormond M. WC1 ....5A 38
Ormond Yd. SW1 ....2C 86
Ormrod Ct. W11 ....4A 52
Ormsby St. E2 ....5B 20
Ormside St. SE15 ....3B 144
Orpen Ho. SW5 ....4E 109
Orpheus Ho. W10 ....4B 30
Orsett M. W2 ....3A 54
  (not continuous)
Orsett St. SE11 ....5C 116
Orsett Ter. W2 ....3A 54
Orsman Rd. N1 ....4F 19
Orton St. E1 ....3D 93
Orwell Ct. E8 ....4E 21
Osbert St. SW1 ....4D 115
Osborn Cl. E8 ....3D 21
Osborne Ho. E16 ....2E 101
Osborne Rd. E9 ....4C 4
Osborn St. E1 ....2C 64
Oscar Ct. SE16 ....5A 96
Oscar Faber Pl. N1 ....2A 20
Osier Ct. E1 ....5D 45
Osier La. SE10 ....2C 128
Osier St. E1 ....5C 44
Oslo Ct. NW8 ....1F 33
Oslo Ho. E9 ....5C 4
Oslo Sq. SE16 ....1A 124
Osmani Youth Cen. **5E 43**
Osman Rd. W6 ....1C 106
Osmington Ho. SW8 ....5C 138

Osmunda Ct. E1 ....2E 65
Osnaburgh St. NW1 ....5A 36
  (Euston Rd.)
  NW1 ....3A 36
  (Robert St.)
Osnaburgh Ter. NW1 ....4A 36
Osprey Cl. E6 ....2F 75
Osprey Ct. E1 ....1D 93
Osprey Est. SE16 ....3E 123
Osprey Ho. E14 ....5A 68
  SE1 ....5F 121
Ospringe Ho. SE1 ....4E 89
Osram Ct. W6 ....2C 106
Osric Path N1 ....1F 41
Ossington Bldgs. W1 ....1D 57
Ossington Cl. W2 ....1E 81
Ossington St. W2 ....1F 81
Ossory Rd. SE1 ....1D 143
Ossulston St. NW1 ....1D 37
Ostend Pl. SE1 ....3B 118
Osten M. SW7 ....2A 110
Osterley Ho. E14 ....3F 69
Oswald Bldg. SW8 ....3F 135
Oswald's Mead E9 ....1A 4
Oswell Ho. E1 ....2A 94
Oswin St. SE11 ....3A 118
Otford Ho. SE1 ....5E 91
  SE15 ....2C 144
Othello Cl. SE11 ....5F 117
Otis St. E3 ....2B 48
Otley Rd. E16 ....3B 74
Ottawa Ho. SE16 ....5C 94
Otterburn Ho. SE5 ....4B 140
Otter Cl. E15 ....4B 26
Otterden Ter. SE1 ....4B 120
Otto St. SE17 ....3F 139
Outer Circ. NW1 ....1A 34
Outram Pl. N1 ....3A 16
Outwich St. EC3 ....3A 64
Oval, The **2C 138**
Oval, The E2 ....5F 21
Ovalhouse Theatre **3D 139**
Oval Mans. SE11 ....2C 138
Oval Pl. SW8 ....4B 138
Oval Rd. NW1 ....2F 13
Oval Way SE11 ....1C 138
Oversley Ho. W2 ....1E 53
Overstone Ho. E14 ....4E 69
Overstone Rd. W6 ....2B 106
Overy Ho. SE1 ....5F 89
Ovex Cl. E14 ....5C 98
Ovington Ct. SW3 ....2A 112
Ovington Gdns. SW3 ....2A 112
Ovington M. SW3 ....2A 112
Ovington Sq. SW3 ....2A 112
Ovington St. SW3 ....2A 112
Owen Mans. W14 ....2A 130
Owen's Row EC1 ....2F 39
Owen St. EC1 ....1F 39
Owgan Cl. SE5 ....5E 141
Oxendon St. SW1 ....1D 87
Oxenham Ho. SE8 ....2E 147
Oxenholme NW1 ....1C 36
Oxestall's Rd. SE8 ....5A 124
Oxford & Cambridge Mans.
  NW1 ....2A 56
Oxford Cir. W1 ....4B 58
Oxford Cir. Av. W1 ....4B 58
Oxford Ct. EC4 ....5D 63
  W9 ....1D 53
Oxford Dr. SE1 ....3F 91
Oxford Gdns. W10 ....4C 50
Oxford Ga. W6 ....3E 107
Oxford Ho. E3 ....1C 68

Oxford Rd. E15 . . . . .5E 7
(not continuous)
NW6 . . . . .1E 31
Oxford Sq. W2 . . . . .4A 56
Oxford St. W1 . . . . .4C 56
Oxleas E6 . . . . .3F 77
Oxley Cl. SE1 . . . . .5C 120
Oxley Sq. E3 . . . . .4A 48
Oxo Tower Wharf SE1 . . . . . . .1E 89
Oxygen, The E16 . . . . .5D 73
Oystercatcher Cl. E16 . . . . . . .3F 73
Oyster Ct. SE17 . . . . .4B 118
Oystergate Wlk. EC4 . . . . .1D 91
Oyster Row E1 . . . . .4B 66
Ozolins Way E16 . . . . .3D 73

P

Pace Pl. E1 . . . . .4A 66
Pacific Ct. E1 . . . . .1C 66
Pacific Ho. E1 . . . . .5E 45
Pacific Rd. E16 . . . . .3D 73
Pacific Wharf SE16 . . . . .2D 95
Packenham Ho. E2 . . . . .2C 42
Packington Sq. N1 . . . . .4B 18
(not continuous)
Packington St. N1 . . . . .3A 18
Padbury SE17 . . . . .1F 141
Padbury Ct. E2 . . . . .3C 42
Padbury Ho. NW8 . . . . .4A 34
Paddenswick Rd. W6 . . . .3A 106
PADDINGTON 4D 55
Paddington Grn. W2 . . . . .1E 55
Paddington Sports Club 4F 31
Paddington St. W1 . . . . .1D 57
Padstone Ho. E3 . . . . .3A 48
Padstow Ho. E14 . . . . .5C 68
Pagden St. SW8 . . . . .5A 136
Pageant Cres. SE16 . . . . .2A 96
Pageantmaster Ct. EC4 . . . . . .4F 61
Page Ho. SE10 . . . . .2B 148
Page St. SW1 . . . . .3E 115
Page's Wlk. SE1 . . . . .3F 119
Paget Ho. E2 . . . . .5B 22
Paget St. EC1 . . . . .2F 39
Pagham Ho. W10 . . . . .5B 28
Pagnell St. SE14 . . . . .4B 146
Painted Hall
  Greenwich 2D 149
Painters M. SE16 . . . . .3E 121
Pakeman Ho. SE1 . . . . .4A 90
Pakenham St. WC1 . . . . .3C 38
Palace Av. W8 . . . . .3A 82
Palace Bingo Club 3B 118
Palace Cl. E9 . . . . .5C 4
Palace Ct. W2 . . . . .5F 53
(not continuous)
Palace Gdns. M. W8 . . . . .2E 81
Palace Gdns. Ter. W8 . . . . . . .2E 81
Palace Ga. W8 . . . . .5B 82
Palace Grn. W8 . . . . .3F 81
Palace Mans. W14 . . . . .3A 108
Palace M. SW1 . . . . .4E 113
  SW6 . . . . .4C 130
Palace Pl. SW1 . . . . .1B 114
Palace Pl. Mans. W8 . . . . .5A 82
Palace St. SW1 . . . . .1B 114
Palace Superbowl 3A 118
Palace Theatre
  Soho 4E 59
Palazzo Apartments N1 . . . . . .1F 19
Palestra Ho. SE1 . . . . .3F 89
Palfrey Pl. SW8 . . . . .5C 138

Palgrave Gdns. NW1 . . . . .4A 34
Palgrave Ho. SE5 . . . . .4B 140
Palissy St. E2 . . . . .3B 42
(not continuous)
Palladium Ct. E8 . . . . .2C 20
Pallant Ho. SE1 . . . . .2E 119
Palliser Ct. W14 . . . . .5F 107
Palliser Ho. E1 . . . . .5E 45
  SE10 . . . . .2E 149
Palliser Rd. W14 . . . . .5F 107
Pall Mall SW1 . . . . .3C 86
Pall Mall E. SW1 . . . . .2E 87
Pall Mall Pl. SW1 . . . . .3C 86
Palm Ct. SE15 . . . . .4C 142
Palmer Ho. SE14 . . . . .5D 145
Palmer Rd. E13 . . . . .1A 74
Palmer's Rd. E2 . . . . .1E 45
Palmerston Ct. E3 . . . . .5E 23
Palmerston Ho. SE1 . . . . .5D 89
  W8 . . . . .3D 81
Palmerston Mans.
  W14 . . . . .3A 130
Palmerston Rd. NW6 . . . . .1C 8
(not continuous)
Palmerston Way SW8 . . . . . . .5A 136
Palmer St. SW1 . . . . .1D 115
(not continuous)
Palyn Ho. EC1 . . . . .3C 40
Pamela Wlk. E8 . . . . .3D 21
Panama Ho. E1 . . . . .1D 67
Pancras La. EC4 . . . . .4C 62
Pancras Rd. N1 . . . . .5E 15
  NW1 . . . . .5D 15
Pancras Sq. N1 . . . . .5F 15
Pancras Way E3 . . . . .5D 25
Pandangle Ho. E8 . . . . .3A 20
Pandora Ct. E16 . . . . .2E 73
Pangbourne NW1 . . . . .3B 36
Pangbourne Av. W10 . . . . .1C 50
Pankhurst Av. E16 . . . . .2A 102
Pankhurst Cl. SE14 . . . . .5D 145
Pankhurst Ho. W12 . . . . .4B 50
Pan Peninsula Sq. E14 . . . . . . .5F 97
Panton St. SW1 . . . . .1D 87
Panyer All. EC1 . . . . .3B 62
Paper Bldgs. EC4 . . . . .5E 61
Paper Mill Wharf E14 . . . . . . .1A 96
Papyrus Ho. N1 . . . . .2B 40
Parade, The SW11 . . . . .4C 134
Paradise Row E2 . . . . .2A 44
Paradise St. SE16 . . . . .5F 93
Paradise Wlk. SW3 . . . . .2C 134
Paragon Cl. E16 . . . . .3D 73
Paragon M. SE1 . . . . .3E 119
Paramount Bldg. EC1 . . . . .4F 39
Paramount Ct. WC1 . . . . .5C 36
Pardoner Ho. SE1 . . . . .1E 119
Pardoner St. SE1 . . . . .1E 119
(not continuous)
Pardon St. EC1 . . . . .4A 40
Parfett St. E1 . . . . .2E 65
(not continuous)
Paris Gdn. SE1 . . . . .2F 89
Paris Ho. E2 . . . . .1F 43
Park App. SE16 . . . . .2A 122
Park Av. E15 . . . . .5F 7
Park Central Bldg. E3 . . . . . . .5E 25
Park Cl. E9 . . . . .3C 22
  SW1 . . . . .5B 84
  W14 . . . . .1C 108
Park Cres. W1 . . . . .5F 35
Park Cres. M. E. W1 . . . . .5A 36
Park Cres. M. W. W1 . . . . .5F 35
Park East Bldg. E3 . . . . .5E 25

Parker Bldg. SE16 . . . . .1D 121
Parker Cl. E16 . . . . .3F 103
Parker Ct. N1 . . . . .3C 18
Parker Ho. E14 . . . . .4E 97
Parker M. WC2 . . . . .3A 60
Parkers Row SE1 . . . . .5C 92
Parker St. E16 . . . . .3F 103
  WC2 . . . . .3A 60
Parkfield Rd. SE14 . . . . .5B 146
Parkfield St. N1 . . . . .5E 17
Parkgate N1 . . . . .3E 19
Parkgate Rd. SW11 . . . . .5F 133
Park Hall SE10 . . . . .5D 149
Park Hgts. Ct. E14 . . . . .4B 68
Parkholme Rd. E8 . . . . .1D 21
Park Ho. E9 . . . . .2B 22
  W1 . . . . .4D 57
Parkhouse St. SE5 . . . . .4E 141
Parkinson Ct. N1 . . . . .3E 41
Parkinson Ho. E9 . . . . .1B 22
  SW1 . . . . .4C 114
Parkland Ct. E15 . . . . .3F 7
  W14 . . . . .4F 79
Park La. E15 . . . . .3D 27
  W1 . . . . .5C 56
Park Lodge NW8 . . . . .2E 11
  W14 . . . . .2C 108
Park Lorne NW8 . . . . .3A 34
Park Mans. NW8 . . . . .1F 33
  SW1 . . . . .5B 84
  SW8 . . . . .2A 138
Park M. SE10 . . . . .5B 128
  W10 . . . . .1A 30
Park Pl. E14 . . . . .2D 97
  N1 . . . . .3E 19
  SW1 . . . . .3B 86
Park Pl. Vs. W2 . . . . .1C 54
Park Rd. NW1 . . . . .2F 33
  NW8 . . . . .2F 33
Park Row SE10 . . . . .1D 149
Park St James NW8 . . . . .4B 12
Parkside NW2 . . . . .4C 84
Parkside Bus. Est. SE8 . . . . . . .2F 145
Parkside Ct. E16 . . . . .4C 102
Parkside Est. E9 . . . . .3C 22
(not continuous)
Parks Info. Cen. 2A 84
Park Sq. E. NW1 . . . . .4F 35
Park Sq. M. NW1 . . . . .5F 35
Park Sq. W. NW1 . . . . .4F 35
Park Steps W2 . . . . .5A 56
Park St. SE1 . . . . .2B 90
  W1 . . . . .5D 57
Park Towers W1 . . . . .3F 85
Park Vw. SE8 . . . . .1E 145
Park Vw. Apartments
  SE16 . . . . .2A 122
Parkview Apartments E14 . . .3A 70
Park Vw. Ct. E3 . . . . .1E 69
Park Vw. Est. E2 . . . . .1D 45
Park Village E. NW1 . . . . .4F 13
Park Village W. NW1 . . . . .5F 13
Parkville Rd. SW6 . . . . .5B 130
Park Vista SE10 . . . . .3E 149
Park Wlk. SE10 . . . . .5D 149
  SW10 . . . . .2C 132
Parkway NW1 . . . . .4F 13
Parkway Cres. E15 . . . . .2C 6
Park West W2 . . . . .3A 56
Park West Bldg. E3 . . . . .5E 25
Park West Pl. W2 . . . . .3A 56
Park Wharf SE8 . . . . .5A 124
Parkwood NW8 . . . . .4B 12
Parliament Ct. E1 . . . . .2A 64

Parliament Sq. SW1 . . . . .5F **87**
Parliament St. SW1 . . . . .5F **87**
Parliament Vw. SE1 . . . . . . .3B **116**
Parmiter St. E2 . . . . .5A **22**
Parmoor Ct. EC1 . . . . .4B **40**
Parnell Ho. WC1 . . . . .3E **59**
Parnell Rd. E3 . . . . .3C **24**
Parnham St. E14 . . . . .3A **68**
        (not continuous)
Parr Ct. N1 . . . . .5D **19**
Parr Ho. E16 . . . . .2F **101**
Parr St. N1 . . . . .5D **19**
Parry Av. E6 . . . . .4B **76**
Parry Ho. E1 . . . . .3A **94**
Parry Rd. W10 . . . . .2A **30**
Parry St. SW8 . . . . .2A **138**
Parsonage St. E14 . . . . .4C **126**
Parsons Ho. W2 . . . . .5D **33**
Parsons Lodge NW6 . . . . .2F **9**
Partridge Cl. E16 . . . . .2D **75**
Partridge Ct. EC1 . . . . .4F **39**
Partridge Ho. E3 . . . . .1C **46**
Partridge Sq. E6 . . . . .1A **76**
Pascall Ho. SE17 . . . . .2B **140**
Pascal St. SW8 . . . . .4E **137**
Pasley Cl. SE17 . . . . .1B **140**
Passfield Dr. E14 . . . . .1A **70**
Passfield Hall WC1 . . . . .4E **37**
Passfields W14 . . . . .1B **130**
Passing All. EC1 . . . . .5A **40**
Passmore Ho. E2 . . . . .4B **20**
Passmore St. SW1 . . . . .4D **113**
Pastel Ct. E1 . . . . .1E **67**
Pastor St. SE11 . . . . .3A **118**
Patent Ho. E14 . . . . .2A **70**
Paternoster La. EC4 . . . . .4A **62**
Paternoster Row EC4 . . . . . . .4B **62**
Paternoster Sq. EC4 . . . . . . .4A **62**
Paterson Ct. EC1 . . . . .3D **41**
Pater St. W8 . . . . .2D **109**
Patina Mans. E20 . . . . .3C **6**
Patmos Lodge SW9 . . . . . . .5F **139**
Patmos Rd. SW9 . . . . .5F **139**
Paton Cl. E3 . . . . .2E **47**
Paton St. EC1 . . . . .3B **40**
Patrick Coman Ho. EC1 . . . . .3F **39**
Patrick Connolly Gdns. E3 . . .3A **48**
Patrick Ct. SE1 . . . . .5A **90**
Patriot Sq. E2 . . . . .1A **44**
Patroni Ct. E15 . . . . .1F **49**
Pat Shaw Ho. E1 . . . . .4D **45**
Patterdale NW1 . . . . .3A **36**
Patterdale Rd. SE15 . . . . . . .4B **144**
Pattern Ho. EC1 . . . . .4F **39**
Pattina Wlk. SE16 . . . . .3A **96**
Pattison Ho. E1 . . . . .3D **67**
    SE1 . . . . .4C **90**
Paul Cl. E15 . . . . .2F **27**
Paul Daisley Ct. NW6 . . . . . . .2A **8**
Paul Ho. W10 . . . . .5F **29**
Pauline Ho. E1 . . . . .1E **65**
Paul Julius Cl. E14 . . . . .1D **99**
Paul Robeson Ho. WC1 . . . .1C **38**
Paul St. E15 . . . . .3E **27**
    EC2 . . . . .5E **41**
Paul's Wlk. EC4 . . . . .5A **62**
Paultons Ho. SW3 . . . . .2E **133**
Paultons Sq. SW3 . . . . .2E **133**
Paultons St. SW3 . . . . .3E **133**
Pavan Ct. E2 . . . . .3C **44**
Paveley Dr. SW11 . . . . .5F **133**
Paveley Ho. N1 . . . . .1B **38**
Paveley St. NW8 . . . . .3F **33**
Pavilion, The SW8 . . . . .4E **137**

Pavilion Apartments NW8 . . . .3E **33**
Pavilion Ct. NW6 . . . . .2D **31**
Pavilion Pde. W12 . . . . .3B **50**
Pavilion Rd. SW1 . . . . .5C **84**
Pavilion St. SW1 . . . . .2C **112**
Pavilion Ter. W12 . . . . .3B **50**
Pavilion Way SE10 . . . . .5F **99**
Pavillion Ho. SE16 . . . . .5D **95**
Paxton Ct. N1 . . . . .1D **17**
Paxton Ho. SE17 . . . . .5C **118**
Paxton Point SE10 . . . . .5F **147**
Paxton Ter. SW1 . . . . .2A **136**
Paymal Ho. E1 . . . . .2C **66**
Payne Ho. N1 . . . . .4C **16**
Payne Rd. E3 . . . . .1F **47**
Payne St. SE8 . . . . .3C **146**
Peabody Av. SW1 . . . . .5F **113**
Peabody Bldgs. E1 . . . . .5D **65**
    EC1 . . . . .5C **40**
    SW3 . . . . .3F **133**
Peabody Cl. SE10 . . . . .5A **148**
    SW1 . . . . .2A **136**
Peabody Ct. EC1 . . . . .5C **40**
Peabody Est. E1 . . . . .5C **66**
    E2 . . . . .1F **43**
    EC1 . . . . .5C **40**
    (Dufferin St., not continuous)
    EC1 . . . . .5E **39**
    (Farringdon La.)
    N1 . . . . .3B **18**
    SE1 . . . . .3E **89**
    (Duchy St.)
    SE1 . . . . .4C **90**
    (Marshalsea Rd.)
    SE1 . . . . .3B **90**
    (Southwark St.)
    SW1 . . . . .3C **114**
    SW3 . . . . .2A **134**
    SW6 . . . . .2C **130**
    W6 . . . . .5C **100**
    W10 . . . . .1C **50**
Peabody Ho. N1 . . . . .3B **18**
Peabody Sq. SE1 . . . . .5F **89**
    (not continuous)
Peabody Ter. EC1 . . . . .5E **39**
Peabody Twr. EC1 . . . . .5C **40**
Peabody Trust SE17 . . . . . . .4D **119**
Peabody Yd. N1 . . . . .5D **17**
Peace Ct. SE1 . . . . .1C **142**
Peach Rd. W10 . . . . .2E **29**
Peachwalk M. E3 . . . . .5E **23**
Peacock Pl. N1 . . . . .1E **17**
Peacock St. SE17 . . . . .4A **118**
Peacock Theatre **4B 60**
Peacock Wlk. E16 . . . . .3F **73**
Peacock Yd. SE17 . . . . .4A **118**
Pearce Ho. SW1 . . . . .4E **115**
Pear Cl. SE14 . . . . .5A **146**
Pear Ct. SE15 . . . . .4B **142**
Pear Cl. E6 . . . . .3D **77**
Pearl St. E1 . . . . .2A **94**
Pearman St. SE1 . . . . .1E **117**
Pearl Pl. SE1 . . . . .4D **89**
Pearse St. SE15 . . . . .3A **142**
Pearson St. E2 . . . . .5B **20**
Pear Tree Cl. E2 . . . . .4B **20**
Pear Tree Ct. EC1 . . . . .5E **39**
Peartree La. E1 . . . . .1C **94**
Pear Tree St. EC1 . . . . .4A **40**
Peartree Way SE10 . . . . .5D **129**
Peary Pl. E2 . . . . .2C **44**
PECKHAM **5B 142**
Peckham Gro. SE15 . . . . . . .4A **142**
Peckham Hill St. SE15 . . . . .4D **143**

Peckham Pk. Rd. SE15 . . . . .4D **143**
Pecks Yd. E1 . . . . .1B **64**
Pedley St. E1 . . . . .5D **43**
Pedworth Gdns. SE16 . . . . . .4B **122**
Peebles Ho. NW6 . . . . .1E **31**
Peel Gro. E2 . . . . .1B **44**
Peel Pas. W8 . . . . .3D **81**
Peel Pct. NW6 . . . . .1D **31**
Peel St. W8 . . . . .3D **81**
Peerless St. EC1 . . . . .3D **41**
Pegasus Ct. NW10 . . . . .2A **28**
Pegasus Ho. E1 . . . . .5D **45**
Pegasus Pl. SE11 . . . . .2D **139**
Pegswood Ct. E1 . . . . .5E **65**
Pekin Cl. E14 . . . . .4E **69**
Pekin St. E14 . . . . .4E **69**
Peldon Wlk. N1 . . . . .3A **18**
Pelham Ct. SW3 . . . . .4F **111**
Pelham Cres. SW7 . . . . .4F **111**
Pelham Ho. SW1 . . . . .2E **115**
    W14 . . . . .4B **108**
Pelham Pl. SW7 . . . . .3F **111**
Pelham St. SW7 . . . . .3E **111**
Pelican Ho. SE8 . . . . .4B **124**
Pelican Pas. E1 . . . . .4B **44**
Pelican Wharf E1 . . . . .2C **94**
Pelier St. SE17 . . . . .2C **140**
Pella Ho. SE11 . . . . .5C **116**
Pellant Rd. SW6 . . . . .3A **130**
Pellew Ho. E1 . . . . .5A **44**
Pelling St. E14 . . . . .5C **68**
Pelter St. E2 . . . . .2B **42**
Pelton Rd. SE10 . . . . .5F **127**
Pember Rd. NW10 . . . . .3D **29**
Pemberton Ct. E1 . . . . .3D **45**
Pemberton Pl. E8 . . . . .2A **22**
Pemberton Row EC4 . . . . . . .3E **61**
Pembridge Cres. W11 . . . . . .5D **53**
Pembridge Gdns. W2 . . . . . . .1D **81**
Pembridge M. W11 . . . . .5D **53**
Pembridge Pl. W2 . . . . .5E **53**
Pembridge Rd. W11 . . . . .1D **81**
Pembridge Sq. W2 . . . . .1E **81**
Pembridge Studios W11 . . . . .5D **53**
Pembridge Vs. W2 . . . . .1D **81**
    W11 . . . . .1D **81**
Pembroke W14 . . . . .4C **108**
Pembroke Av. N1 . . . . .3A **16**
Pembroke Cl. SW1 . . . . .5E **85**
Pembroke Cotts. W8 . . . . . . .2D **109**
Pembroke Ct. W8 . . . . .2D **109**
Pembroke Gdns. W8 . . . . . . .3C **108**
Pembroke Gdns. Cl. W8 . . . .2C **108**
Pembroke Ho. SW1 . . . . .2D **113**
    W2 . . . . .4A **54**
Pembroke M. E3 . . . . .2A **46**
    W8 . . . . .2D **109**
Pembroke Pl. W8 . . . . .2D **109**
Pembroke Rd. E6 . . . . .1B **76**
    W8 . . . . .3C **108**
Pembroke Sq. W8 . . . . .2D **109**
Pembroke St. N1 . . . . .2A **16**
    (not continuous)
Pembroke Studios W8 . . . . . .2C **108**
Pembroke Ter. NW8 . . . . .4D **11**
Pembroke Vs. W8 . . . . .3D **109**
Pembroke Wlk. W8 . . . . .3D **109**
Pemell Cl. E1 . . . . .4C **44**
Pemell Ho. E1 . . . . .4C **44**
Penally Pl. N1 . . . . .5E **19**
Penang Ho. E1 . . . . .2B **94**
Penang St. E1 . . . . .2A **94**
Penarth Cen. SE15 . . . . .2B **144**
Penarth St. SE15 . . . . .2B **144**

Pencombe M. W11	.5C **52**	
Pencraig Way SE15	.3F **143**	
Penda's Mead E9	.1A **4**	
Pendennis Ho. SE8	.4A **124**	
Pendley Ho. E2	.4E **21**	
Pendrell Ho. WC2	.4E **59**	
Penfield Lodge W9	.1E **53**	
Penfold Pl. NW1	.1F **55**	
Penfold St. NW1	.5E **33**	
NW8	.5E **33**	
Pengelly Apartments E14	.5A **126**	
Penhurst Pl. SE1	.2C **116**	
Peninsula Apartments W2	.2E **55**	
Peninsula Ct. E14	.1A **126**	
N1	.3C **18**	
Peninsula Hgts. SE1	.5A **116**	
Peninsular Pk. SE7	.4E **129**	
Peninsular Pk. Rd. SE7	.4E **129**	
Peninsula Sq. SE10	.4F **99**	
Penley Ct. WC2	.5C **60**	
Penmayne Ho. SE11	.5E **117**	
Pennack Rd. SE15	.3C **142**	
Penn Almshouses SE10	.5B **148**	
Pennant M. W8	.3F **109**	
Pennard Mans. W12	.5B **78**	
Pennard Rd. W12	.4B **78**	
Pennethorne Cl. E9	.4B **22**	
Pennethorne Rd. SE15	.5F **143**	
Penn Ho. NW8	.5F **33**	
Pennington Ct. SE16	.2A **96**	
Pennington St. E1	.1E **93**	
Penn St. N1	.4E **19**	
Penny Brookes St. E15	.4D **7**	
E20	.4B **6**	
Pennyfields E14	.5D **69**	
(not continuous)		
Pennyford Ct. NW8	.4D **33**	
Pennymoor Wlk. W9	.4C **30**	
Pennyroyal Av. E6	.4D **77**	
Penrose Gro. SE17	.1B **140**	
Penrose Ho. SE17	.1B **140**	
Penrose St. SE17	.1B **140**	
Penrose Way SE10	.4A **100**	
Penryn Ho. SE11	.5F **117**	
Penryn St. NW1	.5D **15**	
Penry St. SE1	.4A **120**	
Penshurst Ho. SE15	.2C **144**	
Penshurst Rd. E9	.2D **23**	
Pentagram Yd. W11	.4D **53**	
Pentland Rd. NW6	.2D **31**	
Penton Gro. N1	.1D **39**	
Penton Ho. N1	.1D **39**	
Penton Pl. SE17	.4A **118**	
Penton Ri. WC1	.2C **38**	
Penton St. N1	.5D **17**	
PENTONVILLE	.1B **38**	
Pentonville Rd. N1	.2A **38**	
Pentridge St. SE15	.4B **142**	
Penywern Rd. SW5	.5E **109**	
Penzance Pl. W11	.2F **79**	
Penzance St. W11	.2F **79**	
Peony Ct. SW10	.2C **132**	
Peperfield WC1	.3B **38**	
Pepler Ho. W10	.5F **29**	
Pepler M. SE5	.1B **142**	
Peploe Ho. NW6	.1E **29**	
Pepper Cl. E6	.1C **76**	
Pepper St. E14	.1F **125**	
SE1	.4B **90**	
Pepys Cres. E16	.2E **101**	
Pepys Ho. E2	.2C **44**	
Pepys St. EC3	.5A **64**	
Percival St. EC1	.4F **39**	
Percy Cir. WC1	.2C **38**	

Percy M. W1	.2D **59**	
Percy Pas. W1	.2D **59**	
Percy Rd. E16	.1A **72**	
Percy St. W1	.2D **59**	
Percy Yd. WC1	.2C **38**	
Peregrine Ct. SE8	.3D **147**	
Peregrine Ho. EC1	.2A **40**	
Perham Rd. W14	.1A **130**	
Peridot Ct. E2	.3B **42**	
Peridot St. E6	.1A **76**	
Perkins Ho. E14	.2C **68**	
Perkin's Rents SW1	.1D **115**	
Perkins Sq. SE1	.2C **90**	
Perley Ho. E3	.1C **68**	
Perrers Rd. W6	.3A **106**	
Perring Est. E3	.1E **69**	
Perrin Ho. NW6	.2D **31**	
Perronet Ho. SE1	.2A **118**	
Perry Ct. E14	.5E **125**	
Perryn Rd. SE16	.1F **121**	
Perry's Pl. W1	.3D **59**	
Perseverance Pl. SW9	.5E **139**	
Perseverance Works E2	.2A **42**	
Perth Ho. N1	.2B **16**	
Peter Best Ho. E1	.3F **65**	
Peterboat Cl. SE10	.3A **128**	
Peterborough Ct. EC4	.4E **61**	
Peter Butler Ho. SE1	.4D **93**	
Peterchurch Ho. SE15	.3F **143**	
Peter Harrison Planetarium		
	.5E **149**	
Peter Heathfield Ho. E15	.3D **27**	
Peter Hills Ho. SE16	.3D **121**	
Peter Ho. SW8	.4F **137**	
Peterley Bus. Cen. E2	.5A **22**	
Peter Pan Statue	.2D **83**	
Peters Ct. W2	.3A **54**	
Petersham Ho. SW7	.3D **111**	
Petersham La. SW7	.1B **110**	
Petersham M. SW7	.2B **110**	
Petersham Pl. SW7	.1B **110**	
Peter's Hill EC4	.5B **62**	
Peter Shore Ct. E1	.1D **67**	
Peter's La. EC1	.1A **62**	
(not continuous)		
Peter St. W1	.5D **59**	
Petiver Cl. E9	.1C **22**	
Peto Pl. NW1	.4A **36**	
Peto St. Nth. E16	.4B **72**	
Petrie Museum of Egyptian		
Archaeology	.5D **37**	
Petticoat La. E1	.2B **64**	
Petticoat Lane Market	.2A **64**	
(off Middlesex St.)		
Petticoat Sq. E1	.3B **64**	
Petticoat Twr. E1	.3B **64**	
Petty France SW1	.1C **114**	
Petty Wales EC3	.1A **92**	
Petyt Pl. SW3	.3F **133**	
Petyward SW3	.4A **112**	
Pevensey Ho. E1	.2E **67**	
Peverel E6	.3D **77**	
Peveril Ho. SE1	.2E **119**	
Peyton Pl. SE10	.4B **148**	
Pheasant Cl. E16	.3F **73**	
Pheasantry Ho. SW3	.5A **112**	
Phelp St. SE17	.2D **141**	
Phene St. SW3	.2A **134**	
Philadelphia Ct. SW10	.5C **132**	
Philbeach Gdns. SW5	.5D **109**	
Philchurch Pl. E1	.4E **65**	
Philia Ho. NW1	.1B **14**	
Philip Ct. W2	.1D **55**	
Philip Ho. NW6	.4F **9**	

Philip Mole Ho. W9	.4D **31**	
Phillimore Ct. W8	.5E **81**	
Phillimore Gdns. W8	.5D **81**	
Phillimore Gdns. Cl. W8	.1D **109**	
Phillimore Pl. W8	.5D **81**	
Phillimore Ter. W8	.1E **109**	
Phillimore Wlk. W8	.1D **109**	
Phillip Ho. E1	.1C **64**	
Phillipp St. N1	.4F **19**	
Philpot La. EC3	.5F **63**	
Philpot St. E1	.2A **66**	
Phipps Ho. SE7	.5F **129**	
W12	.5A **50**	
Phipp's M. SW1	.2A **114**	
Phipp St. EC2	.4F **41**	
Phoebe Wlk. E16	.4A **74**	
Phoenix Av. SE10	.4A **100**	
Phoenix Cl. E8	.3B **20**	
Phoenix Ct. E1	.4A **44**	
E14	.4E **125**	
NW1	.1E **37**	
SE14	.3F **145**	
Phoenix Hgts. E. E14	.4E **97**	
Phoenix Hgts. W. E14	.4E **97**	
Phoenix Lodge Mans.		
W6	.3C **106**	
Phoenix Pl. WC1	.4C **38**	
Phoenix Rd. NW1	.2D **37**	
Phoenix St. WC2	.4E **59**	
Phoenix Theatre	.4E **59**	
Phoenix Wharf E1	.3A **94**	
Phoenix Wharf Rd. SE1	.5C **92**	
Phoenix Yd. WC1	.3C **38**	
Photographers Gallery	.4B **58**	
Phyllis Hodges Ho. NW1	.1D **37**	
(off Aldenham St.)		
Physical Energy Statue	.3C **82**	
Physic Pl. SW3	.2B **134**	
Piazza, The WC2	.5A **60**	
(not continuous)		
Piccadilly W1	.4F **85**	
Piccadilly Arc. SW1	.2B **86**	
Piccadilly Circus	.1D **87**	
Piccadilly Cir. W1	.1D **87**	
Piccadilly Pl. W1	.1C **86**	
Piccadilly Theatre	.5C **58**	
Pickard Gdns. E3	.1C **68**	
Pickard St. EC1	.2A **40**	
Pickering Cl. E9	.1D **23**	
Pickering Ho. W2	.4B **54**	
Pickering M. W2	.3A **54**	
Pickering Pl. SW1	.3C **86**	
Pickering St. N1	.3A **18**	
Pickfords Wharf N1	.1B **40**	
SE1	.2D **91**	
Pickwick Ho. SE16	.5D **93**	
W11	.2E **79**	
Pickwick St. SE1	.5B **90**	
Pickworth Cl. SW8	.5A **138**	
Picton Pl. W1	.4E **57**	
Picton St. SE5	.5D **141**	
Pied Bull Ct. WC1	.2A **60**	
Pied Bull Yd. N1	.4F **17**	
(off Theberton St.)		
WC1	.2F **59**	
Pier Head E1	.3F **93**	
(not continuous)		
Pierhead Wharf E1	.3F **93**	
Pier Ho. SW3	.3A **134**	
Pier Pde. E16	.3E **105**	
Pierpoint Bldg. E14	.4C **96**	
Pierrepont Arc. N1	.5F **17**	
Pierrepont Row N1	.5F **17**	
Pier Rd. E16	.3E **105**	

Pier St. E14 . . . . .3C 126
(not continuous)
Pier Wlk. SE10 . . . . .4A 100
Pietra Lara Bldg. EC1 . . . . . .4B 40
Piggott Ho. E2 . . . . .5D 23
Pigott St. E14 . . . . .4D 69
Pikemans Ct. SW5 . . . . . . .4D 109
Pilgrimage St. SE1 . . . . .5D 91
Pilgrim Ho. SE1 . . . . .2E 119
SE16 . . . . .5B 94
Pilgrims Cloisters SE5 . . . .5F 141
Pilgrims Cnr. NW6 . . . . .1D 31
Pilgrims M. E14 . . . . .5E 71
Pilgrim St. EC4 . . . . .4F 61
Pillfold Ho. SE11 . . . . .3B 116
Pilot Cl. SE8 . . . . .2B 146
Pilton Pl. SE17 . . . . .5C 118
PIMLICO 1B 136
Pimlico Ho. SW1 . . . . .5F 113
Pimlico Rd. SW1 . . . . .5D 113
Pimlico Wlk. N1 . . . . .2F 41
Pinchin & Johnsons Yd.
E1 . . . . .5E 65
Pinchin St. E1 . . . . .5E 65
Pincombe Ho. SE17 . . . . . .5D 119
Pindar St. EC2 . . . . .1F 63
Pindock M. W9 . . . . .5A 32
Pineapple Ct. SW1 . . . . . . .1B 114
Pine Av. E15 . . . . .2E 7
Pinedene SE15 . . . . .5F 143
Pinefield Cl. E14 . . . . .5D 69
Pine Ho. E3 . . . . .3A 24
SE16 . . . . .4C 94
W10 . . . . .4F 29
Pinehurst Ct. W11 . . . . .4C 52
Pine M. NW10 . . . . .1D 29
Pine St. EC1 . . . . .4D 39
Pinnace Ho. E14 . . . . .1C 126
Pinnacle, The EC3 . . . . .4F 63
Pinnacle Way E14 . . . . .4A 68
Pinner Ct. NW8 . . . . .4D 33
Pinners Pas. EC2 . . . . .3E 63
Pintail Cl. E6 . . . . .2F 75
Pintail Ct. SE8 . . . . .2B 146
Pioneer Cl. E14 . . . . .2F 69
Pioneer Ho. WC1 . . . . .2B 38
Pioneer Way W12 . . . . .4A 50
Pipers Ho. SE10 . . . . .1E 149
Pippin Ct. SW8 . . . . .2B 138
Pippin Ho. W10 . . . . .5D 51
Pippin Mans. E20 . . . . .3C 6
Pique M. E1 . . . . .5D 67
Pirie St. E16 . . . . .3A 102
Pissaro Ho. N1 . . . . .1D 17
Pitcairn Ho. E9 . . . . .1A 22
Pitchford St. E15 . . . . .2E 27
Pitfield Est. N1 . . . . .2F 41
Pitfield St. N1 . . . . .3F 41
Pitman Bldg. SE16 . . . . . . .1D 121
Pitman St. SE5 . . . . .4B 140
Pitsea Pl. E1 . . . . .4E 67
Pitsea St. E1 . . . . .4E 67
Pitt's Head M. W1 . . . . .3E 85
Pitt St. W8 . . . . .4E 81
Pixley St. E14 . . . . .3C 68
Place, The 3E 37
Place, The SE1 . . . . .3E 91
Plaisterers Highwalk EC2 . .2B 62
Plaistow Wharf E16 . . . . . . .3D 101
Planetree Ho. W6 . . . . .3E 107
Plane Tree Ho. SE8 . . . . . . .2A 146
W8 . . . . .4C 80
Plantain Pl. SE1 . . . . .4D 91
Plantation La. EC3 . . . . .5F 63

Plantation Pl. EC3 . . . . .5F 63
Plate Ho. E14 . . . . .5F 125
Platform Theatre 4F 15
Platina St. EC2 . . . . .4E 41
Platinum Ct. E1 . . . . .5C 44
Platt St. NW1 . . . . .5D 15
Plaxdale Ho. SE17 . . . . . . .4F 119
Playfair Ho. E14 . . . . .4E 69
Playfair Mans. W14 . . . . . .3A 130
Playhouse Ct. SE1 . . . . .3B 90
Playhouse Theatre 2A 88
Playhouse Yd. EC4 . . . . .4F 61
Plaza Pde. NW6 . . . . .5F 9
Plaza Shop. Centre, The
W1 . . . . .3C 58
Pleasant Pl. N1 . . . . .2A 18
Pleasant Row NW1 . . . . . . .4A 14
Plender Ct. NW1 . . . . .4C 14
Plender St. NW1 . . . . .4B 14
Plessey Bldg. E14 . . . . .3D 69
Plevna St. E14 . . . . .1B 126
Pleydell Ct. EC4 . . . . .4E 61
Pleydell Est. EC1 . . . . .3C 40
Pleydell Ho. EC4 . . . . .4E 61
(off Pleydell St.)
Pleydell St. EC4 . . . . .4E 61
Plimley Pl. W12 . . . . .4D 79
Plimsoll Cl. E14 . . . . .4F 69
Plough Cl. NW10 . . . . .2A 28
Plough Ct. EC3 . . . . .5E 63
Ploughmans Cl. NW1 . . . . . .3D 15
Plough Pl. EC4 . . . . .3E 61
Plough St. E1 . . . . .3D 65
Plough Way SE16 . . . . .3E 123
Plough Yd. EC2 . . . . .5A 42
Plover Ho. SW9 . . . . .5D 139
Plover Way SE16 . . . . .1F 123
Plowden Bldgs. EC4 . . . . . . .5D 61
(off Middle Temple La.)
Plumber's Row E1 . . . . .2D 65
Plume Ho. SE10 . . . . .3A 148
Plumtree Ct. EC4 . . . . .3F 61
Plymouth Ho. SE10 . . . . . . .5A 148
Plymouth Rd. E16 . . . . .2D 73
Plymouth Wharf E14 . . . . . .3D 127
Plympton Av. NW6 . . . . .2B 8
Plympton Pl. NW8 . . . . .5F 33
Plympton Rd. NW6 . . . . .2B 8
Plympton St. NW8 . . . . .5F 33
Pocock St. SE1 . . . . .4F 89
Poet Ct. E1 . . . . .1E 67
Point, The W2 . . . . .2D 55
Pointers Cl. E14 . . . . .5F 125
Point Hill SE10 . . . . .5C 148
Point West SW7 . . . . .3A 110
Poland St. W1 . . . . .3C 58
Polesworth Ho. W2 . . . . .1E 53
Pollard Cl. E16 . . . . .5D 73
Pollard Ho. N1 . . . . .1B 38
SE16 . . . . .2C 120
Pollard Row E2 . . . . .2E 43
Pollard St. E2 . . . . .2E 43
Pollen St. W1 . . . . .4B 58
Pollitt Dr. NW8 . . . . .4D 33
Pollock Ho. W10 . . . . .4F 29
Pollock's Toy Mus. 1C 58
Polperro Ho. W2 . . . . .2E 53
Polperro M. SE11 . . . . .3E 117
Polychrome Ct. SE1 . . . . . . .5F 89
Polydamas Cl. E3 . . . . .1E 47
Polygon, The NW8 . . . . .3E 11
Polygon Rd. NW1 . . . . .1D 37
(not continuous)
Pomell Way E1 . . . . .3C 64

Pomeroy Ho. E2 . . . . .1D 45
W11 . . . . .4F 51
Pomeroy St. SE14 . . . . .5C 144
Pomona Ho. SE8 . . . . .4F 123
Ponder St. N7 . . . . .1B 16
Pond Ho. SW3 . . . . .4F 111
Pond Pl. SW3 . . . . .4F 111
Pond Rd. E15 . . . . .5F 27
Ponler St. E1 . . . . .4F 65
Ponsard Rd. NW10 . . . . .2A 28
Ponsonby Ho. E2 . . . . .5B 22
(not continuous)
Ponsonby Pl. SW1 . . . . .5E 115
Ponsonby Ter. SW1 . . . . . . .5E 115
Ponsonby Vs. E2 . . . . .5B 22
Pontifex Apartments SE1 . . . .2D 91
(off Stoney St.)
Ponton Rd. SW8 . . . . .3E 137
Pontoon Rd. E16 . . . . .2A 102
Pont St. SW1 . . . . .2B 112
Pont St. M. SW1 . . . . .2B 112
Pontypool Pl. SE1 . . . . .4F 89
Pooja Ct. NW1 . . . . .1C 14
Poole Ct. N1 . . . . .2A 20
Poole Ho. SE11 . . . . .3C 116
Poole Rd. E9 . . . . .1D 23
Pooles Bldgs. WC1 . . . . .5D 39
Pooles La. SW10 . . . . .5B 132
Poole St. N1 . . . . .4D 19
Pooley Ho. E1 . . . . .3F 45
Pool Ho. NW8 . . . . .1E 55
Poolmans St. SE16 . . . . . . .4D 95
Pool St. E20 . . . . .2B 26
Poonah St. E1 . . . . .4C 66
Pope Ho. SE5 . . . . .5D 141
SE16 . . . . .4F 121
Pope's Head All. EC3 . . . . . .4E 63
Pope St. SE1 . . . . .5A 92
Popham Rd. N1 . . . . .3B 18
Popham St. N1 . . . . .3A 10
(not continuous)
POPLAR 5F 69
Poplar Bath St. E14 . . . . . . .5A 70
Poplar Cl. E9 . . . . .2B 4
Poplar Gro. W6 . . . . .5C 78
Poplar High St. E14 . . . . . . .5E 69
Poplar Ho. SE16 . . . . .5D 95
Poplar M. W12 . . . . .3B 78
Poplar Pl. W2 . . . . .5F 53
Poppins Ct. EC4 . . . . .4F 61
Porchester Ct. W2 . . . . .5A 54
Porchester Gdns. W2 . . . . . .5A 54
Porchester Gdns. M. W2 . . .4A 54
Porchester Ga. W2 . . . . .1B 82
(not continuous)
Porchester Ho. E1 . . . . .3F 65
Porchester Leisure Cen. . . .3F 53
Porchester Pl. W2 . . . . .4A 56
Porchester Rd. W2 . . . . .3A 54
Porchester Sq. W2 . . . . .3A 54
Porchester Sq. M. W2 . . . . .3A 54
Porchester Ter. W2 . . . . .4B 54
Porchester Ter. Nth. W2 . . .3A 54
Porchester Wlk. W2 . . . . . . .3A 54
Porlock St. SE1 . . . . .4E 91
Portcullis Ho. SW1 . . . . .5F 87
Port East Apartments E14 . .1E 97
Portelet Ct. N1 . . . . .3F 19
Portelet Rd. E1 . . . . .3D 45
Porten Ho's. W14 . . . . .2F 107
Porten Rd. W14 . . . . .2F 107
Porter Rd. E6 . . . . .3C 76
Porters Lodge, The SW10 . .4B 132
(off Coleridge Gdns.)

Porter St. SE1 . . . . .2C 90
   W1 . . . . .1C 56
Porters Wlk. E1 . . . . .1A 94
Porteus Rd. W2 . . . . .1C 54
Portgate Cl. W9 . . . . .4C 30
Port Ho. E14 . . . . .5F 125
Portia Ct. SE11 . . . . .5F 117
Portia Way E3 . . . . .5B 46
Porticos, The SW3 . . . . .3D 133
Portishead Ho. W2 . . . . .2D 53
Portland Ct. N1 . . . . .2A 20
   SE1 . . . . .1D 119
   SE14 . . . . .3F 145
Portland Ho. SW1 . . . . .2B 114
Portland Mans. W14 . . . . . . .3B 108
Portland M. W1 . . . . .4C 58
Portland Pl. W1 . . . . .5F 35
Portland Rd. W11 . . . . .5F 51
Portland Sq. E1 . . . . .2F 93
Portland St. SE17 . . . . .5D 119
Portland Wlk. SE17 . . . . .2E 141
Portman Cl. W1 . . . . .3C 56
Portman Ga. NW1 . . . . .5A 34
Portman Mans. W1 . . . . .1C 56
Portman M. Sth. W1 . . . . . . .4D 57
Portman Pl. E2 . . . . .3C 44
Portman Sq. W1 . . . . .3D 57
Portman St. W1 . . . . .4D 57
Portman Towers W1 . . . . . . .3C 56
Portnall Ho. W9 . . . . .3B 30
Portnall Rd. W9 . . . . .1B 30
Portobello Ct. W11 . . . . .4C 52
Portobello Grn. W10 . . . . . . .3A 52
Portobello Lofts W10 . . . . . .4F 29
Portobello M. W11 . . . . .1D 81
Portobello Rd. W10 . . . . .5F 29
   W11 . . . . .3B 52
Portobello Road Market *5C 52*
   (off Portobello Rd.)
Portpool La. EC1 . . . . .1D 61
Portree St. E14 . . . . .3E 71
Portsea Hall W2 . . . . .4A 56
Portsea M. W2 . . . . .4A 56
Portsea Pl. W2 . . . . .4A 56
Portsmouth M. E16 . . . . .2A 102
Portsmouth St. WC2 . . . . . . .3B 60
Portsoken St. E1 . . . . .5B 64
Portugal St. WC2 . . . . .4B 60
Pory Ho. SE11 . . . . .4C 116
Poseidon Ct. E14 . . . . .3D 125
Postern, The EC2 . . . . .2C 62
Post Office Ct. EC3 . . . . .4E 63
Post Office Way
   SW8 . . . . .4D 137
Potier St. SE1 . . . . .2E 119
Potter Cl. SE15 . . . . .4A 142
Potters Flds. SE1 . . . . .3A 92
Potters Lodge E14 . . . . .5B 126
Pottery La. W11 . . . . .2A 80
Pottery St. SE16 . . . . .5F 93
Pott St. E2 . . . . .3A 44
Poultry EC2 . . . . .4D 63
Povey Ho. SE17 . . . . .4F 119
Powell Ho. *W2* *5D 55*
   (off Gloucester Ter.)
Powis Ct. W11 . . . . .3C 52
Powis Gdns. W11 . . . . .3C 52
Powis Ho. WC2 . . . . .3A 60
Powis M. W11 . . . . .3C 52
Powis Pl. WC1 . . . . .5A 38
Powis Rd. E3 . . . . .3A 48
Powis Sq. W11 . . . . .3C 52
   (not continuous)
Powis Ter. W11 . . . . .3C 52

Powlesland Ct. *E1* *4F 67*
   (off White Horse Rd.)
Powlett Ho. NW1 . . . . .1F 13
Powlett Pl. NW1 . . . . .1F 13
Pownall Rd. E8 . . . . .4C 20
Poynter Ho. NW8 . . . . .4D 33
   W11 . . . . .2E 79
Poyser St. E2 . . . . .1A 44
Praed M. W2 . . . . .3E 55
Praed St. W2 . . . . .4D 55
Praline Ct. E3 . . . . .1F 47
Pratt M. NW1 . . . . .4B 14
Pratt St. NW1 . . . . .4B 14
Pratt Wlk. SE11 . . . . .3C 116
Preachers Ct. EC1 . . . . .5A 40
Prebend St. N1 . . . . .4B 18
Precinct, The N1 . . . . .4B 18
   (not continuous)
Premier Cnr. W9 . . . . .1B 30
Premiere Pl. E14 . . . . .1D 97
Premier Ho. N1 . . . . .2F 17
Prescot St. E1 . . . . .5C 64
Prescott Ho. SE17 . . . . .3A 140
President Dr. E1 . . . . .2F 93
President Ho. EC1 . . . . .3A 40
President Quay E1 . . . . .2C 92
President St. EC1 . . . . .2B 40
Press Ct. SE1 . . . . .1D 143
Press Ho. E1 . . . . .1E 67
Prestage Way E14 . . . . .1C 98
Preston Cl. SE1 . . . . .3F 119
Preston Ho. SE1 . . . . .3F 119
   (Preston Cl.)
   SE1 . . . . .1B 120
   (St Saviour's Est.)
Preston's Rd. E14 . . . . .1C 98
Preston St. E2 . . . . .1E 45
Prestwood Ho. SE16 . . . . . . .1F 121
Prestwood St. N1 . . . . .1C 40
Priam Ho. E2 . . . . .1A 44
Price Ho. N1 . . . . .4B 18
Price's M. N1 . . . . .4C 16
Price's St. SE1 . . . . .2A 90
Prichard Ho. SE11 . . . . .4D 117
Prideaux Ho. WC1 . . . . .2C 38
Prideaux Pl. WC1 . . . . .2C 38
Priestley Ho. EC1 . . . . .4B 40
Priestman Point E3 . . . . .3F 47
Priest's Ct. EC2 . . . . .3B 62
Prima Rd. SW9 . . . . .4D 139
Prime Meridian Line **4E 149**
Prime Meridian Wlk. E14 . . . .5E 71
PRIMROSE HILL **3D 13**
Primrose Cl. E3 . . . . .1D 47
Primrose Ho. NW8 . . . . .5B 12
Primrose Hill EC4 . . . . .4E 61
Primrose Hill Ct. NW3 . . . . . .2B 12
Primrose Hill Rd. NW3 . . . . . .1A 12
Primrose Hill Studios
   NW1 . . . . .3D 13
Primrose M. NW1 . . . . .2C 12
Primrose Sq. E9 . . . . .2C 22
Primrose St. EC2 . . . . .1F 63
Primrose Wlk. SE14 . . . . .4A 146
Prince Albert Ct. NW8 . . . . . .4B 12
Prince Albert Rd. NW1 . . . . . .2F 33
   NW8 . . . . .2F 33
Prince Charles Cinema **5E 59**
Prince Consort Rd. SW7 . . . .1C 110
Princedale Rd. W11 . . . . .2F 79
Prince Edward Mans. W2 . . . .5E 53
Prince Edward Rd. E9 . . . . . . .5C 4
Prince Edward Theatre **4E 59**
Princelet St. E1 . . . . .1C 64

Prince of Orange Ct.
   SE16 . . . . .2C 122
Prince of Orange La.
   SE10 . . . . .4B 148
Prince of Wales Dr. SW8 . . . .5A 136
   SW11 . . . . .5E 135
Prince of Wales Mans.
   SW11 . . . . .5E 135
Prince of Wales Pas. NW1 . . .3B 36
Prince of Wales Rd. E16 . . . . .4C 74
Prince of Wales Ter. W8 . . . . .5A 82
Prince of Wales Theatre **1D 87**
Prince Regent Ct. NW8 . . . . .5A 12
   SE16 . . . . .1A 96
Prince Regent La. E13 . . . . . .1B 74
   E16 . . . . .3B 74
Prince Regent M. NW1 . . . . . .3B 36
Princes Arc. SW1 . . . . .2C 86
Princes Cir. WC2 . . . . .3F 59
Prince's Ct. SE16 . . . . .2B 124
   SW3 . . . . .1B 112
Princes Ct. Bus. Cen. E1 . . . .1A 94
Prince's Gdns. SW7 . . . . .1E 111
Prince's Ga. SW7 . . . . .5E 83
   (not continuous)
Prince's Ga. Ct. SW7 . . . . . . .5E 83
Prince's Ga. M. SW7 . . . . . . .1E 111
Princes Ho. W11 . . . . .1C 80
Princes M. W2 . . . . .5F 53
   W6 . . . . .5A 106
Princes Pl. SW1 . . . . .2C 86
   W11 . . . . .2F 79
Princes Riverside Rd.
   SE16 . . . . .2D 95
Princess Alice Ho. W10 . . . . .5C 28
Princess Ct. NW6 . . . . .1F 9
   W1 . . . . .2B 56
   W2 . . . . .5A 54
Princess Louise Bldg.
   SE8 . . . . .5D 147
Princess Louise Cl. W2 . . . . .1E 55
Princess Mary Ho. SW1 . . . . .3E 115
Princess of Wales Memorial
   Fountain **4E 83**
Princes Sq. W2 . . . . .5E 53
   (not continuous)
Princess Rd. NW1 . . . . .3D 13
   NW6 . . . . .1D 31
Princess St. SE1 . . . . .2A 118
Princes St. EC2 . . . . .4D 63
   W1 . . . . .4A 58
Prince's Twr. SE16 . . . . .4B 94
Prince St. SE8 . . . . .2C 146
Prince's Yd. W11 . . . . .3A 80
Princethorpe Ho. W2 . . . . . . .1F 53
Princeton St. WC1 . . . . .2B 60
Printers Inn Ct. EC4 . . . . .3D 61
Printers M. E3 . . . . .4A 24
Printer St. EC4 . . . . .3E 61
Printing Ho. Yd. E2 . . . . .3A 42
Printon Ho. E14 . . . . .2C 68
Print Room, The **4E 53**
Printwork Apartments
   SE1 . . . . .1F 119
Prioress Ho. E3 . . . . .2A 48
Prioress St. SE1 . . . . .2E 119
Prior St. SE10 . . . . .5B 148
Priory Ct. EC4 . . . . .4A 62
Priory Grn. N1 . . . . .5B 16
Priory Grn. Est. N1 . . . . .5C 16
Priory Hgts. N1 . . . . .5C 16
Priory Ho. E1 . . . . .1B 64
   EC1 . . . . .4F 39
   SW1 . . . . .5D 115

Priory Mans. SW10 . . . . . .1C 132
Priory Pk. Rd. NW6 . . . . . . .3C 8
Priory Rd. NW6 . . . . .3F 9
Priory St. E3 . . . . .2A 48
Priory Ter. NW6 . . . . .3F 9
Priory Wlk. SW10 . . . . . .1C 132
Pritchard Ho. E2 . . . . .5F 21
Pritchard's Rd. E2 . . . . . . .4E 21
Priter Rd. SE16 . . . . .2E 121
Priter Rd. Hostel SE16 . . .2E 121
Priter Way SE16 . . . . . . .2E 121
Prize Wlk. E20 . . . . .3B 6
Probyn Ho. SW1 . . . . . . .3E 115
Procter Ho. SE1 . . . . .5D 121
   SE5 . . . . .5E 141
Procter St. WC1 . . . . .2B 60
Project Pk. E16 . . . . .4E 49
Prologis Pk. E3 . . . . .5C 48
Prospect Ho. E3 . . . . .3F 47
   N1 . . . . .1D 39
   SE1 . . . . .2F 117
   SE16 . . . . .1D 121
   W10 . . . . .4E 51
Prospect Pl. E1 . . . . .2B 94
   (not continuous)
   SE8 . . . . .2B 146
Prospect St. SE16 . . . . . . .5A 94
Prospect Wharf E1 . . . . . . .1C 94
Prospero Ho. E1 . . . . .5B 64
Prothero Rd. SW6 . . . . . .4A 130
Proton Twr. E14 . . . . .5E 71
Proud Ho. E1 . . . . .3F 65
Provence St. N1 . . . . .5B 18
Providence Cl. E9 . . . . .3E 23
Providence Ct. W1 . . . . . . .5E 57
Providence Ho. E14 . . . . . .4C 68
Providence Pl. N1 . . . . .4F 17
Providence Row N1 . . . . . . .1B 38
Providence Row Cl. E2 . . . .3A 44
Providence Sq. SE1 . . . . . .4D 93
Providence Twr. SE16 . . . . .4D 93
Providence Yd. E2 . . . . . . .2D 43
Province Dr. SE16 . . . . . . .5C 94
Province Sq. E14 . . . . .1C 98
Provost Ct. NW3 . . . . .1B 12
Provost Est. N1 . . . . .2D 41
Provost Rd. NW3 . . . . .1C 12
Provost St. N1 . . . . .1D 41
Prowse Pl. NW1 . . . . .1B 14
Prudent Pas. EC2 . . . . .4C 62
Prusom's Island E1 . . . . . .2B 94
Prusom St. E1 . . . . .2A 94
Pryce Ho. E3 . . . . .3E 47
Pudding La. EC3 . . . . .1E 91
Pudding Mill La. E15 . . . . .4A 26
Puddle Dock EC4 . . . . .5A 62
   (not continuous)
Pugin Ct. N1 . . . . .2E 17
Pulham Ho. SW8 . . . . . . .5B 138
Pullen's Bldgs. SE17 . . . . .5A 118
Pulteney Cl. E3 . . . . .4B 24
Pulteney Ter. N1 . . . . .4C 16
   (not continuous)
Pultney St. N1 . . . . .4C 16
Pulton Pl. SW6 . . . . .5D 131
Puma Ct. E1 . . . . .1B 64
Pump Ct. EC4 . . . . .4D 61
Pump Ho. Cl. SE16 . . . . . . .5C 94
Pumphouse Educational
   Museum, The 2A 96
Pump House Gallery 5D 135
Pump Ho. M. E1 . . . . .5D 65
Pumping Ho. E14 . . . . . . .5D 71
Pump La. SE14 . . . . .4C 144

Punderson's Gdns. E2 . . . .2A 44
Purbeck Ho. SW8 . . . . . . .5B 138
Purbrook Est. SE1 . . . . . . .5A 92
Purbrook St. SE1 . . . . . . .1A 120
Purcell Ho. SW10 . . . . . . .3D 133
Purcell Mans. W14 . . . . . .3A 130
Purcell Room 2C 88
Purcell St. N1 . . . . .5F 19
Purchese St. NW1 . . . . . . .5D 15
Purday Ho. W10 . . . . .3A 30
Purdy St. E3 . . . . .4F 47
Purley Pl. N1 . . . . .1F 17
Purves Rd. NW10 . . . . . . .2A 28
Pusey Ho. E14 . . . . .4E 69
Puteaux Ho. E2 . . . . .1D 45
Pynfolds SE16 . . . . .5A 94

Q Building, The E15 . . . . . . .5F 7
Quad Ct. SE1 . . . . .1A 120
Quadrangle, The W2 . . . . . .3F 55
Quadrangle Cl. SE1 . . . . . .3F 119
Quadrant, The W10 . . . . . .3E 29
Quadrant Arc. W1 . . . . . . .1C 86
Quadrant Bus. Cen.
   NW6 . . . . .3A 8
Quadrant Ho. E1 . . . . .1D 93
   E15 . . . . .2F 49
   SE1 . . . . .3F 89
Quadrant Wlk. E14 . . . . . .1F 125
Quain Mans. W14 . . . . . . .3A 130
Quaker Ct. E1 . . . . .5B 42
   EC1 . . . . .4C 40
Quaker St. E1 . . . . .5B 42
Quality Ct. WC2 . . . . .3D 61
Quarterdeck, The E14 . . . .5D 97
Quastel Ho. SE1 . . . . .5D 91
Quay Ho. E14 . . . . .4E 97
Quayside Cotts. E1 . . . . . .2D 93
Quayside Ct. SE16 . . . . . . .2D 95
Quayside Ho. E14 . . . . . . .3D 97
   W10 . . . . .4F 29
Quay Vw. Apartments
   E14 . . . . .2E 125
Quebec M. W1 . . . . .4C 56
Quebec Way SE16 . . . . . . .5E 95
Quebec Way Ind. Est.
   SE16 . . . . .1F 123
   (not continuous)
Quebec Wharf E8 . . . . .3A 20
   E14 . . . . .3C 68
Quedgeley Ct. SE15 . . . . . .3B 142
Queen Alexandra Mans.
   WC1 . . . . .2F 37
Queen Anne Alcove 1D 83
Queen Anne Ho. E16 . . . . .2E 101
Queen Anne M. W1 . . . . . .2A 58
Queen Anne Rd. E9 . . . . . .1D 23
Queen Anne's Ct. SE10 . . .1D 149
Queen Anne's Ga. SW1 . . . .5D 87
Queen Annes Sq. SE1 . . . .3D 121
Queen Anne St. W1 . . . . . .3F 57
Queen Anne's Wlk. WC1 . . .5A 38
Queen Anne Ter. E1 . . . . . .1A 94
Queen Caroline St. W6 . . . .4C 106
Queen Catherine Ho.
   SW6 . . . . .4A 132
Queen Ct. WC1 . . . . .5A 38
   (off Queen Sq.)
Queen Elizabeth Bldgs.
   EC4 . . . . .5D 61
Queen Elizabeth Hall 2B 88

Queen Elizabeth II Conference Cen.
   . . . . .5E 87
Queen Elizabeth Olympic Pk.
   . . . . .1F 25
Queen Elizabeth's Coll.
   SE10 . . . . .4B 148
Queen Elizabeth St. SE1 . . .4B 92
Queenhithe EC4 . . . . .5C 62
Queen Isabella Way EC1 . . .3A 62
Queen Margaret Flats E2 . . .2A 44
Queen Mary Ho. E16 . . . . .2F 101
   (off Wesley Av.)
Queen Marys Bldgs.
   SW1 . . . . .3C 114
Queen Mary's Ct. SE10 . . . .2D 149
Queen Mary University of London
   Charterhouse Square
   . . . . .5A 40
   Lincoln's Inn Fields Campus
   . . . . .3B 60
   Mile End Campus 4E 45
   West Smithfield Campus
   . . . . .2A 62
Queen Mother Memorial . . .3D 87
Queen Mother Sports Centre, The
   . . . . .3B 114
Queen of Denmark Ct.
   SE16 . . . . .1B 124
Queensberry Mews W.
   SW7 . . . . .3D 111
Queensberry Pl. SW7 . . . . .3D 111
Queensberry Way SW7 . . . .3D 111
Queensborough M. W2 . . . .5B 54
Queensborough Pas. W2 . . .5B 54
Queensborough Studios
   W2 . . . . .5A 54
Queensborough Ter. W2 . . . .5A 54
Queensbridge Ct. E2 . . . . .5C 20
Queensbridge Rd. E2 . . . . .4C 20
   E8 . . . . .3C 20
Queensbridge Sports
   & Community Cen. 1C 20
Queensbury St. N1 . . . . . . .2C 18
Queen's Cir. SW8 . . . . . . .5F 135
Queen's Club Gdns. W14 . . .2A 130
Queen's Club, The (Tennis Courts)
   . . . . .1A 130
Queens Club Ter. W14 . . . .2B 130
   (off Normand Rd.)
Queens Ct. NW8 . . . . .5D 11
   W2 . . . . .1A 82
Queensdale Cres. W11 . . . .2E 79
   (not continuous)
Queensdale Pl. W11 . . . . . .3F 79
Queensdale Rd. W11 . . . . . .3E 79
Queensdale Wlk. W11 . . . . .3F 79
Queen's Elm Pde. SW3 . . . .5E 111
   (off Old Church St.)
Queen's Elm Sq. SW3 . . . .1E 133
Queen's Gallery 5A 86
Queen's Gdns. W2 . . . . . . .5B 54
Queen's Ga. SW7 . . . . .5C 82
Queen's Ga. Gdns. SW7 . . .2B 110
Queensgate Ho. E3 . . . . . .1C 46
Queen's Ga. M. SW7 . . . . .5C 82
Queen's Ga. Pl. SW7 . . . . .2C 110
Queensgate Pl. NW6 . . . . . .2D 9
Queen's Ga. Pl. M. SW7 . . .2C 110
Queen's Ga. Ter. SW7 . . . .1B 110
Queens Ga. Vs. E9 . . . . . . .2F 23
Queen's Gro. NW8 . . . . . . .4D 11
Queen's Gro. Studios
   NW8 . . . . .4D 11
Queen's Head Pas. EC4 . . . .3B 62

Queen's Head St. N1 . . . . .4A **18**
Queen's Head Yd. SE1 . . . . . .3D **91**
Queen's House, The 3D **149**
Queens Ho. SE17 . . . . .2D **141**
  SW8 . . . . .4A **138**
  W2 . . . . .5A **54**
Queen's Ice & Bowl 1A **82**
Queensland Ho. E16 . . . . . .3D **105**
Queen's Mans. W6 . . . . . .3D **107**
Queensmead NW8 . . . . .3E **11**
Queen's M. W2 . . . . .5F **53**
QUEENS PARK **5A 8**
Queens Pk. Ct. W10 . . . . . . .3E **29**
Queen's Park Rangers FC . . .2A **78**
Queen Sq. WC1 . . . . .5A **38**
Queen Sq. Pl. WC1 . . . . . . .5A **38**
Queen's Quay EC4 . . . . .5C **62**
Queen's Row SE17 . . . . . . .2D **141**
Queens Ter. E1 . . . . .5B **44**
  NW8 . . . . .4D **11**
Queen's Theatre
  Westminster **5D 59**
Queens Tower **1D 111**
Queenstown Rd. SW8 . . . . . .3F **135**
Queen St. EC4 . . . . .5C **62**
  (not continuous)
  W1 . . . . .2F **85**
Queen St. Pl. EC4 . . . . .1C **90**
Queen's Wlk. SW1 . . . . .2B **86**
Queen's Walk, The SE1 . . . . .1A **94**
  (Oxo Tower Wharf)
  SE1 . . . . .2E **91**
  (Tooley St.)
  SE1 . . . . .2C **88**
  (Waterloo Rd.)
Queensway W2 . . . . .3A **54**
Queens Yd. E9 . . . . .5D **5**
  WC1 . . . . .5C **36**
Queen Victoria Memorial . .**5B 86**
Queen Victoria Seaman's Rest
  E14 . . . . .4F **69**
Queen Victoria Statue . . .**3B 82**
Queen Victoria St. EC4 . . . . .5F **61**
Queen Victoria Ter. E1 . . . . .1A **94**
Quendon Ho. W10 . . . . .5B **28**
Quenington Ct. SE15 . . . . . . .3B **142**
Quentin Ho. SE1 . . . . .4F **89**
  (not continuous)
Quest, The W11 . . . . .1A **80**
Quex Ct. NW6 . . . . .3F **9**
Quex M. NW6 . . . . .3E **9**
Quex Rd. NW6 . . . . .3E **9**
Quick St. N1 . . . . .1A **40**
Quick St. M. N1 . . . . .1F **39**
Quickswood NW3 . . . . .1A **12**
Quill Ho. E2 . . . . .4D **43**
Quilp St. SE1 . . . . .4B **90**
  (not continuous)
Quilter St. E2 . . . . .2D **43**
Quilting Ct. SE16 . . . . .4D **95**
Quinn Cl. E2 . . . . .1B **44**
Quinton Ho. SW8 . . . . .4F **137**
Quixley St. E14 . . . . .5D **71**

R

Rabbit Row W8 . . . . .2E **81**
Raby St. E14 . . . . .3F **67**
Rackstraw Ho. NW3 . . . . . . .1B **12**
Racton Rd. SW6 . . . . .3D **131**
RADA
  Chenies St. **1D 59**
  Gower St. **1D 59**

RADA Studios **1D 59**
Radcliff Ct. E3 . . . . .5C **46**
Radcliffe Ho. SE16 . . . . .4F **121**
Radcliffe Rd. SE1 . . . . .1A **120**
Radcot St. SE11 . . . . .1E **139**
Raddington Rd. W10 . . . . . .2A **52**
Radford Ct. SE15 . . . . .4A **144**
Radford Ho. E14 . . . . .2A **70**
Radipole Rd. SW6 . . . . .5B **130**
Radisson Ct. SE1 . . . . .1F **119**
  (off Long La.)
Radius Apartments N1 . . . . .1A **38**
Radland Rd. E16 . . . . .4C **72**
Radlett Pl. NW8 . . . . .4F **11**
Radley Ct. SE16 . . . . .4E **95**
Radley Ho. NW1 . . . . .4B **34**
Radley M. W8 . . . . .2F **109**
Radley Ter. E16 . . . . .1B **72**
Radnor Ho. EC1 . . . . .3C **40**
Radnor Lodge W2 . . . . .4E **55**
Radnor M. W2 . . . . .4E **55**
Radnor Pl. W2 . . . . .4F **55**
Radnor Rd. NW6 . . . . .4A **8**
  SE15 . . . . .4D **143**
Radnor St. EC1 . . . . .3C **40**
Radnor Ter. W14 . . . . .3B **108**
Radnor Wlk. E14 . . . . .3E **125**
  SW3 . . . . .1A **134**
Radstock St. SW11 . . . . . . .5F **133**
  (not continuous)
Radway Ho. W2 . . . . .1E **53**
RAF Bomber Command Memorial
  . . . .**4F 85**
Ragged School Mus. **1A 68**
Rahere Ct. E1 . . . . .5F **45**
Railway App. SE1 . . . . .2E **91**
Railway Arches E1 . . . . .4D **67**
  (Barnardo St.)
  E1 . . . . .5F **65**
  (Chapman St.)
  E2 . . . . .1B **42**
  (off Cremer St.)
  E2 . . . . .5B **20**
  (Geffrye St.)
  E2 . . . . .4B **20**
  (Laburnum St.)
  E3 . . . . .5C **46**
  E8 . . . . .2A **22**
  E16 . . . . .2D **101**
  W6 . . . . .1B **106**
  W12 . . . . .4B **78**
Railway Av. SE16 . . . . .4C **94**
  (not continuous)
Railway Cotts. E15 . . . . .5F **27**
  W6 . . . . .5C **78**
Railway Gro. SE14 . . . . .4B **146**
Railway M. W10 . . . . .3A **52**
Railway Sidings Rd.
  SE16 . . . . .2E **121**
Railway St. N1 . . . . .1A **38**
Rainbow Av. E14 . . . . .5F **125**
Rainbow Ct. SE14 . . . . .3F **145**
Rainbow Quay SE16 . . . . . .2B **124**
  (not continuous)
Rainbow St. SE5 . . . . .5F **141**
Raine St. E1 . . . . .2A **94**
Rainham Ho. NW1 . . . . .4C **14**
Rainham Rd. NW10 . . . . . . .3C **28**
Rainhill Way E3 . . . . .2E **47**
  (not continuous)
Rainsborough Av. SE8 . . . . .4F **123**
Rainsford St. W2 . . . . .3F **55**
Rainton Rd. SE7 . . . . .5E **129**
Rajsee Apartments E2 . . . . .3D **43**

Raleana Rd. E14 . . . . .2C **98**
Raleigh Ct. SE8 . . . . .5F **123**
  SE16 . . . . .3D **95**
  W12 . . . . .5B **78**
Raleigh Ho. E14 . . . . .4F **97**
  SW1 . . . . .2D **137**
Raleigh M. N1 . . . . .4A **18**
Raleigh St. N1 . . . . .4A **18**
Ralph Bayer Ct. E3 . . . . .1D **69**
Ralph Brook Ct. N1 . . . . .2E **41**
Ralph Ct. W2 . . . . .3A **54**
Ralston St. SW3 . . . . .1B **134**
Ramac Ind. Est. SE7 . . . . . .5F **129**
Ramac Way SE7 . . . . .4F **129**
Ramar Ho. E1 . . . . .1D **65**
Ramillies Pl. W1 . . . . .4B **58**
Ramillies St. W1 . . . . .4B **58**
Rampart St. E1 . . . . .4F **65**
Rampayne St. SW1 . . . . . . .5D **115**
Ramsay Ho. NW8 . . . . .5F **11**
Ramsay M. SW3 . . . . .2F **133**
Ramsay Rd. E7 . . . . .1F **7**
Ramsey Ho. SW9 . . . . .5E **139**
Ramsey St. E2 . . . . .4E **43**
Ramsfort Ho. SE16 . . . . . . .4F **121**
Ramsgate Cl. E16 . . . . .3F **101**
Randall Pl. SE10 . . . . .4B **148**
Randall Rd. SE11 . . . . .4B **116**
Randall Row SE11 . . . . .4B **116**
Randalls Rents SE16 . . . . . .1B **124**
Randell's Rd. N1 . . . . .3A **16**
Randolph App. E16 . . . . . . .4C **74**
Randolph Av. W9 . . . . .1F **31**
Randolph Ct. NW8 . . . . .4B **10**
Randolph Cres. W9 . . . . . . .5B **32**
Randolph Gdns. NW6 . . . . . .1F **31**
Randolph M. W9 . . . . .5C **32**
Randolph Rd. W9 . . . . .5B **32**
Randolph St. NW1 . . . . .2C **14**
Ranelagh Bri. W2 . . . . .2A **54**
Ranelagh Cotts. SW1 . . . . . .5E **113**
Ranelagh Gro. SW1 . . . . . . .5E **113**
Ranelagh Ho. SW3 . . . . .5B **112**
Ranelagh Rd. SW1 . . . . .1C **136**
Rangoon St. EC3 . . . . .4B **64**
Rankine Ho. SE1 . . . . .2B **118**
Ransome's Dock Bus. Cen.
  SW11 . . . . .5A **134**
Ranston St. NW1 . . . . .1F **55**
Ranwell Cl. E3 . . . . .4B **24**
Ranwell Ho. E3 . . . . .4B **24**
Raphael Ct. SE16 . . . . .5A **122**
Raphael St. SW7 . . . . .5B **84**
Raphen Apartments
  E3 . . . . .1A **46**
Rapley Ho. E2 . . . . .3D **43**
Raquel Ct. SE1 . . . . .4F **91**
Rashleigh Ho. WC1 . . . . . . .3F **37**
RATCLIFF **2F 67**
Ratcliffe Ct. SE1 . . . . .5C **90**
Ratcliffe Cross St. E1 . . . . . .4E **67**
Ratcliffe Ho. E14 . . . . .3F **67**
Ratcliffe La. E14 . . . . .4F **67**
Ratcliffe Orchard E1 . . . . . .5E **67**
Rathbone Ho. E16 . . . . .3B **72**
  NW6 . . . . .4D **9**
Rathbone Mkt. E16 . . . . .2B **72**
Rathbone Pl. W1 . . . . .2D **59**
Rathbone St. E16 . . . . .3B **72**
  W1 . . . . .2C **58**
Rathmore Rd. SE7 . . . . .5F **129**
Rathnew Ct. E2 . . . . .3D **45**
Raven Ho. SE16 . . . . .3D **123**
Raven Row E1 . . . . .1A **66**

Raven Row Contemporary Art Cen.
. . . . .2B 64
Ravensbourne Ho. NW8 . . . . .1F 55
Ravensbourne Mans.
  SE8 . . . . .3E 147
Ravenscar NW1 . . . . .4B 14
Ravenscourt Pk. Mans.
  W6 . . . . .2A 106
Ravenscroft Cl. E16 . . . . .1D 73
Ravenscroft Pk. E2 . . . . .2C 42
Ravenscroft Rd. E16 . . . . .1E 73
Ravenscroft St. E2 . . . . .1C 42
Ravensdon St. SE11 . . . . . . .1E 139
Ravenstone SE17 . . . . .1A 142
Ravens Wlk. E20 . . . . .4A 6
Ravensworth Ct. SW6 . . . . . .5C 130
Ravensworth Rd.
  NW10 . . . . .2A 28
Raven Wharf SE1 . . . . .4B 92
Ravey St. EC2 . . . . .4F 41
Rawalpindi Ho. E16 . . . . .1B 72
Rawlings St. SW3 . . . . .3B 112
Rawreth Wlk. N1 . . . . .3C 18
Rawsthorne Cl. E16 . . . . . . .3B 104
Rawstorne Pl. EC1 . . . . .2F 39
Rawstorne St. EC1 . . . . .2F 39
  (not continuous)
Rayburne Ct. W14 . . . . .1F 107
Ray Gunter Ho. SE17 . . . . . .1A 140
Ray Ho. N1 . . . . .4E 19
  W10 . . . . .3E 51
Rayleigh Rd. E16 . . . . .2A 102
Raymede Towers W10 . . . . . .1F 51
Raymond Bldgs. WC1 . . . . . . .1C 60
Raymouth Rd. SE16 . . . . . . .3A 122
Rayne Ho. W9 . . . . .4F 31
Rayner Ct. W12 . . . . .5C 78
Rayners Ter. E14 . . . . .3A 68
Raynham W2 . . . . .3A 56
Raynham Ho. E1 . . . . .4D 45
Raynham Rd. W6 . . . . .3A 106
Raynor Pl. N1 . . . . .3C 18
Ray St. EC1 . . . . .5E 39
Ray St. Bri. EC1 . . . . .5E 39
Raywood Mans. E20 . . . . .4B 6
Reachview Cl. NW1 . . . . .2C 14
Reader Ho. SE11 . . . . .2D 139
Read Ho. SE11 . . . . .2D 139
Reading Ho. SE15 . . . . .3E 143
  W2 . . . . .4B 54
Reapers Cl. NW1 . . . . .3D 15
Reardon Ho. E1 . . . . .2A 94
Reardon Path E1 . . . . .3A 94
  (not continuous)
Reardon St. E1 . . . . .2A 94
Reaston St. SE14 . . . . .4C 144
Rebecca Ho. E3 . . . . .4C 46
Record St. SE15 . . . . .2B 144
Rector St. N1 . . . . .4B 18
Rectory Chambers
  SW3 . . . . .2F 133
Rectory Sq. E1 . . . . .1E 67
Reculver Ho. SE15 . . . . .2C 144
Reculver Rd. SE16 . . . . .5D 123
Redan Pl. W2 . . . . .4F 53
Redan St. W14 . . . . .1E 107
Redbourne Ho. E14 . . . . .3B 68
Redbourn Ho. W10 . . . . .5B 28
Redbridge Gdns. SE5 . . . . . .5A 142
Redbridge Ho. E16 . . . . .1F 105
Redburn St. SW3 . . . . .2B 134
Redcar St. SE5 . . . . .5B 140
Redcastle Cl. E1 . . . . .5B 66

Redchurch St. E2 . . . . .4B 42
Redcliffe Cl. SW5 . . . . .1F 131
Redcliffe Gdns. SW10 . . . . . .1A 132
Redcliffe M. SW10 . . . . .1A 132
Redcliffe Pl. SW10 . . . . .3B 132
Redcliffe Rd. SW10 . . . . .1B 132
Redcliffe Sq. SW10 . . . . .1A 132
Redcliffe St. SW10 . . . . .2A 132
Redclyf Ho. E1 . . . . .4C 44
Red Cow La. EC1 . . . . .4B 40
Red Cross Cotts. SE1 . . . . . . .4C 90
Redcross Way SE1 . . . . .4C 90
Reddins Rd. SE15 . . . . .3D 143
Rede Pl. W2 . . . . .4E 53
Redesdale St. SW3 . . . . .2A 134
Redfern Ho. NW8 . . . . .3D 11
Redfield La. SW5 . . . . .3E 109
Redfield M. SW5 . . . . .3E 109
Redford Wlk. N1 . . . . .3A 18
Redgrave Ter. E2 . . . . .3E 43
Redhill St. NW1 . . . . .1A 36
Red Ho. Sq. N1 . . . . .1C 18
Redington Ho. N1 . . . . .5C 16
Red Lion Cl. SE17 . . . . .2D 141
Red Lion Ct. EC4 . . . . .4E 61
  SE1 . . . . .2C 90
Red Lion Row SE17 . . . . .2C 140
Red Lion Sq. WC1 . . . . .2B 60
Red Lion St. WC1 . . . . .1B 60
Red Lion Yd. W1 . . . . .2F 85
Redlynch Ct. W14 . . . . .5A 80
Redman Ho. EC1 . . . . .1D 61
  SE1 . . . . .5C 90
Redman's Rd. E1 . . . . .1B 66
Redmead La. E1 . . . . .3D 93
Redmill Ho. E1 . . . . .5A 44
Redmond Ho. N1 . . . . .4C 16
Redmore Rd. W6 . . . . .3A 106
Red Path E9 . . . . .4A 4
Red Pl. W1 . . . . .5D 67
Redriff Est. SE16 . . . . .1B 124
Redriff Rd. SE16 . . . . .3D 123
Redrup Ho. SE14 . . . . .3D 145
Redruth Rd. E9 . . . . .3C 22
Redshank Ho. SE1 . . . . .5C 120
Redstart Cl. E6 . . . . .1F 75
  SE14 . . . . .4F 145
Redvers St. N1 . . . . .2A 42
Redwald Rd. E5 . . . . .1A 4
Redwing Ct. SE1 . . . . .5C 90
Redwood Cl. E3 . . . . .5D 25
  SE16 . . . . .3A 96
Redwood Ct. NW6 . . . . .2A 8
Redwood Mans. W8 . . . . . . .2F 109
Reece M. SW7 . . . . .4D 111
Reed Cl. E16 . . . . .2D 73
Reed's Pl. NW1 . . . . .1B 14
Reedworth St. SE11 . . . . . . .4E 117
Reef Ho. E14 . . . . .1C 126
Rees St. N1 . . . . .4C 18
Reeves Ho. SE1 . . . . .5D 89
Reeves M. W1 . . . . .1D 85
Reeves Rd. E3 . . . . .4F 47
Reflection, The E16 . . . . . . .4F 105
Reflection Ho. E2 . . . . .4D 43
Regal Bldg. W10 . . . . .2E 29
Regal Cl. E1 . . . . .1E 65
Regal Ct. NW6 . . . . .1C 30
  SW6 . . . . .4D 131
Regal La. NW1 . . . . .4E 13
Regal Pl. E3 . . . . .3C 46
  SW6 . . . . .5A 132
Regan Way N1 . . . . .1F 41
Regatta Point E14 . . . . .4D 97

Regency Ct. E3 . . . . .1B 46
  E9 .3C 22
  SE8 . . . . .5C 146
Regency Ho. E16 . . . . .2E 101
  SW1 . . . . .3E 115
Regency Lodge NW3 . . . . . . .2D 11
Regency M. SW9 . . . . .5A 140
Regency Pde. NW3 . . . . .2D 11
Regency Pl. SW1 . . . . .3E 115
Regency St. SW1 . . . . .3D 115
Regency Ter. SW7 . . . . .5D 111
Regeneration House 4F 15
Regeneration Rd. SE16 . . . . .4D 123
Regent Ct. NW6 . . . . .1B 8
  NW8 . . . . .3F 33
  W8 . . . . .1F 109
Regent Ho. W14 . . . . .3F 107
Regent Pl. W1 . . . . .5C 58
Regent's Bri. Gdns.
  SW8 . . . . .4A 138
Regents Canal Ho.
  E14 . . . . .4A 68
Regents Ct. E8 . . . . .4C 20
Regents Ga. Ho. E14 . . . . . . .5F 67
Regents M. NW8 . . . . .5C 10
REGENT'S PARK 3A 36
Regent's Park 1C 34
Regent's Park Barracks 1A 36
Regents Pk. Est. NW1 . . . . . .2B 36
Regent's Pk. Gdns. M.
  NW1 . . . . .3C 12
Regent's Pk. Ho. NW8 . . . . .3A 34
Regent's Park Open Air Theatre
  . . . . .3D 35
Regent's Pk. Rd. NW1 . . . . . .2C 12
  (not continuous)
Regent's Pk. Ter. NW1 . . . . . .3F 13
Regents Pl. NW1 . . . . .4A 36
Regent's Pl. Plaza NW1 . . . . .4B 36
Regents Plaza NW6 . . . . .5F 9
Regent Sq. E3 . . . . .3F 47
  WC1 . . . . .3A 38
Regent's Row E8 . . . . .4D 21
Regent St. NW10 . . . . .3E 29
  SW1 . . . . .1D 87
  W1 . . . . .3A 58
Regent's University London
  . . . . .4D 35
Regents Wharf E2 . . . . .4F 21
  N1 .5B 16
Regent Ter. SW8 . . . . .3A 138
Reginald Pl. SE8 . . . . .5D 147
Reginald Rd. SE8 . . . . .5D 147
Reginald Sq. SE8 . . . . .5D 147
Regina Point SE16 . . . . .1C 122
Regis Ct. NW1 . . . . .1B 56
Regis Ho. W1 . . . . .1E 57
Regnart Bldgs. NW1 . . . . .3C 36
Regnum Apartments E1 . . . . .5B 42
Reid Bldg. E3 . . . . .5B 46
Relay Rd. W12 . . . . .1C 78
Reliance Sq. EC2 . . . . .4A 42
Reliance Wharf N1 . . . . .3A 20
Relton M. SW7 . . . . .1A 112
Rembrandt Cl. E14 . . . . .2D 127
  SW1 . . . . .5D 113
Rembrandt Ct. SE16 . . . . . . .5A 122
Remington Rd. E6 . . . . .3F 75
Remington St. N1 . . . . .1A 40
Remnant St. WC2 . . . . .3B 60
Remsted Ho. NW6 . . . . .4F 9
Remus Building, The
  EC1 . . . . .3E 39
Remus Rd. E3 . . . . .2D 25

Renaissance Wlk. SE10 . . . .1C 128
Renbold Ho. SE10 . . . . . . .5B 148
Rendle Ho. W10 . . . . .5F 29
Renforth St. SE16 . . . . .5C 94
Renfrew Cl. E6 . . . . .5D 77
Renfrew Ho. NW6 . . . . .1F 31
Renfrew Rd. SE11 . . . . .3F 117
Rennie Cotts. E1 . . . . .4C 44
Rennie Ct. SE1 . . . . .2F 89
Rennie Est. SE16 . . . . .4A 122
Rennie Ho. SE1 . . . . .2B 118
Rennie St. SE1 . . . . .2F 89
　　　　　(not continuous)
Renoir Cinema
　　Brunswick Square 5A 38
Renoir Ct. SE16 . . . . .5A 122
Renovation, The E16 . . . . . .4F 105
Rephidim St. SE1 . . . . .2F 119
Reporton Rd. SW6 . . . . .5A 130
Repton Ho. SW1 . . . . .4C 114
Repton St. E14 . . . . .3A 68
Reservoir Studios E1 . . . . . .4E 67
Resolution Way SE8 . . . .4D 147
Restell Cl. SE3 . . . . .2F 149
Reston Pl. SW7 . . . . .5B 82
Restormel Ho. SE11 . . . . . . .4E 117
Retford St. N1 . . . . .1A 42
Reunion Row E1 . . . . .1A 94
Reuters Plaza E14 . . . . .3F 97
Reveley Sq. SE16 . . . . .5A 96
Reverdy Rd. SE1 . . . . .4D 121
Rewell St. SW6 . . . . .5B 132
Rex Pl. W1 . . . . .1E 85
Reynard Pl. SE14 . . . . .3A 146
Reynolah Gdns. SE7 . . . . . .5F 129
Reynolds Ho. E2 . . . . .5C 22
　NW8 . . . . .1E 33
　SW1 . . . . .4E 115
Rheidol M. N1 . . . . .5B 18
Rheidol Ter. N1 . . . . .5A 18
Rhoda St. E2 . . . . .4C 42
Rhodes Ho. N1 . . . . .2D 41
Rhodeswell Rd. E14 . . . . . .1A 68
　　　　　(not continuous)
Rhodium Ct. E14 . . . . .2E 69
Rhondda Gro. E3 . . . . .3A 46
Ribblesdale Ho. NW6 . . . . . .3E 9
Ribbons Wlk. E20 . . . . .3C 6
Ricardo St. E14 . . . . .4F 69
Riceyman Ho. WC1 . . . . . . .3D 39
Richard Anderson Ct.
　SE14 . . . . .4D 145
Richard Fielden Ho. E1 . . . .3F 45
Richard Ho. SE16 . . . . .4C 122
Richard Ho. Dr. E16 . . . . . . .4E 75
Richard Neale Ho. E1 . . . . . .5A 66
Richard Robert Residence, The
　E15 . . . . .5E 7
Richardson Cl. E8 . . . . .3B 20
Richardson Rd. E15 . . . . . . .5F 27
Richardson's M. W1 . . . . . . .5B 36
Richard's Pl. SW3 . . . . .3A 112
Richard St. E1 . . . . .3F 65
Richbell WC1 . . . . .1B 60
Richbell Pl. WC1 . . . . .1B 60
Richborne Ter. SW8 . . . . . . .4B 138
Richborough Ho. SE15 . . . . .3C 144
Richbourne Ct. W1 . . . . .3A 56
　　　　　(off Harrowby St.)
Richford Ga. W6 . . . . .1B 106
Richford St. W6 . . . . .5B 78
Rich Ind. Est. SE1 . . . . .2A 120
　SE15 . . . . .3A 144
Rich La. SW5 . . . . .1F 131

Richman Ho. SE8 . . . . .1B 146
Richmix Sq. E1 . . . . .4C 42
Richmond, The American
　International University in
　London Kensington Campus,
　Ansdell Street 1A 110
　Kensington Campus,
　St Albans Grove 1A 110
　Kensington Campus,
　Young Street 5F 81
Richmond Av. N1 . . . . .3C 16
Richmond Bldgs. W1 . . . . . . .4D 59
Richmond Cotts. W14 . . . . . .3A 108
Richmond Ct. E8 . . . . .1A 22
　SW1 . . . . .5C 84
　W14 . . . . .3F 107
Richmond Cres. N1 . . . . . . .3C 16
Richmond Gro. N1 . . . . .2F 17
　　　　　(not continuous)
Richmond Ho. NW1 . . . . . . .1A 36
　SE17 . . . . .5D 119
Richmond Mans. SW5 . . . . . .5F 109
Richmond M. W1 . . . . .4D 59
Richmond Rd. E8 . . . . .1B 20
Richmond Ter. SW1 . . . . . . .4F 87
Richmond Way W12 . . . . . . .4E 79
　W14 . . . . .4E 79
Rich St. E14 . . . . .5C 68
Rickett St. SW6 . . . . .2E 131
Rickman Ho. E1 . . . . .3C 44
Rickman St. E1 . . . . .3C 44
Rick Roberts Way E15 . . . . .4C 26
Riddell Ct. SE5 . . . . .5B 120
Ridgdale St. E3 . . . . .1E 47
Ridgewell Cl. N1 . . . . .3C 18
Ridgmount Gdns. WC1 . . . . . .5D 37
Ridgmount Pl. WC1 . . . . .1D 59
Ridgmount St. WC1 . . . . .1D 59
Ridgwell Rd. E16 . . . . .1C 70
Riding Ho. St. W1 . . . . .2A 58
Ridley Ho. SW1 . . . . .2E 115
Rifle Ct. SE11 . . . . .2E 139
Rifle St. E14 . . . . .2A 70
Riga M. E1 . . . . .3D 65
Rigden St. E14 . . . . .4F 69
Riley Ho. E3 . . . . .4D 47
　SW10 . . . . .4D 133
Riley Rd. SE1 . . . . .1A 120
Riley St. SW10 . . . . .3D 133
Rill Ho. SE5 . . . . .5E 141
Rima Ho. SW3 . . . . .2D 133
Ring, The SW7 . . . . .5E 83
　W2 . . . . .5F 55
Ring Ct. SE1 . . . . .4F 89
Ring Ho. E1 . . . . .5B 66
Ringlet Cl. E16 . . . . .2F 73
Ring Rd. W12 . . . . .1B 78
　　　　　(not continuous)
Ringsfield Ho. SE17 . . . . . . .1C 140
Ringwood Gdns. E14 . . . . . .3E 125
Ripley Bldgs. SE1 . . . . .4A 90
Ripley Ho. SW1 . . . . .2B 136
Ripley Rd. E16 . . . . .3B 74
Ripley's Believe it or Not . . .1D 87
　　　(within London Pavilion)
Ripplevale Gro. N1 . . . . .2C 16
Risborough Ho. NW8 . . . . . .4A 34
Risborough St. SE1 . . . . . . .4A 90
Risdon Ho. SE16 . . . . .5C 94
Risdon St. SE16 . . . . .5B 94
Riseholme Ct. E9 . . . . .5B 4
Risinghill St. N1 . . . . .1D 17
Rising Sun Ct. EC1 . . . . .2A 62
Rita Rd. SW8 . . . . .3A 138

Ritchie Ho. E14 . . . . .4D 71
　SE16 . . . . .1B 122
Ritchie St. N1 . . . . .5E 17
Ritson Ho. N1 . . . . .4B 16
Riven Ct. W2 . . . . .4A 54
River Barge Cl. E14 . . . . . . .5C 98
River Ct. SE1 . . . . .1F 89
Riverfleet WC1 . . . . .2A 38
Riverford Ho. W2 . . . . .2D 53
Riverlight Development
　SW8 . . . . .3C 136
River Lodge SW1 . . . . .2C 136
Rivermead Ho. E9 . . . . .2A 4
River Pl. N1 . . . . .2B 18
Riverside E3 . . . . .3E 25
　SE7 . . . . .2F 129
　SW11 . . . . .4A 134
　WC1 . . . . .2A 38
Riverside Ct. SW8 . . . . .2E 137
Riverside Gdns. W6 . . . . . . .5A 106
Riverside Ho. N1 . . . . .1B 18
Riverside Mans. E1 . . . . .2B 94
Riverside Rd. E15 . . . . .1C 48
Riverside Wlk. SE10 . . . . . . .2F 127
　　　　　(Morden Wharf Rd.)
　SE10 . . . . .5E 99
　　　　　(Tunnel Av.)
Riverside Wharf E3 . . . . .3E 25
River St. EC1 . . . . .2D 39
River St. M. EC1 . . . . .2D 39
River Ter. WC2 . . . . .1B 88
Riverton Cl. W9 . . . . .3C 30
Riverview Ct. E14 . . . . .2D 125
River Vw. Hgts. SE16 . . . . . .4D 93
Riverwalk Ho. SW1 . . . . . . .5F 115
River Way SE10 . . . . .1B 128
Rivet Ho. SE1 . . . . .5C 120
Riviera Ct. E1 . . . . .3D 93
Rivington Pl. EC2 . . . . .3A 42
Rivington St. EC2 . . . . .3F 41
Rivington Wlk. E8 . . . . .3E 21
Roach Rd. E3 . . . . .1D 25
Roan St. SE10 . . . . .3B 148
Robert Adam St. W1 . . . . . . .3D 57
Roberta St. E2 . . . . .2D 43
Robert Bell Ho. SE16 . . . . . .3D 121
Robert Cl. W9 . . . . .5C 32
Robert Dashwood Way
　SE17 . . . . .4B 118
Robert Gentry Ho. W14 . . . .1A 130
Robert Jones Ho. SE16 . . . . .3D 121
Robert Lowe Cl. SE14 . . . . .4E 145
Robert Morton Ho. NW8 . . . .3C 10
Robert Owen Ho. E2 . . . . . .2C 42
Roberts Cl. SE16 . . . . .5E 95
Roberts Ct. N1 . . . . .4A 18
Roberts M. SW1 . . . . .2D 113
Robertson Rd. E16 . . . . .2E 73
Roberts Pl. EC1 . . . . .4E 39
Robert St. E16 . . . . .3F 105
　NW1 . . . . .3A 36
　WC2 . . . . .1A 88
Robert Sutton Ho. E1 . . . . . .4B 66
Robeson St. E3 . . . . .1C 68
Robin Ct. E14 . . . . .1C 126
　SE16 . . . . .3D 121
Robin Cres. E6 . . . . .1E 75
Robin Hood Ct. EC4 . . . . . . .3E 61
Robin Hood Gdns. E14 . . . . .5B 70
　　　　　(not continuous)
Robin Hood La. E14 . . . . . . .5C 70
Robin Ho. NW8 . . . . .1F 33
Robin Howard Dance Theatre
　. . . . . .3E 37

Robinson Ct. N1 . . . . .3A 18
Robinson Ho. E14 . . . . .2D 69
W10 . . . . .4D 51
Robinson Rd. E2 . . . . .1B 44
Robinson St. SW3 . . . . . . .2B 134
Robson Cl. E6 . . . . .3F 75
Roby Ho. EC1 . . . . .4B 40
Rochdale Way SE8 . . . . . . .4D 147
(not continuous)
Roche Ho. E14 . . . . .5C 68
Rochelle St. E2 . . . . .3B 42
(not continuous)
Rochemont Wlk. E8 . . . . . . .4D 21
Rochester Ct. E2 . . . . .4F 43
NW1 . . . . .1C 14
Rochester Ho. SE1 . . . . .5D 91
SE15 . . . . .3C 144
Rochester M. NW1 . . . . . . .1C 14
Rochester Pl. NW1 . . . . . . .1B 14
Rochester Rd. NW1 . . . . . . .1B 14
Rochester Row SW1 . . . . . .3C 114
Rochester Sq. NW1 . . . . . . .1C 14
Rochester St. SW1 . . . . . . .2D 115
Rochester Ter. NW1 . . . . . . .1B 14
Rochester Wlk. SE1 . . . . . . .2D 91
Rochford Wlk. E8 . . . . .1E 21
Rochfort Ho. SE18 . . . . . . .1B 146
Rockfield Ho. SE10 . . . . . . .2B 148
Rock Gro. Way SE16 . . . . . .3E 121
(not continuous)
Rockingham St. SE1 . . . . . .2B 118
Rockley Ct. W14 . . . . .5D 79
Rockley Rd. W14 . . . . .4D 79
Rockwood Pl. W12 . . . . .4C 78
Rocliffe St. N1 . . . . .1A 40
Rocque Ho. SW6 . . . . .4B 130
Rodborough Ct. W9 . . . . . . .5D 31
Roderick Ho. SE16 . . . . . . .3B 122
Rodin Ct. N1 . . . . .4F 17
Roding Ho. N1 . . . . .4D 17
Roding M. E1 . . . . .2E 93
Roding Rd. E6 . . . . .1F 77
Rodmarton St. W1 . . . . .2C 56
Rodmell WC1 . . . . .3A 38
Rodmere St. SE10 . . . . . . .5A 128
Rodney Ct. W9 . . . . .4C 32
Rodney Ho. E14 . . . . .4F 125
N1 . . . . .1C 38
SW1 . . . . .1C 136
W11 . . . . .5D 53
Rodney Pl. SE17 . . . . .3C 118
Rodney Point SE16 . . . . . . .5B 96
Rodney Rd. SE17 . . . . .3C 118
(not continuous)
Rodney St. N1 . . . . .5C 16
Roebourne Way E16 . . . . . .3D 105
Roffey St. E14 . . . . .5B 98
Roger Dowley Ct. E2 . . . . . .5B 22
Rogers Ct. E14 . . . . .1D 97
Rogers Est. E2 . . . . .3C 44
(not continuous)
Rogers Ho. SW1 . . . . .3E 115
Rogers Rd. E16 . . . . .3C 72
Roger St. WC1 . . . . .5C 38
Rohere Ho. EC1 . . . . .2B 40
Rokeby Ho. WC1 . . . . .5B 38
Rokeby St. E15 . . . . .3E 27
Roland Gdns. SW7 . . . . . . .5C 110
Roland Ho. SW7 . . . . .5C 110
Roland Mans. SW7 . . . . . . .4C 110
Roland M. E1 . . . . .1D 67
Roland Way SE17 . . . . .1E 141
SW7 . . . . .5C 110
Rollins St. SE15 . . . . .2C 144

Rolls Bldgs. EC4 . . . . .3D 61
Rolls Pas. EC4 . . . . .3D 61
Rolls Rd. SE1 . . . . .5C 120
Rolt St. SE8 . . . . .2F 145
(not continuous)
Roman Ho. EC2 . . . . .2C 62
Roman Rd. E2 . . . . .3B 44
E3 . . . . .1F 45
Roman Way N7 . . . . .1C 16
SE15 . . . . .5B 144
Roman Way Ind. Est. N7 . . .1C 16
Romford Rd. E15 . . . . .1F 27
Romford St. E1 . . . . .2E 65
Romilly Ho. W11 . . . . .1F 79
Romilly St. W1 . . . . .5E 59
Romney Cl. SE14 . . . . .5C 144
Romney Ct. W12 . . . . .4C 78
Romney Ho. SW1 . . . . .2E 115
Romney M. W1 . . . . .1D 57
Romney Rd. SE10 . . . . .3C 148
Romney St. SW1 . . . . .2E 115
Ronald Buckingham Ct.
    SE16 . . . . .4C 94
Ronald St. E1 . . . . .4C 66
Rood La. EC3 . . . . .5F 63
Roof Ter. Apartments, The
    EC1 . . . . .5A 40
(off Gt. Sutton St.)
Rooke Way SE10 . . . . .5B 128
Rook Wlk. E6 . . . . .3F 75
Ropemaker Rd. SE16 . . . . . .1F 123
Ropemaker's Flds. E14 . . . .1B 96
Ropemaker St. EC2 . . . . . . .1D 63
Roper La. SE1 . . . . .4A 92
Ropers Orchard SW3 . . . . .3F 133
Ropery St. E3 . . . . .5B 46
Rope St. SE16 . . . . .3F 123
Rope Wlk. Gdns. E1 . . . . . . .3E 65
Ropewalk M. E8 . . . . .2D 21
Ropley St. E2 . . . . .1D 43
Rosalind Ho. N1 . . . . .1A 42
Rosaline Rd. SW6 . . . . .5A 130
Rosaline Ter. SW6 . . . . .5A 130
Rosa Parks Ho. SE17 . . . . .3C 118
Rosary Gdns. SW7 . . . . . . .4B 110
Rosaville Rd. SW6 . . . . .5B 130
Roscoe St. EC1 . . . . .5C 40
(not continuous)
Roscoe St. Est. EC1 . . . . . . .5C 40
Rose All. EC2 . . . . .2A 64
SE1 . . . . .2C 90
Rose & Crown Ct. EC2 . . . . .3B 62
Rose & Crown Yd. SW1 . . . .3C 86
Rose Apartments SE11 . . . . .3E 139
Rosebank Gdns. E3 . . . . . . .1A 46
Rosebank Wlk. NW1 . . . . . . .1E 15
Rosebay Ho. E3 . . . . .1E 69
Roseberry Mans. N1 . . . . . .3F 15
Roseberry St. SE16 . . . . . . .4F 121
Rosebery Av. EC1 . . . . .5D 39
Rosebery Ct. EC1 . . . . .4D 39
W1 . . . . .2F 85
Rosebery Ho. E2 . . . . .5C 22
Rosebery Sq. EC1 . . . . .5D 39
Rose Ct. E1 . . . . .2B 64
E8 . . . . .1C 20
N1 . . . . .4F 17
SE8 . . . . .3E 123
Rosedale Ter. W6 . . . . .2A 106
Rosefield Gdns. E14 . . . . . .5D 69
Roseford Ct. W12 . . . . .5D 79
Rosegate Ho. E3 . . . . .1C 46

Rosehart M. W11 . . . . .4D 53
Rosekey Ct. SE8 . . . . .5C 146
Rosemary Branch Theatre . . 3E 19
Rosemary Ct. SE8 . . . . .2B 146
SE15 . . . . .5A 142
Rosemary Dr. E14 . . . . .4D 71
Rosemary Ho. N1 . . . . .4E 19
Rosemary Rd. SE15 . . . . . . .4C 142
Rosemary St. N1 . . . . .3E 19
Rosemoor St. SW3 . . . . . . .4B 112
Roserton St. E14 . . . . .5B 98
Rose Sq. SW3 . . . . .4E 111
Rose Stapleton Ter.
    SE1 . . . . .2A 120
Rose St. EC4 . . . . .3A 62
WC2 . . . . .5F 59
(not continuous)
Rose Theatre, The 2C 90
Rosetta Cl. SW8 . . . . .5A 138
Rosewood Ct. E11 . . . . .1E 7
Rosewood Ho. SW8 . . . . . . .2A 138
Rosher Cl. E15 . . . . .2D 27
Roslin Ho. E1 . . . . .5D 67
Rosmead Rd. W11 . . . . .5A 52
Rosoman Pl. EC1 . . . . .4E 39
Rosoman St. EC1 . . . . .3E 39
Ross Apartments E16 . . . . . .5D 73
Rosscourt Mans. SW1 . . . . .1A 114
Rossendale Way NW1 . . . . .2C 14
Rossetti Ct. WC1 . . . . .1D 59
Rossetti Gdn. Mans.
    SW3 . . . . .2B 134
Rossetti Ho. SW1 . . . . .4E 115
Rossetti M. NW8 . . . . .4E 11
Rossetti Rd. SE16 . . . . .5F 121
Rossetti Studios SW3 . . . . .2A 134
Ross Ho. E1 . . . . .3A 94
Rosslyn Mans. NW6 . . . . . . .1C 10
Rossmore Cl. NW1 . . . . .5A 34
Rossmore Ct. NW1 . . . . .4B 34
Rossmore Rd. NW1 . . . . . . .5A 34
Ross Way E14 . . . . .4A 68
Roswell Apartments E3 . . . .1C 68
(off Joseph St.)
Rotary St. SE1 . . . . .1F 117
Rothay NW1 . . . . .2A 36
Rothbury Cotts. SE10 . . . . .4A 128
Rothbury Rd. E9 . . . . .1C 24
Rotheley Ho. E9 . . . . .2C 22
Rotherfield Ct. N1 . . . . .2D 19
(not continuous)
Rotherfield St. N1 . . . . .2B 18
Rotherham Wlk. SE1 . . . . . .3F 89
ROTHERHITHE 5B 94
Rotherhithe Bus. Est.
    SE16 . . . . .4B 122
Rotherhithe New Rd.
    SE16 . . . . .1E 143
Rotherhithe Old Rd.
    SE16 . . . . .3D 123
Rotherhithe St. SE16 . . . . . .4B 94
Rotherhithe Tunnel
    SE16 . . . . .3D 95
Rotherwick Ho. E1 . . . . .1D 93
Rothery St. N1 . . . . .3A 18
Rothery Ter. SW9 . . . . .5F 139
Rothesay Ct. SE11 . . . . .3D 139
Rothley Ct. NW8 . . . . .4D 33
Rothsay St. SE1 . . . . .1F 119
Rothsay Wlk. E14 . . . . .3E 125
Rothwell St. NW1 . . . . .3C 12
Rotten Row SW1 . . . . .4B 84
SW7 . . . . .4E 83
Rotterdam Dr. E14 . . . . .2C 126

Rouel Rd. SE16 ....2D **121**
   (Dockley Rd.)
  SE16 ....3D **121**
   (Southwark Pk. Rd.)
Roundhouse, The 1D **13**
Roundhouse La. E20 ......5B **6**
Roundwood Ct. E2 ....3E **45**
Rounton Rd. E3 ....3E **47**
Roupell St. SE1 ....3E **89**
Rousden St. NW1 ....2B **14**
Routh St. E6 ....2C **76**
Rover Ho. N1 ....4A **20**
Rowallan Rd. SW6 ....5A **130**
Rowan Ct. SE15 ....4B **142**
Rowan Ho. E3 ....3B **24**
  SE16 ....5D **95**
   (off Woodland Cres.)
Rowan Lodge W8 ....2F **109**
Rowan Rd. W6 ....4D **107**
Rowan Ter. W6 ....3D **107**
Rowan Wlk. W10 ....4F **29**
Rowcross St. SE1 ....5B **120**
Rowington Cl. W2 ....1F **53**
Rowland Hill Ho. SE1 ....4F **89**
Rowley Ho. SE8 ....1D **147**
Rowley Way NW8 ....3A **10**
Rowse Cl. E15 ....3C **26**
Roxburghe Mans. W8 ....5A **82**
Roxby Pl. SW6 ....2E **131**
Roxford Ho. E3 ....4A **48**
Roxwell NW1 ....1F **13**
Royal Academy of Arts
  (Burlington House) ...1B 86
Royal Academy of Music Mus.
  ....5E 35
Royal Air Force Memorial ...3A 88
Royal Albert Hall 5D 83
Royal Albert Rdbt. E16 .....5F **75**
Royal Albert Way E16 .....5C **74**
Royal Arc. W1 ....1B **86**
Royal Archer SE14 .....5E **145**
Royal Av. SW3 ....5B **112**
Royal Av. Ho. SW3 ......5B **112**
Royal Belgrave Ho. SW1 ...4A **114**
Royal Cl. SE8 ....2B **146**
Royal College of Art 5C 82
Royal College of Music ...1D 111
Royal College of Obstetricians
  & Gynaecologists 4B 34
Royal College of Physicians
  ....4A 36
Royal College of Physicians Mus.
  ....4A 36
Royal College of Surgeons
  ....3C 60
Royal Coll. St. NW1 ....1B **14**
Royal Connaught Apartments
  E16 ....2E **103**
Royal Ct. EC3 ....4E **63**
  SE16 ....1B **124**
Royal Courts of Justice 4D 61
Royal Court Theatre 4D 113
Royal Cres. W11 ....4E **79**
Royal Cres. M. W11 ......4E **79**
Royal Docks Rd. E6 ......2F **77**
Royal Exchange 4E 63
Royal Exchange Av. EC3 ...4E **63**
Royal Exchange Bldgs.
  EC3 ....4E **63**
Royal Festival Hall 3C 88
Royal Fusiliers Mus. 1B 92
Royal Geographical Society
  ....5D 83
Royal Hill SE10 ....4C **148**

Royal Hill Ct. SE10 ......4B **148**
Royal Holloway
  (University of London)
  Gower Street 1E 59
Royal Hospital Chelsea Mus.
  ....1D 135
Royal Hospital Rd. SW3 ...3B **134**
Royal Institution Mus. 1B 86
Royal Langford Apartments
  NW6 ....5F 9
   (off Greville Rd.)
Royal London Bldgs.
  SE15 ....2F **143**
Royal London Hospital
  Archives & Museum 2F 65
Royal Mews, The 1A 114
Royal M. SW1 ....1A **114**
Royal Mint Ct. EC3 ......1C **92**
Royal Mint Pl. E1 ....5C **64**
Royal Mint St. E1 ....5C **64**
Royal Naval Pl. SE14 .....4B **146**
Royal Oak Ct. N1 ....2F **41**
Royal Oak Yd. SE1 ......5F **91**
Royal Observatory Greenwich
  ....4E 149
Royal Opera Arc. SW1 ....2D **87**
Royal Opera House 4A 60
Royal Pde. SW6 ....4A **130**
Royal Pl. SE10 ....5C **148**
Royal Rd. E16 ....4D **75**
  SE17 ....2F **139**
Royal St. SE1 ....1C **116**
Royal Twr. Lodge E1 ......1D **93**
Royalty Mans. W1 ......4D **59**
Royalty M. W1 ....4D **59**
Royalty Studios W11 .....4A **52**
Royal Veterinary College
  Camden Town 4D 15
Royal Victoria Docks
  Watersports Cen. 1D 101
Royal Victoria Pl. E16 ....2F **101**
Royal Victoria Sq. E16 ....1F **101**
Royal Victor Pl. E3 ......5E **23**
Royal Westminster Lodge
  SW1 ....3D **115**
Royle Bldg. N1 ....5B **18**
Royley Ho. EC1 ....4C **40**
Roy Sq. E14 ....5A **68**
Royston Ct. *W8 ....2E 81*
   (off Kensington Chu. St.)
Royston Ho. SE15 ......3F **143**
Royston St. E2 ....1C **44**
Rozel Ct. N1 ....3F **19**
Rubicon Ct. N1 ....3F **15**
Ruby Ct. E15 ....3C **26**
Ruby St. SE15 ....2F **143**
Ruby Triangle SE15 ......2F **143**
Ruckholt Rd. E10 ....1E **5**
Rudbeck Ho. SE15 ......4D **143**
Rudge Ho. SE16 ....1E **121**
Rudgwick Ter. NW8 ......4A **12**
Rudolf Pl. SW8 ....3A **138**
Rudolph Rd. NW6 ......1E **31**
Rudstone Ho. E3 ....2F **47**
Rudyard Ct. SE1 ....5E **91**
Rufford St. N1 ....3A **16**
Rufford St. M. N1 ....2A **16**
Rufus Ho. SE1 ....1B **120**
Rufus St. N1 ....3F **41**
Rugby Mans. W14 ......3A **108**
Rugby St. WC1 ....5B **38**
Rugg St. E14 ....5D **69**
Rugless Ho. E14 ....5B **98**
Rugmere NW1 ....1E **13**

Rumball Ho. SE5 ....5F **141**
Rumbold Rd. SW6 ......5A **132**
Rum Cl. E1 ....1B **94**
Rumford Ho. SE1 ....2B **118**
Runacres Ct. SE17 ......1B **140**
Runcorn Pl. W11 ....5F **51**
Runnymede Ho. E9 ......1A **4**
Rupack St. SE16 ....5B **94**
Rupert Ct. W1 ....5D **59**
Rupert Ho. SE11 ....4E **117**
  SW5 ....4D **109**
Rupert Rd. NW6 ....1C **30**
Rupert St. W1 ....5D **59**
Ruscoe Rd. E16 ....3B **72**
Ruscombe NW1 ....4A **14**
Rushcutters Ct. SE16 ....3A **124**
Rushmead E2 ....3F **43**
Rushmore Ho. W14 ......2A **108**
Rushton St. N1 ....5E **19**
Rushworth St. SE1 ......4A **90**
Ruskin Ho. SW1 ....4E **115**
Ruskin Mans. W14 ......3A **130**
Russell Chambers WC1 ...2A **60**
Russell Ct. SW1 ....3C **86**
  WC1 ....5F **37**
Russell Flint Ho. *E16 .....2A 102*
   (off Pankhurst Av.)
Russell Gdns. W14 ......1F **109**
Russell Gdns. M. W14 ....5F **79**
Russell Gro. SW9 ......5E **139**
Russell Ho. E14 ....4E **69**
  SW1 ....5B **114**
Russell Lodge SE1 ......1D **119**
Russell Mans. WC1 ......1A **60**
Russell Pl. SE16 ....2F **123**
Russell Rd. E16 ....3E **73**
  W14 ....1A **108**
Russell Sq. WC1 ....5F **37**
Russell Sq. Mans. WC1 ...1A **60**
Russell St. WC2 ....5A **60**
Russell's Wharf Flats W10 ..4B **30**
Russia Dock Rd. SE16 ....3A **96**
Russia La. E2 ....5B **22**
Russia Row EC2 ....4C **62**
Russia Wlk. SE16 ....5E **95**
Rustic Wlk. E16 ....3F **73**
Ruston M. W11 ....4F **51**
Ruston St. E3 ....3C **24**
Rust Sq. SE5 ....4D **141**
Ruth Ct. E3 ....1A **46**
Rutherford Ho. E1 ....5F **43**
Rutherford St. SW1 ......3D **115**
Ruth Ho. W10 ....4F **29**
Ruthven St. E9 ....3D **23**
Rutland Ct. SW7 ....5A **84**
Rutland Gdns. SW7 ......5A **84**
Rutland Gdns. M. SW7 ....5A **84**
Rutland Ga. SW7 ....5A **84**
Rutland Ga. M. SW7 ......5F **83**
Rutland Gro. W6 ....5A **106**
Rutland Ho. W8 ....2F **109**
Rutland M. NW8 ....4A **10**
Rutland M. E. SW7 ......1A **112**
Rutland M. Sth. SW7 .....1F **111**
Rutland M. W. SW7 ......1F **111**
Rutland Pl. EC1 ....1A **62**
Rutland Rd. E9 ....3D **23**
Rutland St. SW7 ....1A **112**
Rutley Cl. SE17 ....2F **139**
Rydal Water NW1 ....3B **36**
Ryde Ho. NW6 ....3D **9**
Ryder Ct. SW1 ....2C **86**
Ryder Dr. SE16 ....1F **143**
Ryder Ho. E1 ....4C **44**

Ryder's Ter. NW8 . . . . .5B 10
Ryder St. SW1 . . . . .2C 86
Ryder Yd. SW1 . . . . .2C 86
Rydon St. N1 . . . . .3C 18
Rydston Cl. N7 . . . . .1B 16
Rye Ho. SE16 . . . . .4C 94
  SW1 . . . . .5F 113
Rye Mans. E20 . . . . .3B 6
Rylston Rd. SW6 . . . . .3B 130
Rymill St. E16 . . . . .3D 105
Rysbrack St. SW3 . . . . .1B 112

S

Saatchi Gallery 5C 112
Sabella Ct. E3 . . . . .1C 46
Sable Ho. E20 . . . . .3A 6
Sable St. N1 . . . . .1A 18
Sackville St. W1 . . . . .1C 86
Saddlers Ho. E20 . . . . .3C 6
Saddlers M. SW8 . . . . .5A 138
Saddle Yd. W1 . . . . .2F 85
Sadler Ho. E3 . . . . .2A 48
  EC1 . . . . .2F 39
Sadler Pl. E9 . . . . .3A 4
Sadlers Ct. SE1 . . . . .1F 119
Sadler's Wells Theatre 2E 39
Saffron Av. E14 . . . . .5D 71
Saffron Ct. E15 . . . . .3F 7
Saffron Hill EC1 . . . . .5E 39
Saffron St. EC1 . . . . .1E 61
Saffron Wharf SE1 . . . . . . .4C 92
Sage Cl. E6 . . . . .2B 76
Sage St. E1 . . . . .5B 66
Sage Way WC1 . . . . .3B 38
Saigasso Cl. E16 . . . . .4D 75
Sailacre Ho. SE10 . . . . . . .5B 128
Sail Ct. E14 . . . . .5E 71
Sail St. SE11 . . . . .3C 116
Sainsbury Wing 1E 87
St Agnes Cl. E9 . . . . .3B 22
St Agnes Ho. E3 . . . . .1C 46
St Agnes Pl. SE11 . . . . .3E 139
St Agnes Well EC1 . . . . .4E 41
St Albans Ct. EC2 . . . . .3C 62
St Alban's Gro. W8 . . . . . . .1A 110
St Albans Mans. W8 . . . . . .1A 110
St Albans Pl. N1 . . . . .4F 17
St Alban's St. SW1 . . . . . . .1D 87
St Albans Studios W8 . . . . .1A 110
St Alfege Pas. SE10 . . . . . . .3B 148
St Alphage Gdn. EC2 . . . . . .2C 62
St Alphage Highwalk EC2 . . .2C 62
St Andrews Chambers W1 . . .2C 58
St Andrews Cl. SE16 . . . . . .1A 144
St Andrew's Hill EC4 . . . . . .5A 62
  (not continuous)
St Andrews Ho. SE16 . . . . . .2A 122
St Andrews Mans. W1 . . . . .2D 57
  W14 . . . . .2A 130
St Andrew's Pl. NW1 . . . . . .4A 36
St Andrew's Rd. W14 . . . . . .2A 130
St Andrews Sq. W11 . . . . . .4F 51
St Andrew St. EC4 . . . . .2E 61
St Andrews Way E3 . . . . . . .4F 47
St Andrew's Wharf SE1 . . . .4C 92
St Anne's Ct. NW6 . . . . .4A 8
  W1 . . . . .4D 59
St Anne's Flats NW1 . . . . . .2D 37
St Anne's Pas. E14 . . . . . . .4B 68
St Anne's Row E14 . . . . . . .4C 68
St Anne's Trad. Est. E14 . . . .4C 68
St Anne St. E14 . . . . .4C 68

St Ann's Ho. WC1 . . . . .3D 39
St Ann's La. SW1 . . . . .2E 115
St Ann's Rd. W11 . . . . .1E 79
St Ann's St. SW1 . . . . .1E 115
St Ann's Ter. NW8 . . . . .5E 11
St Ann's Vs. W11 . . . . .3E 79
St Anselm's Pl. W1 . . . . .5F 57
St Anthony's Cl. E1 . . . . .2D 93
  E9 . . . . .5C 4
St Anthony's Flats NW1 . . . . .1D 37
St Aubins Ct. N1 . . . . .3E 19
St Augustine's Ct. SE1 . . . . .5F 121
St Augustine's Ho. NW1 . . . .2D 37
St Augustine's Mans.
  SW1 . . . . .4C 114
St Augustine's Rd. NW1 . . . .1D 15
St Barnabas M. SW1 . . . . . .5E 113
St Barnabas St. SW1 . . . . . .5E 113
St Bartholomew's Hospital Mus.
  .2A 62
St Benet's Pl. EC3 . . . . .5E 63
St Bernards Ho. E14 . . . . . .1B 126
St Botolph Row EC3 . . . . . . .4B 64
St Botolphs E1 . . . . .3B 64
St Botolph St. EC3 . . . . .3B 64
St Brelades Ct. N1 . . . . .3E 19
St Bride's Av. EC4 . . . . .4F 61
St Bride's Crypt Mus. 4F 61
St Bride's Ho. E3 . . . . .1D 47
St Bride's Pas. EC4 . . . . . . .4F 61
St Bride St. EC4 . . . . .3F 61
St Catherine's Apartments
  E3 . . . . .2F 47
St Catherines M. SW3 . . . . . .3B 112
St Chad's Pl. WC1 . . . . .2A 38
St Chad's St. WC1 . . . . .2A 38
  (not continuous)
St Charles Pl. W10 . . . . .2F 51
St Charles Sq. W10 . . . . . . .1E 51
St Chloe's Ho. E3 . . . . .1D 47
St Christopher's Ho. NW1 . . .1C 36
St Christopher's Pl. W1 . . . . .3E 57
St Clair Ho. E3 . . . . .3C 46
St Clare St. EC3 . . . . .4B 64
St Clements Ct. EC4 . . . . . . .5E 63
  SE14 . . . . .2D 145
  W11 . . . . .1E 79
St Clements Ho. E1 . . . . .2B 64
St Clement's La. WC2 . . . . . .4B 60
St Clements St. N7 . . . . .1D 17
St Columba's Ct. E15 . . . . . .1F 7
St Columb's Ho. W10 . . . . . .2A 52
St Cross St. EC1 . . . . .1E 61
St Davids Cl. SE16 . . . . .1A 144
St Davids M. E3 . . . . .3A 46
  (off Morgan St.)
St Davids Sq. E14 . . . . .5A 126
St Dunstan's All. EC3 . . . . . .1F 91
St Dunstan's Ct. EC4 . . . . . .4E 61
St Dunstans Hill EC3 . . . . . .1F 91
St Dunstan's La. EC3 . . . . . .1F 91
St Dunstans M. E1 . . . . .2F 67
St Dunstan's Rd. W6 . . . . . .5E 107
St Edmund's Cl. NW8 . . . . . .4B 12
St Edmund's Ct. NW8 . . . . . .4B 12
St Edmund's Ter. NW8 . . . . .5A 12
St Elmos Rd. SE16 . . . . .5F 95
St Ermin's Hill SW1 . . . . . . .1D 115
St Ervan's Rd. W10 . . . . .1A 52
St Eugene Ct. NW6 . . . . .4A 8
St Francis' Ho. NW1 . . . . . . .1D 37
St Frideswide's M. E14 . . . . .4B 70
St Gabriel's Cl. E14 . . . . . . .2F 69
St George's Bldgs. SE1 . . . .2F 117

St George's Cathedral 2A 36
St George's Cir. SE1 . . . . . .1F 117
St Georges Ct. EC4 . . . . . . .3F 61
  SE1 . . . . .2F 117
  SW1 . . . . .5B 114
  SW3 . . . . .3F 111
  SW7 . . . . .1B 110
St George's Dr. SW1 . . . . . .4A 114
St George's Flds. W2 . . . . . .4A 56
St George's Ho. NW1 . . . . . .1D 37
St George's La. EC3 . . . . . . .5E 63
St George's Leisure Cen. . . .5A 66
St George's Mans. SW1 . . . .5E 115
St George's M. NW1 . . . . . . .2C 12
  SE1 . . . . .1E 117
  SE8 . . . . .3B 124
St George's RC Cathedral
  .1E 117
St George's Rd. SE1 . . . . . .1E 117
St Georges Sq. E14 . . . . . . .5F 67
  SE8 . . . . .3B 124
  (not continuous)
  SW1 . . . . .5D 115
St George's Sq. M. SW1 . . . .1D 137
St George's Ter. NW1 . . . . . .3C 12
  SE15 . . . . .4D 143
St George St. W1 . . . . .4A 58
St George's Way SE15 . . . . .3F 141
St George's Wharf SE1 . . . . .4C 92
St George Wharf SW8 . . . . .2F 137
St Giles Cir. W1 . . . . .3E 59
St Giles High St. WC2 . . . . .3E 59
St Giles Pas. WC2 . . . . .4E 59
St Giles Rd. SE5 . . . . .5F 141
St Giles Ter. EC2 . . . . .2C 62
St Gilles Ho. E2 . . . . .1D 45
St Helena Ho. WC1 . . . . .3D 39
St Helena Rd. SE16 . . . . . . .4D 123
St Helena St. WC1 . . . . .3D 39
St Helen's Gdns. W10 . . . . .2D 51
St Helen's Pl. EC3 . . . . .2F 63
St Helier Ct. N1 . . . . .3F 19
  SE16 . . . . .4D 95
St Hilda's Wharf E1 . . . . . . .2B 94
St Hubert's Ho. E14 . . . . . . .1D 125
St James SE14 . . . . .5A 146
St James Ct. E2 . . . . .3E 43
  SW1 . . . . .1C 114
St James Hall N1 . . . . .4B 18
St James Ind. M. SE1 . . . . . .1E 143
St James Mans. NW6 . . . . . .1E 9
  SE1 . . . . .1D 117
St James M. E14 . . . . .2C 126
St James Residences W1 . . .5D 59
ST JAMES'S 3C 86
St James's App. EC2 . . . . . .5F 41
St James's Av. E2 . . . . .5C 22
St James's Chambers
  SW1 . . . . .2C 86
St James's Cl. NW8 . . . . . . .4B 12
St James's Gdns. W11 . . . . .2F 79
  (not continuous)
St James's Ho. SE1 . . . . . . .4E 121
St James's Mkt. SW1 . . . . . .1D 87
St James's Palace 4C 86
St James's Park 4D 87
St James's Pas. EC3 . . . . . . .4A 64
St James's Pl. SW1 . . . . .3B 86
St James's Rd. SE1 . . . . . . .5E 121
  SE16 . . . . .1E 121
St James's Sq. SW1 . . . . . . .2C 86
St James's St. SW1 . . . . .2B 86
St James's Ter. NW8 . . . . . . .5B 12
St James's Ter. M. NW8 . . . .4B 12

St James's Wlk. EC1 . . . . . . .4F 39
St James Theatre 1B 114
St Joan's Ho. NW1 . . . . . . .2D 37
St John's Cl. SW6 . . . . . . .4D 131
St John's Concert Hall 2F 115
St Johns Ct. E1 . . . . .3F 93
  SW10 . . . . .4C 132
  W6 . . . . .3A 106
St John's Est. N1 . . . . .1E 41
  SE1 . . . . .4B 92
St John's Gdns. W11 . . . . .1A 80
St John's Gate 5F 39
St Johns Ho. E14 . . . . . . .3C 126
  SE17 . . . . .2D 141
St John's La. EC1 . . . . .5F 39
St John's Lodge NW3 . . . . .2F 11
St John's Mans. EC1 . . . . . .2F 39
St John's M. W11 . . . . . . .4D 53
St John's Path EC1 . . . . . . .5F 39
St John's Pl. EC1 . . . . .5F 39
St John's Rd. E16 . . . . . . .3D 73
St John's Sq. EC1 . . . . .5F 39
St John's Ter. W10 . . . . . . .4E 29
St John St. EC1 . . . . .1E 39
St John's Vs. W8 . . . . .2A 110
ST JOHN'S WOOD 1E 33
St John's Wood Ct. NW8 . . .3E 33
St John's Wood High St.
  NW8 . . . . .1E 33
St John's Wood Pk. NW8 . . .3D 11
St John's Wood Rd. NW8 . . .4D 33
St John's Wood Ter. NW8 . . .5E 11
St Josephs Almshouses
  W6 . . . . .3E 107
St Joseph's Cl. W10 . . . . . .2A 52
St Joseph's Cotts. SW3 . . .4B 112
St Joseph's Flats NW1 . . . .2D 37
St Joseph's Ho. W6 . . . . . .3E 107
St Joseph's St. SW8 . . . . . .5A 136
St Jude's Rd. E2 . . . . .1A 44
St Julian's Rd. NW6 . . . . . . .2C 8
St Katharine Docks 1C 92
St Katharine's Pct. NW1 . . .5F 13
St Katharine's Way E1 . . . . .2C 92
  (not continuous)
St Katharine's Yacht Haven
  . . . . .1D 93
St Katherine's Row EC3 . . . .4A 64
St Katherines Wlk. W11 . . . .2E 79
St Lawrence Cotts. E14 . . . .2C 98
St Lawrence Ct. N1 . . . . . . .3E 19
St Lawrence Ho. SE1 . . . . .1A 120
St Lawrence St. E14 . . . . . .2C 98
St Lawrence Ter. W10 . . . . .1F 51
St Leonard M. N1 . . . . .5F 19
St Leonard's Ct. N1 . . . . . . .2E 41
St Leonard's Rd. E14 . . . . .2A 70
  (not continuous)
St Leonard's St. E3 . . . . . . .2A 48
St Leonard's Studios SW3 . .1B 134
St Leonard's Ter. SW3 . . . . .1B 134
St Loo Av. SW3 . . . . .2A 134
St Loo Ct. SW3 . . . . .2A 134
ST LUKE'S 4C 40
St Luke's Cl. EC1 . . . . .4C 40
St Lukes Ct. W11 . . . . .3C 52
St Luke's Est. EC1 . . . . . . .3D 41
St Lukes M. E14 . . . . .5E 97
  W11 . . . . .3B 52
St Luke's Rd. W11 . . . . . . .2C 52
St Luke's Sq. E16 . . . . .4C 72
St Luke's St. SW3 . . . . . . .5A 114
St Luke's Yd. W9 . . . . .1B 30
  (not continuous)

St Margarets Cl. EC2 . . . . . .3D 63
St Margarets Ct. SE1 . . . . . .3D 91
St Margaret's Ho. NW1 . . . .1D 37
  (off Polygon Rd.)
St Margaret's La. W8 . . . . . .2F 109
St Margaret's Rd. NW10 . . . .2B 28
St Margaret St. SW1 . . . . . .5F 87
St Mark's Cl. SE10 . . . . . . .5B 148
  W11 . . . . .4F 51
St Marks Ct. NW8 . . . . .1C 32
St Mark's Cres. NW1 . . . . . .3E 13
St Mark's Ga. E9 . . . . .2C 24
St Marks Gro. SW10 . . . . . .4A 132
St Marks Ho. SE17 . . . . . . .2D 141
St Marks Ind. Est. E16 . . . . .3D 103
St Mark's Pl. W11 . . . . .4A 52
St Mark's Rd. W10 . . . . . . .1D 51
  W11 . . . . .4F 51
St Mark's Sq. NW1 . . . . . . .4D 13
St Mark St. E1 . . . . .4C 64
St Martin-in-the-Fields Church
  . . . . .1F 87
St Martin's Almshouses
  NW1 . . . . .3B 14
St Martin's Cl. NW1 . . . . . . .3B 14
St Martins Ct. EC4 . . . . .3B 62
  N1 . . . . .3A 20
  WC2 . . . . .5F 59
St Martin's Courtyard WC2 . .5F 59
St Martin's Ho. NW1 . . . . . .2D 37
  (off Polygon Rd.)
St Martin's La. WC2 . . . . . . .5F 59
St Martin's Le-Grand EC1 . . .3B 62
St Martin's Pl. WC2 . . . . . . .1F 87
St Martin's St. WC2 . . . . . . .1E 87
  (not continuous)
St Martin's Theatre 5F 59
St Mary Abbot's Ct. W14 . . .2B 108
St Mary Abbot's Pl. W8 . . .2C 108
St Mary Abbot's Ter.
  W14 . . . . .2C 108
St Mary at Hill EC3 . . . . . . .1F 91
St Mary Axe EC3 . . . . .4F 63
St Marychurch St. SE16 . . . .4B 94
St Mary Graces Ct. E1 . . . . .5C 64
St Mary le-Park Ct.
  SW11 . . . . .5A 134
St Mary Newington Cl.
  SE17 . . . . .5A 120
St Mary's Ct. E3 . . . . .2F 47
St Mary's Est. SE16 . . . . . . .5B 94
St Mary's Flats NW1 . . . . . .2D 37
St Mary's Gdns. SE11 . . . . .3E 117
St Mary's Ga. W8 . . . . .2F 109
St Mary's Ho. N1 . . . . .3A 18
St Mary's Mans. W2 . . . . . .1D 55
St Mary's M. NW6 . . . . .2F 9
St Mary's Path E1 . . . . .3D 65
  N1 . . . . .3F 17
St Mary's Pl. W8 . . . . .2F 109
St Mary's Sq. W2 . . . . .1D 55
St Mary's Ter. W2 . . . . .1C 54
St Mary's Twr. EC1 . . . . . . .5C 40
St Mary's Wlk. SE11 . . . . . .3E 117
St Matthews Ct. SE1 . . . . . .2B 118
St Matthews Ho. SE17 . . . . .2D 141
St Matthew's Lodge NW1 . . .5C 14
St Matthew's Row E2 . . . . . .3D 43
St Matthew St. SW1 . . . . . .2D 115
St Michael's All. EC3 . . . . . .4E 63
St Michaels Cl. E16 . . . . . . .2D 75
St Michaels Ct. E14 . . . . . . .2B 70
  SE1 . . . . .5C 90
St Michael's Flats NW1 . . . .1D 37

St Michael's Gdns. W10 . . . .2F 51
St Michael's M. SW1 . . . . . .4D 113
St Michael's St. W2 . . . . . . .3E 55
St Mildred's Ct. EC2 . . . . . . .4D 63
St Nicholas' Flats NW1 . . . . .1D 37
St Nicholas Ho. SE8 . . . . . . .2E 147
St Olaf Ho. SE1 . . . . .2E 91
St Olaf's Rd. SW6 . . . . .5A 130
St Olaf Stairs SE1 . . . . .2E 91
St Olave's Ct. EC2 . . . . .4D 63
St Olave's Est. SE1 . . . . . . .4A 92
St Olave's Gdns. SE11 . . . . .3D 117
St Olaves Ho. SE11 . . . . . . .3D 117
St Olave's Mans. SE11 . . . . .3D 117
St Olav's Sq. SE16 . . . . . . .5B 94
St Oswald's Pl. SE11 . . . . . .5B 116
St Oswalds Studios SW6 . . .2D 131
St Oswulf St. SW1 . . . . .4E 115
St Owen Ho. SE1 . . . . .1A 120
ST PANCRAS 3F 37
St Pancras Commercial Cen.
  NW1 . . . . .3C 14
St Pancras Way NW1 . . . . . .1B 14
St Paul's All. EC4 . . . . .4A 62
  (off St Paul's Chyd.)
St Paul's Av. SE16 . . . . .2E 95
St Paul's Bldgs. EC1 . . . . . .4A 40
St Paul's Cathedral
  London 4B 62
St Paul's Chyd. EC4 . . . . . . .4A 62
St Pauls Courtyard SE8 . . . .4D 147
St Paul's Cres. NW1 . . . . . . .1E 15
  (not continuous)
St Paul's Dr. E15 . . . . .3D 7
St Paul's M. NW1 . . . . .1E 15
St Paul's Studios W14 . . . . .5F 107
St Pauls Ter. SE17 . . . . .2A 140
St Paul St. N1 . . . . .4B 18
  (not continuous)
St Pauls Vw. Apartments
  EC1 . . . . .3D 39
St Paul's Way E3 . . . . .2B 68
St Peter's All. EC3 . . . . .4E 63
St Peter's Av. E2 . . . . .1E 43
St Petersburgh M. W2 . . . . .5F 53
St Petersburgh Pl. W2 . . . . .5F 53
St Peter's Cen. E1 . . . . .2A 94
  (off Reardon St.)
St Peter's Chu. Ct. N1 . . . . .5A 18
St Peter's Cl. E2 . . . . .1E 43
St Peters Ct. E1 . . . . .4C 44
  WC1 . . . . .3A 38
St Peters Ho. SE17 . . . . . . .2D 141
  WC1 . . . . .3A 38
St Peters Pl. W9 . . . . .5F 31
St Peter's Sq. E2 . . . . .1E 43
St Peter's St. N1 . . . . .4A 18
St Peter's St. M. N1 . . . . . . .5A 18
St Peter's Ter. SW6 . . . . . . .5B 130
St Peter's Way N1 . . . . .2A 20
St Philip Ho. WC1 . . . . .3D 39
St Philip's Rd. E8 . . . . .1D 21
St Philip's Way N1 . . . . .3C 18
St Quintin Av. W10 . . . . .2C 50
St Quintin Gdns. W10 . . . . . .2C 50
St Quintin Vw. W10 . . . . . . .2B 50
St Richard's Ho. NW1 . . . . . .2D 37
St Saviour's Est. SE1 . . . . . .1B 120
St Saviour's Wharf SE1 . . . . .4C 92
  (Mill St.)
  SE1 . . . . .4C 92
  (off Shad Thames, Shad Thames)
St Stephen's Av. W12 . . . . . .3A 78
  (not continuous)

St Stephen's Cl. NW8 . . . . . .4A **12**
St Stephen's Cres. W2 . . . . .3E **53**
St Stephen's Gdns. W2 . . . . .3D **53**
    (not continuous)
St Stephens Ho. SE17 . . . .2D **141**
St Stephen's M. W2 . . . . . . .2E **53**
St Stephen's Rd. E3 . . . . . . .4A **24**
St Stephen's Row EC4 . . . . . .4D **63**
St Stephen's Ter. SW8 . . . . .5B **138**
St Stephen's Wlk. SW7 . . . . .3B **110**
St Swithins La. EC4 . . . . . . .5D **63**
St Theresa's Cl. E9 . . . . .1D **5**
St Thomas Ct. NW1 . . . . . . .2C **14**
St Thomas Ho. E1 . . . . .3D **67**
St Thomas Rd. E16 . . . . . . .3D **73**
St Thomas's Pl. E9 . . . . .1B **22**
St Thomas's Sq. E9 . . . . . . .1A **22**
St Thomas St. SE1 . . . . .3D **91**
St Thomas's Way SW6 . . . . .4B **130**
St Vincent De Paul Ho. E1 . .2B **66**
St Vincent Ho. SE1 . . . . . . .1B **120**
St Vincent St. W1 . . . . .2E **57**
St Williams Ct. N1 . . . . .2A **16**
Salamanca Pl. SE1 . . . . . . .4B **116**
Salamanca Sq. SE1 . . . . . . .4B **116**
Salamanca St. SE1 . . . . . . .4B **116**
    SE11 . . . . .4B **116**
Salem Rd. W2 . . . . .5A **54**
Sale Pl. W2 . . . . .2F **55**
Sale St. E2 . . . . .4E **43**
Salford Ho. E14 . . . . .3C **126**
Salisbury Cl. SE17 . . . . . . .3D **119**
Salisbury Ct. E9 . . . . .3A **4**
    EC4 . . . . .4F **61**
    SE16 . . . . .2E **121**
Salisbury Ho. E14 . . . . .3F **69**
    EC2 . . . . .2E **63**
    N1 . . . . .3F **17**
    SW1 . . . . .5E **115**
    SW9 . . . . .1E **139**
Salisbury M. SW6 . . . . .5B **130**
Salisbury Pas. SW6 . . . . . . .4B **130**
Salisbury Pavement SW6 . . .4B **130**
Salisbury Pl. SW9 . . . . .5A **140**
    W1 . . . . .1B **56**
Salisbury Sq. EC4 . . . . .4E **61**
Salisbury St. NW8 . . . . .5E **33**
Salmon La. E14 . . . . .3F **67**
Salmon St. E14 . . . . .3B **68**
Salomons Rd. E13 . . . . .1B **74**
Salter Rd. SE16 . . . . .3D **95**
Salters Ct. EC4 . . . . .4C **62**
Salter's Hall Ct. EC4 . . . . . . .5D **63**
Salters Rd. W10 . . . . .5D **29**
Salter St. E14 . . . . .5D **69**
Saltley Cl. E6 . . . . .3A **76**
Salton Sq. E14 . . . . .4B **68**
Saltram Cres. W9 . . . . .2C **30**
Saltwell St. E14 . . . . .5E **69**
Saltwood Gro. SE17 . . . . . .1D **141**
Saltwood Ho. SE15 . . . . . . .3C **144**
Salusbury Rd. NW6 . . . . .3A **8**
Salutation Rd. SE10 . . . . . .3A **128**
Salway Pl. E15 . . . . .5E **7**
Salway Rd. E15 . . . . .5E **7**
Samaras Mans. E20 . . . . . . .3C **6**
Sambourne Family Home, The
    18 Stafford Terrace 1D 109
Sambrook Ho. E1 . . . . .2B **66**
    SE11 . . . . .4D **117**
Samford Ho. N1 . . . . .4D **17**
Samford St. NW8 . . . . .5F **33**
Sam Manners Ho. SE10 . . .1F **149**
Sam March Ho. E14 . . . . . . .4D **71**

Samphire Hgts. E20 . . . . .3B **6**
Sampson Ho. SE1 . . . . .2A **90**
Sampson St. E1 . . . . .3E **93**
Samuda Est. E14 . . . . .1C **126**
Samuel Cl. E8 . . . . .3C **20**
    SE14 . . . . .3D **145**
Samuel Ct. N1 . . . . .3F **41**
Samuel Ho. E8 . . . . .4B **20**
Samuel Jones Ct. SE15 . . . .5A **142**
Samuel Lewis Bldgs. N1 . . . .1E **17**
Samuel Lewis Trust Dwellings
    SW3 . . . . .4F **111**
    SW6 . . . . .4E **131**
    W14 . . . . .3B **108**
Samuel Richardson Ho.
    W14 . . . . .4B **108**
Samuel's Cl. W6 . . . . .3C **106**
Samuel St. SE15 . . . . .4B **142**
Samuel Wallis Lodge
    SE10 . . . . .4A **128**
Sanchia Ct. E2 . . . . .2D **43**
Sancroft Ho. SE11 . . . . .5C **116**
Sancroft St. SE11 . . . . .5C **116**
Sanctuary, The SW1 . . . . . .1E **115**
Sanctuary St. SE1 . . . . .4C **90**
Sandall Ho. E3 . . . . .5A **24**
Sandal St. E15 . . . . .3F **27**
Sandalwood Cl. E1 . . . . .5F **45**
Sandalwood Mans. W8 . . . .2F **109**
Sandbourne NW8 . . . . .4F **9**
    W11 . . . . .3D **53**
Sandby Ct. NW10 . . . . .2A **28**
Sandby Ho. NW6 . . . . .4D **9**
Sandell St. SE1 . . . . .4D **89**
Sanderling Ct. SE8 . . . . . . .3B **146**
Sanderling Lodge E1 . . . . . .1C **92**
Sanders Ho. WC1 . . . . .2D **39**
Sanderson Ho. SE8 . . . . . . .1B **146**
Sandfield WC1 . . . . .3A **38**
Sandford Row SE17 . . . . . . .5D **119**
Sandford St. SW6 . . . . .5A **132**
Sandgate St. SE15 . . . . . . .2F **143**
Sandgate Trad. Est.
    SE15 . . . . .2F **143**
Sandhills, The SW10 . . . . . .2C **132**
Sandhurst Ho. E1 . . . . .2B **66**
Sandland St. WC1 . . . . .2C **60**
Sandover Ho. SE16 . . . . . . .2D **121**
Sandpiper Cl. SE16 . . . . . . .4B **96**
Sandpiper Ct. E1 . . . . .1D **93**
    E14 . . . . .1C **126**
    SE8 . . . . .3D **147**
Sandringham Bldgs.
    SE17 . . . . .3D **119**
Sandringham Ct. SE16 . . . . .2E **95**
    W1 . . . . .4C **58**
    W9 . . . . .3C **32**
Sandringham Flats WC2 . . . .5E **59**
Sandringham Ho. W14 . . . . .3F **107**
Sandstone La. E16 . . . . .5F **73**
Sandwich Ho. SE16 . . . . . . .4C **94**
    WC1 . . . . .3F **37**
Sandwich St. WC1 . . . . .3F **37**
Sandys Row E1 . . . . .2A **64**
Sanford St. SE14 . . . . .2F **145**
Sanford Wlk. SE14 . . . . . . .2F **145**
Sankey Ho. E2 . . . . .5C **22**
Sansom St. SE5 . . . . .5E **141**
Sans Wlk. EC1 . . . . .4E **39**
Santa Maria Ct. E1 . . . . .1F **67**
Sant Ho. SE17 . . . . .4C **118**
Santiago Ct. E1 . . . . .1F **67**
Santley Ho. SE1 . . . . .5E **89**
Saperton Wlk. SE11 . . . . . . .3C **116**

Saphire Ct. E15 . . . . .3C **26**
Sapperton Ct. EC1 . . . . .4B **40**
Sapperton Ho. W2 . . . . .2D **53**
Sapphire Cl. E6 . . . . .3C **76**
Sapphire Ct. E1 . . . . .5D **65**
Sapphire Rd. SE8 . . . . .4F **123**
Saracens Head Yd. EC3 . . . .4B **64**
Saracen St. E14 . . . . .4E **69**
Sarah Ho. E1 . . . . .3F **65**
Sarah Swift Ho. SE1 . . . . . . .4E **91**
Sara La. Ct. N1 . . . . .5A **20**
Sardinia St. WC2 . . . . .4B **60**
Sark Wlk. E16 . . . . .3F **73**
Sarnesfield Ho. SE15 . . . . . .3F **143**
Sarratt Ho. W10 . . . . .1B **50**
Sarum Ho. W11 . . . . .5C **52**
Sarum Ter. E3 . . . . .5B **46**
Satanita Cl. E16 . . . . .3D **75**
Satchwell Rd. E2 . . . . .3D **43**
Satchwell St. E2 . . . . .3D **43**
Saturn Ho. E3 . . . . .4D **25**
    E15 . . . . .3D **27**
Saunders Apartments E3 . . .3D **47**
Saunders Cl. E14 . . . . .1C **96**
Saunders Ho. SE16 . . . . . . .5E **95**
Saunders Ness Rd. E14 . . . .3D **127**
Saunders St. SE11 . . . . . . .3D **117**
Savage Gdns. E6 . . . . .4C **76**
    EC3 . . . . .5A **64**
    (not continuous)
Savannah Cl. SE15 . . . . . . .5B **142**
Savile Row W1 . . . . .5B **58**
Saville Rd. E16 . . . . .3A **104**
Savill Ho. E16 . . . . .3F **105**
Savona Ho. SW8 . . . . .5B **136**
Savona St. SW8 . . . . .5B **136**
Savoy Bldgs. WC2 . . . . .1B **88**
Savoy Chapel **1B 88**
Savoy Cl. E15 . . . . .3F **27**
Savoy Ct. SW5 . . . . .3E **109**
    WC2 . . . . .1A **88**
Savoy Hill WC2 . . . . .1B **88**
Savoy Pl. W12 . . . . .3D **79**
    WC2 . . . . .1A **88**
Savoy Row WC2 . . . . .5B **60**
Savoy Steps WC2 . . . . .1B **88**
Savoy St. WC2 . . . . .5B **60**
Savoy Theatre **1B 88**
Savoy Way WC2 . . . . .1B **88**
Sawmill Yd. E3 . . . . .4A **24**
Sawyer St. SE1 . . . . .4B **90**
Saxon Ct. N1 . . . . .3F **15**
Saxon Hall W2 . . . . .1F **81**
Saxon Ho. E1 . . . . .2C **64**
Saxon Lea Ct. E3 . . . . .1B **46**
Saxon Rd. E3 . . . . .1B **46**
Sayes Ct. SE8 . . . . .2C **146**
Sayes Ct. St. SE8 . . . . .2C **146**
Scafell NW1 . . . . .2B **36**
Scala **2A 38**
    (off Pentonville Rd.)
Scala St. W1 . . . . .1C **58**
Scampston M. W10 . . . . . . .3E **51**
Scandrett St. E1 . . . . .3F **93**
Scarab Cl. E16 . . . . .1B **100**
Scarborough St. E1 . . . . . . .4C **64**
Scarlet Cl. E20 . . . . .3A **6**
Scarsdale Pl. W8 . . . . .1F **109**
Scarsdale Studios W8 . . . . .2E **109**
Scarsdale Vs. W8 . . . . .2E **109**
Scawen Rd. SE8 . . . . .5F **123**
Scawfell St. E2 . . . . .1C **42**
Sceptre Ct. EC3 . . . . .5C **64**
Sceptre Ho. E1 . . . . .4B **44**

Sceptre Rd. E2 . . . . .3B 44
Schafer Ho. NW1 . . . . .4B 36
Scholars Ho. NW6 . . . . .3D 9
Schomberg Ho. SW1 . . . . . .3E 115
School App. E2 . . . . .2A 42
Schoolbank Rd. SE10 . . . . . .3B 128
Schoolbell M. E3 . . . . .1A 46
School Ho. SE1 . . . . .3F 119
Schoolhouse La. E1 . . . . . . .5D 67
School M. E1 . . . . .5F 65
School Sq. SE10 . . . . .2C 128
Schooner Cl. E14 . . . . .2D 127
   SE16 . . . . .4D 95
Science Mus.
   Knightsbridge 2D 111
Sclater St. E1 . . . . .4B 42
Scoop, The 3A 92
Scoresby St. SE1 . . . . .3F 89
Scorton Ho. N1 . . . . .5A 20
SCOTCH HOUSE 5B 84
Scoter Ct. SE8 . . . . .3B 146
Scotia Bldg. E1 . . . . .5E 67
Scotia Ct. SE16 . . . . .5C 94
Scotland Pl. SW1 . . . . .2F 87
Scotney Ho. E9 . . . . .1C 22
Scotson Ho. SE11 . . . . .4D 117
Scotswood St. EC1 . . . . .4E 39
Scott Ellis Gdns. NW8 . . . . . .3D 33
Scott Ho. E14 . . . . .4E 97
   NW8 . . . . .5F 33
   SE8 . . . . .5B 124
Scott Lidgett Cres. SE16 . . . .5D 93
Scott Russell Pl. E14 . . . . . .5F 125
Scotts Cl. W12 . . . . .5B 78
Scott's Rd. W12 . . . . .5A 78
Scott's Sufferance Wharf
   SE1 . . . . .5C 92
Scott St. E1 . . . . .5F 43
Scott's Yd. EC4 . . . . .5D 63
Scoulding Ho. E14 . . . . .1D 125
Scoulding Rd. E16 . . . . .3C 72
Scouler St. E14 . . . . .5D 71
Scovell Cres. SE1 . . . . .5B 90
Scovell Rd. SE1 . . . . .5B 90
Screen on Baker Street (Cinema)
   . . . . .1C 56
Screen on the Green Cinema
   . . . . .4F 17
Scriven Ct. E8 . . . . .3C 20
Scriven St. E8 . . . . .3C 20
Scrope Ho. EC1 . . . . .1D 61
Scrubs La. NW10 . . . . .5A 28
   W10 . . . . .1A 50
Scrutton St. EC2 . . . . .5F 41
Sculpture Ho. E1 . . . . .1E 67
Seabright St. E2 . . . . .3F 43
Sea Containers Ho. SE1 . . . .1E 89
Seacon Twr. E14 . . . . .5D 97
Seaford Ho. SE16 . . . . .4C 94
Seaford St. WC1 . . . . .3A 38
Seaforth Pl. SW1 . . . . .1C 114
Seagrave Cl. E1 . . . . .2D 67
Seagrave Lodge SW6 . . . . . .2E 131
Seagrave Rd. SW6 . . . . .2E 131
Seagull La. E16 . . . . .5D 73
Seal Ho. SE1 . . . . .1E 119
Sea Life London Aquarium
   . . . . .4B 88
Searles Cl. SW11 . . . . .5A 134
Searles Dr. E6 . . . . .2F 77
Searles Rd. SE1 . . . . .3E 119
Searson Ho. SE17 . . . . .4A 118
Sears St. SE5 . . . . .4D 141
Seasalter Ho. SW9 . . . . .5D 139

Seasons Ho. E20 . . . . .4C 6
Seaton Cl. SE11 . . . . .5E 117
Sebastian Ho. N1 . . . . .1F 41
Sebastian St. EC1 . . . . .3A 40
Sebbon St. N1 . . . . .2A 18
Sebright Ho. E2 . . . . .5E 21
Sebright Pas. E2 . . . . .1E 43
Secker St. SE1 . . . . .3D 89
Second Av. W10 . . . . .4A 30
Sedan Way SE17 . . . . .5F 119
Sedding St. SW1 . . . . .3D 113
Sedding Studios SW1 . . . . . .3D 113
Seddon Highwalk EC1 . . . . . .1B 62
   (off Aldersgate St.)
Seddon Ho. EC2 . . . . .1B 62
Seddon St. WC1 . . . . .3C 38
Sedgmoor Pl. SE5 . . . . .5A 142
Sedgwick Ho. E3 . . . . .1E 69
Sedlescombe Rd. SW6 . . . . .3C 130
Sedley Ho. SE11 . . . . .5D 117
Sedley Pl. W1 . . . . .4F 57
Sedona Ho. E20 . . . . .4A 6
Seething La. EC3 . . . . .5A 64
Sekforde St. EC1 . . . . .5F 39
Selbourne Ho. SE1 . . . . .5D 91
Selby Cl. E6 . . . . .2F 75
Selby Rd. E13 . . . . .1A 74
Selby Sq. W10 . . . . .2A 30
Selby St. E1 . . . . .5E 43
Selcroft Ho. SE10 . . . . .5B 128
Seldon Ho. SW1 . . . . .1B 136
   SW8 . . . . .5B 136
Selfridges 4E 57
Selina Ho. NW8 . . . . .4E 33
Selkirk Ho. N1 . . . . .3B 16
Selman Ho. E9 . . . . .5A 4
Selsdon Way E14 . . . . .2A 126
Selsey WC1 . . . . .3A 38
Selsey St. E14 . . . . .1D 69
Selway Ho. SW8 . . . . .5A 138
Selwood Pl. SW7 . . . . .5D 111
Selwood Ter. SW7 . . . . .5D 111
Selwyn Rd. E3 . . . . .1B 46
Semley Ga. E9 . . . . .4C 4
   (not continuous)
Semley Ho. SW1 . . . . .4F 113
Semley Pl. SW1 . . . . .4E 113
Senators Lodge E3 . . . . .1F 45
Senior St. W2 . . . . .1F 53
Senrab St. E1 . . . . .3D 67
Seraph Ct. EC1 . . . . .2B 40
Seren Pk. Gdns. SE3 . . . . . .2F 149
Serica Ct. SE10 . . . . .4C 148
Serjeants Inn EC4 . . . . .4E 61
Serlby Ct. W14 . . . . .1B 108
Serle St. WC2 . . . . .3C 60
Sermon La. EC4 . . . . .4B 62
Serpentine, The 3F 83
Serpentine Ct. SE16 . . . . . . .4D 95
Serpentine Gallery 3D 83
Serpentine Rd. W2 . . . . .3F 83
Serpentine Sackler Gallery
   . . . . .2F 83
Setchell Rd. SE1 . . . . .3B 120
Setchell Way SE1 . . . . .3B 120
Seth St. SE16 . . . . .5C 94
Settlers Ct. E14 . . . . .5E 71
Settles St. E1 . . . . .2E 65
Seven Dials WC2 . . . . .4F 59
Seven Dials Ct. WC2 . . . . . . .4F 59
Seven Islands Leisure Cen.
   . . . . .2B 122
Seven Seas Gdns. E3 . . . . . .1F 69
Seven Stars Yd. E1 . . . . .1C 64

Severnake Cl. E14 . . . . .3E 125
Severn Av. W10 . . . . .2A 30
Seville Ho. E1 . . . . .3E 93
Seville M. N1 . . . . .2F 19
Seville St. SW1 . . . . .5C 84
Sevington St. W9 . . . . .5F 31
Sewardstone Rd. E2 . . . . . . .5B 22
Seward St. EC1 . . . . .4A 40
Sextant Av. E14 . . . . .3D 127
Sexton Ct. E14 . . . . .5E 71
Sextons Ho. SE10 . . . . .3B 148
Seymore M. SE14 . . . . .5B 146
Seymour Ho. E16 . . . . .2E 101
   NW1 . . . . .2E 37
   WC1 . . . . .4F 37
Seymour Leisure Cen. 2B 56
Seymour M. W1 . . . . .3D 57
Seymour Pl. W1 . . . . .2B 56
Seymour St. W1 . . . . .4B 56
   W2 . . . . .4B 56
Seymour Wlk. SW10 . . . . . . .2B 132
Seyssel St. E14 . . . . .3C 126
Shabana Rd. W12 . . . . .2A 78
Shackleton Ct. E14 . . . . .5E 125
   W12 . . . . .5A 78
Shackleton Ho. E1 . . . . .2B 94
Shacklewell St. E2 . . . . .4C 42
Shad Thames SE1 . . . . .3B 92
   (Anchor Brewhouse)
   SE1 . . . . .5C 92
   (Jamaica Rd.)
SHADWELL 1A 94
Shadwell Gdns. E1 . . . . .5B 66
Shadwell Pierhead E1 . . . . . .1C 94
Shadwell Pl. E1 . . . . .5B 66
Shaftesbury Av. W1 . . . . .1D 87
   WC1 . . . . .3F 59
   WC2 . . . . .3F 59
Shaftesbury Cen. W10 . . . . . .5D 29
Shaftesbury Ct. E6 . . . . .3D 77
   N1 . . . . .1D 41
   SE1 . . . . .1D 119
Shaftesbury Ho. E16 . . . . . . .4C 72
Shaftesbury Lodge E14 . . . . .4F 69
Shaftesbury M. W8 . . . . .2E 109
Shaftesbury St. N1 . . . . .1C 40
   (not continuous)
Shaftesbury Theatre 3F 59
Shaftesbury Vs. W8 . . . . .1E 109
Shafto M. SW1 . . . . .2C 112
Shafton M. E9 . . . . .3D 23
Shafton Rd. E9 . . . . .3E 23
Shafts Ct. EC3 . . . . .4F 63
Shahjalal Ho. E2 . . . . .5E 21
Shakespeare Ct. NW6 . . . . . .2C 10
Shakespeare Ho. E9 . . . . . . .1B 22
Shakespeare's Globe & Exhibition
   . . . . .1B 90
Shakespeare Twr. EC2 . . . . . .1C 62
Shalbourne Sq. E9 . . . . .4B 4
Shalcomb St. SW10 . . . . . . .3C 132
Shalfleet Dr. W10 . . . . .5D 51
Shalford Ct. N1 . . . . .5F 17
Shalford Ho. SE1 . . . . .1E 119
Shand St. SE1 . . . . .4F 91
Shandy St. E1 . . . . .1E 67
Shan Ho. WC1 . . . . .5B 38
Shannon Ct. SE15 . . . . .4B 142
Shannon Pl. NW8 . . . . .5A 12
Shard, The 3E 91

Shard's Sq. SE15 . . . . .3E **143**
Sharnbrook Ho. W14 . . .2D **131**
Sharon Gdns. E9 . . . . .3B **22**
Sharpleshall St. NW1 . . .2C **12**
Sharpley Ct. SE1 . . . . .4F **89**
Sharratt St. SE15 . . . . . .2C **144**
Sharsted St. SE17 . . . . . . .1F **139**
Sharwood WC1 . . . . .1C **38**
Shaver's Pl. SW1 . . . . .1D **87**
Shaw Cres. E14 . . . . .3A **68**
Shawfield St. SW3 . . . . .1A **134**
Shaw Ho. E16 . . . . .4E **105**
Shaw Theatre **3E 37**
Shead Ct. *E1* 4A *66*
(off James Voller Way)
Shearsmith Ho. E1 . . . . . . .5E **65**
Shearwater Ct. *E1* 1D *93*
(off Star Pl.)
SE8 . . . . .2C **146**
Sheba Pl. E1 . . . . .5C **42**
Sheen Gro. N1 . . . . .3D **17**
Sheep La. E8 . . . . .4F **21**
Sheerness M. E16 . . . . . . .4F **105**
Sheerwater Rd. E16 . . . . .1D **75**
Sheffield Sq. E3 . . . . .2C **46**
Sheffield St. WC2 . . . . . . .4B **60**
Sheffield Ter. W8 . . . . .4D **81**
Sheldon Ct. SW8 . . . . .5F **137**
Sheldon Ho. N1 . . . . .3A **20**
Sheldon Pl. E2 . . . . .1E **43**
(not continuous)
Sheldon Sq. W2 . . . . .2C **54**
Sheldrake Cl. E16 . . . . . . .3B **104**
Sheldrake Ho. SE16 . . . . .3E **123**
Sheldrake Pl. W8 . . . . .4C **80**
Shelduck Ct. SE8 . . . . . . .2B **146**
Shell Cen. SE1 . . . . .3C **88**
Shelley Ct. SW3 . . . . . . .2C **134**
Shelley Ho. E2 . . . . .3B **44**
SE17 . . . . .5O **110**
SW1 . . . . .2B **136**
Shelmerdine Cl. E3 . . . . . .1D **69**
Shelton St. WC2 . . . . .4F **59**
(not continuous)
Shene Ho. EC1 . . . . .1D **61**
Shenfield St. N1 . . . . .1A **42**
(not continuous)
Shepherdess Pl. N1 . . . . . .2C **40**
Shepherdess Wlk. N1 . . . .5C **18**
Shepherd Ho. E14 . . . . . . .4F **69**
E16 . . . . .1F **105**
Shepherd Mkt. W1 . . . . . .3F **85**
SHEPHERD'S BUSH **4C 78**
Shepherd's Bush Empire Theatre
. . . .**4C 78**
Shepherd's Bush Grn.
W12 . . . . .4C **78**
Shepherd's Bush Mkt.
W12 . . . . .4B **78**
(not continuous)
Shepherd's Bush Pl. W12 . .4D **79**
Shepherd's Bush Rd. W6 . .5C **78**
Shepherds Cl. W1 . . . . . . .5D **57**
Shepherds Ct. W12 . . . . . .4D **79**
Shepherds Pl. W1 . . . . . . .5D **57**
Shepherd St. W1 . . . . .3F **85**
Sheppard Dr. SE16 . . . . . .5F **121**
Sheppard Ho. E2 . . . . .1E **43**
Shepperton Rd. N1 . . . . . .3C **18**
Shepton Ho's. E2 . . . . .2C **44**
Sherard Ho. E9 . . . . .2C **22**
Sheraton Ho. SW1 . . . . .2A **136**
Sheraton St. W1 . . . . .4D **59**
Sherborne NW1 . . . . .2D **15**

Sherborne Ho. SW1 . . . . . .5A **114**
SW8 . . . . .4B **138**
Sherborne La. EC4 . . . . . . .5D **63**
Sherborne St. N1 . . . . .3D **19**
Sherbourne Ct. SW5 . . . . .3F **109**
Sherbrooke Ho. E2 . . . . . . .5B **22**
SW1 . . . . .2E **115**
Sherbrooke Rd. SW6 . . . . .5A **130**
Sherbrooke Ter. SW6 . . . . .5A **130**
Shere Ho. SE1 . . . . .1D **119**
Sheridan Bldgs. WC2 . . . . .4A **60**
Sheridan Ct. NW6 . . . . .2C **10**
SW5 . . . . .4F **109**
Sheridan Hgts. E1 . . . . .4A **66**
Sheridan Ho. SE11 . . . . . .4E **117**
Sheringham NW8 . . . . .3E **11**
Sheringham Ho. NW1 . . . . .1F **55**
Sherlock Ho. N8 . . . . .3D **11**
Sherlock Holmes Mus. **5C 34**
Sherlock M. W1 . . . . .1D **57**
Sherman Ho. E14 . . . . .3C **70**
Sherren Ho. E1 . . . . .5C **44**
Sheriff Ct. NW6 . . . . .1E **9**
Sheriff Rd. NW6 . . . . .1D **9**
Sherrington Ct. E16 . . . . . .2B **72**
Sherston Ct. SE1 . . . . .3A **118**
WC1 . . . . .3D **39**
Sherwin Ho. SE11 . . . . . . .2D **139**
Sherwood NW6 . . . . .1A **8**
Sherwood Ct. W1 . . . . .2B **56**
Sherwood Gdns. E14 . . . . .3E **125**
SE16 . . . . .1E **143**
Sherwood St. W1 . . . . .5C **58**
Sherwood Ter. E16 . . . . . . .3B **74**
Shetland Rd. E3 . . . . .1B **46**
Shillibeer Pl. W1 . . . . .2A **56**
Shillingford Ho. E3 . . . . . . .3A **48**
Shillingford St. N1 . . . . .3A **18**
Shillingshaw Lodge E16 . . .4D **73**
Shinfield St. W12 . . . . .4B **50**
Ship & Mermaid Row SE1 . .4E **91**
Shiplake Ho. E2 . . . . .3B **42**
Shipman Rd. E16 . . . . .4A **74**
Ship Tavern Pas. EC3 . . . . .5F **63**
Shipton Ho. E2 . . . . .1C **42**
Shipton St. E2 . . . . .2C **42**
Shipwright Rd. SE16 . . . . . .5A **96**
Shipwright Yd. SE1 . . . . . . .3F **91**
Ship Yd. E14 . . . . .5F **125**
Shire Ho. E3 . . . . .3B **48**
EC1 . . . . .5D **41**
Shirland M. W9 . . . . .3C **30**
Shirland Rd. W9 . . . . .3B **30**
Shirlbutt St. E14 . . . . .5F **69**
Shirley Ho. SE5 . . . . .5E **141**
Shirley St. E16 . . . . .3B **72**
Shoe La. EC4 . . . . .3E **61**
Shona Ho. E13 . . . . .1B **74**
Shore Bus. Cen. E9 . . . . . . .2B **22**
SHOREDITCH **2F 41**
Shoreditch Ct. E8 . . . . .2C **20**
Shoreditch High St. E1 . . . .3A **42**
Shoreditch Ho. N1 . . . . .3E **41**
Shore M. E9 . . . . .2B **22**
Shore Pl. E9 . . . . .2B **22**
Shore Rd. E9 . . . . .2B **22**
Shorncliffe Rd. SE1 . . . . . . .5B **120**
Shorrold's Rd. SW6 . . . . . . .4C **130**
Shorter St. E1 . . . . .5C **64**
Shortlands W6 . . . . .4D **107**
Shorts Gdns. WC2 . . . . .4F **59**
Short St. SE1 . . . . .4E **89**
Short Wall E15 . . . . .2C **48**

Shortwave Cinema **1A 120**
Shottendane Rd. SW6 . . . . .5D **131**
Shottsford W2 . . . . .3D **53**
Shoulder of Mutton All.
E14 . . . . .5A **68**
Shouldham St. W1 . . . . . . .2A **56**
Shrewsbury Ct. EC1 . . . . . .5C **40**
Shrewsbury Ho. SW3 . . . . .3F **133**
SW8 . . . . .2C **138**
Shrewsbury M. W2 . . . . . . .2D **53**
Shrewsbury Rd. W2 . . . . . .3D **53**
Shrewsbury St. W10 . . . . . .5C **28**
Shropshire Pl. WC1 . . . . . . .5D **37**
Shroton St. NW1 . . . . .1F **55**
Shrubbery Cl. N1 . . . . .4C **18**
Shrubland Rd. E8 . . . . .3C **20**
Shurland Gdns. SE15 . . . . .4C **142**
Shuters Sq. W14 . . . . .1B **130**
Shuttle St. E1 . . . . .5D **43**
Sicilian Av. WC1 . . . . .2A **60**
Siddons La. NW1 . . . . .5C **34**
Sidford Ho. SE1 . . . . .2D **117**
Sidford Pl. SE1 . . . . .2C **116**
Sidings Apartments, The
E16 . . . . .4D **105**
Siding St. E20 . . . . .3A **26**
Sidmouth Ho. SE15 . . . . . .4E **143**
W1 . . . . .3A **56**
Sidmouth M. WC1 . . . . .3B **38**
Sidmouth St. WC1 . . . . .3A **38**
Sidney Boyd Ct. NW6 . . . . .2E **9**
Sidney Est. E1 . . . . .3B **66**
(Bromhead St.)
E1 . . . . .2B **66**
(Lindley St.)
Sidney Godley (VC) Ho.
E2 . . . . .2C **44**
Sidney Gro. EC1 . . . . .1F **39**
Sidney Ho. E2 . . . . .1D **45**
Sidney Sq. E1 . . . . .2B **66**
Sidney St. E1 . . . . .1A **66**
(not continuous)
Sidney Webb Ho. SE1 . . . . .1E **119**
Sidworth St. E8 . . . . .2A **22**
Siege Ho. E1 . . . . .3A **66**
Siemens Brothers Way
E16 . . . . .1C **100**
Sienna Ho. E20 . . . . .4A **6**
Signal Ho. E8 . . . . .2A **22**
SE1 . . . . .5B **90**
Signmakers Yd. NW1 . . . . . .4A **14**
Sikorski Mus. **5E 83**
Silbury St. N1 . . . . .2D **41**
Silchester Rd. W10 . . . . . . .4E **51**
Silesia Bldgs. E8 . . . . .1A **22**
Silex St. SE1 . . . . .5A **90**
Silicon Way N1 . . . . .3E **41**
Silk Ct. E2 . . . . .2E **43**
Silkin M. SE15 . . . . .5E **143**
Silk M. SE11 . . . . .1E **139**
Silk Mills Sq. E9 . . . . .4C **4**
Silk St. EC2 . . . . .1C **62**
Silk Weaver Way E2 . . . . . . .5A **22**
Sillitoe Ho. N1 . . . . .4E **19**
Silsoe Ho. NW1 . . . . .1A **36**
Silver Cl. SE14 . . . . .4F **145**
Silverdale NW1 . . . . .2B **36**
Silverdale Ct. EC1 . . . . .4A **40**
Silverland St. E16 . . . . .3C **104**
Silver Pl. W1 . . . . .5C **58**
Silver Rd. W12 . . . . .1D **79**
Silverthorn NW8 . . . . .4A **10**
Silverthorne Loft Apartments
SE5 . . . . .3D **141**

SILVERTOWN 3B 102
Silvertown Sq. E16 . . . . .2B 72
Silvertown Viaduct E16 . . . .4B 72
Silvertown Way E16 . . . . . . .3A 72
            (Clarkson Rd.)
E16 . . . . .2D 101
           (Hanover Av.)
Silver Wlk. SE16 . . . . .3B 96
Silvester Ho. E1 . . . . .3A 66
  E2 . . . . .3B 44
  W11 . . . . .3B 52
Silvester St. SE1 . . . . .5D 91
Silvocea Way E14 . . . . .4E 71
Silwood Est. SE16 . . . . .4C 122
Silwood St. SE16 . . . . .4C 122
Simla Ct. N7 . . . . .1F 15
Simla Ho. SE1 . . . . .5E 91
Simmonds Ct. SW5 . . . . . . .4F 109
Simms Rd. SE1 . . . . .4D 121
Simon Cl. W11 . . . . .5C 52
Simon Ct. W9 . . . . .3D 31
Simons Wlk. E15 . . . . .3E 7
Simpson Ho. NW8 . . . . .3F 33
  SE11 . . . . .1C 138
Simpson's Rd. E14 . . . . .1A 98
Sinclair Gdns. W14 . . . . .5E 79
Sinclair Ho. WC1 . . . . .3F 37
Sinclair Mans. W12 . . . . .5E 79
Sinclair Rd. W14 . . . . .5E 79
Sinclairs Ho. E3 . . . . .1B 46
Singer St. EC2 . . . . .3E 41
Siobhan Davis Dance Studios
 . . . . .2F 117
Sir Christopher France Ho.
  E1 . . . . .3F 45
Sirdar Rd. W11 . . . . .1E 79
Sir Francis Drake Ct.
  SE10 . . . . .5F 127
Sirinham Point SW8 . . . . . . .3C 138
Sirius Bldg. E1 . . . . .5E 67
Sir John Kirk Cl. SE5 . . . . .4B 140
Sir John Lyon Ho. EC4 . . . . .5B 62
Sir John Soane's Mus. . . .3B 60
Sir Nicholas Garrow Ho.
  W10 . . . . .4A 30
Sir Oswald Stoll Foundation, The
  SW6 . . . . .4F 131
Sir Oswald Stoll Mans.
  SW6 . . . . .4F 131
Sir Walter Raleigh Ct.
  SE10 . . . . .5F 127
Sise La. EC4 . . . . .4D 63
Siskin Ho. SE16 . . . . .3E 123
Sissinghurst Ho. SE15 . . . . .3C 144
Sister Mabel's Way SE15 . . .4D 143
Sitarey Ct. W12 . . . . .2A 78
Sivill Ho. E2 . . . . .2C 42
Six Bridges Ind. Est. SE1 . .1E 143
        (not continuous)
Sixth Av. W10 . . . . .2F 29
Skeggs Ho. E14 . . . . .1B 126
Skegness Ho. N7 . . . . .1B 16
Skenfrith Ho. SE15 . . . . . . .3F 143
Sketch Apartments E1 . . . . .1E 67
Sketchley Gdns. SE16 . . . .5D 123
Skiers St. E15 . . . . .4F 27
Skinner Pl. SW1 . . . . .4D 113
Skinners La. EC4 . . . . .5C 62
Skinner St. EC1 . . . . .3E 39
Skipwith Ho. EC1 . . . . .1D 61
Skipworth Rd. E9 . . . . .3C 22
Skua Ct. SE8 . . . . .2B 146
Skylark Ct. SE1 . . . . .5C 90
Skyline Ct. SE1 . . . . .2B 120

Skyline Plaza Bldg. E1 . . . . .3E 65
Skylines E14 . . . . .5B 98
Skylines Village E14 . . . . . .5B 98
Sky Studios E16 . . . . .4D 105
Slade Wlk. SE17 . . . . .3A 140
Slaidburn St. SW10 . . . . . .3C 132
Sleaford Ho. E3 . . . . .5E 47
Sleaford Ind. Est. SW8 . . . .5C 136
Sleaford St. SW8 . . . . .4B 136
Sleat Ho. E3 . . . . .5B 24
Sleigh Ho. E2 . . . . .2C 44
Sligo Ho. E1 . . . . .5D 45
Slingsby Pl. WC2 . . . . .5F 59
Slippers Pl. SE16 . . . . .1A 122
Slipway Ho. E14 . . . . .5F 125
Sloane Av. SW3 . . . . .4F 111
Sloane Av. Mans. SW3 . . . .4B 112
Sloane Ct. E. SW3 . . . . . . .5D 113
Sloane Ct. W. SW3 . . . . . . .5D 113
Sloane Gdns. SW1 . . . . . . .4D 113
Sloane Ga. Mans. SW1 . . . .3D 113
Sloane Ho. E9 . . . . .1B 22
Sloane Sq. SW1 . . . . .4C 112
Sloane St. SW1 . . . . .5C 84
Sloane Ter. SW1 . . . . .3C 112
Sloane Ter. Mans. SW1 . . .3D 113
Sly St. E1 . . . . .4F 65
Smallbrook M. W2 . . . . .4D 55
Smart's Pl. WC2 . . . . .3A 60
Smeaton Ct. SE1 . . . . .2B 118
Smeaton St. E1 . . . . .2F 93
Smeed Rd. E3 . . . . .2D 25
Smith Cl. SE16 . . . . .3D 95
Smithfield (Central Markets)
 . . . . .2F 61
Smithfield Ct. E1 . . . . .5E 65
Smithfield St. EC1 . . . . .2F 61
Smith's Ct. W1 . . . . .5D 59
Smith Sq. SW1 . . . . .2F 115
Smith St. SW3 . . . . .5B 112
Smith Ter. SW3 . . . . .1B 134
Smithy St. E1 . . . . .1B 66
Smokehouse Yd. EC1 . . . . .1A 62
Smyrk's Rd. SE17 . . . . .1A 142
Smyrna Mans. NW6 . . . . .2E 9
Smyrna Rd. NW6 . . . . .2E 9
Smythe St. E14 . . . . .5A 70
Snarsgate St. W10 . . . . . . .2B 50
Snowberry Cl. E15 . . . . .1E 7
Snowden St. EC2 . . . . .5F 41
Snowdon Aviary 4C 12
Snow Hill EC1 . . . . .2F 61
Snow Hill Ct. EC1 . . . . .3A 62
Snowman Ho. NW6 . . . . . . .3A 10
Snowsfields SE1 . . . . .4E 91
Soane Ct. NW1 . . . . .1C 14
Soane Ho. SE17 . . . . .1E 141
Soda Studios E8 . . . . .3B 20
SOHO 4D 59
Soho Sq. W1 . . . . .3D 59
Soho St. W1 . . . . .3D 59
Soho Theatre & Writers Cen.
 . . . . .4D 59
Sojourner Truth Cl. E8 . . . . .1A 22
Solander Gdns. E1 . . . . .5A 66
           (Cable St.)
E1 .5B 66
        (The Highway)
Solar Ct. SE16 . . . . .5D 93
Solar Ho. E6 . . . . .1E 77
  E15 . . . . .5F 7
Solarium Ct. SE1 . . . . .3C 120
Solebay St. E1 . . . . .5F 45

Solent Ho. E1 . . . . .2F 67
Soley M. WC1 . . . . .2D 39
Solway Ho. E1 . . . . .5E 45
Somer Ct. SW6 . . . . .3D 131
Somerfield St. SE16 . . . . . .5D 123
Somerford St. E1 . . . . .5F 43
Somerford Way SE16 . . . . . .5F 95
Somers Cl. NW1 . . . . .5D 15
Somers Cres. W2 . . . . .4F 55
Somerset Ct. NW1 . . . . .1D 37
Somerset House 5B 60
Somerset Sq. W14 . . . . .1A 108
Somerston Ho. NW1 . . . . . . .3C 14
SOMERS TOWN 1D 37
Somers Town Community
     Sports Cen. 1D 37
Somerton Ho. WC1 . . . . .3E 37
Somerville Point SE16 . . . . .4B 96
Sondes St. SE17 . . . . .2D 141
Sonning Ho. E2 . . . . .3B 42
Sophia Ho. W6 . . . . .5B 106
Sophia Rd. E16 . . . . .3F 73
Sophia Sq. SE16 . . . . .1F 95
Sopwith Way SW8 . . . . .4F 135
Sorrel Gdns. E6 . . . . .1F 75
Sorrel La. E14 . . . . .4E 71
Sorrell Cl. SE14 . . . . .4F 145
Sotheran Cl. E8 . . . . .3E 21
Sotherby Lodge E2 . . . . . . .5C 22
Sotheron Pl. SW6 . . . . .5A 132
Souldern Rd. W14 . . . . .2E 107
Sounding All. E3 . . . . .3D 25
Southacre W2 . . . . .4F 55
Sth. Africa Rd. W12 . . . . . . .2A 78
Southall Pl. SE1 . . . . .5D 91
Southam Ho. W10 . . . . .5A 30
Southampton Bldgs. WC2 . .2D 61
Southampton M. E16 . . . . . .2F 101
Southampton Pl. WC1 . . . . .2A 60
Southampton Row WC1 . . . .1A 60
Southampton St. WC2 . . . . .5A 60
Southampton Way SE5 . . . .4E 141
Southam St. W10 . . . . .5A 30
Sth. Audley St. W1 . . . . .1E 85
Southbank Bus. Cen.
  SW8 . . . . .3E 137
Southbank Cen. 2C 88
South Block SE1 . . . . .5B 88
Sth. Bolton Gdns. SW5 . . . .5A 110
Southborough Ho. SE17 . . . .5F 119
Southborough Rd. E9 . . . . . .3C 22
SOUTH BROMLEY 5C 70
Southbury NW8 . . . . .3C 10
Sth. Carriage Dr. SW1 . . . . .5E 83
  SW7 . . . . .5E 83
South City Ct. SE15 . . . . . .4A 142
Sth. Colonnade, The E14 . . .2E 97
        (not continuous)
Southcombe St. W14 . . . . . .3F 107
Southcott Ho. E3 . . . . .3F 47
  W9 . . . . .5C 32
Southcott M. NW8 . . . . .1F 33
South Cres. E16 . . . . .5D 49
  WC1 . . . . .2D 59
Sth. Crescent M. WC1 . . . . .4F 37
Sth. Eaton Pl. SW1 . . . . . . .3E 113
Sth. Edwardes Sq. W8 . . . . .2C 108
South End W8 . . . . .1A 110
South End Row W8 . . . . . . .1A 110
Southerngate Way SE14 . . .4F 145
Southern Gro. E3 . . . . .3B 46
Southern Row W10 . . . . .5F 29
Southern St. N1 . . . . .5B 16
Southern Way SE10 . . . . . . .3C 128

Southernwood Retail Pk.
SE1 . . . . .5B 120
Southerton Rd. W6 . . . . . .2B 106
Southey Ho. SE17 . . . . . . .5C 118
Southey M. E16 . . . . .2E 101
Southey Rd. SW9 . . . . . .5D 139
Southgate Ct. N1 . . . . . . .2E 19
Southgate Gro. N1 . . . . . .2E 19
Southgate Rd. N1 . . . . . . .3E 19
SOUTH HACKNEY 2D 23
SOUTH HAMPSTEAD 1C 10
Southill St. E14 . . . . .3A 70
Sth. Island Pl. SW9 . . . . . .5C 138
SOUTH KENSINGTON 3E 111
Sth. Kensington Sta. Arc.
SW7 . . . . .3E 111
SOUTH LAMBETH 5A 138
Sth. Lambeth Pl. SW8 . . . . .2A 138
Sth. Lambeth Rd. SW8 . . . . .3A 138
South Lodge E16 . . . . . . .2F 101
(off Audley Dr.)
NW8 . . . . .2D 33
SW7 . . . . .5A 84
Sth. Molton La. W1 . . . . . .4F 57
Sth. Molton Rd. E16 . . . . . .3E 73
Sth. Molton St. W1 . . . . . .4F 57
Southmoor Way E9 . . . . . .3C 4
South Pde. SW3 . . . . .5E 111
South Pl. EC2 . . . . .1E 63
South Pl. M. EC2 . . . . . . .2E 63
Sth. Quay Plaza E14 . . . . . .4F 97
Sth. Quay Sq. E14 . . . . . . .4F 97
South Ri. W2 . . . . .5A 56
South Sea St. SE16 . . . . . .1B 124
Southside Halls SW7 . . . . .1E 111
Southside Ind. Est. SW8 . . .5B 136
South Sq. WC1 . . . . .2D 61
South St. W1 . . . . .2E 85
Sth. Tenter St. E1 . . . . . . .5C 64
South Ter. SW7 . . . . .5F 111
SOUTHWARK 3A 90
Southwark Bri. SE1 . . . . . .1C 90
Southwark Bri. Bus. Cen.
SE1 . . . . .3C 90
(off Southwark Bri. Rd.)
Southwark Bri. Rd. SE1 . . . .1A 118
Southwark Cathedral 2D 91
Southwark Pk. Est. SE16 . . .3A 122
Southwark Pk. Rd. SE16 . . .3C 120
Southwark Pk. Sports Cen. Track
. . . . .3C 122
Southwark Pk. Sports Complex
. . . . .3C 122
Southwark Playhouse 1B 118
Southwark St. SE1 . . . . . . .2F 89
Southwater Cl. E14 . . . . . .3B 68
Southway Cl. W12 . . . . . . .5A 78
Southwell Gdns. SW7 . . . . .3B 110
Southwell Ho. SE16 . . . . . .4F 121
South W. India Dock Entrance
E14 . . . . .4C 98
Sth. Wharf Rd. W2 . . . . . .3D 55
Southwick M. W2 . . . . . . .3E 55
Southwick Pl. W2 . . . . . . .4F 55
Southwick St. W2 . . . . . . .3F 55
Southwick Yd. W2 . . . . . . .4F 55
Southwold Mans. W9 . . . . .3E 31
Southwood Ct. EC1 . . . . . .2F 39
Southwood Ho. W11 . . . . . .5F 51
Southwood Smith Ho. E2 . . .2F 43
Southwood Smith St. N1 . . .4E 17
Sovereign Cl. E1 . . . . .1A 94
Sovereign Ct. W8 . . . . . . .1F 109
Sovereign Cres. SE16 . . . . .1F 95

Sovereign Ho. E1 . . . . . . .5A 44
Sovereign M. E2 . . . . .5B 20
Space Arts Centre, The 3E 125
Spa Ct. SE16 . . . . .2D 121
Spafield St. EC1 . . . . .4D 39
Spa Grn. Est. EC1 . . . . . . .2F 39
Spanby Rd. E3 . . . . .5E 47
Spanish Pl. W1 . . . . .3E 57
Sparkes Cotts. SW1 . . . . . .4D 113
Spa Rd. SE16 . . . . .2B 120
Sparrick's Row SE1 . . . . . .4E 91
Sparrow Ho. E1 . . . . .5C 44
Speakers' Corner 5C 56
Spearman Ho. E14 . . . . . . .4E 69
Spear M. SW5 . . . . .4E 109
Spectrum Pl. SE17 . . . . . . .2D 141
Speed Highwalk EC2 . . . . .1C 62
Speed Ho. EC2 . . . . .1C 62
Speedwell St. SE8 . . . . . . .5D 147
Speedy Pl. WC1 . . . . .3F 37
Speke's Monument 2C 82
Speldhurst Rd. E9 . . . . . . .2D 23
Spellbrook Wlk. N1 . . . . . .3C 18
Spelman Ho. E1 . . . . .2D 65
Spelman St. E1 . . . . .1D 65
(not continuous)
Spence Cl. SE16 . . . . .5B 96
Spencer Ct. NW8 . . . . . . .1B 32
Spencer House 3B 86
Spencer Mans. W14 . . . . . .2A 130
Spencer M. W6 . . . . .2A 130
Spencer Pl. N1 . . . . .1F 17
Spencer St. EC1 . . . . .3F 39
Spencer Way E1 . . . . .4A 66
Spenlow Ho. SE16 . . . . . . .5E 93
Spenser St. SW1 . . . . .1C 114
Spens Ho. WC1 . . . . .5B 38
Spert St. E14 . . . . .5F 67
Spey St. E14 . . . . .2B 70
Sphere, The E10 . . . . .4D 72
Spice Ct. E1 . . . . .2E 93
Spice Quay Hgts. SE1 . . . . .3C 92
Spindrift Av. E14 . . . . .4E 125
Spinnaker Ho. E14 . . . . . . .4D 97
Spire Ho. W2 . . . . .5C 54
Spirit Quay E1 . . . . .2E 93
SPITALFIELDS 1B 64
Spitalfields City Farm 5D 43
Spital Sq. E1 . . . . .1A 64
Spital St. E1 . . . . .1D 65
Spital Yd. E1 . . . . .1A 64
Splendour Wlk. SE16 . . . . .1B 144
Spode Ho. SE11 . . . . .2D 117
SportsDock 5F 77
Sportsman Pl. E2 . . . . .4D 21
Spriggs Ho. N1 . . . . .1A 18
Sprimont Pl. SW3 . . . . . . .5B 112
Springall St. SE15 . . . . . . .5A 144
Springalls Wharf SE16 . . . . .4D 93
Springbank Wlk. NW1 . . . . .1E 15
Spring Ct. NW6 . . . . .1B 8
Springfield Ct. NW3 . . . . . .1F 11
Springfield La. NW6 . . . . . .4F 9
Springfield Rd. NW8 . . . . . .4B 10
Springfield Wlk. NW6 . . . . .4F 9
Spring Gdns. SW1 . . . . . . .2E 87
(not continuous)
Spring Ho. WC1 . . . . .3D 39
Spring M. W1 . . . . .1C 56
Spring St. W2 . . . . .4D 55
Springvale Ter. W14 . . . . . .2E 107
Spring Wlk. E1 . . . . .1E 65
Springwater WC1 . . . . .1B 60
Springwood Cl. E3 . . . . . . .1D 47

Spruce Ho. SE16 . . . . .5D 95
Spurgeon St. SE1 . . . . . . .1D 119
Spur Rd. SE1 . . . . .4D 89
SW1 . . . . .5B 86
Square, The W6 . . . . .5C 106
Squire Gdns. NW8 . . . . . . .3D 33
Squirries St. E2 . . . . .2E 43
SS Robin 2E 97
Stable Ct. EC1 . . . . .5A 40
Stables Lodge E8 . . . . .1A 22
Stables Market, The NW1 . . .2F 13
Stable St. N1 . . . . .4F 15
Stables Way SE11 . . . . . . .5D 117
Stable Yd. SW1 . . . . .5C 86
Stable Yd. Rd. SW1 . . . . . .3C 86
(not continuous)
Stacey St. WC2 . . . . .4E 59
Stack Ho. SW1 . . . . .4E 113
Stackhouse St. SW3 . . . . . .1B 112
Stacy Path SE5 . . . . .5F 141
Stadium, The
Queen Elizabeth Olympic Pk.
. . . . .2F 25
Stadium St. SW10 . . . . . . .5C 132
Stafford Cl. NW6 . . . . .3D 31
Stafford Ct. SW8 . . . . .5F 137
W8 . . . . .1D 109
Stafford Cripps Ho. E2 . . . . .3C 44
SW6 . . . . .3C 130
Stafford Ho. SE1 . . . . .5C 120
Stafford Mans. SW1 . . . . . .1B 114
SW11 . . . . .5B 134
W14 . . . . .2D 107
Stafford Pl. SW1 . . . . .1B 114
Stafford Rd. E3 . . . . .1B 46
NW6 . . . . .2D 31
Stafford St. W1 . . . . .2B 86
Stafford Ter. W8 . . . . .1D 109
Stoff St. EC1 . . . . .3E 11
Stainer St. SE1 . . . . .3E 91
Staining La. EC2 . . . . .3C 62
Stainsbury St. E2 . . . . .1C 44
Stainsby Rd. E14 . . . . .3D 69
Stalbridge Flats W1 . . . . . .4E 57
Stalbridge Ho. NW1 . . . . . .1B 36
Stalbridge St. NW1 . . . . . .1A 56
Stalham St. SE16 . . . . .2A 122
Stamford Bridge 4F 131
Stamford Bri. Studios
SW6 . . . . .4A 132
(off Wandon Rd.)
Stamford Bldgs. SW8 . . . . .4A 138
Stamford Cotts. SW10 . . . . .4A 132
Stamford Ga. SW6 . . . . . . .4A 132
Stamford Rd. N1 . . . . .1A 20
Stamford St. SE1 . . . . .3D 89
Stamp Pl. E2 . . . . .2B 42
Stanborough Ho. E3 . . . . . .5A 48
Standard Ind. Est. E16 . . . . .4C 104
Standard Pl. EC2 . . . . .3A 42
Stanesgate Ho. SE15 . . . . . .4E 143
Stanfield Ho. NW8 . . . . . . .4E 33
Stanford Ct. W8 . . . . .2A 110
Stanford Pl. SE17 . . . . .4F 119
Stanford Rd. W8 . . . . .2A 110
Stanford St. SW1 . . . . .4D 115
Stangate SE1 . . . . .1C 116
Stanhope Cl. SE16 . . . . . . .4E 95
Stanhope Gdns. SW7 . . . . .3C 110
Stanhope Ga. W1 . . . . .3E 85
Stanhope Ho. SE8 . . . . . . .4C 146
Stanhope M. E. SW7 . . . . . .3C 110
Stanhope M. Sth. SW7 . . . . .4C 110

Stanhope M. W. SW7 . . . . .3C 110
Stanhope Pde. NW1 . . . . . . .2B 36
Stanhope Pl. W1 . . . . .4B 56
Stanhope Row W1 . . . . .3F 85
Stanhope St. NW1 . . . . .1B 36
Stanhope Ter. W2 . . . . .5E 55
Stanier Cl. W14 . . . . .1C 130
Stanlake M. W12 . . . . .3B 78
Stanlake Rd. W12 . . . . .2A 78
Stanlake Vs. W12 . . . . .3B 78
Stanley Bri. Studios SW6 . .5A 132
Stanley Cl. SW8 . . . . .3B 138
Stanley Cohen Ho. EC1 . . . . .5B 8
Stanley Cres. W11 . . . . .5B 52
Stanley Gdns. W11 . . . . .5B 52
Stanley Gdns. M. W11 . . . . . .5C 52
Stanley Holloway Ct. E16 . . . .4E 73
Stanley Ho. E14 . . . . .4E 69
   SW10 . . . . .4B 132
Stanley Mans. SW10 . . . .2C 132
Stanley M. SW10 . . . . . . .4B 132
Stanley St. SE8 . . . . .5C 146
Stanley Studios SW10 . . . .2C 132
Stanliff Ho. E14 . . . . .1E 125
Stanmore Pl. NW1 . . . . .3A 14
Stanmore St. N1 . . . . .3B 16
Stannard Cotts. E1 . . . . .4C 44
Stannary Pl. SE11 . . . . .1E 139
Stannary St. SE11 . . . . .2E 139
Stansbury Sq. W10 . . . . .2A 30
Stansfeld Ho. SE1 . . . . .4C 120
Stansfeld Rd. E6 . . . . .2E 75
   E16 . . . . .5F 75
Stanstead WC1 . . . . .3A 38
Stanstead Ho. E3 . . . . .4B 48
Stanswood Gdns. SE5 . . . .5A 142
Stanton Ho. SE10 . . . . .2B 148
   SE16 . . . . .4B 96
Stanway Ct. N1 . . . . .1A 42
   (not continuous)
Stanway St. N1 . . . . .5A 20
Stanwick Rd. W14 . . . . . . .4B 108
Stanworth St. SE1 . . . . .5B 92
Staple Inn WC1 . . . . .2D 61
Staple Inn Bldgs. WC1 . . . . . .2D 61
Staples Cl. SE16 . . . . .2F 95
Staples Ho. E6 . . . . .3D 77
Staple St. SE1 . . . . .5E 91
Stapleton Ho. E2 . . . . .2F 43
Star All. EC3 . . . . .5A 64
Starboard Way E14 . . . . . . .1E 125
Starcross St. NW1 . . . . .3C 36
Star La. E16 . . . . .4A 50
   E16 . . . . .1A 72
Starling Ho. NW8 . . . . .5F 11
Star Pl. E1 . . . . .1C 92
Star Rd. W14 . . . . .2B 130
Star St. W2 . . . . .3E 55
Star Wharf NW1 . . . . .3C 14
Star Yd. WC2 . . . . .3D 61
Staten Bldg. E3 . . . . .5E 25
Statham Ho. SW8 . . . . . . .5B 136
Station App. NW1 . . . . .5C 34
Station App. Rd. SE1 . . . . . .5D 89
Station Arc. W1 . . . . .5A 36
Stationer's Hall Ct. EC4 . . . . .4A 62
Station Pas. SE15 . . . . .5B 144
Station St. E15 . . . . .1D 27
   E16 . . . . .3F 105
Station Ter. NW10 . . . . .1C 28
Staunton Ho. SE17 . . . . .4F 119
Staunton St. SE8 . . . . .2C 146
Stave Hill Ecological Pk. 4F 95
Staveley NW1 . . . . .2B 36

Staveley Cl. SE15 . . . . .5A 144
Stavers Ho. E3 . . . . .1C 46
Stave Yd. Rd. SE16 . . . . . . .3F 95
Stavordale Lodge W14 . . .1C 108
Stayner's Rd. E1 . . . . .4D 45
Steadman Ct. EC1 . . . . .4C 40
Stead St. SE17 . . . . .4D 119
Stean St. E8 . . . . .3B 20
Stebbing Ho. W11 . . . . .2E 79
Stebondale St. E14 . . . . . . .5C 126
Stedham Pl. WC1 . . . . .3F 59
Steedman St. SE17 . . . . . . .4B 118
Steele Rd. E11 . . . . .1F 7
Steele's Rd. NW3 . . . . .1B 12
Steel's La. E1 . . . . .4C 66
Steelyard Pas. EC4 . . . . . . .1D 91
Steeple Ct. E1 . . . . .4A 44
Steeple Wlk. N1 . . . . .3C 18
Steers Way SE16 . . . . .5A 96
Stelfox Ho. WC1 . . . . .2C 38
Stephan Cl. E8 . . . . .3E 21
Stephen M. W1 . . . . .2D 59
Stephenson Cl. E3 . . . . .3F 47
Stephenson Ho. SE1 . . . . . .1B 118
Stephenson St. E16 . . . . . . .5F 49
Stephenson Way NW1 . . . . . .4C 36
Stephen St. W1 . . . . .2D 59
STEPNEY 2E 67
Stepney C'way. E1 . . . . .4D 67
Stepney City Apartments
   E1 . . . . .2C 66
Stepney Grn. E1 . . . . .5C 44
Stepney Grn. Ct. E1 . . . . . . .1D 67
Stepney High St. E1 . . . . . . .2E 67
Stepney Way E1 . . . . .2F 65
Stepping City Farm 2E 67
Sterling Gdns. SE14 . . . . . . .3F 145
Sterling St. SW7 . . . . .1A 112
Sterndale Rd. W14 . . . . . . .2D 107
Sterne St. W12 . . . . .4D 79
Sterry St. SE1 . . . . .5D 91
Steve Biko Ct. W10 . . . . . . .4E 29
Stevedore St. E1 . . . . .2F 93
Stevenson Cres. SE16 . . . . .5F 121
Stevenson Ho. NW8 . . . . . . .3B 10
Stevens St. SE1 . . . . .1A 120
Steward Ho. E3 . . . . .3E 47
Steward St. E1 . . . . .2A 64
Stewart Rd. E15 . . . . .1C 6
Stewart's Gro. SW3 . . . . . . .5E 111
Stewart's Rd. SW8 . . . . . . .5B 136
Stewart St. E14 . . . . .5C 98
Stew La. EC4 . . . . .5B 62
Stibbington Ho. NW1 . . . . . . .5C 14
Stifford Ho. E1 . . . . .2C 66
Stileman Ho. E3 . . . . .1C 68
Stillington St. SW1 . . . . .3C 114
Stirling Ct. EC1 . . . . .4F 39
Stockbeck NW1 . . . . .1C 36
Stockholm Apartments
   NW1 . . . . .1E 13
Stockholm Ho. E1 . . . . .5E 65
Stockholm Rd. SE16 . . . . . . .1C 144
Stockholm Way E1 . . . . .2D 93
Stockleigh Hall NW8 . . . . . . .5A 12
Stocks Pl. E14 . . . . .5C 68
Stockton Ct. SW1 . . . . .2D 115
Stockton Ho. E2 . . . . .2F 43
Stockwell St. SE10 . . . . .3C 148
Stoddart Ho. SW8 . . . . .3C 138
Stone Bldgs. WC2 . . . . .2C 60
Stonechat Sq. E6 . . . . .1A 76
Stonecutter St. EC4 . . . . . . .3F 61
Stonefield Mans. N1 . . . . . . .4D 17

Stonefield St. N1 . . . . .3E 17
Stone Hall W8 . . . . .2F 109
Stone Hall Gdns. W8 . . . . . . .2F 109
Stone Hall Pl. W8 . . . . .2F 109
Stonehouse NW1 . . . . .4C 14
Stone Ho. Ct. EC3 . . . . .3A 64
Stonehouse Ho. W2 . . . . . . .2D 53
Stoneleigh M. E3 . . . . .1A 46
Stoneleigh Pl. W11 . . . . .1E 79
Stoneleigh St. W11 . . . . .1E 79
Stonemason Ct. SE1 . . . . . . .5B 90
Stones End St. SE1 . . . . .5B 90
Stonewall E6 . . . . .2D 77
Stoneyard La. E14 . . . . .1F 97
Stoney La. E1 . . . . .3A 64
Stoney St. SE1 . . . . .2D 91
Stonor Rd. W14 . . . . .4B 108
Stopes St. SE15 . . . . .5C 142
Stopford Rd. SE17 . . . . .1A 140
Stopher Ho. SE1 . . . . .5A 90
Storehouse M. E14 . . . . .1D 97
Store Rd. E16 . . . . .4D 105
Storers Quay E14 . . . . .4D 127
Store St. E15 . . . . .3E 7
   WC1 . . . . .2D 59
Storey Ct. NW8 . . . . .3D 33
Storey Ho. E14 . . . . .5A 70
Storey's Ga. SW1 . . . . .5E 87
Storey St. E16 . . . . .3E 105
Stork's Rd. SE16 . . . . .2E 121
Storrington WC1 . . . . .3A 38
Story St. N1 . . . . .2B 16
Stothard Ho. E1 . . . . .4C 44
Stothard Pl. E1 . . . . .1A 64
Stothard St. E1 . . . . .4B 44
Stoughton Cl. SE11 . . . . .4C 116
Stourcliffe Cl. W1 . . . . .3B 56
Stourcliffe St. W1 . . . . .4B 56
Stourhead Ho. SW1 . . . . .5D 115
Stour Rd. E3 . . . . .2D 25
Stowage SE8 . . . . .2E 147
Stowe Rd. W12 . . . . .4A 78
Strafford Ho. SE8 . . . . .1B 146
Strafford St. E14 . . . . .4D 97
Strahan Rd. E3 . . . . .2F 45
Straightsmouth SE10 . . . . . . .4A 148
Strait Rd. E6 . . . . .5F 75
Strale Ho. N1 . . . . .4F 19
Strand WC2 . . . . .2F 87
Strand La. WC2 . . . . .5C 60
Strang Ho. N1 . . . . .4B 18
Strangways Ter. W14 . . . . . . .1B 108
Stranraer Way N1 . . . . .2A 16
Strata SE1 . . . . .3B 118
STRATFORD 1E 27
Stratford Centre, The E15 . . .1E 27
Stratford Circus
(Performing Arts Cen.)
   .5E 7
Stratford Eye E15 . . . . .5E 7
STRATFORD NEW TOWN 4E 7
Stratford Office Village, The
   E15 . . . . .1F 27
Stratford Picture House
   London 5E 7
Stratford Pl. E20 . . . . .5C 6
   W1 . . . . .4F 57
Stratford Rd. W8 . . . . .3E 109
Stratford Studios W8 . . . . . .2E 109
Stratford Theatre Royal 5E 7
Stratford Vs. NW1 . . . . .1C 14
Stratford Workshops E15 . . . .3E 27
Strathearn Ho. W2 . . . . .5F 55
Strathearn Pl. W2 . . . . .5F 55

Strathmore Ct. NW8 . . . . .2F **33**
Strathmore Gdns. W8 . . . . . . .2E **81**
Strathnairn St. SE1 . . . . .4E **121**
(not continuous)
Strathray Gdns. NW3 . . . . . . .1F **11**
Stratton Ct. N1 . . . . .1A **20**
Strattondale St. E14 . . . . . . .1B **126**
Stratton St. W1 . . . . .2A **86**
Streatham St. WC1 . . . . .3F **59**
Streatley Rd. NW6 . . . . .2B **8**
Street, The E20 . . . . .5B **6**
Streimer Rd. E15 . . . . .5C **26**
Stretton Mans. SE8 . . . . .2E **147**
Strickland Ho. E2 . . . . .3C **42**
Stringer Ho. N1 . . . . .4A **20**
Strode Rd. SW6 . . . . .4A **130**
Strome Ho. NW6 . . . . .1F **31**
Strood Ho. SE1 . . . . .5E **91**
Stroudley Wlk. E3 . . . . .2F **47**
Strouts Pl. E2 . . . . .2B **42**
Strutton Ct. SW1 . . . . .2D **115**
Strutton Ground SW1 . . . . . .1D **115**
Strype St. E1 . . . . .2B **64**
Stuart Ho. E9 . . . . .1D **23**
E16 . . . . .2F **101**
W14 . . . . .3F **107**
Stuart Mill Ho. N1 . . . . .1B **38**
Stuart Rd. NW6 . . . . .3D **31**
Stuart Twr. W9 . . . . .3C **32**
Stubbs Dr. SE16 . . . . .5F **121**
Stubbs Ho. E2 . . . . .2D **45**
SW1 . . . . .4E **115**
Stubbs Point E13 . . . . .1E **73**
Stucley Pl. NW1 . . . . .2A **14**
Studd St. N1 . . . . .3F **17**
Studholme St. SE15 . . . . . . .5F **143**
Studio Pl. SW1 . . . . .5C **84**
Studios, The W8 . . . . .2E **81**
Studland SE17 . . . . .5D **119**
Studland Ho. E14 . . . . .3F **67**
Studland St. W6 . . . . .4A **106**
Studley Cl. E5 . . . . .3A **4**
Studley Ct. E14 . . . . .1E **99**
Stukeley St. WC2 . . . . .3A **60**
Stunell Ho. SE14 . . . . .3D **145**
Sturdee Ho. E2 . . . . .1D **43**
Sturdy Ho. E3 . . . . .1F **45**
Sturgeon Rd. SE17 . . . . .1B **140**
Sturge St. SE1 . . . . .4B **90**
Sturminster NW1 . . . . .1D **15**
Sturminster Ho. SW8 . . . . . .5B **138**
Sturry St. E14 . . . . .4F **69**
Sturt St. N1 . . . . .1C **40**
Stutfield St. E1 . . . . .4E **65**
Stuttle Ho. E1 . . . . .5D **43**
Styles Ho. SE1 . . . . .3F **89**
Stylus Ho. E1 . . . . .4C **66**
Success Ho. SE1 . . . . .1C **142**
Sudbury E6 . . . . .3E **77**
Sudeley St. N1 . . . . .1A **40**
Sudrey St. SE1 . . . . .5B **90**
Suffield Ho. SE17 . . . . .5A **118**
Suffolk La. EC4 . . . . .5D **63**
Suffolk Pl. SW1 . . . . .2E **87**
Suffolk St. SW1 . . . . .1E **87**
Sugar Bakers Ct. EC3 . . . . . .4A **64**
Sugar Ho. E1 . . . . .4D **65**
Sugar Ho. La. E15 . . . . .5B **26**
Sugar Loaf Wlk. E2 . . . . .2B **44**
Sugar Quay EC3 . . . . .1A **92**
Sugar Quay Wlk. EC3 . . . . . .1A **92**
Sulgrave Gdns. W6 . . . . .5C **78**
Sulgrave Rd. W6 . . . . .1C **106**
Sulkin Ho. E2 . . . . .2D **45**

Sullivan Av. E16 . . . . .1D **75**
Sullivan Ct. E3 . . . . .5B **46**
SW5 . . . . .3E **109**
Sullivan Ho. SE11 . . . . .4C **116**
SW1 . . . . .2A **136**
Sullivan Rd. SE11 . . . . .3E **117**
Sultan Ho. SE1 . . . . .5E **121**
Sultan St. SE5 . . . . .4B **140**
Sumeria Ct. SE16 . . . . .4C **122**
Summercourt Rd. E1 . . . . . . .3C **66**
Summerfield Av. NW6 . . . . . . .5A **8**
Summers St. EC1 . . . . .5D **39**
Sumner Bldgs. SE1 . . . . .2B **90**
Sumner Ct. SW8 . . . . .5F **137**
Sumner Est. SE15 . . . . .5C **142**
Sumner Ho. E3 . . . . .1F **69**
Sumner Pl. SW7 . . . . .4D **111**
Sumner Pl. M. SW7 . . . . .4E **111**
Sumner Rd. SE15 . . . . .3C **142**
Sumner St. SE1 . . . . .2A **90**
Sunbeam Cres. W10 . . . . . . .5C **28**
Sunbury Ho. E2 . . . . .3B **42**
SE14 . . . . .2D **145**
Sunbury Workshops E2 . . . . .3B **42**
Sun Ct. EC3 . . . . .4E **63**
Sunderland Ho. W2 . . . . .2D **53**
Sunderland Ter. W2 . . . . .3F **53**
Sundial Ct. EC1 . . . . .1C **62**
Sundra Wlk. E1 . . . . .5D **45**
Sundridge Ho. E9 . . . . .2D **23**
Sunguard Ct. SE1 . . . . .2F **89**
Sunlight Sq. E2 . . . . .3A **44**
Sunningdale Cl. SE16 . . . . . .1F **143**
Sunningdale Gdns. W8 . . . . .2E **109**
Sunny M. NW1 . . . . .2E **13**
Sun Pas. SE16 . . . . .1D **121**
Sunrise Cl. E20 . . . . .2B **6**
Sun Rd. W14 . . . . .1B **130**
Sun St. EC2 . . . . .1E **63**
(Finsbury Sq.)
EC2 . . . . .1F **63**
(Primrose St.)
Sun St. Pas. EC2 . . . . .2F **63**
Sun Wlk. E1 . . . . .1C **92**
Sun Wharf SE8 . . . . .4F **147**
Supreme Court
Westminster 5F 87
Surma Cl. E1 . . . . .5F **43**
Surrendale Pl. W9 . . . . .5E **31**
Surrey Canal Rd. SE14 . . . . .2C **144**
SE15 . . . . .2C **144**
Surrey County Cricket Club
. .2C 138
Surrey Docks Farm 5B 96
Surrey Docks Watersports Cen.
. .2F 123
Surrey Gro. SE17 . . . . .1F **141**
Surrey Ho. SE16 . . . . .3D **95**
Surrey Quays Rd.
SE16 . . . . .1C **122**
Surrey Quays Shop. Cen.
SE16 . . . . .2D **123**
Surrey Row SE1 . . . . .4F **89**
Surrey Sq. SE17 . . . . .5F **119**
Surrey Steps WC2 . . . . .5C **60**
Surrey St. WC2 . . . . .5C **60**
Surrey Ter. SE17 . . . . .5A **120**
Surrey Water Rd. SE16 . . . . .3E **95**
Susan Constant Ct. E14 . . . .1E **99**
Susan Lawrence Ho. E3 . . . .5F **23**
Susannah St. E14 . . . . .4A **70**
Sussex Ct. SE10 . . . . .3B **148**
W2 . . . . .4D **55**
Sussex Gdns. W2 . . . . .5D **55**

Sussex Ho. NW1 . . . . .5D **15**
Sussex Lodge W2 . . . . .4E **55**
Sussex Mans. SW7 . . . . .4D **111**
WC2 . . . . .5A **60**
Sussex M. E. W2 . . . . .4E **55**
Sussex M. W. W2 . . . . .5E **55**
Sussex Pl. NW1 . . . . .4B **34**
W2 . . . . .4E **55**
W6 . . . . .5C **106**
Sussex Sq. W2 . . . . .5E **55**
Sussex St. SW1 . . . . .1A **136**
Sutherland Av. W9 . . . . .5E **31**
Sutherland Ct. W9 . . . . .5E **31**
Sutherland Ho. W8 . . . . .2F **109**
Sutherland Pl. W2 . . . . .3D **53**
Sutherland Rd. E3 . . . . .5B **24**
Sutherland Row SW1 . . . . . .5A **114**
Sutherland Sq. SE17 . . . . . .1B **140**
Sutherland St. SW1 . . . . . . .5F **113**
Sutherland Wlk. SE17 . . . . . .1C **140**
Sutterton St. N7 . . . . .1B **16**
Sutton Est. EC1 . . . . .3E **41**
SW3 . . . . .5A **112**
W10 . . . . .1B **50**
Sutton Estate, The N1 . . . . . .1F **17**
Sutton La. EC1 . . . . .5A **40**
Sutton Row W1 . . . . .3E **59**
Sutton St. E1 . . . . .5B **66**
Sutton's Way EC1 . . . . .5C **40**
Sutton Wlk. SE1 . . . . .3C **88**
Sutton Way W10 . . . . .1B **50**
SW1 Gallery 1B 114
Swain St. NW8 . . . . .4F **33**
Swallow Ct. SE1 . . . . .5C **90**
W9 . . . . .1E **53**
Swallowfield NW1 . . . . .3A **36**
Swallow Ho. NW8 . . . . .5F **11**
Swallow Pas. W1 . . . . .4B **58**
Swallow Pl. E14 . . . . .4B **68**
W1 . . . . .4A **58**
Swallow St. E6 . . . . .2A **76**
W1 . . . . .1C **86**
Swallowtail Ho. E20 . . . . .3B **6**
Swanage Ct. N1 . . . . .1A **20**
Swanage Ho. SW8 . . . . .5B **138**
Swan App. E6 . . . . .2F **75**
Swanbourne Ho. NW8 . . . . . .4F **33**
Swan Cl. E1 . . . . .1D **93**
E14 . . . . .3C **68**
SW3 . . . . .1A **134**
SW6 . . . . .5D **131**
Swanfield St. E2 . . . . .3B **42**
Swan Ho. E15 . . . . .1F **27**
N1 . . . . .1D **19**
Swan La. EC4 . . . . .1D **91**
Swanley Ho. SE17 . . . . .5A **120**
Swan Mead SE1 . . . . .2F **119**
Swanne Ho. SE10 . . . . .4C **148**
Swan Pas. E1 . . . . .5D **65**
Swan Rd. SE16 . . . . .4C **94**
Swanscombe Ho. W11 . . . . . .2E **79**
Swanscombe Rd. W11 . . . . . .2E **79**
Swansea Ct. E16 . . . . .3F **105**
Swan St. SE1 . . . . .1C **118**
Swan Wlk. SW3 . . . . .2B **134**
Swaton Rd. E3 . . . . .5E **47**
Swedeland Ct. E1 . . . . .2A **64**
Swedenborg Gdns. E1 . . . . . .5E **65**
Sweden Ga. SE16 . . . . .2A **124**
Swedish Quays SE16 . . . . . .2A **124**
(not continuous)
Sweeney Cres. SE1 . . . . .5C **92**
Swift Ho. E3 . . . . .4B **24**
NW6 . . . . .5C **8**

Swift Lodge W9 . . . . .1E 53	Talbot Ho. E14 . . . . .3F 69	Tasso Yd. W6 . . . . .3A 130
Swinbrook Rd. W10 . . . . .1A 52	Talbot Rd. W2 . . . . .3D 53	Tate Apartments E1 . . . . .3F 65
Swinburne Ho. E2 . . . . .3B 44	W11 . . . . .4B 52	Tate Britain 4F 115
Swindon St. W12 . . . . .2A 78	(not continuous)	Tate Ho. E2 . . . . .1D 45
Swingfield Ho. E9 . . . . .3B 22	Talbot Sq. W2 . . . . .4E 55	Tate Modern 2A 90
Swinley Ho. NW1 . . . . .2A 36	Talbot Wlk. W11 . . . . .4F 51	Tate Rd. E16 . . . . .3B 104
Swinnerton St. E9 . . . . .3A 4	Talbot Yd. SE1 . . . . .3D 91	(not continuous)
Swinton Pl. WC1 . . . . .2B 38	Talgarth Mans. W14 . . . . . .5F 107	Tatham Pl. NW8 . . . . .5E 11
Swinton St. WC1 . . . . .2B 38	Talgarth Rd. W6 . . . . .5D 107	Tatsfield Ho. SE1 . . . . .1E 119
SWISS COTTAGE 1D 11	W14 . . . . .5D 107	Tatum St. SE17 . . . . .4E 119
Swiss Cottage Sports Cen.	Talia Ho. E14 . . . . .1C 126	Taunton Ho. W2 . . . . .4B 54
. . . . .2E 11	Tallis Cl. E16 . . . . .4F 73	Taunton M. NW1 . . . . .5B 34
Swiss Ct. W1 . . . . .1E 87	Tallis St. EC4 . . . . .5E 61	Taunton Pl. NW1 . . . . .4B 34
Swiss Ter. NW6 . . . . .1D 11	Talwin St. E3 . . . . .3A 48	Tavern Ct. SE1 . . . . .2C 118
Switch Ho. E14 . . . . .5E 71	Tamar Cl. E3 . . . . .4C 24	Taverners Cl. W11 . . . . .3F 79
Sybil Phoenix Cl. SE8 . . . . . .5E 123	Tamar Ho. E14 . . . . .5B 98	Taverners Ct. E3 . . . . .3A 46
Sybil Thorndike Casson Ho.	SE11 . . . . .5E 117	Tavern Quay SE16 . . . . .3F 123
SW5 . . . . .1E 131	Tamarind Ct. SE1 . . . . .4C 92	Tavistock Ct. WC1 . . . . .4E 37
Sycamore Av. E3 . . . . .3B 24	W8 . . . . .2F 109	WC2 . . . . .5A 60
Sycamore Cl. E16 . . . . .5F 49	Tamarind Ho. SE15 . . . . . . .4D 143	(off Tavistock St.)
Sycamore Ct. NW6 . . . . .3E 9	Tamarind Yd. E1 . . . . .2E 93	Tavistock Cres. W11 . . . . .2B 52
SE1 . . . . .5F 91	Tamworth St. SW6 . . . . .2D 131	(not continuous)
Sycamore Gdns. W6 . . . . .5A 78	Tangerine Ho. SE1 . . . . .5E 91	Tavistock Ho. WC1 . . . . .4E 37
Sycamore Ho. SE16 . . . . .5D 95	Tangmere WC1 . . . . .3B 38	Tavistock M. W11 . . . . .3B 52
W6 . . . . .5B 78	Tan Ho. E9 . . . . .4A 4	Tavistock Pl. WC1 . . . . .4F 37
Sycamore Lodge W8 . . .2F 109	Tankerton Ho's. WC1 . . . . . .3A 38	Tavistock Rd. W11 . . . . .3B 52
(off Stone Hall Pl.)	(off Tankerton St.)	(not continuous)
Sycamore St. EC1 . . . . .5B 40	Tankerton St. WC1 . . . . .3A 38	Tavistock Sq. WC1 . . . . .4E 37
Sycamore Wlk. W10 . . . . .4F 29	Tanner Ho. E1 . . . . .1E 67	Tavistock St. WC2 . . . . .5A 60
Sydney Cl. SW3 . . . . .4E 111	SE1 . . . . .5A 92	Tavistock Twr. SE16 . . . . .2F 123
Sydney M. SW3 . . . . .4E 111	Tanneries, The E1 . . . . .5C 44	Taviton St. WC1 . . . . .4D 37
Sydney Pl. SW7 . . . . .4E 111	Tanner's Hill SE8 . . . . .5D 147	Tavy Cl. SE11 . . . . .5E 117
Sydney St. SW3 . . . . .4F 111	Tanner St. SE1 . . . . .5A 92	Tawny Way SE16 . . . . .3D 123
Sylvan Ct. NW6 . . . . .3F 9	Tanners Yd. E2 . . . . .1F 43	Tayberry Ho. E20 . . . . .4A 6
Sylvan Gro. SE15 . . . . .3A 144	Tannery, The SE1 . . . . .4A 92	Tay Bldgs. SE1 . . . . .1F 119
Sylvan Ter. SE15 . . . . .4A 144	Tanswell Est. SE1 . . . . .1D 65	Tayburn Cl. E14 . . . . .3B 70
Sylvia Ct. N1 . . . . .1E 41	Tanswell St. SE1 . . . . .5D 89	Tay Ct. E2 . . . . .3E 45
Symes M. NW1 . . . . .5B 14	Tansy Cl. E6 . . . . .4E 77	SE1 . . . . .1F 119
Symington Ho. SE1 . . . . .2D 119	Tant Av. E16 . . . . .3B 72	Tay Ho. E3 . . . . .5B 24
Symister M. N1 . . . . .3F 41	Tapestry Bldg. EC2 . . . . .2A 64	Tayler Ct. NW8 . . . . .3D 11
Symons St. SW3 . . . . .4C 112	Tapley Ho. SE1 . . . . .5D 93	Taylor Cl. SE8 . . . . .2B 146
Symphony M. W10 . . . . .2A 30	Taplow NW3 . . . . .2E 11	Taylor Ho. E14 . . . . .1D 97
	SE17 . . . . .5E 119	Taylor Pl. E3 . . . . .1F 47
	Taplow Ho. E2 . . . . .3B 42	Taylors Yd. E1 . . . . .5C 42
T	Taplow St. N1 . . . . .1C 40	Tayport Cl. N1 . . . . .2A 16
	Tapper Wlk. N1 . . . . .3F 15	Tazzeta Ho. E20 . . . . .3B 6
Tabard Ct. E14 . . . . .4B 70	Tapp St. E1 . . . . .4F 43	Teak Cl. SE16 . . . . .3A 96
Tabard Gdn. Est. SE1 . . . . . .1D 119	Tara Ho. E14 . . . . .4E 125	Teal Cl. E16 . . . . .2D 75
Tabard Ho. SE1 . . . . .1E 119	Tarbert Wlk. E1 . . . . .5B 66	Teal Ct. E1 . . . . .1D 93
Tabard St. SE1 . . . . .4C 90	Tariff Cres. SE8 . . . . .3B 124	SE8 . . . . .2B 146
Tabernacle, The 3C 52	Tarling Rd. E16 . . . . .4C 72	Teale St. E2 . . . . .5E 21
Tabernacle St. EC2 . . . . .5E 41	Tarling St. E1 . . . . .4A 66	Teal St. SE10 . . . . .1C 128
Tabor Rd. W6 . . . . .2A 106	Tarling St. Est. E1 . . . . .4B 66	Teasel Way E15 . . . . .2F 49
Tachbrook Est. SW1 . . . . . . .1D 137	Tarnbrook Ct. SW1 . . . . . . .4D 113	Tea Trade Wharf SE1 . . . . . . .4C 92
Tachbrook M. SW1 . . . . .3B 114	Tarns, The NW1 . . . . .2B 36	Ted Roberts Ho. E2 . . . . .1A 44
Tachbrook St. SW1 . . . . .4C 114	Tarn St. SE1 . . . . .2B 118	Tedworth Gdns. SW3 . . . . . . .1B 134
Tadema Ho. NW8 . . . . .5E 33	Tarplett Ho. SE14 . . . . .3C 144	Tedworth Sq. SW3 . . . . .1B 134
Tadema Rd. SW10 . . . . .4C 132	Tarragon Cl. SE14 . . . . .4F 145	Teesdale Cl. E2 . . . . .1E 43
Tadmor St. W12 . . . . .3D 79	Tarranbrae NW6 . . . . .1A 8	Teesdale St. E2 . . . . .1F 43
Tadworth Ho. SE1 . . . . .5F 89	Tarrant Ho. E2 . . . . .2B 44	Teesdale Yd. E2 . . . . .1F 43
Taeping St. E14 . . . . .3F 125	W14 . . . . .1F 107	Telegraph Pl. E14 . . . . .3F 125
Taffeta Ho. E20 . . . . .4C 6	Tarrant Pl. W1 . . . . .2B 56	Telegraph St. EC2 . . . . .3D 63
Taffrail Ho. E14 . . . . .5F 125	Tartan Ho. E14 . . . . .3C 70	Telephone Pl. SW6 . . . . .2C 130
Taft Way E3 . . . . .2A 48	Tarver Rd. SE17 . . . . .1A 140	Telfer Ho. EC1 . . . . .3B 40
Tagwright Ho. N1 . . . . .2D 41	Tarves Way SE10 . . . . .4A 148	Telford Ho. SE1 . . . . .1B 118
Tailor Ho. WC1 . . . . .5F 37	(Lit. Cottage Pl.)	W10 . . . . .1F 51
Tailworth St. E1 . . . . .2D 65	SE10 . . . . .4A 148	Telford Rd. W10 . . . . .1F 51
Tait Ct. E3 . . . . .4A 24	(Norman Rd.)	Telfords Yd. E1 . . . . .1E 93
SW8 . . . . .5E 137	Tasker Ho. E14 . . . . .2C 68	Telford Ter. SW1 . . . . .2B 136
Tait Ho. SE1 . . . . .3E 89	Tasker Lodge W8 . . . . .4D 81	Temair Ho. SE10 . . . . .4A 148
Tait St. E1 . . . . .4F 65	Tasman Ct. E14 . . . . .4F 125	Temeraire St. SE16 . . . . .4C 94
Taj Apartments E1 . . . . .1C 64	Tasman Ho. E1 . . . . .2A 94	Templar Ct. NW8 . . . . .3D 33
Talbot Ct. EC3 . . . . .5E 63	Tasman Wlk. E16 . . . . .4D 75	Templars Ho. E16 . . . . .1F 105
Talbot Gro. Ho. W11 . . . . . . .4F 51	Tasso Rd. W6 . . . . .2A 130	Temple Av. EC4 . . . . .5E 61

Temple Bar 4D 61
Temple Bar Gate 4A 62
Temple Chambers EC4 . . . . .5E 61
Templecombe Rd. E9 . . . . . .3B 22
Temple Ct. E1 . . . . .1E 67
SW8 . . . . .5F 137
Temple Dwellings E2 . . . . . .2F 43
(off Temple St.)
Temple Gdns. EC4 . . . . . . .5D 61
Temple La. EC4 . . . . .4E 61
Templemead Ho. E9 . . . . . . .1A 4
Temple Mills La. E10 . . . . . .1A 6
E15 . . . . .2C 6
E20 . . . . .1A 6
Temple of Mithras (remains)
. . . . .4D 63
Temple Pl. WC2 . . . . .5C 60
Temple St. E2 . . . . .1F 43
Templeton Pl. SW5 . . . . . .4E 109
Temple West M. SE11 . . . . .2F 117
Temple Yd. E2 . . . . .1F 43
Tempus Apartments
EC1 . . . . .2F 39
Tempus Wharf SE16 . . . . . .4D 93
Tenby Ho. W2 . . . . .4B 54
Tenby Mans. W1 . . . . .1E 57
Tench St. E1 . . . . .2F 93
Tenda Rd. SE16 . . . . .4F 121
Tenison Ct. W1 . . . . .5B 58
Tenison Way SE1 . . . . .3D 89
Tenniel Cl. W2 . . . . .5A 54
Tennis St. SE1 . . . . .4D 91
Tennyson Ct. NW1 . . . . . . .5B 34
Tennyson Ho. SE17 . . . . . .5C 118
Tennyson Mans. SW3 . . . . .3F 133
W14 . . . . .2A 130
Tennyson Rd. E15 . . . . . . .1F 27
NW6 . . . . .3B 8
Tenterden Ho. SE17 . . . . . .1F 141
Tenterden Ct. W1 . . . . .1A 58
Tenter Ground E1 . . . . .2B 64
Tenter Pas. E1 . . . . .4C 64
Tent St. E1 . . . . .4F 43
Tenzing Ct. E14 . . . . .1A 70
Tequila Wharf E14 . . . . . . .4A 68
Teredo St. SE16 . . . . .2E 123
Terence McMillan Stadium
. . . . .1C 74
Terling Ho. W10 . . . . .1B 50
Terling Wlk. N1 . . . . .3B 18
Terminus St. SW1 . . . . . . .2A 114
Terrace, The E2 . . . . .2B 44
EC4 . . . . .4D 61
NW6 . . . . .3D 9
SE8 . . . . .4B 124
Terrace Rd. E9 . . . . .1C 22
Terraces, The E2 . . . . .1E 43
(off Garner St.)
NW8 . . . . .5D 11
Terrace Wlk. SW11 . . . . . .4B 134
Terretts Pl. N1 . . . . .2F 17
Terrick St. W12 . . . . .4A 50
Territorial Ho. SE11 . . . . . .4E 117
Testerton Rd. W11 . . . . . . .5E 51
Testerton Wlk. W11 . . . . . .5E 51
Tetbury Pl. N1 . . . . .4F 17
Tetcott Rd. SW10 . . . . . . .4B 132
(not continuous)
Tevatree Ho. SE1 . . . . . . .1D 143
Teversham La.
SW8 . . . . .5A 138
Teviot Est. E14 . . . . .1A 70
Teviot St. E14 . . . . .5B 48
Texryte Ho. N1 . . . . .3E 19

Thackeray Ct. NW6 . . . . . . .2C 10
SW3 . . . . .5B 112
W14 . . . . .2F 107
Thackeray Ho. WC1 . . . . . . .4F 37
Thackeray St. W8 . . . . .5A 82
Thackery Ct. EC1 . . . . .1F 61
Thalia Cl. SE10 . . . . .2E 149
Thalia Ct. E8 . . . . .2B 20
Thame Rd. SE16 . . . . .4E 95
Thames Barrier 5D 103
Thames Barrier Pk. 4B 102
Thamesbrook SW3 . . . . . . .1F 133
Thames Circ. E14 . . . . . . .3E 125
Thames Ct. NW6 . . . . .1C 30
SE15 . . . . .4B 142
Thames Exchange Bldg.
EC4 . . . . .5C 62
Thames Hgts. SE1 . . . . . . .4B 92
Thames Ho. EC4 . . . . .5C 62
SW1 . . . . .3F 115
Thameside Ind. Est. E16 . . .3E 103
Thames Path SE7 . . . . . . .2E 129
SE10 . . . . .3A 100
Thames Quay E14 . . . . . . .4A 98
Thames Rd. E16 . . . . .3D 103
Thames Rd. Ind. Est.
E16 . . . . .3D 103
Thames St. SE10 . . . . .2A 148
Thames Tunnel Mills SE16 . . .4B 94
Thames Wlk. SW11 . . . . . .4F 133
Thanet Ho. WC1 . . . . .3F 37
Thanet Lodge NW2 . . . . . . .1A 8
Thanet St. WC1 . . . . .3F 37
Thanet Wharf SE8 . . . . . . .3F 147
Thavie's Inn EC4 . . . . .3E 61
Thaxted Ct. N1 . . . . .1E 41
Thaxted Ho. SE16 . . . . . . .3B 122
Thaxton Rd. W14 . . . . .2C 130
Thayer St. W1 . . . . .2E 57
Tho . . . .
Names prefixed with 'The' for
example 'The Academy' are
indexed under the main name
such as 'Academy, The'
Theatre Bldg. E3 . . . . .2E 47
Theatre Pl. SE8 . . . . .5D 147
Theatre-Rites 5F 89
Theatre Royal
Drury Lane 4B 60
Haymarket 1E 87
Stratford 5E 7
Theatre Sq. E15 . . . . .5E 7
Theatre Vw. Apartments
SE1 . . . . .4E 89
Theatro Technis 4C 14
Theatro Twr. SE8 . . . . .3E 147
Theberton St. N1 . . . . .3E 17
Theed St. SE1 . . . . .3D 89
Thelbridge Ho. E3 . . . . .3F 47
Theobald's Rd. WC1 . . . . . .2B 60
Theobald St. SE1 . . . . .2D 119
Thermopylae Ga. E14 . . . . .4A 126
Theseus Wlk. N1 . . . . .1A 40
Thessaly Ho. SW8 . . . . . . .5B 136
Thessaly Rd. SW8 . . . . . . .5B 136
(not continuous)
Thesus Ho. E14 . . . . .4C 70
Thetford Ho. SE1 . . . . .1B 120
Theven St. E1 . . . . .4C 44
Third Av. W10 . . . . .2F 29
Thirleby Rd. SW1 . . . . .2C 114
Thirlmere NW1 . . . . .2A 36
Thirza Ho. E1 . . . . .4C 66
Thistle Gro. SW10 . . . . . . .5C 110

Thistle Ho. E14 . . . . .3C 70
Thistley Ct. SE8 . . . . .2F 147
Thomas Burt Ho. E2 . . . . . .2F 43
Thomas Cribb M. E6 . . . . . .3C 76
Thomas Darby Ct. W11 . . . . .4F 51
Thomas Doyle St. SE1 . . . .1A 118
Thomas Frye Ct. E15 . . . . . .1A 48
Thomas Fyre Dr. E3 . . . . . . .1E 47
Thomas Hollywood Ho. E2 . . .1B 44
Thomas More Highwalk
EC2 . . . . .2B 62
Thomas More Ho. EC2 . . . . .2B 62
Thomas More Sq. E1 . . . . . .1D 93
Thomas More St. E1 . . . . . .1D 93
Thomas Neal's Cen. WC2 . . .4F 59
Thomas Nth. Ter. E16 . . . . . .2B 72
Thomas Pl. W8 . . . . .2F 109
Thomas Rd. E14 . . . . .3C 68
Thomas Rd. Ind. Est. E14 . . .2D 69
(not continuous)
Thompson Ho. SE14 . . . . . .3C 144
W10 . . . . .5F 29
Thompson's Av. SE5 . . . . . .4B 140
Thomson Ho. E14 . . . . .4E 69
SE17 . . . . .4F 119
SW1 . . . . .1E 137
Thorburn Ho. SW1 . . . . . . .5C 84
Thorburn Sq. SE1 . . . . .4D 121
Thoresby St. N1 . . . . .2C 40
Thornaby Ho. E2 . . . . .2F 43
Thorn Apartments E3 . . . . . .1D 69
Thornbill Ho. SE15 . . . . . . .4D 143
Thornbury Ct. W11 . . . . . . .5D 53
Thorncroft St. SW8 . . . . . . .5F 137
Thorndike Cl. SW10 . . . . . .4B 132
Thorndike Ho. SW1 . . . . . . .5D 115
Thorndike St. SW1 . . . . . . .4D 115
Thorne Cl. E16 . . . . .3C 72
Thorne Ho. E2 . . . . .2C 44
F14 . . . . .1R 126
Thorne Rd. SW8 . . . . .5F 137
Thornewill Ho. E1 . . . . .5C 66
Thorney Ct. W8 . . . . .5B 82
Thorney Cres. SW11 . . . . . .5E 133
Thorney St. SW1 . . . . .3F 115
Thornfield Ho. E14 . . . . . . .5D 69
Thornfield Rd. W12 . . . . . . .4A 78
(not continuous)
Thorngate Rd. W9 . . . . .4E 31
Thornham Gro. E15 . . . . . . .3D 7
Thornham Ind. Est. E15 . . . . .3D 7
Thornham St. SE10 . . . . . . .3A 148
Thornhaugh M. WC1 . . . . . .5E 37
Thornhaugh St. WC1 . . . . . .5E 37
Thornhill Bri. N1 . . . . .5B 16
Thornhill Bri. Wharf N1 . . . .4B 16
Thornhill Cres. N1 . . . . .2C 16
Thornhill Gro. N1 . . . . .2C 16
Thornhill Ho's. N1 . . . . .1D 17
Thornhill Rd. N1 . . . . .1D 17
Thornhill Sq. N1 . . . . .2C 16
Thornley Pl. SE10 . . . . .1F 149
Thornton Ho. SE17 . . . . . . .4F 119
Thornton Pl. W1 . . . . .1C 56
Thornton St. E20 . . . . .2A 26
Thornwood Gdns. W8 . . . . .4D 81
Thornwood Lodge W8 . . . . .4D 81
Thorogood Gdns. E15 . . . . . .3F 7
Thorold Ho. SE1 . . . . .4B 90
Thorparch Rd. SW8 . . . . . .5E 137
Thorpe Cl. W10 . . . . .3A 52
Thorpe Ho. N1 . . . . .4C 16
Thoydon Rd. E3 . . . . .1F 45
Thrale St. SE1 . . . . .3C 90

Thrasher Cl. E8 . . . . .3B 20
Thrawl St. E1 . . . . .2C 64
Threadneedle St. EC2 . . . . . .4D 63
Threadneedle Wlk. EC2 . . .3E 63
Three Barrels Wlk. EC4 . . . .1C 90
Three Colts Cnr. E2 . . . . . . .5D 43
Three Colts La. E2 . . . . .4F 43
Three Colt St. E14 . . . . .5C 68
Three Cranes Wlk. EC4 . . . . .1C 90
Three Cups Yd. WC1 . . . . . .2C 60
Three Kings Yd. W1 . . . . . . .5F 57
Three Mill La. E3 . . . . .1B 48
Three Mills Studios E3 . . .2C 48
Three Nun Ct. EC2 . . . . .3C 62
Three Oak La. SE1 . . . . .4B 92
Three Quays EC3 . . . . .1A 92
Three Quays Wlk. EC3 . . . . .1A 92
Threshers Pl. W11 . . . . .5F 51
Throckmorten Rd. E16 . . . . .4A 74
Throgmorton Av. EC2 . . . . . .3E 63
(not continuous)
Throgmorton St. EC2 . . . . . .3E 63
Thrush St. SE17 . . . . .5A 118
Thurland Ho. SE16 . . . . .4F 121
Thurland Rd. SE16 . . . . .1D 121
Thurloe Cl. SW7 . . . . .3F 111
Thurloe Ct. SW3 . . . . .4F 111
Thurloe Pl. SW7 . . . . .3E 111
Thurloe Pl. M. SW7 . . . . .3E 111
Thurloe Sq. SW7 . . . . .3F 111
Thurloe St. SW7 . . . . .3E 111
Thurlow St. SE17 . . . . .5E 119
(not continuous)
Thurlow Wlk. SE17 . . . . .5F 119
(not continuous)
Thurnscoe NW1 . . . . .4B 14
Thurso Ho. NW6 . . . . .1F 31
Thurstan Dwellings WC2 . . .3A 60
Thurston Ho. N1 . . . . .4C 16
Thurtle Rd. E2 . . . . .4C 20
Tibbatt's Rd. E3 . . . . .4F 47
Tibberton Sq. N1 . . . . .2B 18
Tiber Cl. E3 . . . . .4D 25
Tiber Gdns. N1 . . . . .4A 16
Tickford Ho. NW8 . . . . .3F 33
Tidal Basin Rd. E16 . . . . .1C 100
(not continuous)
Tidbury Ct. SW8 . . . . .5B 136
Tidemill Way SE8 . . . . .4E 147
Tideway Ct. SE16 . . . . .2E 95
Tideway Ho. E14 . . . . .4E 97
Tideway Ind. Est. SW8 . . .3C 136
Tideway Wlk. SW8 . . . . .3C 136
Tidey St. E3 . . . . .1E 69
Tidworth Rd. E3 . . . . .4D 47
Tiger Ho. WC1 . . . . .3E 37
Tilbury Cl. SE15 . . . . .4C 142
Tilbury Ho. SE14 . . . . .2D 145
Tile Ho. N1 . . . . .3F 15
Tilehurst NW1 . . . . .3A 36
Tileyard Rd. N7 . . . . .1F 15
Tiller Ho. N1 . . . . .4A 20
Tiller Leisure Cen. 1E 125
Tiller Rd. E14 . . . . .1D 125
Tillett Sq. SE16 . . . . .5A 96
Tillet Way E2 . . . . .2D 43
Tillman St. E1 . . . . .4A 66
Tilloch St. N1 . . . . .2B 16
Tillotson Ct. SW8 . . . . .5E 137
Tilney Ct. EC1 . . . . .4C 40
Tilney St. W1 . . . . .2E 85
Tilson Cl. SE5 . . . . .4F 141
Tilton St. SW6 . . . . .3A 130
Timberland Cl. SE15 . . . . . . .5D 143

Timberland Rd. E1 . . . . .4A 66
Timber Pond Rd. SE16 . . . . .3E 95
Timber St. EC1 . . . . .4B 40
Timber Wharf E2 . . . . .4B 20
Timber Wharves Est.
E14 . . . . .3E 125
Timber Yard, The N1 . . . . . .3A 42
Timbrell Pl. SE16 . . . . .3B 96
Times Sq. E1 . . . . .4D 65
Timor Ho. E1 . . . . .5F 45
Tindal St. SW9 . . . . .5F 139
Tinsley Rd. E1 . . . . .1C 66
Tintagel Ct. EC1 . . . . .4F 39
Tintern Ho. NW1 . . . . .1A 36
SW1 . . . . .4F 113
Tinto Rd. E16 . . . . .1E 73
Tinworth St. SE11 . . . . .5A 116
Tiptree NW1 . . . . .1F 13
Tisbury Ct. W1 . . . . .5D 59
Tisdall Ho. SE17 . . . . .4E 119
Tisdall Pl. SE17 . . . . .4E 119
Tissington Ct. SE16 . . . . . . .4D 123
Titan Bus. Est. SE8 . . . . . . .4D 147
Titan Ho. E20 . . . . .3B 6
Titchborne Row W2 . . . . . . .4F 55
Titchfield Rd. NW8 . . . . .4B 12
Tite St. SW3 . . . . .1B 134
Titian Hgts. E20 . . . . .3A 6
Titmuss St. W12 . . . . .5A 78
Tiverton St. SE1 . . . . .2B 118
Tivoli Ct. SE16 . . . . .3B 96
Tobacco Dock E1 . . . . .1A 94
Tobacco Quay E1 . . . . .1F 93
Tobago St. E14 . . . . .4D 97
Tobin Cl. NW3 . . . . .1A 12
Toby La. E1 . . . . .5F 45
Todber Ho. W14 . . . . .1F 107
Tokenhouse Yd. EC2 . . . . . .3D 63
Tolchurch W11 . . . . .3C 52
Tolhurst Dr. W10 . . . . .2A 30
Tollard Ho. W14 . . . . .2B 108
Tollbridge Cl. W10 . . . . .4A 30
Tollet St. E1 . . . . .4D 45
Tollgate Gdns. NW6 . . . . . . .5F 9
Tollgate Ho. NW6 . . . . .5F 9
Tollgate Rd. E6 . . . . .2E 75
E16 . . . . .2B 74
Tollgate Sq. E6 . . . . .1B 76
Tolmers Sq. NW1 . . . . .4C 36
(not continuous)
Tolpaide Ho. SE11 . . . . .4D 117
Tolpuddle St. N1 . . . . .5D 17
Tom Groves Cl. E15 . . . . . . .3E 7
Tom Hood Cl. E15 . . . . .3E 7
Tom Jenkinson Rd.
E16 . . . . .2E 101
Tomkyns Ho. SE11 . . . . .4D 117
Tomline Ho. SE1 . . . . .3B 90
Tomlin's Gro. E3 . . . . .2E 47
Tomlinson Cl. E2 . . . . .3C 42
Tomlins Ter. E14 . . . . .3A 68
Tom Nolan Cl. E15 . . . . .1F 49
Tompion Ho. EC1 . . . . .4A 40
Tompion St. EC1 . . . . .3A 40
(not continuous)
Tom Smith Cl. SE10 . . . . . . .2F 149
Tomson Ho. SE1 . . . . .1B 120
Tom Williams Ho. SW6 . . .3B 130
Tonbridge Ho's. WC1 . . . . . .3F 37
(not continuous)
Tonbridge St. WC1 . . . . .2F 37
Tonbridge Wlk. WC1 . . . . . . .2F 37
Toneborough NW8 . . . . .4A 10
Tony Cannell M. E3 . . . . .3B 46

Took's Ct. EC4 . . . . .3D 61
Tooley St. SE1 . . . . .2E 91
Toomey Cen. E16 . . . . .2A 102
Topham Ho. SE10 . . . . .5B 148
Topham St. EC1 . . . . .4D 39
Topmast Point E14 . . . . .5D 97
Torbay Ct. NW1 . . . . .1A 14
Torbay Mans. NW6 . . . . .2B 8
Torbay Rd. NW6 . . . . .2B 8
Torbay St. NW1 . . . . .1A 14
Tor Ct. W8 . . . . .4E 81
Toreno Mansion E20 . . . . . .3A 6
Tor Gdns. W8 . . . . .4D 81
Tornay Ho. E9 . . . . .2C 22
N1 . . . . .5B 16
Toronto Ho. SE16 . . . . .5D 95
Torquay St. W2 . . . . .2F 53
Torrens St. EC1 . . . . .1F 39
Torrent Lodge SE10 . . . . . . .5F 147
Torres Sq. E14 . . . . .5E 125
Torridon Ho. NW6 . . . . .1F 31
Torrington Pl. E1 . . . . .2E 93
WC1 . . . . .1D 59
Torrington Sq. WC1 . . . . . . .5E 37
Tortington Ho. SE15 . . . . . . .4E 143
Tothill Ho. SW1 . . . . .3E 115
Tothill St. SW1 . . . . .5D 87
Tottan Ter. E1 . . . . .3E 67
Tottenhall NW1 . . . . .1E 13
Tottenham Ct. Rd. W1 . . . . .5C 36
Tottenham M. W1 . . . . .1C 58
Tottenham St. W1 . . . . .2C 58
Totters Ct. SE17 . . . . .2D 141
Touchard Ho. N1 . . . . .3E 41
Toulmin St. SE1 . . . . .5B 90
Toulon St. SE5 . . . . .4B 140
Toulouse Ct. SE16 . . . . .5A 122
Tounson Ct. SW1 . . . . .4E 115
Tourist Info. Cen.
City of London 4B 62
Greenwich 2C 148
Leicester Square 1E 87
(off Leicester Sq.)
Tournay Rd. SW6 . . . . .4C 130
Toussaint Wlk. SE16 . . . . . . .1E 121
Tovy Ho. SE1 . . . . .1D 143
Towcester Rd. E3 . . . . .5A 48
Tower, The SW8 . . . . .2F 137
Tower 42 . . . . .3F 63
Tower Bri. SE1 . . . . .3B 92
Tower Bri. App. E1 . . . . .2B 92
Tower Bri. Bus. Complex
SE16 . . . . .2F 121
Tower Bri. Bus. Sq.
SE16 . . . . .3F 121
Tower Bridge Exhibition 2B 92
Tower Bri. Plaza SE1 . . . . . .3B 92
Tower Bri. Rd. SE1 . . . . .2F 119
Tower Bri. Sq. SE1 . . . . .4B 92
Tower Bri. Wharf E1 . . . . . . .3D 93
Tower Bldgs. E1 . . . . .3A 94
Tower Ct. N1 . . . . .2B 18
NW8 . . . . .5A 12
WC2 . . . . .4F 59
Towergate SE1 . . . . .3F 119
Towergate Ho. E3 . . . . .1C 46
TOWER HILL 1B 92
Tower Hill EC3 . . . . .1A 92
Tower Hill Ter. EC3 . . . . .1A 92
Tower Ho. E1 . . . . .2E 65
Tower Mans. SE1 . . . . .2B 120
Tower M. E5 . . . . .2A 4
Tower Mill Rd. SE15 . . . . . . .4F 141
Tower of London, The 1B 92

Tower of London Welcome Cen.
. . . . .1A **92**
Tower Pl. EC3 . . . . .1A **92**
Tower Pl. E. EC3 . . . . .1A **92**
Tower Pl. W. EC3 . . . . .1A **92**
Tower Royal EC4 . . . . .5C **62**
Tower St. WC2 . . . . .4E **59**
Tower Wlk. SE1 . . . . .3F **119**
Tower Wharf SE1 . . . . .4B **92**
Tower Workshops SE1 . . . . .5B **92**
Townley St. SE17 . . . . .5D **119**
 (not continuous)
Townsend Ho. SE1 . . . . . . .4E **121**
Townsend St. SE17 . . . . . . .4E **119**
Townshend Ct. NW8 . . . . . .5A **12**
Townshend Est. NW8 . . . . . .5F **11**
Townshend Rd. NW8 . . . . . .4F **11**
 (not continuous)
Towpath Wlk. E9 . . . . .2B **4**
Toynbee St. E1 . . . . .2B **64**
Toynbee Studios 3C **64**
Tracy Ho. E3 . . . . .3B **46**
Trader Rd. E6 . . . . .4F **77**
Tradescant Ho. E9 . . . . . . .1B **22**
Tradescant Rd. SW8 . . . . . .5A **138**
Tradewind Hgts. SE16 . . . . .3D **95**
Tradewinds Ct. E1 . . . . .2E **93**
Trafalgar Av. SE15 . . . . . . .1C **142**
Trafalgar Chambers
 SW3 . . . . .5E **111**
Trafalgar Cl. SE16 . . . . .3F **123**
Trafalgar Ct. E1 . . . . .2C **94**
Trafalgar Gdns. E1 . . . . . . .1E **67**
 W8 . . . . .1A **110**
Trafalgar Gro. SE10 . . . . . .2E **149**
Trafalgar Ho. SE17 . . . . . . .5D **119**
Trafalgar M. E9 . . . . .4B **4**
Trafalgar Point N1 . . . . .2E **19**
Trafalgar Quarters
 CL10 . . . . .1D **149**
Trafalgar Rd. SE10 . . . . . . .5A **128**
 SE10 . . . . .2E **149**
Trafalgar Square 2E **87**
Trafalgar Sq. SW1 . . . . . . .2E **87**
 WC2 . . . . .2E **87**
Trafalgar St. SE17 . . . . .5D **119**
Trafalgar Studios 2F **87**
Trafalgar Way E14 . . . . . . .2B **98**
Trafford Ho. N1 . . . . .1E **41**
Trahorn Cl. E1 . . . . .5E **43**
Traitors' Gate 2B **92**
Tralee Ct. SE16 . . . . .5F **121**
Tramway Av. E15 . . . . .1E **27**
Tramway Ct. E1 . . . . .1A **68**
Transenna Works N1 . . . . . .1F **17**
Transept St. NW1 . . . . .2A **56**
Transom Cl. SE16 . . . . .3A **124**
Transom Sq. E14 . . . . .5F **125**
Tranton Rd. SE16 . . . . .1E **121**
Trappes Ho. SE16 . . . . .4F **121**
Travers Ho. SE10 . . . . .2E **149**
Treadgold Ho. W11 . . . . . . .5E **51**
Treadgold St. W11 . . . . . . .5E **51**
Treadway St. E2 . . . . .1F **43**
Treasury Pas. SW1 . . . . . . .4F **87**
Treaty St. N1 . . . . .4B **16**
Trebeck St. W1 . . . . .2F **85**
Trebovir Rd. SW5 . . . . .5E **109**
Treby St. E3 . . . . .5B **46**
Tredegar Ho. E3 . . . . .2D **47**
Tredegar M. E3 . . . . .2B **46**
Tredegar Rd. E3 . . . . .1B **46**
Tredegar Sq. E3 . . . . .2B **46**
Tredegar Ter. E3 . . . . .2B **46**

Trederwen Rd. E8 . . . . .3E **21**
Tree Rd. E16 . . . . .3B **74**
Treetop M. NW6 . . . . .2A **8**
Trego Rd. E9 . . . . .1C **24**
Tregunter Rd. SW10 . . . . . .2A **132**
Trehurst St. E5 . . . . .1A **4**
Trelawney Ho. SE1 . . . . . . .4B **90**
Trellick Twr. W10 . . . . .5B **30**
Trellis Sq. E3 . . . . .2C **46**
Trematon Ho. SE11 . . . . . . .5E **117**
Trenchard St. SE10 . . . . . . .1E **149**
Trenchold St. SW8 . . . . . . .3F **137**
Trendell Ho. E14 . . . . .3D **69**
Trenmar Gdns. NW10 . . . . .2A **28**
Tresco Ho. SE11 . . . . .5D **117**
Tresham Cres. NW8 . . . . . . .4F **33**
Tresham Ho. WC1 . . . . .1B **60**
 (off Red Lion Sq.)
Tressell Cl. N1 . . . . .2A **18**
Tress Pl. SE1 . . . . .2F **89**
Trevanion Rd. W14 . . . . . . .5A **108**
Trevelyan Ho. E2 . . . . .3D **45**
 SE5 . . . . .4A **140**
Treveris St. SE1 . . . . .3A **90**
Treverton St. W10 . . . . .5E **29**
Treverton Towers W10 . . . . .1E **51**
Treves Ho. E1 . . . . .5E **43**
Trevithick Ho. SE16 . . . . . . .4A **122**
Trevithick St. SE8 . . . . .2D **147**
Trevithick Way E3 . . . . .3E **47**
Trevor Pl. SW7 . . . . .5A **84**
Trevor Sq. SW7 . . . . .5B **84**
Trevor St. SW7 . . . . .5A **84**
Trevor Wlk. SW7 . . . . .5B **84**
 (not continuous)
Trevose Ho. SE11 . . . . .5C **116**
Tria Apartments E2 . . . . . . .2E **43**
Triangle, The E8 . . . . .3A **22**
 EC1 . . . . .4A **40**
Triangle Ct. E16 . . . . .1C **74**
 SE1 . . . . .3C **90**
Triangle Est. SE11 . . . . .1D **139**
Triangle Ho. SE1 . . . . .4B **92**
Triangle Rd. E8 . . . . .3F **21**
Tribeca Apartments E1 . . . . .1C **64**
 (off Heneage St.)
Tricycle Cinema, The 2C **8**
Tricycle Theatre, The 2C **8**
Trident Ho. E14 . . . . .4C **70**
Trident Pl. SW3 . . . . .2E **133**
Trident St. SE16 . . . . .3E **123**
Trig La. EC4 . . . . .5B **62**
Trigon Rd. SW8 . . . . .4C **138**
Trimdon NW1 . . . . .4C **14**
Trim St. SE14 . . . . .3B **146**
Trinidad Ho. E14 . . . . .5C **68**
Trinidad St. E14 . . . . .5C **68**
Trinity Buoy Wharf
 E14 . . . . .1A **100**
Trinity Chu. Sq. SE1 . . . . . .5C **90**
Trinity College of Music 2C **148**
Trinity Ct. N1 . . . . .3F **19**
 SE8 . . . . .5A **124**
 W2 . . . . .3B **54**
 W9 . . . . .3C **30**
 WC1 . . . . .4C **38**
Trinity Gdns. E16 . . . . .1C **72**
 (not continuous)
Trinity Grn. E1 . . . . .1B **66**
Trinity Hospital (Almshouses)
 SE10 . . . . .1E **149**
Trinity Ho. EC3 . . . . .5B **64**
 SE1 . . . . .1C **118**
 W14 . . . . .3B **108**

Trinity M. E1 . . . . .1B **66**
 W10 . . . . .3E **51**
Trinity Pl. EC3 . . . . .1B **92**
Trinity Sq. EC3 . . . . .1A **92**
Trinity St. E16 . . . . .2D **73**
 SE1 . . . . .5C **90**
 (not continuous)
Trinity Twr. E1 . . . . .1D **93**
Trio Pl. SE1 . . . . .5C **90**
Tristan Ct. SE8 . . . . .2B **146**
Triton Ct. E16 . . . . .2E **73**
Triton Ho. E14 . . . . .4F **125**
Triton Sq. NW1 . . . . .4B **36**
Triton St. NW1 . . . . .4B **36**
Triumph Rd. E6 . . . . .3C **76**
Trocette Mans. SE1 . . . . . . .1F **119**
Trojan Ct. NW6 . . . . .2A **8**
Troon Cl. SE16 . . . . .5A **122**
Troon Ho. E1 . . . . .3F **67**
Troon St. E1 . . . . .3F **67**
Tropical Ct. W10 . . . . .2E **29**
Trothy Rd. SE1 . . . . .3E **121**
Trotwood Ho. SE16 . . . . . . .5F **93**
Troughton Rd. SE7 . . . . . . .5F **129**
Troutbeck NW1 . . . . .3A **36**
Trowbridge Est. E9 . . . . . . .4C **4**
Trowbridge Ho. E9 . . . . .5C **4**
Trowbridge Rd. E9 . . . . .5C **4**
Troy Ct. W8 . . . . .1D **109**
Truesdale Rd. E6 . . . . .4C **76**
Truman Wlk. E3 . . . . .4A **48**
Trump St. EC2 . . . . .4C **62**
Trundle Ho. SE1 . . . . .4B **90**
Trundle St. SE1 . . . . .4B **90**
Trundleys Rd. SE8 . . . . .4E **123**
Trundley's Ter.
 SE8 . . . . .4E **123**
Truro Ho. W2 . . . . .2D **53**
Trussley Rd. W6 . . . . .2B **106**
Tryon Cres. E9 . . . . .3B **22**
Tryon St. SW3 . . . . .5B **112**
Tucana Ct. E1 . . . . .4C **42**
 (off Cygnet St.)
Tucana Hgts. E20 . . . . .3C **6**
Tudor Cl. SE16 . . . . .2D **95**
Tudor Gro. E9 . . . . .2B **22**
Tudor Ho. E9 . . . . .2B **22**
 E16 . . . . .2E **101**
 W14 . . . . .3E **107**
Tudor Rd. E9 . . . . .3A **22**
Tudor St. EC4 . . . . .5E **61**
Tufnell Ct. E3 . . . . .4B **24**
Tufton Ct. SW1 . . . . .2F **115**
Tufton St. SW1 . . . . .1E **115**
Tulip Cl. E6 . . . . .2B **76**
Tullis Ho. E9 . . . . .1C **22**
Tunbridge Ho. EC1 . . . . . . .2F **39**
Tunis Rd. W12 . . . . .2A **78**
Tunley Grn. E14 . . . . .2C **68**
Tunnan Leys E6 . . . . .3E **77**
Tunnel App. E14 . . . . .5F **67**
 SE10 . . . . .5F **99**
 SE16 . . . . .5B **94**
Tunnel Av. SE10 . . . . .4E **99**
 (not continuous)
Tunnel Av. Trad. Est.
 SE10 . . . . .5E **99**
Tunnel Rd. SE16 . . . . .4B **94**
Tupman Ho. SE16 . . . . .1D **121**
Turin St. E2 . . . . .3D **43**
Turk's Head Yd.
 EC1 . . . . .1F **61**
Turk's Row SW3 . . . . .5C **112**
Turley Cl. E15 . . . . .4F **27**

Turnagain La. EC4 . . . . . . .3F **61**
Turnberry Cl. SE16 . . . . . . .1A **144**
Turnberry Quay
  E14 . . . . .1A **126**
Turnbull Ho. N1 . . . . .4A **18**
Turner Cl. SW9 . . . . .5A **140**
Turner Ct. SE16 . . . . .5C **94**
Turner Ho. E14 . . . . .5E **97**
  NW8 . . . . .5F **11**
  SW1 . . . . .4E **115**
Turner Pde. N1 . . . . .1D **17**
Turners Ct. E15 . . . . .1D **7**
Turners Rd. E3 . . . . .2B **68**
Turner St. E1 . . . . .2F **65**
  E16 . . . . .4C **72**
Turneville Rd. W14 . . . . . . .2B **130**
Turnmill St. EC1 . . . . .5E **39**
Turnour Ho. E1 . . . . .4F **65**
Turnpike Cl. SE8 . . . . .4C **146**
Turnpike Ho. EC1 . . . . .3A **40**
Turnpin La. SE10 . . . . .3C **148**
Turnstone Ho. *E1* *1D 93*
  (off Star Pl.)
Turpentine La.
  SW1 . . . . .5A **114**
Turpin Cl. E1 . . . . .5D **67**
Turpins Yd. SE10 . . . . .5C **148**
Turquand St. SE17 . . . . .4C **118**
Turville Ho. NW8 . . . . .4F **33**
Turville St. E2 . . . . .4C **42**
Tuscan Ho. E2 . . . . .2C **44**
Tuskar St. SE10 . . . . .1F **149**
Tussah Ho. E2 . . . . .5B **22**
Tustin Est. SE15 . . . . .4B **144**
Tuttle Ho. SW1 . . . . .1D **137**
Tweezer's All. WC2 . . . . .5D **61**
Twelvetrees Bus. Pk.
  E3 . . . . .4D **49**
Twelvetrees Cres. E3 . . . . . .4B **48**
  (not continuous)
  E16 . . . . .5D **49**
Twig Folly Cl. E2 . . . . .1E **45**
Twine Ct. E1 . . . . .5B **66**
Twine Ter. E3 . . . . .5B **46**
Twycross M. SE10 . . . . . . .4A **128**
Twyford Pl. WC2 . . . . .3B **60**
Twyford St. N1 . . . . .3B **16**
Tyas Rd. E16 . . . . .1B **72**
Tyburn Ho. NW8 . . . . .4E **33**
Tyburn Tree (site of) 5B **56**
Tyburn Way W1 . . . . .5C **56**
Tyers Est. SE1 . . . . .4F **91**
Tyer's Ga. SE1 . . . . .5F **91**
Tyers St. SE11 . . . . .1B **138**
Tyers Ter. SE11 . . . . .1B **138**
Tyler Cl. E2 . . . . .5B **20**
Tyler's Ct. W1 . . . . .4D **59**
Tyler St. SE10 . . . . .1F **149**
  (not continuous)
Tylney Ho. E1 . . . . .3A **66**
Tyndale Ct. E9 . . . . .5A **4**
  E14 . . . . .5F **125**
Tyndale Ho. N1 . . . . .1F **17**
Tyndale La. N1 . . . . .1F **17**
Tyndale Mans. N1 . . . . .1F **17**
Tyndale Ter. N1 . . . . .1F **17**
Tynemouth Cl. E6 . . . . .4F **77**
Tyne St. E1 . . . . .3C **64**
Tynte Ct. E9 . . . . .3A **4**
Type St. E2 . . . . .1D **45**
Tyrawley Rd. SW6 . . . . .5F **131**
Tyrian Pl. E1 . . . . .2D **65**
Tyrrell Ho. SW1 . . . . .2C **136**
Tysoe St. EC1 . . . . .3E **39**

Tyssen St. N1 . . . . .5A **20**
Tytherton E2 . . . . .1B **44**

U

Uamvar St. E14 . . . . .1A **70**
Udall St. SW1 . . . . .4C **114**
Udimore Ho. W10 . . . . .1B **50**
Ufford St. SE1 . . . . .4E **89**
Ufton Gro. N1 . . . . .1E **19**
Ufton Rd. N1 . . . . .2E **19**
  (not continuous)
Ullin St. E14 . . . . .2B **70**
Ullswater Ho. SE15 . . . . . . .3B **144**
Ulster Pl. NW1 . . . . .5F **35**
Ulster Ter. NW1 . . . . .5F **35**
Umberston St. E1 . . . . .3F **65**
Underhill Ho. E14 . . . . .2D **69**
Underhill Pas. NW1 . . . . .3A **14**
Underhill St. NW1 . . . . .4A **14**
Undershaft EC3 . . . . .4F **63**
Underwood Ho. W6 . . . . . . .1A **106**
Underwood Rd. E1 . . . . .5D **43**
Underwood Row N1 . . . . .2C **40**
Underwood St. N1 . . . . .2C **40**
Undine Rd. E14 . . . . .3A **126**
Unex Twr. E15 . . . . .2D **27**
Unicorn Bldg. E1 . . . . .5E **67**
Unicorn Theatre
  London 3A **92**
Union Ct. EC2 . . . . .3F **63**
  W9 . . . . .1D **53**
Union Dr. E1 . . . . .4A **46**
Union Pk. SE10 . . . . .5B **128**
Union Sq. N1 . . . . .4B **18**
Union St. SE1 . . . . .3F **89**
Union Theatre 3A **90**
Union Wlk. N1 . . . . .2A **42**
Union Wharf N1 . . . . .4C **18**
  (Arlington Av.)
  N1 . . . . .5A **18**
  (Wenlock Rd.)
Union Yd. W1 . . . . .4A **58**
United Ho. SE16 . . . . .5B **94**
Unit Workshops E1 . . . . .3D **65**
Unity Ct. SE1 . . . . .1C **142**
Unity M. NW1 . . . . .5D **15**
Unity Wharf SE1 . . . . .4C **92**
University College London
  Art Museum 4D **37**
  Bloomsbury Campus 4D **37**
  Department of Geological
  Collections 5D **37**
  Institute of Neurology . . .5A **38**
  (off Queen Sq.)
  Slade School of Fine Art
  .4D **37**
  Windeyer Institute 1C **58**
University of East London
  Docklands Campus 5E **77**
  Duncan House 2D **27**
University of Greenwich
  Greenwich Campus, King
  William Wlk. 3C **148**
  Maritime Greenwich Campus
  . . . . .2D **149**
University of London
  Birkbeck College 5E **37**
  Heythrop College 1F **109**
  School of Hygiene
  & Tropical Medicine 1E **59**
  School of Oriental
  & African Studies 5E **37**

University of London
  Senate House 1E **59**
  Warburg Institute 5E **37**
University of London Institute
  of Education &
  Institute of Advanced
  Legal Studies 5E **37**
University of the Arts London
  Chelsea College of Art
  & Design 5E **115**
  London College of Fashion -
  Golden La. 5B **40**
  London College of Fashion -
  Mare St. 1A **22**
University of Westminster
  Cavendish Campus, Hanson St.
  . . . . .1B **58**
  Cavendish Campus, Lit.
  Titchfield St. 2B **58**
  Marylebone Campus 1D **57**
  Regent Campus, Regent St.
  .3A **58**
  Regent Campus, Wells St.
  .2C **58**
University St. WC1 . . . . .5C **36**
University Way E16 . . . . .1E **105**
Unwin Cl. SE15 . . . . .3D **143**
Unwin Mans. W14 . . . . .2B **130**
Unwin Rd. SW7 . . . . .1D **111**
Up at The O2 . . . . .3A **100**
Upbrook M. W2 . . . . .4C **54**
Upcerne Rd. SW10 . . . . .5B **132**
Upcott Ho. E3 . . . . .3F **47**
  E9 . . . . .1B **22**
Upnall Ho. SE15 . . . . .3C **144**
Upnor Way SE17 . . . . .5A **120**
Up. Addison Gdns. W14 . . . .4F **79**
Up. Bank St. E14 . . . . .3F **97**
  (not continuous)
Up. Belgrave St. SW1 . . . . . .1E **113**
Up. Berenger Wlk. *SW10* . . .4D **133**
  (off Berenger Wlk.)
Up. Berkeley St. W1 . . . . .4B **56**
Up. Blantyre Wlk. *SW10* 4D **133**
  (off Blantyre Wlk.)
Up. Brook St. W1 . . . . .1D **85**
Up. Caldy Wlk. *N1* *1C 18*
  (off Caldy Wlk.)
Up. Camelford Wlk. W11 . . . .5F **51**
Up. Cheapside Pas. *EC2* *4B 62*
  (off Cheapside)
Up. Cheyne Row SW3 . . . . .3F **133**
Up. Clarendon Wlk. W11 . . . .4F **51**
Up. Dartrey Wlk. *SW10* 4C **132**
  (off Whistler Wlk.)
Up. Dengie Wlk. *N1* *3B 18*
  (off Baddow Wlk.)
Upper Feilde W1 . . . . .5D **57**
Up. Grosvenor St. W1 . . . . . .1D **85**
Upper Ground SE1 . . . . .2D **89**
Up. Gulland Wlk. N1 . . . . .1C **18**
Up. Hawkwell Wlk. *N1* *3C 18*
  (off Maldon Cl.)
Up. James St. W1 . . . . .5C **58**
Up. John St. W1 . . . . .5C **58**
Upper Lodge W8 . . . . .3A **82**
Upper Marsh SE1 . . . . .1C **116**
Up. Montagu St. W1 . . . . .1B **56**
Upper Nth. St. E14 . . . . .2E **69**
Up. Phillimore Gdns.
  W8 . . . . .5D **81**
Up. Rawreth Wlk. *N1* *3C 18*
  (off Basire St.)
Up. St Martin's La. WC2 . . . . .5F **59**

Upper St. N1 . . . . .1F 17
Up. Tachbrook St. SW1 . . . .3B 114
Up. Talbot Wlk. W11 . . . . . . .4F 51
Up. Thames St. EC4 . . . . .5A 62
Up. Whistler Wlk. SW10 . . .4C 132
(off Worlds End Est.)
Up. Wimpole St. W1 . . . . . . .1E 57
Up. Woburn Pl. WC1 . . . . . .3E 37
Upton Ho. E9 . . . . .3A 4
Upwey Ho. N1 . . . . .4F 19
Urdang, The 3E 39
Urlwin St. SE5 . . . . .3B 140
Urmston Ho. E14 . . . . .3C 126
Ursa Mans. E20 . . . . .3B 6
Ursula Gould Way E14 . . . . .2E 69
Usborne M. SW8 . . . . .4C 138
Usher Rd. E3 . . . . .4C 24
(not continuous)
Usk St. E2 . . . . .2D 45
Utopia Village NW1 . . . . . . .3D 13
Uverdale Rd. SW10 . . . . . . .4C 132
Uxbridge Rd. W12 . . . . .3A 78
Uxbridge St. W8 . . . . .2D 81

V

Vaine Ho. E9 . . . . .5A 4
Vale, The SW3 . . . . .2D 133
Vale Cl. W9 . . . . .3B 32
Vale Ct. W9 . . . . .3C 32
Valentine Ho. E3 . . . . .4C 24
Valentine Pl. SE1 . . . . .4F 89
Valentine Rd. E9 . . . . .1D 23
Valentine Row SE1 . . . . .5F 89
Valerian Way E15 . . . . .3F 49
Vale Royal N7 . . . . .2F 15
Vale Royal Ho. WC2 . . . . . . .5E 59
Valiant Ho. E14 . . . . .5B 98
Valiant Way E6 . . . . .2R 76
Vallance Rd. E1 . . . . .5E 43
E2 . . . . .3E 43
Valois Ho. SE1 . . . . .1B 120
V & A Museum of Childhood
. . . . .2B 44
Vanbrugh Castle SE10 . . . . .3F 149
Vanbrugh Cl. E16 . . . . .2D 75
Vanbrugh Ct. SE11 . . . . .4E 117
Vanbrugh Hill SE10 . . . . . .5B 128
Vanbrugh Ho. E9 . . . . .1C 22
Vanburgh Ho. E1 . . . . .1B 64
Vancouver Ho. E1 . . . . .3A 94
SE16 . . . . .5D 95
Vanderbilt Vs. W12 . . . . .4D 79
Vandome Cl. E16 . . . . .4F 73
Vandon St. SW1 . . . . .1C 114
Vandon Pas. SW1 . . . . .1C 114
Vandon St. SW1 . . . . .1C 114
Vandy St. EC2 . . . . .5F 41
Vane St. SW1 . . . . .3C 114
Vange Ho. W10 . . . . .1B 50
Van Gogh Ct. E14 . . . . .2D 127
Vanguard Bldg. E14 . . . . . . .4D 97
Vanguard Cl. E16 . . . . .2E 73
Vanguard Ho. E8 . . . . .1A 22
Vanilla & Sesame Ct.
SE1 . . . . .4C 92
Vansittart St. SE14 . . . . .4A 146
Vanstone Ct. N7 . . . . .1D 17
Vantage M. E14 . . . . .3C 98
Vantage Pl. W8 . . . . .2E 109
Vantrey Ho. SE11 . . . . .4D 117
Varcoe Rd. SE16 . . . . .1A 144

Varden St. E1 . . . . .3F 65
Varley Ho. NW6 . . . . .4D 9
SE1 . . . . .2C 118
Varley Rd. E16 . . . . .3F 73
Varna Rd. SW6 . . . . .4A 130
Varndell St. NW1 . . . . .2B 36
Vassall Ho. E3 . . . . .2A 46
Vassall Rd. SW9 . . . . .5D 139
Vat Ho. SW8 . . . . .4A 138
Vauban Est. SE16 . . . . .2C 120
Vauban St. SE16 . . . . .2C 120
Vaudeville Theatre 1A 88
Vaughan Est. E2 . . . . .2B 42
Vaughan Ho. SE1 . . . . .4F 89
Vaughan St. SE16 . . . . .5B 96
Vaughan Way E1 . . . . .1D 93
Vaughan Williams Cl.
SE8 . . . . .5D 147
VAUXHALL 1A 138
Vauxhall Bri. SW1 . . . . .5E 115
Vauxhall Bri. Rd. SW1 . . . . .2B 114
Vauxhall City Farm 1B 138
VAUXHALL CROSS 1A 138
Vauxhall Gro. SW8 . . . . .2A 138
Vauxhall St. SE11 . . . . .5C 116
Vauxhall Wlk. SE11 . . . . . . .1B 138
Vawdrey Cl. E1 . . . . .5B 44
Vega Ho. E20 . . . . .3B 6
Velletri Ho. E2 . . . . .1D 45
Velodrome
Queen Elizabeth Olympic Pk.
. . . . .2F 5
Velo Pl. E20 . . . . .2A 6
Venables St. NW8 . . . . .5E 33
Venerable Ho. E3 . . . . .5B 46
Venice Ct. SE5 . . . . .4C 140
Venice Wlk. W2 . . . . .2C 54
Venn Ho. N1 . . . . .4C 16
Ventnor Rd. SE14 . . . . .5E 145
Venture Ct. SE1 . . . . .1A 120
Venture Ho. W10 . . . . .4E 51
(off Bridge Cl.)
Venue St. E14 . . . . .1B 70
Venus Ho. E3 . . . . .4D 25
E14 . . . . .3D 125
Vera Ct. E3 . . . . .3A 48
Verdi Cres. W10 . . . . .1A 30
Vereker Rd. W14 . . . . .1A 130
Vere Ct. W2 . . . . .3F 53
Vere St. W1 . . . . .4F 57
Verity Cl. W11 . . . . .4F 51
Verity Ho. E3 . . . . .3C 46
Vermeer Ct. E14 . . . . .2D 127
Verna Ho. E20 . . . . .3B 6
Verney Ho. NW8 . . . . .4F 33
Verney Rd. SE16 . . . . .2E 143
Verney Way SE16 . . . . .1F 143
Vernon Ho. SE11 . . . . .1C 138
WC1 . . . . .2A 60
Vernon Mans. W14 . . . . .2B 130
Vernon M. W14 . . . . .4A 108
Vernon Pl. WC1 . . . . .2A 60
Vernon Ri. WC1 . . . . .2C 38
Vernon Rd. E3 . . . . .5C 24
E15 . . . . .1F 27
Vernon Sq. WC1 . . . . .2C 38
Vernon St. W14 . . . . .4F 107
Vernon Yd. W11 . . . . .5B 52
Verona Ct. SE14 . . . . .2D 145
Veronica Ho. E3 . . . . .3A 48
Verulam Bldgs. WC1 . . . . . . .1C 60
Verulam Ho. W6 . . . . .5A 78
Verulam St. WC1 . . . . .1D 61

Vervian Ho. SE15 . . . . .4D 143
Verwood Ho. SW8 . . . . .5C 138
Verwood Lodge E14 . . . . . . .2D 127
Vesage Ct. EC1 . . . . .2E 61
Vesey Path E14 . . . . .4A 70
Vesta Ct. SE1 . . . . .5F 91
Vesta Ho. E3 . . . . .4D 25
E20 . . . . .3B 6
Vestry Ct. SW1 . . . . .2E 115
Vestry St. N1 . . . . .2D 41
Vesuvius Apartments E3 . . .5C 24
(off Centurion La.)
Viaduct Bldgs. EC1 . . . . .2E 61
Viaduct Pl. E2 . . . . .3F 43
Viaduct St. E2 . . . . .3F 43
Vibart Wlk. N1 . . . . .3A 16
Vibeca Apartments E1 . . . . .2C 64
Vicarage Ct. W8 . . . . .4F 81
Vicarage Gdns. W8 . . . . .3E 81
Vicarage Ga. W8 . . . . .3F 81
Vicar's Cl. E9 . . . . .4B 22
Viceroy Ct. NW8 . . . . .5A 12
Vicinity Ho. E14 . . . . .1D 97
(off Storehouse M.)
Vic Johnson Ho. E3 . . . . .4C 24
Vickery Ct. EC1 . . . . .4C 40
Vickery's Wharf E14 . . . . . . .3D 69
Victor Cazalet Ho. N1 . . . . . .3F 17
(off Gaskin St.)
Victoria & Albert Mus. 2E 111
Victoria Arc. SW1 . . . . .2A 114
Victoria Av. EC2 . . . . .2A 64
Victoria Bldgs. E8 . . . . .4A 22
Victoria Chambers EC2 . . . .4F 41
Victoria Colonnade WC1 . . .2A 60
Victoria Cotts. E1 . . . . .1D 65
Victoria Ct. SE1 . . . . .4A 120
Victoria Dock Rd. E16 . . . . .5C 72
Victoria Emb. EC4 . . . . .5A 88
SW1 . . . . .5A 88
WC2 . . . . .5A 88
Victoria Gdns. W11 . . . . .2D 81
Victoria Gro. W8 . . . . .1B 110
Victoria Gro. M. W2 . . . . . . .1F 81
Victoria Hall E16 . . . . .2E 101
(not continuous)
Victoria Ho. E6 . . . . .3D 77
SW1 . . . . .5F 113
(Ebury Bri. Rd.)
SW1 . . . . .3C 114
(Francis St.)
SW8 . . . . .4A 138
Victoria Mans. SW8 . . . . . . .4A 138
W14 . . . . .2B 130
Victoria M. NW6 . . . . .3D 9
Victoria Mills Studios
E15 . . . . .3D 27
Victoria Palace Theatre 2B 114
Victoria Park
Hackney 3F 23
Victoria Pk. Ct. E9 . . . . .1C 22
Victoria Pk. Ind. Cen. E9 . . .1C 24
Victoria Pk. Rd. E9 . . . . .4A 22
Victoria Pk. Sq. E2 . . . . .2B 44
Victoria Pk. Studios E9 . . . .1C 22
(off Milborne St.)
Victoria Pas. NW8 . . . . .4D 33
Victoria Pl. Shop. Cen.
SW1 . . . . .3A 114
Victoria Ri. NW6 . . . . .2C 10
Victoria Rd. E11 . . . . .1E 7
NW6 . . . . .5B 8
W8 . . . . .5B 82
Victoria Sq. SW1 . . . . .1A 114

Victoria St. E15 . . . . .1F 27
   SW1 . . . . .2A 114
Victoria Way SE7 . . . . .5F 129
Victoria Wharf E2 . . . . .1E 45
   E14 . . . . .5A 68
   SE8 . . . . .5B 124
Victoria Yd. E1 . . . . .4E 65
Victor Rd. NW10 . . . . .2A 28
Victor Wharf *SE1* *2D 91*
              (off Clink St.)
Victory Ct. W9 . . . . .5D 31
Victory Pde. E20 . . . . .4A 6
Victory Pl. E14 . . . . .5A 68
   SE17 . . . . .3C 118
Victory Way SE16 . . . . .5A 96
Vida Ho. SE8 . . . . .5E 123
Vigers Ct. NW10 . . . . .2A 28
Vigo St. W1 . . . . .1B 86
Viking Cl. E3 . . . . .1A 46
Viking Ct. SW6 . . . . .2E 131
Viking Gdns. E6 . . . . .1F 75
Villa St. SE17 . . . . .1E 141
Villa Wlk SE17 . . . . .1E 141
Villiers St. WC2 . . . . .1F 87
Vince Ct. N1 . . . . .3E 41
Vincent Cl. SE16 . . . . .5F 95
Vincent Ct. W1 . . . . .3B 56
Vincent Ho. SW1 . . . . .3E 115
            (Regency St.)
   SW1 . . . . .4D 115
           (Vincent Sq.)
Vincent M. E3 . . . . .5D 25
Vincent Sq. SW1 . . . . .2C 114
Vincent Sq. Mans. *SW1* *3C 114*
         (off Walcott St.)
Vincent St. E16 . . . . .3C 72
   SW1 . . . . .3D 115
Vincent Ter. N1 . . . . .5F 17
Vince St. EC1 . . . . .3E 41
Vine Cotts. E1 . . . . .3B 66
Vine Ct. E1 . . . . .2E 65
Vinegar St. E1 . . . . .2F 93
Vinegar Yd. SE1 . . . . .4F 91
Vine Hill EC1 . . . . .5D 39
Vine La. SE1 . . . . .3A 92
Vinery, The SW8 . . . . .4A 138
Vinery Row W6 . . . . .1A 106
Vine Sq. W14 . . . . .1C 130
Vine St. EC3 . . . . .4B 64
   W1 . . . . .1C 86
Vine St. Bri. EC1 . . . . .5E 39
Vine Yd. SE1 . . . . .4C 90
Vineyard Wlk. EC1 . . . . .4D 39
Vinopolis **2C 90**
Vinson Ho. N1 . . . . .1E 41
Vintner's Ct. EC4 . . . . .5C 62
Vintner's Pl. EC4 . . . . .5C 62
Vintry Ct. SE1 . . . . .5E 91
Violet Cl. E16 . . . . .5F 49
   SE8 . . . . .2B 146
Violet Ct. E15 . . . . .1F 27
Violet Hill NW8 . . . . .1B 32
Violet Hill Ho.
   NW8 . . . . .1B 32
Violet Rd. E3 . . . . .5F 47
Violet St. E2 . . . . .4A 44
Virgil Pl. W1 . . . . .2B 56
Virgil St. SE1 . . . . .1C 116
Virgin Active
   Barbican **1B 62**
   City **2B 62**
   Fulham *3A 130*
      (within Fulham Pools)
   Hammersmith **4D 107**

Virgin Active
   Islington, Essex Road . . .**4F 17**
   Islington, Goswell Road
     . . . .**1F 39**
   Kensington **5A 82**
   Mayfair **5D 57**
   Moorgate **5D 41**
   Notting Hill **4F 51**
   The Strand **1A 88**
Virginia Ct. SE16 . . . . .4D 95
   WC1 . . . . .4E 37
Virginia Ho. E14 . . . . .5B 70
Virginia Rd. E2 . . . . .3B 42
Virginia St. E1 . . . . .1E 93
Viridian Apartments SW8 . .5B 136
Visage NW3 . . . . .2E 11
Viscount Ct. W2 . . . . .4E 53
Viscount Dr. E6 . . . . .1B 76
Viscount St. EC1 . . . . .5B 40
Vista Bldg. E3 . . . . .3D 47
Vista Ct. E1 . . . . .1F 67
Vittoria Ho. N1 . . . . .4C 16
Vivian Ct. W9 . . . . .5F 9
Vivian Rd. E3 . . . . .5F 23
Vixen M. E8 . . . . .2B 20
Vogans Mill SE1 . . . . .4C 92
Vogler Ho. E1 . . . . .5B 66
Vollasky Ho. E1 . . . . .1D 65
Voss St. E2 . . . . .3E 43
Voyager Bus. Est. SE16 . . .1D 121
Voyager Ct. E16 . . . . .2E 73
Voysey Sq. E3 . . . . .1F 69
Vue Cinema
   Apollo **1D 87**
   Fulham Broadway **4E 131**
   Islington **5E 17**
   Leicester Square **5E 59**
   Shepherds Bush **4D 79**
   Westfield **2C 78**
Vulcan Cl. E6 . . . . .4E 77
Vulcan Sq. E14 . . . . .4E 125
Vulcan Wharf E15 . . . . .1A 48
Vyner St. E2 . . . . .5A 22

W

Wadding St. SE17 . . . . .4D 119
Waddington Rd. E15 . . . . .3E 7
Waddington St. E15 . . . . .4E 7
Wade Ho. SE1 . . . . .5D 93
Wadeson St. E2 . . . . .5A 22
Wade's Pl. E14 . . . . .5F 69
Wadham Gdns. NW3 . . . . . . .3F 11
Wadhurst Rd. SW8 . . . . .5B 136
Wager St. E3 . . . . .5B 46
Wagner St. SE15 . . . . .4B 144
Wainwright Ho. E1 . . . . .2B 94
Waite St. SE15 . . . . .2B 142
Waithman St. EC4 . . . . .4F 61
Wakefield M. WC1 . . . . .3A 38
Wakefield St. WC1 . . . . .3A 38
Wakeling St. E14 . . . . .4F 67
Wakelin Ho. N1 . . . . .2F 17
Wakelin Rd. E15 . . . . .5F 27
Wakeman Ho. NW10 . . . . . . .2D 29
Wakeman Rd. NW10 . . . . . . .3C 28
Wakerley Cl. E6 . . . . .4B 76
Wakley St. EC1 . . . . .2F 39
Walberswick St. SW8 . . . . .5A 138
Walbrook EC4 . . . . .5D 63
           (not continuous)
Walbrook Ct. N1 . . . . .5F 19
Walbrook Wharf EC4 . . . . . . .1C 90

Walburgh St. E1 . . . . .4F 65
Walcorde Av. SE17 . . . . .4C 118
Walcot Gdns. SE11 . . . . . . .3D 117
Walcot Sq. SE11 . . . . .3E 117
Walcott St. SW1 . . . . .3C 114
Waldair Ct. E16 . . . . .4F 105
Walden Ho. SW1 . . . . .4E 113
Walden St. E1 . . . . .3F 65
           (not continuous)
Waldo Ho. NW10 . . . . .2A 28
Waldo Rd. NW10 . . . . .2A 28
Waldron M. SW3 . . . . .2E 133
Waleran Flats SE1 . . . . .3F 119
Wales Cl. SE15 . . . . .3A 144
Waley St. E1 . . . . .1E 67
Walford Ho. E1 . . . . .4F 65
Walham Grn. Ct. SW6 . . . . . .5F 131
Walham Gro. SW6 . . . . .4D 131
Walham Yd. SW6 . . . . .4D 131
Walker Ho. NW1 . . . . .1D 37
   SE16 . . . . .1B 124
Walker's Ct. W1 . . . . .5D 59
Walkers Lodge E14 . . . . .4B 98
Walkie-Talkie, The **5F 63**
Walkinshaw Ct. N1 . . . . .2C 18
Wallace Bldg. NW8 . . . . .5E 33
Wallace Collection **3D 57**
Wallace Ct. NW1 . . . . .2A 56
Waller Way SE10 . . . . .4A 148
Wallgrave Rd. SW5 . . . . .3F 109
Wallingford Av. W10 . . . . . . .2D 51
Wallis All. SE1 . . . . .4C 90
Wallis Rd. E9 . . . . .1C 24
Wallpaper Apartments, The
   N1 . . . . .1D 17
Wallside EC2 . . . . .2C 62
Wallwood St. E14 . . . . .2C 68
Walmer Ho. W10 . . . . .4E 51
Walmer Pl. W1 . . . . .1B 56
Walmer Rd. W10 . . . . .4C 50
   W11 . . . . .5F 51
Walmer St. W1 . . . . .1B 56
Walnut Cl. SE8 . . . . .3C 146
Walnut Ct. *W8* *2F 109*
         (off St Mary's Ga.)
Walnut Gdns. E15 . . . . .2F 7
Walnut Ho. E3 . . . . .4B 24
Walnut Tree Ho. SW10 . . . . .2A 132
Walnut Tree Rd. SE10 . . . . . .1F 149
           (not continuous)
Walnut Tree Wlk. SE11 . . . . .3D 117
Walpole Ct. NW6 . . . . .1C 10
   W14 . . . . .2E 107
Walpole Ho. SE1 . . . . .5D 89
Walpole M. NW8 . . . . .4D 11
Walpole St. SW3 . . . . .5B 112
Walsham Ho. SE17 . . . . .5D 119
Walsingham NW8 . . . . .3E 11
Walsingham Mans. SW6 . . .4A 132
Walston Ho. SW1 . . . . .5D 115
Walter Besant Ho. E1 . . . . . . .3D 45
Walter Ho. *SW10* *4D 133*
            (off Riley St.)
Walter Langley Ct. *SE16* *4C 94*
         (off Brunel Rd.)
Walters Cl. SE17 . . . . .4C 118
Walters Ho. N1 . . . . .3A 18
   SE17 . . . . .3F 139
Walter Sickert Hall N1 . . . . . .1B 40
Walter St. E2 . . . . .3D 45
Walter Ter. E1 . . . . .3E 67
Walterton Rd. W9 . . . . .5C 30
Waltham Ho. NW8 . . . . .3B 10
Walton Cl. SW8 . . . . .4A 138

Walton Ct. NW6 . . . . .2C **10**
Walton Ho. E2 . . . . .4B **42**
  NW1 . . . . .4A **36**
  SW3 . . . . .2B **112**
Walton Pl. SW3 . . . . .1B **112**
Walton St. SW3 . . . . .3A **112**
Walton Vs. N1 . . . . .2A **20**
WALWORTH 5C **118**
Walworth Pl. SE17 . . . . .1C **140**
Walworth Rd. SE1 . . . . .3B **118**
  SE17 . . . . .3B **118**
Wandle Ho. NW8 . . . . .1F **55**
Wandon Rd. SW6 . . . . .5A **132**
Wandsworth Rd. SW8 . . . . . .5E **137**
Wansbeck Rd. E9 . . . . .1C **24**
Wansdown Pl. SW6 . . . . .4F **131**
Wansey St. SE17 . . . . .4B **118**
WAPPING 2A **94**
Wapping Dock St. E1 . . . . . . .3A **94**
Wapping High St. E1 . . . . . . .3D **93**
Wapping La. E1 . . . . .1A **94**
Wapping Wall E1 . . . . .2B **94**
Warbeck Rd. W12 . . . . .3A **78**
Warburton Ho. E8 . . . . .3F **21**
Warburton Rd. E8 . . . . .3A **22**
Warburton St. E8 . . . . .3F **21**
Wardall Gro. SE14 . . . . .4C **144**
Wardalls Ho. SE8 . . . . .2C **146**
Wardell Ho. SE10 . . . . .2B **148**
Wardens Gro. SE1 . . . . .3B **90**
Ward La. E9 . . . . .3A **4**
Wardour M. W1 . . . . .4C **58**
Wardour St. W1 . . . . .3C **58**
Ward Point SE11 . . . . .4D **117**
Ward Rd. E15 . . . . .3D **27**
Wardrobe Pl. EC4 . . . . .4A **62**
Wardrobe Ter. EC4 . . . . .5A **62**
Wardroper Ho. SE1 . . . . .2A **118**
Wards Wharf App. E16 . . . . .4D **103**
Worcham Ct. N1 . . . . .1A **20**
Wareham Ho. SW8 . . . . .4B **138**
Warehouse Way E16 . . . . . . .1F **101**
Warfield Rd. NW10 . . . . .3D **29**
Warfield Yd. NW10 . . . . .3D **29**
Wargrave Ho. E2 . . . . .3B **42**
Warham St. SE5 . . . . .4A **140**
Warley St. E2 . . . . .2D **45**
Warlock Rd. W9 . . . . .4C **30**
Warmsworth NW1 . . . . .3B **14**
Warndon St. SE16 . . . . .4C **122**
Warneford St. E9 . . . . .3A **22**
Warner Ho. NW8 . . . . .2B **32**
Warner Pl. E2 . . . . .1E **43**
Warner St. EC1 . . . . .5D **39**
Warner Ter. E14 . . . . .2E **69**
Warner Yd. EC1 . . . . .5D **39**
Warnford St. EC2 . . . . .3E **63**
Warnham WC1 . . . . .3B **38**
Warren Ct. NW1 . . . . .4B **36**
Warren Gdns. E15 . . . . .3D **7**
Warren Ho. E3 . . . . .2F **47**
  W14 . . . . .3C **108**
Warren M. W1 . . . . .5B **36**
Warren Pl. E1 . . . . .4E **67**
Warren St. W1 . . . . .5B **36**
Warrington Cres. W9 . . . . . . .5B **32**
Warrington Gdns. W9 . . . . . .5B **32**
  (not continuous)
Warspite Ho. E14 . . . . .4F **125**
Warton Ct. E1 . . . . .5D **67**
Warton Ho. E15 . . . . .4C **26**
Warton Rd. E15 . . . . .3B **26**
Warwall E6 . . . . .3F **77**
Warwick W14 . . . . .4C **108**

Warwick Av. W2 . . . . .5A **32**
  W9 . . . . .5A **32**
Warwick Bldg. SW8 . . . . .3F **135**
Warwick Chambers
  W8 . . . . .1D **109**
Warwick Cl. W8 . . . . .2C **108**
Warwick Ct. EC4 . . . . .4A **62**
  WC1 . . . . .2C **60**
Warwick Cres. W2 . . . . .1B **54**
Warwick Est. W2 . . . . .2A **54**
Warwick Gdns. W14 . . . . . . .2C **108**
Warwick Ho. E16 . . . . .2E **101**
  (off Wesley Av.)
Warwick Ho. St. SW1 . . . . . .2E **87**
Warwick La. EC4 . . . . .3A **62**
Warwick Mans. SW5 . . . . . . .3D **109**
Warwick Pas. EC4 . . . . .3A **62**
Warwick Pl. W9 . . . . .1B **54**
Warwick Pl. Nth. SW1 . . . . . .4B **114**
Warwick Rd. SW5 . . . . .2B **108**
  W14 . . . . .2B **108**
Warwick Row SW1 . . . . .1A **114**
Warwickshire Path SE8 . . . . .4C **146**
Warwick Sq. EC4 . . . . .3A **62**
  SW1 . . . . .5B **114**
  (not continuous)
Warwick Sq. M. SW1 . . . . . . .4B **114**
Warwick St. W1 . . . . .5C **58**
Warwick Way SW1 . . . . .5F **113**
Warwick Yd. EC1 . . . . .5C **40**
Wasdale NW1 . . . . .3A **36**
Washington Cl. E3 . . . . .2A **48**
Washington Ho. SW3 . . . . . . .5B **84**
Watercress Pl. N1 . . . . .2A **20**
Waterden Ct. W11 . . . . .3F **79**
Waterden Rd. E20 . . . . .5E **5**
Waterford Ho. W11 . . . . .5B **52**
Waterford Rd. SW6 . . . . .5F **131**
Waterfront M. N1 . . . . .5C **18**
Waterfront Studios Bus. Cen.
  E16 . . . . .1D **101**
Water Gardens, The W2 . . . . .3A **56**
Water Gdns. Sq. SE16 . . . . . .5E **95**
Watergate EC4 . . . . .5F **61**
Watergate St. SE8 . . . . .3D **147**
Watergate Wlk. WC2 . . . . . . .2A **88**
Waterhead NW1 . . . . .2B **36**
Waterhouse Cl. E16 . . . . .1D **75**
  W6 . . . . .5E **107**
Waterhouse Sq. EC1 . . . . . . .2D **61**
Wateridge Cl. E14 . . . . .2D **125**
Water La. E15 . . . . .4F **7**
  EC3 . . . . .1A **92**
  NW1 . . . . .2A **14**
  SE14 . . . . .4C **144**
Waterline Ho. W2 . . . . .2E **55**
Waterloo Bri. WC2 . . . . .1B **88**
Waterloo East Theatre 3E **89**
Waterloo Gdns. E2 . . . . .5B **22**
  N1 . . . . .2F **17**
Waterloo Pas. NW6 . . . . .2C **8**
Waterloo Pl. SW1 . . . . .2D **87**
Waterloo Rd. SE1 . . . . .2C **88**
Waterloo Ter. N1 . . . . .2F **17**
Waterman Bldg. E14 . . . . . . .4D **97**
Watermans Wlk. SE16 . . . . . .3F **95**
Waterman Way E1 . . . . .2F **93**
Watermead Ho. E9 . . . . .2B **4**
Watermead Lodge SE16 . . . . .2E **95**
Waterside N1 . . . . .1B **40**
  W2 . . . . .2D **55**
Waterside Cl. E3 . . . . .3B **24**
  SE16 . . . . .5E **93**
Waterside Hgts. E16 . . . . . . .4C **102**

Waterside Pl. NW1 . . . . .3E **13**
Waterside Point SW11 . . . . .4A **134**
Waterson St. E2 . . . . .2A **42**
Water St. WC2 . . . . .5D **61**
Water Twr. Pl. N1 . . . . .4F **17**
Waterview Ho. E14 . . . . .2A **68**
Watford Rd. E16 . . . . .2E **73**
Watkins Ho. E14 . . . . .5B **98**
Watling Ct. EC4 . . . . .4C **62**
Watling Ho. SE1 . . . . .3C **118**
Watling St. EC4 . . . . .4B **62**
  SE15 . . . . .3A **142**
Watney Mkt. E1 . . . . .4A **66**
Watney St. E1 . . . . .4A **66**
Watson Ct. E3 . . . . .3E **47**
Watsons Ho. N1 . . . . .4A **20**
Watson's M. W1 . . . . .2A **56**
Watsons St. SE8 . . . . .5D **147**
Watts Gro. E3 . . . . .1E **69**
Watts Ho. W10 . . . . .1F **51**
Watts St. E1 . . . . .2A **94**
  SE15 . . . . .5C **142**
Wavel Ct. E1 . . . . .2B **94**
Wavelengths Leisure Cen.
. . . . .4E **147**
Wavel M. NW6 . . . . .2F **9**
Waveney Cl. E1 . . . . .2E **93**
Waverley Ct. NW3 . . . . .1B **12**
  NW6 . . . . .2A **8**
Waverley Gdns. E6 . . . . .2A **76**
Waverley Lodge E15 . . . . .5F **7**
Waverley Pl. NW8 . . . . .5D **11**
Waverton Ho. E3 . . . . .3C **24**
Waverton St. W1 . . . . .2E **85**
Waylett Ho. SE11 . . . . .1D **139**
Wayman Ct. E8 . . . . .1F **21**
Waynflete Ho. SE1 . . . . .3B **90**
Waynflete Sq. W10 . . . . .4D **51**
  (not continuous)
Weald Cl. SE16 . . . . .5F **121**
Wealden Ho. E3 . . . . .3B **48**
Wearmouth Ho. E3 . . . . .5C **46**
Wear Pl. E2 . . . . .3F **43**
  (not continuous)
Weatherbury W2 . . . . .3D **53**
Weatherley Cl. E3 . . . . .1C **68**
Weaver Cl. E6 . . . . .5F **77**
Weaver Ho. E1 . . . . .5D **43**
Weavers La. SE1 . . . . .3A **92**
Weavers Ter. SW6 . . . . .3E **131**
Weaver St. E1 . . . . .5D **43**
  (not continuous)
Weavers Way NW1 . . . . .3D **15**
Webb Cl. W10 . . . . .5C **28**
Webber Row SE1 . . . . .5E **89**
Webber St. SE1 . . . . .4E **89**
Webb Ho. E3 . . . . .3E **47**
  SW8 . . . . .5E **137**
Webb St. SE1 . . . . .2F **119**
Webheath NW6 . . . . .1C **8**
  (not continuous)
Webster Rd. SE16 . . . . .2E **121**
Weddell Ho. E1 . . . . .5E **45**
Wedderburn Ho. SW1 . . . . . .5D **113**
Wedgewood Ho. SW1 . . . . . .1A **136**
Wedgwood Ho. E2 . . . . .3D **45**
  SE11 . . . . .2D **117**
Wedgwood M. W1 . . . . .4E **59**
Wedlake St. W10 . . . . .4A **30**
Weighhouse St. W1 . . . . .5E **57**
Weightman Ho. SE16 . . . . . . .2D **121**
Weir's Pas. NW1 . . . . .2E **37**
Welbeck Ct. W14 . . . . .3B **108**
Welbeck Ho. W1 . . . . .3F **57**

Welbeck St. W1 . . . . .2E **57**
Welbeck Way W1 . . . . .3F **57**
Welbury Ct. E8 . . . . .1A **20**
Welford Ct. NW1 . . . . .1A **14**
  W9 . . . . .1D **53**
Welland M. E1 . . . . .2E **93**
Welland St. SE10 . . . . .3B **148**
Wellclose Sq. E1 . . . . .5E **65**
  (not continuous)
Wellclose St. E1 . . . . .1E **93**
Wellcome Collection **4D 37**
Wellcome Museum, The . . .**3C 60**
(within Royal College of Surgeons)
Well Ct. EC4 . . . . .4C **62**
  (not continuous)
Wellday Ho. E9 . . . . .5A **4**
Weller Ct. W11 . . . . .2B **80**
Weller Ho. SE16 . . . . .5D **93**
Weller St. SE1 . . . . .4B **90**
Welles Ct. E14 . . . . .1D **97**
Wellesley Av. W6 . . . . .2A **106**
Wellesley Ct. *SE1* *2B 118*
  (off Rockingham St.)
  W9 . . . . .2B **32**
Wellesley Ho. NW1 . . . . .3D **37**
  SW1 . . . . .5F **113**
Wellesley Mans. W14 . . . . . .5B **108**
Wellesley Pl. NW1 . . . . .3D **37**
Wellesley St. E1 . . . . .2D **67**
Wellesley Ter. N1 . . . . .2C **40**
Wellington Arch **4E 85**
Wellington Bldgs. E3 . . . . . .3D **47**
  SW1 . . . . .1E **135**
Wellington Cl. W11 . . . . .4D **53**
Wellington Ct. NW8 . . . . . . .1D **33**
  SW1 . . . . .5B **84**
Wellington Gro. SE10 . . . . . .5D **149**
Wellington Ho. E16 . . . . .2E **101**
  SE17 . . . . .2C **140**
Wellington Lodge SE1 . . . . .5E **89**
Wellington Mans.
  W14 . . . . .2B **130**
Wellington Monument **4E 85**
Wellington Pl. NW8 . . . . . . .2E **33**
Wellington Rd. NW8 . . . . . . .5E **11**
  NW10 . . . . .3E **29**
Wellington Row E2 . . . . .2C **42**
Wellington Sq. N1 . . . . .3A **16**
  SW3 . . . . .5B **112**
Wellington St. WC2 . . . . .5A **60**
Wellington Ter. E1 . . . . .2F **93**
  W2 . . . . .1F **81**
Wellington Way E3 . . . . .3D **47**
Wells Ct. NW6 . . . . .5E **9**
Wells Ho. EC1 . . . . .2E **39**
  SE16 . . . . .1C **122**
  W10 . . . . .5F **29**
Wells M. W1 . . . . .2C **58**
Wellspring Cl. E14 . . . . .1B **70**
Wells Ri. NW8 . . . . .4B **12**
Wells Rd. W12 . . . . .5B **78**
Wells Sq. WC1 . . . . .3B **38**
Wells St. W1 . . . . .2B **58**
Well St. E9 . . . . .2A **22**
  E15 . . . . .4F **7**
Wells Way SE5 . . . . .2E **141**
  SW7 . . . . .1D **111**
Welsford St. SE1 . . . . .5D **121**
  (not continuous)
Welsh Ho. E1 . . . . .2A **94**
Welshpool Ho. E8 . . . . .3E **21**
Welshpool St. E8 . . . . .3E **21**
  (not continuous)
Welstead Ho. E1 . . . . .4F **65**

Welton Ho. E1 . . . . .2D **67**
Welwyn St. E2 . . . . .2C **44**
Wendle Ct. SW8 . . . . .3F **137**
Wendon St. E3 . . . . .3C **24**
Wendover SE17 . . . . .5F **119**
  (not continuous)
Wendover Ct. W1 . . . . .2D **57**
Wendover Ho. W1 . . . . .2D **57**
Wenham Ho. SW8 . . . . .5B **136**
Wenlake Ho. EC1 . . . . .4B **40**
Wenlock Barn Est. N1 . . . . . .1D **41**
Wenlock Ct. N1 . . . . .1E **41**
Wenlock Rd. N1 . . . . .5B **18**
Wenlock St. N1 . . . . .1C **40**
Wennington Rd. E3 . . . . .5E **23**
Wentworth Ct. SW1 . . . . .1F **135**
  W6 . . . . .3A **130**
Wentworth Cres. SE15 . . . . .5E **143**
Wentworth Dwellings E1 . . . .3B **64**
Wentworth M. E3 . . . . .4A **46**
Wentworth St. E1 . . . . .3B **64**
Werrington St. NW1 . . . . .1C **36**
Wesley Av. E16 . . . . .2E **101**
Wesley Cl. SE17 . . . . .4A **118**
Wesley Ct. SE16 . . . . .2F **121**
Wesley's Chapel & Museum
  of Methodism **4E 41**
Wesley's House **4E 41**
Wesley Sq. W11 . . . . .4F **51**
Wesley St. W1 . . . . .2E **57**
Wesse Ho. SE1 . . . . .5C **120**
Wessex St. E2 . . . . .3C **44**
Wesson Mead SE5 . . . . .5C **140**
West 12 Shop. Cen. W12 . . . .4D **79**
W. Arbour St. E1 . . . . .3C **66**
WEST BECKTON **4E 75**
West Block SE1 . . . . .5B **88**
Westbourne Bri. W2 . . . . .2B **54**
Westbourne Ct. W2 . . . . .3B **54**
Westbourne Cres. W2 . . . . . .5D **55**
Westbourne Cres. M. W2 . . .5D **55**
Westbourne Gdns. W2 . . . . . .3F **53**
WESTBOURNE GREEN **1E 53**
Westbourne Gro. W2 . . . . . . .4E **53**
  W11 . . . . .5B **52**
Westbourne Gro. M. W11 . . .4D **53**
Westbourne Gro. Ter. W2 . . . .3F **53**
Westbourne Ho. SW1 . . . . . .5F **113**
Westbourne Pk. Pas. W2 . . . .1E **53**
Westbourne Pk. Rd. W2 . . . . .2E **53**
  W11 . . . . .4A **52**
Westbourne Pk. Vs. W2 . . . . .2E **53**
Westbourne Rd. N7 . . . . .1D **17**
Westbourne St. W2 . . . . .5D **55**
Westbourne Ter. W2 . . . . .3B **54**
Westbourne Ter. M. W2 . . . . .3B **54**
Westbourne Ter. Rd. W2 . . . . .2B **54**
Westbourne Ter. Rd. Bri.
  W2 . . . . .1B **54**
Westbridge Rd. SW11 . . . . . .5F **133**
WEST BROMPTON **1F 131**
Westbrook Ho. E2 . . . . .2B **44**
Westbury Ho. W11 . . . . .2D **53**
Westbush Ct. W12 . . . . .5A **78**
W. Carriage Dr. W2 . . . . .4E **83**
  (North Ride)
  W2 . . . . .4E **83**
  (Rotten Row)
W. Central St. WC1 . . . . .3F **59**
Westcliffe Apartments
  W2 . . . . .2E **55**
Westcombe Hill SE10 . . . . . .5D **129**
Westcombe Pk. Rd. SE3 . . . .3F **149**
Westcott Ho. E14 . . . . .5E **69**

Westcott Rd. SE17 . . . . .2F **139**
W. Cromwell Rd. W14 . . . . . .5B **108**
W. Cross Route W10 . . . . . . .5D **51**
  W11 . . . . .1D **79**
  W12 . . . . .1D **79**
Westdown Rd. E15 . . . . .1C **6**
W. Eaton Pl. SW1 . . . . .3D **113**
W. Eaton Pl. M. SW1 . . . . . .3D **113**
West End Ct. NW6 . . . . .1F **9**
West End La. NW6 . . . . .2E **9**
  (not continuous)
West End Quay W2 . . . . .2E **55**
Westerham NW1 . . . . .4B **14**
Westerham Ho. SE1 . . . . . . .1E **119**
Western Beach Apartments
  E16 . . . . .2D **101**
Western Ct. NW6 . . . . .1C **30**
Western Courtyard EC2 . . . . .2A **64**
Western Gateway E16 . . . . . .5C **72**
Western M. W9 . . . . .5C **30**
Western Pl. SE16 . . . . .4C **94**
Western Transit Shed N1 . . . .4F **15**
Westferry Cir. E14 . . . . .2D **97**
Westferry Rd. E14 . . . . .2D **97**
Westfield Av. E20 . . . . .5F **5**
Westfield Cl. SW10 . . . . .5B **132**
Westfield Ct. NW10 . . . . .2E **29**
Westfield Ho. SE16 . . . . .3E **123**
  SW10 . . . .*4D 133*
  (off Cremorne Est.)
Westfield Shop. Cen. E20 . . . .5C **6**
  W12 . . . . .3D **79**
Westfield Way E1 . . . . .3F **45**
West Gdn. Pl. W2 . . . . .4A **56**
West Gdns. E1 . . . . .1A **94**
Westgate Apartments
  E16 . . . . .5E **73**
Westgate Centre, The E8 . . . .3F **21**
Westgate M. W10 . . . . .4F **29**
Westgate St. E8 . . . . .3F **21**
Westgate Ter. SW10 . . . . . . .1A **132**
W. Halkin St. SW1 . . . . .1D **113**
West Ham La. E15 . . . . .1E **27**
W. Hampstead M. NW6 . . . . . .1F **9**
W. Handyside Canopy N1 . . . .4F **15**
W. Harding St. EC4 . . . . .3E **61**
Westhill Ct. W11 . . . . .5C **52**
Westhope Ho. E2 . . . . .4E **43**
W. India Av. E14 . . . . .2D **97**
W. India Dock Rd. E14 . . . . . .4C **68**
W. India Ho. E14 . . . . .5D **69**
W. Kensington Ct. W14 . . . . .5B **108**
W. Kensington Mans.
  W14 . . . . .1B **130**
WEST KILBURN **3B 30**
Westlake SE16 . . . . .4C **122**
Westland Ho. E16 . . . . .3D **105**
Westland Pl. N1 . . . . .2D **41**
West La. SE16 . . . . .5F **93**
West Lodge *E16* *2E 101*
  (off Britannia Ga.)
W. London Crematorium
  NW10 . . . . .4A **28**
W. London Studios SW6 . . . .4A **132**
Westmacott Ho. NW8 . . . . . . .5E **33**
West Mall W8 . . . . .2E **81**
W. Mersea Cl. E16 . . . . .3F **101**
West M. SW1 . . . . .4B **114**
WESTMINSTER **5F 87**
Westminster Abbey **1F 115**
Westminster Abbey Chapter House
  . . . .**1F 115**
Westminster Abbey Mus.
  . . . .**1F 115**

Westminster Abbey Pyx Chamber
. . . . .1F 115
Westminster Boating Base & Pier
. . . . .2D 137
Westminster Bri. SW1 . . . . .5A 88
Westminster Bri. Ho.
SE1 . . . . .1F 117
Westminster Bri. Rd. SE1 . . .5B 88
Westminster Bus. Sq.
SE11 . . . . .2B 138
Westminster Ct. NW8 . . . . .5D 33
SE16 . . . . .2E 95
Westminster Gdns. SW1 . . .3F 115
Westminster Hall 5F 87
Westminster Mans.
SW1 . . . . .1E 115
Westminster Pal. Gdns.
SW1 . . . . .2D 115
Westminster RC Cathedral
. . . . .2B 114
Westmoreland Ho. E16 . . . .2E 101
(off Gatcombe Rd.)
Westmoreland Pl. SW1 . . . .1A 136
Westmoreland Rd. SE17 . . .2C 140
(not continuous)
Westmoreland St. W1 . . . . .2E 57
Westmoreland Ter. SW1 . . .5A 114
Westmoreland Wlk.
SE17 . . . . .2D 141
(not continuous)
Westonbirt Ct. SE15 . . . . . .3B 142
West One Ho. W1 . . . . .2B 58
West One Shop. Cen. W1 . . .4E 57
Weston Ho. E9 . . . . .3B 22
NW6 . . . . .2A 8
Weston Ri. WC1 . . . . .1C 38
Weston St. SE1 . . . . .3E 91
(not continuous)
Weston Wlk. E8 . . . . .2A 22
West Parkside SE10 . . . . . .5A 100
West Pk. Wlk. E20 . . . . .3B 6
West Point E14 . . . . .5C 68
SE1 . . . . .5D 121
Westport Rd. E13 . . . . .1F 73
Westport St. E1 . . . . .3E 67
W. Poultry Av. EC1 . . . . . . .2F 61
West Quay Wlk. E14 . . . . .1F 125
West Ri. W2 . . . . .5A 56
West Rd. SE1 . . . . .4C 88
SW3 . . . . .1C 134
Westrovia Ct. SW1 . . . . . .4D 115
West Row W10 . . . . .4F 29
Westside Ct. W9 . . . . .4E 31
West Smithfield EC1 . . . . . .2F 61
West Sq. SE11 . . . . .2F 117
West St. E2 . . . . .1A 44
WC2 . . . . .4E 59
W. Tenter St. E1 . . . . .4C 64
West Twr. E14 . . . . .4F 97
W. View Apartments N7 . . .1F 15
Westview Cl. W10 . . . . .3C 50
W. Warwick Pl. SW1 . . . . .4B 114
Westway W2 . . . . .1D 53
W9 . . . . .1C 52
W10 . . . . .3F 51
W12 . . . . .4A 50
Westway Lodge W9 . . . . .1E 53
Westway Sports Cen. 4D 51
Westway Travellers Site
W12 . . . . .5D 51
Westwick Gdns. W14 . . . . .5D 79
West Wintergarden 3F 97
Westwood Ho. W12 . . . . . .3C 78
Westwood M. E3 . . . . .2D 47

Westwood Rd. E16 . . . . . . .3F 101
Wetherby Gdns. SW5 . . . . .4B 110
Wetherby Mans. SW5 . . . . .5F 109
Wetherby M. SW5 . . . . .5F 109
Wetherby Pl. SW7 . . . . . . .4B 110
Wetherell Rd. E9 . . . . .3E 23
Wevco Wharf SE15 . . . . . .2F 143
Wexford Ho. E1 . . . . .2B 66
Wexner Bldg. E1 . . . . .2B 64
Weybridge Ct. SE16 . . . . . .1F 143
Weyhill Rd. E1 . . . . .3E 65
Wey Ho. NW8 . . . . .5E 33
Weymouth Cl. E6 . . . . .4F 77
Weymouth Ct. E2 . . . . .5C 20
Weymouth Ho. SW8 . . . . . .4B 138
Weymouth M. W1 . . . . .1F 57
Weymouth St. W1 . . . . .2E 57
Weymouth Ter. E2 . . . . .5C 20
Whalebone Ct. EC2 . . . . . . .3D 63
Whalebone La. E15 . . . . . . .2F 27
Whales Yd. E15 . . . . .2F 27
Wharf, The EC3 . . . . .2A 92
Wharfdale Rd. N1 . . . . .5A 16
Wharfedale Ho. NW6 . . . . . . .3F 9
Wharfedale St. SW10 . . . . .1F 131
Wharfedale Yd. N1 . . . . . . .5A 16
Wharf La. E14 . . . . .4B 68
Wharf Pl. E2 . . . . .4E 21
Wharf Rd. E16 . . . . .2C 102
N1 . . . . .1B 40
(Baldwin Ter.)
N1 . . . . .4F 15
(York Way)
Wharfside Point Nth. E14 . .1B 98
Wharfside Point Sth. E14 . .1B 98
Wharfside Rd. E16 . . . . .2F 71
SE8 . . . . .1E 147
Wharf St. E16 . . . . .2F 71
Wharf Vw. Ct. E14 . . . . .4C 70
Wharton Cotts. WC1 . . . . . .2D 39
Wharton Ho. SE1 . . . . .1B 120
Wharton St. WC1 . . . . .3C 38
Whatman Ho. E14 . . . . .3C 68
Wheatfield Ho. NW6 . . . . . .3E 31
Wheatfields E6 . . . . .3F 77
Wheatley Ct. E3 . . . . .2A 48
Wheatley St. W1 . . . . .2E 57
Wheat Sheaf Cl. E14 . . . . . .3F 125
Wheatsheaf La. SW8 . . . . . .4F 137
Wheatsheaf Ter. SW6 . . . . .5C 130
Wheatstone Ho. SE1 . . . . . .2C 118
W10 . . . . .1F 51
Wheatstone Rd. W10 . . . . . .1A 52
Wheeler Gdns. N1 . . . . .3A 16
Wheel Ho. E14 . . . . .5F 125
Wheelwright St. N7 . . . . . . .1B 16
Wheler Ho. E1 . . . . .5B 42
Wheler St. E1 . . . . .5B 42
Whetstone Pk. WC2 . . . . . . .3B 60
Whidborne Bldgs. WC1 . . . .3A 38
Whidborne St. WC1 . . . . . . .3A 38
(not continuous)
Whippingham Ho. E3 . . . . . .3C 46
Whiskin St. EC1 . . . . .3F 39
Whistler M. SE15 . . . . .5C 142
Whistlers Av. SW11 . . . . . . .5E 133
Whistler Twr. SW10 . . . . . .4D 133
Whistler Wlk. SW10 . . . . . .4C 132
Whiston Ho. N1 . . . . .1A 18
Whiston Rd. E2 . . . . .5B 20
Whitacre M. SE11 . . . . .1E 139
Whitby Ho. NW8 . . . . .4B 10
Whitby St. E1 . . . . .4B 42
(not continuous)

Whitcher Cl. SE14 . . . . .3F 145
Whitcher Pl. NW1 . . . . .1C 14
Whitchurch Ho. W10 . . . . . .4E 51
Whitchurch Rd. W11 . . . . . .5E 51
Whitcomb Ct. WC2 . . . . . . .1E 87
Whitcomb St. WC2 . . . . .1E 87
Whiteadder Way E14 . . . . . .3A 126
Whitear Wlk. E15 . . . . .4E 7
Whitebeam Cl. SW9 . . . . . . .5C 138
Whitebeam Ho. E15 . . . . . . .2F 49
White Bear Yd. EC1 . . . . . . .5D 39
WHITECHAPEL 2D 65
Whitechapel Art Gallery . . .2C 64
Whitechapel High St. E1 . . .3C 64
Whitechapel Rd. E1 . . . . . . .3D 65
Whitechapel Sports Cen. . . .1F 65
White Church La. E1 . . . . . . .3D 65
White Church Pas. E1 . . . . . .3D 65
WHITE CITY 5A 50
WHITE CITY 4B 50
White City Cl. W12 . . . . .1B 78
White City Est. W12 . . . . . . .5A 50
White City Rd. W12 . . . . . . .5B 50
White Conduit St. N1 . . . . . .5E 17
Whitecross Pl. EC2 . . . . .1E 63
Whitecross St. EC1 . . . . .4C 40
Whitefriars St. EC4 . . . . .4E 61
Whitehall SW1 . . . . .2F 87
Whitehall Ct. SW1 . . . . .3F 87
(not continuous)
Whitehall Gdns. SW1 . . . . . .3F 87
Whitehall Pl. SW1 . . . . .3F 87
White Hart Ct. EC2 . . . . .2F 63
White Hart St. EC4 . . . . .3A 62
SE11 . . . . .5E 117
White Hart Yd. SE1 . . . . .3D 91
Whitehaven St. NW8 . . . . . . .5F 33
Whiteheads Gro. SW3 . . . . .5A 112
White Heather Ho. WC1 . . . .3A 38
(off Cromer St.)
White Horse All. EC1 . . . . . . .1F 61
White Horse La. E1 . . . . .5D 45
Whitehorse M. SE1 . . . . .1E 117
White Horse Rd. E1 . . . . .4F 67
(not continuous)
White Horse St. W1 . . . . .3A 86
White Horse Yd. EC2 . . . . . . .3D 63
White House, The NW1 . . . . .4A 36
Whitehouse Apartments
SE1 . . . . .3C 88
White Kennett St. E1 . . . . . . .3A 64
Whitelands Ho. SW3 . . . . . .5B 112
Whiteleys Cen. (Shop. Cen.)
W2 . . . . .4A 54
White Lion Ct. EC3 . . . . .4F 63
SE15 . . . . .3C 144
White Lion Hill EC4 . . . . .5A 62
White Lion St. N1 . . . . .1D 39
White Lyon Ct. EC2 . . . . .1B 62
White Post La. E9 . . . . .1C 24
White Post St. SE15 . . . . . . .4C 144
Whites Grounds SE1 . . . . . . .5A 92
White's Grounds Est. SE1 . . .4A 92
White's Row E1 . . . . .2B 64
Whitethorn Ho. E1 . . . . .2B 94
Whitethorn Pas. E3 . . . . .5E 47
Whitethorn St. E3 . . . . .5D 47
White Twr. Way E1 . . . . .1F 67
Whitfield Ho. NW8 . . . . .5F 33
Whitfield Pl. W1 . . . . .5B 36
Whitfield St. W1 . . . . .5B 36
Whitgift Ho. SE11 . . . . .3B 116
Whitgift St. SE11 . . . . .3B 116
Whitings Way E6 . . . . .1D 77

Whitley Ho. SW1 . . . . .2C **136**
Whitman Ho. E2 . . . . .3B **44**
Whitman Rd. E3 . . . . .4A **46**
Whitmore Est. N1 . . . . .4A **20**
Whitmore Gdns. NW10 . . . .1B **28**
Whitmore Ho. N1 . . . . .4A **20**
Whitmore Rd. N1 . . . . .4F **19**
Whitstable Ho. W10 . . . . . . .4E **51**
Whittaker St. SW1 . . . . .4D **113**
Whittaker Way SE1 . . . . .4E **121**
Whittington Apartments
    E1 .3D **67**
Whittington Av. EC3 . . . . . . .4F **63**
Whittlesey St. SE1 . . . . .3E **89**
Whitton NW3 . . . . .2B **12**
Whitton Wlk. E3 . . . . .1D **47**
    (not continuous)
Whitworth Ho. SE1 . . . . .2C **118**
Whitworth St. SE10 . . . . . . .5A **128**
Whytlaw Ho. E3 . . . . .1C **68**
Wicker St. E1 . . . . .4F **65**
Wickfield Apartments E15 . .4E **7**
Wickfield Ho. SE16 . . . . .5E **93**
Wickford Ho. E1 . . . . .4B **44**
Wickford St. E1 . . . . .4B **44**
Wickham Cl. E1 . . . . .2C **66**
Wickham Ho. *N1* *4F 19*
    (off Halcomb St.)
Wickham St. SE11 . . . . .5B **116**
Wick La. E3 . . . . .2C **24**
Wicklow St. WC1 . . . . .2B **38**
Wick Rd. E9 . . . . .5A **4**
Wicksteed Ho. SE1 . . . . .2C **118**
Wickway Ct. SE15 . . . . .3B **142**
Widdin St. E15 . . . . .2E **27**
Widegate St. E1 . . . . .2A **64**
Widford NW1 . . . . .1F **13**
Widford Ho. N1 . . . . .1F **39**
Widgeon Cl. E16 . . . . .3F **73**
Widley Rd. W9 . . . . .3E **31**
Wigmore Hall **3F 57**
Wigmore Pl. W1 . . . . .3F **57**
Wigmore St. W1 . . . . .4D **57**
Wigram Ho. E14 . . . . .5F **69**
Wigton Pl. SE11 . . . . .1E **139**
Wilbraham Ho. SW8 . . . . . . .5F **137**
Wilbraham Mans. *SW1* *3D 113*
    (off Wilbraham Pl.)
Wilbraham Pl. SW1 . . . . .3C **112**
Wilby M. W11 . . . . .2C **80**
Wilcox Cl. SW8 . . . . .4A **138**
    (not continuous)
Wilcox Ho. E3 . . . . .1C **68**
Wilcox Pl. SW1 . . . . .2C **114**
Wilcox Rd. SW8 . . . . .4F **137**
Wild Ct. WC2 . . . . .4B **60**
Wilde Cl. E8 . . . . .3D **21**
Wilde Ho. *W2* *5D 55*
    (off Gloucester Ter.)
Wilder Wlk. W1 . . . . .1C **86**
Wild's Rents SE1 . . . . .1F **119**
Wild St. WC2 . . . . .4A **60**
Wilfred St. SW1 . . . . .1B **114**
Wilfred Wood Ct. *W6* *3C 106*
    (off Samuel's Cl)
Wilkes St. E1 . . . . .1C **64**
Wilkie Ho. SW1 . . . . .5E **115**
Wilkins Ho. SW1 . . . . .2A **136**
Wilkinson Ho. N1 . . . . .1E **41**
Wilkinson Rd. E16 . . . . .3C **74**
Wilkinson St. SW8 . . . . .5B **138**
Wilks Pl. N1 . . . . .1A **42**
Willesden La. NW6 . . . . .1A **8**
William IV St. WC2 . . . . .1F **87**

William Booth Ho. E14 . . . . .3D **69**
William Caslon Ho. E2 . . . . .1A **44**
William Channing Ho. E2 . . .2F **43**
William Cobbett Ho. W8 . . . .1F **109**
William Congreve M. N1 . . . .4B **18**
William Cotton Ct. E14 . . . . .1D **69**
William Ct. NW8 . . . . .2C **32**
    SE10 . . . . .5F **147**
William Dromey Ct. NW6 . . . .1C **8**
William Dunbar Ho. NW6 . . .1C **30**
William Ellis Way SE16 . . . .2E **121**
William Evans Ho. SE8 . . . . .4E **123**
William Fenn Ho. E2 . . . . . . .1D **43**
William Fry Ho. E1 . . . . .3D **67**
William Gibbs Ct. SW1 . . . . .2D **115**
William Guy Gdns. E3 . . . . . .3A **48**
William Henry Wlk. SW8 . . .3D **137**
William M. N1 . . . . .2F **19**
    SW1 . . . . .5C **84**
William Owston Ct. E16 . . . .3F **103**
William Pl. E3 . . . . .5B **24**
William Rathbone Ho. E2 . . .2F **43**
William Rd. NW1 . . . . .3B **36**
William Rushbrooke Ho.
    SE16 . . . . .3D **121**
William Saville Ho. NW6 . . . .1C **30**
William's Bldgs. E2 . . . . .4B **44**
Williams Cl. SW6 . . . . .4A **130**
Williams Ho. E3 . . . . .2D **47**
    E9 .3A **22**
    SW1 . . . . .4E **115**
William Smith Ho. E3 . . . . . .3D **47**
Williamson Cl. SE10 . . . . . . .5B **128**
Williamson Ct. SE17 . . . . . . .1B **140**
William Sq. SE16 . . . . .2A **96**
William St. SW1 . . . . .5C **84**
William Whiffin Sq. E3 . . . . .5C **46**
Willis Ho. E14 . . . . .5F **69**
Willis St. E14 . . . . .4A **70**
Willoughby Highwalk EC2 . .2D **63**
Willoughby Ho. E1 . . . . .3F **93**
    EC2 . . . . .2D **63**
Willoughby Pas. E14 . . . . . . .2D **97**
Willoughby St. WC1 . . . . . . .2F **59**
Willoughby Way SE7 . . . . . . .3F **129**
Willow Bri. Rd. N1 . . . . .1B **18**
    (not continuous)
Willowbrook Est. SE15 . . . . .5D **143**
Willow Brook Rd. SE15 . . . . .3C **142**
Willow Ct. EC2 . . . . .4F **41**
    NW6 . . . . .2A **8**
    W9 .1E **53**
Willowdene SE15 . . . . .5F **143**
Willow Ho. SE1 . . . . .3B **120**
    W10 . . . . .4E **29**
Willow Pl. SW1 . . . . .3C **114**
Willows, The SE1 . . . . .3A **120**
Willow St. EC2 . . . . .4F **41**
Willow Tree Cl. E3 . . . . .4B **24**
Willow Wlk. N1 . . . . .5A **18**
    SE1 . . . . .3A **120**
Willow Way W11 . . . . .1E **79**
Willsbridge Ct. SE15 . . . . . . .3B **142**
Will Wyatt Ct. N1 . . . . .1F **41**
Wilman Gro. E8 . . . . .1E **21**
Wilmcote Ho. W2 . . . . .1F **53**
Wilmer Gdns. N1 . . . . .4F **19**
    (not continuous)
Wilmer Ho. E3 . . . . .5A **24**
Wilmer Lea Cl. E15 . . . . .2C **26**
Wilmington Sq. WC1 . . . . . . .3D **39**
    (not continuous)
Wilmington St. WC1 . . . . . . .3D **39**
Wilmington Ter. SE16 . . . . . .4F **121**

Wilmot Cl. SE15 . . . . .5D **143**
Wilmot Ho. SE11 . . . . .4F **117**
Wilmot Pl. NW1 . . . . .1B **14**
    (not continuous)
Wilmot St. E2 . . . . .4F **43**
Wilsham St. W11 . . . . .2E **79**
Wilshaw Ho. SE8 . . . . .5E **147**
Wilshaw St. SE14 . . . . .5D **147**
Wilson Gro. SE16 . . . . .5F **93**
Wilson Ho. NW6 . . . . .2B **10**
Wilson's Rd. W6 . . . . .5E **107**
Wilson St. EC2 . . . . .1E **63**
Wilton Ct. E1 . . . . .3A **66**
Wilton Cres. SW1 . . . . .5D **85**
Wilton M. SW1 . . . . .1E **113**
Wilton Pl. SW1 . . . . .5D **85**
Wilton Plaza SW1 . . . . .3B **114**
Wilton Rd. SW1 . . . . .2A **114**
Wilton Row SW1 . . . . .5D **85**
Wiltons Music Hall **5E 65**
Wilton Sq. N1 . . . . .3D **19**
Wilton St. SW1 . . . . .1F **113**
Wilton Ter. SW1 . . . . .1D **113**
Wilton Vs. N1 . . . . .4D **19**
Wiltshire Cl. SW3 . . . . .4B **112**
Wiltshire Row N1 . . . . .4D **19**
Wimbolt St. E2 . . . . .2D **43**
Wimborne Ho. E16 . . . . .5C **72**
    NW1 . . . . .5A **34**
    SW8 . . . . .5C **138**
Wimbourne Ct. N1 . . . . .5D **19**
Wimbourne St. N1 . . . . .5D **19**
Wimpole M. W1 . . . . .1F **57**
Wimpole St. W1 . . . . .1F **57**
Winant Ho. E14 . . . . .1A **98**
Winchelsea Ho. SE16 . . . . . .4C **94**
Winchendon Rd. SW6 . . . . . .5B **130**
Winchester Av. NW6 . . . . . . .3A **8**
Winchester Bldgs. SE1 . . . . .4B **90**
Winchester Cl. E6 . . . . .4A **76**
    SE17 . . . . .4A **118**
Winchester Ct. W8 . . . . .4E **81**
Winchester Ho. E3 . . . . .3C **46**
    SW3 . . . . .3E **133**
    SW9 . . . . .4E **139**
    W2 .4B **54**
Winchester M. NW3 . . . . .1E **11**
Winchester Palace **2D 91**
Winchester Rd. NW3 . . . . . . .1E **11**
Winchester Sq. SE1 . . . . .2D **91**
Winchester St. SW1 . . . . .5A **114**
Winchester St. SE1 . . . . .2D **91**
Winchester Wlk. SE1 . . . . . . .2D **91**
Winchester Wharf SE1 . . . . .2D **91**
Winch Ho. E14 . . . . .1F **125**
    SW10 . . . . .4C **132**
Winchilsea Ho. NW8 . . . . . . .3D **33**
Winckworth Ct. N1 . . . . .3E **41**
Wincott Pde. SE11 . . . . .3E **117**
Wincott St. SE11 . . . . .3E **117**
Windermere NW1 . . . . .3A **36**
Windermere Av. NW6 . . . . . .4A **8**
Windermere Ho. E3 . . . . .4B **46**
Windermere Point SE15 . . . .4B **144**
Windlass Pl. SE8 . . . . .4A **124**
Windmill WC1 . . . . .1B **60**
Windmill Cl. SE1 . . . . .3E **121**
Windmill Ho. E14 . . . . .3D **125**
    SE1 . . . . .3E **89**
Windmill La. E15 . . . . .4E **7**
Windmill Row SE11 . . . . .1D **139**
Windmill St. W1 . . . . .2D **59**
    (not continuous)
Windmill Wlk. SE1 . . . . .3E **89**
Windrose Cl. SE16 . . . . .4D **95**

Windrush Cl. E8 . . . . .2E 21
Windrush Ho. NW8 . . . . . .5E 33
Windsock Cl. SE16 . . . . . . .3B 124
Windsor Centre, The
  N1 . . . . .3A 18
Windsor Cotts. SE14 . . . . . .4B 146
Windsor Ct. E3 . . . . .1D 47
  SE16 . . . . .1E 95
  SW3 . . . . .5A 112
  W2 . . . . .5F 53
  W10 . . . . .4D 51
Windsor Gdns. W9 . . . . . . .5D 31
Windsor Hall E16 . . . . .2F 101
Windsor Ho. E2 . . . . .2D 45
  N1 . . . . .5C 18
  NW1 . . . . .2A 36
  NW2 . . . . .1A 8
Windsor Pl. SW1 . . . . .3C 114
Windsor St. N1 . . . . .3A 18
Windsor Ter. N1 . . . . .2C 40
Windsor Way W14 . . . . . . .3E 107
Windsor Wharf E9 . . . . .3C 4
Windspoint Dr. SE15 . . . . .3F 143
Windward Ct. E16 . . . . . . .1F 105
Wine Cl. E1 . . . . .1B 94
  (not continuous)
Wine Office Ct. EC4 . . . . . . .3E 61
Winford Ho. E3 . . . . .2C 24
Winforton St. SE10 . . . . . .5B 148
Wingate Ho. E3 . . . . .3F 47
Wingfield Ct. E14 . . . . .1D 99
Wingfield Ho. E2 . . . . .3B 42
  NW6 . . . . .5F 9
Wingfield Rd. E15 . . . . .1F 7
Wingrad Ho. E1 . . . . .2B 66
Wingreen NW8 . . . . .3A 10
Winicotte Ho. W2 . . . . . . .1E 55
Winifred St. E16 . . . . .3C 104
Winkley St. E2 . . . . .1F 43
Winkworth Cotts. E1 . . . . . .4C 44
Winnett St. W1 . . . . .5D 59
Winnington Ho. SE5 . . . . .4B 140
  W10 . . . . .5F 29
Winsham Ho. NW1 . . . . . . .2E 37
Winsland M. W2 . . . . .3D 55
Winsland St. W2 . . . . .3D 55
Winsley St. W1 . . . . .3B 58
Winslow SE17 . . . . .1F 141
WINSOR PARK 2F 77
Winsor Ter. E6 . . . . .2D 77
Winston Ho. WC1 . . . . .4E 37
Winterbourne Ho. W11 . . . .1F 79
Wintergreen Cl. E6 . . . . . . .2F 75
Winterleys NW6 . . . . .1C 30
Winter Lodge SE16 . . . . . .1E 143
Winterton Ho. E1 . . . . .4B 66
Winterton Pl. SW10 . . . . . .2C 132
Winthrop Ho. W12 . . . . . . .5A 50
Winthrop St. E1 . . . . .1F 65
Winton Ct. N1 . . . . .5B 16
Wireworks Ct. SE1 . . . . . . .5A 90
Wisden Ho. SW8 . . . . .3C 138
Wise Rd. E15 . . . . .3D 27
Wisley Ho. SW1 . . . . .5D 115
Wistow Ho. E2 . . . . .4D 21
Witan St. E2 . . . . .3A 44
Withers Pl. EC1 . . . . .4C 40
Withy Ho. E1 . . . . .5D 45
Witley Ct. WC1 . . . . .5F 37
Woburn Ct. SE16 . . . . .5A 122
  WC1 . . . . .5F 37
  (off Bernard St.)
Woburn Mans. WC1 . . . . . .1D 59
Woburn M. WC1 . . . . .4E 37

Woburn Pl. WC1 . . . . .4E 37
Woburn Sq. WC1 . . . . .5E 37
  (not continuous)
Woburn Wlk. WC1 . . . . . . .3E 37
Wodeham Gdns. E1 . . . . . .1E 65
Wodehouse Av. SE5 . . . . .5B 142
Wolcot Ho. NW1 . . . . .1C 36
Wolfe Cres. SE16 . . . . .5D 95
Wolfe Ho. W12 . . . . .5A 50
  W14 . . . . .3B 108
Wollaston Cl. SE1 . . . . .3B 118
Wollaton Ho. N1 . . . . .5E 17
Wollett Ct. NW1 . . . . .1C 14
Wolseley St. SE1 . . . . .5C 92
Wolsey Ct. NW6 . . . . .1C 10
  SW11 . . . . .5F 133
Wolsey St. E1 . . . . .2B 66
Wolverley St. E2 . . . . .3F 43
Wolverton SE17 . . . . .5E 119
  (not continuous)
Wolverton Gdns. W6 . . . . .3D 107
Wontner Cl. N1 . . . . .2B 18
Woodall Cl. E14 . . . . .5A 70
Woodbridge St. EC1 . . . . . .4F 39
  (not continuous)
Woodchester Ho. E14 . . . . .1A 126
Woodchester Sq. W2 . . . . . .1F 53
Woodchurch Rd. NW6 . . . . .2E 9
Wood Cl. E2 . . . . .4D 43
Woodcock Ho. E14 . . . . . . .2D 69
Woodcocks E16 . . . . .2C 74
Woodcote Ho. SE8 . . . . . .2C 146
Woodcroft M. SE8 . . . . . . .4F 123
Woodfall St. SW3 . . . . . . .1B 134
Woodfield Pl. W9 . . . . .5C 30
Woodfield Rd. W9 . . . . . . .1C 52
Woodford Ct. W12 . . . . . . .4D 79
Woodger Rd. W12 . . . . . . .5C 78
Woodget Cl. E6 . . . . .3F 75
Woodhall NW1 . . . . .3B 36
Woodhatch Cl. E6 . . . . . . .2F 75
Wood Ho. NW6 . . . . .1C 30
Woodland Cres. SE10 . . . . .2F 149
  SE16 . . . . .5D 95
Woodland Gro. SE10 . . . . .1F 149
Woodlands, The SW9 . . . . .5A 140
Woodlands Pk. Rd. SE10 . . .2F 149
  (not continuous)
Wood La. W12 . . . . .3B 50
Wood La. Studios W12 . . . .4B 50
Woodman Pde. E16 . . . . . .3E 105
Woodman's M. W12 . . . . . .2A 50
Woodman St. E16 . . . . . . .3E 105
Woodpecker Rd. SE14 . . . . .3F 145
Woodrush Cl. SE14 . . . . . .4F 145
Wood's Bldgs. E1 . . . . .1F 65
Woodseer St. E1 . . . . .1C 64
Woodsford SE17 . . . . .1D 141
Woodsford Sq. W14 . . . . . .4A 80
Woods Ho. SW1 . . . . .1F 135
Woods M. W1 . . . . .5C 56
Woods Pl. SE1 . . . . .2A 120
Woodstar Ho. SE15 . . . . . .4D 143
Woodstock Ct. SE11 . . . . . .5C 116
Woodstock Gro. W12 . . . . . .4E 79
Woodstock M. W1 . . . . . . .2E 57
Woodstock St. W1 . . . . . . .4F 57
Woodstock Studios W12 . . .5E 79
Woodstock Ter. E14 . . . . . .5A 70
Wood St. EC2 . . . . .4C 62
  (not continuous)
Woodville Ho. SE1 . . . . . . .1B 120
Woodville Rd. NW6 . . . . . . .5C 8
Wood Wharf SE10 . . . . . . .2A 148

Wood Wharf Bus. Pk.
  E14 . . . . .3A 98
Woolcombes Ct. SE16 . . . .2D 95
Wooler St. SE17 . . . . .1D 141
Woolf M. WC1 . . . . .4E 37
Woollon Ho. E1 . . . . .3B 66
Woolmore St. E14 . . . . . . .5B 70
Woolridge Way E9 . . . . . . .1C 22
Woolstaplers Way
  SE16 . . . . .2D 121
Woolstone Ho. E2 . . . . . . .4D 21
Woolwich Mnr. Way E6 . . .1D 77
  E16 . . . . .1F 105
Woolwich Rd. SE7 . . . . . . .5E 129
  SE10 . . . . .5B 128
Wooster Gdns. E14 . . . . . .3D 71
Wooster Pl. SE1 . . . . .3E 119
Wootton St. SE1 . . . . .3E 89
Worcester Ct. W9 . . . . .1D 53
Worcester Ho. SE11 . . . . . .2D 117
  SW9 . . . . .4E 139
  W2 . . . . .4B 54
Worcester Point EC1 . . . . . .3B 40
Wordsworth Ho. NW6 . . . . .2D 31
Wordsworth Mans. W14 . . .2B 130
  (off Queens Club Gdns.)
Wordsworth Rd. SE1 . . . . . .4C 120
Worfield St. SW11 . . . . . . .5A 134
Worgan St. SE11 . . . . .5B 116
  SE16 . . . . .2E 123
Worlds End Est. SW10 . . . .4D 133
World's End Pas. SW10 . . . .4D 133
World's End Pl. SW10 . . . . .4C 132
Worlidge St. W6 . . . . .5B 106
Wormwood Scrubs Pk.
(Local Nature Reserve)
  . . . . .1A 50
Wormwood St. EC2 . . . . . . .3F 63
Wornington Rd. W10 . . . . . .5F 29
  (not continuous)
Woronzow Rd. NW8 . . . . . .4E 11
Worship St. EC2 . . . . .5E 41
  (not continuous)
Worth Gro. SE17 . . . . .1D 141
Worthing Cl. E15 . . . . .4F 27
Worthington Ho. EC1 . . . . . .2E 39
Wotton Ct. E14 . . . . .1E 99
Wotton Rd. SE8 . . . . .3C 146
Wouldham Rd. E16 . . . . . . .3B 72
Wraxall Rd. E3 . . . . .4B 46
Wrayburn Ho. SE16 . . . . . .5E 93
Wren Cl. E16 . . . . .3C 72
Wren Ho. E3 . . . . .1F 45
  SW1 . . . . .1D 137
Wren Landing E14 . . . . . . .2E 97
Wren St. WC1 . . . . .4C 38
Wrestlers Ct. EC3 . . . . .3F 63
Wrexham Rd. E3 . . . . .1E 47
Wrigglesworth St.
  SE14 . . . . .4D 145
Wright's La. W8 . . . . .5F 81
Wright's Rd. E3 . . . . .5B 24
  (not continuous)
Wrotham Ho. SE1 . . . . . . .1E 119
Wrotham Rd. NW1 . . . . . . .2C 14
Wrottesley Rd. NW10 . . . . .1A 28
Wyatt Cl. SE16 . . . . .5B 96
Wyatt Ho. NW8 . . . . .5D 33
Wybert St. NW1 . . . . .4B 36
Wyclif Ct. EC1 . . . . .3F 39
Wyclif St. EC1 . . . . .3F 39
Wycombe Ho. NW8 . . . . . . .4F 33
Wycombe Sq. W8 . . . . .3D 81
Wyfold Rd. SW6 . . . . .5A 130

Wykeham Ho. SE1 . . . . .3B **90**
Wyke Rd. E3 . . . . .2D **25**
Wyllen Cl. E1 . . . . .5B **44**
Wymering Mans. W9 . . . . . .3E **31**
Wymering Rd. W9 . . . . .3E **31**
Wymondham Ct.
 NW8 . . . . .3E **11**
Wynan Rd. E14 . . . . .5F **125**
Wyndham Deedes Ho.
 E2 .1E **43**
Wyndham Est. SE5 . . . . . . .4C **140**
Wyndham Ho. E14 . . . . .4A **98**
 SW1 . . . . .4D **113**
Wyndham M. W1 . . . . .2B **56**
Wyndham Pl. W1 . . . . .2B **56**
Wyndham Rd. SE5 . . . . .5A **140**
Wyndhams Ct. E8 . . . . .2B **20**
Wyndham's Theatre 5F **59**
Wyndham St. W1 . . . . .1B **56**
Wyndham Yd. W1 . . . . .2B **56**
Wynford Rd. N1 . . . . .5B **16**
Wynnstay Gdns. W8 . . . . . . .1E **109**
Wynyard Ho. SE11 . . . . .5C **116**
Wynyard Ter. SE11 . . . . .5C **116**
Wynyatt St. EC1 . . . . .3F **39**
Wytham Ho. NW8 . . . . .5E **33**
Wythburn Ct. W1 . . . . .3B **56**
Wythburn Pl. W1 . . . . .4B **56**
Wythes Rd. E16 . . . . .3F **103**
Wyvil Rd. SW8 . . . . .4F **137**
Wyvis St. E14 . . . . .1A **70**

Y

Yabsley St. E14 . . . . .2C **98**
Yaldham Ho. SE1 . . . . .4F **119**
Yalding Rd. SE16 . . . . .2D **121**
Yard, The N1 . . . . .1A **38**
Yardley St. WC1 . . . . .3D **39**
 (not continuous)
Yarmouth Pl. W1 . . . . .3F **85**
Yarrell Mans. W14 . . . . . . .2B **130**

Yarrow Cres. E6 . . . . .1F **75**
Yarrow Ho. E14 . . . . .1C **126**
 W10 . . . . .1C **50**
Yatesbury Ct. E5 . . . . .3A **4**
Yates Ct. SE1 . . . . .5C **92**
Yates Ho. E2 . . . . .2E **43**
Yatton Ho. W10 . . . . .1C **50**
Yeadon Ho. W10 . . . . .1C **50**
Yearby Ho. W10 . . . . .5C **28**
Yeate St. N1 . . . . .2D **19**
Yeldham Ho. W6 . . . . .5D **107**
Yeldham Rd. W6 . . . . .5D **107**
Yeldham Vs. W6 . . . . .5D **107**
Yeoman Cl. E6 . . . . .5F **77**
Yeoman's Row
 SW3 . . . . .2A **112**
Yeoman St. SE8 . . . . .3F **123**
Yeoman's Yd. E1 . . . . .5C **64**
Yeo St. E3 . . . . .1F **69**
Yeovil Ho. W10 . . . . .5B **28**
Yew Ho. SE16 . . . . .5D **95**
 (off Woodland Cres.)
York Av. SE17 . . . . .5C **118**
York Bri. NW1 . . . . .4D **35**
York Bldgs. WC2 . . . . .1A **88**
York Cl. E6 . . . . .4B **76**
York Ga. NW1 . . . . .5D **35**
York Hall Leisure Cen.
 . . . . .1A **44**
York Ho. E16 . . . . .2E **101**
 SE1 . . . . .2C **116**
 SW3 . . . . .5C **112**
 W1 . . . . .1B **56**
 W8 . . . . .4F **81**
York Ho. Pl. W8 . . . . .4F **81**
Yorkley Ho. W10 . . . . .5B **28**
York Mans. SE17 . . . . .5C **118**
 SW5 . . . . .5F **109**
 W1 . . . . .1D **57**
York Pas. W8 . . . . .4F **81**
York Pl. WC2 . . . . .1A **88**
York Pl. Mans. W1 . . . . .1C **56**
York Rd. SE1 . . . . .4C **88**

Yorkshire Grey Yd.
 WC1 . . . . .2B **60**
Yorkshire Rd. E14 . . . . .4F **67**
York Sq. E14 . . . . .4F **67**
York St. W1 . . . . .2B **56**
York St. Chambers
 W1 . . . . .1B **56**
York Ter. E. NW1 . . . . .5E **35**
York Ter. W. NW1 . . . . .5D **35**
Yorkton St. E2 . . . . .1D **43**
York Way N1 . . . . .1F **15**
 N7 . . . . .1F **15**
York Way Ct. N1 . . . . .4A **16**
 (not continuous)
Young Ct. NW6 . . . . .1A **8**
Young Rd. E16 . . . . .2B **74**
Youngs Bldgs.
 EC1 . . . . .4C **40**
Young St. W8 . . . . .5F **81**
Young Vic Theatre, The
 . . . . .4E **89**
Yoxall Ho. W10 . . . . .5B **28**

Z

Zachary Ct. SW1 . . . . .4E **115**
Zahra Ho. NW10 . . . . .3C **28**
Zampa Rd. SE16 . . . . .1B **144**
Zander Ct. E2 . . . . .2E **43**
Zangwill Ho. NW6 . . . . .1C **30**
Zapotec Ho. SE8 . . . . .4E **123**
Zealand Rd. E3 . . . . .5F **23**
Zeller Ho. E20 . . . . .3A **6**
Zenobia Mans.
 W14 . . . . .2B **130**
Zetland Ho. W8 . . . . .1F **109**
Zetland St. E14 . . . . .2A **70**
Zinnia Mans. E20 . . . . .4A **6**
Zion Ho. E1 . . . . .3B **66**
Zoar St. SE1 . . . . .2B **90**
Zodiac Ho. E3 . . . . .4D **47**
Zona Ct. SE1 . . . . .2B **120**

SAFETY CAMERA INFORMATION

PocketGPSWorld.com's CamerAlert is a self-contained speed and red light camera warning system for
SatNavs and Android or Apple iOS smartphones/tablets. Visit www.cameralert.com to download.

Safety camera locations are publicised by the Safer Roads Partnership which operates them in order to encourage drivers to comply
with speed limits at these sites. It is the driver's absolute responsibility to be aware of and to adhere to speed limits at all times.

By showing this safety camera information it is the intention of Geographers' A-Z Map Company Ltd. to encourage
safe driving and greater awareness of speed limits and vehicle speed. Data accurate at time of printing.

HOSPITALS, HOSPICES and selected HEALTHCARE FACILITIES covered by this atlas.

N.B. Where it is not possible to name these facilities on the map, the reference given is for the road in which they are situated.

BECKTON CYGNET HOSPITAL 3E **77**
  23 Tunnan Leys
  LONDON
  E6 6ZB
  Tel: 020 7511 2299

BMI CITY MEDICAL 3F **63**
  17 St Helen's Place
  LONDON
  EC3A 6DG
  Tel: 0845 123 5380

CAMDEN MEWS DAY HOSPITAL 1C **14**
  1-5 Camden Mews
  LONDON
  NW1 9DB
  Tel: 020 3317 4740

CHELSEA & WESTMINSTER HOSPITAL 2C **132**
  369 Fulham Road
  LONDON
  SW10 9NH
  Tel: 020 3315 8000

CHURCHILL CAMBIAN HOSPITAL 1E **117**
  Barkham Terrace
  Lambeth Road
  LONDON
  SE1 7PW
  Tel: 0800 138 1418

CROMWELL BUPA HOSPITAL 3F **109**
  162-174 Cromwell Road
  LONDON
  SW5 0TU
  Tel: 020 7460 2000

EASTMAN DENTAL HOSPITAL & DENTAL INSTITUTE 4B **38**
  256 Gray's Inn Road
  LONDON
  WC1X 8LD
  Tel: 020 3456 7899

EVELINA CHILDREN'S HOSPITAL 1B **116**
  St Thomas' Hospital
  Westminster Bridge Road
  LONDON
  SE1 7EH
  Tel: 020 7188 7188

FITZROY SQUARE BMI HOSPITAL 5B **36**
  14 Fitzroy Square
  LONDON
  W1T 6AH
  Tel: 020 7388 4954

GENERAL MEDICAL WALK-IN CENTRE (LIVERPOOL STREET) 1A **64**
  Exchange Arcade
  Bishopsgate
  LONDON
  EC2M 3WA
  Tel: 0845 437 0691

GORDON HOSPITAL 4D **115**
  Bloomburg Street
  LONDON
  SW1V 2RH
  Tel: 020 8746 8733

GREAT ORMOND STREET HOSPITAL FOR CHILDREN 5A **38**
  Great Ormond Street
  LONDON
  WC1N 3JH
  Tel: 020 7405 9200

GUY'S HOSPITAL 4D **91**
  Great Maze Pond
  LONDON
  SE1 9RT
  Tel: 020 7188 7188

GUY'S NUFFIELD HOUSE 4D **91**
  Guy's Hospital
  Newcomen Street
  LONDON
  SE1 1YR
  Tel: 020 7188 5282

HAMMERSMITH HOSPITAL 3A **50**
  Du Cane Road
  LONDON
  W12 0HS
  Tel: 020 3313 1000

HARLEY STREET CLINIC 1F **57**
  35 Weymouth Street
  LONDON
  W1G 8BJ
  Tel: 020 7935 7700

HEART HOSPITAL 2E **57**
  16-18 Westmoreland Street
  LONDON
  W1G 8PH
  Tel: 020 3456 7898

HOSPITAL FOR TROPICAL DISEASES 5C **36**
  Mortimer Market
  Capper Street
  LONDON
  WC1E 6JB
  Tel: 020 3456 7891

HOSPITAL OF ST JOHN & ST ELIZABETH 1D **33**
  60 Grove End Road
  LONDON
  NW8 9NH
  Tel: 020 7806 4000

KING EDWARD VII'S HOSPITAL SISTER AGNES 1E **57**
  5-10 Beaumont Street
  LONDON
  W1G 6AA
  Tel: 020 7486 4411

LISTER HOSPITAL 1F **135**
  Chelsea Bridge Road
  LONDON
  SW1W 8RH
  Tel: 020 7730 3417

LONDON BRIDGE HOSPITAL 2E **91**
  27 Tooley Street
  LONDON
  SE1 2PR
  Tel: 0845 602 7906

LONDON CHEST HOSPITAL 5C **22**
  Bonner Road
  LONDON
  E2 9JX
  Tel: 020 3146 5000

LONDON CLINIC 5E **35**
  20 Devonshire Place
  LONDON
  W1G 6BW
  Tel: 020 7935 4444

LONDON EYE HOSPITAL 3F **57**
  8-10 Harley Street
  LONDON
  W1G 9PF
  Tel: 0800 612 2021

LONDON INDEPENDENT BMI HOSPITAL 1D **67**
  1 Beaumont Square
  LONDON
  E1 4NL
  Tel: 020 7780 2400

LONDON WELBECK HOSPITAL 2F **57**
  27 Welbeck Street
  LONDON
  W1G 8EN
  Tel: 020 7224 2242

MILDMAY HOSPITAL 3B **42**
  Austin Street
  LONDON
  E2 7NA
  Tel: 020 7613 6300

MILE END HOSPITAL 4E **45**
  Bancroft Road
  LONDON
  E1 4DG
  Tel: 020 3416 5000

MOORFIELDS EYE HOSPITAL 3D **41**
  162 City Road
  LONDON
  EC1V 2PD
  Tel: 020 7253 3411

NATIONAL HOSPITAL FOR NEUROLOGY & NEUROSURGERY 5A **38**
  Queen Square
  LONDON
  WC1N 3BG
  Tel: 020 3456 7890

NHS WALK-IN CENTRE (ANGEL MEDICAL PRACTICE) 5E **17**
Ritchie Street Group Practice
34 Ritchie Street
LONDON
N1 0DG
Tel: 020 7837 1663

NHS WALK-IN CENTRE (SOHO). 4D **59**
1 Frith Street
LONDON
W1D 3HZ
Tel: 020 7534 6500

NHS WALK-IN CENTRE (WALDRON HEALTH CENTRE) 5B **146**
Amersham Vale
LONDON
SE14 6LD
Tel: 020 3049 2370

NIGHTINGALE CAPIO HOSPITAL 1A **56**
11-19 Lisson Grove
LONDON
NW1 6SH
Tel: 020 7535 7700

OLD BROAD STREET PRIVATE MEDICAL CENTRE 3F **63**
31 Old Broad Street
LONDON
EC2N 1HT
Tel: 020 7496 3555

PEMBRIDGE PALLIATIVE CARE CENTRE 1D **51**
St Charles Hospital
Exmoor Street
LONDON
W10 6DZ
Tel: 020 8962 4410

PORTLAND HOSPITAL FOR WOMEN & CHILDREN 5A **36**
205-209 Great Portland Street
LONDON
W1W 5AH
Tel: 020 7580 4400

PRINCESS GRACE HOSPITAL 5E **35**
42-52 Nottingham Place
LONDON
W1M 3FD
Tel: 020 7486 1234

QUEEN CHARLOTTE'S & CHELSEA HOSPITAL 3A **50**
Du Cane Road
LONDON
W12 0HS
Tel: 020 3313 1111

RICHARD DESMOND CHILDREN'S EYE CENTRE 3D **41**
3 Peerless Street
LONDON
EC1V 9EZ
Tel: 020 7253 3411

RICHARD HOUSE CHILDREN'S HOSPICE 5E **75**
Richard House Drive
LONDON
E16 3RG
Tel: 020 7511 0222

ROYAL BROMPTON HOSPITAL 5F **111**
Sydney Street
LONDON
SW3 6NP
Tel: 020 7352 8121

ROYAL BROMPTON HOSPITAL (OUTPATIENTS) 5E **111**
Fulham Road
LONDON
SW3 6HP
Tel: 020 7351 8011

ROYAL LONDON HOSPITAL 2F **65**
Whitechapel Road
LONDON
E1 1BB
Tel: 020 3416 5000

ROYAL LONDON HOSPITAL FOR INTEGRATED MEDICINE 1A **60**
60 Great Ormond Street
LONDON
WC1N 3HR
Tel: 020 3456 7890

ROYAL MARSDEN HOSPITAL (FULHAM) 5E **111**
Fulham Road
LONDON
SW3 6JJ
Tel: 020 7352 8171

ROYAL NATIONAL ORTHOPAEDIC HOSPITAL
(CENTRAL LONDON OUTPATIENT DEPT.) 5A **36**
45-51 Bolsover Street
LONDON
W1W 5AQ
Tel: 020 8954 2300

ROYAL NATIONAL THROAT, NOSE & EAR HOSPITAL 2B **38**
330 Gray's Inn Road
LONDON
WC1X 8DA
Tel: 020 3456 7890

ST BARTHOLOMEW'S HOSPITAL 2A **62**
West Smithfield
LONDON
EC1A 7BE
Tel: 020 3416 5000

ST CHARLES CENTRE FOR WELL BEING 1E **51**
Exmoor Street
LONDON
W10 6DZ
Tel: 020 8962 4656

ST CHARLES HOSPITAL 1D **51**
Exmoor Street
LONDON
W10 6DZ
Tel: 020 8206 7343

ST JOHN'S HOSPICE 1D **33**
Hospital of St John & St Elizabeth
60 Grove End Road
LONDON
NW8 9NH
Tel: 020 7806 4050

ST JOSEPH'S HOSPICE 3A **22**
Mare Street
LONDON
E8 4SA
Tel: 020 8525 6047

ST MARY'S HOSPITAL 3E **55**
Praed Street
LONDON
W2 1NY
Tel: 020 3312 6666

ST PANCRAS HOSPITAL 4D **15**
4 St Pancras Way
LONDON
NW1 0PE
Tel: 020 7530 3500

ST THOMAS' HOSPITAL 1B **116**
Westminster Bridge Road
LONDON
SE1 7EH
Tel: 020 7188 7188

TOWER HAMLETS CENTRE FOR MENTAL HEALTH 4E **45**
Bancroft Road
Mile End
LONDON
E1 4DG
Tel: 020 8121 5001

UCH MACMILLAN CANCER CENTRE 5C **36**
Huntley Street
LONDON
WC1E 6DH
Tel: 020 3456 7016

UNIVERSITY COLLEGE HOSPITAL 4C **36**
235 Euston Road
LONDON
NW1 2BU
Tel: 020 3456 7890

URGENT CARE CENTRE (GUY'S HOSPITAL) 4E **91**
Great Maze Pond
LONDON
SE1 9RT
Tel: 020 3049 8970

URGENT CARE CENTRE (ST MARY'S HOSPITAL) 3D **55**
Praed Street
LONDON
W2 1NY
Tel: 020 3312 6666

WELLINGTON HOSPITAL 1E **33**
8a Wellington Place
LONDON
NW8 9LE
Tel: 020 7483 5148

WESTERN EYE HOSPITAL 1B **56**
171 Marylebone Road
LONDON
NW1 5QH
Tel: 020 3312 6666

WEYMOUTH BMI HOSPITAL, THE 1E **57**
42-46 Weymouth Street
LONDON
W1G 6NP
Tel: 020 7935 1200

RAIL, DOCKLANDS LIGHT RAILWAY, RIVERBUS, CABLE CAR, UNDERGROUND STATIONS and OVERGROUND STATIONS

with their map square reference

A

Abbey Road (DLR)	5F 27
Aldgate East (Underground)	3C 64
Aldgate (Underground)	4B 64
All Saints (DLR)	5A 70
Angel (Underground)	5E 17

B

Baker Street (Underground)	5C 34
Bankside Pier (River Bus & Tours)	1B 90
Bank (Underground & DLR)	4D 63
Barbican (Underground)	1B 62
Barons Court (Underground)	5F 107
Battersea Park (Rail)	5F 135
Bayswater (Underground)	5A 54
Beckton Park (DLR)	5B 76
Beckton (DLR)	2D 77
Bermondsey (Underground)	1E 121
Bethnal Green (Rail)	4F 43
Bethnal Green (Underground)	3B 44
Blackfriars Millennium Pier (River Bus)	5E 61
Blackfriars (Rail & Underground)	5F 61
Blackwall (DLR)	1C 98
Bond Street (Underground)	4F 57
Borough (Underground)	5C 90
Bow Church (DLR)	2E 47
Bow Road (Underground)	3D 47
Bromley-by-Bow (Underground)	3B 48
Brondesbury Park (Overground)	3A 8
Brondesbury (Overground)	1C 8

C

Cable Car	5B 100
Cadogan Pier (River Bus)	3A 134
Caledonian Road & Barnsbury (Overground)	1C 16
Cambridge Heath (Rail)	1A 44
Camden Road (Overground)	2B 14
Camden Town (Underground)	3A 14
Canada Water (Underground & Overground)	1C 122
Canary Wharf Pier (River Bus)	2C 96
Canary Wharf (Underground & DLR)	2E 97
Canning Town (Underground & DLR)	3A 72
Cannon Street (Rail & Underground)	5D 63
Chalk Farm (Underground)	1D 13
Chancery Lane (Underground)	2D 61
Charing Cross (Rail & Underground)	2F 87
City Thameslink (Rail)	3F 61
Covent Garden (Underground)	4A 60
Crossharbour (Underground & DLR)	1A 126
Custom House for ExCeL (DLR)	5F 73
Cutty Sark for Maritime Greenwich (DLR)	3B 148
Cyprus (DLR)	5E 77

D

Deptford Bridge (DLR)	5E 147
Deptford (Rail)	4D 147
Devons Road (DLR)	4F 47

E

Earl's Court (Underground)	5E 109
East India (DLR)	5D 71
Edgware Road (Underground)	2F 55
Elephant & Castle (Rail & Underground)	3B 118
Embankment Pier (River Bus & Tours)	2A 88
Embankment (Underground)	2A 88
Emirates Air Line	
Emirates Greenwich Peninsula	4B 100
Emirates Royal Docks	1D 101
Essex Road (Rail)	2B 18
Euston Square (Underground)	4C 36
Euston (Rail, Underground & Overground)	3D 37

F

Farringdon (Rail & Underground)	1F 61
Fenchurch Street (Rail)	5A 64
Festival Pier (River Tours)	2B 88
Fulham Broadway (Underground)	5E 131

G

Gallions Reach (DLR)	5F 77
Gloucester Road (Underground)	3B 110
Goldhawk Road (Underground)	5B 78
Goodge Street (Underground)	1D 59
Great Portland Street (Underground)	5A 36
Greenland Pier (River Bus)	2C 124
Green Park (Underground)	2A 86
Greenwich Pier (River Bus & Tours)	1C 148
Greenwich (Rail & DLR)	4A 148

H

Hackney Wick (Overground)	5D 5
Haggerston (Overground)	3B 20
Hammersmith (Underground)	4C 106
Heron Quays (DLR)	3E 97
High Street Kensington (Underground)	5F 81
Hilton Docklands Pier (River Bus)	3B 96
Holborn (Underground)	2B 60
Holland Park (Underground)	3B 80
Hoxton (Overground)	1B 42
Hyde Park Corner (Underground)	4E 85

I

Island Gardens (DLR)	5B 126

K

Kennington (Underground)	5F 117
Kensal Green (Underground & Overground)	2B 28
Kensal Rise (Overground)	1D 29
Kensington Olympia (Rail, Underground & Overground)	2A 108
Kilburn High Road (Overground)	4E 9
Kilburn Park (Underground)	5E 9
King George V (DLR)	3D 105
King's Cross (Rail & Underground)	1F 37
King's Cross St Pancras (Underground)	2F 37
Knightsbridge (Underground)	5C 84

L

Ladbroke Grove (Underground) 3A 52
Lambeth North (Underground) 1D 117
Lancaster Gate (Underground) 5D 55
Langdon Park (DLR) 3A 70
Latimer Road (Underground) 5E 51
Leicester Square (Underground) 5E 59
Limehouse (Rail & DLR) 4F 67
Liverpool Street (Rail & Underground) 2F 63
London Bridge City Pier (River Bus) 2F 91
London Bridge (Rail & Underground) 3E 91
London City Airport (DLR) 2A 104
London Eye Millennium Pier (River Bus & Tours) . . .4B 88
London Fields (Rail) 1A 22

M

Maida Vale (Underground) 2A 32
Mansion House (Underground) 4C 62
Marble Arch (Underground) 4C 56
Maryland (Rail) 4F 7
Marylebone (Rail & Underground) 5B 34
Masthouse Terrace Pier (River Bus) 5E 125
Maze Hill (Rail) 2F 149
Mile End (Underground) 3B 46
Millbank Millennium Pier (River Bus) 4A 116
Monument (Underground) 5E 63
Moorgate (Rail & Underground) 2D 63
Mornington Crescent (Underground) 5B 14
Mudchute (DLR) 4A 126

N

New Cross Gate (Rail & Overground) 5F 145
New Cross (Rail & Overground) 5B 146
North Greenwich Pier (River Bus & Tours) 3B 100
North Greenwich (Underground) 4F 99
North Terminal (Riverbus) 5D 105
Notting Hill Gate (Underground) 2D 81

O

Old Street (Rail & Underground) 4E 41
Oval (Underground) 3D 139
Oxford Circus (Underground) 3B 58

P

Paddington (Rail & Underground) 3D 55
Piccadilly Circus (Underground) 1D 87
Pimlico (Underground) .5D 115
Pontoon Dock (DLR) 3B 102
Poplar (DLR) 1F 97
Prince Regent (DLR) 5C 74
Pudding Mill Lane (DLR) 4A 26

Q

Queen's Park (Underground & Overground) 1B 30
Queensway (Underground) 1A 82

R

Regent's Park (Underground) 5F 35
Rotherhithe (Overground) 4C 94

Royal Albert (DLR) 5F 75
Royal Oak (Underground) 2A 54
Royal Victoria (DLR) 5D 73
Russell Square (Underground) 5F 37

S

Shadwell (Overground & DLR) 5A 66
Shepherd's Bush Market (Underground) 3B 78
Shepherd's Bush (Rail, Underground & Overground) . . 4D 79
Shoreditch High Street (Overground) 4B 42
Sloane Square (Underground) 4D 113
South Bermondsey (Rail) 5B 122
South Hampstead (Overground) 2C 10
South Kensington (Underground) 3E 111
South Quay (DLR) 5A 98
Southwark (Underground) 3F 89
Star Lane (DLR) 5F 49
Stepney Green (Underground) 5D 45
St George Wharf Pier (River Bus) 1F 137
St James's Park (Underground) 1D 115
St John's Wood (Underground) 5D 11
St Katharine's Pier (River Tours) 2C 92
St Pancras International (Rail) 1F 37
St Paul's (Underground) 3B 62
Stratford High Street (DLR) 2D 27
Stratford International (Rail & DLR) 4B 6
Stratford (Rail, Underground, Overground & DLR) 1D 27
Surrey Quays (Overground) 3D 123
Swiss Cottage (Underground) 1D 11

T

Temple (Underground) 5C 60
Tottenham Court Road (Underground) 3E 59
Tower Gateway (DLR) 5B 64
Tower Hill (Underground) 5B 64
Tower Millennium Pier (River Bus & Tours) 2A 92

V

Vauxhall (Rail & Underground) 1A 138
Victoria (Coach) 4A 114
Victoria (Rail & Underground) 2A 114

W

Wapping (Overground) 3B 94
Warren Street (Underground) 4C 36
Warwick Avenue (Underground) 5B 32
Waterloo East (Rail) 4D 89
Waterloo (Rail & Underground) 4D 89
Westbourne Park (Underground) 1C 52
West Brompton (Underground & Overground) 1E 131
Westferry (DLR) 5C 68
West Ham (DLR) 2F 49
West Ham (Rail & Underground) 2F 49
West India Quay (DLR) 1E 97
West Kensington (Underground) 5B 108
Westminster Millennium Pier (River Tours) 4A 88
Westminster (Underground) 5A 88
West Silvertown (DLR) 3E 101
Whitechapel (Underground & Overground) 1F 65
White City (Underground) 1C 78
Wood Lane (Underground) 1C 78

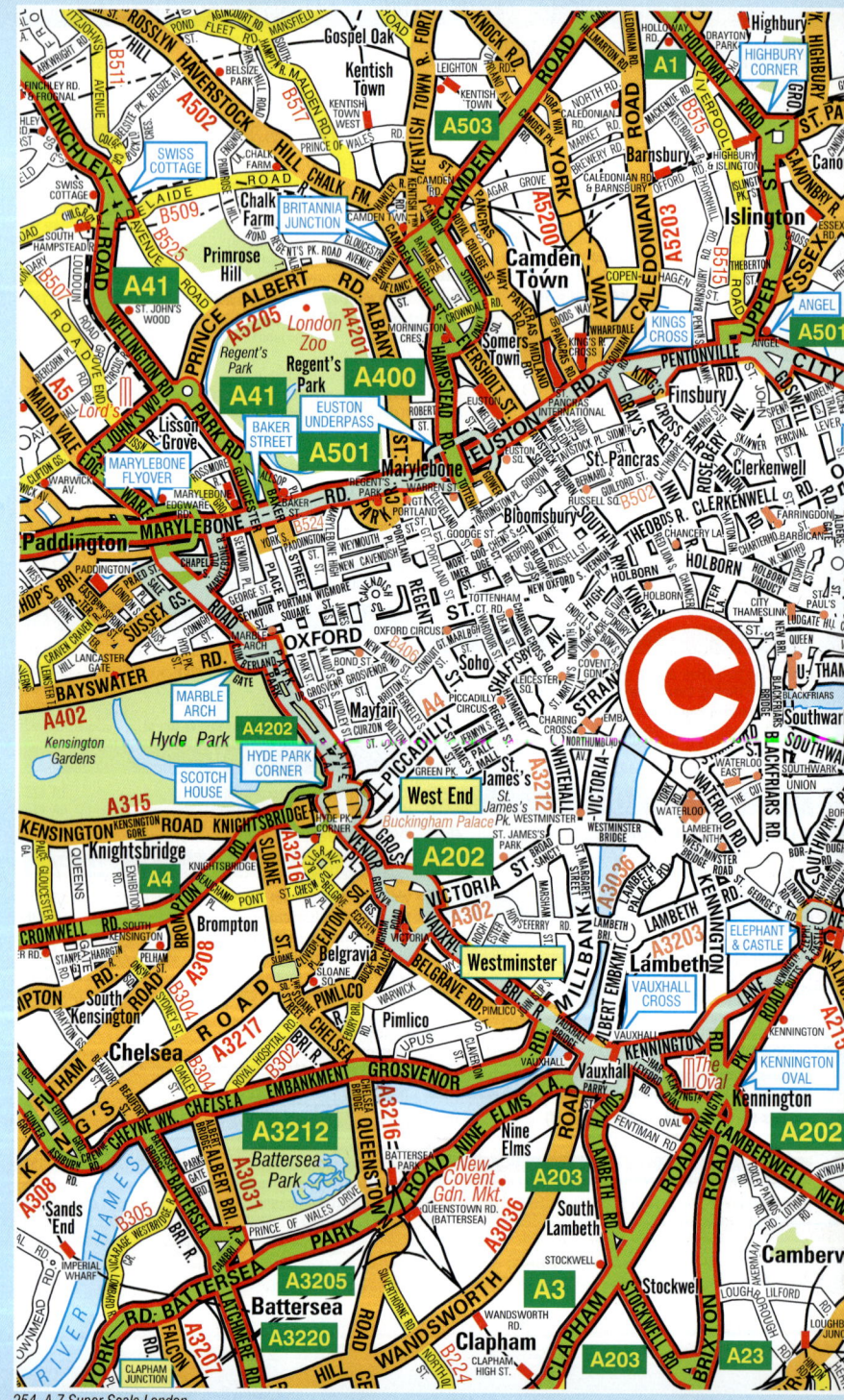

Congestion Charging Zone

■ The daily charge applies Mon.-Fri. 7-00am to 6-00pm excluding English bank and public holidays and designated non-charging days.

■ Payment of the daily charge allows you to drive in, around, leave and re-enter the charging zone as many times as required.

■ Payment must be made before or on the day of travel by midnight. Drivers who forget to pay the charge for the previous day's journey can pay a late payment charge the next day up until midnight by telephone or online and avoid a Penalty Charge.

■ You can pay using Congestion Charging Auto Pay (registration required), online (www.cclondon.com), by telephone (0343 222 2222), by SMS text message (registration required) or by post (10 days in advance).

■ Exemptions include motorcycles, mopeds and bicycles.
Registration for discount schemes, including Congestion Charging Auto Pay, Fleet Auto Pay, Blue Badge holders, residents & Ultra Low Emission Vehicles, is available from Transport for London.

■ Penalty charge for non-payment of the daily charge by midnight on the day after the day of travel.

This information is correct at the time of publication.

For further information www.tfl.gov.uk

WEST END CINEMAS

WEST END THEATRES

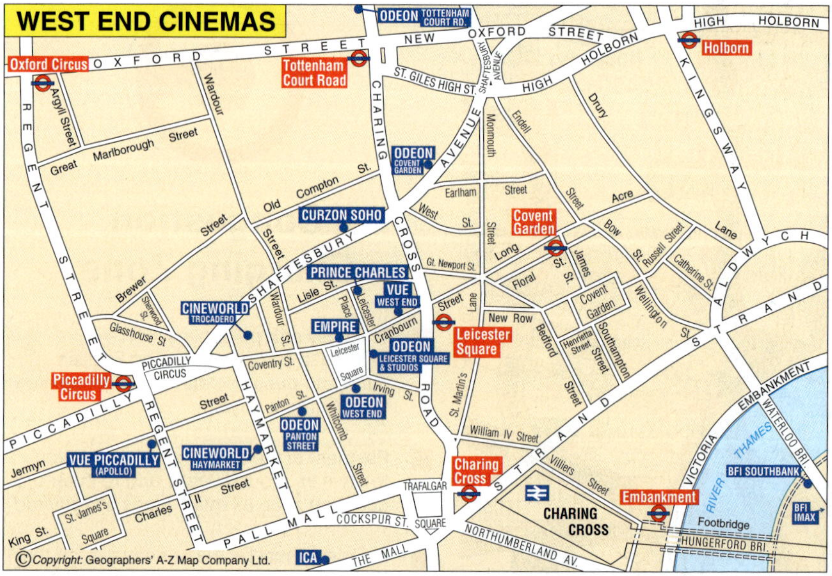

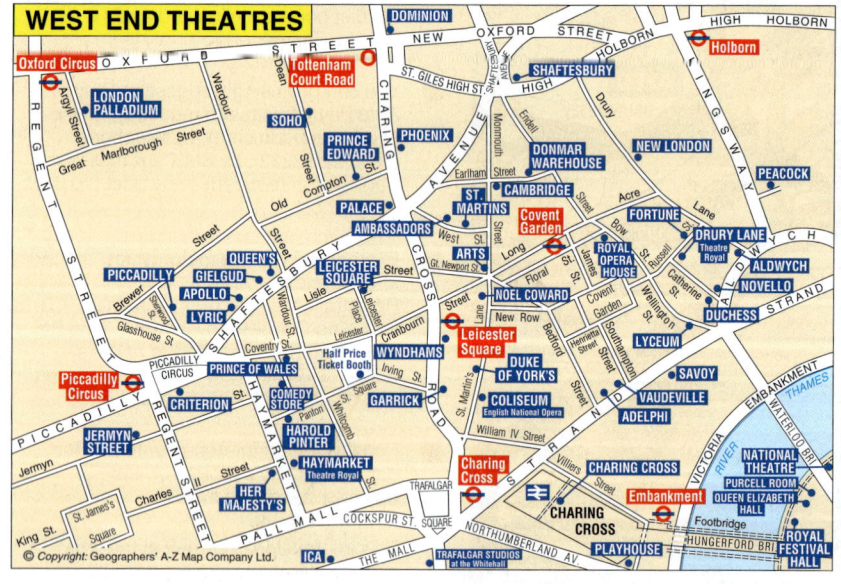